Complete Curriculum

Grade 3

Harcourt Family Learning™

For more information, please visit flashkids.com
Please submit all inquiries to Flashkids@sterlingpublishing.com

ISBN 978-1-4114-9882-2

Manufactured in Canada

Lot#:
29 31 33 35 37 36 34 32 30
11/20

FlashKids
New York

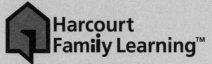

Dear Parent,

Beginning a new grade is a milestone for your child, and each new subject is bound to present some challenges that may require some attention out of the classroom. With this comprehensive third-grade book at hand, you and your child can work together on any skill that he or she is finding difficult to master. Here to help are hundreds of fun, colorful pages for learning and practicing reading, spelling, math, language arts, writing, and test preparation.

In the reading section, the wide range of high-interest stories will hold your child's attention and help develop his or her proficiency in reading. Each of the six units focuses on a different reading comprehension skill: finding facts, detecting a sequence, learning new vocabulary through context, identifying the main idea, drawing conclusions, and making inferences. Mastering these skills will ensure that your child has the necessary tools for a lifetime love of reading.

Lessons in the spelling section present third-grade words in lists grouped by vowel sound, suffix, or related forms, like plurals and contractions. This order will clearly show your child the different ways that similar sounds can be spelled. Your child will learn to sort words, recognize definitions, synonyms, and base words, as well as use capitalization and punctuation. Each lesson also features a short passage containing spelling and grammar mistakes that your child will proofread and correct.

The math section starts with basics like place value and number comparison, followed by addition and subtraction with multiple digits and regrouping. Next your child is introduced to multiplication, division, and simple fractions, as well as units reviewing geometry, time, and measurement. Each section begins with clear examples that illustrate new skills, and then practice drills, problem-solving lessons, and unit reviews encourage your child to master each new technique.

More than 100 lessons in the language arts section provide clear examples of and exercises in language skills such as parts of speech, sentences, mechanics, vocabulary and usage, writing, and research skills. Grammar lessons range from using nouns and verbs to constructing better sentences. Writing exercises include the friendly letter and the book report. These skills will help your child improve his or her communication abilities, excel in all academic areas, and increase his or her scores on standardized tests.

Each of the six units in the writing section focuses on a unique type of writing: personal narrative, informative writing, descriptive writing, opinion and comparative writing, story, and short report. The first half of each unit reinforces writing aspects such as putting ideas in a sequence and using descriptive details, in addition to providing fun, inspirational writing ideas for your child to explore alone or with a friend. In the second half of each unit, your child will read a practice paragraph, analyze it, prepare a writing plan for his or her own paper or paragraph, and then write and revise.

Lastly, the test prep section employs your child's knowledge in reading, math, and language to the basic standardized test formats that your child will encounter throughout his or her school career. Each unit in the first half of this section teaches specific test strategies for areas such as word study skills, reading comprehension, and mathematics. The second half of the section allows your child to apply these test-taking skills in a realistic testing environment. By simulating the experience of taking standardized tests, these practice tests can lessen feelings of intimidation during school tests.

As your child works through the test prep section, help him or her keep in mind these four important principles of test-taking:

1. *Using Time Wisely*

All standardized tests are timed, so your child should learn to work rapidly but comfortably. He or she should not spend too much time on any one question, and mark items to return to if possible. Use any remaining time to review answers. Most importantly, use a watch to keep on track!

2. *Avoiding Errors*

When choosing the correct answers on standardized tests, your child should pay careful attention to directions, determine what is being asked, and mark answers in the appropriate place. He or she should then check all answers and not make stray marks on the answer sheet.

3. *Reasoning*

To think logically toward each answer, your child should read the entire question or passage and all the answer choices before answering a question. It may be helpful to restate questions or answer choices in his or her own words.

4. *Guessing*

When the correct answer is not clear right away, your child should eliminate answers that he or she knows are incorrect. If that is not possible, skip the question. Then your child should compare the remaining answers, restate the question, and then choose the answer that seems most correct.

An answer key at the back of this workbook allows you and your child to check his or her work in any of the subject sections. Remember to give praise and support for each effort. Also, learning at home can be accomplished at any moment—you can ask your child to read aloud to you, write grocery lists, keep a journal, or measure the ingredients for a recipe. Use your imagination! With help from you and this workbook, your child is well on the way to completing the third grade with flying colors!

TABLE OF CONTENTS

Reading Skills

Spelling Skills

Math Skills

Language Arts

Writing Skills

Test Prep

Reading Skills

unit 1

What Are Facts?

Facts are sometimes called details. They are small bits of information. Facts are in true stories, such as those in the newspaper. There are facts in stories that people make up, too.

How to Read for Facts

You can find facts by asking yourself questions. Ask *who*, and your answer will be a fact about a person. Ask *what*, and your answer will be a fact about a thing. Ask *where*, and your answer will be a fact about a place. Ask *when*, and your answer will be a fact about a time. Ask *how many* or *how much*, and your answer will be a fact about a number or an amount.

Try It!

Read this story and look for facts as you read. Ask yourself *what* and *where*.

Coober Pedy

Opals are stones that sparkle with many colors. Some of the most beautiful opals come from a town in South Australia. This town is called Coober Pedy. Opals were first found there in 1915. People like to visit this town. They come to buy opals and to see the unusual buildings. Coober Pedy gets very hot in the summer, so most people build their homes underground. In this way the homes stay cool in the summer and warm in the winter. Tourists can stay in an underground hotel.

Did you find these facts when you read the story? Write the facts on the lines below.

- What are opals?

Fact: yes

- Where is Coober Pedy?

Fact: yes

Practice Finding Facts

Below are some practice questions. The first two are already answered. You can do the third one on your own.

B 1. When were opals first found at Coober Pedy?

A. in 1991
B. in 1915
C. in summer
D. in winter

Look at the question and answers again. The word *when* is asking for a time. Reread the story and look for times. Find the sentence that says, "Opals were first found there in 1915." So the correct answer is B.

C 2. Tourists like to visit Coober Pedy

A. to swim
B. to dig
C. to buy opals
D. to learn to cook

Look at the question. It has the words *tourists like to visit.* Look for these words in the story. You will find this sentence: "People like to visit this town." Read the next sentence. It says, "They come to buy opals and to see the unusual buildings." The correct answer is C.

Now it's your turn to practice. Answer the next question. Write the letter of the correct answer on the line.

D 3. Where can tourists stay?

A. in a camp
B. in a house
C. in an apartment
D. in an underground hotel

Lesson 1

Read each story. After each story you will answer questions about the facts in the story. Remember, a fact is something that you know is true.

Secret Sharks

Most people think of sharks as the ones they see in the movies. These "movie stars" are usually the great white sharks. However, the great whites are just one of about 350 kinds of sharks. There are some sharks that have never been seen alive. They live deep in the ocean. They are like the sharks that lived 300 million years ago.

One example is the goblin shark. It lives hundreds of feet under the sea. Scientists do not believe that it could live if it came to the ocean surface. People in Japan have built a small submarine to learn more about goblin sharks.

Another unusual shark is the megamouth. *Mega* means large and strong. One megamouth that scientists have seen was 15 feet long. Its mouth was 4 feet long.

______ **1.** The sharks usually seen in movies are
- **A.** gray sharks
- **B.** goblin sharks
- **C.** megamouth sharks
- **D.** great white sharks

______ **2.** How many kinds of sharks are there?
- **A.** about 300
- **B.** about 15
- **C.** about 4,500
- **D.** about 350

______ **3.** The goblin shark will be studied using a
- **A.** submarine
- **B.** telescope
- **C.** library
- **D.** museum

______ **4.** *Mega* means large and
- **A.** mean
- **B.** rare
- **C.** strong
- **D.** hungry

______ **5.** The mouth of one megamouth was about
- **A.** 3 feet long
- **B.** 4 feet long
- **C.** 15 feet long
- **D.** 60 feet long

Scientists are trying to learn more about other unusual sharks. One is the frilled shark. This creature has a body like an eel. It has frills on its neck. Scientists want to know what the frilled shark eats. They think it may eat squid.

There are many interesting kinds of small sharks, too. The cookie-cutter shark is only 16 inches long, but it has very large teeth. This shark also has strong lips. It holds a larger fish with its lips while it scoops out big bites.

Many small sharks hunt together. This way they can kill fish much larger than themselves. One kind of shark that does this is the cigar shark. You can probably guess how this shark got its name. It is the size and shape of a cigar. It is even small enough for you to hold in your hand!

______ **6.** Scientists are studying

A. large sharks **C.** unusual sharks
B. unkind sharks **D.** common sharks

______ **7.** The shark that looks like an eel is the

A. cigar shark **C.** eel shark
B. goblin shark **D.** frilled shark

______ **8.** The cookie-cutter shark is

A. little **C.** tasty
B. huge **D.** fishy

______ **9.** The cookie-cutter shark has strong

A. cookies **C.** eyes
B. fins **D.** lips

______ **10.** One shark that hunts in groups is the

A. goblin shark **C.** frilled shark
B. cigar shark **D.** ghost shark

LESSON 2

The Sound Machine's Deaf Inventor

Thomas Edison was one of the greatest inventors of all time. One of his best-known works was the phonograph. He built it in 1877. It was the first machine to record and play sound. Any inventor of this sound machine could be called great. For Edison, it was a very great deed. That's because he was partly deaf.

When Tom was a teen, he worked on a train. One day he was late for work. He ran for the train just as it was pulling out of the station. The conductor tried to help the boy. He grabbed Tom by the ears and pulled him up. "I felt something snap inside my head," Edison said later. From that point on, he grew more and more deaf.

_____ **1.** Thomas Edison was a great

A. doctor **C.** inventor
B. writer **D.** president

_____ **2.** One of Edison's best-known works was the

A. telephone **C.** television
B. phonograph **D.** photograph

_____ **3.** The phonograph was built in

A. 1887 **C.** 1877
B. 1787 **D.** 1777

_____ **4.** Edison was

A. totally blind **C.** partly blind
B. totally deaf **D.** partly deaf

_____ **5.** Tom was hurt when his ears were pulled by a

A. teacher **C.** singer
B. conductor **D.** bully

Despite his hearing loss, Edison went on to invent many things. His favorite was the phonograph. Edison tested it once it was built. He spoke into the mouth of the machine. He said, "Mary had a little lamb." The machine played back his words.

How could Edison build a sound machine if he was deaf? He had a trick. He pressed his ear up to the machine to feel it vibrate.

Edison could have had an operation so he could hear again, but he chose not to. He said that being deaf helped him. He said it let him think better. Outside noises did not distract him at work. That was another part of his genius!

______ **6.** The phonograph was Edison's

- **A.** only invention
- **B.** first invention
- **C.** last invention
- **D.** favorite invention

______ **7.** Edison's phonograph

- **A.** did not work
- **B.** helped Mary
- **C.** made words louder
- **D.** repeated his words

______ **8.** Edison could hear by pressing his ear to

- **A.** a paper cup
- **B.** another person
- **C.** a hearing aid
- **D.** the phonograph

______ **9.** Edison did not have an ear operation because he

- **A.** had no choice
- **B.** chose not to
- **C.** was afraid
- **D.** was too busy

______ **10.** Edison said that being deaf

- **A.** hurt him
- **B.** annoyed him
- **C.** made him tired
- **D.** aided him

Lesson 3

The Oldest Toy

One of the very first toys was simple and round. It was a ball. The first balls were just rocks that were round and smooth. People liked kicking rocks to see how far the rocks would go. They also threw rocks to see if they could hit certain things with them.

Bowling was first played thousands of years ago in Egypt. A ball made of rock was rolled through a short tunnel. People tried to knock down the nine rock pieces at the other end of the tunnel.

Later bowling was played in Germany. At first people used a stone ball and one wooden pin. Then they used a ball made of wood. The number of pins also changed. Sometimes people used three pins. Other times people used as many as 17 pins.

_____ **1.** One of the very first toys was

A. round **C.** square
B. sharp **D.** flat

_____ **2.** People liked kicking rocks to see how

A. soft they were **C.** high they would go
B. hard they were **D.** far they would go

_____ **3.** The first bowling game was played

A. in Egypt **C.** in the United States
B. in Germany **D.** with one wooden pin

_____ **4.** In Egypt, a rock ball was rolled through a

A. field **C.** tunnel
B. street **D.** sidewalk

_____ **5.** At first in Germany people used

A. three pins **C.** one wooden pin
B. 17 pins **D.** 100 pins

Native Americans made up games that used balls. Some of them played a game that was like basketball. They even had a ball made of rubber. They got the rubber from the trees where they lived.

Handball games started in Europe. Children liked to bounce small balls made of animal skin against the sides of buildings. They especially liked the high stone walls of churches. Later people started hitting the ball to each other over a net. At first they used only their hands. Then they began to wrap their hands with string. They also added a stick. The game of tennis started from the game of handball.

______ 6. Some Native Americans had a ball that

A. didn't bounce
B. fell apart
C. they hit with a bat
D. was made of rubber

______ 7. Rubber comes from

A. rivers
B. trees
C. animal skins
D. the ground

______ 8. Handball was first played in

A. prisons
B. Japan
C. Europe
D. churches

______ 9. People first hit balls over nets with their

A. gloves
B. feet
C. hands
D. shoes

______ 10. Tennis came from the game of

A. handball
B. basketball
C. bowling
D. skin ball

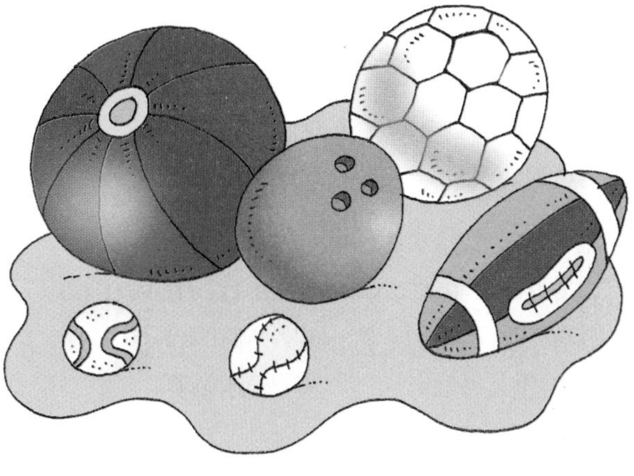

Lesson 4

Save the Turkeys!

Turkeys are interesting birds. They don't take off and fly smoothly like other birds. Turkeys take off like helicopters. They go almost straight up and can fly fast. One wild turkey was timed flying at 55 miles per hour.

Turkeys differ from most birds in other ways, too. Male turkeys have snoods and wattles. The snood is a flap of skin above the beak. It can grow to be 5 inches long. Male turkeys use their snoods to attract females.

A turkey's wattle is the bumpy skin on his neck. It can grow very large. It can also turn from red to white and back again. Some people think that this happens when the turkey wants to send a message. He may be trying to attract a female. He might be sending a signal to another male that says, "Stay away!"

______ **1.** When a turkey takes off, it flies

A. slowly **C.** straight up
B. smoothly **D.** near the ground

______ **2.** One turkey was timed flying

A. 5 feet per hour **C.** 10 miles per hour
B. 15 feet per hour **D.** 55 miles per hour

______ **3.** A turkey's snood can be found

A. on its back **C.** under the wing
B. above the beak **D.** above the eye

______ **4.** A wattle is part of the turkey's

A. neck **C.** foot
B. feathers **D.** beak

______ **5.** A turkey's wattle can turn from red to

A. black **C.** white
B. blue **D.** brown

Turkeys were once threatened birds. Wild turkeys lived in the woods. People cut down the woods to make roads, towns, and farms. The turkeys had no place to live. People liked to eat turkeys, so hunters killed many of these birds. By the 1900s the number of turkeys in America had dropped. Very few were left.

Leaders in each state knew that something had to be done. They passed laws to solve the problem. Some laws placed limits on the number of turkeys that hunters could kill. Also, laws allowed some turkeys to be moved to areas where others had vanished. The new laws helped turkeys, and people learned that passing laws to help them is one way to take care of wild animals.

______ **6.** As people changed the land, wild turkeys
A. flew straight up **C.** lost their homes
B. lived in towns **D.** enjoyed people

______ **7.** Hunters killed many turkeys for
A. food **C.** wattles
B. beaks **D.** feathers

______ **8.** The turkeys were finally helped by
A. experts **C.** lawmakers
B. hunters **D.** soldiers

______ **9.** Turkeys were saved by being moved to
A. zoos **C.** rolling hills
B. other areas **D.** cages

______ **10.** The new laws
A. helped hunters **C.** were not passed
B. did not work **D.** saved the turkeys

Lesson 5

Shivering Is Not Just Quivering

Have you ever shivered on a cold day? You may not have noticed, but as you shivered, your body warmed up. Shivering is one way your body stays warm. It happens when signals are sent from the nervous system to the muscles. This is how it works.

The nervous system has two parts. One part is the nerves. They look like long, thin threads. Their job is to carry messages to all parts of the body. The spinal cord and the brain make up the other part of the nervous system. The spinal cord is a large bundle of nerves inside the backbone. Signals from the brain travel down the spinal cord. They go to the rest of the body through the nerves. Muscles receive these signals.

______ **1.** Shivering helps your body

- **A.** keep calm
- **B.** stay warm
- **C.** cool down
- **D.** stand up straight

______ **2.** Signals go from the nervous system to

- **A.** the muscles
- **B.** a certain cell
- **C.** the legs
- **D.** the nerves

______ **3.** The nervous system has

- **A.** one part
- **B.** three parts
- **C.** two parts
- **D.** many parts

______ **4.** Nerves look like

- **A.** muscles
- **B.** threads
- **C.** blood cells
- **D.** small trees

______ **5.** The spinal cord is a large bundle of

- **A.** muscles
- **B.** brain cells
- **C.** nerves
- **D.** signals

Imagine waiting for a bus on a street corner. It's a cold day, the bus is late, and you feel chilled. Here's what happens.

A control center in your brain senses that you're cold. It sends a message down the spinal cord to all the nerves. The message races through nerves that connect to other nerves. Then it goes from the nerves to the muscles. The message says, "Warning! Prepare for action!"

When a muscle moves, it makes heat. That is why you get warm when you run or play soccer. When your muscles get the signal that you are cold, they get busy. First they become tight, then they loosen. They tighten then loosen over and over again. This makes you shiver. You also get warmer.

_____ **6.** Your brain's signal travels first to the

A. bus **C.** heart

B. spinal cord **D.** muscles

_____ **7.** Nerves tell the muscles to

A. stop **C.** get ready

B. relax **D.** cool down

_____ **8.** When a muscle moves, it becomes

A. warm **C.** stiff

B. cool **D.** heavy

_____ **9.** When you become cold, your muscles

A. relax **C.** stop moving

B. stretch **D.** tighten and loosen

_____ **10.** When you shiver, you get

A. weaker **C.** stronger

B. colder **D.** warmer

Lesson 6

Good Night, Don't Bite!

There's nothing quite like falling sound asleep after a full day of work. Like people, animals need to rest after working hard. Some animals sleep floating in water. Others dig holes under the ground. Some even sleep high in trees or under leaves. But they all find a way to rest.

Animals sleeping in the sea can be a strange sight. Fish sleep with their eyes open. They do not have eyelids, so they seem to stare into the depths while they nap. Sea otters sometimes sleep in beds of seaweed. This keeps them from floating away. Parrotfish blow a clear gel from their mouths when they are ready to snooze. The gel forms a bubble around them. The bubble protects them from harm while they sleep.

______ **1.** Like people, animals need to

A. cry **C.** rest
B. talk **D.** tell time

______ **2.** Fish do not have

A. scales **C.** tails
B. bubbles **D.** eyelids

______ **3.** Sea otters sometimes sleep in

A. holes **C.** boats
B. seaweed **D.** caves

______ **4.** Parrotfish make a clear gel with their

A. mouths **C.** skin
B. scales **D.** fins

______ **5.** Parrotfish sleep in a bubble that

A. shrinks **C.** grows large
B. glows **D.** protects them

Other animals sleep under the ground. Chipmunks sleep curled up in a ball. Their beds are made of leaves and grass. They wake up now and then to snack on food stored nearby. Some desert frogs dig underground holes during the hot, dry season. A frog may stay in its hole for months.

High above the ground, monkeys make leafy nests in trees each evening before they retire. The tree's high branches help to keep the monkeys safe during the night. Even the insects buzzing around their heads rest. Some sleep under a leaf that will be their next meal. A bee may crawl down into a blossom to rest. When it crawls out the next morning, it is rested and ready to buzz off to work.

______ **6.** Chipmunks sleep in beds made of

A. nets **C.** leaves and grass
B. mud **D.** sticks and twigs

______ **7.** Desert frogs stay underground during

A. morning **C.** the night
B. winter **D.** the hot, dry season

______ **8.** Monkeys make beds using material from

A. insects **C.** the ground
B. water **D.** trees

______ **9.** Some insects rest

A. while eating **C.** while buzzing
B. under leaves **D.** curled up in a ball

______ **10.** A bee might sleep in

A. a flower **C.** a bubble
B. mud **D.** clear gel

LESSON 7

Stop That Pacing, Fido!

If you are planning a picnic, watch your pets. If your dog paces and your cat twitches, make other plans. It may rain that day. If you want to wash your car, go outside early in the day and look for a spider. If you see a spider spinning a web, get out your soap and bucket. There will most likely be fair weather.

If you would rather fly a kite, look at the stars the night before. If they are bright, find your kite and string. It will be windy the next day. But if you are more in the mood for a swim, listen to the crickets. By counting their chirps, you can tell if it is warm enough.

______ **1.** If your cat twitches as you plan a picnic,

A. wash your car
B. go swimming
C. take more food
D. make other plans

______ **2.** A spider spinning a web means

A. rain
B. clouds
C. fair weather
D. snow

______ **3.** If you want to fly a kite, look at the

A. dust
B. crickets
C. grass
D. stars

______ **4.** If you want to swim, listen to the

A. crickets
B. dogs
C. cats
D. spiders

______ **5.** To tell about weather, count a cricket's

A. legs
B. chirps
C. eyes
D. wings

What do animals know about weather? Dampness collects in the air before rain. It makes each hair in an animal's fur swell. That is why your pets move about restlessly. Spiders do not like dampness in the air, either. A spiderweb will not stick to a damp surface. So if a spider is spinning a web, the air must be dry.

How can stars help you plan your fun? Stars are most easily seen when winds high in the air blow dust and clouds away. These winds will drop to the ground the next day, making it windy. What about those crickets? Count the number of times a cricket chirps in 15 seconds. Then add 37 to find out how warm it is. If you hear 35 chirps, it is 72 degrees.

______ **6.** Dampness in the air makes an animal
- **A.** hungry
- **B.** warm
- **C.** restless
- **D.** smaller

______ **7.** If a spider is spinning a web, the air must be
- **A.** damp
- **B.** fresh
- **C.** dry
- **D.** hot

______ **8.** Strong winds high in the air blow away
- **A.** fur
- **B.** webs
- **C.** stars
- **D.** clouds

______ **9.** If you see bright stars, there will be wind
- **A.** in a month
- **B.** in a week
- **C.** the following day
- **D.** in two days

______ **10.** A cricket's chirps can help tell if it's
- **A.** warm
- **B.** rainy
- **C.** cloudy
- **D.** dusk

LESSON 8

Louis Braille

Louis Braille was born in a small French town. When he was three, he lost his sight. At ten he went to a school for children who were blind. The books at his school were written with raised letters. He moved his fingers over the letters to read the books. Letters like *A* and *H* felt the same. He had a hard time understanding what he read.

Then Louis learned of a different way to read. It was used by soldiers who had to read messages in the dark. To write the messages, people punched dots in paper. Since the dots were raised, people could feel them.

______ **1.** Louis Braille was born in

A. Spain **C.** England
B. France **D.** the United States

______ **2.** Louis lost his sight when he was

A. two **C.** ten
B. three **D.** fifteen

______ **3.** To read books Louis used

A. his fingers **C.** a machine
B. his eyes **D.** his mother's help

______ **4.** Louis had a hard time understanding

A. his friends **C.** what he heard
B. his teachers **D.** what he read

______ **5.** The system with raised dots was used by

A. miners **C.** doctors
B. soldiers **D.** forest rangers

Louis liked the idea of reading with raised dots, but he thought it could be made simpler. So when Louis was fifteen, he made up a new way of writing. He used raised dots, but he made up his own alphabet.

All of Louis's friends at school liked his idea, but many teachers did not want to use it. They thought the old way worked just fine. Then in 1844, this new way of reading and writing was shown to the public. When more people saw how it worked, they liked it. Today people all over the world read books written in Braille.

______ **6.** Louis decided to use the idea of reading

A. old books **C.** raised dots

B. aloud **D.** picture books

______ **7.** Louis's new system used

A. small letters **C.** no raised dots

B. a machine **D.** a new alphabet

______ **8.** Louis's friends thought his system

A. was strange **C.** worked well

B. was too hard **D.** did not work

______ **9.** At first the new system was not used by

A. parents **C.** the government

B. students **D.** people who taught school

______ **10.** Today Braille's system

A. is not used **C.** does not work

B. is well liked **D.** is used only in France

Writing Roundup

Read the story below. Think about the facts. Then answer the questions in complete sentences.

Have you ever seen a comet? It looks like a fuzzy star with a tail. It travels along a path in the sky. When the comet comes near the Sun, its tail looks long and bright.

Long ago most people thought that comets appeared by chance. They did not think comets traveled on a set path or time. But Edmond Halley disagreed. He was an English scientist. He claimed that comets came near the Sun at set times. Halley mapped the path of one comet. He had seen it in 1682. He predicted it would appear again in 1758. He was right. Today that comet is known as Halley's Comet. It is seen about every 77 years.

1. What does a comet look like?

____

____

2. When does a comet's tail look long and bright?

____

____

3. How often can Halley's Comet be seen?

____

____

Prewriting

Think of an idea you might write about, such as a planet or a way to travel in space. Write the idea in the center of the idea web below. Then fill out the rest of the web with facts.

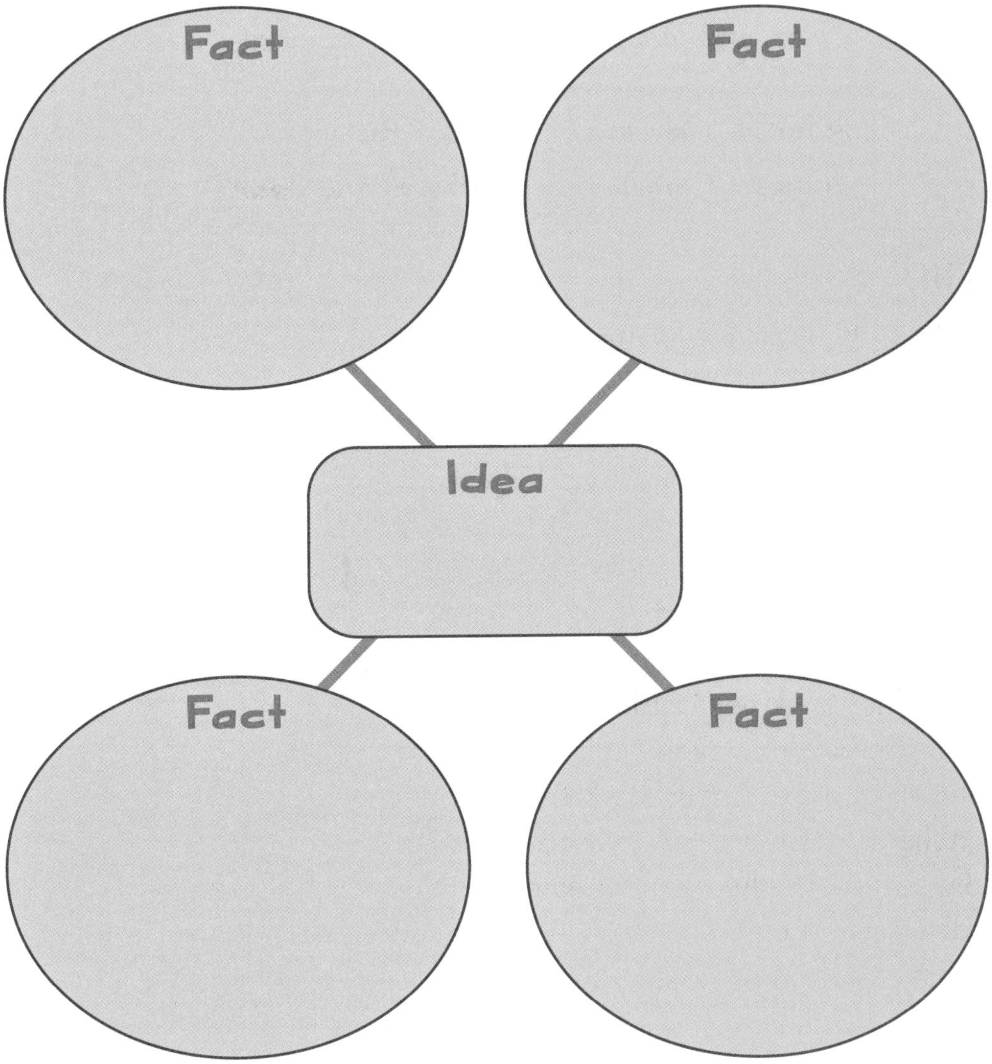

On Your Own

Now use another sheet of paper to write a story about your idea. Use the facts from your idea web.

unit 2

What Is Sequence?

Sequence means time order. Events in a story happen in a sequence. Something happens first. Then other things happen.

How can you find the sequence in a story? Look for time words, such as *first*, *next*, and *last*. Here is a list of time words:

later	**during**	**days of the week**
today	**while**	**months of the year**

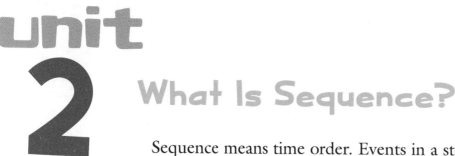

Try It!

Follow the sequence in this story. Circle all the time words.

Long ago a woodcutter and his wife lived in the forest. One day he found a lovely white crane caught in a trap. He freed the crane and went back to work. That night a young girl knocked on the couple's door. They took her inside. The next day she gave them a beautiful woven cloth and told them to sell it for a high price. Each day she gave them a new cloth. On the seventh night, the woodcutter woke up. He saw a crane at the loom weaving cloth from its feathers. The crane said, "I came here to repay you for saving me. But now I must go." It said good-bye and then flew away.

Try putting these events in the order that they happened. What happened first? Write the number **1** on the line by that sentence. Then write the number **2** by the sentence that tells what happened next. Write the number **3** by the sentence that tells what happened last.

_____ A young girl knocked on the couple's door.

_____ The woodcutter freed the crane from a trap.

_____ The girl gave the couple beautiful cloth.

Practice with Sequence

Here are some practice sequence questions. The first two are already answered. You can do the third one on your own.

__C__ **1.** When did the woodcutter see the crane at the loom?

A. that evening
B. at noon on the second day
C. on the seventh night

Look at the question. Find the words *at the loom* in the story. They are in the sentence "He saw a crane at the loom weaving cloth from its feathers." The sentence before this one will tell you when he saw the crane. It says, "On the seventh night, the woodcutter woke up." So **C** is the correct answer. The man saw the crane at the loom on the seventh night.

__B__ **2.** What happened just before the crane flew away?

A. The crane gave a cry of pain.
B. The crane said good-bye.
C. The crane wove cloth from its feathers.

Look at the question carefully. Notice the time word *before.* Also notice the word *just.* The question asks what happened *just before* the crane flew away. The sentence "It said good-bye and then flew away" tells you. The last thing the crane did before flying away was to say good-bye. So **B** is the correct answer.

_____ **3.** When did the crane weave the cloth?

A. during the night
B. in the morning
C. in the afternoon

Can you find the answer?

Lesson 1

Read each story. After each story you will answer questions about the sequence of events in the story. Remember, sequence is the order of things.

Long-Lost Note

Have you ever sealed a note inside of a bottle and thrown it into the sea? Many people have done this. Some have done it for fun, and others have done it for more serious reasons.

In 1784, a young Japanese sailor threw a bottle with a message into the sea. The sailor had been on a treasure hunt in the Pacific Ocean. A storm had come up, and his small ship had been wrecked. He and the other crew members had landed on a tiny island.

At first the men were happy. They were safe from the rough waves and the terrible wind. They waited for the storm to end. Finally the Sun came out. The men looked around. A few palm trees lay on the ground. There was nothing to eat except for some tiny crabs. Even worse, there wasn't any water to drink.

Soon the sailor was afraid that he and his friends would never leave the island. They would never see their families again. "Still," thought the sailor, "I might be able to send them a message."

He found a bottle in the wrecked ship. He cut thin pieces of wood from one of the trees. These pieces of wood would serve as paper. Slowly the sailor carved the story about the wreck into the wood. Then he put the message in the bottle and sealed it well. He tossed the bottle as far as he could into the ocean.

The sailor and his friends never left the island, but the bottle did. It rode the ocean waves for many years. Then one day the bottle washed up on the shore. A man found it tangled in some seaweed. He was very surprised! The bottle had landed in the very same village that was the sailor's home. The year was now 1935. The sailor's message had floated at sea for 150 years!

1. Put these events in the order that they happened. What happened first? Write the number **1** on the line by that sentence. Then write the number **2** by the sentence that tells what happened next. Write the number **3** by the sentence that tells what happened last.

_____ A big storm came up.

_____ The sailors landed on an island.

_____ The sailors hunted for buried treasure.

_____ 2. When was the ship wrecked?
- A. before 1784
- B. during 1784
- C. after 1784

_____ 3. When did the sailors look for food?
- A. after the storm
- B. before they reached the shore
- C. before they sailed away

_____ 4. When did the sailor write his message?
- A. while the storm was coming
- B. after he had cut some wood
- C. after 1935

_____ 5. When was the bottle found in the sailor's village?
- A. right after the sailor threw it into the sea
- B. 15 years after the sailor threw it into the sea
- C. 150 years after the sailor threw it into the sea

LESSON 2

Dogs That Guide

In 1918, a doctor and his pet dog walked with a soldier who was blind. They were outside a German hospital. The doctor had to go in the building for a short time. The soldier and dog waited outside. When the doctor came out, the soldier and dog weren't there.

The doctor looked all around. He found them on the other side of the hospital yard. The doctor saw that his pet had led the soldier there safely. He thought a trained dog might be able to do more, so he taught a dog to lead a person. It worked out well. The German government helped start a program to teach dogs to be guides.

Dorothy Eustis went to Germany to find out about the guide dog course. When she came back to the United States, she wrote about it for a magazine. Soon more people knew of the guide dogs.

The best dogs for the job are smart and fit. They behave well and make good choices. It takes more than two years to train a puppy to be a guide dog. When the dog is 14 months old, it learns many commands. It learns to know right and left. It learns to cross a busy street, or not to cross if that puts its owner in danger. A dog is trained for months. Then the owner and the dog meet, and they practice for four weeks.

The first U.S. school for guide dogs opened in 1929. Now there are many schools, and there are more than 6,000 people with guide dogs.

1. Put these events in the order that they happened. What happened first? Write the number **1** on the line by that sentence. Then write the number **2** by the sentence that tells what happened next. Write the number **3** by the sentence that tells what happened last.

_____ The doctor saw the soldier and dog on the other side of the yard.

_____ The doctor taught a dog to lead a person.

_____ The doctor couldn't find the soldier and dog.

_____ **2.** When did the doctor go in the building?

A. after he walked with the soldier
B. after he looked all around
C. after he found his pet dog

_____ **3.** What did Eustis do after she returned from Germany?

A. found out about a guide dog course
B. trained a dog
C. wrote about the guide dog course

_____ **4.** When did the German government start a program to teach dogs to be guides?

A. after Eustis went to Germany
B. after the United States opened a guide dog school
C. after the doctor taught a dog to lead a person

_____ **5.** When was the first guide dog school started in the United States?

A. 1981
B. 1929
C. 1918

LESSON 3

Traveling the Western Trail

Long ago moving west was not easy. There were no trains to Oregon or Washington. There were no airplanes or cars. People had to ride in covered wagons. They left their old way of life behind.

First people sold their farms. They took only their tools, seeds, and clothes with them. A fine horse or nice clothes were often left behind. They said good-bye to their families and friends forever.

The people rode a boat down a river to Independence, Missouri. From all across the East, people came to this town because it was located at the edge of the plains. There they bought wagons and mules. Then they loaded these wagons with food and supplies.

The people with wagons waited until spring. They waited for the grass to grow. The green grass would feed the mules during the trip. Once the plains turned green, everyone began the trip west in their wagons.

After three days they had to cross a river. Since it was spring, the river ran high. People made their mules jump into the cold water. Sometimes a family's food fell into the water. Many times the mules fell and could not get up. Still people had to keep moving forward.

The trip had to be made in six months. If it lasted longer, people would be trapped in the mountains during the winter. If they were trapped, they would freeze to death. The trip west was 2,000 miles long. Yet most people walked beside their wagons all the way to their new homes.

1. Put these events in the order that they happened. What happened first? Write the number **1** on the line by that sentence. Then write the number **2** by the sentence that tells what happened next. Write the number **3** by the sentence that tells what happened last.

_____ People rode a boat to Independence, Missouri.

_____ People sold their farms.

_____ People had to cross a river.

_____ **2.** When did people buy mules?

A. after they rode the boat
B. before they sold their farms
C. during the summer

_____ **3.** When did the wagons start the trip west?

A. in the fall
B. during the spring
C. in the winter

_____ **4.** How long did the trip take?

A. fifteen months
B. six months
C. twelve months

_____ **5.** When did families sometimes lose their food?

A. during the boat trip
B. before crossing the plains
C. when crossing a river

Lesson 4

The Space Shuttle

Space shuttles go back and forth between Earth and space. The first one flew on April 12, 1981. A space shuttle has four main parts. They are the orbiter, the fuel tank, and two rocket boosters.

The orbiter looks like an airplane. It carries the crew. A huge tank is attached to the orbiter. It holds fuel for the orbiter's engines. A rocket booster is on each side of the tank. These fire on liftoff. In two minutes, the rockets run out of fuel and fall off. Parachutes slow their drop to the sea. Then boats tow them to shore. Rockets can be used as many as 20 times. The big tank runs out of fuel in eight minutes. It falls and breaks apart over the sea. Now the orbiter enters its orbit.

There may be up to seven crew members on board the orbiter. They do tests. They might launch satellites. In 1999, a shuttle went up to fix the Hubble telescope. The Hubble is as big as a bus. The shuttle caught it. The telescope was held in the cargo bay. That's an open place like the back of a pickup truck. The crew worked out in space to make repairs. They wore space suits. They were attached to the shuttle by a long line. A robot arm put the Hubble back in orbit.

When it's time to come home, the orbiter's engines fire. This slows the shuttle, and it drops from orbit. Tiles protect the shuttle from heat caused by entering Earth's atmosphere. The shuttle then acts like an airplane. It glides to a landing on a runway.

1. Put these events in the order that they happened. What happened first? Write the number **1** on the line by that sentence. Then write the number **2** by the sentence that tells what happened next. Write the number **3** by the sentence that tells what happened last.

_____ The shuttle drops from orbit.

_____ The orbiter's engines fire.

_____ The shuttle glides to a landing.

_____ 2. When do the rocket boosters fire?
- A. while the orbiter is circling Earth
- B. right before landing
- C. on liftoff

_____ 3. When does the orbiter enter its orbit?
- A. after the big fuel tank falls to the sea
- B. when the parachutes open
- C. after a satellite is launched

_____ 4. When was the telescope held in the cargo bay?
- A. before 1999
- B. after the shuttle caught it
- C. after a robot arm put it in orbit

_____ 5. When do the orbiter's engines fire?
- A. when it's time to return to Earth
- B. before it reaches orbit
- C. when the crew works out in space

Lesson 5

How a Grizzly Spends the Winter

Imagine that it is a fall day in the Northwest. You are following a female grizzly bear. She walks through the woods looking for mice, berries, fruit, ant eggs, and honey. When she comes to a stream, she stops and swipes at fish. She catches a trout with one paw and swallows it quickly.

For days she is constantly on the move, searching for food. She may put on as many as 4 inches of fat at this time. Something tells the bear to stock up. She knows winter is coming.

As the days grow colder, the big bear begins looking for something else. She must find a place for her winter den. She digs a tunnel into the dirt on the side of a mountain. The hole is just a little larger than she is. She lines the den with moss, grass, or tree branches.

As winter comes closer, the grizzly begins to move more slowly. She drags herself from place to place. She looks as if she is half asleep. Finally one day when the snow is swirling around her, the grizzly crawls into her den. The snow soon covers the entrance. A person could stand 5 feet away and not know that the grizzly is there.

Sometime during the winter, the bear gives birth to two cubs. The cubs are very small and helpless. The mother bear takes good care of them. She nurses them and keeps them warm. In the spring they are old enough to leave the den. She teaches them to hunt for food. The young cubs stay with their mother for a year and a half.

1. Put these events in the order that they happened. What happened first? Write the number **1** on the line by that sentence. Then write the number **2** by the sentence that tells what happened next. Write the number **3** by the sentence that tells what happened last.

_____ The mother grizzly teaches the cubs to hunt.

_____ The cubs leave their mother.

_____ The baby cubs are born.

_____ **2.** When do grizzlies eat constantly?

A. after they have cubs
B. during winter
C. in the fall

_____ **3.** When do grizzlies look for a place to dig their winter dens?

A. when the days get colder
B. while they are helpless
C. in the spring

_____ **4.** When do grizzlies crawl into their dens?

A. when it is very humid
B. when it begins snowing
C. when it begins raining

_____ **5.** When do grizzlies give birth to their cubs?

A. during the summer
B. in the spring
C. during the winter

Lesson 6

Black Widow Spiders

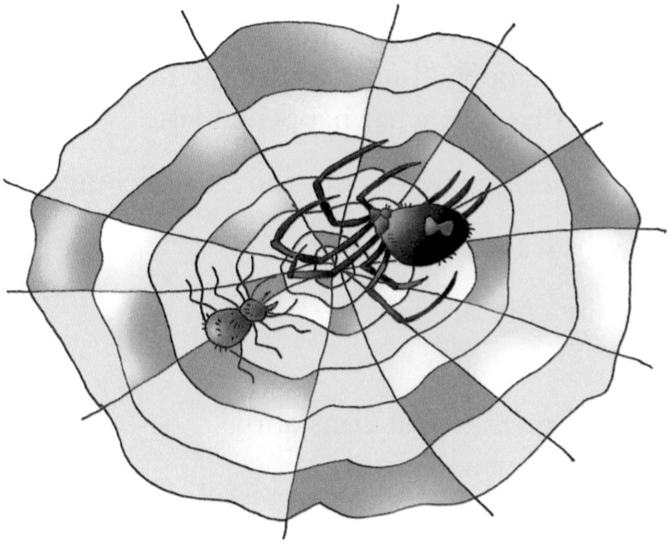

Did you know that the black widow spider is one of the most poisonous spiders in the world? But only the females can hurt you. The males are harmless. The female's poison is much stronger than that of a rattlesnake. A person who has been bitten can die if he or she does not get treatment.

The female black widow is about $\frac{1}{2}$ inch long. She is black and has red marks on her belly. The black widow gets her name from the fact that she sometimes eats her mate. The male is $\frac{1}{3}$ of the female's size. He doesn't have any red marks.

Let's observe one black widow female. When we first see her, she is hanging upside down in her web. She stays there for three days without moving. Her skin becomes too small, so she sheds it. She grows a new, larger skin. This is called molting, and it happens about eight times during her life.

One day a male black widow comes to the edge of the female's web. He strums on the web. If the female is ready to mate, she will strum also. If not, she may chase and eat him. It is unsafe to be a male black widow.

After mating, the female weaves a small silk sac. This is where she will lay from 250 to 750 eggs. Black widows lay their eggs in the spring. The female guards the egg sac for about a month. Then baby spiders, or spiderlings, hatch. The spiderlings are small and helpless when they come out of the egg sac. Many are eaten by birds or insects. Some are even eaten by their mother. Most, however, live and become adults.

1. Put these events in the order that they happened. What happened first? Write the number **1** on the line by that sentence. Then write the number **2** by the sentence that tells what happened next. Write the number **3** by the sentence that tells what happened last.

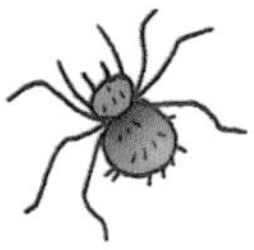

_____ The spiderlings hatch.

_____ The female makes the egg sac.

_____ The male black widow strums on the web.

_____ **2.** When does the female black widow hang in her web without moving?

A. after eating
B. before laying eggs
C. while she is molting

_____ **3.** When does the female black widow strum on her web?

A. when she is ready to mate
B. when she is hungry
C. when she is sleepy

_____ **4.** When does the female make an egg sac?

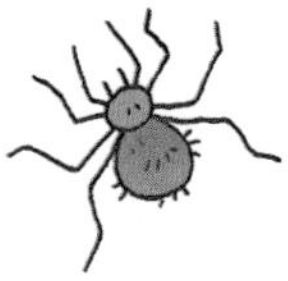

A. when she is molting
B. after mating
C. before biting someone

_____ **5.** When do black widows lay their eggs?

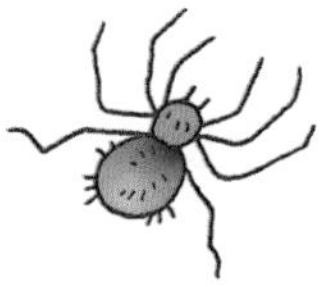

A. in the spring
B. during summer
C. before the first snow

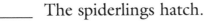

Lesson 7 Trains of the Past

In the early 1800s, horses pulled wagons over wooden rails. These were the first American trains. These trains could go only a short distance. Only a few cars could be pulled at once.

A big improvement was made in the 1830s. The first steam engines were used. They used wood as fuel to feed a fire. The fire burned and turned the water inside the engine into steam. The steam made pistons move back and forth. The pistons moved rods that turned the wheels. Wood was used for about the next 40 years.

After the Civil War, steam engines used coal instead of wood. Coal burned longer and made a better fuel. It was burned to heat water and make steam in the same way that wood was used.

From 1900 to 1935, the design of trains did not change much. Trains from these years are called the classic trains. Some people think these are the best trains ever made. Many passengers rode on trains at this time. A classic train had a dining car, a lounge, and Pullman cars. The seats in a Pullman car changed into beds. Passengers could get a good night's sleep on their long trips.

Trains used the steam engine for about 60 years. In the 1930s the diesel engine appeared. The classic trains were replaced by streamliner trains. Today you might ride on a double-deck superliner train.

1. Put these events in the order that they happened. What happened first? Write the number **1** on the line by that sentence. Then write the number **2** by the sentence that tells what happened next. Write the number **3** by the sentence that tells what happened last.

_____ The diesel engine appeared.

_____ Steam engines used wood as fuel.

_____ Steam engines used coal as fuel.

_____ **2.** When did horses pull trains?
- **A.** during the Revolutionary War
- **B.** in the early 1800s
- **C.** around 1935

_____ **3.** When were steam engines first used?
- **A.** from 1900 to 1935
- **B.** after the Civil War
- **C.** around 1830

_____ **4.** When did the classic trains run?
- **A.** when superliners appeared
- **B.** in the early 1800s
- **C.** from 1900 to 1935

_____ **5.** When did diesel engines appear?
- **A.** in the 1930s
- **B.** from 1900 to 1935
- **C.** before the Civil War

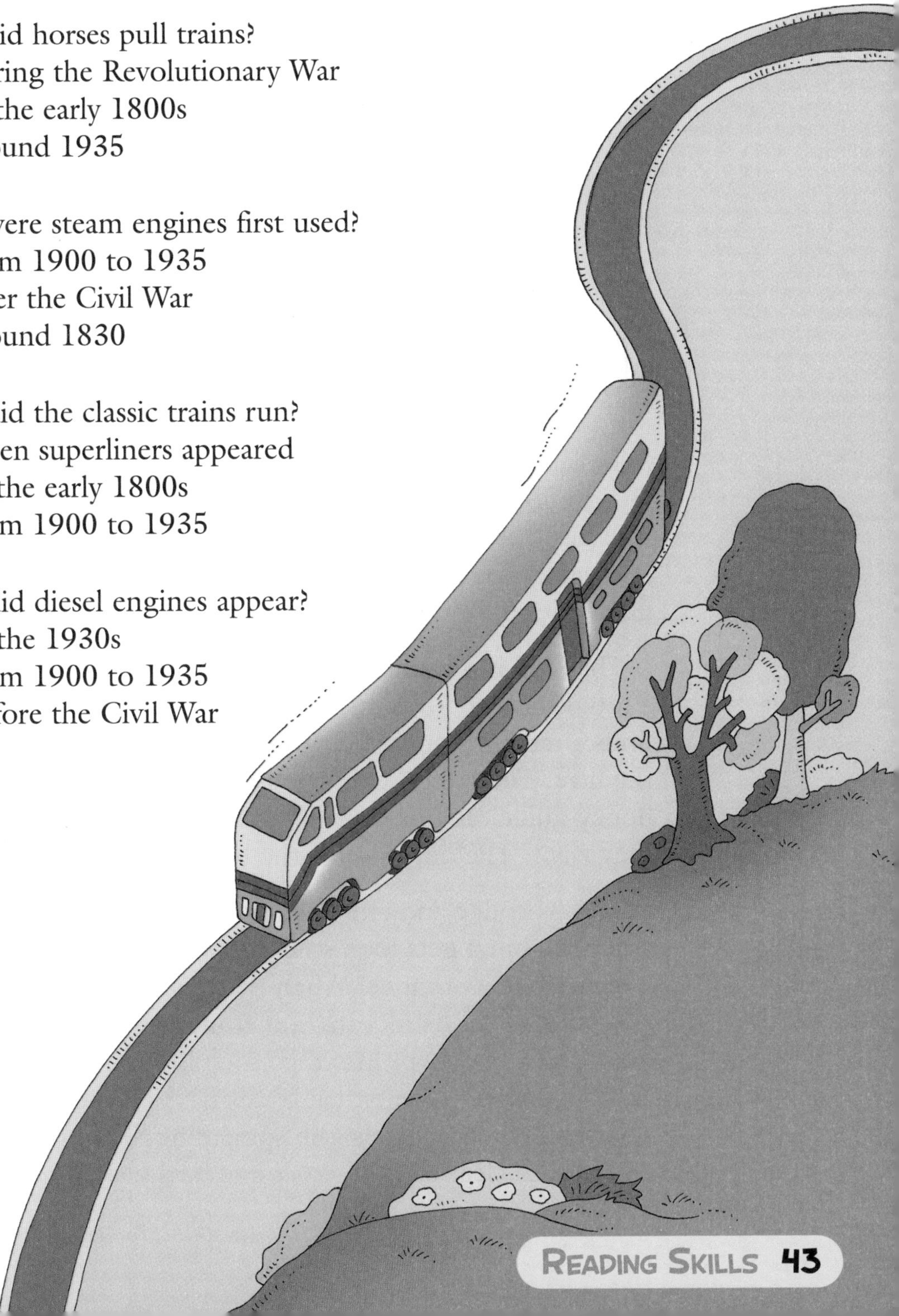

Lesson 8

Animal Partners

What would you do if your back itched in a place you couldn't reach? What if you couldn't get a jar open? You would probably ask someone to help you. Did you know that animals also help each other? Sometimes they form strange partnerships.

Two animals in Africa are partners. They help each other get their favorite food. A small bird called the honey guide likes to eat beeswax. The bird has a good sense of smell. It can find a hive from far away. Its beak is not strong enough to break into the hive, so the honey guide flies off in search of its partner—the ratel.

The ratel is a mammal. It loves honey! It has sharp claws and a tough hide to keep it from getting stung. When the honey guide finds a ratel, it hops and chatters. The ratel follows the honey guide to the hive. The ratel breaks open the hive and eats the honey. Then the honey guide eats the wax and grubs inside. Both animals get what they want. The only loser is the bee!

The crocodile and crocodile bird are also good partners. The crocodile often gets food stuck between its teeth when it is eating. Leeches bite its tongue. When the crocodile bird is around, the crocodile opens its mouth. Sometimes it leaves its mouth open for hours. The bird hops into the crocodile's mouth. It eats the leeches and bits of food. The bird also eats ticks on the crocodile's back. In this partnership both animals gain something. The crocodile has its back and mouth cleaned. The crocodile bird has dinner.

1. Put these events in the order that they happened. What happened first? Write the number **1** on the line by that sentence. Then write the number **2** by the sentence that tells what happened next. Write the number **3** by the sentence that tells what happened last.

_____ The honey guide eats the beeswax.

_____ The honey guide smells a beehive.

_____ The honey guide searches for a ratel.

_____ 2. When does a honey guide look for a ratel?

A. when it needs protection
B. before it makes its nest
C. when it finds a beehive

_____ 3. When does the honey guide eat the beeswax?

A. after the ratel has broken the hive open
B. before looking for the ratel
C. when it first smells the hive

_____ 4. When does the crocodile need to have its mouth cleaned?

A. when it is hungry
B. after it has eaten
C. when it is sleeping

_____ 5. When does the crocodile hold open its mouth?

A. when it is tired
B. when the crocodile bird is cleaning
C. when it has ticks

Writing Roundup

Read the story below. Think about the sequence, or time order. Answer the questions in complete sentences.

During lunch, Leo said that he had a rock collection. Later Jonelle thought of what to get him for his birthday. She told Duane her idea. Duane told two more friends. At his party Leo first unwrapped Jonelle's gift. It was a piece of quartz. Next Duane gave him a piece of marble. After that he got flint and slate. Leo smiled and said thanks. He didn't tell his friends he collected rock music.

1. When did Leo say he had a rock collection?

____

____

2. After opening his rock gifts, what did Leo do?

____

____

3. When did Jonelle think of a gift for Leo?

____

____

4. When did Leo open Duane's present?

____

____

Prewriting

Think about something that you have done, such as wrapping a gift, playing baseball, or going through a cafeteria line. Write the events in sequence below.

What I Did

First

Next

Then

Last

On Your Own

Now use another sheet of paper to write a story about what you have done. Write the events in the order that they happened. Use time order words.

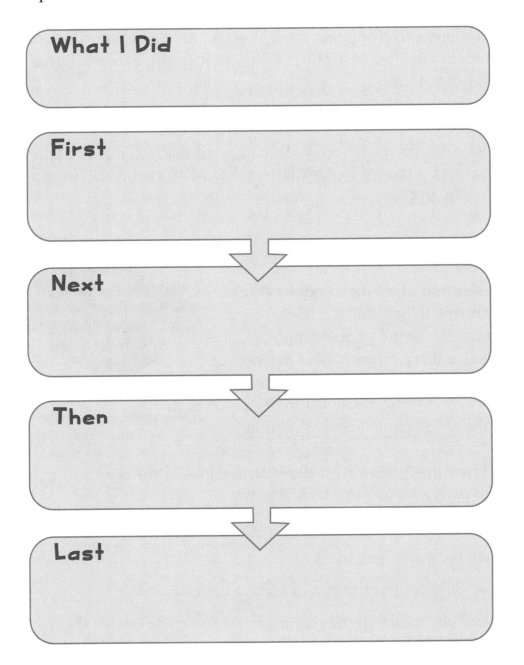

unit 3

What Is Context?

Context means all the words in a sentence or all the sentences in a paragraph. If you find a word you do not know, look at the words around it. These other words can help you figure out what the word means.

Try It!

Read the paragraph below. It has a word that you may not know. The word is printed in **dark letters**. See whether you can find out what the word means.

Sheena's best friend gave her a present. It looked like a book on the outside. But the pages were blank. It was a **diary**. Sheena liked the idea of making her own book. She writes in it every day. She writes about her family and friends. She writes about training her dog.

If you don't know what **diary** means, look at the context. This paragraph contains these words:

Clue: looked like a book on the outside

Clue: the pages were blank

Clue: Sheena liked the idea of making her own book.

Find these clues in the paragraph. Draw a circle around them. What words do you think of when you read the clues? Write the words below:

____

Did you write *journal*? The context clue words tell you that a **diary** is a journal or record of what you do every day.

Working with Context

This unit asks questions that you can answer by using context clues in paragraphs. There are two kinds of paragraphs. The paragraphs in the first part of this book have blank spaces in them. You can use the context clues in the paragraphs to decide which word should go in each space. Here is an example:

Animals have different kinds of feet. Squirrels have long toes with sharp __1__ that help them climb trees. A mountain goat's __2__ help it go up steep cliffs.

__B__ **1.** **A.** fingers **B.** claws **C.** gloves **D.** knives

______ **2.** **A.** hooves **B.** hands **C.** nails **D.** boots

Look at the answer choices for question 1. Treat the paragraph as a puzzle. Which pieces don't fit? Which piece fits best? Try putting each word in the blank. See which one makes the most sense. Squirrels don't have sharp *fingers* or *gloves* or *knives. Claws* (answer **B**) is the only choice that makes sense. Now try to answer question 2 on your own.

The paragraphs in the second part of this unit are different. For these you figure out the meaning of a word that is printed in **dark letters** in the paragraph. Here is an example:

The Inuit people use **kayaks** to travel the icy waters where they live. Kayaks are like canoes, but they have room for only one person.

The word in dark type is **kayaks**. Find the context clues. Then choose a word that means the same as **kayaks**.

______ **3.** In this paragraph, the word **kayaks** means

A. sleds **C.** boats

B. skis **D.** planes

Lesson 1

Read the passages and answer the questions about context. Remember, context is a way to learn new words by thinking about the other words used in a story.

The California condor is dying out. Only 27 of these large birds were still living in 1987. Some people started raising condors in a zoo. They took eggs from condor nests. The eggs ___1___. Then the baby birds lived in the zoo. It took ___2___ years for the condors to grow up. Then they were turned loose.

______ **1.** **A.** sang **B.** behaved **C.** locked **D.** hatched

______ **2.** **A.** several **B.** bad **C.** bent **D.** deep

---

Some wasps build their nests out of paper. They chew wood. They ___3___ it with juice in their mouths. Then they ___4___ out the wet mixture and make their nests.

______ **3.** **A.** mix **B.** paste **C.** hurt **D.** bake

______ **4.** **A.** kick **B.** spit **C.** shoot **D.** hug

---

Magic Johnson was a basketball superstar. He practiced every day when he was a ___5___. He practiced bouncing the ball. He practiced ___6___the ball. Magic said that it's hard to practice every day, but that's how to become a winner!

______ **5.** **A.** teacher **B.** coach **C.** batter **D.** youth

______ **6.** **A.** sliding **B.** hunting **C.** shooting **D.** sitting

---

Guide dogs are helpful to people who are blind. The dog wears a ___7___ with a long handle. The owner holds the handle. Then the person gives ___8___. The dog obeys them. It carefully guides its owner across streets.

______ **7.** **A.** coat **B.** harness **C.** shirt **D.** belt

______ **8.** **A.** fences **B.** jars **C.** toys **D.** commands

People in Russia give eggs as gifts. They do not give just plain white eggs. The eggs are painted with pictures. Many of the pictures have ___9___ meanings, such as "good luck" and "long life." In Russia, ___10___ eggs become little works of art!

______ **9.** **A.** special **B.** cold **C.** small **D.** purple

______**10.** **A.** lizard **B.** ordinary **C.** red **D.** broken

---

A man wondered whether bees know which flowers to go to. So he drew flowers on a large ___11___ of paper. Half the flowers were blue. The other half were yellow. On each blue flower, he put a big cup of sugar water. He put a ___12___ cup on each yellow flower. The bees stopped going to the yellow flowers.

______**11.** **A.** test **B.** row **C.** sheet **D.** pencil

______**12.** **A.** big **B.** tiny **C.** glass **D.** slow

---

Some plants don't have seeds. How can you grow a seedless grape plant? First cut off a piece of ___13___ from a grape plant. Put it in water. Soon it begins to grow roots. Plant it in the ___14___ . It will grow into a new grape plant.

______**13.** **A.** stem **B.** tree **C.** spoon **D.** stone

______**14.** **A.** step **B.** dirt **C.** green **D.** road

---

Sounds can move through air or water. Sounds bounce back if they hit a ___15___ object. Then you can hear them a second time. These ___16___ sounds are called echoes.

______**15.** **A.** solid **B.** mean **C.** burned **D.** eager

______**16.** **A.** fair **B.** forty **C.** pink **D.** repeated

Lesson 2

Animals have different ways to escape from ___1___. Some run very fast. Others climb trees. Some are safe because they are hard to see. They may be the same color as the ground. They may look like plants. They may have ___2___ or spots that look like the shadows of trees. Instead of running, these animals stand very still.

_____ **1. A.** mice **B.** danger **C.** clouds **D.** help

_____ **2. A.** stripes **B.** teeth **C.** string **D.** soup

---

Every year in Thailand, people have Elephant Day. They bring their elephants to one ___3___. Everyone comes to see whose elephant is the best. The elephants run a race. They also carry big logs and ___4___ them in a pile.

_____ **3. A.** bit **B.** fault **C.** location **D.** paper

_____ **4. A.** think **B.** climb **C.** stack **D.** sneeze

---

Have you ever ___5___ a pill bug? These animals are not pills or bugs! They got the name *pill* because they can roll up into a ball. They got the name *bug* because of their small ___6___. Pill bugs belong to the same family as crabs.

_____ **5. A.** counted **B.** run **C.** cried **D.** observed

_____ **6. A.** answers **B.** size **C.** day **D.** park

A giant toad finds ___7___ in a cool, damp place. At night the toad comes out. It needs food for its huge ___8___. The toad eats as many insects as it can find.

_____ **7. A.** cows **B.** magic **C.** money **D.** shelter

_____ **8. A.** leg **B.** appetite **C.** suit **D.** rule

A man used an airplane to cover his gas __9__. He hoped people would then stop to buy gas. He bought a B-17 airplane. It took three big machines to __10__ the plane onto poles. Then he put lights under the wings. People could look up at the plane while they filled their cars up with gas.

______ **9.** **A.** well **B.** hole **C.** tank **D.** station

______ **10.** **A.** fly **B.** elevate **C.** begin **D.** drive

---

Turtles __11__ to be very slow animals. Many turtles are really very __12__. Sea turtles can swim quickly. The green turtle can swim as fast as 20 miles per hour for a short time.

______ **11.** **A.** appear **B.** alarm **C.** nibble **D.** hide

______ **12.** **A.** young **B.** huge **C.** plain **D.** speedy

---

The moray eel lives in warm ocean waters. It is a strong fish with very sharp teeth. The eel hides in a hole or cave. It can catch fish with __13__ speed. The moray eel will not __14__ out from its hole to look for food until it is night.

______ **13.** **A.** brave **B.** dry **C.** lightning **D.** half

______ **14.** **A.** blink **B.** venture **C.** list **D.** roll

---

Some people think Lincoln wrote the Gettysburg Address on a __15__ of paper. This is __16__. He wrote it carefully on a whole sheet of paper. He changed the words four times. Every time he changed the words, he copied it over again.

______ **15.** **A.** letter **B.** scrap
C. ship **D.** chain

______ **16.** **A.** incorrect **B.** sad
C. large **D.** useful

LESSON 3

Totem poles are tall wooden poles with animals painted on them. The animals look ___1___. Parts of them look like people. One part of each animal sticks out. Bears have huge claws. Beavers have long front teeth. Crows have long, straight ___2___.

______ **1.** **A.** better **B.** unreal **C.** orange **D.** unhappy

______ **2.** **A.** noses **B.** arms **C.** buttons **D.** beaks

---

The first Ferris wheel was taller than a building 20 stories high. George Ferris made the giant wheel ride for the 1893 World's Fair. It had 36 cars. It held many ___3___. At the top of the wheel, everyone could see for ___4___.

______ **3.** **A.** passengers **B.** puppets **C.** rulers **D.** balls

______ **4.** **A.** glasses **B.** animals **C.** miles **D.** hours

---

The numbat has sharp claws on its front feet. The numbat uses these to tear open ___5___ logs. Then it puts its long, sticky ___6___ inside to catch termites. A numbat eats only termites.

______ **5.** **A.** yellow **B.** square **C.** red **D.** rotten

______ **6.** **A.** brain **B.** tongue **C.** fin **D.** eye

---

There is gold in ocean water. The ___7___ is getting it out. Since the gold there is ___8___, taking it out of the ocean costs a lot of money. Maybe one day someone will find an easy way to do it.

______ **7.** **A.** bank **B.** team **C.** number **D.** problem

______ **8.** **A.** scarce **B.** light **C.** free **D.** nickel

Harriet Tubman was a slave who escaped to ___9___ in the North. She worried about the slaves still in the South, so she returned many times. Each time, she helped slaves escape. A huge ___10___ was offered to anyone who caught her. No one ever did.

______ **9. A.** nowhere **B.** rains **C.** us **D.** freedom

______ **10. A.** reward **B.** trunk **C.** cave **D.** seal

---

In the spring some fish leave the ___11___ where they live. They swim ___12___ in rivers to ponds where they were born. These fish can find their way even when their eyes are covered. They get lost if their noses are covered. The fish use their noses to find their way!

______ **11. A.** ocean **B.** valley **C.** basket **D.** leaf

______ **12. A.** everywhere **B.** hardly **C.** upstream **D.** here

---

Smog is usually a mix of smoke and fog. It can also come from the sun acting on ___13___ in the air. Smog can ___14___ a person's health and kill plant life. Smog can be very thick, making it hard to see things.

______ **13. A.** stars **B.** fumes **C.** pals **D.** pens

______ **14. A.** fix **B.** save **C.** give **D.** damage

Puffins are birds that live on northern coasts. ___15___ of puffins stay at sea most of the time. They swim and dive to catch fish. They come on land to nest on high ___16___.

______ **15. A.** Pans **B.** Friends **C.** Flocks **D.** Barns

______ **16. A.** cliffs **B.** seas **C.** nets **D.** pits

LESSON 4

Peanut butter was first made by George Washington Carver. He also ___1___ many other ways to use peanuts. Carver wanted to help farmers. He hoped they could make money raising peanuts. His wish came true. Farmers started making money. Kids started ___2___ peanut butter!

______ **1.** **A.** carried **B.** discovered **C.** filled **D.** raked

______ **2.** **A.** enjoying **B.** losing **C.** wearing **D.** drinking

---

In Florida it's too warm for snow. One year people there had a Snow Day. They got a snow machine. The machine made a snow pile that was two ___3___ high. The people had so much fun they ___4___ to have a Snow Day every year.

______ **3.** **A.** plants **B.** heads **C.** books **D.** stories

______ **4.** **A.** decided **B.** believed **C.** blinked **D.** drove

---

Dark ___5___ on the Sun are called sunspots. They look dark because they are cooler than the rest of the Sun. Large spots may take weeks to fade away, while small ones ___6___ in just hours.

______ **5.** **A.** patches **B.** dust **C.** kits **D.** leaves

______ **6.** **A.** remember **B.** swim **C.** vanish **D.** use

---

Water lilies grow year after year. Their roots ___7___ to the bottom of a lake or stream. Their large leaves float. Strong stems hold the flowers above water. Some water lilies bloom during the day. Others bloom ___8___ at night.

______ **7.** **A.** see **B.** cling **C.** thaw **D.** pierce

______ **8.** **A.** loudly **B.** solely **C.** wisely **D.** barely

You may think of beavers as the ___9___ of the animal world. Beavers have strong front teeth. They cut down many trees. They use the branches to build ___10___ for homes in the water. Beavers use the bark for food.

______ 9. A. keepers B. lumberjacks C. pilots D. knights

______10. A. lodges B. pillows C. motors D. porches

The elf owl is most often found in dry areas of the country. It sits still in its nest during the day. Then the owl flies out to feed at ___11___. It uses its ___12___ senses to find food.

______11. A. market B. sundown C. breakfast D. feather

______12. A. flat B. outside C. fat D. keen

BOLD is a group that helps people who are blind learn to ski. The helpers tell how the ski trail looks. They follow the skiers. They say when to turn. They teach other skiing ___13___. The blind people ski on the same trails as ___14___ else.

______13. A. skills B. fiddles C. hairs D. stairs

______14. A. all B. somebody C. everyone D. someone

The king or queen of England owns the crown jewels. These ___15___ include crowns, rings, bracelets, ___16___, and swords. They are kept safe in the Tower of London.

______15. A. treasures B. monkeys C. carts D. trails

______16. A. tribes B. doors C. thoughts D. necklaces

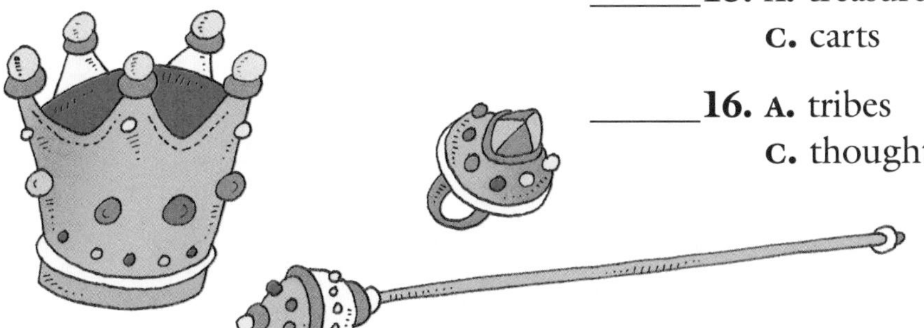

LESSON 5

Larry Nyce builds tiny railroads. He makes the trains himself instead of **purchasing** them from a store. He lays the tracks on tiny wooden railroad ties. He makes tiny trees from sticks and little mountains from rocks.

______ **1.** In this paragraph, the word **purchasing** means

A. selling   **C.** buying
B. riding   **D.** carrying

One kind of lizard changes colors to match the thing it is standing on. These lizards can be green like leaves. They can be brown like tree bark. If you put one on an apple, the lizard will not turn **scarlet**. It can match only the colors in its outdoor home.

______ **2.** In this paragraph, the word **scarlet** means

A. shiny   **C.** red
B. spotted   **D.** juicy

The Inca people lived 500 years ago. Today some people remember the old Incan ways by dressing in Incan **costumes**. They wear hats with feathers on top and gold chains hanging down.

______ **3.** In this paragraph, the word **costumes** means

A. clothes   **C.** kings
B. parades   **D.** faces

The polar bear is a large bear with white fur. The polar bear's color helps it. The white fur blends with the white snow. The bear can **sneak** up on a seal without being seen.

______ **4.** In this paragraph, the word **sneak** means

A. spill   **C.** arrange
B. creep   **D.** hang

Running is fun. Some people like to run against each other. Most people **prefer** to run against themselves. They may try to run more and more miles each day, or they may try to run for longer and longer times.

______ **5.** In this paragraph, the word **prefer** means

A. help	**C.** measure
B. shop	**D.** like

Many animals live in shell houses, but they get their shells in different ways. A turtle's shell is really part of its skeleton. It wears its bones on the outside. A **clam** has no bones. It makes its shell from salt in the ocean.

______ **6.** In this paragraph, the word **clam** means

A. shark	**C.** small land animal
B. fish	**D.** kind of sea animal

Babe Ruth was the home-run king for a long time. He hit a record 714 home runs. Ruth played his last game in 1935. Then he **retired**. It took almost 40 years for someone to break his record.

______ **7.** In this paragraph, the word **retired** means

A. quit work	**C.** went to sleep
B. played songs	**D.** forgot something

There are giant ships more than 700 feet long. These ships were built to carry tons of wheat from place to place. They have a road folded up in back. When they get to shore, the road unfolds. The **cargo** is moved on and off.

______ **8.** In this paragraph, the word **cargo** means

A. truck	**C.** load
B. garbage	**D.** flower

Lesson 6

Sherlock Holmes is a great detective, but he lives only in books. The **tales** about him have been written in 57 languages.

______ **1.** In this paragraph, the word **tales** means

A. places **C.** stories
B. names **D.** pens

The most important part of a running shoe is the part under your foot. This bottom part must be thick and soft. That is so it will **cushion** your foot as you run. A good shoe can keep you running well for a long time.

______ **2.** In this paragraph, the word **cushion** means

A. bring **C.** protect
B. tie **D.** enter

Birds **perch** on a tree even while they sleep. Their toes grab the branch so they don't fall. Three toes point forward. One toe points backward. The toes lock tightly onto the branch.

______ **3.** In this paragraph, the word **perch** means

A. fly **C.** vanish
B. sit **D.** promise

Doctors studied thousands of people. Some of the people spent most of their time alone. Many of these people had weak hearts. They were more likely to have a heart attack. Other people spent much time with their families and friends. Most of these **social** people had strong hearts.

______ **4.** In this paragraph, the word **social** means

A. lonely **C.** strange
B. friendly **D.** sick

Car builders might make a new kind of car. The car will have a kind of **vision**. It will warn you if something is in your way. The car will be able to see a small child. It will be able to see a wall that is too close when you are parking.

______ **5.** In this paragraph, the word **vision** means

A. smell	**C.** sight
B. light	**D.** window

Sugar **arrived** in Europe hundreds of years ago. Traders brought it from the East. At first people used sugar as medicine. It was many years before people used sugar to make desserts.

______ **6.** In this paragraph, the word **arrived** means

A. read	**C.** nodded
B. appeared	**D.** tested

Tears are good for your eyes. They wash away dirt and help keep germs out of your eyes. Tears **bathe** your eyes all the time to keep them from getting too dry.

______ **7.** In this paragraph, the word **bathe** means

A. wash	**C.** kiss
B. dry	**D.** lift

The armadillo can swim across a river. It **gulps** air into its stomach to make it float. Then it just paddles toward the other side!

______ **8.** In this paragraph, the word **gulps** means

A. heats	**C.** shakes
B. plows	**D.** swallows

LESSON 7

Ferns are plants without flowers. Most ferns live in **mild** climates, but some ferns can grow in cold places.

______ **1.** In this paragraph, the word **mild** means

A. warm **C.** noisy
B. cheerful **D.** sour

A man wanted to be the first to see a desert that had never been explored. He bought two camels and set out. The trip took 19 days. He got lost and ran out of water. He was **exhausted** from walking in the heat. He lost 60 pounds, but he finally made it!

______ **2.** In this paragraph, the word **exhausted** means

A. very shy **C.** very afraid
B. very tired **D.** very ready

Some jungle animals travel by air. They may look as if they are flying, but they're not. They're gliding. They leap from a high branch and **descend** to a lower branch.

______ **3.** In this paragraph, the word **descend** means

A. go down **C.** jump up
B. fly by **D.** cross over

The tiger cat lives in Australia. It runs fast and also climbs trees well. The tiger cat looks for small animals at night. This cat hunts **restlessly** until it catches its dinner.

______ **4.** In this paragraph, the word **restlessly** means

A. in cities **C.** while sleeping
B. under water **D.** without stopping

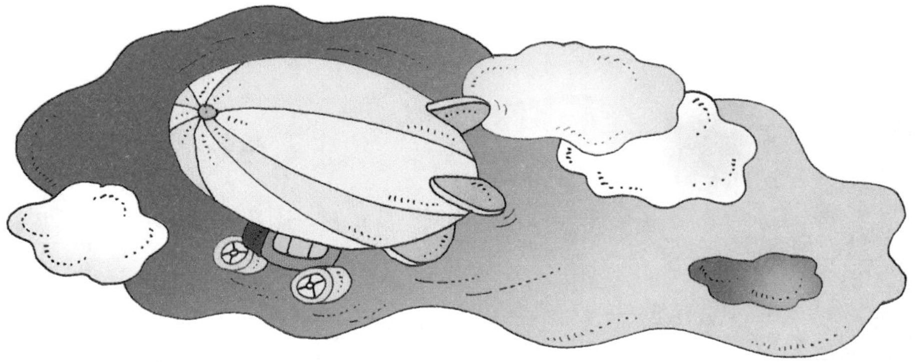

A blimp is a small airship. It doesn't have a metal frame to give it shape. But a blimp does have a strong bag that is filled with gas. The gas makes the blimp float. When the gas is taken out, the blimp **collapses**.

______ **5.** In this paragraph, the word **collapses** means

A. falls down **C.** flies off
B. works out **D.** takes over

Trees are important. Their roots help hold soil in place and keep it from being washed away by rains. Tree roots also help hold **moisture** in the ground and keep it from drying out.

______ **6.** In this paragraph, the word **moisture** means

A. cloth **C.** dampness
B. morning **D.** safety

There is a huge copper mine in Utah. The mine is an open pit. It is about $1/2$ mile deep and more than 2 miles wide at the top. This mine has **yielded** more copper than any other mine.

______ **7.** In this paragraph, the word **yielded** means

A. bowed **C.** stretched
B. supplied **D.** divided

Baby geese are called goslings. The mother goose does not have to teach them how to behave like geese. The goslings can swim and dive without **instruction**.

______ **8.** In this paragraph, the word **instruction** means

A. frogs **C.** crowns
B. books **D.** lessons

Lesson 8

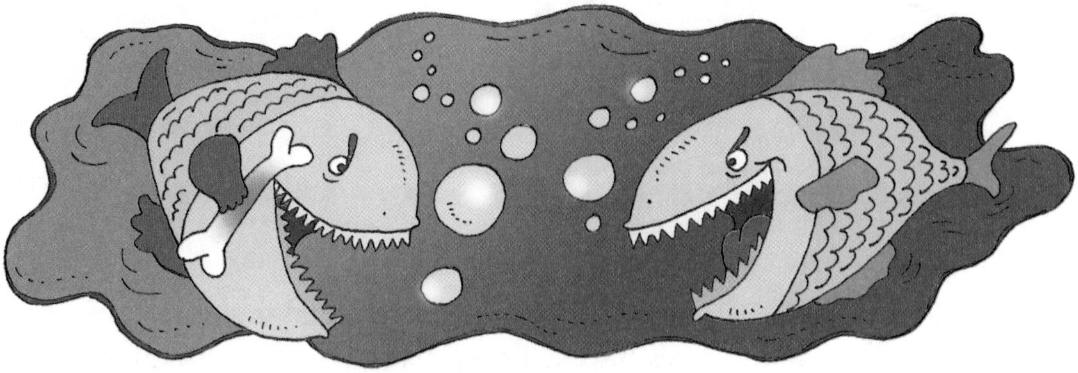

Piranhas are fish. They live in South American rivers. These fish tend to swim in large groups. They will tear the flesh off an animal or person that gets in the water. In just minutes all that is left is the **skeleton**.

______ **1.** In this paragraph, the word **skeleton** means

A. key **C.** butter
B. pie **D.** bones

A cartoon is a **humorous** way to tell a story or make a point. A cartoon can be one drawing or a set of drawings. A cartoon may have words with the picture, but words aren't always needed.

______ **2.** In this paragraph, the word **humorous** means

A. cozy **C.** dangerous
B. funny **D.** thirsty

Usually Pluto is the planet farthest from the Sun. Not much is known about this **distant** planet. It is quite cold there since it is so far from the Sun. Scientists don't think that there is any life on Pluto.

______ **3.** In this paragraph, the word **distant** means

A. faraway **C.** lucky
B. nearby **D.** pleasant

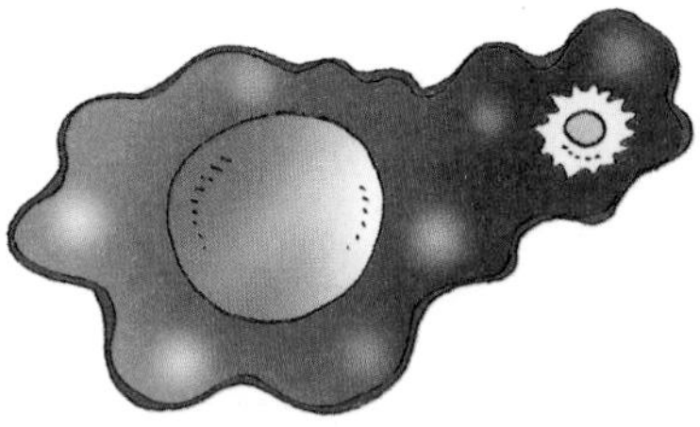

Long ago, **vessels** crossed the water from northern Europe to other countries. They carried Viking warriors. At first the Vikings fought with people. Then the Vikings decided to trade. They set up many new trade centers.

______ **4.** In this paragraph, the word **vessels** means

A. whales **C.** ships
B. bottles **D.** horses

The bluebonnet is one flower that really helps bees. A bluebonnet has a white spot on it. After a bee has visited this flower and taken nectar, the white spot turns red. The other bees don't waste time. They know they will be **disappointed** if they go to the blue flowers with red spots.

______ **5.** In this paragraph, the word **disappointed** means

A. pretty **C.** large
B. hot **D.** sorry

The Negev Desert covers half of Israel. The soil in this desert is **fertile**. People can grow crops there. They use water from a nearby sea. Special hoses spray water on the crops.

______ **6.** In this paragraph, the word **fertile** means

A. rich **C.** greedy
B. glad **D.** sharp

The Aztecs lived long ago. They were a great tribe. They built a **glorious** city. Now this city is known as Mexico City.

______ **7.** In this paragraph, the word **glorious** means

A. foolish **C.** corner
B. grand **D.** helpless

Plants can be grown without soil. They grow in special water. The water has everything that plants need to grow. This **style** of farming is called hydroponics. It can be used in space.

______ **8.** In this paragraph, the word **style** means

A. center **C.** rush
B. garden **D.** type

Writing Roundup

Read each paragraph. Write a word that makes sense on each line.

Sara got out the water hose and bucket and gave her dog Dusty a bath. Dusty did not like to be (1) ________________. As soon as his bath was over, he rolled in the (2) ________________.

Our family likes to go camping. It's fun to sit outside the tent at night and look up at the (3) ________________. I wish we could go camping every (4) ________________.

A new boy came to our (5) ________________ today. We wanted to be friendly, so we asked him to (6) ________________ with us.

Read each paragraph. Complete each sentence with a word or words that make sense in the paragraph.

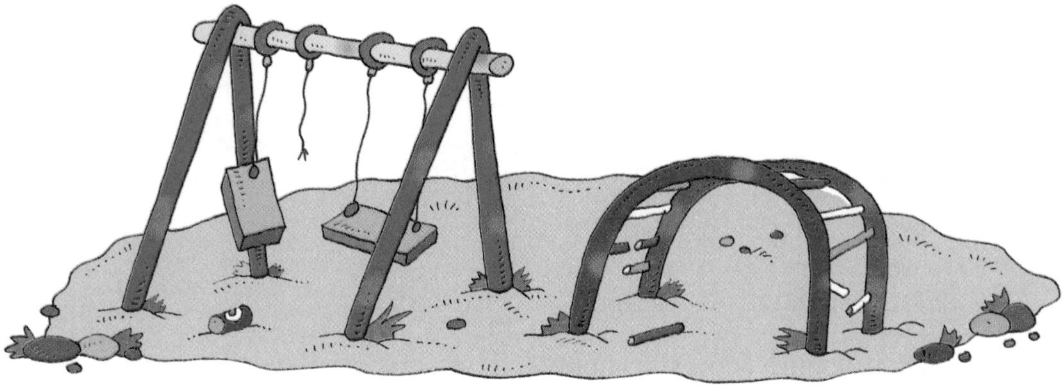

One corner of the school playground did not look pretty. Mr. Jackson's class wanted to make it look better. At first they thought about

(1) ____________________________________.

Then they talked to **(2)** ____________________

____________________________________.

Now they knew they would **(3)** ______________

____________________________________.

Jamal went shopping for a gift for his mother. First he went to **(4)** ____________________

____________________________________.

Nothing that he found seemed just right. Then he saw **(5)** ____________________________.

"I know!" he cried. "I'll get her **(6)** __________

____________________________________!"

unit 4

What Is a Main Idea?

The main idea of a story tells what it is about. The other sentences add details to the main idea. Often the main idea is stated in the first or last sentence of the paragraph. Sometimes you may find the main idea in the middle of the paragraph.

This example may help you think about main ideas:

5	+	6	+	7	=	18
detail	+	detail	+	detail	=	main idea

The *5*, *6*, and *7* are like details. They are smaller than their sum, *18*. The *18*, like a main idea, is bigger. It is made of several smaller parts.

Try It!

Read the story below. Draw a line under the main idea.

Jazz is an American form of music. Jazz was first based on the work songs of slaves. It began in the South and spread to other parts of the country.

The main idea sentence is the first sentence in the story. All the other sentences are details. They give more facts about jazz.

The main idea could come at the end of the story:

Jazz was first based on the work songs of slaves. It began in the South and spread to other parts of the country. Jazz is an American form of music.

Practice Finding the Main Idea

This unit asks you to find main ideas. Read the story and answer the question below.

There are more than 3,000 kinds of frogs. The grass frog is so small it can sit on an acorn. The goliath frog of West Africa is the largest frog in the world. It is the size of a cat. The water-holding frog uses the skin it has shed to make a bag around itself. This bag holds in water and keeps the frog cool.

__C__ **1.** The story mainly tells
- **A.** about the goliath frog
- **B.** about a tiny frog
- **C.** that there are many kinds of frogs
- **D.** about the water-holding frog

The correct answer is **C**. The story includes details about three kinds of frogs. These details support the first sentence.

Sometimes a story does not have a main idea sentence. You can figure out the main idea by reading the details. Read the story below.

The Sahara is a desert found in North Africa. The desert gets from 5 to 10 inches of rain per year. Sometimes there are dry periods that last for years. It may reach 135 degrees during the day.

______ **2.** The story mainly tells
- **A.** how hot the Sahara is
- **B.** facts about the Sahara
- **C.** where the Sahara is found
- **D.** how much rainfall the Sahara gets

Lesson 1

Read each passage. After each passage you will answer a question about the main idea of the passage. Remember, the main idea is the main point in a story.

1. An iguana is part of the lizard family. Marine iguanas are strange lizards. They are called diving dragons. They jump off rocks and dive into the water to find food. Now scientists have found an amazing fact about marine iguanas. Some can make themselves shrink when food is hard to find! When their food supply returns, they grow back to normal size.

_____ **1.** The story mainly tells
- **A.** why marine iguanas are strange lizards
- **B.** what a diving dragon eats
- **C.** how iguanas shrink
- **D.** how an iguana finds food

---

2. Buttons are useful. At first buttons were used only as ornaments. Once, a king of France had a coat with thousands of gold buttons sewn on it. Then someone had a new thought. Why not make a slit in cloth and push a button through it? Buttons began to hold pants up and keep shirts closed. Some buttons are tiny works of art. Collectors search for them.

_____ **2.** The story mainly tells
- **A.** that buttons are useful
- **B.** where gold buttons were sewn
- **C.** how shirts stay closed
- **D.** what collectors search for

3. Horse shows are the place to see beautiful horses. The riders and horses get scores for each event. First all the riders walk their horses around the ring. Then they trot the horses, making them go faster and faster. Finally they gallop. When they jump over logs or ponds, the riders must not fall. The best riders and horses get ribbons and prizes.

______ **3.** The story mainly tells

- **A.** which kinds of horses jump the highest
- **B.** who gets prizes for galloping
- **C.** what horses and riders do in horse shows
- **D.** how the horses jump fences

---

4. Many people are afraid of flying in airplanes. Sometimes they're so afraid that they get sick. This is a problem. These people can never visit friends who live far away. Doctors have started classes that teach people about planes. The people practice flying in planes. Many people have learned to get over their fear of flying this way!

______ **4.** The story mainly tells

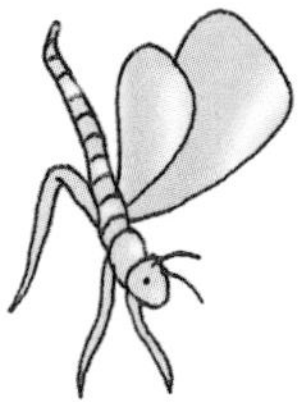

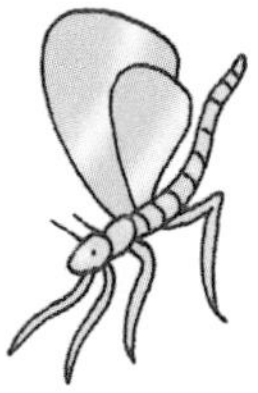

- **A.** why people are afraid of the dark
- **B.** how people learn to get over their fear of flying
- **C.** why people are afraid of flying
- **D.** how these people learn to fly airplanes

---

5. Mayflies are insects. They begin life underwater. As they grow older, mayflies leave the water and grow wings. When their wings are strong, they fly with thousands of other mayflies near the water. You can often see them by ponds. They look like a dark cloud hanging over the water.

______ **5.** The story mainly tells

- **A.** why mayflies have no wings
- **B.** what looks like a cloud
- **C.** about the life of mayflies
- **D.** how mayflies grow on land

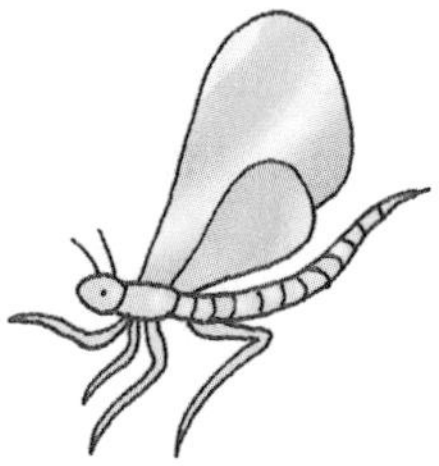

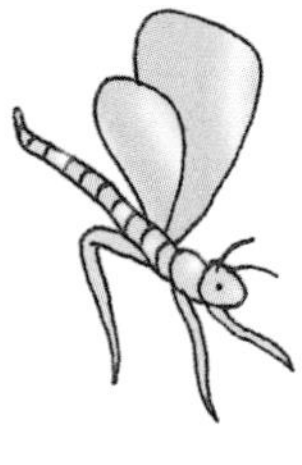

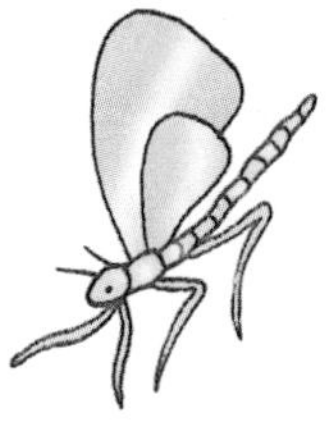

Lesson 2

1. Kings and queens had the earliest zoos. They wanted to show off their money by keeping strange animals. Later, people kept animals in zoos because they wanted to learn about them. Students could take classes at the zoo. Today zoos try to help certain animals. These animals are disappearing from their wild homes. Zoos help keep these animals safe.

______ **1.** The story mainly tells

A. how rulers showed off their money
B. which people learned about zoo animals
C. how zoos have changed over the years
D. how animals will never disappear

---

2. Some butterflies lay their eggs on just one kind of plant. By tasting the plant, they know which one is right. Sometimes butterflies taste the wrong plant, so they fly to another plant and taste again. When they find the right plant, they lay their eggs there. Soon the eggs hatch. The hungry babies eat the plant their mother chose!

______ **2.** The story mainly tells

A. when baby butterflies come out of eggs
B. how butterflies choose where to lay eggs
C. what flies from one plant to another
D. how butterflies always taste the right plant

---

3. Airplanes have changed our lives. Long ago, people traveled in ships. They spent weeks or even months getting from one country to another. Today airplanes carry people halfway around the world in 15 hours. So we spend less time going places and more time doing things.

______ **3.** The story mainly tells

A. how small the world was long ago
B. how fast ships sailed around the world
C. how airplanes changed our lives
D. how people still travel on ships

4. A man in Florida can talk to fish. He spent a long time learning how to do this. First he watched fish very closely. Then he listened to the noises they made. Finally he learned to make the same sounds. Sometimes the fish listen to him. At times he can even make them do things. This man thinks that someday fishermen might be able to call fish to their nets.

______ **4.** The story mainly tells

- **A.** why fish listen to sounds
- **B.** who likes to fish
- **C.** how a man talks to fish
- **D.** how the fish never listen to this man

---

5. John Chapman planted apple trees in Ohio in the early 1800s. He carried the seeds all over the country. He sold the seeds or just gave them away to people. Chapman was a very kind man. He loved people, animals, and trees. The story of Johnny Appleseed is the story of his life.

______ **5.** The story mainly tells

- **A.** how apple trees grow from seeds
- **B.** where we get the story of Johnny Appleseed
- **C.** when Chapman lived in Ohio
- **D.** how Chapman traveled the country

Lesson 3

1. Back in the 1700s, people often ate with their fingers. In England, the fourth Earl of Sandwich liked to keep his hands clean. One day he asked to have his food placed between two slices of bread. The sandwich was born. It was a great idea. Without it, lunches might be different today. We could be spreading our peanut butter and jelly on broccoli!

______ **1.** The story mainly tells
- **A.** how the sandwich was born
- **B.** how people used to eat
- **C.** why lunches might be different
- **D.** where to put peanut butter

---

2. The first dollhouses were built for grown-ups. These houses were as tall as people. They were also filled with pretty things. Rich people made these dollhouses look like their own homes. Only later did they build smaller dollhouses for children. Some of these are still around. They help us learn what real houses looked like long ago.

______ **2.** The story mainly tells
- **A.** when people made dollhouses for children
- **B.** which dollhouses were the tallest
- **C.** what the first dollhouses were like
- **D.** which people didn't build dollhouses

3. Mother ducks take baby ducks away from each other. This is the way it happens. The mother ducks take their babies swimming. Soon the pond is full of ducks. The mother ducks quack. They swim around the baby ducks. The mother duck that quacks loudest gets the greatest number of babies. Some mother ducks may have 40 baby ducks. Others may have only two or three.

______ **3.** The story mainly tells

- A. which duck quacks the loudest
- B. how mother ducks take babies away
- C. when the ducks go swimming
- D. how baby ducks choose their mother

---

4. Cats are very much like lions and tigers. They can jump high in the air. Cats can jump 7 feet straight up. They have padded feet. That way they can sneak up on their prey. Cats have 18 claws on their feet. They can push out and draw back their claws.

______ **4.** The story mainly tells

- A. how a cat looks
- B. about special things that a cat can do
- C. how high a cat can jump
- D. why a cat is a better pet than a dog

5. Aardvarks are strange animals. They have short stumpy legs and huge donkey ears. Termites are their favorite feast. Aardvarks break open the termites' mounds with their strong claws. Humans would have to use a pickax to break these mounds. Soldier termites try to save the mound by biting the aardvarks, but it is useless. Aardvarks' stiff hair and tough skin help keep them safe.

______ **5.** The story mainly tells

- A. why aardvarks are strange animals
- B. what aardvarks eat
- C. why soldier termites bite
- D. about aardvarks' stiff hair

Lesson 4

1. Children learn their first lessons in banking when they use piggy banks. Children put pennies in their banks and wait for the number of pennies to grow. The money is safe there. When the bank is full, the child can buy something with the money. In the same way, children's parents put their money in a real bank. It's safe there. They can add more money every month. Later they can use it to buy the things they need.

______ **1.** The story mainly tells
- **A.** how children spend their money
- **B.** how a piggy bank is a lesson in banking
- **C.** when grown people put money in a bank
- **D.** why grown people don't use piggy banks

---

2. Zoo elephants get very good care. Each morning zookeepers give them a special bath. They wash the elephants with water and a brush. Then they paint oil on their skin and rub oil on their feet. This is very important in elephant care. It helps the elephants stay healthy.

______ **2.** The story mainly tells
- **A.** why zookeepers have happy lives
- **B.** who paints oil on elephants
- **C.** how zookeepers give elephants special care
- **D.** how much elephants eat

---

3. Not long ago, people raised their own chickens. They fed the chickens leftover food. They also gathered fresh eggs every day. Every morning the roosters awakened everybody. Sometimes the family cooked a chicken for dinner. Today life has changed. Most people buy chickens and eggs at stores. They have clocks to wake them.

______ **3.** The story mainly tells
- **A.** that people once raised chickens
- **B.** why chickens give fresh eggs
- **C.** when the family cooked a chicken
- **D.** where the chicken pens were found

4. All winter long bears do nothing but sleep. To get ready for their winter sleep, they eat. They eat much food to get fat. The fat will become food their bodies will use while they sleep. Bears choose sleeping places such as caves. They might also choose a hollow log or even a big pile of brush. If it gets warm on a winter day, the bears may come out to walk around. They don't stay out long. Only in the spring do they finally get up and look for food.

______ **4.** The story mainly tells

- **A.** what kind of life a bear leads
- **B.** who likes caves for sleeping
- **C.** where bears sleep in the summer
- **D.** why bears love honey

---

5. Many farmers today grow fields of yellow sunflowers. People have many uses for sunflower seeds. After the seeds are dried and salted, people buy them to eat. Some sunflower seeds are pressed to make cooking oil. Some seeds are also ground to make a kind of butter.

______ **5.** The story mainly tells

- **A.** why people eat salty seeds
- **B.** how sunflower seeds are of great value
- **C.** who uses cooking oil
- **D.** who likes sunflower butter

Lesson 5

1. A new thread is being made from seashells. This thread is very strong. Doctors can use it to fix cuts in people's skin. The thread helps bring the cut skin back together. Also, it never has to be taken out. After some time the thread becomes part of the body.

______ **1.** The story mainly tells

- **A.** why thread made of seashells is used to fix cuts
- **B.** how thread is made into cloth
- **C.** how cuts in the skin get well
- **D.** how doctors take out the thread

---

2. Neil Armstrong was an astronaut. In 1969, he did something no one else had done before. He set foot on the Moon. He said, "That's one small step for a man, one giant leap for mankind." Edwin Aldrin followed Armstrong. They placed an American flag on the Moon.

______ **2.** The story mainly tells

- **A.** what Neil Armstrong said on the Moon
- **B.** who first walked on the Moon
- **C.** how Armstrong and Aldrin reached the Moon
- **D.** what clothing Armstrong wore on the Moon

3. Baseball players have to step up to get onto the field. They must step down when their side is out. Their dugouts are built half below the ground. They are made like that for good reasons. If dugouts were tall, the fans who sit behind them could not see the game. Lower dugouts would be a problem for the players. They would need a stepladder to see the game.

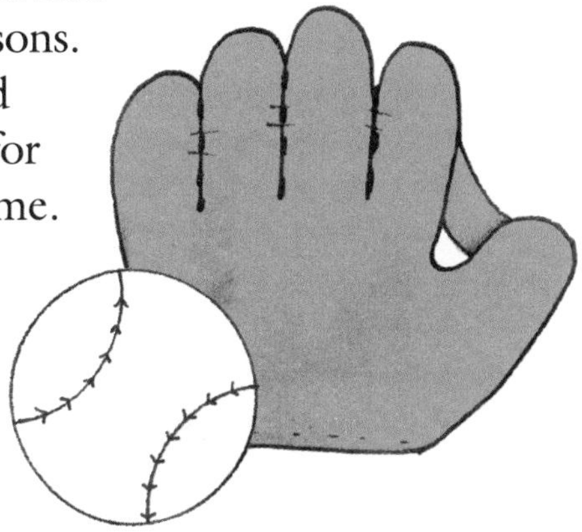

______ **3.** The story mainly tells

A. where baseball players sit
B. when baseball players must step down
C. why dugouts are built the way they are
D. who needs a stepladder

---

4. We all know that babies make funny sounds. Little by little, babies learn that some sounds will call their mother and father. Other sounds will get them food. Yet some sounds will bring them nothing at all. Babies learn to talk by finding out which sounds work best.

______ **4.** The story mainly tells

A. which babies make the loudest noises
B. how babies learn to talk
C. when babies first start to make noise
D. how babies aren't smart

---

5. Centipedes are not insects, but they look like insects. They are long animals with short legs. *Centipede* means "hundred feet," but centipedes have 350 legs! Millipedes also have many legs. *Millipede* means "thousand feet," but they have about 700 legs!

______ **5.** The story mainly tells

A. how many legs centipedes and millipedes have
B. what kind of animal a centipede is
C. that centipedes have one hundred legs
D. that millipedes have one thousand legs

Lesson 6

1. The bee hummingbird is the size of a bee. This bird is 2 1/2 inches long. It weighs the same as a lump of sugar. It has a long beak. This tiny bird lives in Cuba.

______ **1.** The story mainly tells
- **A.** about a kind of bee
- **B.** how a hummingbird is like a bee
- **C.** about the smallest insect
- **D.** about the bee hummingbird

---

2. One kind of spider makes a web underwater. It weaves its web in water plants. Then it carries bubbles of air down to fill the web. The water spider lies still on its web. Soon a water insect swims near it. The spider dashes out and catches the insect. It brings its catch back to the air-filled web to eat.

______ **2.** The story mainly tells
- **A.** what a water spider looks like
- **B.** how a water spider builds its web
- **C.** what the spider does with water insects
- **D.** how one kind of spider lives under the water

---

3. A fly has six feet. Each foot has a plump little pad on the bottom. The pads flatten out when the fly walks on a smooth surface. They give off a sticky liquid that holds the fly to the wall or the ceiling. The liquid acts like glue so that the fly doesn't fall.

______ **3.** The story mainly tells
- **A.** how many legs a fly has
- **B.** about the fly's special feet
- **C.** how flies make glue
- **D.** about different types of flies

4. One day Frank Baum was telling a story to some children. He told about a girl named Dorothy. She was swept from her home to a strange land. It was a magical place. One of the children asked Baum about the name of the strange land. He looked around the room. He saw a filing cabinet. One drawer was labeled A–G. The next was labeled H–N. The last drawer was O–Z. He looked at the last drawer and named the land Oz. Baum later wrote the book *The Wonderful Wizard of Oz.*

______ **4.** This story mainly tells
- **A.** how Baum named the land of Oz
- **B.** where Dorothy lived
- **C.** how Baum named Dorothy
- **D.** when Baum wrote *The Wonderful Wizard of Oz*

---

5. A chameleon is a kind of lizard. Its skin is clear, but it can change color. Under its skin are layers of cells. These cells have yellow, black, and red color in them. Anger makes these colors darken. Fear makes them lighten. Fear also makes yellow spots appear. Temperature and light can also cause these colors to change. These changes make the chameleon hard to see, because chameleons change to blend with their surroundings. Changing colors can save a chameleon's life.

______ **5.** The story mainly tells
- **A.** that a chameleon has clear skin
- **B.** how a chameleon's skin can change color
- **C.** where chameleons live
- **D.** that sometimes a chameleon has yellow spots

Lesson 7

1. Sometimes deep in the ocean, an earthquake shakes the ocean floor. The movement starts a tidal wave. At first the wave is small. But it can move toward the shore at a speed of up to 500 miles per hour. It makes a huge wave as it reaches the coast. The tidal wave hits the land with great force. It can destroy everything in its path.

______ **1.** The story mainly tells

- **A.** that earthquakes happen on the ocean floor
- **B.** how fast a tidal wave moves
- **C.** another name for a tidal wave
- **D.** how a tidal wave is formed

2. Camels have one or two humps on their backs. The humps are made of fat. The fat stores energy. When there isn't much food, the camel lives off the energy from its humps.

______ **2.** The story mainly tells

- **A.** about the humps of camels
- **B.** how many humps a camel has
- **C.** how much fat is in a camel's humps
- **D.** how heavy a camel's humps can be

3. A person who sews clothes is a tailor. One kind of bird is good at sewing. This bird is called the tailor bird. It sews a nest for itself. The tailor bird uses its beak to punch holes in the edges of leaves. Then it threads a piece of spiderweb through the holes. It pulls the leaves together and knots the thread. This makes a cup-shaped nest. The tailor bird lines the nest with cotton or grass.

______ **3.** The story mainly tells
- **A.** why this bird is called a tailor bird
- **B.** how the tailor bird lines its nest
- **C.** what a tailor bird's nest is called
- **D.** where the tailor bird is found

---

4. Pumice is a rock that can float on water. Pumice is not solid. It has bubbles of air inside. Pumice is formed from lava. Lava is the liquid rock that pours from a volcano. The lava bubbles and then cools to form pumice.

______ **4.** The story mainly tells
- **A.** what lava is
- **B.** how pumice is used
- **C.** why pumice can float
- **D.** how pumice looks

---

5. Pigskin is very sensitive. It sunburns very easily. This is why pigs don't lie in the sun. They lie in the shade. They roll around in the mud to cover their skin from the sun.

______ **5.** The story mainly tells
- **A.** how pigs keep from getting sunburned
- **B.** what pigs do in the sun
- **C.** where pigs live
- **D.** how pigskin is made

Lesson 8

1. Louis XIV, king of France, was a short man. He wanted to look taller, so he ordered high heels for his shoes. Then he had his shoes trimmed with lace, bows, and jewels. One pair of shoes had bows that were 16 inches wide. He had artists paint scenes on the heels of his shoes. Soon other men in France wore high-heeled shoes with flowers and bows.

______ **1.** The story mainly tells
- **A.** about King Louis XIV's high heels
- **B.** how tall King Louis XIV was
- **C.** how the king painted his heels
- **D.** about shoes that men wear today

---

2. When an io moth is resting, its wings are folded. If the moth sees a hungry bird, it unfolds its wings. The wings have markings called eyespots. Each spot looks like a big eye. The eyespots scare the bird away.

______ **2.** The story mainly tells
- **A.** which animals have eyespots
- **B.** about the size of eyespots
- **C.** how an io moth protects itself
- **D.** about the color of an io moth

---

3. People pick the ripe fruit of the soapberry tree. They cut up the fruit. Then they mix it with cold water from a stream or lake. The fruit fills the water with suds. These suds are used to wash clothes.

______ **3.** The story mainly tells
- **A.** where soapberry trees are found
- **B.** about a natural laundry soap
- **C.** about the many uses of the soapberry tree
- **D.** about washing clothes

4. The Loch Ness monster has been seen many times. It lives in a lake in Scotland called Loch Ness. The waters of Loch Ness are the color of coffee. So no one has been able to take a clear picture of the monster or catch it. The monster is said to be about 20 feet long with a tiny head and a long neck. Its big body has flippers and many humps.

______ **4.** The story mainly tells

- **A.** that the monster does not exist
- **B.** how many people have seen the monster
- **C.** where Loch Ness is located
- **D.** how no one has proved that the monster is real

---

5. Trees are cut down and chopped into tiny chips. The wood chips are cooked in water and chemicals. They make a pulp that looks like oatmeal. The pulp is squeezed until it is very thin and flat. It is dried to make a giant sheet of paper. Paper can also be made from cotton fibers.

______ **5.** The story mainly tells

- **A.** how paper is made
- **B.** what wood pulp is
- **C.** how many trees it takes to make a sheet of paper
- **D.** how cotton fibers are turned into paper

Writing Roundup

Read each story. Think about the main idea. Write the main idea in your own words.

1. Mary Myers liked to go up in balloons. She wanted to be her own pilot. In 1880 she did just that. Her balloon took off from Little Falls, New York. Mary became the first woman balloon pilot. After that many women flew alone in their own balloons.

What is the main idea of this story?

____

____

2. Beto lived in the city. One summer he visited his Uncle Alex on the farm. That summer Beto learned how to ride horses. Now Beto is grown up. He rides horses in races. He is a famous jockey. He says he owes it all to his Uncle Alex.

What is the main idea of this story?

____

____

3. People have learned much about the oceans. They learned through exploring oceans. Oceans are huge, and they are very deep. There is much more to learn. There still are many questions about life in the oceans.

What is the main idea of this story?

____

____

Prewriting

Think of a main idea that you would like to write about, such as visiting a farm, flying in a balloon, or exploring the ocean. Fill in the chart below.

Main Idea

Detail

Detail

Detail

On Your Own

Now use another sheet of paper to write your story. Underline the sentence that tells the main idea.

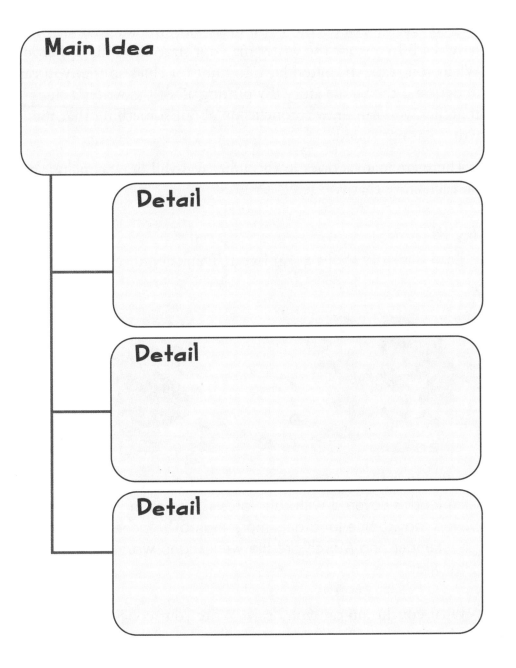

unit 5

What Is a Conclusion?

A conclusion is a decision you make after thinking about what you have read. In a story the writer may not state all of his or her ideas. When you read, you often have to hunt for clues so that you can understand the whole story. By putting all of the writer's clues together, you can draw a conclusion about something that the writer has not stated.

There are many stories in this unit. You will draw conclusions based on each story that you read.

Try It!

Read this story about a rain forest. Think about what it tells you.

The climate around the equator is always warm. Much of the land is covered with rain forests. It rains in these areas every day. Some land gets more than 500 inches per year. September and March are the wettest and warmest times of the year.

What conclusion can you draw? Write your conclusion on the lines.

____

____

You may have written something such as, "It is warm and wet in the rain forests" or "It is never cold in the rain forests." You can draw these conclusions from the paragraph. The first sentence tells about the warm climate around the equator. The second sentence says that it rains every day. From those clues, you can draw these conclusions.

Using What You Know

Let's say that animals can talk. Several animals are describing themselves in the stories below. Hunt for clues that tell which animal is talking. Answer the questions by writing the name of each animal.

I have black-and-white stripes. The horse is my cousin. I live in a herd and like to graze on grass. I live on the huge plains of Africa. When I'm frightened, I run away as fast as I can. I can run 40 miles per hour.

What am I? ______________________________

I'm the largest animal on land. I weigh 250 pounds at birth. I'm gray and have large ears. I'm also one of the smartest animals. I live in a group. If a member of my group gets hurt, I try to help. I eat and drink with my long trunk.

What am I? ______________________________

I'm the tallest animal in the world. I could easily look into your second-story window. My long neck lets me eat the fruit and leaves that no other animal can reach. Lions, cheetahs, and hyenas are my enemies.

What am I? ______________________________

I live in the ocean. The whale is my cousin. I have a long, pointed nose. I'm very intelligent, and I'm friendly to people. In fact, sometimes I even let people ride on my back. I'm playful and like to learn tricks. I'm often trained to perform for crowds.

What am I? ______________________________

Lesson 1

Read each passage. After each passage you will answer a question that will require you to draw a conclusion about the story. Remember, a conclusion is a decision you make after putting together all the clues you are given.

1. Baseball is a big sport in Japan. The rules are the same as those in America, but the customs are different. Players in Japan don't show their anger when they're *out.* They don't try to hurt the player from the other team as the player slides into second base. Also, when the fans clap, the players bow to them.

______ **1.** From this story you can tell that

A. Japanese players do not slide into second base
B. American players show their anger
C. Japanese players can play better
D. Japanese players wave when the fans clap

---

2. The knight in chess is different from the other pieces. The knight is the only piece that can jump over the other ones. This move comes from the days of the knights. Knights traveled far and wide in search of adventure. They traveled off the regular road. There they often met enemies. The knight in chess also does not have a regular move. The knight's move in chess is like the life of the knight of long ago.

______ **2.** From this story you can tell that

A. all chess pieces move in the same way
B. the knight in chess has a regular move
C. chess pieces move in different ways
D. the knight in chess does not move

3. How fast can you run? At top speed a human can run about 20 miles per hour. A snake can travel 2 miles per hour. The fastest mammal is the cheetah. It can run up to 70 miles per hour. A golden eagle can fly 120 miles per hour, and a duck hawk can fly up to 180 miles per hour.

______ **3.** From this story you can tell that
- **A.** eagles fly faster than duck hawks
- **B.** snakes move very fast
- **C.** cheetahs run faster than humans
- **D.** humans are the fastest mammals

---

4. Years ago in England, many people became sick. Nobody knew why. Then a doctor found out that all the sick people lived near each other. He noticed that they all drank water from the same water well. The doctor took the handle off the well pump. People could no longer draw and drink the water. Suddenly they stopped getting sick.

______ **4.** From this story you can tell that
- **A.** everyone in England got sick
- **B.** the doctors at that time were not very smart
- **C.** the water was making the people sick
- **D.** there weren't enough doctors to help the sick

---

5. Long ago, Spanish ships sailed to America. They landed in a warm part of the country. The sun shone brightly there. Flowers bloomed even in the winter. There wasn't any snow. The Spanish people called the land Florida. It is the Spanish word for "blooming." That's how the state got its name.

______ **5.** From this story you can tell that
- **A.** American states can have Spanish names
- **B.** the Spanish people came in the spring
- **C.** *Florida* means "snow" in Spanish
- **D.** the Spanish ships landed in Texas

Lesson 2

1. About 200 years ago, a doctor climbed a mountain in Europe. In those days people never climbed mountains. They did not know what the tops of mountains were like. In fact they thought the doctor would meet many terrible monsters along the way. He came back down, safe and sound. He hadn't seen a single monster. Today many people enjoy the sport of mountain climbing.

______ **1.** From this story you can tell that

A. there are monsters living on mountains
B. there were trees on top of the mountain
C. others began climbing mountains after the doctor returned
D. the doctor was hurt during his climb

2. Ants help keep one tree in South America safe. This tree has thorns that are hollow. The ants live inside the thorns. When animals try to eat the tree's leaves, the ants rush out from the thorns. Hundreds of ants bite the animal. The thorns also stick the animal until it moves away.

______ **2.** From this story you can tell that

A. the tree and the ants need each other
B. ants eat other animals for food
C. the tree in this story is very tall
D. the thorns don't hurt the animals

---

3. Long ago in Europe, there were no police. Instead there were only town watchpersons. A watchperson walked the streets at night. Troublemakers stayed away. A watchperson walked for a length of time called a watch. Then someone else took over the next watch. How did a watchperson know when to stop walking? The watchperson carried a small clock. Today the name of the small clock reminds us of the watchpersons of Europe.

______ **3.** From this story you can tell that

A. a length of time was called a *stretch*
B. the name of the clock is *timer*
C. the name of the clock is *watch*
D. the watchpersons ran races on the streets

4. Baby Dee woke up and started crying loudly. Scott ran to her from the kitchen. He held Dee and talked to her. Scott didn't know why she was crying. He had fed Dee earlier. He checked to see if the baby's clothes were wet. They were dry. Then Scott noticed an open safety pin lying in Dee's bed.

______ **4.** From this story you can tell that

- **A.** the baby was probably very hungry
- **B.** the safety pin probably hurt Dee
- **C.** Scott had to take care of only one child
- **D.** Scott was not a good father

---

5. The largest fish on Earth is the whale shark. This giant shark can grow twice as large as an elephant. The whale shark can weigh up to 12 tons. This shark is big, but it is not harmful to people. It stays alive by eating only small water plants and animals.

______ **5.** The story suggests that the whale shark

- **A.** is larger than an elephant
- **B.** attacks people
- **C.** is smaller than an elephant
- **D.** is not a fish

Lesson 3

1. Many people don't like bugs. Some bugs bite or sting people. Other bugs eat people's plants and fruits. People poison bugs to get rid of them. Now scientists are finding new ways to kill bugs with germs. The germs make the bugs sick, and then they die. Scientists also use some bugs to fight the other bugs. The ladybug is an example. It eats bugs that hurt fruit.

_____ **1.** From this story you can tell that
- **A.** poison is not the only way to get rid of bugs
- **B.** people need to stay away from ladybugs
- **C.** most bugs like to eat fruit trees
- **D.** the germs make the bugs stronger

2. Laughing makes people feel great. Some people think that laughing is the best thing in life. Now scientists have shown that laughing is good for the body too. Laughing makes the heart beat faster. It brings more air into the body. Many people keep fit by running, but laughing is easier on the feet!

_____ **2.** From this story you can tell that
- **A.** laughing is good for your health
- **B.** swimming is very good for your body
- **C.** crying is like laughing
- **D.** laughing makes the heart beat slower

3. Mark Twain was a famous writer. One night he was going to give a talk in a small town. He went to the barbershop to get a shave. The barber asked, "Are you going to hear that famous writer tonight? It's sold out, you know. If you go, you'll have to stand."

"Just my luck," said Twain. "I always have to stand when that man gives a talk!"

______ **3.** From this story you can tell that

- **A.** the barber did not like to hear writers talk
- **B.** the barber wasn't going to the talk
- **C.** the barber didn't know he was shaving Twain
- **D.** the barber only cut hair

---

4. How do people put out forest fires? Machines are used to knock down trees that aren't burning. Other machines remove the fallen trees. This clears some of the land. The fire can't cross this land because there is nothing to burn. The firefighters also start small fires nearby to clear more land. Airplanes help to put out the bigger fires by pouring clay on them.

______ **4.** From this story you can tell that

- **A.** it is easy to stop a big fire
- **B.** clay burns very easily when it gets hot
- **C.** there are many ways to fight forest fires
- **D.** firefighters make big fires to clear more land

---

5. Have you ever heard people call money by the name of *bits*? There was once a Mexican coin called a bit. It was worth 12 1/2 cents. This coin was also used in parts of the United States. So the people began calling American coins by the name of bits too. Today a quarter is sometimes known as two bits. A half-dollar is called four bits.

______ **5**. From this story you can conclude that

- **A.** Mexican coins are used in the United States
- **B.** today a bit is worth less than a nickel
- **C.** the name of the Mexican coin is still used for money
- **D.** Mexican coins are now used for horse bridles

1. Did you know you can start a campfire with ice? First find a large piece of very clear ice. Then melt it down in the palms of your hands. When it is ready, the ice should look like a lens. It should have smooth curves on both sides. Finally use the ice to direct the sun's rays onto paper or wood shavings. This will start the fire.

______ **1.** The story suggests that

- **A.** ice burns
- **B.** the ice will freeze the fire
- **C.** the warmth of your hands melts the ice
- **D.** the ice should be curved on one side only

---

2. Nat Love was a special breed of man. He was a restless cowboy who helped settle the Wild West. As a young man, Love was a slave in Tennessee. Set free by the Civil War, Love learned to herd cattle. In Deadwood, South Dakota, Love won a big cowboy contest. There he gained his nickname, Deadwood Dick.

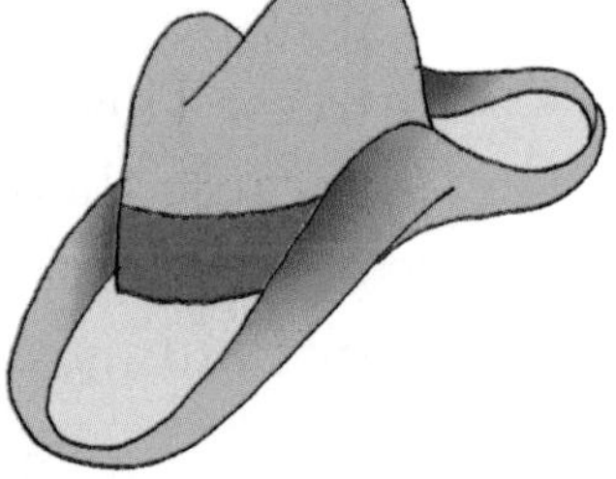

______ **2.** You can tell from the story that Nat Love

- **A.** drove a fast car
- **B.** was a slave all his life
- **C.** grew up in Texas
- **D.** was a skilled cowboy

---

3. For years people longed to fly in space. They wanted to visit the Moon. In 1957, the Soviet Union launched a satellite. Its name was *Sputnik*. The name means "fellow wayfarer." *Sputnik* was the first spacecraft to orbit Earth. *Sputnik* had no crew. But it paved the way for later spaceflights.

______ **3.** The story tells that *Sputnik*

- **A.** was the first satellite in space
- **B.** crashed when it was launched
- **C.** was full of potatoes
- **D.** was launched by South Dakota

4. Most whales survive by eating small sea creatures known as krill. Some companies were planning to harvest krill. Mary Cahoon and Mary McWhinnie were afraid that this harvest would cause whales to starve. They went to the South Pole to study the problem. They were the first women to spend a whole winter at the cold South Pole.

______ **4.** The story suggests that the companies
- **A.** planned to harvest wheat
- **B.** weren't worried about whales
- **C.** liked warm weather
- **D.** went ice-skating often

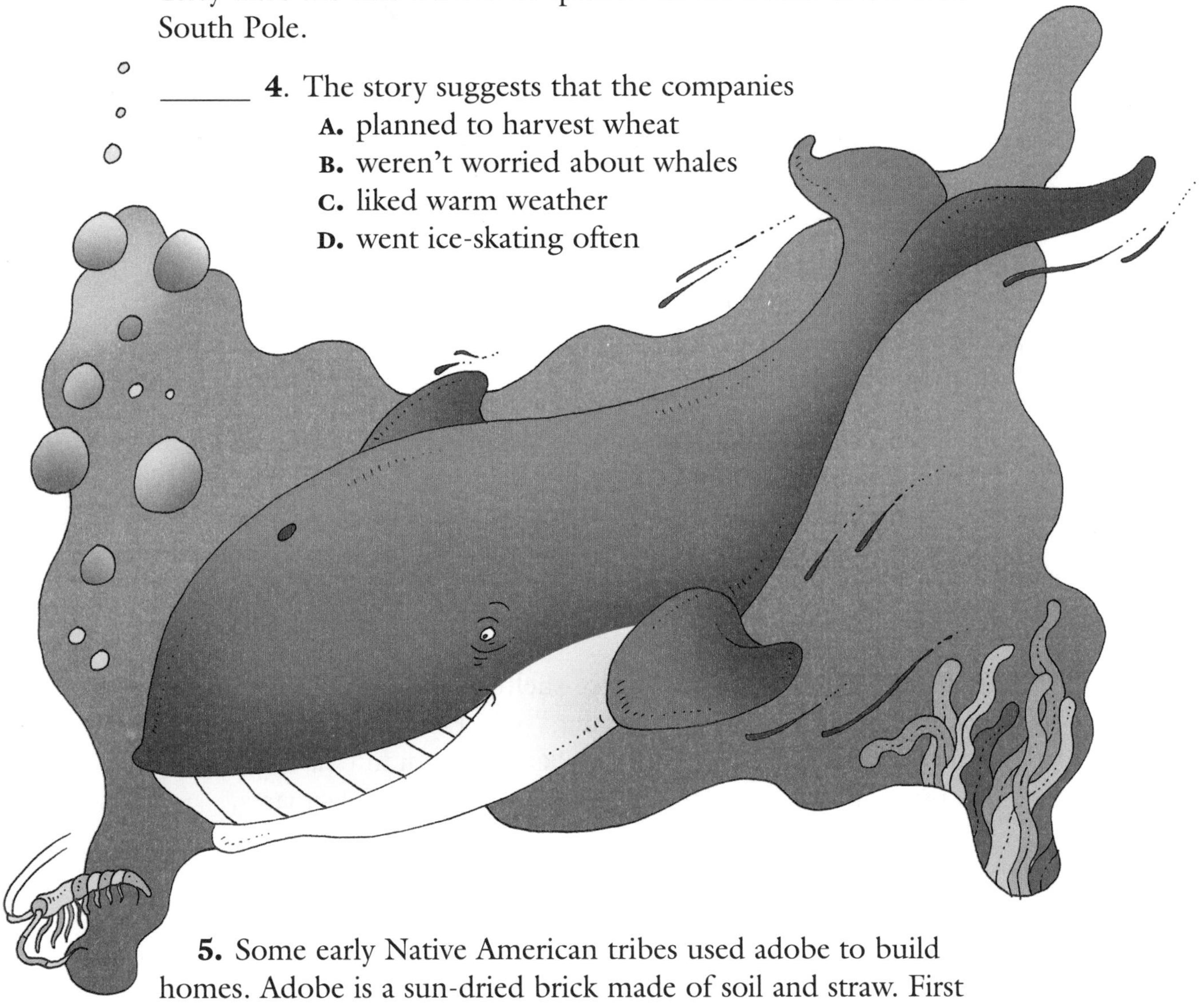

5. Some early Native American tribes used adobe to build homes. Adobe is a sun-dried brick made of soil and straw. First they mixed soil and water to make mud. Next they added straw for strength. Then they put the mixture into a brick-shaped mold. Finally the brick was placed in the sun to dry. The dried bricks were used to build the walls of houses.

______ **5.** From the story you can tell that adobe
- **A.** was made from concrete
- **B.** contained straw that weakened the brick
- **C.** was placed in the rain to dry
- **D.** was a useful building material

1. The water made a splashing sound as it ran past the big gray rocks. In some places it formed little pools. A small branch bobbed by as the water hurried down the hill. A skunk sat on the mossy bank and watched.

______ **1.** You can tell that the skunk is sitting near
- **A.** a bathtub
- **B.** a fountain
- **C.** a stream
- **D.** a lake

---

2. Flo and Mike were at the animal shelter. Flo wanted a kitten. Mike wanted a puppy. "Cats are cleaner," said Flo. "You don't have to give them baths or take them for walks." Mike didn't care about that. He thought that cats sleep too much to be good playmates.

______ **2.** This story does not tell
- **A.** what Flo wanted
- **B.** what Mike wanted
- **C.** why Flo likes cats better than dogs
- **D.** what Flo and Mike decided to get

3. When Tony woke up, he looked out the window. What luck! The mountain was covered with snow. Quickly he pulled on his long underwear and other warm clothes. He ate a good, hot breakfast so that he'd have plenty of energy. Then he checked his equipment. He clomped in his heavy boots toward the door and looked at the slopes.

______ **3.** In this story the mood is

- A. angry
- B. dangerous
- C. happy
- D. silly

---

4. Nina was walking down a long hall. She kept turning corners and looking for a certain door. But all the doors she found were the wrong ones. Suddenly a bell rang, and Nina thought, "Oh, I must run or I'll be late." But the bell kept ringing, and Nina couldn't run. Instead, she opened her eyes. The telephone beside her bed was ringing loudly.

______ **4.** From this story you can tell that

- A. the telephone woke Nina from her dream
- B. Nina was in school
- C. Nina didn't want to answer the telephone
- D. Nina was glad the telephone rang

---

5. A dog was carrying a bone in his mouth. As he walked over a bridge, he saw his reflection in the water. He thought it was another dog with another bone. "I'll bark and scare that dog away," he thought. "Then I'll have two bones!" After the dog barked, he found out that it doesn't pay to be greedy.

______ **5.** The dog learned his lesson when

- A. the other dog ran away
- B. he had no bone at all
- C. he went home with a bone
- D. he jumped off the bridge

1. A popular part of Yellowstone Park is Old Faithful. This geyser shoots out thousands of gallons of steam and water every hour. The water is heated deep in the ground. It works its way up through cracks in the ground. Then it bursts high into the air. Yellowstone Park has more geysers than anyplace else on Earth.

______ **1.** You cannot tell from the story

- **A.** how often Old Faithful erupts
- **B.** where Old Faithful can be found
- **C.** how the water shoots from a geyser
- **D.** where Yellowstone Park is located

---

2. Evelyn Cheesman loved to study bugs. She worked as a helper in the Insect House at the London Zoo. In the 1920s she began to go on field trips. Most of her trips were to Asia. During her life she was able to collect 40,000 insects.

______ **2.** The story suggests that Evelyn Cheesman

- **A.** was afraid of insects
- **B.** made most of her field trips to Africa
- **C.** worked with insects all her life
- **D.** did not collect insects

---

3. A great white building stands in Agra, India. It is called the Taj Mahal. It was built by a ruler named Shah Jahan. He wanted a special place to bury his dead wife. Twenty thousand men worked for 20 years to build the Taj Mahal.

______ **3.** You can tell that the Taj Mahal

- **A.** was built to be a grave
- **B.** is found in Indiana
- **C.** was built of granite
- **D.** took 30 years to build

4. Lewis Latimer was an African American man. When he was young, he learned the skill of drafting. Then he met Alexander Bell. Bell invented the telephone. He used a design drawn by Latimer. Not long after that, Latimer invented a special lamp. It was called the Latimer Lamp. Later he worked with the great inventor Thomas Edison.

_____ **4.** The story does <u>not</u> tell if Lewis Latimer
- **A.** learned drafting
- **B.** invented more than one thing
- **C.** worked with Thomas Edison
- **D.** invented a special lamp

---

5. Rosita put the flag up in front of her home. She had read about the correct way to do this. She knew that the flag can be flown from the top of a flag pole. She didn't have a flag pole, though. She also knew that the flag can be hung on a staff. That was how Rosita flew the flag.

_____ **5.** From this story you can tell that
- **A.** Rosita's flag is new
- **B.** Rosita lives in an apartment
- **C.** there is more than one right way to fly a flag
- **D.** Rosita lives in a house

1. There was war in the Middle East. The country of Israel had just been formed. Its Arab neighbors were upset. Ralph Bunche worked in the State Department of the United States. He was sent to help end the war. Bunche knew the war would not be easy to stop. At last he gained peace between the two sides. In 1950, he became the first African American to win the Nobel Peace Prize.

______ **1.** You can tell from the story that Bunche
- **A.** worked for the Israeli government
- **B.** was honored for his hard work
- **C.** solved the Middle East conflict easily
- **D.** did not go to the Middle East

---

2. The Iditarod is a sled-dog race across Alaska. Each team has one person to drive the sled and a group of about 12 dogs to pull it. The person, called a musher, rides on the sled with the food and supplies. The team must cross more than 1,000 miles in cold and often snowy weather. It takes about two weeks. The musher puts special socks on each dog's paws. The musher also feeds and cares for the dogs on the long ride. The dogs run fast and pull the musher all the way to the finish line.

______ **2.** The story tells that
- **A.** mushers and their dogs work together to finish the race
- **B.** sled dogs take care of themselves during the race
- **C.** mushers don't worry about the sled dogs
- **D.** mushers and dogs ride on the sled together

3. Leonardo da Vinci was a great artist. He lived about 500 years ago. His most famous work is the painting *Mona Lisa.* He also liked to learn about all sorts of things. He knew much about the human body. He loved to invent things, too. He even drew plans for a flying machine.

______ **3.** You <u>cannot</u> tell from the story
- **A.** when Leonardo lived
- **B.** the name of Leonardo's most famous painting
- **C.** if Leonardo's flying machine could fly
- **D.** that Leonardo was a famous painter

---

4. In Aztec legends the new world needed light and warmth. Two sons of the Aztec god wanted to jump into the fire. They wanted to become the Sun. The first brother jumped into the fire. He became the Sun. But the other brother was afraid. When he jumped into the fire, he became only the Moon.

______ **4.** The story suggests that
- **A.** fear kept one brother from becoming the Sun
- **B.** the Aztec god had five sons
- **C.** only one brother jumped into the fire
- **D.** the first brother never jumped into the fire

---

5. The smallest flower on Earth is on the duckweed plant. Its blossom can barely be seen with the naked eye. The small duckweed plants float free on still water. These plants are a popular food for ducks.

______ **5.** From the story you <u>cannot</u> tell
- **A.** on what plant the smallest flower grows
- **B.** what animal likes to eat the duckweed plant
- **C.** how small these flowers are
- **D.** what color the smallest flowers are

Lesson 8

1. It is almost spring. Latwanda is not looking forward to the change of season. That is because some flowering plants make her sick. In the spring the air is full of pollens. When Latwanda starts sneezing, her friends know that spring is here.

_____ **1.** This story suggests that
- **A.** Latwanda catches colds from her friends
- **B.** pollens make Latwanda sneeze
- **C.** dust mites make Latwanda sneeze
- **D.** medicine helps Latwanda get well

---

2. Tina called her friend Eva in Maryland. Eva sounded very sleepy when she said hello. The two girls talked for 10 minutes. Then Eva said she had to go. "School starts early, you know," she said. "I need my sleep." It was then that Tina knew what she had done. She forgot that Maryland's time zone was not the same as California's.

_____ **2.** You can conclude from the story that
- **A.** Eva did not enjoy talking to Tina
- **B.** Tina did not enjoy talking to Eva
- **C.** Tina and Eva talk often on the phone
- **D.** Eva was asleep when Tina called

---

3. Stars do not last forever. After billions of years, they just burn out. Some stars suddenly brighten before they dim. These stars are called novas. *Nova* means "new" in Latin. The novas seem to be new stars. The last great nova was in 1054. It could be seen even in the daytime. It outshone everything in the sky except the Sun and Moon.

_____ **3.** You can tell from the story that
- **A.** novas are not seen very often
- **B.** great novas happen all the time
- **C.** all stars become novas
- **D.** the nova of 1054 was not very bright

4. Mary Bethune had a dream. She wanted to start a school for African American children. She had a teaching degree, but she had no building, and she had no money. Still Mary had hope. She received donations. At last her school opened in 1904. Through her hard work, the school was a big success. It became known as Bethune-Cookman College. The school, located in Florida, is still open.

______ **4.** The story does <u>not</u> tell

A. what Mary Bethune's dream was
B. when Mary Bethune's school opened
C. where Mary Bethune's school was located
D. who gave Mary Bethune donations

---

5. There are more than six billion people on Earth. But scientists think there are four billion insects in each square mile of land. That means there are more than 150 million insects for each person. Luckily, very few insects harm people.

______ **5.** This story does <u>not</u> tell

A. how many people are on Earth
B. how many insects are in each square mile
C. which insects are most dangerous to people
D. how many more insects there are than people

Writing Roundup

Read each story. Think about a conclusion you can draw. Write your conclusion in a complete sentence.

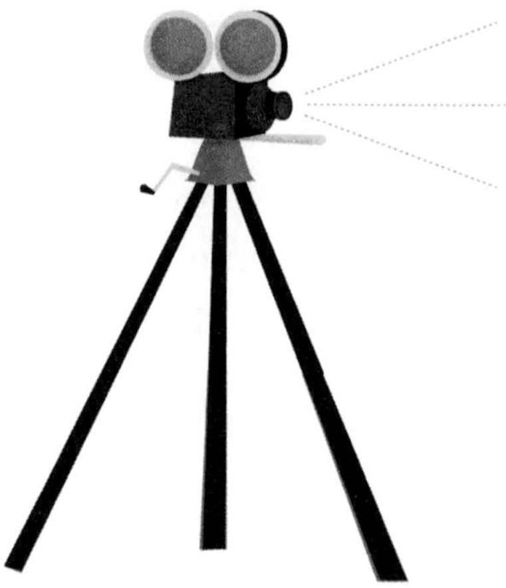

1. The first movie with people talking was shown in 1927. It was a big hit. Some movies made after that did not have talking in them. Some people still wanted to see the kind of movies they had been watching for years.

What conclusion can you draw from this story?

____

____

____

2. A family in England got a goldfish in 1956. It lived until 1999. One book claims it lived longer than any other goldfish kept in a fish tank. Who knows if that's true? Some people may want to keep the age of their goldfish a secret.

What conclusion can you draw from this story?

____

____

3. By the year 2000, 34 Super Bowls had been played. This football game draws big crowds, but many more football fans watch it on television. The game that had the most TV watchers was Super Bowl 16. In it, San Francisco beat Cincinnati.

What conclusion can you draw from this story?

____

____

Read the story below. What conclusions can you draw? Use the clues in the story to answer the questions in complete sentences.

Raul is from Cuba. He came to America with his mom. At first they lived in Florida. Raul liked Florida. He did not want to move, but his mom found out she had an uncle in New Jersey. He helped her find a good job. Raul and his mom moved in with Raul's granduncle. Raul went to high school. There he got a surprise. Many of the students were Cuban Americans. They spoke Spanish and English. Raul decided he was going to like New Jersey.

1. Was Raul born in America? How do you know?

____

____

2. When Raul lived in Cuba, did he meet his granduncle? How do you know?

____

____

3. Do Raul and his mom live alone? How do you know?

____

____

4. Does Raul want to move back to Florida? How do you know?

____

____

unit 6

What Is an Inference?

An inference is a guess you make after thinking about what you already know. Suppose a friend invites you to a picnic. From what you know about picnics, you might infer that there will be food and drinks, and that you will eat outside.

An author does not write every detail in a story. If every detail were told, a story would be long and boring, and the main point would be lost. Suppose you read, "Lynn went to a restaurant." The writer does not have to tell you what a restaurant is. You already know that it is a place where people go to eat a meal. From what you know, you might imagine that Lynn looked at a menu. Then a server took her order. By filling in these missing details, you could infer that Lynn went to the restaurant to eat. You can infer this by putting together what you read and what you already know.

Try It!

Read this story. Think about the facts in the story.

Earthquakes can cause a lot of damage. This is especially true in places where the soil is loose and damp. An earthquake can turn loose, damp soil into thick mud. Buildings will sink or fall down. Many people may be hurt.

What can you infer? Write an inference on the line below.

____

____

You may have written something such as, "An earthquake can harm a city." You can make this inference from what the story tells you about earthquakes and what you already know.

Practice Making Inferences

In lessons 1 through 4 of this unit, you will be asked to answer the question, "Which of these sentences is probably true?" Read the following story and answer the question.

Red-crowned cranes are beautiful birds. They are known for their trumpeting call. Many of these cranes live on an island in Japan. They live in marshes and are protected by law, but there are fewer than 2,000 cranes left. They are in danger of disappearing.

B **1.** Which of these sentences is probably true?

- **A.** The Japanese don't care about these cranes.
- **B.** People in Japan want to help the cranes.
- **C.** Red-crowned cranes live in the desert.
- **D.** There are too many cranes in Japan.

Answer **B** is the best choice. The story says that these cranes are protected by law. From the story you can infer that people in Japan want to help these cranes.

In lessons 5 through 8 of this unit you will do a new kind of exercise. Each story is followed by statements. Some of the statements are inferences. Others are facts. Decide whether each statement is an inference or a fact.

Ben moved from England to Maine. In England he was taught to stand up when answering a question. In his new class, he stood up when the teacher called on him. Some of the other students laughed at him. After class the teacher told him that he could stay in his seat when she called on him.

Fact	Inference	
○	●	**2. A.** Ben was a polite person.
●	○	**B.** Ben moved from England to Maine.
○	●	**C.** The teacher wanted to help Ben.
●	○	**D.** Some students laughed at Ben.

You can find statements **B** and **D** in the story, so they are facts. We can infer from the way he acts that Ben is a polite person, but this isn't stated in the story. So **A** is an inference. We can guess from the teacher's actions that she wanted to help Ben. So **C** is also an inference.

Lesson 1

Read the passages. Use what you know about inference to answer the questions. Remember, an inference is a guess you make by putting together what you know and what you read or see in the stories.

1. John loved to fish. He went fishing anytime he could. The weather was very hot and dry. John sat on the shore, thinking about catching fish. All day John waited patiently. The fish just would not bite. He was hungry and thirsty, but did not move even as the Sun went down.

______ **1.** Which of these sentences is probably true?

A. There were no fish in the water.
B. John wanted to stay until he caught a fish.
C. Other people were fishing at the pond.
D. John went home early for dinner.

---

2. The village people chose a boy to guard the sheep. It was an important job. If a wolf came near, the boy was supposed to call the people in the village. Then they would come to help him. The boy watched the sheep for a little while. Then he decided to have some fun. He cried out loudly, "Wolf! Wolf!" The people rushed out to fight the wolf. When they arrived the boy was laughing at them. There was no wolf.

______ **2.** Which of these sentences is probably true?

A. Everyone thought the joke was funny.
B. Several of the sheep got lost.
C. The people were angry at the boy.
D. The boy was very kind.

3. You have probably seen a rainbow in the sky. What does it take to form a rainbow? There are three conditions for a rainbow to form. First, there must be many raindrops in the sky. Second, the sunlight must be shining on the raindrops. Third, the Sun must be behind you. Then the rainbow will be in front of you.

______ **3.** Which of these sentences is probably true?

A. Rainbows are only seen in the West.
B. Rainbows always appear during storms.
C. Rainbows never appear when there are clouds.
D. Rainbows rarely appear at night.

---

4. A pet store owner in Maine noticed a strange thing. He found that he could tell when the country was having good times or bad. He looked at what kind of dogs people wanted to buy. People bought small dogs when they had enough money. People bought big dogs when they felt sad or needed protection.

______ **4.** Which of these sentences is probably true?

A. People bought big dogs during bad times.
B. Pet store owners don't like dogs.
C. People bought big dogs during good times.
D. Dogs make better pets than cats do.

---

5. The cowbird does not build a nest of its own. The mother cowbird lays her eggs in the nest of another bird. Then the cowbird leaves the eggs. She hopes the other bird will take care of her babies when they hatch.

______ **5.** Which of these sentences is probably true?

A. The cowbird is lazy.
B. Nests are easy to build.
C. The cowbird is very caring.
D. Baby cowbirds eat much food.

LESSON 2

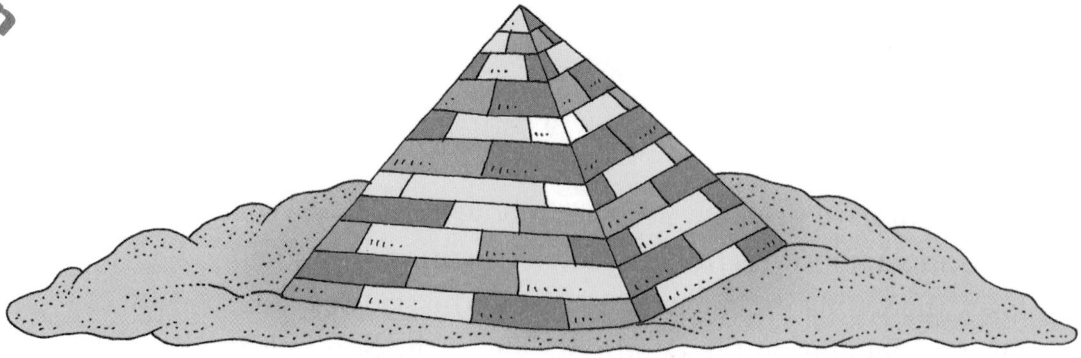

1. The Pyramids in Egypt were built more than 5,000 years ago. The Pyramids are made of large blocks of stone. They are stacked on top of each other. The blocks are very heavy. People moved the blocks by placing logs under them. The logs acted like wheels to make the blocks easier to move. The stones were then pulled into place.

______ 1. Which of these sentences is probably true?
- A. The Pyramids in Egypt are very old.
- B. The Pyramids were built from large trees.
- C. Large rocks are easy to move.
- D. The Pyramids were discovered recently.

---

2. The day was sunny and hot. Ava stood happily at the side of the swimming pool. She thought about the clear, blue water. Then she jumped in. As she began swimming, she started shaking, and her skin began to turn blue.

______ 2. Which of these sentences is probably true?
- A. The water was very hot.
- B. Ava forgot to wear her coat.
- C. The water was very cold.
- D. Ava didn't know how to swim.

---

3. Fingernails grow faster on the right hand of people who are right-handed. The nails grow faster on the left hand of left-handed people. They grow faster in the day than at night. Ray has to trim the nails on his left hand more than the ones on his right hand.

______ 3. Which of these sentences is probably true?
- A. Ray is a right-handed person.
- B. Painted nails grow very slowly.
- C. Ray is a left-handed person.
- D. At night Ray's nails grow quickly.

4. One day Sam found a library book under his bed. He realized he was late in taking it back. Sam decided to return the book the next day. The next day, he could not find the book. Two days later Sam found the book again, so he hurried to the library. When he arrived, there was a sign on the door. He walked home again with the book in his hand.

______ **4.** Which of these sentences is probably true?

A. Sam didn't like the book very much.

B. The book could move by itself.

C. Sam did not know where the library was.

D. When Sam went to the library, it was closed.

5. One day Ann heard her friend Tom talking. Tom was telling everybody how smart his dog was. Tom said his dog could do tricks and could even ride a bicycle. Ann knew that Tom's dog was just like any other dog. Ann just smiled as Tom went on talking.

______ **5.** Which of these sentences is probably true?

A. Ann didn't understand Tom's story.

B. Tom wanted to make Ann mad at him.

C. Ann didn't want to hurt Tom's feelings.

D. Tom had two dogs and a cat.

LESSON 3

1. Nick sat trembling behind the couch as a storm roared outside. Lightning flashed and thunder rumbled. Each time the thunder rolled, Nick screamed loudly. Nick's dad tried to get the boy to come out, but Nick would not move.

______ **1.** Which of these sentences is probably true?
- **A.** Storms made Nick's dad afraid.
- **B.** Nick liked to play hide and seek.
- **C.** Nick's dad made him feel better.
- **D.** Nick was afraid of thunder and lightning.

---

2. Bill Stanton found a skunk in his garage. He asked the city of Chicago for help. He wanted to get rid of the skunk, but the city would not help him. Bill bought a trap to catch the skunk himself. Then he learned he had broken the law several times. First he had brought a trap into the city. Then he had trapped an animal without the city's permission. The city laws stated that he could not keep the skunk in his garage. They also said he could not kill the skunk or let it go free, either!

______ **2.** Which of these sentences is probably true?
- **A.** The skunk became Bill's best friend.
- **B.** Bill didn't know what to do with the skunk.
- **C.** The skunk was moved to the city leaders' office.
- **D.** Bill was glad the skunk was in his garage.

3. The sport of softball began as indoor baseball. The first game of softball was played on a cold day in November 1887. It took place in a Chicago boat club. The men used an old boxing glove for a ball and a broomstick for a bat.

______ **3.** Which of these sentences is probably true?

- **A.** The men wanted to play baseball in the winter.
- **B.** Real baseballs cost a lot of money in 1887.
- **C.** The men didn't know how to play baseball.
- **D.** People first played softball outside.

---

4. When you think of dinosaurs, you likely think of large animals. Not all dinosaurs were large. The smallest dinosaurs were about the size of a chicken. They were fast runners. They probably ate insects, frogs, and lizards.

______ **4.** Which of these sentences is probably true?

- **A.** Dinosaurs were many different sizes.
- **B.** Dinosaurs ate only plants.
- **C.** Some dinosaurs looked like chickens.
- **D.** Dinosaurs were all about the same size.

---

5. The speed limit on the road was 30 miles per hour. But drivers always went faster than that. The neighbors who lived on the road were angry about the speeders. So they talked to the city leaders. The leaders soon took action. They raised the speed limit to 35 miles per hour.

______ **5.** Which of these sentences is probably true?

- **A.** The neighbors disliked the new speed limit.
- **B.** The neighbors were glad the leaders took action.
- **C.** After hearing the leaders' decision, the neighbors moved away.
- **D.** Drivers started going 30 miles per hour.

Lesson 4

1. Bob Hope was playing golf with a friend. His friend missed an easy shot. The angry friend threw his golf club into the tall grass. Bob secretly got the golf club back and started using it himself. Bob hit the ball a long way with his friend's club. The friend thought Bob's golf club was very good. He offered to buy it for $50. Bob sold the man the club he had just thrown away. Later Bob told his friend what had happened.

______ **1.** Which of these sentences is probably true?
- **A.** Bob decided to keep his friend's golf club.
- **B.** Bob's friend felt silly for buying back his own club.
- **C.** Bob used the money to open a golf shop.
- **D.** Bob's friend never played golf again.

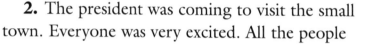

---

2. The president was coming to visit the small town. Everyone was very excited. All the people worked hard to clean up their town. They mowed the grass and swept the sidewalks. They fixed up the old houses. They even painted the water tower.

______ **2.** Which of these sentences is probably true?
- **A.** The president was moving to the town.
- **B.** The people were trying to fool the president.
- **C.** The president only liked big towns.
- **D.** The people wanted their town to look nice.

---

3. Jim carefully lifted the eggs from their box. He handed two eggs to his mother. Then Jim measured a cup of milk, being careful not to spill any. He rubbed the pan with butter and watched as his mother poured in the batter. Then Jim and his mother cleaned up.

______ **3.** Which of these sentences is probably true?
- **A.** Jim was a good helper.
- **B.** Jim's mother was a bad cook.
- **C.** Jim was hungry.
- **D.** Jim's mother was lazy.

4. Jan was always playing basketball. In fact, she almost never left the basketball court. Jan started practicing early every morning. As the Sun went down, Jan was still bouncing the basketball.

______ **4.** Which of these sentences is probably true?

A. Jan slept at the basketball court.
B. Tennis was very important to Jan.
C. Jan wanted to be a great basketball player.
D. The basketball was too big to bounce inside.

---

5. When he was a boy, George Washington Carver had a garden. He loved to study the plants and flowers growing there. He knew how to make the flowers bloom. George could also cure sick plants. People began to call him the "plant doctor."

______ **5.** Which of these sentences is probably true?

A. George became a plant scientist later in life.
B. The neighbors didn't like George's garden.
C. George chopped down all the plants.
D. His mother called George the "animal doctor."

Lesson 5

1. People have been eating cheese for more than 4,000 years. Cheese is made from milk. As milk turns to cheese, solid clumps form. When the liquid is taken out, the cheese becomes even harder. The cheese is then allowed to *age*. This means it has to sit for a while before it's ready. Sometimes the cheese is ready to be eaten in two weeks. For other types of cheese, aging takes up to two years.

Fact	Inference	
○	○	**1. A.** Cheese is made from milk.
○	○	**B.** There are different kinds of cheeses.
○	○	**C.** Aging cheese can take two years.
○	○	**D.** Cheese hardens when liquid is removed.

2. Have you ever caught fireflies on a warm summer night? Fireflies are interesting little insects. They make light with their bodies, but the light is not hot. Fireflies use their lights to send signals to other fireflies.

Fact	Inference	
○	○	**2. A.** Fireflies come out in summer.
○	○	**B.** The light of fireflies is not hot.
○	○	**C.** Fireflies send signals with their lights.
○	○	**D.** Fireflies can only send signals at night.

3. If you watch the sky at night, you may see a shooting star. Shooting stars are actually meteors. Meteors are small bits of rock that enter the atmosphere. When this happens, they burn up. They look like streaks of light. Sometimes Earth passes through a place with many small rocks. When this happens, the sky is filled with meteors. Since there are so many meteors, these events are called meteor showers.

Fact	Inference	
○	○	**3. A.** Meteors are small bits of rock.
○	○	**B.** Meteors are not really stars.
○	○	**C.** Most meteors never reach the ground.
○	○	**D.** Meteor showers are made up of many meteors.

---

4. Drew's team was tied with the other soccer team. The game was almost over. Drew had scored all his team's goals in the game so far. His friend Brian had never scored a goal. As Drew ran up the field, he saw that Brian was in a great position to kick the ball into the goal. Drew quickly kicked the ball to Brian.

Fact	Inference	
○	○	**4. A.** Drew wanted Brian to make a goal.
○	○	**B.** Drew was a thoughtful person.
○	○	**C.** Drew was a good soccer player.
○	○	**D.** Brian had never scored a goal.

---

5. Mount St. Helens is a volcano in Washington. In 1980, it erupted for the first time in more than 100 years. Fire and melting rock poured out of the volcano. This caused rivers to flood. Four states were covered with ash. More than 60 people were killed.

Fact	Inference	
○	○	**5. A.** Mount St. Helens erupted in 1980.
○	○	**B.** The volcano did not erupt often.
○	○	**C.** People lived near Mount St. Helens.
○	○	**D.** Mount St. Helens is in Washington.

LESSON 6

1. Marta and her cousin Pilar set up a lawn-mowing service. They made quite a bit of money over the summer. Mr. Lee was their neighbor. He had been sick lately, and his lawn had not been mowed. Marta and Pilar decided to mow the lawn for him. When Mr. Lee offered to pay them, they wouldn't take his money.

Fact	Inference	
○	○	**1. A.** Marta and Pilar wanted to help Mr. Lee.
○	○	**B.** Mr. Lee had been sick lately.
○	○	**C.** Marta and Pilar were hard workers.
○	○	**D.** Mr. Lee offered to pay the girls.

---

2. Popcorn is one of the oldest kinds of corn. It was first grown by people in North America and South America. Today most popcorn is grown in Nebraska and Indiana.

Fact	Inference	
○	○	**2. A.** Popcorn is grown in Indiana.
○	○	**B.** People in South America grew popcorn.
○	○	**C.** Popcorn doesn't grow well everywhere.
○	○	**D.** People still eat popcorn.

---

3. Dana loved computers. Once or twice a week, she went to the computer store near her house. The owner was glad to let Dana use the computers, but he told her not to bring drinks inside. One day Dana carried a can of apple juice into the store.

Fact	Inference	
○	○	**3. A.** Dana spilled the apple juice.
○	○	**B.** The owner was angry with Dana.
○	○	**C.** Dana liked apple juice.
○	○	**D.** The store was near Dana's house.

4. Mammoths lived thousands of years ago. They looked a little like elephants. They had trunks and long teeth called tusks. Some had hair all over their bodies. They were called woolly mammoths. The bones of mammoths have been found in Siberia. The last mammoths died about 10,000 years ago.

Fact	Inference	
○	○	**4. A.** Woolly mammoths had hair on their bodies.
○	○	**B.** Mammoths had trunks and tusks.
○	○	**C.** Woolly mammoths died long ago.
○	○	**D.** Mammoths lived in Siberia.

---

5. Andy watched his mother take his training wheels off. He was excited to try out his bike. Without the training wheels, he kept falling off. Then his older brother Jeff came outside. Jeff had an idea. He ran beside Andy as Andy pedaled the bike. Andy rode faster and faster. Soon Jeff couldn't keep up. Andy was riding the bike by himself!

Fact	Inference	
○	○	**5. A.** Andy fell off his bike.
○	○	**B.** Jeff wanted to help Andy.
○	○	**C.** Andy's mother took off his training wheels.
○	○	**D.** Jeff was Andy's older brother.

Lesson 7

1. Mushrooms grow under piles of fallen leaves or on dead logs. People eat mushrooms in spaghetti or on pizza, but not all mushrooms are good to eat. Some mushrooms have poison in them. The poisonous ones are called toadstools.

Fact	Inference	
○	○	**1. A.** Some mushrooms are poisonous.
○	○	**B.** People eat mushrooms on pizza.
○	○	**C.** Mushrooms grow on dead logs.
○	○	**D.** People should not eat toadstools.

---

2. One man made a pizza so big it could feed 30,000 people. The pizza was more than 100 feet across. It was cut into more than 90,000 slices! The man's name was Mr. Avato. He set a world record.

Fact	Inference	
○	○	**2. A.** The pizza was more than 100 feet across.
○	○	**B.** The pizza set a world record.
○	○	**C.** Mr. Avato likes pizza.
○	○	**D.** There were more than 90,000 pieces.

3. Rob heard a rooster crow. He opened his eyes and felt the sun shining through the window. It was his first day on his cousin's farm. He jumped out of bed and began putting on his jeans. When his aunt called him to breakfast, he ran downstairs eagerly.

Fact	Inference	
○	○	**3. A.** Rob liked farm life.
○	○	**B.** The sun was shining.
○	○	**C.** Rob was hungry.
○	○	**D.** A rooster crowed.

4. Think about this the next time you brush your teeth. Before people had toothbrushes, they used twigs. They would smash the end to make it like a brush. About 600 years ago, the toothbrush was invented in China. It was made from hog hair. Hog hairs are very stiff and are called bristles. The bristles were attached to a wooden stick. Today, toothbrushes are not made with hog hairs. They have nylon bristles.

Fact	Inference	
○	○	**4. A.** Toothbrushes have changed over time.
○	○	**B.** People first used twigs to clean their teeth.
○	○	**C.** Modern toothbrushes have nylon bristles.
○	○	**D.** The first toothbrushes used wooden sticks and hog hair.

5. When we think of windmills, we often think of Holland. The people there used windmills to take water off their land. That way they had more land for farming. Now windmills are used to make electricity.

Fact	Inference	
○	○	**5. A.** There is not enough farmland in Holland.
○	○	**B.** Farmland must be fairly dry.
○	○	**C.** Holland has many windmills.
○	○	**D.** Now windmills make electricity.

LESSON 8

1. A compass is used as a guide. The needle of a compass always points north. The needle is really just a small magnet. The needle is balanced so that it turns freely. When the compass is turned, the needle continues to point north. The compass was invented in China about 2,000 years ago. It was used to guide ships on long trips.

Fact	Inference	
○	○	**1. A.** If a compass is turned, the needle still points one direction.
○	○	**B.** A compass could help a ship when the sky is cloudy.
○	○	**C.** A compass always points north.
○	○	**D.** Ship captains found the compass helpful.

---

2. The Venus flytrap is a strange plant. An insect that flies near it doesn't have much of a chance. When an insect touches the leaves in the center of the plant, the leaves snap shut. The insect gets trapped inside. It takes a few days for the Venus flytrap to finish eating the insect.

Fact	Inference	
○	○	**2. A.** A Venus flytrap is a plant.
○	○	**B.** The Venus flytrap's leaves snap shut.
○	○	**C.** The leaves trap the insect.
○	○	**D.** Venus flytraps eat insects.

---

3. A coral reef is a strange and beautiful place. It has towers, tunnels, caves, and castles, but it is under the sea. The coral is made of shells from tiny animals. It looks like rock. Different kinds of fish swim around the reef. They make the reef look like a rainbow of color.

Fact	Inference	
○	○	**3. A.** Coral reefs are beautiful.
○	○	**B.** Fish swim around a coral reef.
○	○	**C.** The fish are colorful.
○	○	**D.** A coral reef is made of shells.

4. Koko was a gorilla. Penny, her owner, had taught the ape sign language. One day Penny asked Koko what she wanted for her birthday. "Cat," Koko answered. Penny bought a toy cat for Koko. When Koko opened her present, she threw it down. Koko had wanted a real cat. A few months later, Penny gave Koko a real cat. Then Koko was happy.

Fact	Inference	
○	○	**4. A.** Penny was Koko's owner.
○	○	**B.** Koko wanted a cat for her birthday.
○	○	**C.** The real cat made Koko happy.
○	○	**D.** Koko was upset when she didn't get a cat.

---

5. Dodo birds once lived on some islands in the Indian Ocean. They were about the same size as a turkey. Dodos could not fly. They had a hooked beak, short legs, and a short neck. Dodo eggs were eaten by other animals on the islands. The last dodos died out more than 200 years ago.

Fact	Inference	
○	○	**5. A.** A dodo was the size of a turkey.
○	○	**B.** The dodos died more than 200 years ago.
○	○	**C.** A dodo was larger than a chicken.
○	○	**D.** Other animals ate dodo eggs.

Writing Roundup

Read each story. Then read the question that follows it. Write your answers on the lines below each question.

1. Karen watered the rose plant. It was in a pot. Then she spotted water leaking under the pot. She did not want water stains on the shelf, so she put some old newspapers under the pot. As she did this, the sun hit her and the rose. Tomorrow the rose would be in a new pot.

Where did Karen keep the flowerpot?

____

____

2. Leon pulled his pencil out of the sharpener. Then he shook the shavings off the pencil. It looked fine. He was ready to start writing again.

Why did Leon stop writing?

____

____

3. The dog looked up and down the street. The man waited until the dog stepped off the curb. Then the man followed the dog. They crossed the street.

Why did the man wait for the dog?

____

____

Read the paragraph below. Then answer the questions.

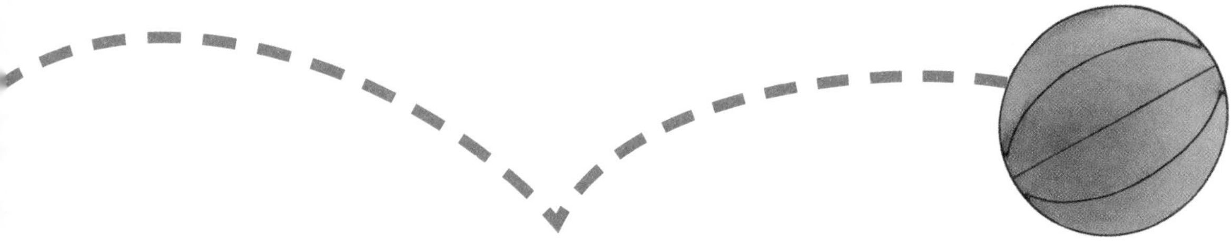

Mary grew 6 inches in her first year in high school. Now she wants to join the basketball team. Mary knows she must build her skills over the summer. Every day she practices her shooting and dribbling. Some days she gets her little brother to help. She practices passing the ball to him. Soon Mary plans to visit the playground. There she can practice with players who are on the team. She can learn how she is doing. She can also find out what else she needs to learn.

1. Why didn't Mary join the team in her first year?

____

____

2. What skill does Mary's little brother need to help Mary?

____

____

3. What kind of person is Mary?

____

____

4. How does Mary feel about her skills?

____

____

Spelling Skills

Spelling Strategies

What can you do when you aren't sure how to spell a word?

Say the word aloud. Make sure you say it correctly. Listen to the sounds in the word. Think about letters and patterns that might spell the sounds.

Look in the Spelling Table on page 265 to find common spellings for sounds in the word.

Think about related words. They may help you spell the word you're not sure of.

child—children

Guess the spelling of the word and check it in a dictionary.

Write the word in different ways. Compare the spellings and choose the one that looks correct.

trane tran (train) trayn

Think about any spelling rules you know that can help you spell the word.

Most plural words are formed by adding -s.

Choose a rhyming helper and use it. A rhyming helper is a word that rhymes with the word and is spelled like it.

strong—song

Break the word into syllables and think about how each syllable might be spelled.

No-vem-ber
for-got

Create a memory clue, such as a rhyme.

Write *i* before *e*, except after *c*.

Proofreading Marks

Mark	Meaning	Example
	spell correctly	I liek dogs.
	add period	They are my favorite kind of pet.
	add question mark	What kind of pet do you have?
	capitalize	My dog's name is scooter.
	take out	He likes to ~~to~~ run and play.
	indent paragraph	¶ I love my dog Scooter. He is the best pet I have ever had. Every morning he wakes me with a bark. Every night he sleeps with me.
	add quotation marks	"You are my best friend," I tell him.

Words with Short *a*

ask	matter	black	add
match	Saturday	class	apple
subtract	laugh	thank	catch
January	after	hammer	half

Say and Listen

Say each spelling word. Listen for the short *a* sound.

Think and Sort

Look at the letters in each word. Think about how short *a* is spelled. Spell each word aloud.

Short *a* can be shown as /ă/. How many spelling patterns for /ă/ do you see?

1. Write the **fifteen** spelling words that have the *a* pattern, like *match.*
2. Write the **one** spelling word that has the *au* pattern.

1. a Words

________________ ________________

________________ ________________

________________ ________________

________________ ________________

________________ ________________

________________ ________________

____

____

____

2. au Word

____

Definitions

Write the spelling word for each definition. Use a dictionary if you need to.

1. to find the sum ____________
2. problem ____________
3. to look alike ____________
4. group of students ____________
5. following ____________
6. to say one is grateful ____________
7. one of two equal parts ____________
8. to request ____________

Classifying

Write the spelling word that belongs in each group.

9.	banana	orange	pear	____________
10.	add	multiply	divide	____________
11.	screwdriver	saw	drill	____________
12.	white	green	yellow	____________
13.	chuckle	grin	smile	____________
14.	March	April	September	____________
15.	run	throw	pitch	____________

Words with Short *a*

ask	matter	black	add
match	Saturday	class	apple
subtract	laugh	thank	catch
January	after	hammer	half

Proofreading

Proofread the ad for apple juice below. Use proofreading marks to correct five spelling mistakes, three capitalization mistakes, and two punctuation mistakes. See the chart on page 131 to learn how to use the proofreading marks.

It's Janary You have the sniffles. did you cach a cold? to feel better fast, drink this.

It is the finest fruit juice ever made. Look for the aple on the bottle. you will feel great affter only haf a glass

Alphabetical Order

When words are in alphabetical order, they are in **ABC** order.

This group of words is in alphabetical order.

bend *friend* *horse*

This group of words is not in alphabetical order.

egg *animal* *chicken*

Write the following groups of words in alphabetical order.

1. matter January hammer

____
____
____

2. add match class

____
____
____

3. thank ask Saturday

____
____
____

4. black subtract laugh

____
____
____

Words with Long a

gray	page	great	change
April	face	save	away
break	ate	place	pay
late	safe	May	came

April

Say and Listen

Say each spelling word. Listen for the long *a* sound.

Think and Sort

Look at the letters in each word. Think about how long *a* is spelled. Spell each word aloud.

Long *a* can be shown as /ā/ . How many spelling patterns for /ā/ do you see?

1. Write the **nine** spelling words that have the *a*-consonant-*e* pattern, like *face.*
2. Write the **four** spelling words that have the *ay* pattern, like *May.*
3. Write the **two** spelling words that have the *ea* pattern, like *break.*
4. Write the **one** spelling word that has the *a* pattern.

1. a-consonant-e Words

____
____
____
____
____
____
____
____
____

2. ay Words

____
____
____
____

3. ea Words

____
____

4. a Word

____

Synonyms

Synonyms are words that have the same meaning. Write the spelling word that is a synonym for each word below.

1. arrived __________
2. unhurt __________
3. absent __________
4. put __________
5. messenger __________
6. wonderful __________
7. switch __________
8. silvery __________

Anagrams

An anagram is a word whose letters can be used to make another word. Write the spelling word that contains the letters of the underlined anagram in each sentence.

9. Jenna's birthday is in the month of <u>yaM</u>. __________
10. The team <u>tea</u> pizza after the game. __________
11. Please do not <u>brake</u> my pencil. __________
12. Ten dollars is too much to <u>yap</u>. __________
13. The bus was <u>tale</u> this morning. __________
14. Let's <u>vase</u> the best for last. __________
15. The baby had a big smile on her <u>cafe</u>. __________

Words with Long a

gray	page	great	change
April	face	save	away
break	ate	place	pay
late	safe	May	came

Proofreading

Proofread these directions for planting a tree. Use proofreading marks to correct five spelling mistakes, three capitalization mistakes, and two unnecessary words.

How to Plant a Tree

To plant a tree, first choose a saif spot. it should be a playce far from houses and awey from from strong winds. Plant the tree laete in the day when the sun is low. dig a deep hole and save the soil. then put the tree in the hole and water it well. Be careful not to to brek any branches on the tree. Last, pack the soil around the tree.

Sentences

Begin the first word of each sentence with a capital letter.

My sister collects postage stamps.

Put a period at the end of a sentence that tells something.

The first postage stamp was made in England.

Use the spelling words in the boxes below to complete the story. Then use proofreading marks to correct mistakes in the use of capital letters and periods.

May | face | save | great | page | gray | away

heather likes to ______________ stamps She must keep them ______________ from Scooter, her ______________ puppy. last ______________ a ______________ fell out of Heather's stamp book She looked all over for it. then she looked at Scooter The fur on his ______________ was stuck together. he had a ______________ time eating her stamps.

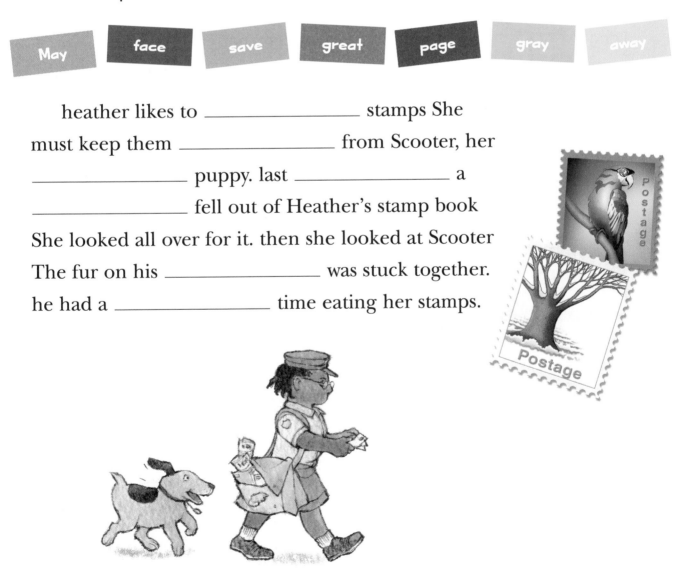

weigh

More Words with Long *a*

fable	rain	danger	sail
afraid	table	aid	train
eight	wait	able	aim
weigh	they	paint	paper

Say and Listen

Say each spelling word. Listen for the long *a* sound.

Think and Sort

Look at the letters in each word. Think about how long *a* is spelled. Spell each word aloud.

Long *a* can be shown as /ā/ . How many spelling patterns for /ā/ do you see?

1. Write the **eight** spelling words that have the *ai* pattern, like *rain.*
2. Write the **five** spelling words that have the *a* pattern, like *paper.*
3. Look at the word *eight.* The spelling pattern for this word is *eigh.* The *g* and *h* are silent. Write the **two** spelling words that have the *eigh* pattern, like *weigh.*
4. Write the **one** spelling word that has the *ey* pattern.

1. ai Words

2. a Words

3. eigh Words

4. ey Word

Antonyms

Antonyms are words that have opposite meanings. Write the spelling word that is an antonym of each word below.

1. hurt ______________
2. fearless ______________
3. go ______________
4. safety ______________
5. unable ______________

Analogies

An analogy shows that one pair of words is like another pair. Write the spelling word that completes each analogy.

6. *Bedspread* is to *bed* as *tablecloth* is to ______________.
7. *Two* is to *four* as *four* is to ______________.
8. *Car* is to *road* as ______________ is to *track.*
9. *Engine* is to *car* as ______________ is to *sailboat.*
10. *Story* is to ______________ as *animal* is to *dog.*
11. *Silk* is to *smooth* as ______________ is to *wet.*
12. *We* is to *us* as ______________ is to *them.*
13. *Oven* is to *bake* as *scale* is to ______________.
14. *Ink* is to *pen* as ______________ is to *brush.*
15. *Easy* is to *simple* as ______________ is to *point.*

fable	*rain*	*danger*	*sail*
afraid	*table*	*aid*	*train*
eight	*wait*	*able*	*aim*
weigh	*they*	*paint*	*paper*

Proofreading

Proofread the paragraph below. Use proofreading marks to correct five spelling mistakes, three capitalization mistakes, and two unnecessary words.

Mr. sanchez is the art teacher at our school. He teaches the third grade once a week. each class is abel to make many things. This week we are making things out of paper. our class has made a boat with with a large paper sail. Mrs. Digg's class has made a trane that that is aight feet long. Thay cannot wate to paint it.

Dictionary Skills

Using the Spelling Table

Suppose that you need to find a word in a dictionary, but you're not sure how to spell one of the sounds. What can you do? You can use a spelling table to find the different ways that the sound can be spelled.

Let's say that you're not sure how to spell the last consonant sound in *sock*. Is it *k, c, ck,* or *ch*? First, find the pronunciation symbol for the sound in the Spelling Table on page 265. Then read the first spelling listed for /k/ and look up *sok* in a dictionary. Look for each spelling in the dictionary until you find the correct one.

Sound	Spellings	Examples
/k/	k c ck ch	keep, coat, kick, school

Write the correct spelling for /k/ in each word below. Use the Spelling Table entry above and a dictionary.

1. kable ____________
2. karton ____________
3. koarse ____________
4. blak ____________
5. blok ____________
6. skeme ____________
7. komb ____________
8. subtrakt ____________
9. klok ____________
10. kard ____________
11. korn ____________
12. soks ____________

Words with Short e

next	egg	says	ready
end	help	spent	again
second	forget	dress	said
address	read	test	head

egg

Say and Listen

Say each spelling word. Listen for the short e sound.

Think and Sort

Look at the letters in each word. Think about how short e is spelled. Spell each word aloud.

Short e can be shown as /ĕ/. How many spelling patterns for /ĕ/ do you see?

1. Write the **ten** spelling words that have the *e* pattern, like *dress.*
2. Write the **three** spelling words that have the *ea* pattern, like *head.*
3. Write the **two** spelling words that have the *ai* pattern, like *said.*
4. Write the **one** spelling word that has the *ay* pattern.

1. e Words

2. ea Words

3. ai Words

4. ay Word

Clues

Write the spelling word for each clue.

1. includes a ZIP code ______
2. once more ______
3. what is done to a book ______
4. opposite of *remember* ______
5. used your money ______
6. all set ______
7. aid ______
8. I say, you say, he ___ ______

Classifying

Write the spelling word that belongs in each group.

9. hour minute ______
10. exam quiz ______
11. spoke told ______
12. first then ______
13. stop quit ______
14. blouse skirt ______
15. toast juice ______

next	egg	says	ready
end	help	spent	again
second	forget	dress	said
address	read	test	head

Proofreading

Proofread the journal entry below. Use proofreading marks to correct five spelling mistakes, two capitalization mistakes, and three punctuation mistakes.

October 18

Today I forgot to take my lunch to school. I often forgit things Mom sezs that i need to use my hed. she gave me some string and told me about a trick that will healp I will use the string to tie a bow around my secund finger The bow will help me remember my lunch.

Multiple Meanings

Many words have more than one meaning. If an entry word in a dictionary has more than one meaning, the different meanings are numbered. Read the dictionary entry below.

then (*th*ĕn) *adverb* **1.** At the time: *I used to sleep with a teddy bear, but I was only a baby then.* **2.** After that: *We saw lightning flash, and then we heard the thunder roar.* **3.** A time mentioned: *Go finish your homework, and by then dinner will be ready.*

1. What is the entry word? ____________
2. How many meanings does the word have? ____________

Write the words *egg, address, next,* and *help* in alphabetical order. Then look them up in the dictionary. Write the page on which each entry appears. Then write the number of meanings each word has.

	Word	Page	Number of Meanings
3.	____________	____________	____________
4.	____________	____________	____________
5.	____________	____________	____________
6.	____________	____________	____________

Plural Words

tests	pages	papers	dresses
hammers	tables	clowns	classes
paints	apples	eggs	matches
hands	trains	addresses	places

Say and Listen

Say the spelling words. Listen for the ending sounds.

Think and Sort

All of the spelling words are plural words. **Plural** words name more than one thing. Most plural words are formed by adding *-s*.

boy + **s** = boy**s**   page + **s** = page**s**

Singular words name one thing. If a singular word ends in *s, ss, ch,* or *x, -es* is added to form the plural.

glass + **es** = glass**es**

1. Write the **twelve** spelling words that are formed by adding *-s*, like *tests.*
2. Write the **four** spelling words that are formed by adding *-es*, like *dresses.*

1. -s Plurals

______________________ ______________________
______________________ ______________________
______________________ ______________________
____
____
____
____
____
____

2. -es Plurals

____
____
____
____

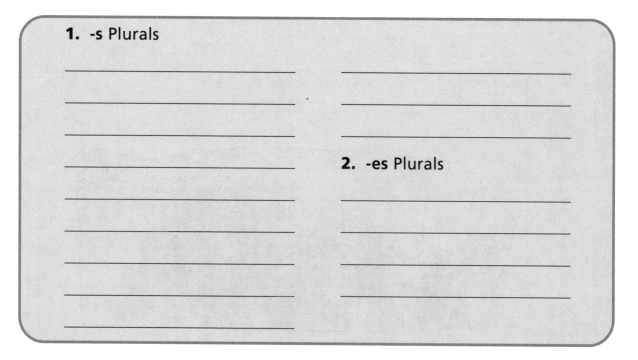

Making Connections

Complete each sentence with the spelling word that goes with the workers.

1. Artists use brushes and ______________.
2. Carpenters work with nails and ______________.
3. Fruit farmers grow oranges and ______________.
4. Cooks work with milk and ______________.
5. Teachers grade projects and ______________.
6. Writers work with ______________ in books.
7. Tailors sew skirts and ______________.
8. Mail carriers work with names and ______________.

Definitions

Write the spelling word for each definition. Use a dictionary if you need to.

9. questions that measure knowledge ______________
10. small sticks of wood used to light fires ______________
11. connected railroad cars ______________
12. part of the arms below the wrists ______________
13. particular areas ______________
14. circus performers who make people laugh ______________
15. groups of students taught by the same teacher ______________

Plural Words

tests	pages	papers	dresses
hammers	tables	clowns	classes
paints	apples	eggs	matches
hands	trains	addresses	places

Proofreading

Proofread the movie review below. Use proofreading marks to correct five spelling mistakes, three capitalization mistakes, and two punctuation mistakes.

Proofreading Marks

- ○ spell correctly
- ≡ capitalize
- ⊙ add period

MOVIE REVIEW

Do you like funny movies? If you do, you will love *Pagess from Our Lives*. it is the story of a group of clownes as they travel to different playces all over the world They use apples and egges to teach juggling to children at a school in France. they also dance on tabels at a park in China. you will have a great time at this movie Your parents will like it, too.

Base Words

A base word is a word from which other words are formed. For example, *apple* is the base word in *apples*, and *test* is the base word in *tests*.

Many entry words in a dictionary are base words. Different forms of a base word may be listed in the entry. The different forms are printed in dark type. Look up the word *dress* in a dictionary. How many different forms of *dress* does the entry show? What are they?

Write the following words in alphabetical order. Write the base word for each word. Then find the base word in the dictionary. Write the number of different forms given for the word.

hands addresses trains pages paints

	Word	Base Word	Number of Word Forms
1.	____________	____________	____________
2.	____________	____________	____________
3.	____________	____________	____________
4.	____________	____________	____________
5.	____________	____________	____________

Unit 1 Review
Lessons 1–5

Lesson 1

subtract
catch
January
laugh
half

Words with Short *a*

Write the spelling word that completes each analogy.

1. *Grab* is to ________________ as *pitch* is to *throw.*
2. *Ten* is to *five* as *whole* is to ________________.
3. *Chuckle* is to ________________ as *cry* is to *sob.*
4. *Multiply* is to *divide* as *add* is to ________________.
5. *Snow* is to ________________ as *rain* is to *April.*

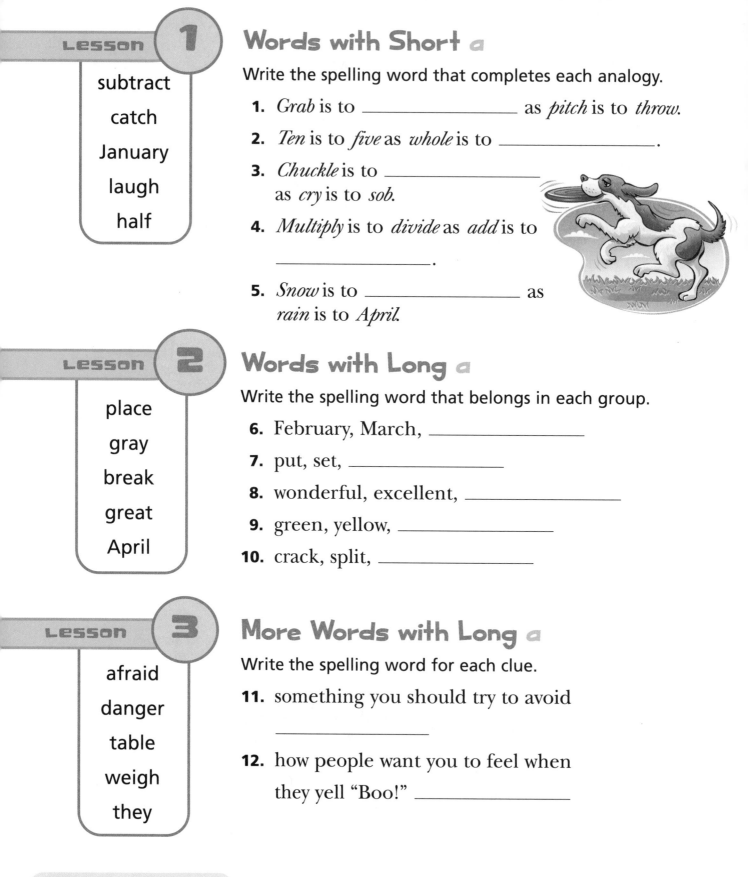

Lesson 2

place
gray
break
great
April

Words with Long *a*

Write the spelling word that belongs in each group.

6. February, March, ________________
7. put, set, ________________
8. wonderful, excellent, ________________
9. green, yellow, ________________
10. crack, split, ________________

Lesson 3

afraid
danger
table
weigh
they

More Words with Long *a*

Write the spelling word for each clue.

11. something you should try to avoid ________________
12. how people want you to feel when they yell "Boo!" ________________

13. a word that can be used to name others

____

14. what scales are used for _______________

15. what you set before a meal and sit at to eat the meal _______________

LESSON 4

address
second
ready
again
says

Words with Short e

Write the spelling word that completes each sentence.

16. Are you _______________ for school?

17. If my hair is still messy, I need to comb it _______________.

18. My mother _______________, "Clean up your room, please."

19. At the end of the race, Mario was in _______________ place.

20. Your street, town, and ZIP code are parts of your _______________

LESSON 5

eggs
hammers
places
apples
matches

Plural Words

Write the spelling word that answers each question.

21. What are red, round, and juicy? _______________

22. What do hens lay? _______________

23. What tools are good for pounding nails?

____

24. Which word rhymes with *spaces*?

____

25. What can be used to light fires?

____

More Words with Short e

slept	February	them	never
when	many	sent	kept
September	best	friend	then
cents	Wednesday	guess	better

Say and Listen

Say each spelling word. Listen for the short *e* sound.

Think and Sort

Look at the letters in each word. Think about how short *e* is spelled. Spell each word aloud.

Short *e* can be shown as /ĕ/. How many spelling patterns for /ĕ/ do you see?

1. Write the **thirteen** spelling words that have the *e* pattern, like *best.*
2. Write the **one** spelling word that has the *ie* pattern.
3. Write the **one** spelling word that has the *a* pattern.
4. Write the **one** spelling word that has the *ue* pattern.

1. e Words

______________________ ______________________

______________________ ______________________

______________________ ______________________

______________________ ______________________

____

____

____

____

____

2. ie Word

____

3. a Word

____

4. ue Word

____

Classifying

Write the spelling word that belongs in each group.

1. lots several ____________
2. pal buddy ____________
3. July August ____________
4. Monday Tuesday ____________
5. rested napped ____________
6. December January ____________
7. good better ____________
8. mailed shipped ____________
9. who what ____________

Rhymes

Write the spelling word that completes each sentence and rhymes with the underlined word.

10. If you don't have a <u>pen</u>, ____________ I will lend you one.
11. No one <u>slept</u> because the dog ____________ us up.
12. Tell ____________ to <u>hem</u> the curtains.
13. Have you ever read a ____________ <u>letter</u>?
14. Let me ____________ who made this <u>mess</u>.
15. I ____________ knew you were so <u>clever</u>.

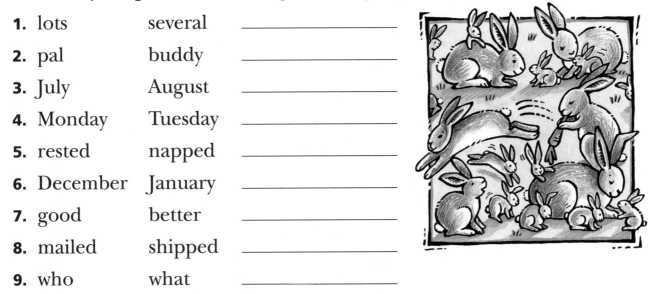

slept	February	them	never
when	many	sent	kept
September	best	friend	then
cents	Wednesday	guess	better

Proofreading

Proofread the e-mail below. Use proofreading marks to correct five spelling mistakes, three capitalization mistakes, and two punctuation mistakes.

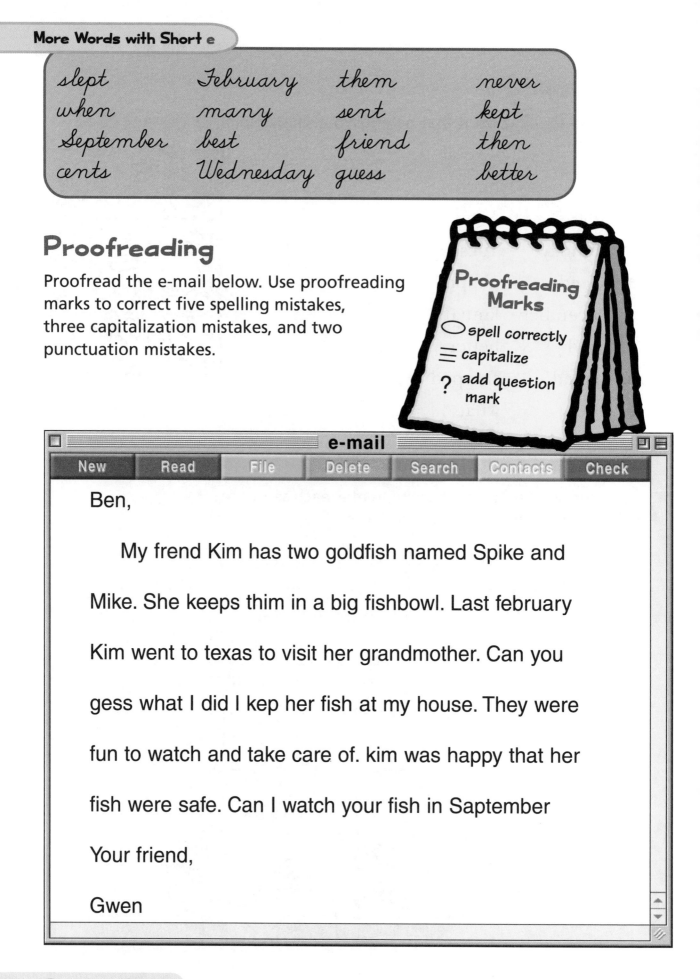

e-mail

New | Read | File | Delete | Search | Contacts | Check

Ben,

My frend Kim has two goldfish named Spike and Mike. She keeps thim in a big fishbowl. Last february Kim went to texas to visit her grandmother. Can you gess what I did I kep her fish at my house. They were fun to watch and take care of. kim was happy that her fish were safe. Can I watch your fish in Saptember

Your friend,

Gwen

Capital Letters

Use a capital letter to begin the names of people and pets and to write the word *I*. Also use a capital letter to begin the first word of a sentence.

The following sentences have capitalization errors. Write each sentence correctly.

1. the book i like best was written by fred gibson.

   ____

2. it is about a dog called old yeller.

   ____

3. travis and old yeller have many adventures.

   ____

4. carl anderson wrote about a horse named blaze.

   ____

5. blaze was kept by a boy named billy.

   ____

6. a horse named thunderbolt became friends with billy and blaze.

   ____

Words with Long e

street	please	free	wheel
read	queen	each	sneeze
people	meet	team	sea
need	dream	sleep	meat

queen

Say and Listen

Say each spelling word. Listen for the long e sound.

Think and Sort

Look at the letters in each word. Think about how long e is spelled. Spell each word aloud.

Long e can be shown as /ē/. How many spelling patterns for /ē/ do you see?

1. Write the **eight** spelling words that have the *ee* pattern, like *meet.*
2. Write the **seven** spelling words that have the *ea* pattern, like *team.*
3. Write the **one** spelling word that has the *eo* pattern.

1. e Words

____

____

____

____

____

____

____

____

2. ea Words

____

____

____

____

____

____

____

3. eo Word

____

Analogies

Write the spelling word that completes each analogy.

1. *Sit* is to *chair* as ________________ is to *bed.*
2. *Train* is to *track* as *car* is to ________________.
3. *Hives* are to *bees* as *houses* are to ________________.
4. *Cough* is to *mouth* as ________________ is to *nose.*
5. *Book* is to ________________ as *movie* is to *watch.*
6. *Rectangle* is to *door* as *circle* is to ________________.
7. *Bush* is to *shrub* as *ocean* is to ________________.

Definitions

Write the spelling word for each definition.
Use a dictionary if you need to.

8. food from the flesh of animals ________________
9. a group of people playing on the same side ________________
10. to think, feel, or see during sleep ________________
11. to come together ________________
12. without cost ________________
13. to give pleasure or happiness to ________________
14. every one ________________
15. must have ________________

street	please	free	wheel
read	queen	each	sneeze
people	meet	team	sea
need	dream	sleep	meat

Proofreading

Proofread the book jacket below. Use proofreading marks to correct five spelling mistakes, three capitalization mistakes, and two unnecessary words.

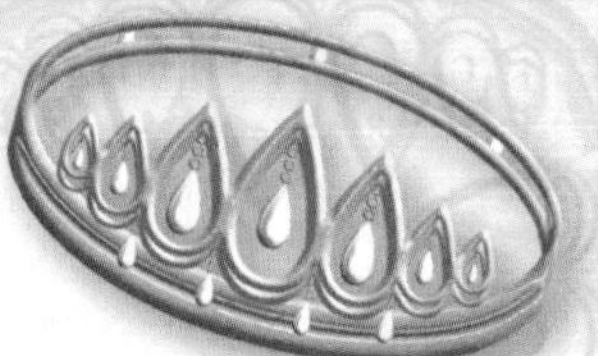

Readers will love this new story about a young queen. one day she has a a strange dream. In the dream, she is on a baseball teme. each time she gets up to bat, a sea of of peeple cheer her. The queen hits four home runs. after the game, she wants to mete ech fan. Rede this exciting tale to learn what happens when the queen wakes up.

Language Connection

Nouns

A noun is a word that names a person, place, thing, or idea. The following words are nouns.

Person	Place	Thing	Idea
boy	seashore	toy	beauty
girl	forest	dog	peace

Write the sentences below, completing them with the correct nouns from the boxes.

meat | wheel | sea | dream | people | street

1. I had a wonderful ___ last night.

2. All the ___ who live on my ___ were in it.

3. I used a big ___ to steer our big ship out to ___.

4. We had a feast of fruit and roasted ___ on an island.

More Words with Long e

only	story	key	family
sleepy	carry	sunny	these
funny	very	every	city
penny	even	happy	busy

city

Say and Listen

Say each spelling word. Listen for the long e sound.

Think and Sort

Look at the letters in each word. Think about how long e is spelled. Spell each word aloud.

Long e can be shown as /ē/. How many spelling patterns for /ē/ do you see?

1. Write the **one** spelling word that has the *e* pattern.
2. Write the **thirteen** spelling words that have the *y* pattern, like *story.*
3. Write the **one** spelling word that has the *e*-consonant-*e* pattern.
4. Write the **one** spelling word that has the *ey* pattern.

1. e Word

____

2. y Words

____

____

____

____

____

____

____

____

____

____

____

____

____

3. e-consonant-e Word

____

4. ey Word

____

Definitions

Write the spelling word for each definition.
Use a dictionary if you need to.

1. to take from one place to another ________
2. extremely ________
3. the most important part ________
4. laughable ________
5. each ________
6. one cent ________
7. nearby items ________
8. a telling of something that happened ________
9. just ________

Antonyms

Write the spelling word that is an antonym of the underlined word.

10. Seth was <u>sad</u> when summer camp began. ________
11. We will go to the zoo on a <u>cloudy</u> day. ________
12. Saturday was a <u>lazy</u> day for everyone. ________
13. Life in the <u>country</u> can be very exciting. ________
14. Kara felt <u>lively</u> after reading a book. ________
15. Twelve is an <u>odd</u> number. ________

only	story	key	family
sleepy	carry	sunny	these
funny	very	every	city
penny	even	happy	busy

Proofreading

Proofread the letter below. Use proofreading marks to correct five spelling mistakes, three capitalization mistakes, and two punctuation mistakes.

306 Maple Drive
Campbell, CA 95011
November 10, 2004

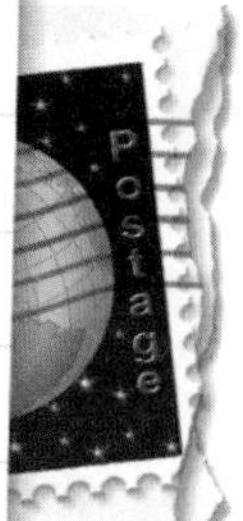

Dear Tina,

My mom got a new job. she is going to be a firefighter in the big citty of Chicago, Illinois Our familee is very hapy. we have been buzy packing since early thursday morning I will write again verry soon and tell you more.

Your cousin,

Tasha

Alphabetical Order

The words in a dictionary are in alphabetical order.
Use a dictionary to complete the following sentences.

1. Words that begin with **A** start on page ________________ and end on page ________________.
2. Words that begin with **M** start on page ________________ and end on page ________________.
3. Words that begin with **W** start on page ________________ and end on page ________________.

Write the words below in alphabetical order. Then find each one in the dictionary and write its page number.

funny even carry key

	Word	**Page**
4.	________________	________________
5.	________________	________________
6.	________________	________________
7.	________________	________________

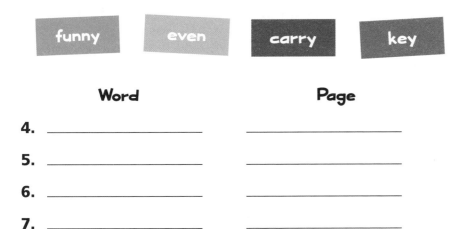

Words with Short u

from	Sunday	money	under
nothing	summer	does	mother
lunch	month	such	front
much	sun	other	Monday

Say and Listen

Say each spelling word. Listen for the short *u* sound.

Think and Sort

Look at the letters in each word. Think about how short *u* is spelled. Spell each word aloud.

Short *u* can be shown as /ŭ/. How many spelling patterns for /ŭ/ do you see?

1. Write the **seven** spelling words that have the *u* pattern, like *sun.*
2. Write the **one** spelling word that has the *oe* pattern.
3. Write the **eight** spelling words that have the *o* pattern, like *month.*

1. u Words

____
____
____
____
____
____
____

2. oe Word

____

3. o Words

____
____
____
____
____
____
____
____

Letter Scramble

Unscramble the underlined letters to make a spelling word. Write the word on the line.

1. Kelly was at the <u>tronf</u> of the line. ______________
2. We hid the keys <u>drune</u> the mat. ______________
3. How much <u>noemy</u> is in your pocket? ______________
4. We had never seen <u>chus</u> a mess. ______________
5. We could see <u>honnitg</u> in the dark. ______________
6. When <u>osde</u> the bus come? ______________

Clues

Write the spelling word for each clue.

7. The first one is January. ______________
8. This day comes before Tuesday. ______________
9. This word is the opposite of *to*. ______________
10. When it shines, you feel warmer. ______________
11. This day comes after Saturday. ______________
12. This person has at least one son or daughter. ______________
13. If you have this, you have a lot. ______________
14. This season contains June, July, and August. ______________
15. This word means "different." ______________

Words with Short u

from	Sunday	money	under
nothing	summer	does	mother
lunch	month	such	front
much	sun	other	Monday

Proofreading

Proofread the e-mail message below. Use proofreading marks to correct five spelling mistakes, three capitalization mistakes, and two punctuation mistakes.

e-mail

New | Read | File | Delete | Search

Dear Grandpa,

Thank you for the soccer ball and mony you gave me for my birthday on Munday. Somer begins in only one more month. Can you believe it I am going to play soccer in our frunt yard every day. each sunday I will come to your house. We can sit in the sun and eat lonch. We'll have fun! does that sound good to you

Josh

Language Connection

Question Marks

Use a question mark at the end of a sentence that asks a question.

Do you like riddles? **Can you answer these?**

your teeth

your lap

the letter m

Write each riddle correctly. Then choose one of the answers in the boxes to the right and write it in the space provided.

1. What comes once in a month, twice in a moment, but never in a hundred years

____

____

Answer: ________________

2. What do you lose whenever you stand up

____

Answer: ________________

3. What can you put into the apple pie you have for lunch

____

Answer: ________________

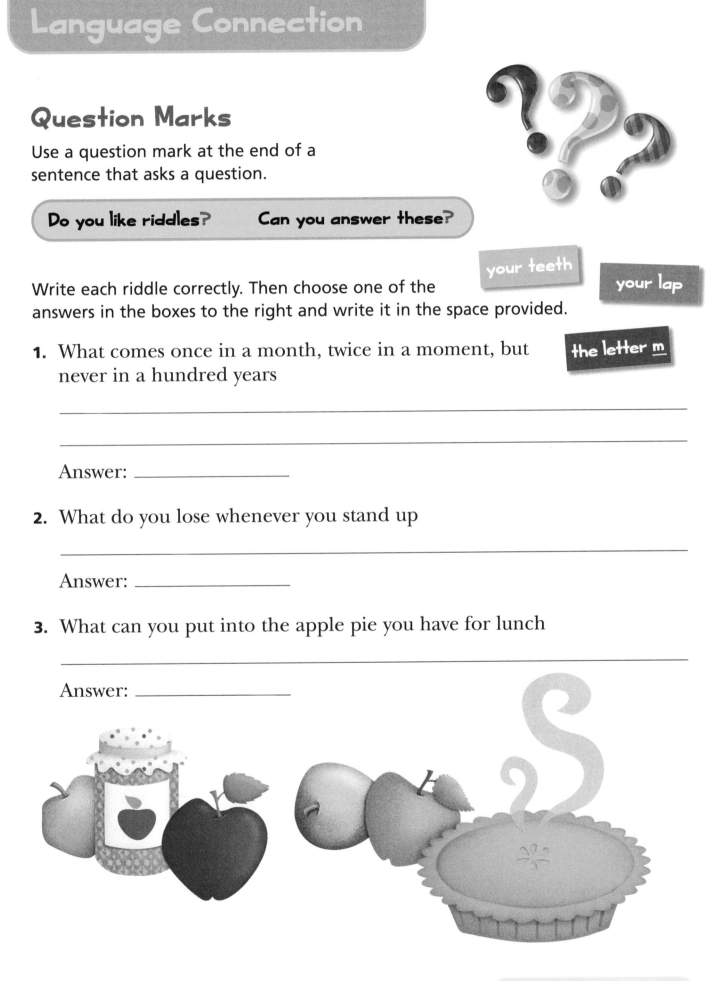

Contractions

she's	they'll	I've	you'll
we've	I'm	I'll	you've
it's	I'd	you'd	we'll
they'd	she'll	they've	he's

Say and Listen

Say the spelling words. Listen to the ending sounds.

Think and Sort

Each spelling word is a **contraction**. Two words are joined, but one or more letters are left out. An apostrophe (') is used in place of the missing letters.

Had and *would* are written the same way in contractions. So are *is* and *has*.

1. Write the **five** spelling words that are *will* contractions, like *we'll.*
2. Write the **four** spelling words that are *have* contractions, like *you've.*
3. Write the **three** spelling words that are *would* or *had* contractions, like *they'd.*
4. Write the **three** spelling words that are *is* or *has* contractions, like *she's.*
5. Write the **one** spelling word that is an *am* contraction.

1. will Contractions

____

____

____

____

____

2. have Contractions

____

____

____

____

3. would or **had** Contractions

____

____

____

4. is or **has** Contractions

____

____

____

5. am Contractions

____

Trading Places

Write the contraction that could be used instead of the underlined words in each sentence.

1. It is time to eat. ________________
2. I have seen the world's tallest building. ________________
3. He is feeling tired. ________________
4. You will like my uncle's farm. ________________
5. You have grown so tall! ________________
6. They would be happy to see you. ________________
7. They have found their ball. ________________
8. We will make dinner together. ________________
9. We have finished painting. ________________

Rhymes

Write the spelling word that completes each sentence and rhymes with the underlined word.

10. A dime is what ________________ looking for.
11. Did you hear Kara sneeze? ________________ got a cold.
12. If the children see a whale, ________________ be excited.
13. The seal is hungry, so ________________ feed it.
14. Let's buy food that ________________ like to eat.
15. While you nap, ________________ read a book.

she's	they'll	I've	you'll
we've	I'm	I'll	you've
it's	I'd	you'd	we'll
they'd	she'll	they've	he's

Proofreading

Proofread the journal entry below. Use proofreading marks to correct five spelling mistakes, two capitalization mistakes, and three punctuation mistakes.

November 14

My friend pete and I found a lost dog today. I'me not sure whose puppy it is. Pete thought that I'dd know because I know all the dogs in the neighborhood He's really worried about the pup. It's white with black spots.

Wev' put up signs about finding a lost puppy. I'v even called Chief collins at the police station

We'l be glad when we find the owner

Language Connection

Contractions

At least one letter and sound are missing from every contraction. An apostrophe (') shows where the letter or letters have been left out. For example, in the contraction *we've*, the apostrophe shows that the letters *ha* have been left out.

I'm = I **am**   we've = we **ha**ve

Write the contraction for each pair of words. Then write the letter or letters that are left out.

	Contraction	Letter or Letters Left Out
1. I will	________	________
2. he is	________	________
3. it is	________	________
4. they have	________	________
5. you had	________	________
6. I am	________	________
7. you would	________	________
8. she has	________	________

Unit 2 Review
Lessons 6–10

Lesson 6

Wednesday
February
friend
many
guess

More Words with Short e

Write the spelling word that completes each analogy.

1. *Pal* is to ______________ as *chilly* is to *cold.*
2. *Saturday* is to *end* as ______________ is to *middle.*
3. *Know* is to *understand* as *suppose* is to ______________.
4. *Little* is to *few* as *much* is to ______________.
5. *Monday* is to *day* as ______________ is to *month.*

Lesson 7

queen
meet
please
team
people

Words with Long e

Write the spelling word that belongs in each group.

6. duchess princess ______________
7. group club ______________
8. persons humans ______________
9. touch join ______________
10. delight cheer ______________

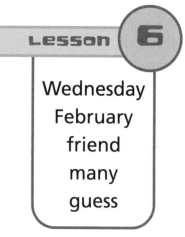

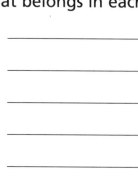

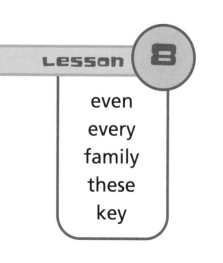

Lesson 8

even
every
family
these
key

More Words with Long e

Write the spelling word for each clue.

11. This has parents and children. ______________
12. If a floor is flat, it is this. ______________
13. You can use this word instead of *each.* ______________

14. This can unlock a door or start a car.

____

15. We use this word to point out a group of nearby things. ______________

LESSON 9

lunch
such
other
month
does

Words with Short u

Write the spelling word that completes each sentence.

16. My cat always ______________ whatever he wants.

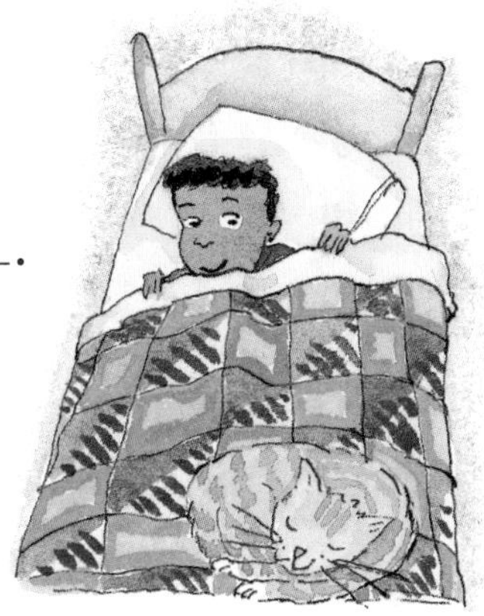

17. Mom and Dad pay our bills at the end of the ______________.

18. Do you want this blouse or the ______________ one?

19. Isaac had soup and a salad for ______________ today.

20. Dad and I had never seen ______________ a big storm.

LESSON 10

she'll
you've
they'd
it's
I'm

Contractions

Write the spelling word for each word pair.

21. I am ______________

22. you have ______________

23. she will ______________

24. they would ______________

25. it is ______________

More Words with Short u

lovely	just	something	hundred
done	some	sum	must
shove	won	butter	cover
supper	none	number	one

supper

Say and Listen

Say each spelling word. Listen for the short *u* sound.

Think and Sort

Look at the letters in each word. Think about how short *u* is spelled. Spell each word aloud.

Short *u* can be shown as /ŭ/. How many spelling patterns for /ŭ/ do you see?

1. Write the **seven** spelling words that have the *u* pattern, like *must.*
2. Write the **two** spelling words that have the *o* pattern, like *won.*
3. Write the **seven** spelling words that have the *o*-consonant-*e* pattern, like *some.*

1. u Words

____
____
____
____
____
____
____

2. o Words

____
____

3. o-consonant-**e** Words

____
____
____
____
____
____
____

Definitions

Write the spelling word for each definition. Use a dictionary if you need to.

1. gained a victory ________
2. to put or lay over ________
3. a particular thing that is not named ________
4. a certain number of ________
5. the answer for an addition problem ________
6. a number, written 1 ________
7. ten groups of ten ________
8. will have to ________
9. amount ________
10. not any ________

Synonyms

Complete each sentence by writing the spelling word that is a synonym for the underlined word.

11. Tan's work will soon be <u>finished</u>. ________
12. Tasha is wearing a <u>beautiful</u> scarf. ________
13. I'll <u>push</u> Mother's surprise in the closet. ________
14. No one could argue with the <u>fair</u> law. ________
15. Kevin ate fish and rice for <u>dinner</u>. ________

lovely	just	something	hundred
done	some	sum	must
shove	won	butter	cover
supper	none	number	one

Proofreading

Proofread the journal entry below. Use proofreading marks to correct five spelling mistakes, three capitalization mistakes, and two punctuation mistakes.

December 15

yesterday was the best day of my life. I jest cannot believe that I won something. rocket and I were nomber one in the show. now we have a lovley ribbon. There were more than two hunderd people watching.

I must enter another horse show soon I've never dun anything as fun as riding in that show. I think Rocket had fun, too. Dad says that he will take us to any show in the state

Homophones

Homophones are words that sound alike but have different spellings and meanings. Look at the homophone pairs in the boxes below. Think about what each homophone means.

one won some sum

ate eight son sun sail sale

Use the homophones above to complete each sentence. Use a dictionary if you need to.

1. The ship must ________________ at sunrise.
2. I bought this lovely jacket on ________________.
3. Jason ________________ some soup and a sandwich for supper.
4. My favorite number is ________________.
5. The hot ________________ made some of us thirsty.
6. We just met Mrs. Lee's daughter and her ________________.
7. Jesse ________________ two blue ribbons at the art contest.
8. Mr. Ono owns ________________ car and two bicycles.
9. Mari found the ________________ of ________________ numbers.

Words with Short i

thing	little	winter	kick
begin	river	been	dish
fill	think	spring	pretty
which	December	build	children

Say and Listen

Say each spelling word. Listen for the short *i* sound.

Think and Sort

Look at the letters in each word. Think about how short *i* is spelled. Spell each word aloud.

Short *i* can be shown as /ĭ/. How many spelling patterns for /ĭ/ do you see?

1. Write the **eleven** spelling words that have the *i* pattern, like *dish.*
2. Write the **two** spelling words that have the *e* pattern, like *pretty.*
3. Write the **one** spelling word that has the *e* and the *i* patterns.
4. Write the **one** spelling word that has the *ui* pattern.
5. Write the **one** spelling word that has the *ee* pattern.

1. i Words

____

____

____

____

____

____

____

____

____

____

____

2. e Words

____

____

3. e and i Word

____

4. ui Word

____

5. ee Word

____

Clues

Write the spelling word for each clue.

1. what you do to a soccer ball ____________
2. young people ____________
3. what you do with a hammer and nails ____________
4. a big stream ____________
5. a season that can be cold ____________
6. a word that rhymes with *fish* ____________
7. the opposite of *end* ____________
8. a word for *beautiful* ____________
9. the opposite of *big* ____________

Rhymes

Write the spelling word that completes each sentence and rhymes with the underlined word.

10. I ____________ I will wear my pink shirt.
11. The coach told the player ____________ pitch was good.
12. If you have not ____________ practicing, you will not win the music contest.
13. I will bring you flowers in the ____________.
14. Jill will climb the hill and ____________ the bucket.
15. Bring that little blue ____________ to me.

thing	little	winter	kick
begin	river	been	dish
fill	think	spring	pretty
which	December	build	children

Proofreading

Proofread the postcard below. Use proofreading marks to correct five spelling mistakes, three capitalization mistakes, and two punctuation mistakes.

Hi, luke!

We had a great time at the pioneer fair. i saw people buld a barn I learned that it was hard to be a pioneer in the winnter. The rivere freezes by Decembr, and then it is hard to fish. Life is easier when springe comes. maybe you can come to the fair with us next year

Dylan

Luke Babb
158 Beach Drive
Austin, TX 78739

Language Connection

Adjectives

An adjective describes a noun or pronoun by telling which one, what kind, or how many.

The spotted pony ate the green grass.

The fresh flowers are lovely.

Use the adjectives in the boxes below to complete the sentences. Then circle all the adjectives in the sentences.

icy | little | hot | every | dangerous | pretty | shallow | many | brown | late

1. A river flows by the simple ______________ cabin.
2. It travels for ______________ miles through the thick forest.
3. In the winter the river is cold and ______________.
4. Thin ice in some places is ______________ for skaters.
5. Many ______________ flowers line the banks in spring.
6. On ______________ summer days, people wade in the river.
7. They walk on large rocks in the ______________ water.
8. In the fall, red and ______________ leaves float down the river.
9. The river changes with ______________ season.

Words with Long i

alike	while	eyes	white
line	lion	size	miles
times	nice	drive	tiny
write	inside	mine	shine

lion

Say and Listen

Say each spelling word. Listen for the long *i* sound.

Think and Sort

Look at the letters in each word. Think about how long *i* is spelled. Spell each word aloud.

Long *i* can be shown as /ī/. How many spelling patterns for /ī/ do you see?

1. Write the **thirteen** spelling words that have the *i*-consonant-*e* pattern, like *nice.*
2. Write the **two** spelling words that have the *i* pattern, like *tiny.*
3. Write the **one** spelling word that has the *eye* pattern.

1. i-consonant-e Words

______________________ ______________________

______________________ ______________________

______________________ ______________________

______________________ ______________________

____

____

____

____

____

2. i Words

____

____

3. eye Word

____

Clues

Write the spelling word for each clue.

1. what people do with a car ________
2. belongs in a group with *feet* and *yards* ________
3. it can be straight or crooked ________
4. a word meaning "at the same time" ________
5. a word that rhymes with eyes ________
6. what people do to some shoes ________

Analogies

Write the spelling word that completes each analogy.

7. *Mean* is to ________ as *weak* is to *strong*.
8. *You* is to *me* as *yours* is to ________.
9. *Add* is to *plus* as *multiply* is to ________.
10. *Light* is to *dark* as ________ is to *black*.
11. *Hear* is to *ears* as *see* is to ________.
12. *Needle* is to *sew* as *pen* is to ________.
13. *Small* is to ________ as *big* is to *huge*.
14. *Different* is to *unlike* as *same* is to ________.
15. *Up* is to *down* as ________ is to *outside*.

alike	while	eyes	white
line	lion	size	miles
times	nice	drive	tiny
write	inside	mine	shine

Proofreading

Proofread the newspaper article below. Use proofreading marks to correct five spelling mistakes, three capitalization mistakes, and two punctuation mistakes.

Lion Land Big Treat

Lion Land opened over the weekend to wild cheers People came from mils away. they stood in linne for hours to become part of this wildlife adventure. once they got insid, they could not believe their eyez. Lions strolled freely and came right up to the cars. We got just a tiney bit nervous when a lion the size of a horse looked at us through our car window. check out Lion Land for yourself. You won't be disappointed

Guide Words

Each page in a dictionary has two words at the top. These words are called guide words. The first guide word is the first entry word on the page. The other guide word is the last entry word on the page. Guide words help you find entry words.

Look at the dictionary page below and find the guide words.

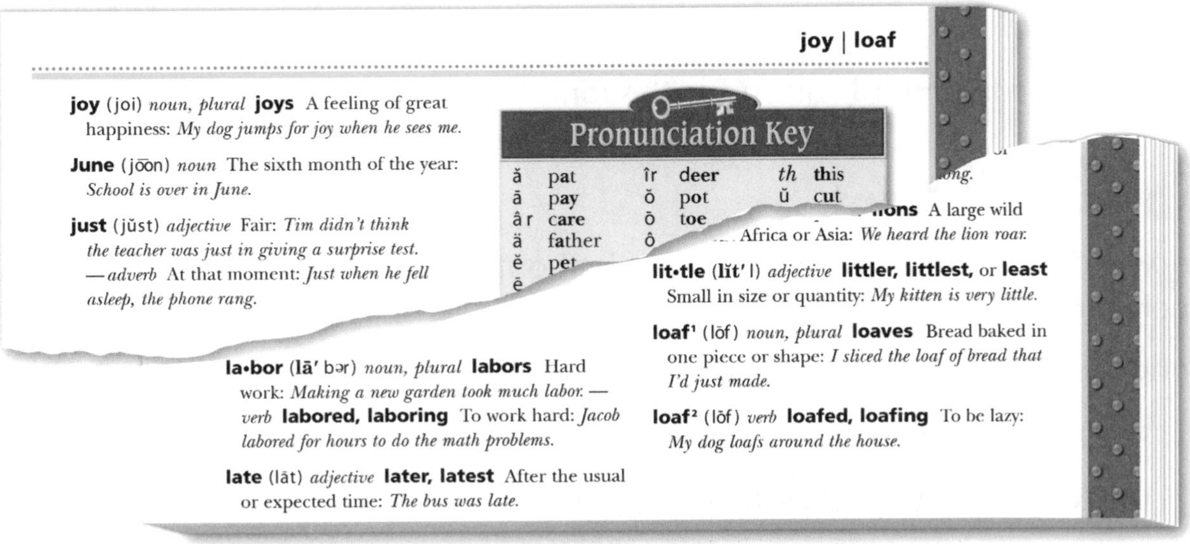

joy | loaf

joy (joi) *noun, plural* **joys** A feeling of great happiness: *My dog jumps for joy when he sees me.*

June (jo͞on) *noun* The sixth month of the year: *School is over in June.*

just (jŭst) *adjective* Fair: *Tim didn't think the teacher was just in giving a surprise test.* —*adverb* At that moment: *Just when he fell asleep, the phone rang.*

la•bor (lā′ bər) *noun, plural* **labors** Hard work: *Making a new garden took much labor.* —*verb* **labored, laboring** To work hard: *Jacob labored for hours to do the math problems.*

late (lāt) *adjective* **later, latest** After the usual or expected time: *The bus was late.*

Pronunciation Key

ă	pat	îr	deer	*th*	this
ā	pay	ŏ	pot	ŭ	cut
âr	care	ō	toe		
ä	father	ô			
ĕ	pet				
ē					

ong.

ons A large wild ... Africa or Asia: *We heard the lion roar.*

lit•tle (lĭt′ l) *adjective* **littler, littlest,** or **least** Small in size or quantity: *My kitten is very little.*

loaf¹ (lōf) *noun, plural* **loaves** Bread baked in one piece or shape: *I sliced the loaf of bread that I'd just made.*

loaf² (lōf) *verb* **loafed, loafing** To be lazy: *My dog loafs around the house.*

Look up these spelling words in a dictionary. Write the guide words and page number for each.

	Guide Words		Page
1. while	______	______	______
2. drive	______	______	______
3. nice	______	______	______
4. size	______	______	______

More Words with Long i

buy	Friday	fly	kind
why	child	mind	try
behind	sky	cry	high
right	by	light	night

Say and Listen

Say each spelling word. Listen for the long *i* sound.

Think and Sort

Look at the letters in each word. Think about how long *i* is spelled. Spell each word aloud.

Long *i* can be shown as /ī/. How many spelling patterns for /ī/ do you see?

1. Write the **five** spelling words that have the *i* pattern, like *kind.*
2. Write the **six** spelling words that have the *y* pattern, like *try.*
3. Write the **four** spelling words that have the *igh* pattern, like *high.*
4. Write the **one** spelling word that has the *uy* pattern.

1. i Words

____

____

____

____

____

2. y Words

____

____

____

____

____

____

3. igh Words

____

____

____

____

4. uy Word

____

Definitions

Write the spelling word for each definition. Use a dictionary if you need to.

1. at the back of ______
2. to move through the air ______
3. day before Saturday ______
4. helpful ______
5. next to ______

Rhymes

Write the spelling word that completes each sentence and rhymes with the underlined word.

6. My ______ shoe feels too <u>tight</u>.
7. The big box of toys was <u>quite</u> ______.
8. The <u>spy</u> climbed ______ in the tree.
9. The young ______ chose a book about <u>wild</u> animals.
10. Wet or <u>dry</u>, these onions make me ______.
11. Turn on the <u>light</u> to see at ______.
12. Here's a fork so you can ______ my apple <u>pie</u>.
13. What should I ______ <u>my</u> mom for her birthday?
14. Do you ______ if I close the <u>blind</u>?
15. Tell me ______ you used purple <u>dye</u>.

buy	Friday	fly	kind
why	child	mind	try
behind	sky	cry	high
right	by	light	night

Proofreading

Proofread the e-mail message below. Use proofreading marks to correct five spelling mistakes, three capitalization mistakes, and two punctuation mistakes.

Proofreading Marks

- ◯ spell correctly
- ≡ capitalize
- ⊙ add period

e-mail

New | Read | File | Delete | Search | Contacts

sam,

Tinker is in trouble again On Frieday he put my hat behinde the couch. That nighte he hid my sock He really has a miend of his own. that is whiy I love him so much.

Are you going to the cat show on Saturday? write me back and let me know. Here is a new picture of Tinker.

Betsy

Tinker

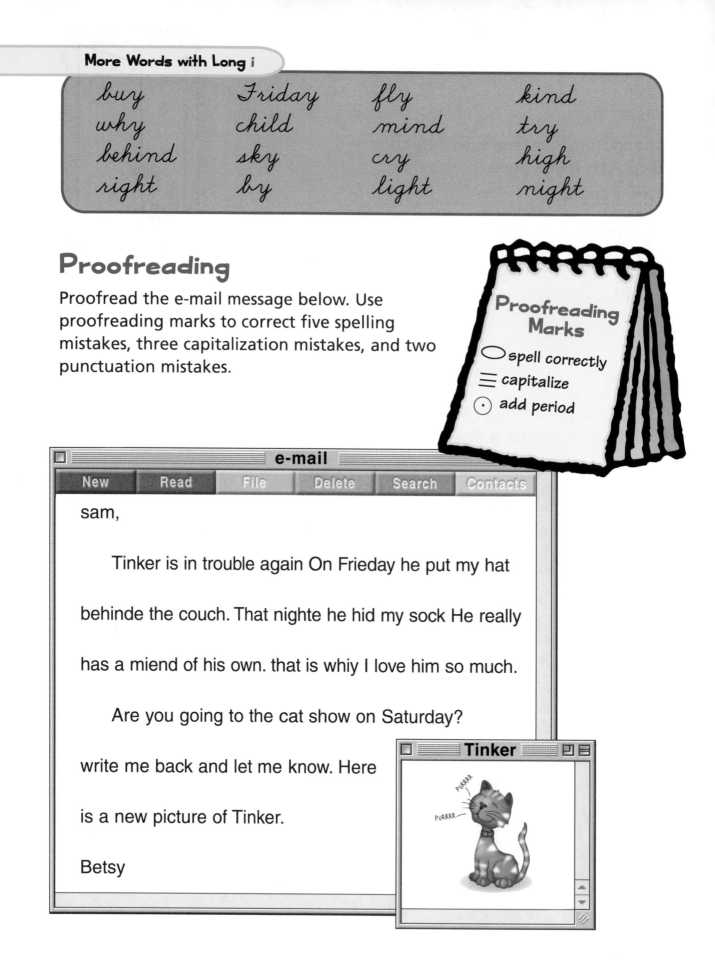

Alphabetical Order

Many words begin with the same letter. To arrange these words in alphabetical order, look at the second letter of each word. Look at the two words below. Then complete the sentences that follow.

sky **story**

1. *Sky* and *story* both start with the letter *s*. To put them in alphabetical order, look at the _______________ letter.
2. The second letter in *sky* is _______________.
3. The second letter in *story* is _______________.
4. In the alphabet, *k* comes before *t*, so the word _______________ comes before the word _______________.

In each list below, the words begin with the same letter. Look at the second letter of each word. Then write the words in alphabetical order.

5. **buy** **behind** **by**

____

____

____

6. **fly** **Friday** **finish**

____

____

____

Words with -ed or -ing

ending	wished	asked	guessing
laughing	dreamed	rained	meeting
sleeping	handed	painted	filled
reading	subtracted	thanked	waited

rained

Say and Listen

Say the spelling words.
Listen for the *-ed* and *-ing* endings.

Think and Sort

Each spelling word is formed by adding *-ed* or *-ing* to a base word. A **base word** is a word from which other words are formed. The base word for *wished* is *wish*. The base word for *ending* is *end*.

Look at each spelling word. Think about the base word and the ending. Spell each word aloud.

1. Write the **ten** spelling words that end in *-ed*, like *painted*.
2. Write the **six** spelling words that end in *-ing*, like *reading*.

1. -ed Words

____
____
____
____
____
____
____
____
____
____

2. -ing Words

____
____
____
____
____
____

Definitions

Write the spelling word for each definition.
Use a dictionary if you need to.

1. passed with one's hands ________
2. said that one was pleased ________
3. stayed ________
4. a coming together for some purpose ________
5. forming an opinion without all the facts ________
6. saw or thought during sleep ________
7. fell in drops of water from the clouds ________

Analogies

Write the spelling word that completes each analogy.

8. *Taught* is to *instructed* as *hoped* is to ________.
9. *Dress* is to *sewed* as *picture* is to ________.
10. *Playing* is to *piano* as ________ is to *book.*
11. *Chair* is to *sitting* as *bed* is to ________.
12. *Told* is to *explained* as *questioned* is to ________.
13. *Happy* is to ________ as *sad* is to *crying.*
14. *Beginning* is to *start* as ________ is to *finish.*
15. *Out* is to *emptied* as *in* is to ________.

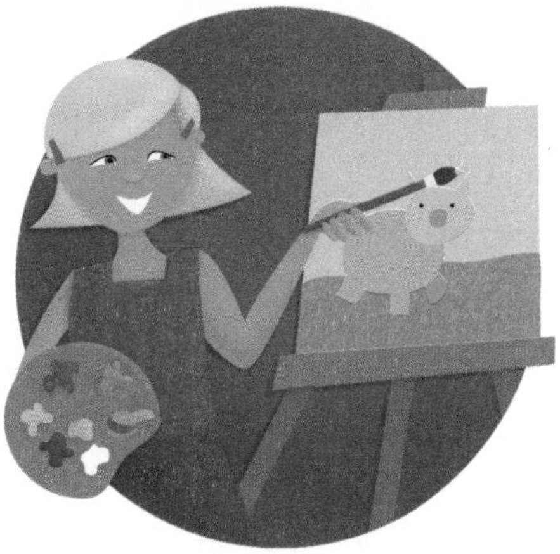

ending	wished	asked	guessing
laughing	dreamed	rained	meeting
sleeping	handed	painted	filled
reading	subtracted	thanked	waited

Proofreading

Proofread the movie review below. Use proofreading marks to correct five spelling mistakes, three capitalization mistakes, and two unnecessary words.

Proofreading Marks

- ○ spell correctly
- ≡ capitalize
- ℓ take out

A Winning Team Is a Winner!

this movie is about a losing hockey team. The coach has tried everything to to help the team win. he called a meating each day before practice. He thankt the players for their hard work but told them he wisht they would do better. He askt the players to run five miles a day, even when it it rained. the surprise endin shows what really worked.

Language Connection

End Punctuation

- Use a **period** at the end of a sentence that tells or explains something.
- Use a **question mark** at the end of a sentence that asks a question.
- Use an **exclamation point** at the end of a sentence that shows strong feeling or surprise.

In sentences that have quotation marks, place the end punctuation inside the quotation marks.

Matt said, "Here comes the team."

The police officer yelled, "Open that door!"

Write the following sentences, using periods, question marks, and exclamation points correctly.

1. Betsy asked Paul, "Who painted this picture"

   ____

2. She saw that Paul was sleeping

   ____

3. Betsy shouted, "Boo"

   ____

4. Paul jumped up fast

   ____

5. "Oh, Betsy," he cried. "Now I'll never know the ending of my dream"

   ____

6. They both started laughing

   ____

Unit 3 Review
Lessons 11–15

Lesson 11

butter
hundred
done
lovely
won

More Words with Short u

Write the spelling word for each clue.

1. People often use this word to describe flowers. ______________
2. This is the sum of 99 and 1. ______________
3. If you came in first, you did this. ______________
4. You can spread this on bread. ______________
5. When you are finished, you are this. ______________

Lesson 12

which
children
pretty
build
been

Words with Short i

Write the spelling word that belongs in each group.

6. where when ______________
7. be being ______________
8. beautiful lovely ______________
9. form make ______________
10. tots youngsters ______________

Lesson 13

while
write
tiny
lion
eyes

Words with Long i

Write the spelling word for each definition.

11. the body parts used for seeing ______________
12. to make letters on a surface ______________
13. a large wild cat ______________

14. although ________________

15. very small ________________

Lesson 14

behind
why
right
night
buy

More Words with Long i

Write the spelling word that has the same meaning as the word or words in dark type.

16. **For what reason** did the pioneers go west?

____

17. Can I **pay for** this toy?

____

18. You were **correct** about the weather.

____

19. Last **evening** I had a strange dream.

____

20. Please stand **in back of** me in line.

____

Lesson 15

wished
thanked
dreamed
guessing
laughing

Words with -ed or -ing

Write the spelling word that completes each sentence.

21. They are ________________ at your joke.

22. Alicia ________________ for a new bicycle.

23. Are you just ________________ the answer?

24. Amad ________________ about winning a trophy.

25. The teacher ________________ the children for the gift.

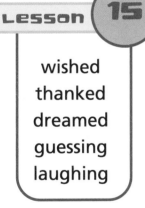

Words with Short o

October	shop	block	bottle
o'clock	sorry	socks	problem
what	jog	wash	was
clock	bottom	forgot	body

shop

Say and Listen

Say each spelling word. Listen for the short *o* sound.

Think and Sort

Look at the letters in each word. Think about how short *o* is spelled. Spell each word aloud.

Short *o* can be shown as /ŏ/. How many spelling patterns for /ŏ/ do you see?

1. Write the **thirteen** spelling words that have the *o* pattern, like *shop.*
2. Write the **three** spelling words that have the *a* pattern, like *was.*

1. o Words

______________________ ______________________

______________________ ______________________

______________________ ______________________

______________________ ______________________

____

____

____

____

____

2. a Words

____

____

____

Clues

Write the spelling word for each clue.

1. clothes that belong on your feet ______________
2. has streets on all sides ______________
3. in a group with *walk* and *run* ______________
4. feeling regret ______________
5. a question word ______________
6. opposite of *remembered* ______________
7. means "of the clock" ______________

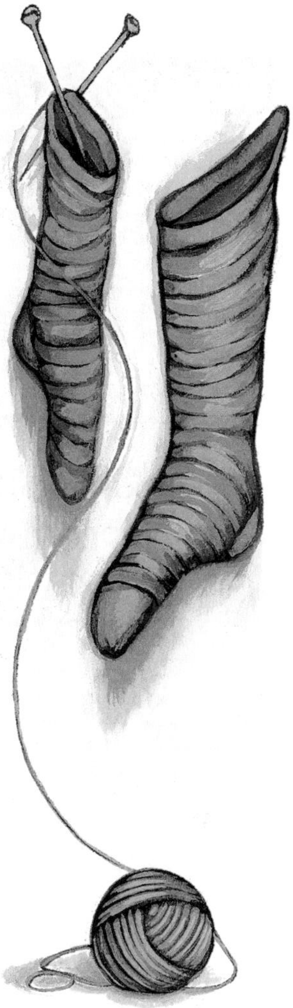

Analogies

Write the spelling word that completes each analogy.

8. *Have* is to *has* as *were* is to ______________.
9. *Month* is to ______________ as *day* is to *Monday.*
10. *Bark* is to *tree* as *skin* is to ______________.
11. *Top* is to ______________ as *up* is to *down.*
12. *Learn* is to *school* as ______________ is to *store.*
13. *Solution* is to ______________ as *answer* is to *question.*
14. *Soap* is to ______________ as *towel* is to *dry.*
15. *Catsup* is to ______________ as *pickle* is to *jar.*

October	shop	block	bottle
o'clock	sorry	socks	problem
what	jog	wash	was
clock	bottom	forgot	body

Proofreading

Proofread the journal entry below. Use proofreading marks to correct five spelling mistakes, three capitalization mistakes, and two punctuation mistakes.

October 18

today I have a mystery to solve. My running sox and hat were at the botom of the stairs when I got home from school Now it is time for my jogg around the blak, but there is a problum. they are both missing. Mom says she didn't move them Nobody is here but Mom and me. Maybe sparky has moved them. I haven't seen that dog since four o'clock.

Alphabetical Order

The words *block*, *bottle*, and *butter* begin with the same letter, *b*. To arrange words that begin with the same letter in alphabetical order, use the second letter.

block bottle butter

Write each group of words in alphabetical order.

1. **cover clock cap children**

   ____
   ____
   ____
   ____

2. **shop salt sorry stack**

   ____
   ____
   ____
   ____

3. **wash wonder west what**

   ____
   ____
   ____
   ____

4. **forgot feed funny farmer**

   ____
   ____
   ____
   ____

Words with Long o

slow	whole	hope	blow
joke	wrote	show	yellow
goes	toe	alone	hole
snow	close	November	know

blow

Say and Listen

Say each spelling word. Listen for the long *o* sound.

Think and Sort

Look at the letters in each word. Think about how long *o* is spelled. Spell each word aloud.

Long *o* can be shown as /ō/. How many spelling patterns for /ō/ do you see?

1. Write the **seven** spelling words that have the *o*-consonant-*e* pattern, like *hope.*
2. Write the **six** spelling words that have the *ow* pattern, like *slow.*
3. Write the **two** spelling words that have the *oe* pattern, like *toe.*
4. Write the **one** spelling word that has the *o* pattern.

1. o-consonant-**e** Words

____
____
____
____
____
____
____

2. ow Words

____
____
____
____
____
____

3. oe Words

____
____

4. o Word

____

Definitions

Write the spelling word for each definition.
Use a dictionary if you need to.

1. moves; travels ________________
2. made words with a pen ________________
3. to wish for something ________________
4. the entire amount ________________
5. to be familiar with ________________
6. by oneself ________________

Analogies

Write the spelling word that completes each analogy.

7. *Shape* is to *square* as *color* is to ________________.
8. *Lose* is to *win* as ________________ is to *open.*
9. *January* is to *February* as ________________ is to *December.*
10. *Hand* is to *finger* as *foot* is to ________________.
11. *Hot* is to *fire* as *cold* is to ________________.
12. *Beat* is to *drum* as ________________ is to *whistle.*
13. *Write* is to *letter* as *dig* is to ________________.
14. *Rabbit* is to *fast* as *tortoise* is to ________________.
15. *Day* is to *night* as ________________ is to *hide.*

slow	whole	hope	blow
joke	wrote	show	yellow
goes	toe	alone	hole
snow	close	November	know

Proofreading

Proofread the letter below. Use proofreading marks to correct five spelling mistakes, three capitalization mistakes, and two punctuation mistakes.

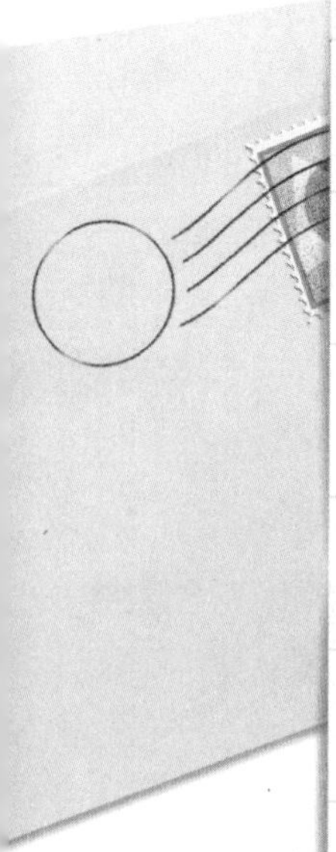

214 Spring Street

Flint Hill, VA 22627

Novemer 29, 2004

Dear Joe,

I kno I haven't written lately. i hoppe you are not mad. thanks for the yello sweater It gose great with my blue jacket.

Here's a good joke. why did the pill wear a blanket? It was a cold tablet

Moe

Language Connection

Verbs

wrote

goes

know

Action words are called verbs. The spelling words in the boxes are verbs.

Unscramble the letters of the spelling words in the sentences below. Write each sentence and then circle the verb.

1. Jack hurt his oet.

____

2. Please wosh me your new shoes.

____

3. nows fell all night long.

____

4. We ate the lewoh pizza.

____

5. Krista bought a loweyl skateboard.

____

6. Scooter dug a lohe in the yard.

____

7. Ming twore a story about a crow.

____

8. Mrs. Sosa egos to lunch with our class.

____

More Words with Long o

most	hello	over	boat
coat	cocoa	comb	both
ago	open	toast	road
hold	loaf	almost	gold

boat

Say and Listen

Say each spelling word. Listen for the long *o* sound.

Think and Sort

Look at the letters in each word. Think about how long *o* is spelled. Spell each word aloud.

Long *o* can be shown as /ō/. How many spelling patterns for /ō/ do you see?

1. Write the **ten** spelling words that have the *o* pattern, like *most.*
2. Write the **five** spelling words that have the *oa* pattern, like *boat.*
3. Write the **one** spelling word that has both the *o* and *oa* patterns.

1. o Words

____
____
____
____
____
____
____
____
____
____

2. oa Words

____
____
____
____
____

3. o and oa Word

____

Definitions

Write the spelling word for each definition.
Use a dictionary if you need to.

1. to arrange the hair ____________
2. a precious metal ____________
3. in the past ____________
4. the one as well as the other ____________
5. a greeting ____________
6. to keep in the hand ____________
7. the greatest amount ____________
8. nearly ____________
9. to cause something to be no longer closed ____________
10. above ____________
11. bread baked in one piece ____________

Classifying

Write the spelling word that belongs in each group.

12. hat	scarf	gloves	____________
13. milk	eggs	cereal	____________
14. street	avenue	lane	____________
15. car	train	airplane	____________

most	hello	over	boat
coat	cocoa	comb	both
ago	open	toast	road
hold	loaf	almost	gold

Proofreading

Proofread the e-mail below. Use proofreading marks to correct five spelling mistakes, three capitalization mistakes, and two punctuation mistakes.

Proofreading Marks

- ⬭ spell correctly
- ≡ capitalize
- ? add question mark

e-mail

New | Read | File | Delete | Search | Contacts | Check

Helo, adam. We went to a lake last week. It had an island in the middle. I thought I had found some goold, but it was only rocks. Are you ready for our trip to the beach We'll combe the beach for seashells early in the morning. we can eat breakfast before we go. Mom baked a lofe of bread. do you like toest with jam

Jasmine

Language Connection

Synonyms

Synonyms are words that have the same meaning. The words *hello, howdy,* and *hi* are synonyms.

Use spelling words from this lesson to write synonym clues for the puzzle.

ACROSS

3. ____________________

4. ____________________

6. ____________________

7. ____________________

DOWN

1. ____________________

2. ____________________

3. ____________________

5. ____________________

6. ____________________

Words with /ŏŏ/

book	took	cook	sure
should	stood	wood	put
poor	foot	shook	would
full	cookies	pull	could

cook

Say and Listen

Say each spelling word. Listen for the vowel sound you hear in *book*.

Think and Sort

Look at the letters in each word. Think about how the vowel sound in *book* is spelled. Spell each word aloud.

The vowel sound in *book* can be shown as /ŏŏ/. How many spelling patterns for /ŏŏ/ do you see?

1. Write the **nine** spelling words that have the *oo* pattern, like *book.*
2. Write the **four** spelling words that have the *u* or *u*-consonant-*e* pattern, like *put.*
3. Write the **three** spelling words that have the *ou* pattern, like *would.*

1. oo Words

____
____
____
____
____
____
____
____
____

2. u, u-consonant-**e** Words

____
____
____
____

3. ou Words

____
____
____

Antonyms

Write the spelling word that is an antonym of each word.

1. push ____________
2. sat ____________
3. uncertain ____________
4. rich ____________
5. empty ____________
6. gave ____________

Clues

Write the spelling word for each clue.

7. You put a shoe on this part of your body. ____________
8. This word means "ought to." ____________
9. Logs are made of this. ____________
10. Most people like these sweet treats. ____________
11. This word means "was able to." ____________
12. You might do this to prepare food. ____________
13. This word means "to set." ____________
14. This word sounds like *wood.* ____________
15. This word is the past tense of *shake.* ____________

Words with /o͝o/

book	took	cook	sure
should	stood	wood	put
poor	foot	shook	would
full	cookies	pull	could

Proofreading

Proofread the story review below. Use proofreading marks to correct five spelling mistakes, three capitalization mistakes, and two unnecessary words.

Story Review

The Lion and the Mouse is an an old story that has stod the test of time. the beginning will pul you into the story. what will happen to that that poer little mouse? Culd the lion be kind enough to let him go? What lesson does the story teach? If you have read the story before, then you know. if not, read it soon. You are shure to enjoy it.

Language Connection

Capital Letters

The names of cities and states always begin with a capital letter.

Phoenix is the capital of Arizona.

Unscramble the spelling words in the sentences below. Then write the sentences, using capital letters correctly.

1. many dowo products come from maine.

   ____

2. i am rues that the largest state is alaska.

   ____

3. everyone dosluh visit chicago, illinois.

   ____

4. dowlu you like to go to new orleans?

   ____

5. san francisco ohsko during an earthquake.

   ____

6. my friend from toronto sent me some okecois.

   ____

More Words with -ed or -ing

sneezed	smiling	beginning	hoped
dropping	shining	stopped	pleased
dropped	liked	taking	driving
closed	jogged	hopping	shopping

hopping

Say and Listen

Say the spelling words. Listen for the *-ed* and *-ing* endings.

Think and Sort

Each spelling word is formed by adding *-ed* or *-ing* to a base word. Look at the letters in each spelling word. Spell each word aloud. Think about how the spelling of the base word changes.

1. If a base word ends in *e*, the *e* is usually dropped before *-ed* or *-ing* is added. Write the **nine** spelling words in which the final *e* of the base word is dropped, like *taking*.
2. If a base word ends in a single vowel and a single consonant, the consonant is often doubled before *-ed* or *-ing* is added. Write the **seven** spelling words in which the final consonant of the base word is doubled, like *beginning*.

1. Final **e** Dropped

____

2. Final Consonant Doubled

Synonyms

Write the spelling word that is a synonym for each word.

1. trotted ____________
2. starting ____________
3. shut ____________
4. wished ____________
5. enjoyed ____________
6. sparkling ____________
7. quit ____________
8. grinning ____________
9. jumping ____________

Rhymes

Write the spelling word that completes each sentence and rhymes with the underlined word.

10. The singer was not pleased when I ____________.
11. Are you ____________ the cake you are making?
12. The bus stopped, and my backpack ____________.
13. To turn diving into ____________, add the letter *r*.
14. Mom was not ____________ when I teased my brother.
15. I keep ____________ the jelly and mopping up the mess.

sneezed	smiling	beginning	hoped
dropping	shining	stopped	pleased
dropped	liked	taking	driving
closed	jogged	hopping	shopping

Proofreading

Proofread the letter below. Use proofreading marks to correct five spelling mistakes, three capitalization mistakes, and two punctuation mistakes.

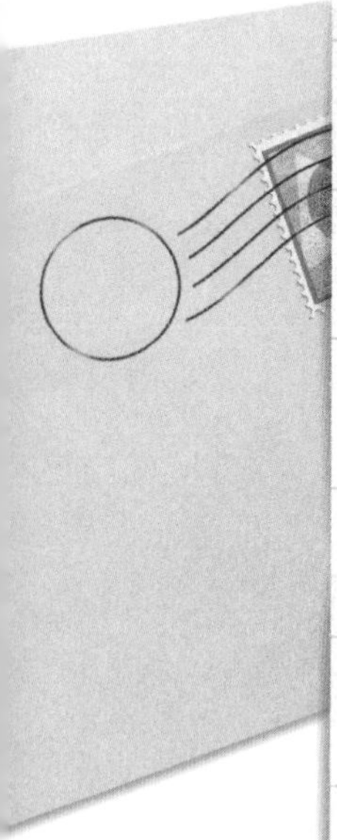

2616 Lakeview Drive
Gilbert, AZ 85234
May 15, 2004

Dear Tyler,

Last week we stoped by the animal shelter. i likd the kittens a lot. my parents said we could get one I was so pleaseed that I couldn't stop smilling. when we were driveing home, I thought of you. Please come see my new kitten soon

Your friend,
Samara

Language Connection

Commas

To make it easy to read a date, use a comma between the day and the year.

July 4, 1776 **December 27, 1998**

Decide which word from the boxes below completes each sentence.
Then write the sentences, using commas correctly.

jogged	closed	dropped	hoped

1. School ___ for vacation on May 28 2004.

____

2. On June 25 1999, Ms. Padden ___ in a race.

____

3. Old friends ___ in to visit us on February 4 2003.

____

4. Ana ___ her party would be on May 17 2006.

____

Unit 4 Review
Lessons 16–20

Lesson 16

socks
bottle
o'clock
wash

Words with Short o

Write the spelling word that belongs in each group.

1. time, watch, ________________
2. jar, can, ________________
3. shoes, gloves, ________________
4. clean, scrub, ________________

Lesson 17

wrote
hole
know
yellow
goes
November

Words with Long o

Write the spelling word for each clue.

5. This is something you might find in your sock. ________________
6. If your shirt is the color of butter, it's this color. ________________
7. If you recorded your thoughts on paper, you did this. ________________
8. Someone who travels does this. ________________
9. If you understand, you do this. ________________
10. If it's the eleventh month, it's this month.

____

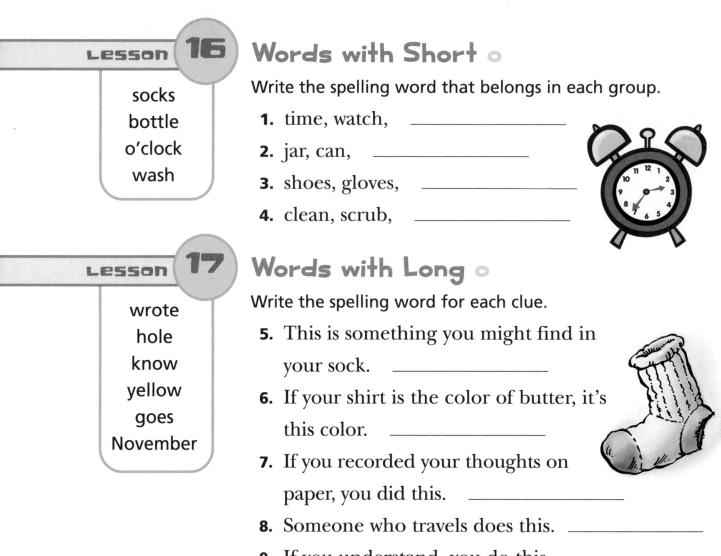

Lesson 18

comb
hello
almost
road
toast

More Words with Long o

Write the spelling word that completes each sentence.

11. Would you like some eggs and ________________ for breakfast?
12. The sun was setting, so it was ________________ dark outside.

13. I use a ______________ and a brush to fix my hair.

14. This ______________ goes all the way to Canada.

15. When I see people I know, I say ______________ to them.

Lesson 19

poor
shook
cookies
sure
should

Words with /o͝o/

Write the spelling word that completes each analogy.

16. *Ice cream* is to *freeze* as ______________ is to *bake.*

17. *Wake* is to *sleep* as *rich* is to ______________.

18. *Little* is to *small* as ______________ is to *must.*

19. *Take* is to *took* as *shake* is to ______________.

20. *Thin* is to *skinny* as *certain* is to ______________.

Lesson 20

hoped
shining
stopped
dropped
hopping

More Words with -ed or -ing

Write the spelling word that is a synonym for each underlined word.

21. The stars were <u>glowing</u> like diamonds.

____

22. The temperature <u>fell</u> twenty degrees in three hours. ______________

23. Cinderella <u>wished</u> she could go to the ball.

____

24. Our washing machine <u>quit</u> working yesterday.

____

25. My little brother was <u>jumping</u> on one foot.

____

Words with /ōō/ or /yōō/

noon	huge	few	used
tooth	blue	school	Tuesday
who	knew	two	true
too	news	move	June

huge

Say and Listen

Say each spelling word. Listen for the vowel sound you hear in *noon* and *huge*.

Think and Sort

The vowel sound in *noon* and *huge* can be shown as /ōō/. In *huge* and some other /ōō/ words, *y* is pronounced before /ōō/.

Look at the letters in each word. Think about how /ōō/ or /yōō/ is spelled. Spell each word aloud.

1. Write the **four** spelling words with the *oo* pattern, like *noon.*
2. Write the **six** spelling words with the *ue* or *ew* pattern, like *true.*
3. Write the **three** spelling words with the *u*-consonant-*e* pattern, like *huge.*
4. Write the **three** spelling words with the *o* or *o*-consonant-*e* pattern, like *move.*

1. oo Words

2. ue, ew Words

3. u-consonant-**e** Words

4. o, o-consonant-**e** Words

Classifying

Write the spelling word that belongs in each group.

1.	lunch time	twelve o'clock	__________
2.	report	information	__________
3.	what	where	__________
4.	mouth	tongue	__________
5.	wiggle	walk	__________
6.	post office	library	__________
7.	red	green	__________

Clues

Write the spelling word for each clue.

8. one of the summer months __________

9. not very many __________

10. the sum of one plus one __________

11. means the same as *also* __________

12. gigantic __________

13. the opposite of *false* __________

14. not new __________

15. sounds like *new* __________

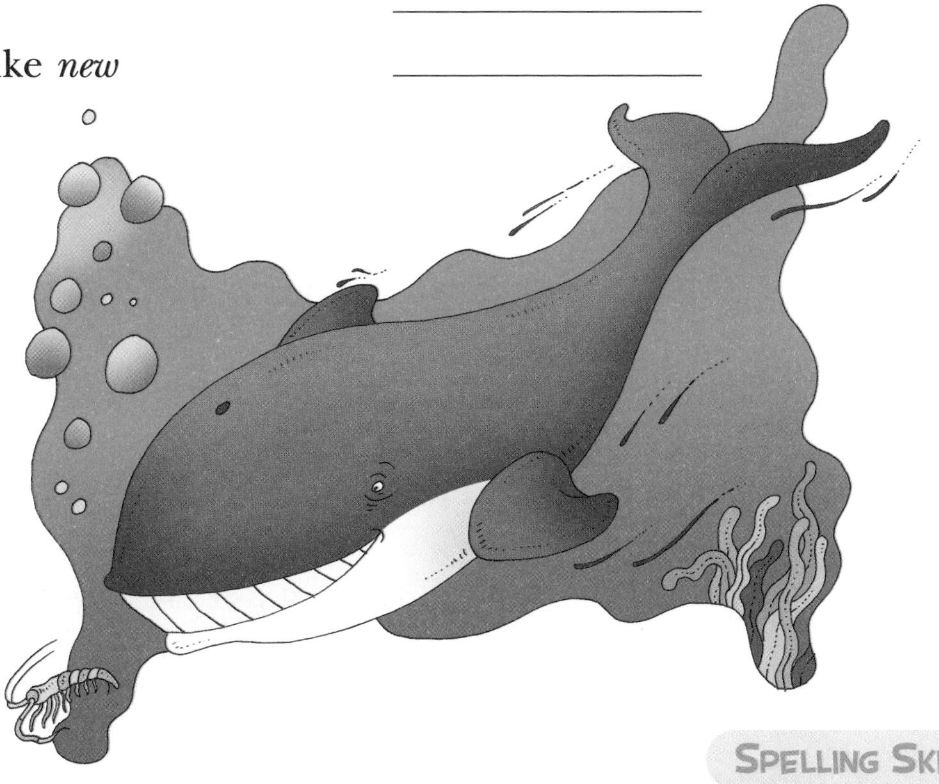

Words with /o͞o/ or /yo͞o/

noon	huge	few	used
tooth	blue	school	Tuesday
who	knew	two	true
too	news	move	June

Proofreading

Proofread the journal entry below. Use proofreading marks to correct five spelling mistakes, three capitalization mistakes, and two punctuation mistakes.

June 2

here is the big news for the week. On Toosday I ran in a race at the school track it started at nune and was tue miles long. I wore my green and bloo shirt. Lots of people ran in the race There were adults, children, and grandparents. Uncle Scott came with Mom to see me run. guess whue won. I did!

Dictionary Skills

Pronunciation

Most dictionary entries show how a word is said. The way a word is said is called its pronunciation.

Entry Word → **noon** (no͞on) *noun* Midday; 12 o'clock in the middle of the day: *We'll eat at noon.*

Pronunciation

Letters and symbols are used to write pronunciations. These letters and symbols can be found in the pronunciation key.

Pronunciation Key

ă	pat	îr	deer	*th*	this
ā	pay	ŏ	pot	ŭ	cut
âr	care	ō	toe	ûr	urge
ä	father	ô	paw, for	ə	about,
ĕ	pet	oi	noise		item,
ē	bee	o͝o	took		edible,
ĭ	pit	o͞o	boot		gallop,
ī	pie	ou	out		circus
		th	thin		

Use the pronunciation key to write the word from the boxes that goes with each pronunciation. Check your answers in the dictionary.

tooth | move | few | huge

1. /fyo͞o/ ________________
2. /to͞oth/ ________________
3. /mo͞ov/ ________________
4. /hyo͞oj/ ________________

Words with /ûr/

curl	world	learn	turn
were	girl	word	bird
work	earth	first	Thursday
dirt	worm	fur	third

Say and Listen

The spelling words for this lesson contain the /ûr/ sound you hear in *curl*. Say each spelling word. Listen for the /ûr/ sound.

Think and Sort

Look at the letters in each word. Think about how the /ûr/ sounds are spelled. Spell each word aloud. How many spelling patterns for /ûr/ do you see?

1. Write the **four** spelling words that have the *ur* pattern, like *curl.*
2. Write the **five** spelling words that have the *ir* pattern, like *first.*
3. Write the **four** spelling words that have the *or* pattern, like *work.*
4. Write the **two** spelling words that have the *ear* pattern, like *earth.*
5. Write the **one** spelling word that has the *ere* pattern.

1. ur Words

____
____
____
____

2. ir Words

____
____
____
____
____

3. or Words

____
____
____
____

4. ear Words

____
____

5. ere Word

____

Definitions

Write the spelling word for each definition. Use a dictionary if you need to.

1. a long, thin creature that crawls ________________
2. a young female child ________________
3. the third planet from the sun ________________
4. coming at the beginning ________________
5. next after second ________________
6. to move around ________________
7. the day between Wednesday and Friday ________________
8. a group of letters that has a meaning ________________
9. soil or earth ________________

Synonyms

Write the spelling word that is a synonym for the underlined word in each sentence.

10. Dinosaurs <u>existed</u> on Earth long ago. ________________
11. Next year I hope to <u>study</u> French. ________________
12. We finished our <u>task</u> in the garden. ________________
13. I will <u>loop</u> my hair around my finger. ________________
14. Wouldn't it be fun to go around the <u>Earth</u>? ________________
15. Our dog's <u>hair</u> is thick and black. ________________

Words with /ûr/

curl	world	learn	turn
were	girl	word	bird
work	earth	first	Thursday
dirt	worm	fur	third

Proofreading

Proofread this paragraph from a story. Use proofreading marks to correct five spelling mistakes, three capitalization mistakes, and two punctuation mistakes.

Four young robins fluttered to the ground. The first bird ate a werm. the second one ate a bug. The therd bird said bugs made his feathers kurl. he saw a berry in the dert and ate it The fourth bird had work to do. For an hour she dug in the erth. the fifth bird slept late that morning He said it was his day off!

Language Connection

Synonyms and Antonyms

Synonyms are words that have the same meaning.
Antonyms are words that have opposite meanings.

small **little** | **thick** **thin**

Write the word from the boxes below that is an antonym of each word.

dirty **add** **huge** **young**

1. subtract add
2. clean dirty
3. tiny huge
4. old young

Each group of four words below has a pair of antonyms and a pair of synonyms. First write the antonyms. Then write the synonyms.

full **turn** **empty** **spin**

5. Antonyms full, empty
6. Synonyms turn spin

Earth **first** **world** **last**

7. Antonyms first, last
8. Synonyms Earth, world

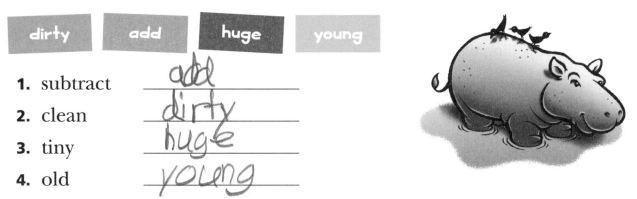

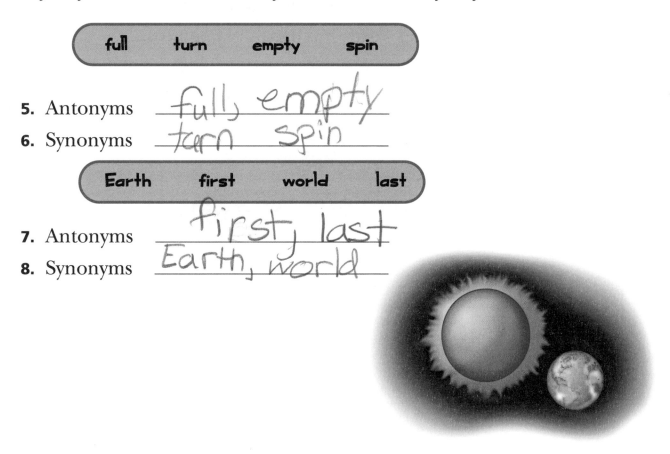

Words with /ä/

dark	yard	art	market
garden	hard	heart	father
March	arm	barn	start
star	card	sharp	bark

garden

Say and Listen

Say each spelling word. Listen for the vowel sound you hear in *dark*.

Think and Sort

Look at the letters in each word. Think about how the vowel sound in *dark* is spelled. Spell each word aloud.

The vowel sound in *dark* can be shown as /ä/. How many spelling patterns for /ä/ do you see?

1. Write the **fifteen** spelling words that have the *a* pattern, like *dark*.
2. Write the **one** spelling word that has the *ea* pattern.

1. a Words

______________________ ______________________

______________________ ______________________

______________________ ______________________

______________________ ______________________

______________________ ______________________

______________________ ______________________

____

____

____

2. ea Word

____

Clues

Write the spelling word for each clue.

1. where flowers grow ________________
2. where to buy fruits and vegetables ________________
3. month after February ________________
4. what you send on someone's birthday ________________
5. where farm animals sleep ________________
6. a place to play near a house ________________
7. what the inside of a cave is ________________
8. what stones are ________________
9. another word for *dad* ________________
10. the kind of knife you need to cut things ________________
11. what the car does when Mom turns the key ________________
12. a drawing or painting ________________

Multiple Meanings

Write the spelling word that has more than one meaning and completes each sentence below.

13. The movie ________________ wished upon a shining ________________.
14. My ________________ pounded as I put all my ________________ into the final leg of the race.
15. I heard Scooter ________________ at the squirrel gnawing on the tree ________________.

Words with /ä/

dark	yard	art	market
garden	hard	heart	father
March	arm	barn	start
star	card	sharp	bark

Proofreading

Proofread the announcement below. Use proofreading marks to correct five spelling mistakes, three capitalization mistakes, and two punctuation mistakes.

Proofreading Marks

- ⬭ spell correctly
- ≡ capitalize
- ? add question mark

Be a Star!

Do you dance or sing Can you do carde tricks? are you good at aret? The Near North neighbors are having a talent show. We will steart practicing next week. we also need someone to paint signs. The show will end with a parade around the Near North Park flower gardin. Would you like to join us Come to mary Wu's yarde on Friday after school!

Dictionary Skills

Multiple Meanings

Some words have more than one meaning. Look at this entry for *heart*. The word *heart* has two meanings. Each is numbered. Read the sample sentence for each meaning of *heart*. The words around the word *heart* give a clue to its meaning.

> **heart** (härt) *noun, plural* **hearts**
> **1.** The organ in the chest that pumps blood through the body: *The doctor listened to my heart.* **2.** Courage and enthusiasm: *He put his heart into winning the game.*

Write **Meaning 1** or **Meaning 2** to indicate which definition of *heart* is used in each sentence. Then write your own sentences showing you understand each meaning of *heart*.

1. Our class lost **heart** when we lost the game. ______________
2. My **heart** beats fast after a race. ______________

____

____

Words with /oi/

coin	boy	choice	spoil
royal	boil	voice	toy
soil	joy	noise	point
broil	enjoy	join	oil

boy

Say and Listen

Say each spelling word. Listen for the vowel sound you hear in *coin*.

Think and Sort

Look at the letters in each word. Think about how the vowel sound in *coin* is spelled. Spell each word aloud.

The vowel sound in *coin* can be shown as /oi/. How many spelling patterns for /oi/ do you see?

1. Write the **eleven** spelling words that have the *oi* pattern, like *coin.*

2. Write the **five** spelling words that have the *oy* pattern, like *toy.*

1. oi Words

coin
Soil
broil
boil
Choice
vaice
noice
Join
spoil
point
oil

2. oy Words

Royal
toy
Joy
enjoy
boy

Classifying

Write the spelling word that belongs in each group of words.

1.	noble	kingly	________
2.	gas	coal	________
3.	doll	yo-yo	________
4.	happiness	pleasure	________
5.	sound	speech	________
6.	rot	decay	________
7.	tie	connect	________
8.	money	dollar bill	________

Analogies

Write the spelling word that completes each analogy.

9. *Man* is to *woman* as boy is to *girl*.

10. *Laugh* is to Happy as *cry* is to *fear*.

11. *Lose* is to *loss* as *choose* is to chose.

12. *Soft* is to *whisper* as *loud* is to Scream.

13. *Ocean* is to *sea* as ________ is to *dirt*.

14. *Cake* is to *bake* as *steak* is to grill.

15. *Finger* is to ________ as *hand* is to *wave*.

Words with /oi/

coin	boy	choice	spoil
royal	boil	voice	toy
soil	joy	noise	point
broil	enjoy	join	oil

Proofreading

Proofread the e-mail below.
Use proofreading marks to correct five spelling mistakes, three capitalization mistakes, and two punctuation mistakes.

Proofreading Marks

- ◯ spell correctly
- ≡ capitalize
- ⊙ add period

e-mail

New | Read | File | Delete | Search

Diego,

Last night I dreamed I lived in a royle castle. I had every toy a boy could want What I had for breakfast, lunch, and dinner was my choic. nothing could spoyal my joi Then I heard a noise. It was the voyce of my brother, james. It was so loud that it woke me up.

Have you ever had a dream like this? I would enjoy reading about it. send me an e-mail.

Tomas

Language Connection

Capital Letters

The following kinds of words begin with a capital letter:

- the first word of a sentence
- the names of streets
- the names of people and pets
- the names of cities and states

Write each sentence below, using capital letters correctly.
Circle the spelling word in the sentence.

1. we will enjoy visiting minneapolis.

____

2. my dog max makes a lot of noise!

____

3. can you point out mallory street?

____

4. this coin was made in colorado.

____

5. mrs. hays bought a toy for her baby.

____

6. kevin and I want to join the baseball team.

____

More Contractions

isn't	weren't	can't	doesn't
hadn't	mustn't	wouldn't	won't
shouldn't	aren't	wasn't	don't
couldn't	didn't	hasn't	haven't

Say and Listen

Say the spelling words. Listen for the sounds at the end of each word.

Think and Sort

All of the spelling words in this lesson are contractions. Each contraction is formed from the word *not* joined with another word. When the two words are joined, one or more letters are left out. An apostrophe (') is used to show the missing letters.

In the contraction *won't*, the spelling of *will* changes to *wo*. One contraction, *can't*, is formed from one word, not two separate words.

1. Write the **fifteen** spelling words that are formed from *not* joined with a separate word, like *isn't.*
2. Write the **one** spelling word that is formed from one word.

1. Two Words

2. One Word

Either . . . or

Write the spelling word that completes each sentence.

1. Either Wags will or he ______________.
2. Either you do or you ______________.
3. Either James could or he ______________.
4. Either Julie would or she ______________.
5. Either Sara does or she ______________.
6. Either Ricky was or he ______________.

Trading Places

Write the contraction that can be used instead of the underlined word or words in each sentence.

7. Marta <u>had not</u> seen the new puppy. ______________
8. You <u>must not</u> touch the wet paint. ______________
9. Lan <u>did not</u> bring his lunch. ______________
10. I <u>cannot</u> believe you ran five miles! ______________
11. The mail <u>has not</u> come yet. ______________
12. I <u>have not</u> finished my homework. ______________
13. Did you know that whales <u>are not</u> fish? ______________
14. We <u>were not</u> home on Saturday. ______________
15. "That <u>is not</u> my car," Ms. Ford said. ______________

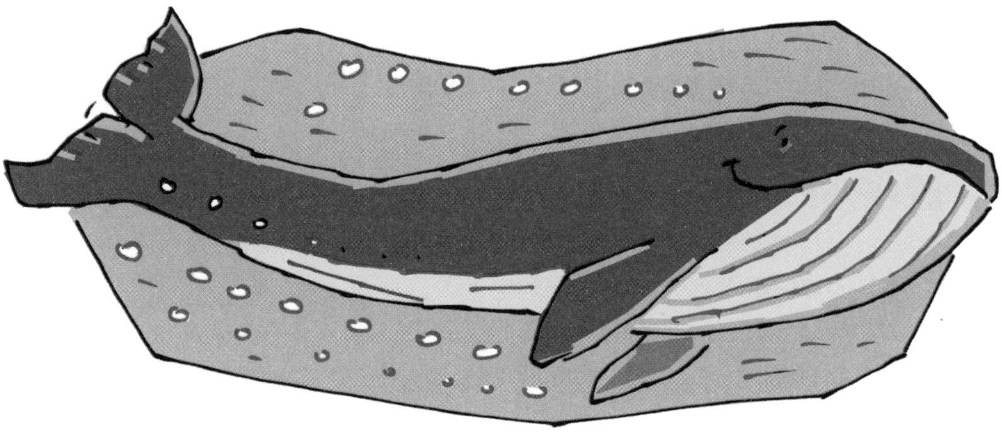

isn't	weren't	can't	doesn't
hadn't	mustn't	wouldn't	won't
shouldn't	aren't	wasn't	don't
couldn't	didn't	hasn't	haven't

Proofreading

Proofread the note below. Use proofreading marks to correct five spelling mistakes, three capitalization mistakes, and two unnecessary words.

Chad,

I couldnt' wait for you to see this game. Open the box and look at the checkerboard. it has'nt been used in in ten years. It's still in great shape! Wouldent you like to play? Well, Aunt rose won'nt let anyone use it except me and one other person. you are that person. I'll come to your house tonight for a game. Doesnt' that sound like like a great plan?

Ling

Language Connection

Be Verbs

There are many different forms of the verb *be*. Some tell what is happening now. Others tell what happened in the past. These forms of *be* are used in *not* contractions.

Present Tense		Contraction
is	The bus **is** late.	isn't
are	They **are** in a hurry.	aren't

Past Tense		Contraction
was	Bart **was** still here.	wasn't
were	Jill and Will **were** on the way.	weren't

Use the correct contraction above to complete each sentence.

1. Toni ________________ here every day.
2. Today the trains ________________ on time.
3. Paige and Wanda ________________ here last Thursday.
4. Last month ________________ the best month for planting a garden.

Unit 5 Review
Lessons 21–25

Lesson 21 Words with /o͞o/ or /yo͞o/

too
true
knew
few
huge
used
two

Write the spelling word that can be used instead of the word or words in dark type in each sentence.

1. The story that we read was **real**. ______________
2. My father's car is **not new**. ______________
3. The sun is **very** hot in the summer. ______________
4. **One plus one** is less than three. ______________
5. Malika **was certain** that she would win. ______________
6. **Not very many** people stood in line. ______________
7. Elephants and whales are **big**. ______________

Lesson 22 Words with /ûr/

curl
girl
worm
earth
were

Write the spelling word that belongs in each group.

8. lady woman ______________
9. are was ______________
10. curve coil ______________
11. soil ground ______________
12. snake eel ______________

LESSON 23

garden
father
sharp
heart

Words with /ä/

Write the spelling word that completes each analogy.

13. *Scissors* is to ______________ as *feather* is to *soft.*

14. *Son* is to ______________ as *daughter* is to *mother.*

15. *Apple* is to *orchard* as *carrot* is to ______________.

16. *Brain* is to *head* as ______________ is to *chest.*

LESSON 24

voice
soil
enjoy
royal

Words with /oi/

Write the spelling word for each clue.

17. People sing with this. ______________

18. This is a synonym for *like.*

____

19. Kings and queens are this.

____

20. People plant seeds in this.

____

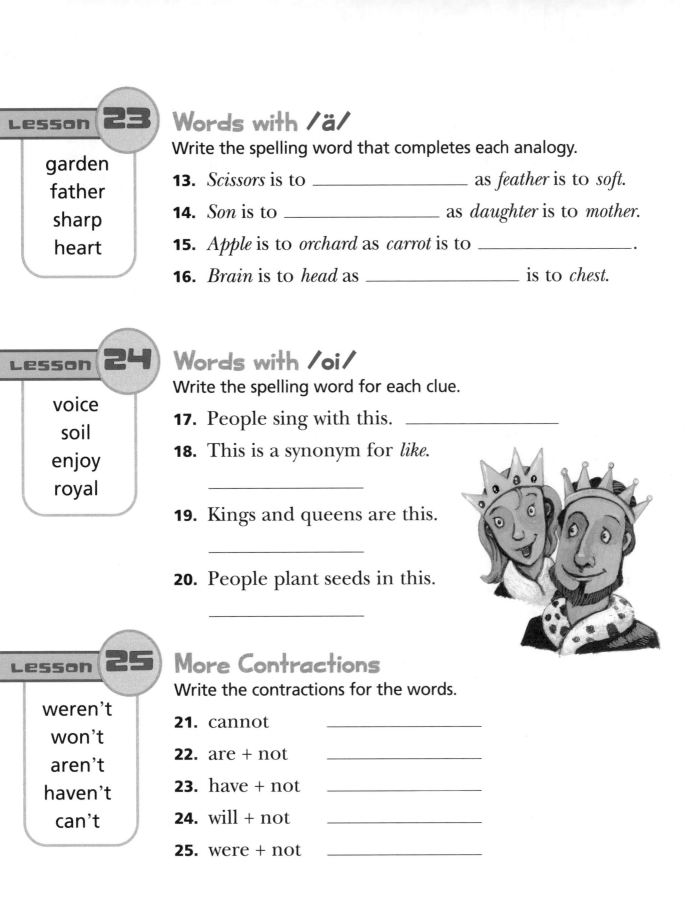

LESSON 25

weren't
won't
aren't
haven't
can't

More Contractions

Write the contractions for the words.

21. cannot ______________

22. are + not ______________

23. have + not ______________

24. will + not ______________

25. were + not ______________

Words with /ô/

draw	walk	bought	because
frog	along	long	water
always	brought	off	belong
mall	strong	tall	talk

strong

Say and Listen

Say each spelling word. Listen for the vowel sound you hear in *draw*.

Think and Sort

Look at the letters in each word. Think about how the vowel sound in *draw* is spelled. Spell each word aloud.

The vowel sound in *draw* can be shown as /ô/. How many spelling patterns for /ô/ do you see?

1. Write the **six** spelling words that have the *o* pattern, like *long*.
2. Write the **six** spelling words that have the *a* pattern, like *talk*.
3. Write the **two** spelling words that have the *ough* pattern, like *bought*.
4. Write the **one** spelling word that has the *au* pattern.
5. Write the **one** spelling word that has the *aw* pattern.

1. o Words

______________________ ______________________
______________________ ______________________
______________________ ______________________
____
____
____

2. a Words

____
____
____

3. ough Words

____
____

4. au Word

____

5. aw Word

____

Antonyms

Write the spelling word that is an antonym of each underlined word.

1. That basketball player is very <u>short</u>. ______
2. Please turn <u>on</u> the light. ______
3. Tina <u>never</u> eats breakfast. ______
4. Elephants are very large and <u>weak</u>. ______
5. Mr. Good gave a <u>brief</u> speech. ______

Clues

Write the spelling word for each clue.

6. what you do on the phone ______
7. what people and animals drink ______
8. place to shop ______
9. past tense of bring ______
10. what artists do ______
11. green thing that sits on a lily pad ______
12. means "to be owned by" ______
13. means almost the same as *beside* ______
14. rhymes with *talk* ______
15. past tense of *buy* ______

Words with /ô/

draw	walk	bought	because
frog	along	long	water
always	brought	off	belong
mall	strong	tall	talk

Proofreading

Proofread the e-mail below. Use proofreading marks to correct five spelling mistakes, four capitalization mistakes, and two unnecessary words.

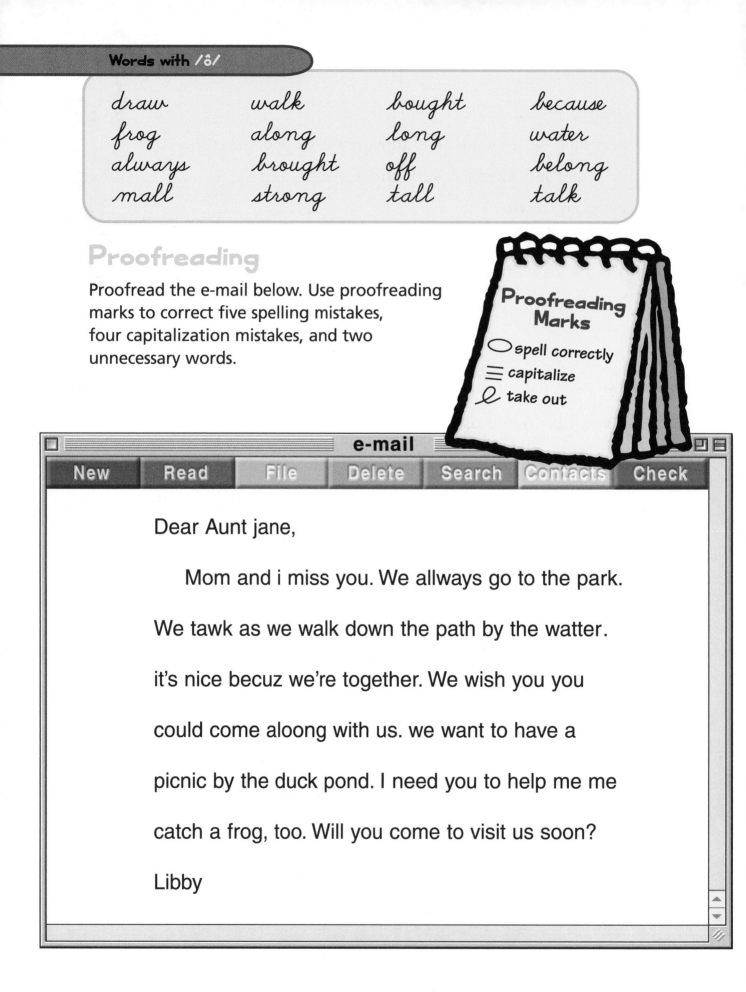

e-mail

New | Read | File | Delete | Search | Contacts | Check

Dear Aunt jane,

Mom and i miss you. We allways go to the park. We tawk as we walk down the path by the watter. it's nice becuz we're together. We wish you you could come aloong with us. we want to have a picnic by the duck pond. I need you to help me me catch a frog, too. Will you come to visit us soon?

Libby

Language Connection

Subject and Predicate

The subject of a sentence tells who or what is doing the action or being talked about. The predicate of a sentence tells what the subject does or did.

Subject	Predicate
Sally	danced.
The cat	had jumped off the chair.

Unscramble the spelling words as you write the sentences below. Then circle the subjects and underline the predicates.

1. My sister hid behind a latl tree.

____

2. Ling tughob a baseball.

____

3. Mrs. Martinez took a nogl vacation.

____

4. I will wrad a picture of you.

____

5. The old clock fell fof the shelf.

____

More Words with /ô/

August	morning	four	quart
pour	popcorn	before	autumn
corner	storm	door	floor
north	born	fork	sport

popcorn

Say and Listen

Say each spelling word. Listen for the first vowel sound you hear in *August* and *morning*.

Think and Sort

Look at the letters in each word. Think about how the first vowel sound in *August* and *morning* is spelled. Spell each word aloud.

The first vowel sound in *August* and *morning* can be shown as /ô/. How many spelling patterns for /ô/ do you see?

1. Write the **two** spelling words that have the *au* pattern, like *August.*
2. Write the **nine** spelling words that have the *o* pattern, like *morning.*
3. Write the **four** spelling words that have the *oo* or *ou* pattern, like *door.*
4. Write the **one** spelling word that has the *a* pattern.

1. **au** Words

____________ ____________

____________ ____________

2. **o** Words

____

____

____

____

____

____

____

3. **oo, ou** Words

____

____

____

____

4. **a** Word

____

Clues

Write the spelling word for each clue.

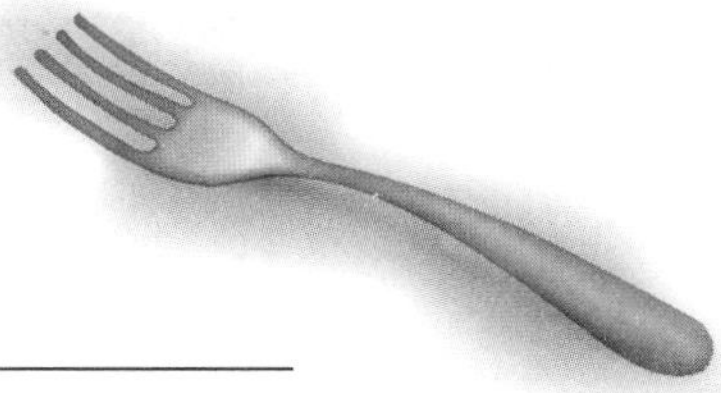

1. snack to eat at the movies ________________
2. spoon, knife, _____ ________________
3. rain or snow and lots of wind ________________
4. where the walls in a room meet ________________
5. how to get milk into a glass ________________

Analogies

Write the spelling word that completes each analogy.

6. *East* is to *west* as ________________ is to *south.*
7. *Summer* is to *winter* as *spring* is to ________________.
8. *Evening* is to *dinner* as ________________ is to *breakfast.*
9. *Cool* is to *warm* as *after* is to ________________.
10. *Foot* is to *yard* as ________________ is to *gallon.*
11. *Above* is to *below* as *ceiling* is to ________________.
12. *Lid* is to *jar* as ________________ is to *house.*
13. *One* is to *two* as *three* is to ________________.
14. *Color* is to *blue* as ________________ is to *hockey.*
15. *Bird* is to *hatched* as *child* is to ________________.

More Words with /ô/

August	morning	four	quart
pour	popcorn	before	autumn
corner	storm	door	floor
north	born	fork	sport

Proofreading

Proofread the paragraph below. Use proofreading marks to correct five spelling mistakes, three capitalization mistakes, and two punctuation mistakes.

Proofreading Marks

- ◯ spell correctly
- ≡ capitalize
- ⊙ add period

Hiking is a great spoort. It can be a lot of fun. here are some things to remember when you go Make sure you are wearing good shoes. Befour you go, put water and snacks in a backpack Trail mix and popcawrn are good snacks. also, bring rain gear in case there is a stourm. It's a good idea to start early in the morening, when you have lots of energy. As you hike along, remember to stop and rest. you will have more fun if you don't get too tired.

Dictionary Skills

Alphabetical Order

Many words begin with the same letter or the same two letters. To put these words in alphabetical order, use the third letter of each word. Look at the two words below.

train **trim**

Both words start with the letters *tr*. To put them in alphabetical order, look at the third letter. The third letter in *train* is *a*. The third letter in *trim* is *i*. In the alphabet, *a* comes before *i*, so *train* comes before *trim*.

In each list below, the words begin with the same two letters. Look at the third letter of each word. Then write the words in alphabetical order.

1. autumn aunt August

____

____

____

2. porch point pour

____

____

____

3. fond four foggy

____

____

____

4. money morning moon

____

____

____

Words with /ou/

house	flower	town	sound
ground	tower	found	brown
about	hour	power	down
around	count	our	owl

house

Say and Listen

Say each spelling word. Listen for the vowel sound you hear in *house*.

Think and Sort

Look at the letters in each word. Think about how the vowel sound in *house* is spelled. Spell each word aloud.

The vowel sound in *house* can be shown as /ou/. How many spelling patterns for /ou/ do you see?

1. Write the **nine** spelling words that have the *ou* pattern, like *house*.
2. Write the **seven** spelling words that have the *ow* pattern, like *brown*.

1. **ou** Words	2. **ow** Words
______	______
______	______
______	______
______	______
______	______
______	______
______	______
______	
______	

Hink Pinks

Hink pinks are pairs of rhyming words that have funny meanings. Read each clue. Write the spelling word that completes each hink pink.

1. a place for mice to live — mouse ________
2. a beagle's bark — hound ________
3. the time to bake — flour ________
4. rain falling on a tall building — ________ shower
5. a night bird's loud sound — ________ howl

Letter Scramble

Unscramble the letters in parentheses.
Then write the spelling word to complete the phrase.

6. (wodn) run ________ the hill
7. (repow) ________ from electricity
8. (boaut) books for and ________ children
9. (wolfer) a ________ in a vase
10. (ungord) on the ________ or in the air
11. (dnofu) lost and ________
12. (nuoct) ________ to ten
13. (wonrb) ________ hair and eyes
14. (ruodna) in, ________, and through
15. (rou) her, their, and ________

Words with /ou/

house	flower	town	sound
ground	tower	found	brown
about	hour	power	down
around	count	our	owl

Proofreading

Proofread the journal entry below. Use proofreading marks to correct five spelling mistakes, three capitalization mistakes, and two unnecessary words.

May 14

Today was a wild day! Dad and I heard a strange sownd. we looked around the inside of the howse. Then we looked outside. Finally we climbed up on the roof. We found an owel stuck in our our chimney. Dad got his gloves and a fishing net. it took us an hour to free the big broun bird, but it seemed all right as it flew away. I can't wait to to tell chris abuot it.

Dictionary Skills

Using the Spelling Table

A spelling table can help you find the spelling of a word in a dictionary. Suppose you are not sure how the vowel sound in *should* is spelled. You can use a spelling table to find the different spellings for the sound. First, find the pronunciation symbol for the sound. Then read the first spelling listed for /o͝o/ and look up *shoold* in a dictionary. Look for each spelling in the dictionary until you find the correct one.

Sound	Spellings	Examples
/o͝o/	oo ou u u_e	book, could, pull, sure

Write the correct spelling for each word. Use the Spelling Table on page 265 and a dictionary. One word has two correct spellings.

1. /brôth/ ________
2. /mān **tān'**/ ________
3. /ăd **mīr'**/ ________
4. /dōm/ ________
5. /fīr/ ________
6. /wīr/ ________
7. /stärch/ ________
8. /dîr/ ________ ________

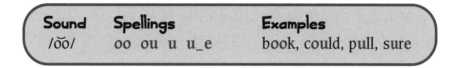

Words with /îr/, /âr/, or /īr/

near	care	fire	where
hear	wire	stairs	deer
ear	year	tire	here
dear	chair	air	hair

Say and Listen

The spelling words for this lesson contain the /îr/, /âr/, and /īr/ sounds that you hear in *near*, *care*, and *fire*. Say the spelling words. Listen for the /îr/, /âr/, and /īr/ sounds.

Think and Sort

Look at the letters in each word. Think about how the /îr/, /âr/, or /īr/ sounds are spelled. Spell each word aloud.

1. Write the **seven** /îr/ spelling words, like *deer*. Circle the letters that spell /îr/ in each word.
2. Write the **six** /âr/ spelling words, like *care*. Circle the letters that spell /âr/ in each word.
3. Write the **three** /īr/ spelling words, like *fire*. Circle the letters that spell /īr/ in each word.

1. /îr/ Words

______________________ ______________________
______________________ ______________________
______________________ ______________________
______________________ ______________________
______________________ ______________________
____
____

2. /âr/ Words

____

3. /īr/ Words

____
____
____

Synonyms

Write the spelling word that is a synonym of the underlined word.

1. Look at the long fur on that dog! ____________
2. These steps go to the attic. ____________
3. Don't trip over that cord. ____________
4. The Rileys are loved family friends. ____________

Clues

Write the spelling word for each clue.

5. You breathe this. ____________
6. This animal can have antlers. ____________
7. When you listen, you do this. ____________
8. If you are concerned, you do this. ____________
9. You hear with this. ____________
10. This equals 12 months. ____________
11. This means the opposite of *far.* ____________
12. This is a question word. ____________
13. A car should have a spare one. ____________
14. Matches can start this. ____________
15. This means the opposite of *there.* ____________

near	care	fire	where
hear	wire	stairs	deer
ear	year	tire	here
dear	chair	air	hair

Proofreading

Proofread the ad for a Cozy Quilt below. Use proofreading marks to correct five spelling mistakes, three capitalization mistakes, and two punctuation mistakes.

Proofreading Marks

- ⬭ spell correctly
- ≡ capitalize
- ? add question mark

Cozy Quilt

are you toasty warm on cold winter nights If not, try a Cozy Quilt. do you like to curl up in a chare and read So do I! With a Cozy Quilt, I don't have to sit nere the fire. The aire outside may be cold, but i don't caire. Even on the coldest night of the yeer, my Cozy Quilt keeps me as snug as a bug in a rug!

Dictionary Skills

Pronunciation

Letters and symbols are used to write pronunciations in a dictionary. The letters and symbols can be found in the pronunciation key.

Pronunciation Key

ă	pat	ĕ	pet	îr	deer	oi	noise	th	thin	ə	about,
ā	pay	ē	bee	ŏ	pot	o͝o	took	*th*	this		item,
âr	care	ĭ	pit	ō	toe	o͞o	boot	ŭ	cut		edible,
ä	father	ī	pie	ô	paw, for	ou	out	ûr	urge		gallop,
											circus

Write the three words from the boxes that go with each pronunciation.

stairs wire where here near

fire year tire hair

1. /âr/ ________ ________ ________
2. /īr/ ________ ________ ________
3. /îr/ ________ ________ ________

Words with -er or -est

taller	tallest	longer	longest
dirtier	dirtiest	hotter	hottest
stronger	strongest	greater	greatest
funnier	funniest	sharper	sharpest

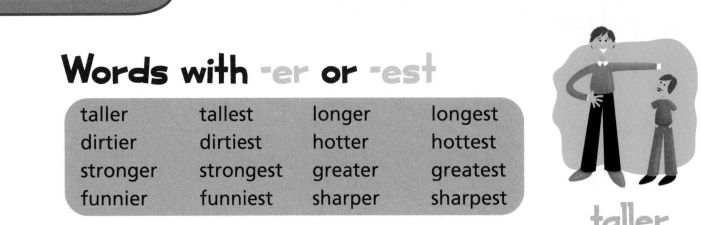

Say and Listen

Say each spelling word. Listen for the ending sounds.

Think and Sort

All of the spelling words end in *-er* or *-est*. Spell each word aloud.

Each spelling word is formed by adding *-er* or *-est* to a base word. Look at the letters of each base word.

1. Write the **ten** spelling words that have no change in the base word, like *taller.*
2. Write the **four** spelling words in which the final *y* of the base word is changed to *i,* like *funnier.*
3. Write the **two** spelling words in which the final consonant of the base word is doubled, like *hotter.*

1. No Change to Base Word

___________________ ___________________

____

____

____

____

____

____

____

____

2. Final **y** Changed to **i**

____

____

____

____

3. Final Consonant Doubled

____

____

Antonyms

Write the spelling word that is an antonym of the underlined word.

1. Turn on the fan if it gets colder. ______________
2. I need the dullest knife for the steak. ______________
3. An owl's eyes are duller than a robin's. ______________
4. The weakest wrestler is most likely to win. ______________
5. I will put the cleanest clothes in the wash. ______________

Comparisons

Write the spelling word that completes each comparison.

6. An oak tree is ______________ than a person.
7. Her joke was the ______________ one I ever heard.
8. Mt. Everest is the ______________ mountain in the world.
9. Four is ______________ than three.
10. A mile is ______________ than a foot.
11. An elephant is ______________ than a mouse.
12. The Nile River is the ______________ river in the world.
13. Summer is usually the ______________ season of the year.
14. Who is the ______________ basketball player of all time?
15. I thought the joke was ______________ than the riddle.

taller	tallest	longer	longest
dirtier	dirtiest	hotter	hottest
stronger	strongest	greater	greatest
funnier	funniest	sharper	sharpest

Proofreading

Proofread this paragraph from a newspaper article. Use proofreading marks to correct five spelling mistakes, three capitalization mistakes, and two punctuation mistakes.

Gabby's Garden Tips

spring is the greatist season of them all The sun shines stronger than in winter. The days are longger. the trees and grass grow taler and faster. Early spring is the time to start a flower garden Digging in the earth might make your hands dirtyer than watching TV, but it will also make you happier! A flower garden is something everyone can enjoy. having lots of bright, colorful flowers will make your spring even grater !

Language Connection

Adjectives

An adjective describes a noun or a pronoun. It tells which, what kind, or how many.

The strong man lifted the box. **Mike is strong.**

Add *-er* to most adjectives to compare two people or things. Add *-est* to compare more than two people or things.

Cliff is stronger than Mike. **Paul is the strongest of all.**

Use the correct word from the boxes to write each sentence.

greater | hotter | funniest | tallest

1. Sharon tells the ___ jokes we've ever heard.

   ____

2. The sun is ___ today than it was yesterday.

   ____

3. Gigi is the ___ girl on the basketball team.

   ____

4. Twenty is ___ than ten.

   ____

Unit 6 Review
Lessons 26–30

Lesson 26

strong
talk
bought
because
draw

Words with /ô/

Unscramble the letters in parentheses. Then write the spelling word to complete the sentence.

1. (thobug) Maria ________________ two tickets to the concert.
2. (abesceu) We could not see ________________ of the tall post.
3. (torsgn) That horse has very ________________ legs.
4. (kalt) Let's ________________ about the game.
5. (ward) Can you ________________ a picture of the house?

Lesson 27

autumn
before
floor
pour
quart

More Words with /ô/

Write the spelling word for each clue.

6. This is a measure for liquids.

   ____

7. You do this with water in a pitcher.

   ____

8. This season comes before winter.

   ____

9. This word is the opposite of *after*.

   ____

10. This can be covered with tile or carpet.

    ____

LESSON 28

count
hour
tower
owl

Words with /ou/

Write the spelling word that completes each analogy.

11. *Days* is to *week* as *minutes* is to ________________.

12. *Terrier* is to *dog* as ________________ is to *bird*.

13. *Read* is to *book* as ________________ is to *money*.

14. *House* is to *garage* as *castle* is to ________________.

LESSON 29

deer
near
here
care
air
where
wire

Words with /îr/, /âr/, or /īr/

Write the spelling word that completes each sentence.

15. The smell of lilacs filled the ________________.

16. The ________________ darted across the road.

17. Do you know ________________ my keys are?

18. We can rest ________________ in the shade.

19. The cage was made of wood and ________________.

20. Our hotel is ________________ the park.

21. Heidi takes good ________________ of her pet.

LESSON 30

greater
sharpest
funnier
hottest

Words with -er or -est

Write the spelling word that belongs in each group.

22. sharp sharper ________________

23. great ________________ greatest

24. hot hotter ________________

25. funny ________________ funniest

commonly misspelled words

about
above
across
again
a lot
always
another
baby
because
been
before
beginning
bought
boy
buy
can
came
children
color
come
cousin
didn't
does
don't
every
family
favorite
finally
friend
friends
from
get
getting
girl
goes
guess
have
hear
her
here
him
his
house
into
know
like
little
made
make
many
name
nice
now
once
one
our
out
outside
party
people
play
please
pretty
read
really
right
said
saw
scared
school
sent
some
store
swimming
teacher
that's
their
then
there
they
though
today
too
two
upon
very
want
was
went
were
when
where
white
with
would
write
writing
wrote
your
you're

Spelling Table

Sound	Spellings	Examples
/ă/	a a_e ai au	ask, have, plaid, laugh
/ā/	a a_e ai ay ea eigh ey	table, save, rain, gray, break, eight, they
/ä/	a ea	father, heart
/âr/	air are ere	chair, care, where
/b/	b bb	best, rabbit
/ch/	ch tch	child, catch
/d/	d dd	dish, add
/ĕ/	e ea ie ue a ai ay	best, read, friend, guess, many, said, says
/ē/	e e_e ea ee ei eo ey y	even, these, each, meet, receive, people, key, city
/f/	f ff gh	fly, off, laugh
/g/	g gg	go, egg
/h/	h wh	hot, who
/ĭ/	i ui e ee u a	inside, build, pretty, been, busy, luggage
/ī/	i i_e ie igh eye uy y	tiny, drive, pie, high, eyes, buy, fly
/îr/	ear eer eir ere	year, deer, weird, here
/j/	j g	jog, danger
/k/	k c ck ch	keep, coat, kick, school
/ks/	x	six
/kw/	qu	quiet
/l/	l ll	late, tell
/m/	m mb mm	much, comb, hammer
/n/	n kn nn	need, know, beginning
/ng/	n ng	thank, bring

Sound	Spellings	Examples
/ŏ/	o a	shop, was
/ō/	o o_e oa oe ou ow	both, hole, road, toe, boulder, slow
/oi/	oi oy	point, enjoy
/ô/	o oa oo ou ough a au aw	off, coarse, door, four, brought, tall, autumn, draw
/ŏŏ/	oo ou u u_e	book, could, pull, sure
/ōō/	oo ou u_e ue ew o	noon, you, June, blue, news, two
/ou/	ou ow	about, owl
/p/	p pp	place, dropped
/r/	r rr wr	rain, sorry, write
/s/	s ss c	safe, dress, city
/sh/	sh s	shook, sure
/t/	t tt ed	take, matter, thanked
/*th*/	th	then
/th/	th	third
/ŭ/	u o oe	such, mother, does
/ûr/	ur ir er or ear ere our	curl, girl, dessert, world, learn, were, flourish
/v/	v f	even, of
/w/	w wh o	walk, when, one
/y/	y	year
/yōō/	u_e ew ue	use, few, Tuesday
/z/	z zz s	sneeze, blizzard, says
/ə/	a e i o u	along, misery, estimate, lion, subtract

Math

Skills

unit 1

Place value and number sense

Tens and Ones

Every two-digit **whole number** has a tens and a ones place.

Count the groups of tens and ones.

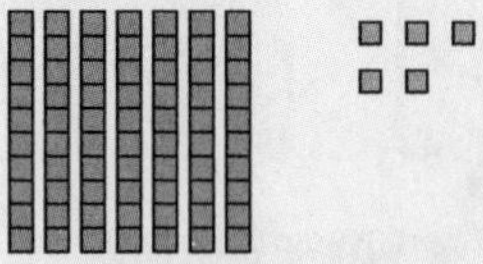

Tens	Ones
7	5

= 75

Write the number.

Count the groups of tens and ones. Then write the numbers.

1. 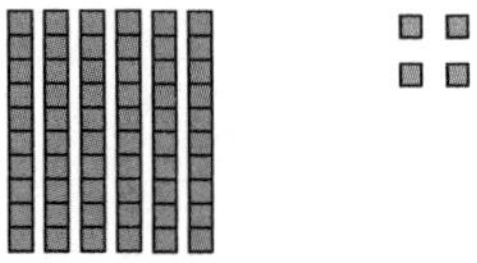

a

Tens	Ones
6	4

b

= 64

2. 

Tens	Ones

= ☐

3. 

Tens	Ones

= ☐

4. 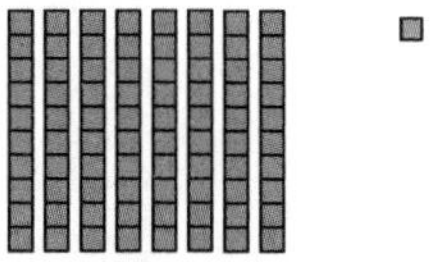

Tens	Ones

= ☐

5. 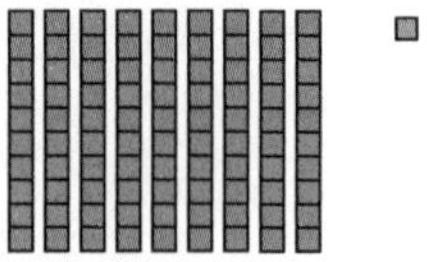

Tens	Ones

= ☐

6. 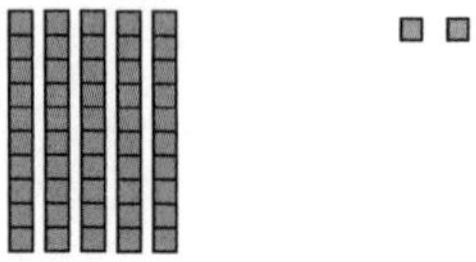

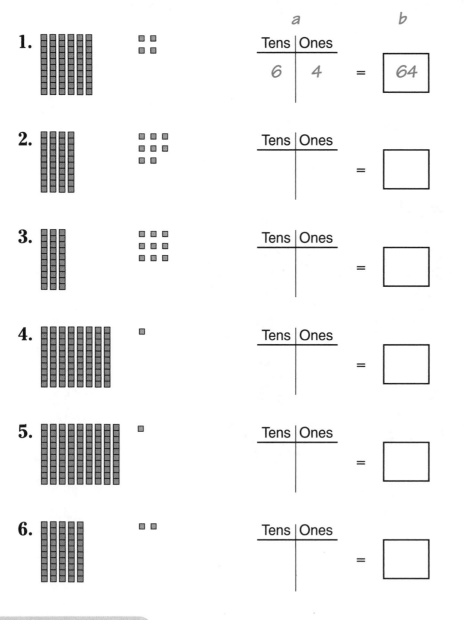

Tens	Ones

= ☐

Hundreds, Tens, and Ones

Every three-digit whole number has a hundreds, a tens, and a ones place.

Count the groups of hundreds, tens, and ones.

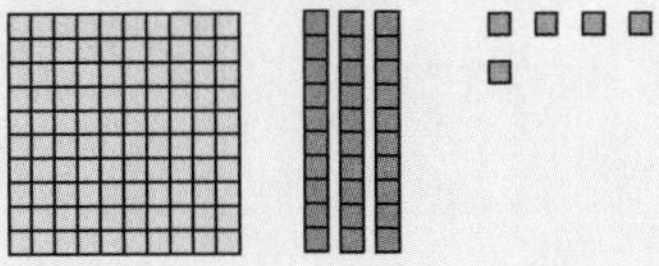

Write the number.

Hundreds	Tens	Ones
1	3	5

= 135

Count the groups of hundreds, tens, and ones. Then write the numbers.

a   b

1. 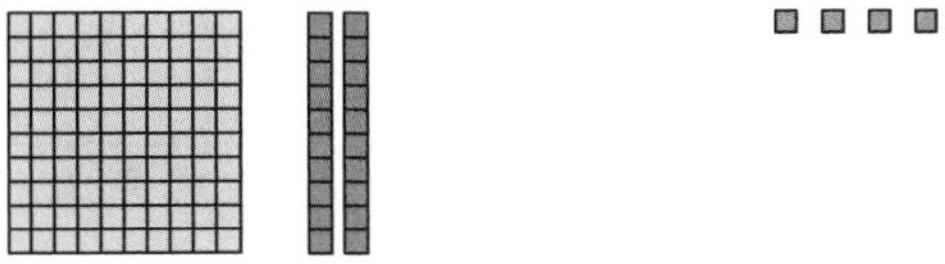

Hundreds	Tens	Ones
1	2	4

= 124

2. 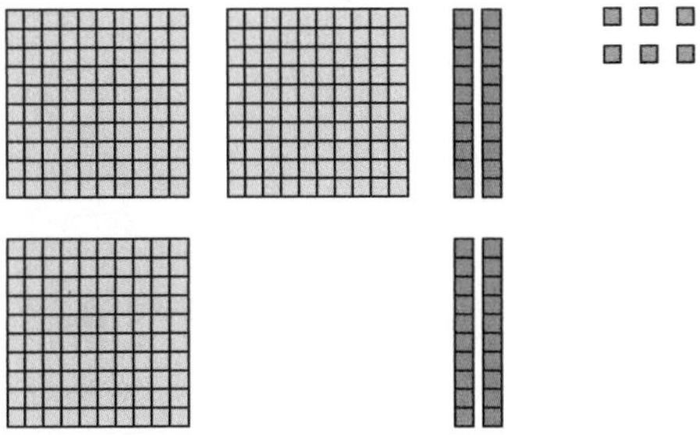

Hundreds	Tens	Ones

= ______

3. 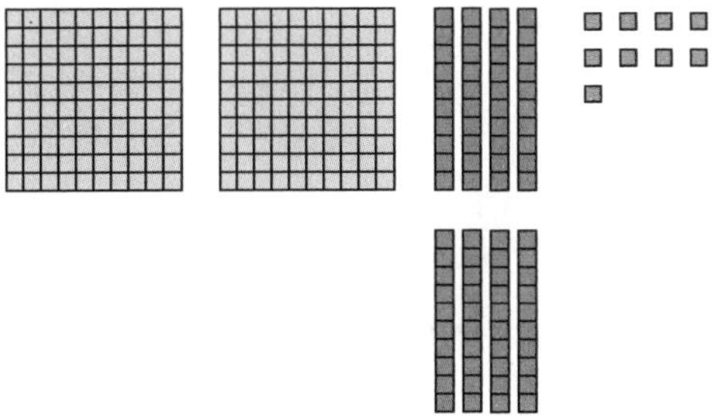

Hundreds	Tens	Ones

= ______

4. 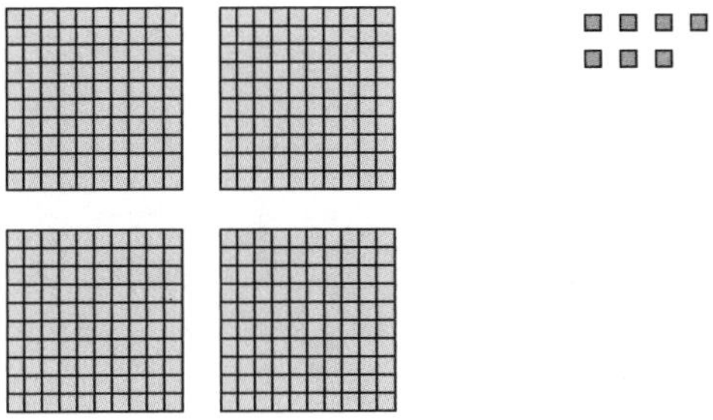

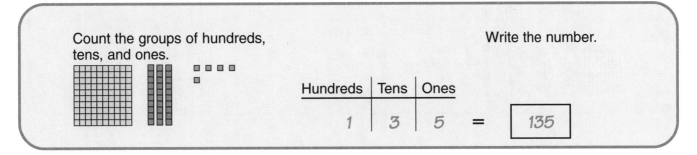

Hundreds	Tens	Ones

= ______

Thousands, Hundreds, Tens, and Ones

Every four-digit whole number has a thousands, a hundreds, a tens, and a ones place.

Count the groups of thousands, hundreds, tens, and ones.

Th	H	T	O
1,	2	3	6

= 1,236

Write the number.

Count the groups of thousands, hundreds, tens, and ones.
Then write the numbers.

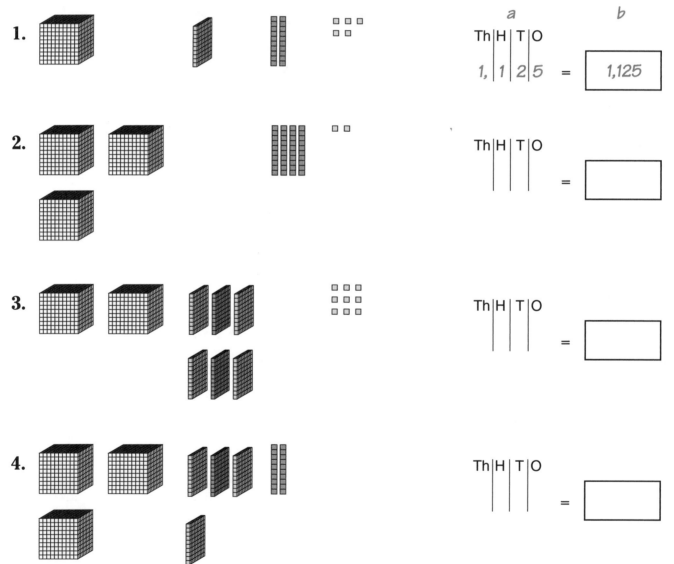

a | b

1. 

Th	H	T	O
1,	1	2	5

= 1,125

2. 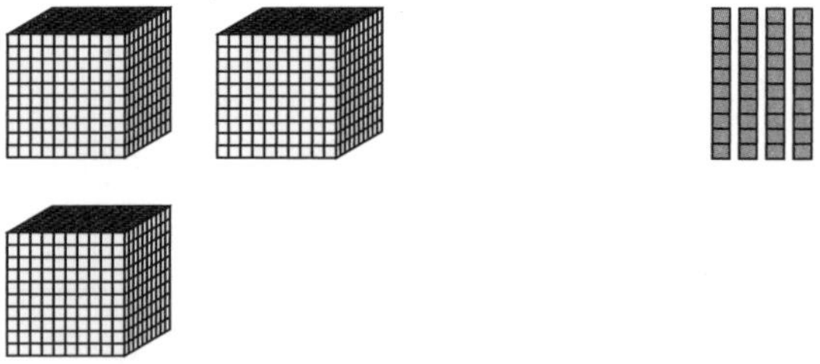

Th	H	T	O

= ______

3. 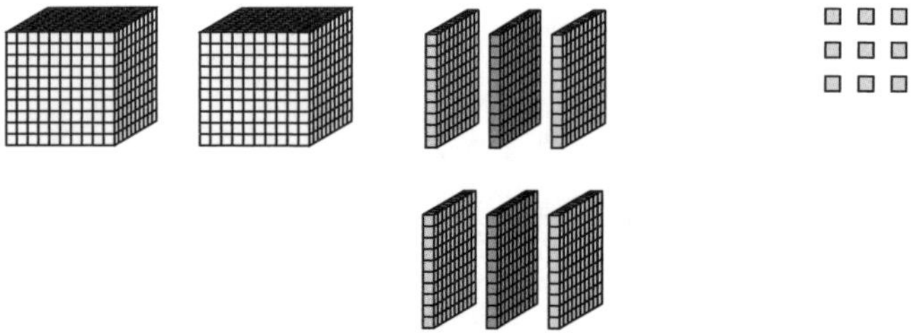

Th	H	T	O

= ______

4. 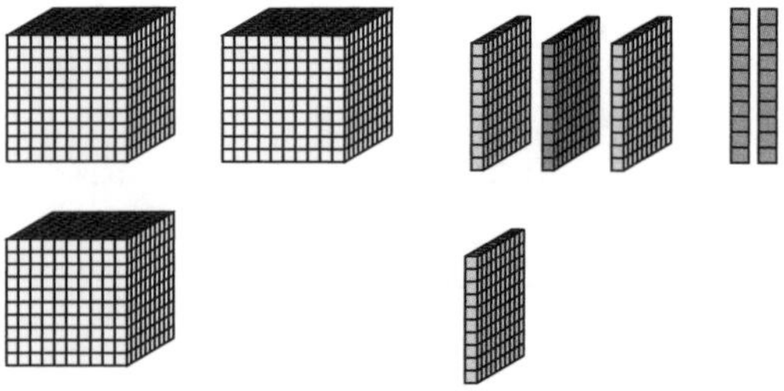

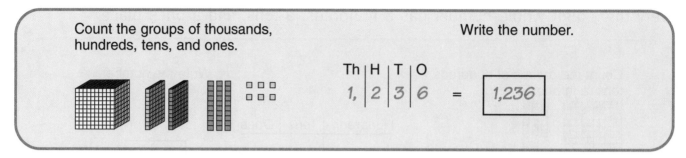

Th	H	T	O

= ______

You can write the groups of thousands, hundreds, tens, and ones in two ways.

> 4,325 = 4 thousands 3 hundreds 2 tens 5 ones
>
> 5 thousands 0 hundreds 6 tens 2 ones = 5,062

Write the numbers.

1. 3,003 = 3 thousands 0 hundreds 0 tens 3 ones
2. 1,807 = ______ thousands ______ hundreds ______ tens ______ ones
3. 8,140 = ______ thousands ______ hundreds ______ tens ______ ones
4. 2,794 = ______ thousands ______ hundreds ______ tens ______ ones
5. 3,682 = ______ thousands ______ hundreds ______ tens ______ ones
6. 4,036 = ______ thousands ______ hundreds ______ tens ______ ones
7. 9,805 = ______ thousands ______ hundreds ______ tens ______ ones
8. 354 = ______ thousands ______ hundreds ______ tens ______ ones

Write the numbers.

9. 5 thousands 0 hundreds 0 tens 6 ones = 5,006
10. 0 thousands 6 hundreds 2 tens 0 ones = ______
11. 5 thousands 2 hundreds 3 tens 6 ones = ______
12. 6 thousands 5 hundreds 7 tens 1 one = ______
13. 3 thousands 1 hundred 5 tens 8 ones = ______
14. 7 thousands 9 hundreds 2 tens 1 one = ______
15. 1 thousand 3 hundreds 2 tens 0 ones = ______
16. 0 thousands 2 hundreds 3 tens 9 ones = ______

Problem-Solving Method: Find a Pattern

Lashad puts the same amount of money in the bank every month. In March, she had $300 in the bank. In April, she had $400. In May, she had $500. How much money will Lashad have in the bank in June?

Understand the problem.

- **What do you want to know?**
  how much money Lashad will have in the bank in June

- **What information do you know?**
  Lashad puts the same amount of money in the bank every month

March	April	May	June
$300	$400	$500	?

Plan how to solve it.

- **What method can you use?**
  You can find and complete a pattern.

Solve it.

- **How can you use this method to solve the problem?**
  Look at the first two numbers. What is the same? What is different? See if this is true for the next number. If it is, you found the pattern to complete.

Find the Pattern.
March: $300 ← Both numbers have 0 ones and 0 tens.
April: $400 ← April had 1 more hundred than March.
May: $500 ← May had 1 more hundred than April.

Complete the Pattern.
June: $600 ← June will have 1 more hundred than May.

- **What is the answer?**
  Lashad will have $600 in the bank in June.

Look back and check your answer.

- **Is your answer reasonable?**
  Find a rule for the pattern: Each month is 1 more.

  The answer is reasonable.

Find the pattern. Write the rule. Then solve.

1. What is the next number?
2, 4, 6, ____

Rule: ____________________

Answer: ____________________

2. What is the next number?
500, 600, 700, ____

Rule: ____________________

Answer: ____________________

3. What is the next number?
5, 10, 15, ____

Rule: ____________________

Answer: ____________________

4. What is the next number?
10, 20, 30, ____

Rule: ____________________

Answer: ____________________

5. What is the missing number?
16, 26, 36, 46, ____, 66

Rule: ____________________

Answer: ____________________

6. What are the next two numbers?
110, 111, 112, ____, ____

Rule: ____________________

Answer: ____________________

Problem Solving

Write how many ones in each number.

1. Every day, 98 astronauts train at the Kennedy Space Center in Florida.

_______________ ones

2. When you speak just one word, you use 72 muscles.

_______________ ones

Write how many tens in the number.

3. The Statue of Liberty weighs 225 tons.

_______________ tens

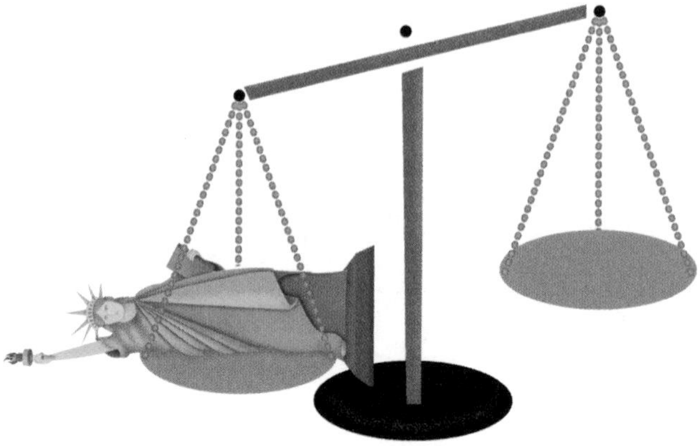

Write how many hundreds in the number.

4. One day on Venus is equal to 243 Earth days.

_______________ hundreds

5. Every day in Canada, around 3,562 people play ice hockey.

_______________ hundreds

Write how many thousands in each number.

6. The border between the United States and Mexico is 1,933 miles long.

_______________ thousands

7. The San Diego Zoo buys 2,825 pounds of peanuts every year to feed the animals.

_______________ thousands

Write each number.

8. "The Viper" is the biggest looping roller coaster. The height of its largest drop is 1 hundred 8 tens 8 ones feet.

____

9. Wilt Chamberlain played in the NBA. In 1962, he set the record for the most points scored in a season. His record is 4 thousands 2 tens 9 ones points.

____

Reading and Writing Numbers

We read and write the number in the **place-value chart** as: eight thousand, twenty-six.

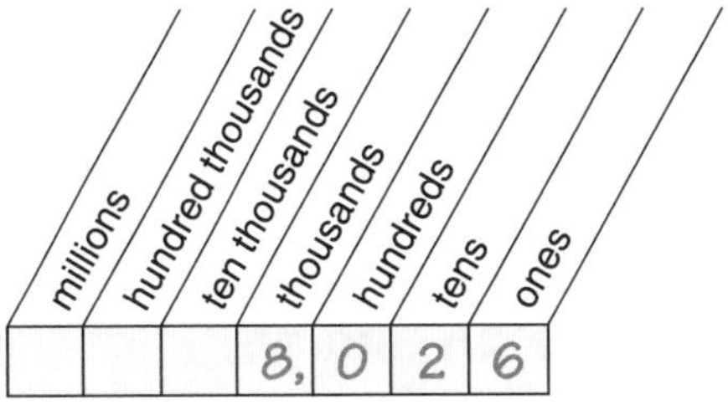

The digit 8 means 8 thousands, or 8,000.
The digit 0 means 0 hundreds, or 0.
The digit 2 means 2 tens, or 20.
The digit 6 means 6 ones, or 6.

Notice that commas are used to separate the digits into groups of three. This helps to make larger numbers easier to read.

Write commas in the numbers.

	a	b	c
1.	2368 2,368	1085 ______	7654 ______
2.	5609 ______	9472 ______	4961 ______

Write the numbers using digits.

3. eight hundred twenty-seven 827

4. one thousand, four hundred thirteen ______

5. five thousand, nine hundred four ______

6. seven hundred thirty-two ______

7. nine thousand, five hundred forty ______

Write the numbers using words.

8. 4,756 four thousand, seven hundred fifty-six

9. 217 ______

10. 6,059 ______

11. 8,112 ______

12. 5,099 ______

Comparing Numbers

To compare two numbers, begin at the left.
Compare the digits in each place.

The symbol $<$ means **is less than.** $5 < 6$

The symbol $>$ means **is greater than.** $9 > 7$

The symbol $=$ means **is equal to.** $3 = 3$

Compare 26 and 38.

2 6
3 8

2 < 3, so 26 < 38.

Compare 147 and 69.

1 4 7
0 6 9

1 > 0, so 147 > 69.

Compare 56 and 51.

5 6
5 1

The tens digits are the same. Compare the ones digits.

6 > 1, so 56 > 51.

Compare. Write <, >, or =.

	a	b	c
1.	37 __>__ 12 3 7 1 2	64 ____ 70 6 4 7 0	75 ____ 75 7 5 7 5
2.	25 ____ 28 2 5 2 8	96 ____ 125 0 9 6 1 2 5	116 ____ 161 1 1 6 1 6 1
3.	31 ____ 48	63 ____ 36	104 ____ 104
4.	83 ____ 208	695 ____ 659	791 ____ 792
5.	13 ____ 7	167 ____ 230	50 ____ 40

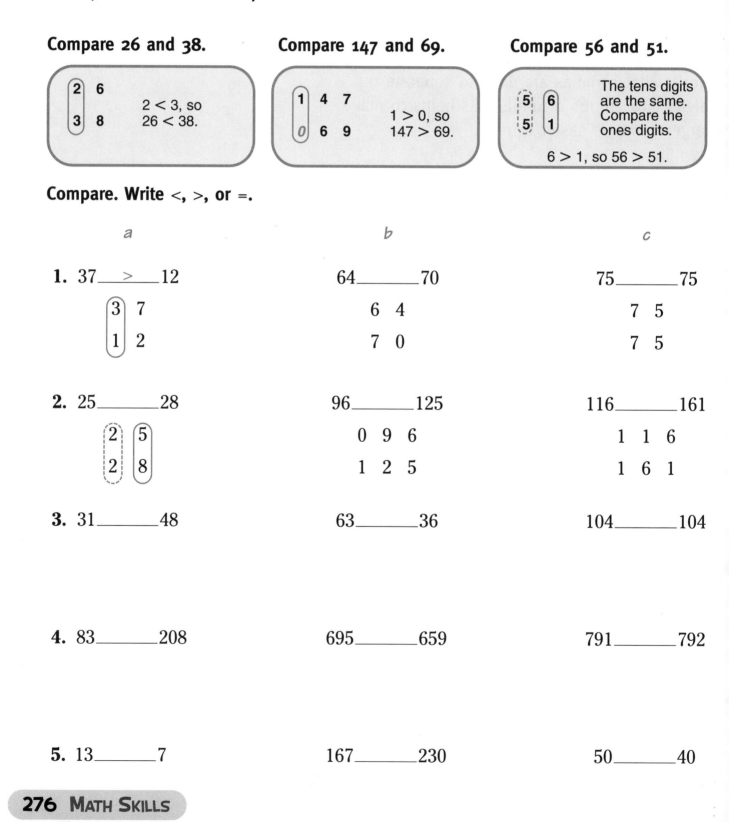

Ordering Numbers

To write numbers in order from least to greatest, compare the numbers. Then write the numbers in order.

Write in order from least to greatest.

32 18 47

Compare the numbers.

3 2
1 8 1 < 3 < 4, so
4 7 18 < 32 < 47.

Write in order from least to greatest.

18 32 47

Write in order from least to greatest.

278 95 163

Compare the numbers.

2 7 8
0 **9 5** 0 < 1 < 2, so
1 6 3 95 < 163 < 278.

Write in order from least to greatest.

95 163 278

Write in order from least to greatest.

	a	*b*	*c*
1.	24 59 36	47 75 19	62 42 22
	2 4 5 9 3 6	4 7 7 5 1 9	6 2 4 2 2 2
	24 36 59	19 < 47 < 75	22 < 42 < 62
2.	17 9 23	25 42 35	267 100 88
	1 7 *0* 9 2 3	2 5 4 2 3 5	2 6 7 1 0 0 *0* 8 8
	________	________	________
3.	108 123 116	759 299 158	278 238 288
	1 0 8 1 2 3 1 1 6	7 5 9 2 9 9 1 5 8	2 7 8 2 3 8 2 8 8
	________	________	________

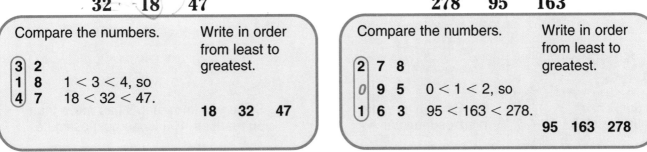

Number Sense

When you cannot count a group of objects, you can use **number sense** to make an estimate.

Compare your objects to a count you know.

Jar A has 50 marbles.

Jar B has a lot more marbles than Jar A.

Choose the most reasonable count.

about 20 marbles

about 50 marbles

about 100 marbles

Since you know Jar B has **more** than 50 marbles, 100 is the best estimate.

Circle the best estimate.

1. The green box has 100 pencils. About how many pencils are in the blue box?

about 50 pencils　　about 100 pencils　　about 1,000 pencils

2. The first fish tank holds 25 gallons of water. About how many gallons of water are in the second fish tank?

about 3 gallons　　about 30 gallons　　about 300 gallons

3. It is 20 miles from Brownsville to Georgetown. About how many miles is it from Brownsville to Sanders?

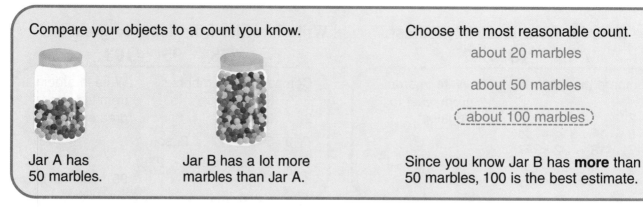

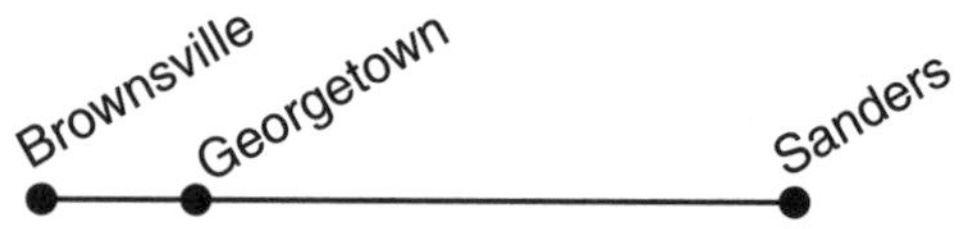

about 2 miles　　about 20 miles　　about 100 miles

Circle the best estimate.

	a		b	
1.	number of books in the City Library		number of windows in a house	
	about 80 books	about 8,000 books	about 10 windows	about 100 windows
2.	length of a pencil		weight of an elephant	
	about 6 inches	about 60 inches	about 90 pounds	about 9,000 pounds
3.	number of students in a classroom		distance across the United States	
	about 30 students	about 300 students	about 25 miles	about 2,500 miles
4.	height of a dog		gallons of water in a lake	
	about 4 feet	about 40 feet	about 60 gallons	about 6,000 gallons
5.	temperature on the Sun		distance you can walk in 1 hour	
	about 87 degrees	about 8,700 degrees	about 4 miles	about 40 miles

Write the numbers.

6. 4 thousands 2 hundreds 1 ten 5 ones = ____________________

7. 0 thousands 3 hundreds 2 tens 4 ones = ____________________

8. 9 thousands 6 hundreds 8 tens 0 ones = ____________________

9. three hundred fifty-one ____________________

10. seventy-nine ____________________

11. six thousand, four hundred twenty-nine ____________________

Problem-Solving Method: Use Logic

A lion, a horse, and a cheetah can all run fast.
One animal runs 43 miles per hour. One runs 50 mph.
One runs 70 mph. The horse runs slower than 50 mph.
Cheetahs run faster than lions.
How fast can each animal run?

Understand the problem.

- **What do you want to know?**
  how fast the animals can run

- **What information is given?**
  Speeds: 43 mph, 50 mph, 70 mph
  Clue 1: The horse runs slower than 50 mph.
  Clue 2: Cheetahs are faster than lions.

Plan how to solve it.

- **What method can you use?**
  You can use logic to organize the information in a table.

Solve it.

- **How can you use this method to solve the problem?**
  Fill in the table using the clues.

	43 mph	50 mph	70 mph
lion	no	**YES**	no
horse	**YES**	no	no
cheetah	no	no	**YES**

- **What is the answer?**
  A lion can run 50 mph.
  A horse can run 43 mph.
  A cheetah can run 70 mph.

Look back and check your answer.

- **Is your answer reasonable?**
  Clue 1: Horses run slower than 50 mph. **Check: $43 < 50$**
  Clue 2: Cheetahs run faster than lions. **Check: $70 > 50$**

  The answer matches the clues.
  The answer is reasonable.

Use logic to solve each problem.

1. Clinton, Kennedy, and Theodore Roosevelt were the three youngest United States presidents. Their ages at election were 42, 43, and 46. Clinton was the oldest. Roosevelt was younger than Kennedy. Who was the youngest president?

   Clue 1: Clinton was the oldest.

   Clue 2: Roosevelt was younger than Kennedy.

	42	43	46
Clinton			
Kennedy			
Roosevelt			

Answer ______________________

2. Elvis Presley, Michael Jackson, and the Beatles had the most number one songs. One had 20. One had 18. One had 13 number one songs. The Beatles had the most. Michael Jackson had fewer than Elvis Presley. How many number one songs did they each have?

Elvis Presley ______________________

The Beatles ______________________

Michael Jackson ______________________

3. Mark, Shawna, and Liz do magic tricks. One does card tricks. One does coin tricks. One makes a rabbit appear out of a hat. Mark uses cards. Liz does not use rabbits. What trick does each person do?

card tricks ______________________

coin tricks ______________________

rabbit tricks ______________________

Unit 1 Review

Write the numbers.

	a	b	c
1.	T | O 8 | 1 = ☐	T | O 4 | 3 = ☐	H | T | O 6 | 7 | 1 = ☐
2.	H | T | O 2 | 6 | 7 = ☐	Th | H | T | O 1, | 3 | 5 | 4 = ☐	Th | H | T | O | 2 | 8 | 3 = ☐

Write the numbers using digits.

3. seven hundred thirty-nine ______________________

4. one thousand, five hundred eighty ______________________

Write the numbers.

5. 47 = ______ thousands ______ hundreds ______ tens ______ ones

6. 629 = ______ thousands ______ hundreds ______ tens ______ ones

7. 7,809 = ______ thousands ______ hundreds ______ tens ______ ones

Write the numbers using words.

8. 119 ______________________

9. 3,065 ______________________

Compare. Write <, >, or =.

	a	b	c
10.	24 ______ 37	96 ______ 69	114 ______ 141

Write the numbers.

11. 0 thousands 0 hundreds 7 tens 3 ones = ________

12. 0 thousands 8 hundreds 3 tens 6 ones = ________

13. 5 thousands 9 hundreds 4 tens 0 ones = ________

14. 1 thousand 0 hundreds 9 tens 1 one = ________

Unit 1 Review

Write in order from least to greatest.

	a			b			c	
15. 31	48	17	64	89	72	325	185	267

a	b	c
31	64	325
48	89	185
17	72	267
______	______	______

Circle the best estimate.

a		b	
16. number of flowers in a vase		weight of a lion	
about 20 flowers	about 2,000 flowers	about 50 pounds	about 500 pounds

Find the pattern. Write the rule. Then solve.

17. What is the next number?
20, 40, 60, ____

Rule ____________________

____

Answer ____________________

18. Anita, Jamie, and Mei are going to the park tomorrow. One will swim, one will play baseball, and one will play tennis. Anita can't swim. Jamie will bring her baseball glove. Who will swim? Who will play baseball? Who will play tennis?

swim ____________________

baseball ____________________

tennis ____________________

Basic Facts

The answer to an addition problem is called the **sum.**

Find: 6 + 1

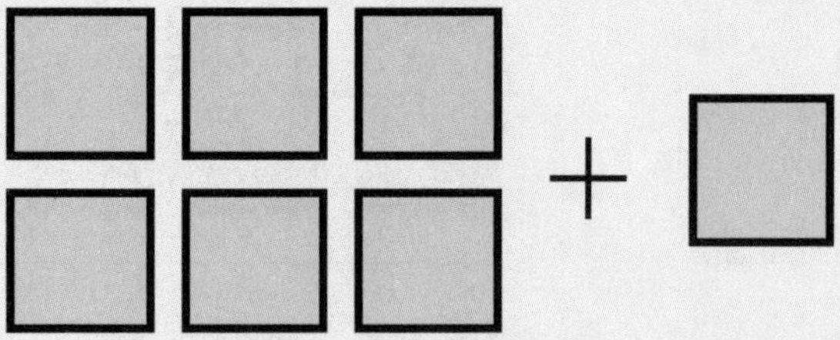

6 + 1 = 7

Find: 4 + 2

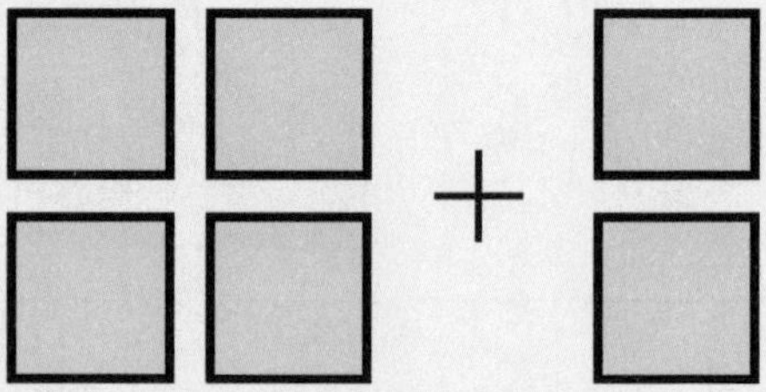

4 + 2 = 6

Add.

	a	b	c
1.	1 + 4 = 5	8 + 9 = ______	6 + 7 = ______
2.	7 + 2 = ______	9 + 0 = ______	9 + 5 = ______
3.	4 + 4 = ______	8 + 2 = ______	0 + 3 = ______
4.	8 + 7 = ______	9 + 6 = ______	3 + 5 = ______
5.	4 + 8 = ______	5 + 1 = ______	4 + 0 = ______
6.	7 + 5 = ______	8 + 6 = ______	6 + 8 = ______
7.	8 + 3 = ______	7 + 0 = ______	5 + 8 = ______
8.	9 + 9 = ______	8 + 1 = ______	0 + 7 = ______
9.	3 + 2 = ______	6 + 3 = ______	7 + 4 = ______
10.	6 + 5 = ______	9 + 8 = ______	2 + 0 = ______
11.	5 + 4 = ______	2 + 1 = ______	9 + 2 = ______

Basic Facts

Addition can be shown two different ways.

Find: 2 + 3

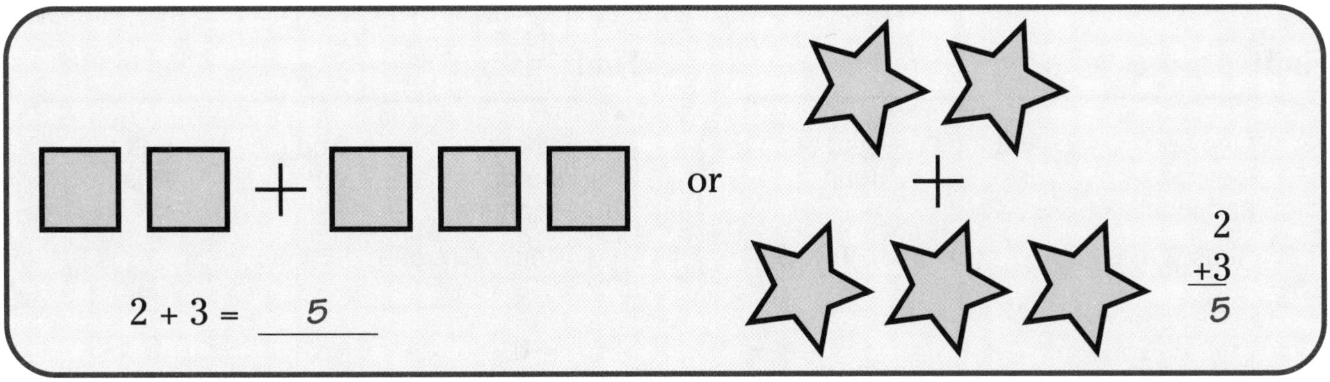

Add.

	a	b	c
1.	9 + 0 = ______	6 + 4 = ______	5 + 9 = ______

Find the sums.

	a	b	c	d	e	f	g
2.	2 +6 8	6 +0	9 +3	1 +8	6 +3	8 +5	4 +7
3.	3 +9	0 +0	8 +8	5 +6	3 +7	5 +2	8 +4
4.	9 +6	7 +7	0 +4	2 +2	3 +0	5 +7	7 +9
5.	1 +5	6 +2	7 +8	3 +3	2 +9	0 +9	5 +5

Two-digit Addition

To add 2-digit numbers, first add the ones.
Then add the tens.

You may need to rewrite a problem by lining up the digits in the ones and tens places.

Find: 61 + 4

Line up the ones and tens.

Tens	Ones
6	1
+	4

Add the ones.

T	O
6	**1**
+	**4**
	5

Add the tens.

T	O
6	1
+	4
6	5

Find: 31 + 67

Line up the ones and tens.

Tens	Ones
3	1
+6	7

Add the ones.

T	O
3	**1**
+6	**7**
	8

Add the tens.

T	O
3	1
+6	7
9	8

Add.

1\.

	a		b		c		d		e		f	
	T	O	T	O	T	O	T	O	T	O	T	O
	8	2	3	0	4	2	2	1	2	2	5	3
	+	3	+	1	+	5	+	2	+	6	+	3
	8	5										

2\.

a	b	c	d	e	f
54	60	31	13	80	11
+44	+32	+58	+61	+19	+80

3\.

a	b	c	d	e	f
62	61	10	31	72	94
+24	+ 6	+43	+67	+ 7	+ 5

Rewrite. Then find the sums.

4\. a. 14 + 5 = ______ b. 14 + 53 = ______

T	O
1	4
+	5

Three-digit Addition

To add three-digit numbers, first add the ones. Then add the tens. Last, add the hundreds.

You may need to rewrite a problem by lining up the digits in the ones, tens, and hundreds places.

Find: 223 + 75

Line up the ones, tens, and hundreds.

	H	T	O
	2	2	3
+		7	5

Add the ones.

	H	T	O
	2	2	**3**
+		7	**5**
			8

Add the tens.

	H	T	O
	2	**2**	3
+		**7**	5
		9	8

Add the hundreds.

	H	T	O
	2	2	3
+		7	5
	2	9	8

Add.

1.

a

	H	T	O
	8	3	3
+		1	4
	8	4	7

b

	H	T	O
	5	8	1
+		1	0

c

	H	T	O
	6	0	7
+		9	1

d

	H	T	O
	1	4	1
+		5	3

e

	H	T	O
	4	6	1
+		2	6

f

	H	T	O
	5	3	1
+		3	5

2. 742 + 246   131 + 862   523 + 435   522 + 257   320 + 309   684 + 110

3. 414 + 572   135 + 21   764 + 31   542 + 34   601 + 148   525 + 304

Rewrite. Then find the sums.

4. *a* 401 + 463 = ________   *b* 917 + 80 = ________

	H	T	O
	4	0	1
+	4	6	3

Two-digit Addition with Regrouping Ones as Tens

Sometimes you have to **regroup** ones as tens when adding.

Find: 48 + 8

Add the ones.

Regroup as 1 ten and 6 ones.

T	O
1	
4	**8**
+	**8**
	6

Add the tens.

T	O
1	
4	8
+	8
5	6

Find: 64 + 27

Add the ones.

Regroup as 1 ten and 1 one.

T	O
1	
6	**4**
+2	**7**
	1

Add the tens.

T	O
1	
6	4
+**2**	7
9	1

Add.

	a	b	c	d	e	f
1.	T O	T O	T O	T O	T O	T O
	1					
	2 2	4 6	7 6	2 9	8 7	3 8
	+ 8	+ 7	+ 5	+ 9	+ 6	+ 3
	3 0					
2.	T O	T O	T O	T O	T O	T O
	2 8	2 8	3 7	1 9	1 7	2 9
	+1 5	+4 2	+5 3	+1 8	+7 8	+3 1
3.	T O	T O	T O	T O	T O	T O
	5 9	3 6	8 7	2 6	2 8	8 5
	+ 2	+2 6	+ 4	+6 8	+1 9	+ 6

Three-digit Addition with Regrouping Ones as Tens

To add three-digit numbers, first add the ones. Sometimes you have to regroup ones as tens. Then add the tens. Last, add the hundreds.

Find: 437 + 23

Line up the digits in each place.

	H	T	O
	4	3	7
+		2	3

Add the ones. Regroup.

	H	T	O
		1	
	4	3	7
+		2	3
			0

Add the tens.

	H	T	O
		1	
	4	3	7
+		2	3
		6	0

Add the hundreds.

	H	T	O
		1	
	4	3	7
+		2	3
	4	6	0

Add.

	a	b	c	d	e	f
1.	619 + 18 = 637	327 + 64 = 391	208 + 42 = 250	526 + 25 = 551	329 + 42 = 371	739 + 24 = 763
2.	645 + 226 = 871	838 + 124 = 962	419 + 342 = 761	128 + 569 = 697	209 + 781 = 990	238 + 118 = 356
3.	714 + 36 = 750	315 + 165 = 480	926 + 58 = 984	204 + 687 = 891	809 + 81 = 890	246 + 516 = 762

Rewrite. Then find the sums.

4. a. 168 + 17 = 175   b. 405 + 546 = 951

	H	T	O
	1	6	8
+		1	7
	1	7	5

Problem-Solving Method: Guess and Check

Neptune and Mars have a total of ten moons. Neptune has six more moons than Mars. How many moons does each planet have?

Understand the problem.

- **What do you want to know?**
  how many moons each planet has

- **What information is given?**
  Clue 1: Neptune moons + Mars moons = 10
  Clue 2: Neptune has 6 more moons than Mars.

Plan how to solve it.

- **What method can you use?**
  You can guess an answer for the first clue.
  Then you can check your guess with the second clue.

Solve it.

- **How can you use this method to solve the problem?**
  You know that Neptune has at least 6 moons. Use 6 as your first guess. Think about what two numbers could equal 10. Make a table to organize your guesses.

Guess	Check	Evaluate
6 + 4 = 10	6 is only 2 more than 4.	6 is too low.
7 + 3 = 10	7 is only 3 more than 4.	7 is too low.
8 + 2 = 10	8 is 6 more than 2.	8 is correct.

- **What is the answer?**
  Neptune has 8 moons.
  Mars has 2 moons.

Look back and check your answer.

- **Is your answer reasonable?**
  Clue 1: Neptune moons + Mars moons = 10
  Check: 8 + 2 = 10

  Clue 2: Mars moons + 6 = Neptune moons
  Check: 2 + 6 = 8

  The answer matches the clues.
  The answer is reasonable.

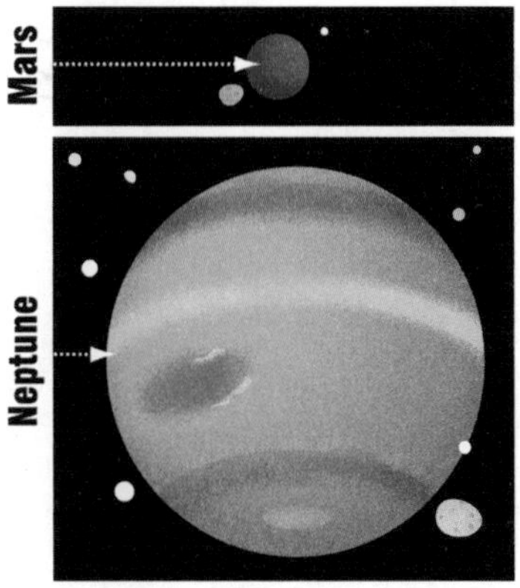

Use guess and check to solve each problem.

1. Jill and Dave work in a shoe store. Last week, Jill sold 5 more pairs of shoes than Dave did. Together they sold 21 pairs. How many pairs of shoes did each person sell?

5 - 21 = 16

Jill ______________ pairs

Dave ______________ pairs

2. Antoine spent \$8 in all on a hot dog and soda at the baseball game. The hot dog cost \$2 more than the soda. How much did the hot dog cost? How much did the soda cost?

hot dog \$______________

soda \$______________

3. Nita is 10 years older than Joe. The sum of their ages is 20 years. How old is Nita? How old is Joe?

Nita ______________ years old

Joe ______________ years old

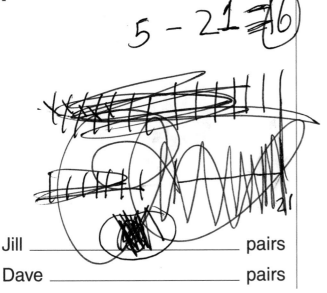

Problem Solving

Solve.

1. A young panda eats about 25 pounds of bamboo a day. An adult panda eats about 35 pounds a day. How much bamboo do they eat in all each day?

________________ pounds

2. By 2000, the United States had won 230 Olympic gold medals in swimming. They also won 46 gold medals in diving. How many gold medals is that altogether?

________________ gold medals

3. Janet had 237 seashells. She found 36 more shells. How many shells does she have now?

________________ shells

4. One shower uses 37 gallons of water. Angela took two showers today. How much water did she use in all?

________________ gallons

5. Jamal collects baseball cards. He has 218 American League cards. He has 172 National League cards. How many baseball cards does Jamal have?

218+172=
200+100=300
10+70=80
8+8=10
390 cards
390

________________ cards

Three-digit Addition with Regrouping Tens as Hundreds

Sometimes you have to regroup tens as hundreds.

Find: 675 + 32

Line up the digits in each place.	Add the ones.	Add the tens. Regroup 10 tens as 1 hundred and 0 tens.	Add the hundreds.
H T O 6 7 5 + 3 2	H T O 6 7 5 + 3 2 7	H T O 1 6 7 5 + 3 2 0 7	H T O 1 6 7 5 + 3 2 7 0 7

Add.

	a	b	c	d	e	f
1.	H T O 1 1 8 0 + 3 9 2 1 9	H T O 5 7 0 + 5 0	H T O 7 9 2 + 1 0	H T O 4 8 1 + 4 5	H T O 6 3 4 + 7 2 706	H T O 5 8 0 + 5 9
2.	675 +132	361 +446	264 +674	291 +218	477 +352	497 +340
3.	382 +150	184 + 43	492 +436	465 +353	193 +795	272 + 65

Rewrite. Then find the sums.

4. a. 365 + 361 = ________ b. 374 + 34 = ________

H T O
3 6 5
+ 3 6 1

Three-digit Addition with Two Regroupings

Sometimes you regroup two times when adding three-digit numbers.

Find: 786 + 17

Add the ones.	Add the tens.	Add the hundreds.
Regroup 13 as 1 ten 3 ones.	Regroup 10 as 1 hundred 0 tens.	

H T O
  1
7 8 6
+ 1 7
    3
	H T O
	1 1
	7 8 6
	+ 1 7
	  0 3
		H T O
		1 1
		7 8 6
		+ 1 7
		8 0 3

Add.

	a	b	c	d	e	f
1.	H T O 1 1 8 6 9 + 9 3 9 6 2	H T O 3 8 9 + 3 9	H T O 6 6 3 + 4 9	H T O 2 8 7 + 1 8	H T O 5 6 8 + 4 6	H T O 6 8 6 + 5 9
2.	389 + 65	138 + 98	679 + 34	457 + 96	849 + 59	387 + 54
3.	388 +546	167 + 65	497 + 54	179 +764	698 +219	249 +272

Rewrite. Then find the sums.

4. *a* 298 + 17 = ________   *b* 772 + 38 = ________

H T O
2 9 8
+ 1 7

Addition Practice: Deciding When to Regroup

Add.

	a	b	c	d	e	f
1.	$\begin{array}{r} 1 \\ 118 \\ +\ 43 \\ \hline 161 \end{array}$	$\begin{array}{r} 889 \\ +\ 73 \\ \hline \end{array}$	$\begin{array}{r} 78 \\ +\ 8 \\ \hline \end{array}$	$\begin{array}{r} 34 \\ +47 \\ \hline \end{array}$	$\begin{array}{r} 758 \\ +\ 64 \\ \hline \end{array}$	$\begin{array}{r} 147 \\ +\ 49 \\ \hline \end{array}$
2.	$\begin{array}{r} 669 \\ +179 \\ \hline \end{array}$	$\begin{array}{r} 23 \\ +\ 8 \\ \hline \end{array}$	$\begin{array}{r} 26 \\ +56 \\ \hline \end{array}$	$\begin{array}{r} 908 \\ +\ 89 \\ \hline \end{array}$	$\begin{array}{r} 467 \\ +189 \\ \hline \end{array}$	$\begin{array}{r} 97 \\ +76 \\ \hline \end{array}$
3.	$\begin{array}{r} 371 \\ +395 \\ \hline \end{array}$	$\begin{array}{r} 656 \\ +\ 79 \\ \hline \end{array}$	$\begin{array}{r} 137 \\ +195 \\ \hline \end{array}$	$\begin{array}{r} 398 \\ +569 \\ \hline \end{array}$	$\begin{array}{r} 46 \\ +\ 5 \\ \hline \end{array}$	$\begin{array}{r} 59 \\ +23 \\ \hline \end{array}$
4.	$\begin{array}{r} 48 \\ +25 \\ \hline \end{array}$	$\begin{array}{r} 257 \\ +\ 98 \\ \hline \end{array}$	$\begin{array}{r} 38 \\ +\ 4 \\ \hline \end{array}$	$\begin{array}{r} 524 \\ +349 \\ \hline \end{array}$	$\begin{array}{r} 108 \\ +\ 76 \\ \hline \end{array}$	$\begin{array}{r} 416 \\ +\ 69 \\ \hline \end{array}$
5.	$\begin{array}{r} 86 \\ +\ 7 \\ \hline \end{array}$	$\begin{array}{r} 496 \\ +297 \\ \hline \end{array}$	$\begin{array}{r} 72 \\ +19 \\ \hline \end{array}$	$\begin{array}{r} 309 \\ +345 \\ \hline \end{array}$	$\begin{array}{r} 65 \\ +25 \\ \hline \end{array}$	$\begin{array}{r} 798 \\ +146 \\ \hline \end{array}$
6.	$\begin{array}{r} 580 \\ +\ 26 \\ \hline \end{array}$	$\begin{array}{r} 17 \\ +33 \\ \hline \end{array}$	$\begin{array}{r} 41 \\ +39 \\ \hline \end{array}$	$\begin{array}{r} 389 \\ +285 \\ \hline \end{array}$	$\begin{array}{r} 25 \\ +\ 8 \\ \hline \end{array}$	$\begin{array}{r} 348 \\ +285 \\ \hline \end{array}$

Rewrite. Then find the sums.

a

7. 47 + 6 = _____

b

692 + 35 = _____

$\begin{array}{r} 47 \\ +\ 6 \\ \hline \end{array}$

Problem-Solving Method: Use Estimation

Jerry Rice and Marcus Allen were professional football players. Rice scored 165 touchdowns. Allen scored 134 touchdowns. About how many touchdowns did they score in all?

Understand the problem.

- **What do you want to know?**
  about how many touchdowns they scored in all

- **What information is given?**
  Jerry Rice scored 165 touchdowns.
  Marcus Allen scored 134 touchdowns.

Plan how to solve it.

- **What method can you use?**
  The question is not asking for an exact answer.
  So, you can use estimation.

Solve it.

- **How can you use this method to solve the problem?**
  Change each number to the closest hundred.
  Then add.

165 →	**Think:** 165 is closer to 200 than 100.	**200**
+134 →	**Think:** 134 is closer to 100 than 200.	**+100**
		300

- **What is the answer?**
  They scored about 300 touchdowns in all.

Look back and check your answer.

- **Is your answer reasonable?**
  You can check your estimate by finding the exact answer.

$$\begin{array}{r} 165 \\ +134 \\ \hline 299 \end{array}$$

The estimate is close to the sum.
The answer is reasonable.

Use estimation to solve each problem.

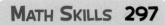

1. Last fall, park workers planted 192 white roses. They also planted 110 yellow roses. About how many roses did they plant in all?

about ____________ roses

2. A gorilla weighs about 485 pounds. A baboon weighs about 99 pounds. About how much do the two animals weigh together?

about ___________ pounds

3. Tawanda drove 287 miles on the first day of her trip. She drove 294 miles on the second day. About how far did she drive on these two days?

about ___________ miles

4. Two scout troops had a car wash. There were 37 Boy Scouts and 52 Girl Scouts working. About how many scouts worked at the car wash?

about ____________ scouts

5. In 1985, a shipwreck near Florida was found filled with treasures. It held 36 tons of gold and silver. It also had about 69 tons of emeralds. About how much did these treasures weigh in all?

about ______________ tons

Unit 2 Review

Add.

	a	b	c	d	e	f
1.	21 + 5	37 + 10	74 + 23	56 + 32	15 + 73	87 + 11
2.	275 + 134	154 + 253	486 + 360	652 + 167	533 + 281	392 + 164
3.	316 + 85	275 + 249	486 + 57	479 + 134	576 + 159	253 + 598
4.	427 + 96	183 + 58	243 + 89	784 + 127	321 + 479	635 + 144

Rewrite. Then find the sums.

	a	b
5.	57 + 39 = ________	375 + 61 = ________
6.	756 + 163 = ________	527 + 281 = ________
7.	598 + 54 = ________	283 + 497 = ________

Unit 2 Review

Use guess and check to solve each problem.

8. Sue and Manuel collect model trains. Sue has 1 more train than Manuel has. Together they have 13 trains. How many trains do they each have?

Sue ______________ trains

Manuel ______________ trains

9. Inez bought 15 pizzas for the party. There were 7 more pepperoni pizzas than cheese pizzas. How many of each kind of pizza did Inez buy?

______________ pepperoni pizzas

______________ cheese pizzas

Use estimation to solve.

10. A humpback whale weighs about 49 tons. A fin whale weighs about 82 tons. About how much do a humpback whale and fin whale weigh in all?

about ______________ tons

unit 3
subtraction

Basic Facts

The answer to a subtraction problem is called the **difference**.

Find: 6 − 1

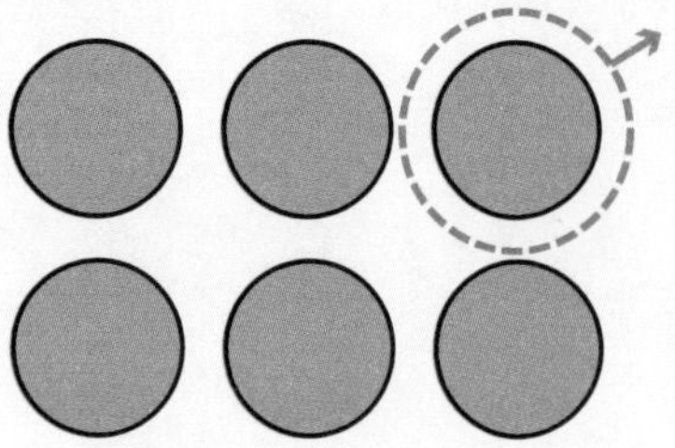

6 − 1 = 5

Find: 7 − 3

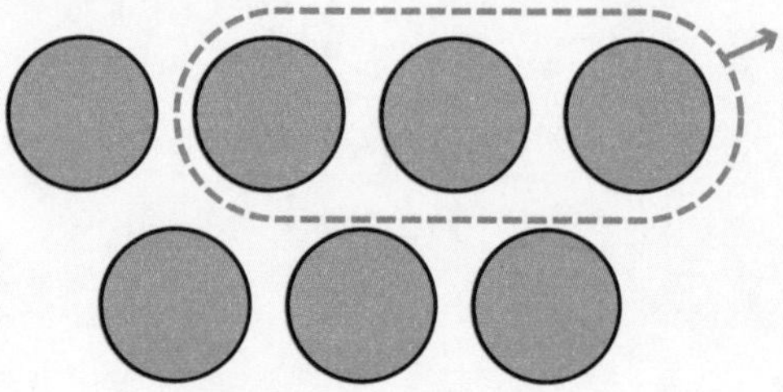

7 − 3 = 4

Subtract.

	a	b	c
1.	6 − 1 = 5	10 − 8 = ______	3 − 0 = ______
2.	7 − 3 = ______	9 − 5 = ______	12 − 8 = ______
3.	8 − 1 = ______	1 − 0 = ______	13 − 6 = ______
4.	12 − 0 = ______	10 − 9 = ______	9 − 7 = ______
5.	4 − 1 = ______	14 − 7 = ______	5 − 0 = ______
6.	12 − 7 = ______	8 − 4 = ______	17 − 8 = ______
7.	2 − 1 = ______	12 − 4 = ______	5 − 2 = ______
8.	8 − 6 = ______	15 − 6 = ______	13 − 8 = ______
9.	14 − 8 = ______	3 − 2 = ______	7 − 4 = ______
10.	16 − 7 = ______	10 − 6 = ______	6 − 3 = ______
11.	4 − 3 = ______	14 − 5 = ______	7 − 5 = ______

Basic Facts

Subtraction can be shown two different ways.

Find: 10 − 4

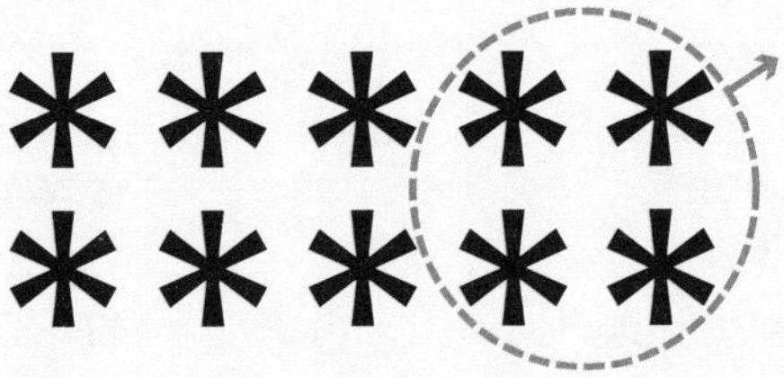

10 − 4 = 6

or

Line up the ones and tens.

Tens	Ones
1	0
−	4
	6

Subtract.

	a	b	c
1.	2 − 0 = ______	11 − 7 = ______	6 − 3 = ______

Find the differences.

	a	b	c	d	e	f	g
2.	T | O	T | O	T | O	T | O	T | O	T | O	T | O
	8	1 1	8	1 1	1 2	9	8
	− 6	− 4	− 2	− 8	− 5	− 2	− 3
	2						

3.	10	6	14	6	8	13	15
	− 4	−0	− 6	−5	−5	− 5	− 7
4.	16	12	13	16	10	4	12
	− 8	− 6	− 9	− 9	− 3	−0	− 9
5.	7	13	4	10	9	14	9
	−6	− 4	−2	− 7	−1	− 9	−6

Two-digit Subtraction

To subtract two-digit numbers, first subtract the ones. Then subtract the tens.

You may need to rewrite a problem by lining up the digits in the ones and tens places.

Find: 29 − 3

Line up the ones and tens.

Tens	Ones
2	9
−	3

Subtract the ones.

T	O
2	**9**
−	**3**
	6

Subtract the tens.

T	O
2	9
−	3
2	6

Find: 84 − 21

Line up the ones and tens.

Tens	Ones
8	4
−2	1

Subtract the ones.

T	O
8	**4**
−2	**1**
	3

Subtract the tens.

T	O
8	4
−2	1
6	3

Subtract.

1.

	a		b		c		d		e		f	
	T	O	T	O	T	O	T	O	T	O	T	O
	3	7	7	4	4	7	1	9	8	9	3	8
	−	3	−	1	−	3	−	4	−	7	−	6
	3	4										

2.

a	b	c	d	e	f
76	59	61	85	29	97
−31	− 2	−30	−61	− 5	−85

Rewrite. Then find the differences.

3. a. 95 − 4 = ________ b. 87 − 41 = ________

T	O
9	5
−	4

Three-digit Subtraction

To subtract three-digit numbers, first subtract the ones. Then subtract the tens. Last, subtract the hundreds.

You may need to rewrite a problem by lining up the digits in the ones, tens, and hundreds places.

Find: 398 – 56

Line up the ones, tens, and hundreds.

	H	T	O
	3	9	8
–		5	6

Subtract the ones.

	H	T	O
	3	9	8
–		5	6
			2

Subtract the tens.

	H	T	O
	3	9	8
–		5	6
		4	2

Subtract the hundreds.

	H	T	O
	3	9	8
–		5	6
	3	4	2

Subtract.

1.

a

	H	T	O
	5	4	9
–		3	6
	5	1	3

b

	H	T	O
	1	2	6
–		1	2

c

	H	T	O
	6	7	5
–		3	4

d

	H	T	O
	2	9	8
–		4	3

e

	H	T	O
	7	6	5
–		5	3

f

	H	T	O
	7	4	9
–		3	6

2. 449 − 27   477 − 326   839 − 521   494 − 73   829 − 14   278 − 15

Rewrite. Then find the differences.

3. *a* 393 − 161 = ________   *b* 576 − 63 = ________

	H	T	O
	3	9	3
–	1	6	1

Two-digit Subtraction with Regrouping Tens as Ones

Sometimes you have to regroup 1 ten as 10 ones to subtract.

Find: 31 – 9

Line up the ones and tens. To subtract the ones, more ones are needed.	Regroup 1 ten as 10 ones. Show 1 less ten. Show 10 more ones.	Subtract the ones.	Subtract the tens.
T O	T O	T O	T O
	2 11	2 11	2 11
3 1	~~3~~ ~~1~~	~~3~~ ~~1~~	~~3~~ ~~1~~
– 9	– 9	– 9	– 9
		2	2 2

Subtract.

	a	b	c	d	e	f
1.	T O 3 17 ~~4~~ ~~7~~ – 9 3 8	T O 9 2 – 3	T O 3 5 – 8	T O 6 2 – 4	T O 2 1 – 2	T O 5 4 – 5
2.	T O 2 2 –1 6	T O 5 1 –2 6	T O 7 5 –3 8	T O 4 1 –1 7	T O 9 4 –5 9	T O 5 2 –3 9
3.	T O 7 6 –4 9	T O 7 2 – 5	T O 7 1 –5 8	T O 6 4 – 7	T O 7 3 – 6	T O 9 1 –6 6

Rewrite. Then find the differences.

	a	b
4.	53 – 18 = ________ T O 5 3 – 1 8	42 – 27 = ________

Three-digit Subtraction with Regrouping Tens as Ones

To subtract three-digit numbers, you may need to regroup 1 ten as 10 ones. Then subtract.

Find: 542 − 37

Line up the ones, tens, and hundreds. To subtract the ones, more ones are needed.

	H	T	O
	5	4	2
−		3	7

Regroup 1 ten as 10 ones. Show 1 less ten. Show 10 more ones.

	H	T	O
		3	12
	5	~~4~~	~~2~~
−		3	7

Subtract the ones.

	H	T	O
		3	12
	5	~~4~~	~~2~~
−		3	7
			5

Subtract the tens.

	H	T	O
		3	12
	5	~~4~~	~~2~~
−		3	7
		0	5

Subtract the hundreds.

	H	T	O
		3	12
	5	~~4~~	~~2~~
−		3	7
	5	0	5

Subtract.

1.

a

	H	T	O
		5	14
	8	~~6~~	~~4~~
−	1	3	7
	7	2	7

b

	H	T	O
	2	7	0
−		4	4

c

	H	T	O
	1	7	2
−		5	6

d

	H	T	O
	7	9	2
−		4	9

e

	H	T	O
	9	5	0
−	3	4	6

f

	H	T	O
	6	3	0
−	4	2	5

	a	*b*	*c*	*d*	*e*	*f*
2.	281 − 48	941 − 339	785 − 208	490 − 63	682 − 367	464 − 36
3.	170 − 38	561 − 243	154 − 17	880 − 255	361 − 135	673 − 29

Rewrite. Then find the differences.

4. *a* 352 − 126 = ______ *b* 632 − 24 = ______

	H	T	O
	3	5	2
−	1	2	6

Problem-Solving Method: Use a Graph

There are about 140 skyscrapers in New York City. A skyscraper is a building taller than 500 feet. How many more skyscrapers are in New York City than in Chicago?

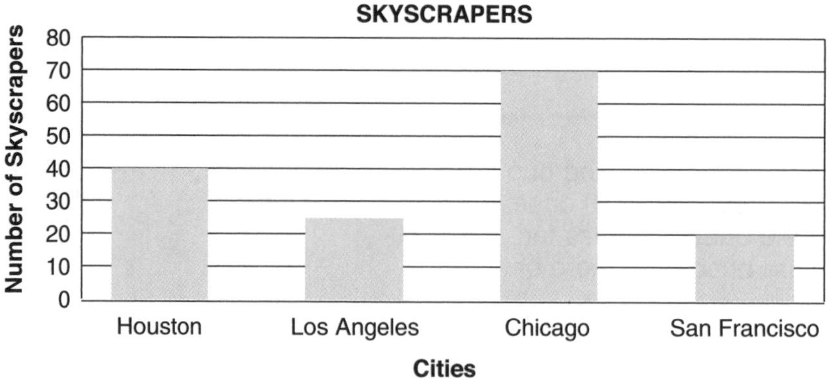

Understand the problem.

- **What do you want to know?**
  How many more skyscrapers are in New York City than in Chicago?

- **What information is given?**
  New York City has about 140 skyscrapers.
  The bar graph shows the number of skyscrapers in four cities.

Plan how to solve it.

- **What method can you use?**
  You can use the bar graph to compare the data.

Solve it.

- **How can you use this method to solve the problem?**
  Find Chicago on the bar graph. Move your finger to the top of its bar. Move across to the left to find the number of skyscrapers in Chicago. Then subtract.

$$\begin{array}{r} 140 \\ -\ 70 \\ \hline 70 \end{array}$$

140 → Number of skyscrapers in New York City
70 → Number of skyscrapers in Chicago

- **What is the answer?**
  New York has 70 more skyscrapers than Chicago.

Look back and check your answer.

- **Is your answer reasonable?**
  You can check subtraction with addition.
  $70 + 70 = 140$
  The answer is reasonable.

Use the bar graph to solve each problem.

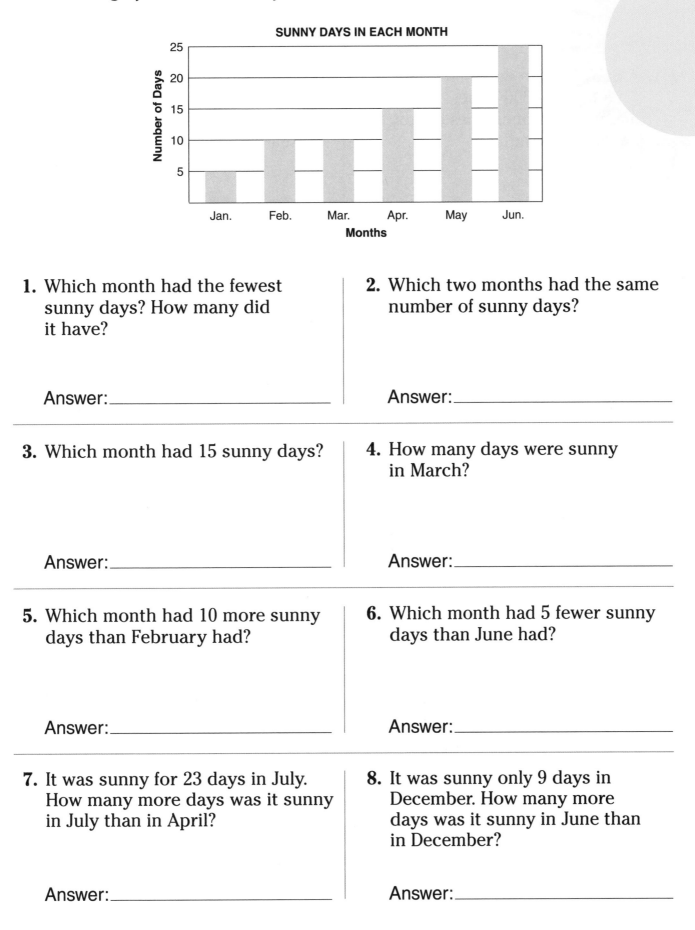

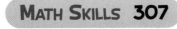

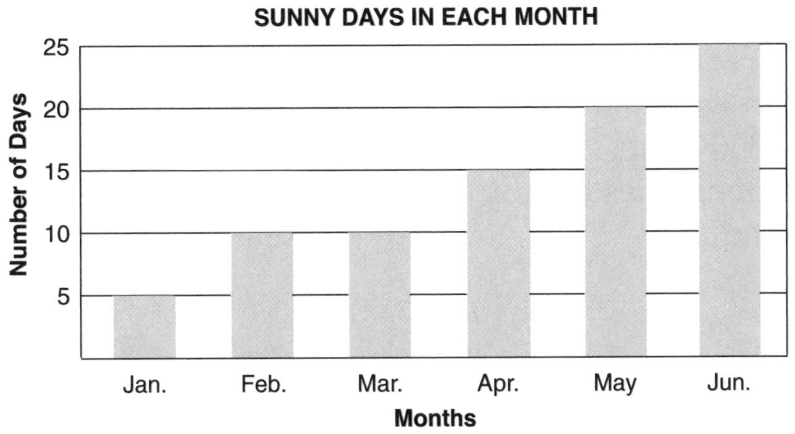

1. Which month had the fewest sunny days? How many did it have?

Answer:____________________

2. Which two months had the same number of sunny days?

Answer:____________________

3. Which month had 15 sunny days?

Answer:____________________

4. How many days were sunny in March?

Answer:____________________

5. Which month had 10 more sunny days than February had?

Answer:____________________

6. Which month had 5 fewer sunny days than June had?

Answer:____________________

7. It was sunny for 23 days in July. How many more days was it sunny in July than in April?

Answer:____________________

8. It was sunny only 9 days in December. How many more days was it sunny in June than in December?

Answer:____________________

Problem Solving

Solve.

1. A baby is born with 350 bones. An adult has 206 bones. How many more bones does a baby have than an adult?

   ______________ bones

2. A jet can carry 217 passengers. Only 108 passengers were on a jet going to Memphis. How many seats were empty?

   ______________ seats

3. Maya drove 372 miles the first day of her trip. She drove 105 fewer miles on the second day. How far did Maya drive on the second day?

   ______________ miles

4. There were 132 men in the stands at the hockey game. There were also 119 women. How many more men than women were in the stands?

   ______________ men

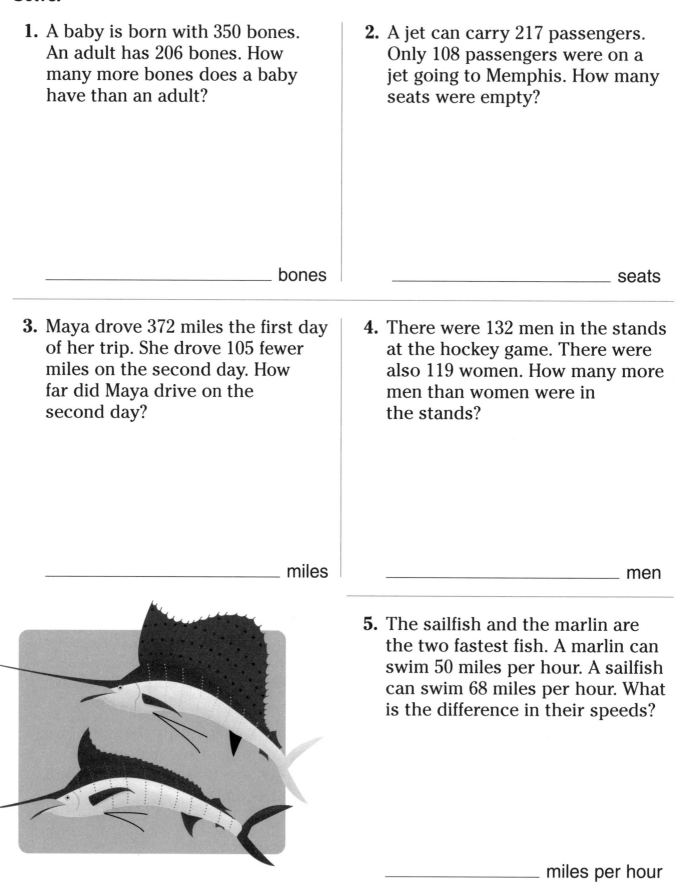

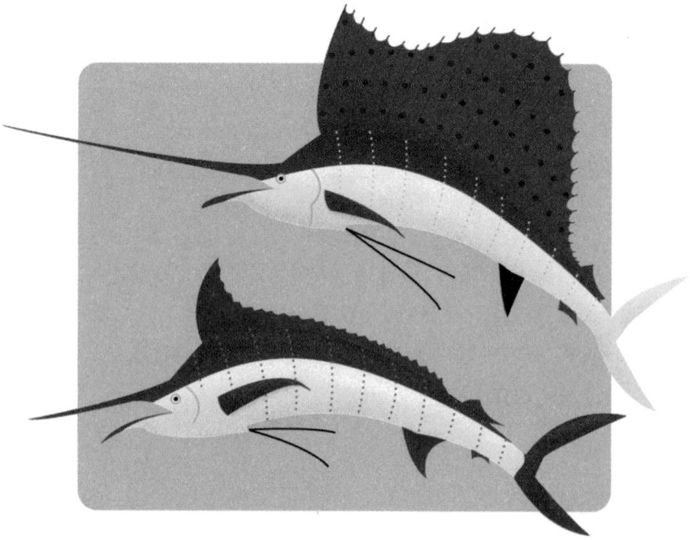

5. The sailfish and the marlin are the two fastest fish. A marlin can swim 50 miles per hour. A sailfish can swim 68 miles per hour. What is the difference in their speeds?

   ______________ miles per hour

Three-digit Subtraction with Regrouping Hundreds as Tens

Sometimes you have to regroup 1 hundred as 10 tens.

Find: 628 − 47

Line up the ones, tens, and hundreds.	Subtract the ones. To subtract the tens, more tens are needed.	Regroup 1 hundred as 10 tens. Show 1 less hundred. Show 10 more tens.	Subtract the tens.	Subtract the hundreds.
H | T | O	H | T | O	H | T | O	H | T | O	H | T | O
		5 | 12 |	5 | 12 |	5 | 12 |
6 | 2 | 8	6 | 2 | 8	~~6~~ | ~~2~~ | 8	~~6~~ | ~~2~~ | 8	~~6~~ | ~~2~~ | 8
− | 4 | 7	− | 4 | 7	− | 4 | 7	− | 4 | 7	− | 4 | 7
| |	| | 1	| | 1	| 8 | 1	5 | 8 | 1

Subtract.

	a	b	c	d	e	f
1.	H T O 1 11 ~~2~~ ~~1~~ 9 − 6 7 1 5 2	H T O 5 3 4 − 6 0	H T O 4 1 7 − 4 1	H T O 7 2 9 − 9 8	H T O 8 1 2 −7 7 0	H T O 8 3 4 −4 9 1
2.	9 2 9 −4 5 8	7 2 8 − 6 5	5 3 2 − 7 0	6 2 5 − 5 3	3 1 4 − 6 4	3 2 9 −2 9 4
3.	5 1 8 −2 4 3	7 3 7 − 8 4	7 1 4 −2 3 2	8 4 1 −4 8 0	9 6 5 − 9 5	4 3 4 −3 4 4

Rewrite. Then find the differences.

	a	b
4.	635 − 172 = __________	876 − 94 = __________

H	T	O
6	3	5
− 1	7	2

Subtraction Practice with One Regrouping

Subtract.

	a	b	c	d	e	f
1.	$\begin{array}{r} \scriptstyle 4\,12 \\ \not{5}\,\not{2} \\ -\ 3\,7 \\ \hline 1\,5 \end{array}$	$\begin{array}{r} 61 \\ -22 \\ \hline \end{array}$	$\begin{array}{r} 31 \\ -16 \\ \hline \end{array}$	$\begin{array}{r} 752 \\ -217 \\ \hline \end{array}$	$\begin{array}{r} 964 \\ -83 \\ \hline \end{array}$	$\begin{array}{r} 93 \\ -75 \\ \hline \end{array}$
2.	$\begin{array}{r} 240 \\ -102 \\ \hline \end{array}$	$\begin{array}{r} 731 \\ -470 \\ \hline \end{array}$	$\begin{array}{r} 817 \\ -397 \\ \hline \end{array}$	$\begin{array}{r} 64 \\ -8 \\ \hline \end{array}$	$\begin{array}{r} 715 \\ -284 \\ \hline \end{array}$	$\begin{array}{r} 451 \\ -27 \\ \hline \end{array}$
3.	$\begin{array}{r} 319 \\ -38 \\ \hline \end{array}$	$\begin{array}{r} 80 \\ -53 \\ \hline \end{array}$	$\begin{array}{r} 927 \\ -466 \\ \hline \end{array}$	$\begin{array}{r} 195 \\ -69 \\ \hline \end{array}$	$\begin{array}{r} 40 \\ -9 \\ \hline \end{array}$	$\begin{array}{r} 658 \\ -387 \\ \hline \end{array}$
4.	$\begin{array}{r} 918 \\ -48 \\ \hline \end{array}$	$\begin{array}{r} 92 \\ -76 \\ \hline \end{array}$	$\begin{array}{r} 247 \\ -19 \\ \hline \end{array}$	$\begin{array}{r} 82 \\ -25 \\ \hline \end{array}$	$\begin{array}{r} 30 \\ -7 \\ \hline \end{array}$	$\begin{array}{r} 654 \\ -36 \\ \hline \end{array}$
5.	$\begin{array}{r} 474 \\ -39 \\ \hline \end{array}$	$\begin{array}{r} 32 \\ -6 \\ \hline \end{array}$	$\begin{array}{r} 826 \\ -455 \\ \hline \end{array}$	$\begin{array}{r} 70 \\ -51 \\ \hline \end{array}$	$\begin{array}{r} 212 \\ -71 \\ \hline \end{array}$	$\begin{array}{r} 251 \\ -43 \\ \hline \end{array}$

Rewrite. Then find the differences.

	a		b
6.	46 − 29 = ________	$\begin{array}{r} 46 \\ -29 \\ \hline \end{array}$	153 − 72 = ________
7.	70 − 13 = ________		885 − 577 = ________

Three-digit Subtraction with Two Regroupings

Sometimes you have to regroup two times when subtracting three-digit numbers.

Find: 322 – 39

Line up the ones, tens, and hundreds. To subtract the ones, more ones are needed.

H	T	O
3	2	2
–	3	9

Regroup 1 ten as 10 ones. Subtract the ones. To subtract the tens, more tens are needed.

H	T	O
	1	12
3	~~2~~	~~2~~
–	3	9
		3

Regroup 1 hundred as 10 tens. Subtract the tens.

H	T	O
	11	
2	~~1~~	12
~~3~~	~~2~~	~~2~~
–	3	9
	8	3

Subtract the hundreds.

H	T	O
	11	
2	~~1~~	12
~~3~~	~~2~~	~~2~~
–	3	9
2	8	3

Subtract.

1.

a

H	T	O
	14	
8	~~4~~	13
~~9~~	~~5~~	~~3~~
–	7	4
8	7	9

b $571 - 98$

c $872 - 95$

d $260 - 66$

e $252 - 65$

f $753 - 369$

2.

a $741 - 484$

b $730 - 149$

c $634 - 377$

d $862 - 284$

e $941 - 757$

f $240 - 76$

Rewrite. Then find the differences.

3. a 511 – 27 = __________

H	T	O
3	1	1
–	2	7

b 325 – 198 = __________

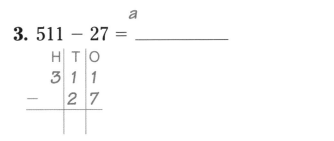

Subtraction Practice: Deciding When to Regroup

Subtract.

	a	b	c	d	e	f
1.	3 10 ~~4~~ ~~0~~ 3 −1 9 1 2 1 2	893 −745	609 − 28	821 − 41	234 − 16	304 − 64
2.	912 −379	650 −322	914 − 88	567 − 96	973 −948	916 −207
3.	275 − 17	952 −497	602 −412	152 − 87	909 −385	940 −263
4.	743 −193	328 − 38	186 − 58	808 −435	414 − 67	827 −353
5.	575 −228	907 −374	727 −509	546 − 55	826 −261	433 − 62
6.	683 − 29	830 −463	562 − 97	792 −769	245 − 90	520 −147

Rewrite. Then find the differences.

7. a. 541 − 76 = ________ b. 127 − 39 = ________

	H	T	O
	5	4	1
−		7	6

Subtraction with Regrouping Across One Zero

Sometimes you have to regroup across zero when subtracting.

Find: 302 − 29

Line up the ones, tens, and hundreds. To subtract the ones, more ones are needed.

	H	T	O
	3	0	2
−		2	9

There are 0 tens. Regroup 1 hundred as 10 tens. Show 1 less hundred and 10 more tens.

	H	T	O
	2	10	
	~~3~~	~~0~~	2
−		2	9

Regroup 1 ten as 10 ones. Show 1 less ten and 10 more ones.

	H	T	O
		9	
	2	~~10~~	12
	~~3~~	~~0~~	~~2~~
−		2	9

Subtract the ones, then the tens, then the hundreds.

	H	T	O
		9	
	2	~~10~~	12
	~~3~~	~~0~~	~~2~~
−		2	9
	2	7	3

Subtract.

1.

a

	H	T	O
		9	
	2	~~10~~	14
	~~3~~	~~0~~	~~4~~
−		1	6
	2	8	8

b

	H	T	O
	1	0	3
−		5	8

c

	H	T	O
	7	0	2
−		4	3

d

	H	T	O
	2	0	2
−		6	7

e

	H	T	O
	4	0	1
−		2	3

f

	H	T	O
	6	0	3
−		5	6

2. $802 - 386$ $\quad$ $701 - 562$ $\quad$ $801 - 424$ $\quad$ $502 - 413$ $\quad$ $806 - 678$ $\quad$ $704 - 65$

3. $901 - 15$ $\quad$ $904 - 879$ $\quad$ $601 - 33$ $\quad$ $804 - 536$ $\quad$ $503 - 99$ $\quad$ $403 - 247$

Rewrite. Then find the differences.

4. a $302 - 76 =$ ________ $\qquad$ b $705 - 98 =$ ________

	H	T	O
	3	0	2
−		7	6

Subtraction with Regrouping Across Two Zeros

Sometimes you have to regroup across two zeros when subtracting.

Find: 300 − 27

Line up the ones, tens, and hundreds. There are 0 ones. To subtract the ones, more ones are needed.	There are 0 tens. Regroup 1 hundred as 10 tens. Show 1 less hundred and 10 more tens.	Regroup 1 ten as 10 ones. Show 1 less ten and 10 more ones.	Subtract the ones, then the tens, then the hundreds.
H T O 3 0 0 − 2 7	H T O 2 10 ~~3~~ ~~0~~ 0 − 2 7	H T O 9 2 ~~10~~ 10 ~~3~~ ~~0~~ ~~0~~ − 2 7	H T O 9 2 ~~10~~ 10 ~~3~~ ~~0~~ ~~0~~ − 2 7 2 7 3

Subtract.

	a	b	c	d	e	f
1.	H T O 9 8 ~~10~~ 10 ~~9~~ ~~0~~ ~~0~~ − 4 6 8 5 4	H T O 6 0 0 −1 6 8	H T O 5 0 0 − 2 1	H T O 8 0 0 − 5 3	H T O 7 0 0 −2 4 7	H T O 4 0 0 − 1 4
2.	500 −232	900 −122	700 − 85	600 − 97	400 − 72	800 −226
3.	400 −112	700 −131	200 − 54	800 −398	300 − 67	500 − 73

Rewrite. Then find the differences.

4. a 900 − 516 = ________ b 800 − 55 = ________

H T O
9 0 0
− 5 1 6

Zeros in Subtraction Practice

Subtract.

	a	b	c	d	e	f
1.	9 3 10 11 4 0 1 −1 1 8 ─── 2 8 3	3 0 1 − 9 4	5 0 1 −3 5 8	5 0 2 −1 6 7	1 0 1 − 6 5	3 0 3 −1 4 4
2.	2 0 1 − 5 8	3 0 2 −2 9 3	9 0 2 − 7 3	8 0 0 − 3 7	7 0 0 −4 1 9	4 0 5 −2 9 7
3.	2 0 0 − 5 4	1 0 0 − 3 9	9 0 0 − 3 8	8 0 1 −7 7 9	4 0 2 − 1 7	9 0 0 −6 5 3
4.	3 0 0 − 3 6	5 0 0 −4 2 7	5 0 3 − 7 4	3 0 5 − 6 7	4 0 0 −2 5 1	8 0 0 −5 4 2

Rewrite. Then find the differences.

a

5. $506 - 228 = $ _____ 5 0 6
−2 2 8

b

$107 - 48 = $ _____

6. $400 - 86 = $ _____ $604 - 95 = $ _____

7. $600 - 573 = $ _____ $802 - 663 = $ _____

Problem-Solving Method: Work Backwards

Manuel had $3 left over after going to the movies. He spent $7 on his ticket and $6 on snacks. How much money did Manuel take to the movies?

Understand the problem.

- **What do you want to know?**
  how much money Manuel took to the movies

- **What information is given?**
  He spent $7 for a ticket and $6 for snacks.
  He had $3 left over.

Plan how to solve it.

- **What method can you use?**
  You can work backwards. Work from the amount he had left to find the amount he started with.

Solve it.

- **How can you use this method to solve the problem?**
  Addition is the opposite of subtraction. So, add the amounts he spent to the amount he had left over.

$$
\begin{array}{rl}
\$\ 3 & \leftarrow \text{amount left over} \\
+\quad 7 & \leftarrow \text{spent on ticket} \\
\hline
10 & \\
+\quad 6 & \leftarrow \text{spent on snacks} \\
\hline
\$16 &
\end{array}
$$

- **What is the answer?**
  Manuel took $16 to the movies.

Look back and check your answer.

- **Is your answer reasonable?**
  You can check by working forwards. Subtract the amounts he spent from the amount he took to the movies.

$$
\begin{array}{rl}
\$16 & \\
-\quad 7 & \leftarrow \text{ticket} \\
\hline
9 & \\
-\quad 6 & \leftarrow \text{snacks} \\
\hline
\$\ 3 &
\end{array}
$$

The amount left over matches.
The answer is reasonable.

Work backwards to solve each problem.

1. Today Jason has 123 stamps in his collection. He got 5 stamps at a show last week. Then he got 4 more stamps at a show this week. How many stamps did Jason have before the two shows?

   128 stamps

2. After the swim meet, Shamal had 58 ribbons. She won 2 first-place ribbons and 3 second-place ribbons at the meet. How many ribbons did she have before the swim meet?

   58 ribbons

3. Aiko has 132 tadpoles in her tank. She had put 47 in the tank on Saturday. She had put 28 in the tank on Sunday. How many tadpoles were in the tank before Saturday?

   ______ tadpoles

4. Vicky had 12 cookies left over after the bake sale. She had sold 75 cookies in the morning and 40 cookies in the afternoon. How many cookies did she have at the beginning of the bake sale?

   ______ cookies

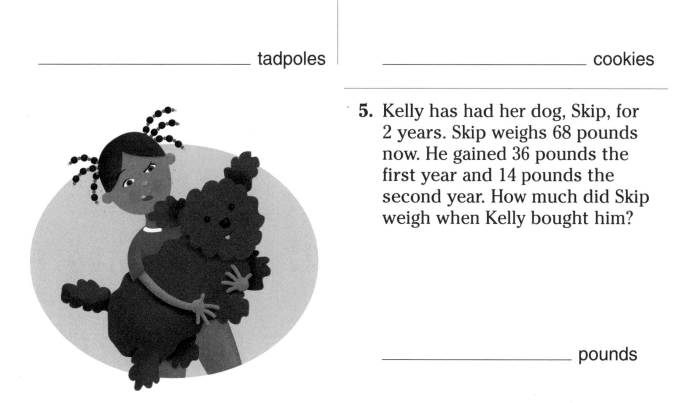

5. Kelly has had her dog, Skip, for 2 years. Skip weighs 68 pounds now. He gained 36 pounds the first year and 14 pounds the second year. How much did Skip weigh when Kelly bought him?

   ______ pounds

Unit 3 Review

Subtract.

	a	b	c	d	e	f
1.	64 − 6	81 −64	45 −29	53 − 9	64 −38	76 − 8
2.	478 − 25	382 − 61	294 −161	635 −113	476 −233	594 −392
3.	234 − 75	654 −257	816 −367	652 −167	533 −287	342 −164
4.	30 −17	205 − 49	406 −157	405 −138	506 −159	850 −528
5.	400 − 96	100 − 58	200 − 89	700 −127	300 −179	600 −344

Rewrite. Then find the differences.

	a	b
6.	136 − 54 = ________	357 − 161 = ________
7.	756 − 69 = ________	527 − 268 = ________

Unit 3 Review

Use the bar graph to solve each problem.

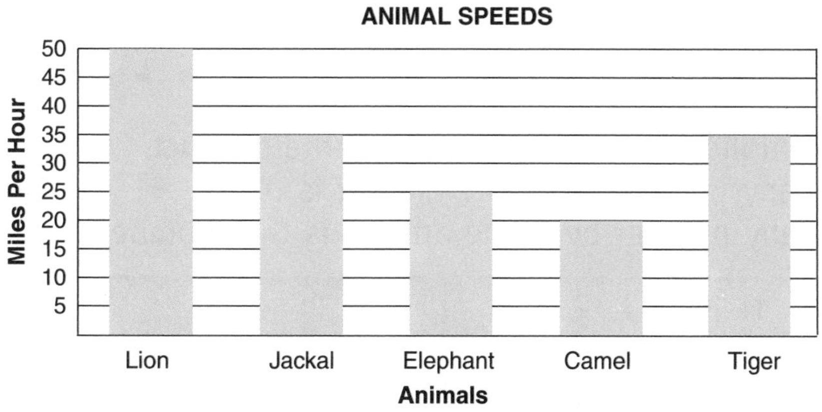

8. Which animal runs the fastest? Which animal runs the slowest?

fastest ____________________

slowest ____________________

9. Which two animals run at the same speed? What is that speed?

animals ____________________

speed ____________________

10. Which animal runs 25 miles per hour?

Answer: ____________________

11. How much faster can a lion run than a tiger?

____________________ miles per hour

Work backwards to solve each problem.

12. Kaya has $25 left over after the football game. She had spent $17 for her ticket. She then bought a team hat for $11. How much money did Kaya bring to the football game?

$ ____________________

13. Antoine has 154 books in his collection. He got 27 books at a sale last year. His sister gave him 16 books this year. How many books did Antoine have in his collection before the book sale?

____________________ books

unit 4
multiplication

Basic Facts to 1

The answer to a multiplication problem is called the **product**.
When you **multiply** any number by 0, the answer is 0.
When you multiply any number by 1, the answer is that number.

$\begin{array}{r} 1 \\ \times 0 \end{array}$	$\begin{array}{r} 1 \\ \times 1 \end{array}$	$\begin{array}{r} 1 \\ \times 2 \end{array}$	$\begin{array}{r} 1 \\ \times 3 \end{array}$	$\begin{array}{r} 1 \\ \times 4 \end{array}$	$\begin{array}{r} 1 \\ \times 5 \end{array}$	$\begin{array}{r} 1 \\ \times 6 \end{array}$	$\begin{array}{r} 1 \\ \times 7 \end{array}$	$\begin{array}{r} 1 \\ \times 8 \end{array}$	$\begin{array}{r} 1 \\ \times 9 \end{array}$
0	1	2	3	4	5	6	7	8	9

Multiply.

	a	*b*	*c*	*d*	*e*	*f*	*g*
1.	$\begin{array}{r} 1 \\ \times 0 \\ \hline 0 \end{array}$	$\begin{array}{r} 1 \\ \times 1 \\ \hline \end{array}$	$\begin{array}{r} 1 \\ \times 2 \\ \hline \end{array}$	$\begin{array}{r} 1 \\ \times 3 \\ \hline \end{array}$	$\begin{array}{r} 1 \\ \times 4 \\ \hline \end{array}$	$\begin{array}{r} 1 \\ \times 5 \\ \hline \end{array}$	$\begin{array}{r} 1 \\ \times 6 \\ \hline \end{array}$
2.	$\begin{array}{r} 1 \\ \times 7 \\ \hline \end{array}$	$\begin{array}{r} 1 \\ \times 8 \\ \hline \end{array}$	$\begin{array}{r} 1 \\ \times 9 \\ \hline \end{array}$	$\begin{array}{r} 0 \\ \times 8 \\ \hline \end{array}$	$\begin{array}{r} 6 \\ \times 0 \\ \hline \end{array}$	$\begin{array}{r} 4 \\ \times 0 \\ \hline \end{array}$	$\begin{array}{r} 1 \\ \times 4 \\ \hline \end{array}$
3.	$\begin{array}{r} 0 \\ \times 1 \\ \hline \end{array}$	$\begin{array}{r} 8 \\ \times 1 \\ \hline \end{array}$	$\begin{array}{r} 0 \\ \times 5 \\ \hline \end{array}$	$\begin{array}{r} 7 \\ \times 1 \\ \hline \end{array}$	$\begin{array}{r} 5 \\ \times 1 \\ \hline \end{array}$	$\begin{array}{r} 0 \\ \times 4 \\ \hline \end{array}$	$\begin{array}{r} 9 \\ \times 0 \\ \hline \end{array}$

Multiplication can be shown two ways. $\begin{array}{r} 4 \\ \times 0 \\ \hline 0 \end{array}$ or $4 \times 0 = \underline{\quad 0 \quad}$

Find the products.

	a	*b*	*c*
4.	$4 \times 0 =$ ______	$8 \times 1 =$ ______	$2 \times 0 =$ ______
5.	$1 \times 4 =$ ______	$0 \times 5 =$ ______	$3 \times 1 =$ ______

Basic Facts to 2

Use these multiplication facts when multiplying with **2**.

2 × 0	2 × 1	2 × 2	2 × 3	2 × 4	2 × 5	2 × 6	2 × 7	2 × 8	2 × 9
0	2	4	6	8	10	12	14	16	18

Multiply.

	a	b	c	d	e	f	g
1.	2 × 0 = 0	2 × 1	2 × 2	2 × 3	2 × 4	2 × 5	2 × 6
2.	2 × 7	2 × 8	2 × 9	2 × 1	4 × 2	1 × 2	6 × 2
3.	8 × 2	9 × 2	2 × 2	0 × 2	5 × 2	3 × 2	7 × 2
4.	0 × 0	1 × 4	0 × 2	3 × 1	0 × 1	6 × 0	1 × 4

Find the products.

	a	b	c
5.	$1 \times 7 =$ ______	$2 \times 6 =$ ______	$4 \times 0 =$ ______

6.

2	× 4	× 1	× 6	× 3	× 0	× 9	× 7	× 2	× 8	× 5
	8									

Basic Facts to 3

Use these multiplication facts when multiplying with **3**.

3 × 0	3 × 1	3 × 2	3 × 3	3 × 4	3 × 5	3 × 6	3 × 7	3 × 8	3 × 9
0	3	6	9	12	15	18	21	24	27

Multiply.

	a	*b*	*c*	*d*	*e*	*f*	*g*
1.	3 × 0 = *0*	3 × 1	3 × 2	3 × 3	3 × 4	3 × 5	3 × 6
2.	3 × 7	3 × 8	3 × 9	3 × 3	6 × 3	9 × 3	3 × 3
3.	1 × 3	7 × 3	8 × 3	4 × 3	0 × 3	2 × 3	5 × 3
4.	1 × 4	7 × 2	2 × 9	0 × 6	5 × 1	9 × 0	9 × 2

5.

×	2	9	4	1	6	5	3	8	0	7
1	*2*	*9*								
2										
3										

Basic Facts to 4

Use these multiplication facts when multiplying with **4**.

$\begin{array}{r}4\\\times 0\end{array}$	$\begin{array}{r}4\\\times 1\end{array}$	$\begin{array}{r}4\\\times 2\end{array}$	$\begin{array}{r}4\\\times 3\end{array}$	$\begin{array}{r}4\\\times 4\end{array}$	$\begin{array}{r}4\\\times 5\end{array}$	$\begin{array}{r}4\\\times 6\end{array}$	$\begin{array}{r}4\\\times 7\end{array}$	$\begin{array}{r}4\\\times 8\end{array}$	$\begin{array}{r}4\\\times 9\end{array}$
0	4	8	12	16	20	24	28	32	36

Multiply.

	a	b	c	d	e	f	g
1.	$\begin{array}{r}4\\\times 0\\\hline 0\end{array}$	$\begin{array}{r}4\\\times 1\\\hline\end{array}$	$\begin{array}{r}4\\\times 2\\\hline\end{array}$	$\begin{array}{r}4\\\times 3\\\hline\end{array}$	$\begin{array}{r}4\\\times 4\\\hline\end{array}$	$\begin{array}{r}4\\\times 5\\\hline\end{array}$	$\begin{array}{r}4\\\times 6\\\hline\end{array}$
2.	$\begin{array}{r}4\\\times 7\\\hline\end{array}$	$\begin{array}{r}4\\\times 8\\\hline\end{array}$	$\begin{array}{r}4\\\times 9\\\hline\end{array}$	$\begin{array}{r}1\\\times 4\\\hline\end{array}$	$\begin{array}{r}8\\\times 4\\\hline\end{array}$	$\begin{array}{r}7\\\times 4\\\hline\end{array}$	$\begin{array}{r}0\\\times 4\\\hline\end{array}$
3.	$\begin{array}{r}2\\\times 4\\\hline\end{array}$	$\begin{array}{r}5\\\times 4\\\hline\end{array}$	$\begin{array}{r}3\\\times 4\\\hline\end{array}$	$\begin{array}{r}6\\\times 4\\\hline\end{array}$	$\begin{array}{r}9\\\times 4\\\hline\end{array}$	$\begin{array}{r}1\\\times 4\\\hline\end{array}$	$\begin{array}{r}4\\\times 4\\\hline\end{array}$

Find the products.

a	b	c
4. $7 \times 2 = $ _____	$3 \times 5 = $ _____	$9 \times 1 = $ _____
5. $3 \times 8 = $ _____	$4 \times 1 = $ _____	$5 \times 2 = $ _____

6.

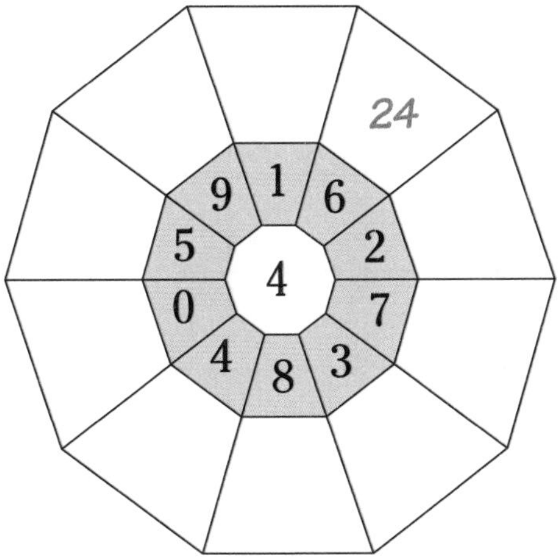

7.

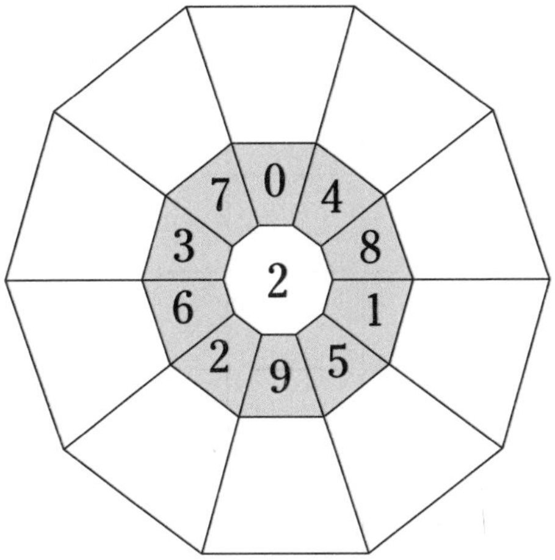

Basic Facts to 5

Use these multiplication facts when multiplying with **5**.

5×0	5×1	5×2	5×3	5×4	5×5	5×6	5×7	5×8	5×9
0	5	10	15	20	25	30	35	40	45

Multiply.

	a	*b*	*c*	*d*	*e*	*f*	*g*
1.	5×0 = *0*	5×1	5×2	5×3	5×4	5×5	5×6
2.	5×7	5×8	5×9	1×5	5×5	4×5	5×5
3.	9×5	2×5	8×5	3×5	7×5	6×5	0×5

Find the products.

	a	*b*	*c*
4.	$7 \times 3 =$ ______	$1 \times 4 =$ ______	$4 \times 8 =$ ______
5.	$2 \times 3 =$ ______	$6 \times 4 =$ ______	$2 \times 0 =$ ______

6.

×	0	1	2	3	4	5	6	7	8	9
5	*0*									
1										
3										
2										
4										

Basic Facts to 6

Use these multiplication facts when multiplying with **6**.

6 × 0	6 × 1	6 × 2	6 × 3	6 × 4	6 × 5	6 × 6	6 × 7	6 × 8	6 × 9
0	6	12	18	24	30	36	42	48	54

Multiply.

	a	*b*	*c*	*d*	*e*	*f*	*g*
1.	6 × 0 = *0*	6 × 1	6 × 2	6 × 3	6 × 4	6 × 5	6 × 6
2.	6 × 7	6 × 8	6 × 9	1 × 6	6 × 6	0 × 6	8 × 6
3.	3 × 6	7 × 6	4 × 6	9 × 6	2 × 6	5 × 6	6 × 7
4.	5 × 7	8 × 3	4 × 8	2 × 7	6 × 5	8 × 1	9 × 0

Find the products.

	a	*b*	*c*
5.	5 × 5 = ______	6 × 8 = ______	3 × 9 = ______

6. 6

× 8	*48*
× 4	
× 6	
× 3	

7. 3

× 4	
× 9	
× 5	
× 7	

8. 5

× 8	
× 6	
× 4	
× 7	

Basic Facts to 7

Use these multiplication facts when multiplying with **7**.

7×0	7×1	7×2	7×3	7×4	7×5	7×6	7×7	7×8	7×9
0	7	14	21	28	35	42	49	56	63

Multiply.

	a	*b*	*c*	*d*	*e*	*f*	*g*
1.	7×0 = *0*	7×1	7×2	7×3	7×4	7×5	7×6
2.	7×7	7×8	7×9	5×7	6×7	1×7	9×7
3.	8×7	2×7	6×7	7×7	4×7	0×7	3×7

Find the products.

	a	*b*	*c*
4.	$6 \times 3 =$ ______	$4 \times 9 =$ ______	$3 \times 0 =$ ______

5.

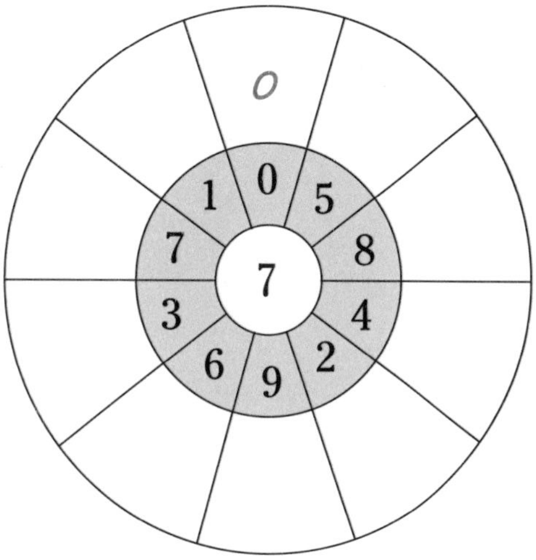

6.

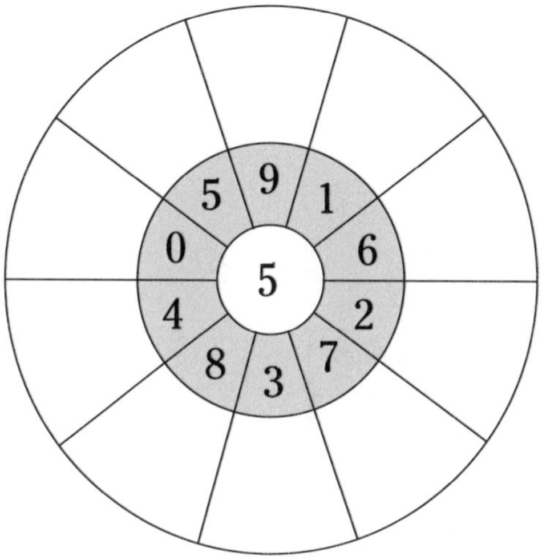

Basic Facts to 8

Use these multiplication facts when multiplying with **8**.

8 ×0	8 ×1	8 ×2	8 ×3	8 ×4	8 ×5	8 ×6	8 ×7	8 ×8	8 ×9
0	8	16	24	32	40	48	56	64	72

Multiply.

	a	b	c	d	e	f	g
1.	8 ×0 = 0	8 ×1	8 ×2	8 ×3	8 ×4	8 ×5	8 ×6
2.	8 ×7	8 ×8	8 ×9	6 ×8	8 ×9	8 ×8	0 ×8
3.	2 ×8	1 ×8	5 ×8	7 ×8	9 ×8	4 ×8	3 ×8
4.	6 ×5	7 ×7	4 ×7	3 ×1	2 ×5	7 ×9	4 ×6

Find the products.

	a	b	c
5.	$9 \times 6 =$ ______	$7 \times 7 =$ ______	$1 \times 9 =$ ______

6. 8

×6	48
×4	
×9	
×5	

7. 6

×1	
×4	
×6	
×2	

8. 7

×6	
×3	
×5	
×2	

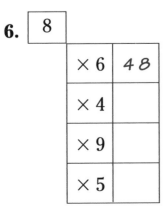

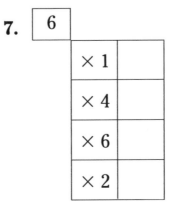

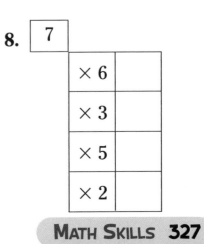

Basic Facts to 9

Use these multiplication facts when multiplying with **9**.

9 × 0	9 × 1	9 × 2	9 × 3	9 × 4	9 × 5	9 × 6	9 × 7	9 × 8	9 × 9
0	9	18	27	36	45	54	63	72	81

Multiply.

	a	b	c	d	e	f	g
1.	9×0 = 0	9×1	9×2	9×3	9×4	9×5	9×6
2.	9×7	9×8	9×9	2×9	7×9	4×9	9×9
3.	5×9	1×9	6×9	8×9	3×9	0×9	9×7
4.	6×6	7×3	5×4	7×8	4×4	4×5	0×7

Find the products.

5. a $5 \times 7 =$ ______ b $7 \times 6 =$ ______ c $4 \times 3 =$ ______

6.

×	2	9	4	1	6	5	3	8	0
9	18								
6									
8									

Basic Facts Practice

Multiply.

	a	b	c	d	e	f	g
1.	6×8 = 48	4×4	8×6	5×5	7×8	9×4	3×7
2.	5×1	3×6	9×5	6×0	4×5	9×2	6×7
3.	4×6	7×5	8×4	6×9	4×2	5×6	9×8
4.	8×7	5×6	8×1	4×7	9×6	7×9	3×5
5.	7×7	4×8	5×9	3×3	7×6	3×9	8×5
6.	5×4	8×8	3×4	7×2	5×8	8×9	6×4
7.	3×8	6×6	9×7	7×4	4×9	9×9	5×7

Problem-Solving Method: Make a Model

Gwen is planning her garden. She wants to plant 4 rows of tulips. In each row she wants to have 7 tulips. How many tulips should Gwen buy?

Understand the problem.

- **What do you want to know?**
  how many tulips Gwen should buy

- **What information is given?**
  She wants 4 rows.
  She wants 7 tulips in each row.

Plan how to solve it.

- **What method can you use?**
  You can make a model of her garden.

Solve it.

- **How can you use this method to solve the problem?**
  Use tiles to make a model of the garden. Use one tile for each tulip in the garden. Then count the tiles.

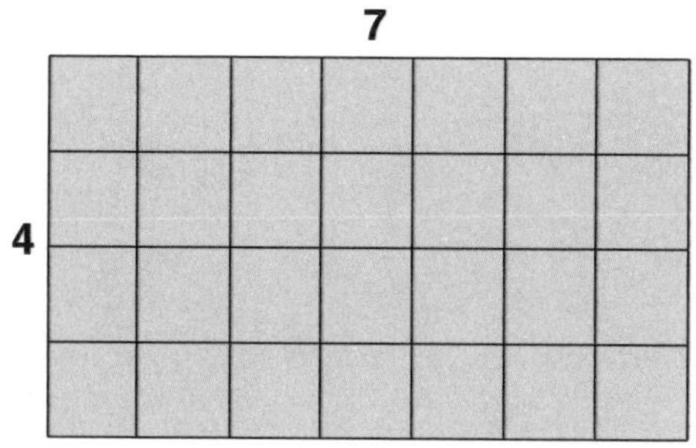

- **What is the answer?**
  Gwen should buy 28 tulips.

Look back and check your answer.

- **Is your answer reasonable?**
  You can check your count with multiplication.

  4 rows of 7 tulips = 28 tulips

  $4 \times 7 = 28$

  The count and the product are the same.
  The answer is reasonable.

Make a model to solve each problem.

1. Brenda put new tiles on her kitchen floor. The floor now has 6 rows with 8 tiles in each row. How many tiles did Brenda use in all?

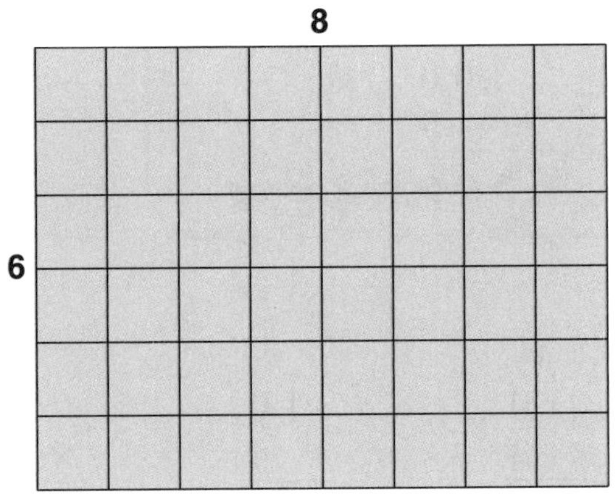

____________________ tiles

2. Calvin wants to make a quilt that has 5 rows. Each row will have 4 squares of fabric. How many squares of fabric does Calvin need to make his quilt?

____________________ squares

3. A sheet of postage stamps has 9 rows. There are 4 stamps in each row. How many stamps are on one sheet?

____________________ stamps

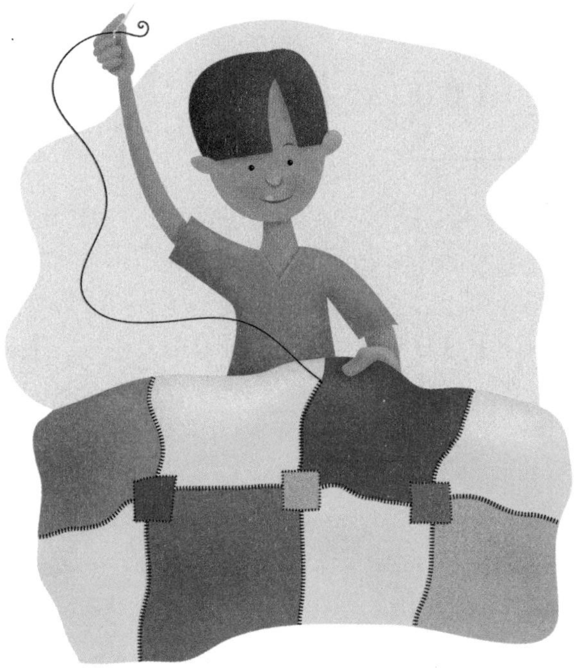

Multiplication of Tens and Hundreds

To multiply a number by 10, multiply the number by 1 and write one zero.

To multiply a number by 100, multiply the number by 1 and write two zeros.

Find: 4×10

Multiply by 4 ones.

$$\begin{array}{r} 10 \\ \times\ 4 \\ \hline 40 \end{array} \leftarrow \text{1 zero}$$

Find: 5×100

Multiply by 5 ones.

$$\begin{array}{r} 100 \\ \times\ \ 5 \\ \hline 500 \end{array} \leftarrow \text{2 zeros}$$

Multiply.

	a	*b*	*c*	*d*	*e*	*f*
1.	10×4 = 40	10×1	10×2	10×3	10×4	10×5
2.	10×6	10×7	10×8	10×9	10×3	10×2
3.	100×5	100×1	100×2	100×3	100×4	100×5
4.	100×2	100×7	100×8	100×6	100×9	100×4
5.	100×1	100×9	100×3	100×7	100×8	100×5

Two-digit Multiplication

To multiply a two-digit number by a one-digit number, first multiply the number in the ones place. Then multiply the number in the tens place.

You may have to rewrite a problem before you multiply by lining up the digits in the ones place.

Find: 4×62

Line up the ones.

Tens	Ones
6	2
×	4

Multiply the 2 ones by 4.

T	O
6	2
×	4
	8

Multiply the 6 tens by 4.

T	O
6	2
×	4
24	8

Multiply.

1.

a

T	O
6	4
×	2
12	8

b

T	O
4	1
×	6

c

T	O
8	3
×	3

d

T	O
7	3
×	2

e

T	O
2	0
×	8

f

T	O
9	1
×	5

2. $\begin{array}{r} 53 \\ \times\ 2 \\ \hline \end{array}$ $\begin{array}{r} 92 \\ \times\ 3 \\ \hline \end{array}$ $\begin{array}{r} 40 \\ \times\ 9 \\ \hline \end{array}$ $\begin{array}{r} 82 \\ \times\ 4 \\ \hline \end{array}$ $\begin{array}{r} 21 \\ \times\ 7 \\ \hline \end{array}$ $\begin{array}{r} 50 \\ \times\ 6 \\ \hline \end{array}$

3. $\begin{array}{r} 11 \\ \times\ 6 \\ \hline \end{array}$ $\begin{array}{r} 80 \\ \times\ 5 \\ \hline \end{array}$ $\begin{array}{r} 71 \\ \times\ 8 \\ \hline \end{array}$ $\begin{array}{r} 72 \\ \times\ 3 \\ \hline \end{array}$ $\begin{array}{r} 62 \\ \times\ 4 \\ \hline \end{array}$ $\begin{array}{r} 84 \\ \times\ 2 \\ \hline \end{array}$

Rewrite. Then find the products.

4. a $94 \times 2 =$ ________ b $60 \times 8 =$ ________

T	O
9	4
×	2

Multiply.

	a	b	c	d	e	f
1.	$\begin{array}{r} 53 \\ \times\ 2 \\ \hline \end{array}$	$\begin{array}{r} 70 \\ \times\ 5 \\ \hline \end{array}$	$\begin{array}{r} 72 \\ \times\ 3 \\ \hline \end{array}$	$\begin{array}{r} 60 \\ \times\ 7 \\ \hline \end{array}$	$\begin{array}{r} 52 \\ \times\ 4 \\ \hline \end{array}$	$\begin{array}{r} 64 \\ \times\ 2 \\ \hline \end{array}$
2.	$\begin{array}{r} 61 \\ \times\ 3 \\ \hline \end{array}$	$\begin{array}{r} 50 \\ \times\ 8 \\ \hline \end{array}$	$\begin{array}{r} 31 \\ \times\ 6 \\ \hline \end{array}$	$\begin{array}{r} 71 \\ \times\ 2 \\ \hline \end{array}$	$\begin{array}{r} 39 \\ \times\ 1 \\ \hline \end{array}$	$\begin{array}{r} 40 \\ \times\ 9 \\ \hline \end{array}$
3.	$\begin{array}{r} 21 \\ \times\ 9 \\ \hline \end{array}$	$\begin{array}{r} 73 \\ \times\ 3 \\ \hline \end{array}$	$\begin{array}{r} 84 \\ \times\ 2 \\ \hline \end{array}$	$\begin{array}{r} 43 \\ \times\ 3 \\ \hline \end{array}$	$\begin{array}{r} 93 \\ \times\ 2 \\ \hline \end{array}$	$\begin{array}{r} 21 \\ \times\ 7 \\ \hline \end{array}$
4.	$\begin{array}{r} 41 \\ \times\ 4 \\ \hline \end{array}$	$\begin{array}{r} 10 \\ \times\ 9 \\ \hline \end{array}$	$\begin{array}{r} 82 \\ \times\ 2 \\ \hline \end{array}$	$\begin{array}{r} 74 \\ \times\ 2 \\ \hline \end{array}$	$\begin{array}{r} 41 \\ \times\ 5 \\ \hline \end{array}$	$\begin{array}{r} 92 \\ \times\ 3 \\ \hline \end{array}$
5.	$\begin{array}{r} 51 \\ \times\ 9 \\ \hline \end{array}$	$\begin{array}{r} 34 \\ \times\ 2 \\ \hline \end{array}$	$\begin{array}{r} 63 \\ \times\ 3 \\ \hline \end{array}$	$\begin{array}{r} 70 \\ \times\ 5 \\ \hline \end{array}$	$\begin{array}{r} 30 \\ \times\ 7 \\ \hline \end{array}$	$\begin{array}{r} 31 \\ \times\ 9 \\ \hline \end{array}$

Rewrite. Then find the products.

	a		b
6.	$83 \times 3 =$ __________	$\begin{array}{r} 83 \\ \times\ 3 \\ \hline \end{array}$	$91 \times 6 =$ __________
7.	$62 \times 4 =$ __________		$81 \times 8 =$ __________

Two-digit Multiplication with Regrouping

Sometimes you have to regroup ones as tens when multiplying.

Find: 7 × 38

Multiply the 8 ones by 7.	Regroup 56 as 5 tens and 6 ones.	Multiply the 3 tens by 7 ones.	Add the regrouped 5 tens.
T | O	T | O	T | O	T | O
	5	5	5
3 | 8	3 | 8	3 | 8	3 | 8
× | 7	× | 7	× | 7	× | 7
	| 6	| 6	26 | 6

Multiply.

	a	b	c	d	e	f
1.	2 64 × 6 38 | 4	96 × 5	87 × 9	75 × 3	59 × 6	16 × 8
2.	89 × 5	98 × 3	23 × 7	78 × 4	37 × 2	36 × 9
3.	25 × 8	18 × 6	95 × 4	67 × 2	88 × 5	46 × 6

Rewrite. Then find the products.

4. a. 83 × 4 = ________

T | O
8 | 3
× | 4

b. 59 × 7 = ________

Multiply.

	a	b	c	d	e	f
1.	98×2	79×3	96×9	47×4	69×8	28×4
2.	68×3	86×2	43×8	99×5	53×7	76×8
3.	65×5	85×3	63×9	45×3	56×4	38×6
4.	87×9	36×4	18×5	26×5	25×6	54×7
5.	84×3	67×7	27×2	73×6	97×8	16×4

Rewrite. Then find the products.

	a		b
6.	$43 \times 5 =$ ______	43×5	$22 \times 9 =$ ______
7.	$57 \times 6 =$ ______		$82 \times 7 =$ ______

Multiplication Practice: Deciding When to Regroup

Multiply.

	a	b	c	d	e	f
1.	$\begin{array}{r} ^{1}\\ 16 \\ \times\ 3 \\ \hline 48 \end{array}$	$\begin{array}{r} 21 \\ \times\ 4 \\ \hline \end{array}$	$\begin{array}{r} 10 \\ \times\ 8 \\ \hline \end{array}$	$\begin{array}{r} 65 \\ \times\ 3 \\ \hline \end{array}$	$\begin{array}{r} 42 \\ \times\ 2 \\ \hline \end{array}$	$\begin{array}{r} 18 \\ \times\ 9 \\ \hline \end{array}$
2.	$\begin{array}{r} 75 \\ \times\ 6 \\ \hline \end{array}$	$\begin{array}{r} 87 \\ \times\ 5 \\ \hline \end{array}$	$\begin{array}{r} 34 \\ \times\ 2 \\ \hline \end{array}$	$\begin{array}{r} 100 \\ \times\ 3 \\ \hline \end{array}$	$\begin{array}{r} 27 \\ \times\ 3 \\ \hline \end{array}$	$\begin{array}{r} 12 \\ \times\ 4 \\ \hline \end{array}$
3.	$\begin{array}{r} 78 \\ \times\ 6 \\ \hline \end{array}$	$\begin{array}{r} 40 \\ \times\ 7 \\ \hline \end{array}$	$\begin{array}{r} 86 \\ \times\ 8 \\ \hline \end{array}$	$\begin{array}{r} 37 \\ \times\ 4 \\ \hline \end{array}$	$\begin{array}{r} 18 \\ \times\ 7 \\ \hline \end{array}$	$\begin{array}{r} 100 \\ \times\ 9 \\ \hline \end{array}$
4.	$\begin{array}{r} 70 \\ \times\ 4 \\ \hline \end{array}$	$\begin{array}{r} 15 \\ \times\ 8 \\ \hline \end{array}$	$\begin{array}{r} 59 \\ \times\ 3 \\ \hline \end{array}$	$\begin{array}{r} 21 \\ \times\ 6 \\ \hline \end{array}$	$\begin{array}{r} 100 \\ \times\ 2 \\ \hline \end{array}$	$\begin{array}{r} 85 \\ \times\ 4 \\ \hline \end{array}$
5.	$\begin{array}{r} 77 \\ \times\ 7 \\ \hline \end{array}$	$\begin{array}{r} 16 \\ \times\ 9 \\ \hline \end{array}$	$\begin{array}{r} 60 \\ \times\ 7 \\ \hline \end{array}$	$\begin{array}{r} 85 \\ \times\ 5 \\ \hline \end{array}$	$\begin{array}{r} 100 \\ \times\ 7 \\ \hline \end{array}$	$\begin{array}{r} 29 \\ \times\ 9 \\ \hline \end{array}$

Rewrite. Then find the products.

	a	b
6.	$41 \times 6 =$ ________	$38 \times 9 =$ ________

	T	O
	4	1
×		6

Problem-Solving Method: Identify Extra Information

The "London Eye" is the largest Ferris wheel in the world. It opened in January 2000. It is 446 feet tall. The wheel is 443 feet wide. Each car on the "London Eye" can carry 25 people. How many people can ride in three cars?

Understand the problem.

- **What do you want to know?**
  how many people can ride in 3 cars

Plan how to solve it.

- **What method can you use?**
  You can identify extra information that is not needed to solve the problem.

Solve it.

- **How can you use this method to solve the problem?**
  Read the problem again. Cross out any extra facts. Then use the needed facts to solve the problem.

~~The "London Eye" is the largest Ferris wheel in the world. It opened in January 2000. It is 446 feet tall. The wheel is 443 feet wide~~. Each car on the "London Eye" can carry 25 people. How many people can ride in three cars?

- **What is the answer?**
  $25 \times 3 = 75$
  75 people can ride in 3 cars.

Look back and check your answer.

- **Is your answer reasonable?**
  You can check multiplication with addition.

$$25 \times 3 = 75$$
$$25 + 25 + 25 = 75$$

The sum matches the product.
The answer is reasonable.

In each problem, cross out the extra information. Then solve the problem.

1. Cougars live in North America. They are about 9 feet long. Cougars are one of the best jumpers. They can cover 45 feet in one jump. How many feet can a cougar go in 5 jumps?

_______________ feet

2. Jupiter is the largest planet. Gravity is different on Jupiter. Things weigh 2 times what they weigh on Earth. Tom weighs 89 pounds. How much would Tom weigh on Jupiter?

_______________ pounds

3. Giant kelp is a huge seaweed. It can grow 18 inches a day. There are giant kelp forests in the ocean. The forests can be 328 feet tall. How many inches can giant kelp grow in 7 days?

_______________ inches

4. The ostrich is the largest bird in the world. Some ostriches are 9 feet tall. They also lay the biggest eggs. An ostrich egg is 7 inches long. It weighs 3 pounds. How much does a dozen ostrich eggs weigh? (1 dozen = 12)

_______________ pounds

5. Little League Baseball started in 1939 in Pennsylvania. There were 3 teams in the first season. Each team had 10 players. By 1998, there were 200,000 teams. How many players were in the first season?

_______________ players

Unit 4 Review

Multiply.

	a	b	c	d	e	f	g
1.	10×4	10×8	10×2	100×7	100×9	100×5	100×3
2.	60×8	71×9	82×4	94×2	51×8	65×1	23×3
3.	59×2	94×9	26×4	45×3	72×6	58×5	27×8
4.	65×6	87×5	16×3	83×4	69×7	48×8	92×5

Rewrite. Then find the products.

	a	b	c
5.	$10 \times 8 =$ ______	$6 \times 10 =$ ______	$100 \times 3 =$ ______
6.	$71 \times 8 =$ ______	$43 \times 3 =$ ______	$54 \times 2 =$ ______
7.	$97 \times 5 =$ ______	$28 \times 6 =$ ______	$74 \times 3 =$ ______
8.	$90 \times 8 =$ ______	$74 \times 8 =$ ______	$53 \times 6 =$ ______

Unit 4 Review

Make a model to solve each problem.

9. Russ needs to replace the glass panes in a large window. There are 6 rows of panes in the window. Each row has 4 panes. How many panes of glass should Russ buy?

__________________ panes

10. Kuang put mirror squares on her bedroom wall. She made 5 rows. Each row had 3 mirror squares. How many mirror squares did she use in all?

__________________ squares

Cross out the extra information in the problem. Then solve the problem.

11. Leatherbacks are the largest turtles. They can weigh 1,100 pounds. Leatherbacks are also the fastest turtles. They can swim about 22 miles per hour. How many miles can the turtle swim in 8 hours?

__________________ miles

Basic Facts to 3

Use your multiplication facts to **divide**.

The answer to a division problem is the **quotient**.

Find: $2\overline{)10}$

$2\overline{)10}$ Think → $2 \times 5 = 10$ Write → $2\overline{)10}$ with quotient 5

Divide.

	a	b	c	d	e
1.	$2\overline{)10}$ (5)	$3\overline{)6}$	$1\overline{)9}$	$3\overline{)24}$	$2\overline{)6}$
2.	$3\overline{)12}$	$1\overline{)6}$	$2\overline{)4}$	$3\overline{)9}$	$2\overline{)14}$
3.	$2\overline{)18}$	$3\overline{)27}$	$1\overline{)1}$	$2\overline{)16}$	$2\overline{)2}$
4.	$3\overline{)15}$	$1\overline{)7}$	$3\overline{)3}$	$1\overline{)5}$	$2\overline{)12}$

Division can be shown two ways. $2\overline{)18}$ (9) or $18 \div 2 =$ 9

Find the quotients.

	a	b	c
5.	$18 \div 2 =$ ______	$9 \div 1 =$ ______	$21 \div 3 =$ ______
6.	$15 \div 3 =$ ______	$6 \div 1 =$ ______	$16 \div 2 =$ ______

Basic Facts to 4

Divide.

	a	b	c	d	e
1.	$\overset{4}{1\overline{)4}}$	$2\overline{)4}$	$3\overline{)9}$	$1\overline{)9}$	$4\overline{)28}$
2.	$3\overline{)6}$	$2\overline{)12}$	$2\overline{)10}$	$4\overline{)16}$	$3\overline{)15}$
3.	$4\overline{)20}$	$3\overline{)18}$	$2\overline{)16}$	$2\overline{)8}$	$4\overline{)36}$
4.	$3\overline{)27}$	$4\overline{)32}$	$1\overline{)7}$	$3\overline{)21}$	$3\overline{)12}$

Find the quotients.

	a	b	c
5.	$8 \div 2 =$ ________	$14 \div 2 =$ ________	$24 \div 3 =$ ________
6.	$18 \div 2 =$ ________	$24 \div 4 =$ ________	$10 \div 2 =$ ________

7.

$9 \div 3$	3
$24 \div 3$	
$3 \div 3$	
$15 \div 3$	
$12 \div 3$	
$18 \div 3$	
$27 \div 3$	
$21 \div 3$	

8.

$16 \div 4$	
$4 \div 4$	
$28 \div 4$	
$36 \div 4$	
$8 \div 4$	
$32 \div 4$	
$20 \div 4$	
$24 \div 4$	

9.

$6 \div 2$	
$18 \div 2$	
$4 \div 2$	
$14 \div 2$	
$10 \div 2$	
$8 \div 2$	
$12 \div 2$	
$2 \div 2$	

Basic Facts to 5

Divide.

	a	b	c	d	e
1.	$\overset{7}{1\overline{)7}}$	$3\overline{)9}$	$4\overline{)24}$	$2\overline{)14}$	$5\overline{)40}$
2.	$5\overline{)35}$	$1\overline{)5}$	$5\overline{)10}$	$4\overline{)32}$	$1\overline{)8}$
3.	$5\overline{)25}$	$4\overline{)4}$	$1\overline{)9}$	$5\overline{)45}$	$3\overline{)15}$
4.	$2\overline{)8}$	$4\overline{)20}$	$2\overline{)10}$	$4\overline{)28}$	$3\overline{)6}$

Find the quotients.

	a	b	c
5.	$3 \div 1 =$ ________	$30 \div 5 =$ ________	$27 \div 3 =$ ________
6.	$18 \div 3 =$ ________	$20 \div 5 =$ ________	$5 \div 5 =$ ________

7.

	÷ 4 =	
12		3
28		
32		
16		
36		
20		
8		
24		

8.

	÷ 3 =	
27		
12		
9		
21		
15		
6		
24		
18		

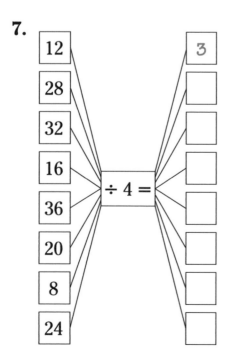

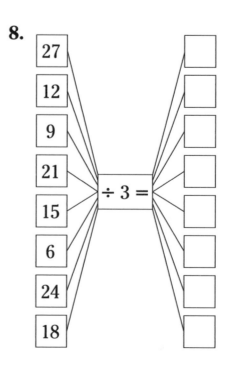

Basic Facts to 6

Divide.

	a	b	c	d	e
1.	$4\overline{)20}$ (5)	$2\overline{)14}$	$6\overline{)24}$	$4\overline{)24}$	$6\overline{)6}$
2.	$6\overline{)18}$	$3\overline{)9}$	$6\overline{)48}$	$5\overline{)5}$	$3\overline{)18}$
3.	$3\overline{)24}$	$5\overline{)40}$	$3\overline{)15}$	$5\overline{)20}$	$3\overline{)12}$
4.	$5\overline{)10}$	$6\overline{)54}$	$4\overline{)16}$	$3\overline{)21}$	$5\overline{)25}$

Find the quotients.

	a	b	c
5.	27 ÷ 3 = ______	36 ÷ 6 = ______	30 ÷ 5 = ______
6.	35 ÷ 5 = ______	32 ÷ 4 = ______	12 ÷ 4 = ______

7.

24 ÷ 6	4
48 ÷ 6	
30 ÷ 6	
18 ÷ 6	
54 ÷ 6	
36 ÷ 6	
12 ÷ 6	
42 ÷ 6	

8.

24 ÷ 4	
36 ÷ 4	
12 ÷ 4	
20 ÷ 4	
32 ÷ 4	
8 ÷ 4	
16 ÷ 4	
28 ÷ 4	

9.

14 ÷ 2	
10 ÷ 2	
4 ÷ 2	
12 ÷ 2	
6 ÷ 2	
18 ÷ 2	
8 ÷ 2	
16 ÷ 2	

10.

25 ÷ 5	
45 ÷ 5	
30 ÷ 5	
20 ÷ 5	
10 ÷ 5	
40 ÷ 5	
15 ÷ 5	
35 ÷ 5	

Problem-Solving Method: Choose an Operation

Sam made 48 chocolate chip cookies for the bake sale. He wants to put the same number of cookies in 6 bags. How many cookies should he put in each bag?

Understand the problem.

- **What do you want to know?**
  how many cookies to put in each bag
- **What information is given?**
  Sam has 48 cookies and 6 bags.
  He will put the same number of cookies in each bag.

Plan how to solve it.

- **What method can you use?**
  You can choose the operation needed to solve it.

Unequal Groups	Equal Groups
Add to combine unequal groups.	**Multiply** to combine equal groups.
Subtract to separate into unequal groups.	**Divide** to separate into equal groups.

Solve it.

- **How can you use this method to solve the problem?**
  You need to separate the total, 48 cookies, into 6 equal groups. So, you should divide to find how many cookies will be in each group.

  $48 \div 6 = 8$

- **What is the answer?**
  Sam should put 8 cookies in each bag.

Look back and check your answer.

- **Is your answer reasonable?**
  You can check division with multiplication.

  $\mathbf{48 \div 6 = 8}$
  $\mathbf{8 \times 6 = 48}$

  The product matches the total.
  The answer is reasonable.

Choose an operation to solve each problem. Then solve the problem.

1. Callie grass grows 6 inches a day. The callie grass is 24 inches tall. How many days has it been growing?

Operation:____________________

Answer:__________________ days

2. There are 376 boys in Kim's school. There are 358 girls in the school. How many students are in Kim's school?

Operation:____________________

Answer:________________ students

3. Killer whales can swim 35 miles per hour. How many miles can a killer whale swim in 8 hours?

Operation:____________________

Answer:__________________ miles

4. A bakery had 650 pounds of flour. The baker used 385 pounds. How much flour was left over?

Operation:____________________

Answer:________________ pounds

5. The pet store has 28 hamsters. They keep the same number of hamsters in each cage. There are 4 cages. How many hamsters are in each cage?

Operation:____________________

Answer:________________ hamsters

Basic Facts to 7

Divide.

	a	b	c	d	e
1.	$\overset{6}{5\overline{)3\,0}}$	$\overset{1}{7\overline{)7}}$	$\overset{7}{4\overline{)2\,8}}$	$\overset{6}{2\overline{)1\,2}}$	$\overset{7}{5\overline{)3\,5}}$
2.	$\overset{9}{3\overline{)2\,7}}$	$\overset{6}{7\overline{)4\,2}}$	$\overset{4}{6\overline{)2\,4}}$	$\overset{6}{3\overline{)1\,8}}$	$\overset{9}{7\overline{)6\,3}}$
3.	$\overset{9}{4\overline{)3\,6}}$	$\overset{5}{5\overline{)2\,5}}$	$\overset{7}{1\overline{)7}}$	$\overset{8}{2\overline{)1\,6}}$	$\overset{}{6\overline{)1\,8}}$
4.	$\overset{9}{2\overline{)1\,8}}$	$\overset{2}{6\overline{)1\,2}}$	$\overset{8}{7\overline{)5\,6}}$	$\overset{4}{5\overline{)2\,0}}$	$\overset{8}{1\overline{)8}}$

Find the quotients.

	a	b	c
5.	$54 \div 6 = \underline{\ 9\ }$	$28 \div 7 = \underline{\ 1\ }$	$24 \div 3 = \underline{\ 7\ }$
6.	$24 \div 4 = \underline{\ 6\ }$	$49 \div 7 = \underline{\ 7\ }$	$48 \div 6 = \underline{\quad}$

Draw a line from each problem to the correct quotient.

7.

$27 \div 3$	8	$7\overline{)1\,4}$
$49 \div 7$	2	$4\overline{)3\,6}$
$40 \div 5$	4	$6\overline{)4\,8}$
$6 \div 3$	9	$5\overline{)3\,5}$
$21 \div 7$	7	$7\overline{)7}$
$2 \div 2$	1	$2\overline{)8}$
$24 \div 6$	3	$5\overline{)1\,5}$

Basic Facts to 8

Divide.

	a	b	c	d	e
1.	9 8)72	6)24	3)27	8)48	5)40
2.	4)32	8)40	2)14	3)15	8)16
3.	7)42	4)20	8)32	1)8	6)48
4.	6)54	8)8	5)35	2)12	8)24

Find the quotients.

	a	b	c
5.	63 ÷ 7 = ______	42 ÷ 6 = ______	72 ÷ 8 = ______
6.	30 ÷ 5 = ______	56 ÷ 8 = ______	45 ÷ 5 = ______
7.	64 ÷ 8 = ______	16 ÷ 2 = ______	28 ÷ 4 = ______

8.

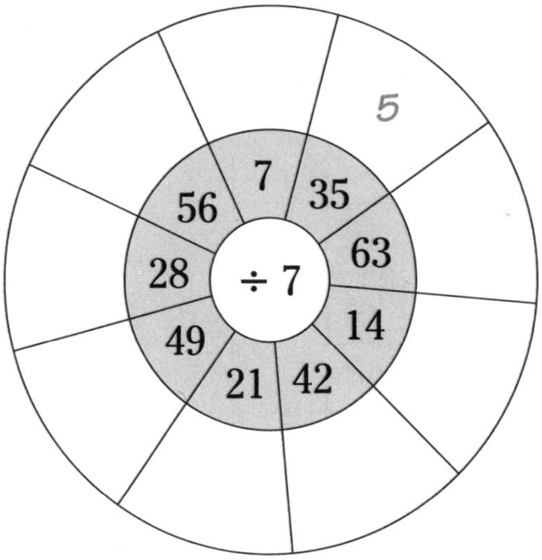

9.

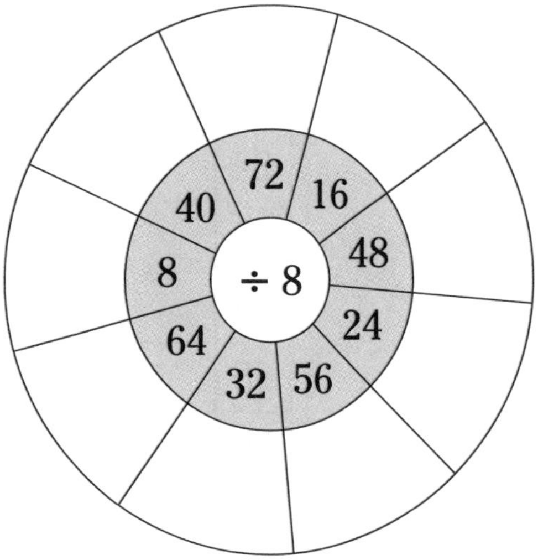

Basic Facts to 9

Divide.

	a	b	c	d	e
1.	$4\overline{)32}$ (8)	$6\overline{)30}$	$8\overline{)48}$	$6\overline{)42}$	$7\overline{)21}$
2.	$2\overline{)10}$	$9\overline{)36}$	$1\overline{)4}$	$5\overline{)25}$	$3\overline{)27}$
3.	$6\overline{)36}$	$7\overline{)42}$	$3\overline{)15}$	$8\overline{)40}$	$2\overline{)16}$
4.	$9\overline{)9}$	$4\overline{)20}$	$7\overline{)56}$	$5\overline{)40}$	$9\overline{)45}$

Find the quotients.

	a	b	c
5.	$21 \div 3 =$ ______	$18 \div 9 =$ ______	$81 \div 9 =$ ______
6.	$54 \div 9 =$ ______	$35 \div 5 =$ ______	$72 \div 9 =$ ______

7.

÷ 9	
27	3
63	
54	
36	
81	
45	

8.

÷ 6	
24	
42	
18	
48	
36	
54	

9.

÷ 4	
24	
32	
20	
28	
36	
16	

10.

÷ 8	
32	
48	
24	
64	
56	
72	

11.

÷ 5	
30	
40	
20	
35	
45	
25	

Divide.

	a	b	c	d	e
1.	$7\overline{)7}$ (0)	$8\overline{)64}$	$4\overline{)12}$ (3)	$9\overline{)54}$	$7\overline{)28}$
2.	$9\overline{)27}$	$5\overline{)15}$ (3)	$9\overline{)72}$	$8\overline{)48}$	$7\overline{)49}$
3.	$7\overline{)21}$ (3)	$9\overline{)81}$ (9)	$7\overline{)35}$	$5\overline{)20}$ (4)	$6\overline{)42}$
4.	$4\overline{)8}$ (2)	$5\overline{)35}$ (7)	$8\overline{)16}$ (2)	$5\overline{)25}$ (5)	$8\overline{)24}$ (3)

Find the quotients.

	a	b	c
5.	$45 \div 9 =$ __________	$56 \div 7 =$ __________	$24 \div 6 =$ __________
6.	$56 \div 8 =$ __________	$30 \div 5 =$ __________	$45 \div 5 =$ __________

Draw a line from each problem to the correct quotient.

7.	$81 \div 9$	7	$8\overline{)24}$
	$42 \div 7$	3	$9\overline{)63}$
	$56 \div 8$	6	$7\overline{)63}$
	$18 \div 6$	9	$6\overline{)36}$
	$40 \div 8$	4	$3\overline{)24}$
	$36 \div 9$	2	$8\overline{)32}$
	$12 \div 6$	8	$4\overline{)8}$
	$48 \div 6$	5	$6\overline{)30}$

Problem-Solving Method: Write a Number Sentence

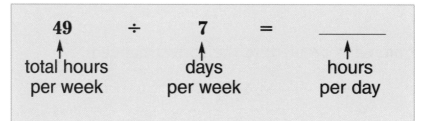

Most people sleep 49 hours each week. There are 7 days in a week. People usually sleep about the same number of hours every day. How many hours do most people sleep each day?

Understand the problem.

- **What do you want to know?**
  how many hours most people sleep each day

- **What information is given?**
  Most people sleep 49 hours a week.
  There are 7 days in a week.

Plan how to solve it.

- **What method can you use?**
  You can write a number sentence to model the problem.

Solve it.

- **How can you use this method to solve the problem?**
  You want to separate the total, 49 hours, into 7 equal groups. So, write a division sentence.

49	÷	**7**	=	______
↑		↑		↑
total hours per week		days per week		hours per day

- **What is the answer?**
  $49 \div 7 = 7$
  Most people sleep 7 hours each day.

Look back and check your answer.

- **Is your answer reasonable?**
  You can check division with multiplication.

  $49 \div 7 = 7$
  $7 \times 7 = 49$

  The product matches the total.
  The answer is reasonable.

Write a number sentence to solve each problem.

1. The lunchroom can seat 64 people at the same time. There are 8 tables. Each table seats the same number of people. How many people can sit at each table?

   Number sentence: ____________

   Answer: ____________ people

2. Carol made 5 pizzas. She cut them into 8 slices each. How many slices of pizza did she make?

   Number sentence: ____________

   Answer: ____________ slices

3. In the human body, there are 68 bones in the face and hands. There are 136 bones in the rest of the body. How many bones are there in all?

   Number sentence: ____________

   Answer: ____________ bones

4. Robert Wadlow was the tallest man in the world. At 8 years old, he was 72 inches tall. At 20 years old, he was 107 inches tall. How much did he grow in those 12 years?

   Number sentence: ____________

   Answer: ____________ inches

5. Each baseball team in the league has 9 players. There are 72 players in all. How many teams are there?

   Number sentence: ____________

   Answer: ____________ teams

Unit 5 Review

Divide.

	a	b	c	d	e
1.	$8\overline{)24}$	$7\overline{)49}$	$9\overline{)36}$	$7\overline{)28}$	$6\overline{)36}$
2.	$9\overline{)63}$	$8\overline{)16}$	$6\overline{)54}$	$7\overline{)56}$	$9\overline{)81}$
3.	$6\overline{)30}$	$8\overline{)8}$	$7\overline{)21}$	$9\overline{)18}$	$8\overline{)72}$
4.	$8\overline{)48}$	$7\overline{)35}$	$6\overline{)24}$	$9\overline{)27}$	$6\overline{)12}$
5.	$9\overline{)72}$	$8\overline{)64}$	$6\overline{)48}$	$9\overline{)54}$	$7\overline{)7}$
6.	$8\overline{)56}$	$7\overline{)42}$	$8\overline{)32}$	$9\overline{)45}$	$6\overline{)18}$

Find the quotients.

	a	b	c
7.	$63 \div 9 =$ ________	$36 \div 6 =$ ________	$36 \div 9 =$ ________
8.	$42 \div 7 =$ ________	$40 \div 8 =$ ________	$9 \div 1 =$ ________
9.	$54 \div 6 =$ ________	$63 \div 7 =$ ________	$14 \div 7 =$ ________

Unit 5 Review

Choose an operation to solve each problem. Then solve the problem.

10. There are 9 elephants in the circus. In all, they eat 72 bales of hay every day. Each animal eats the same amount of hay. How many bales of hay does each elephant eat every day?

Operation: ____________________

Answer: ____________________ bales

11. An elephant drinks 53 gallons of water every day. If it drinks the same amount for 6 days, how many gallons of water will it drink?

Operation: ____________________

Answer: ____________________ gallons

12. At the aquarium, there were 96 fish in one tank. Another tank had 124 fish. How many fish were there in all?

Operation: ____________________

Answer: ____________________ fish

13. Out of 100 questions on the test, Tyler got 88 right. How many of the questions did he get wrong?

Operation: ____________________

Answer: ____________________ questions

Write a number sentence to solve the problem.

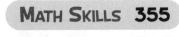

14. A raccoon sleeps 13 hours a day. How many hours will it sleep in 7 days?

Number sentence: ____________________

Answer: ____________________ hours

unit 6
Geometry and Measurement

Lines and Line Segments

A **point** is an exact location in space.

Name a point with a capital letter:

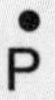

point *P*

A **line** is an endless straight path.

Name a line by any two points on the line:

line *AB* or line *BA*

A **line segment** is a straight path between two points.

Name a line segment by its two endpoints:

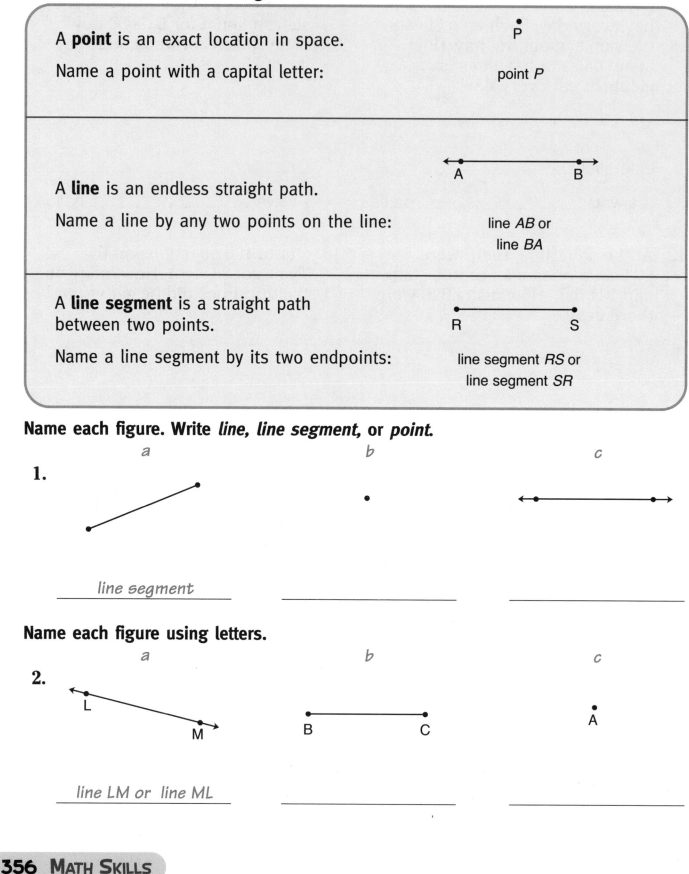

line segment *RS* or line segment *SR*

Name each figure. Write *line, line segment,* or *point.*

1.

a

line segment

b

____

c

____

Name each figure using letters.

2.

a

line LM or line ML

b

____

c

____

Name each figure. Write *line*, *line segment*, or *point*.

1.

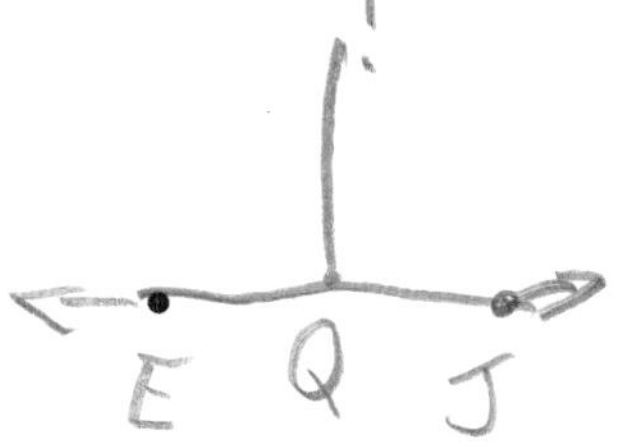

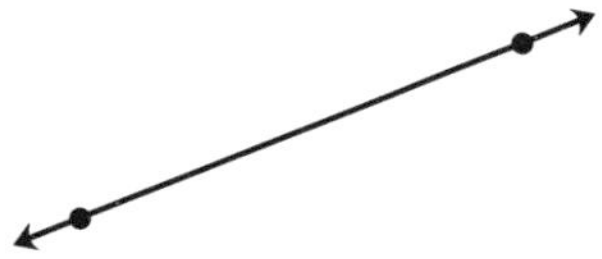

______________ ______________ ______________

Name each figure using letters.

2.

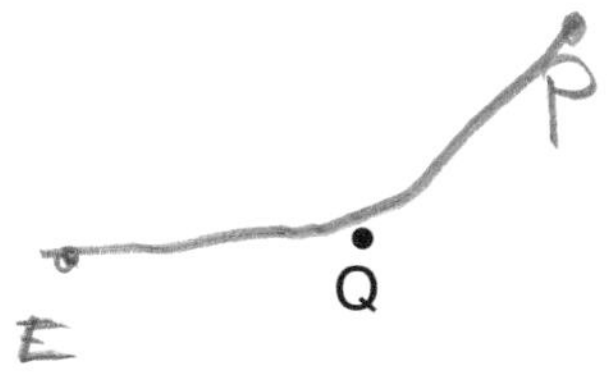

______________ ______________ ______________

3.

______________ ______________ ______________

Use the drawing at right for Exercises 4–6.

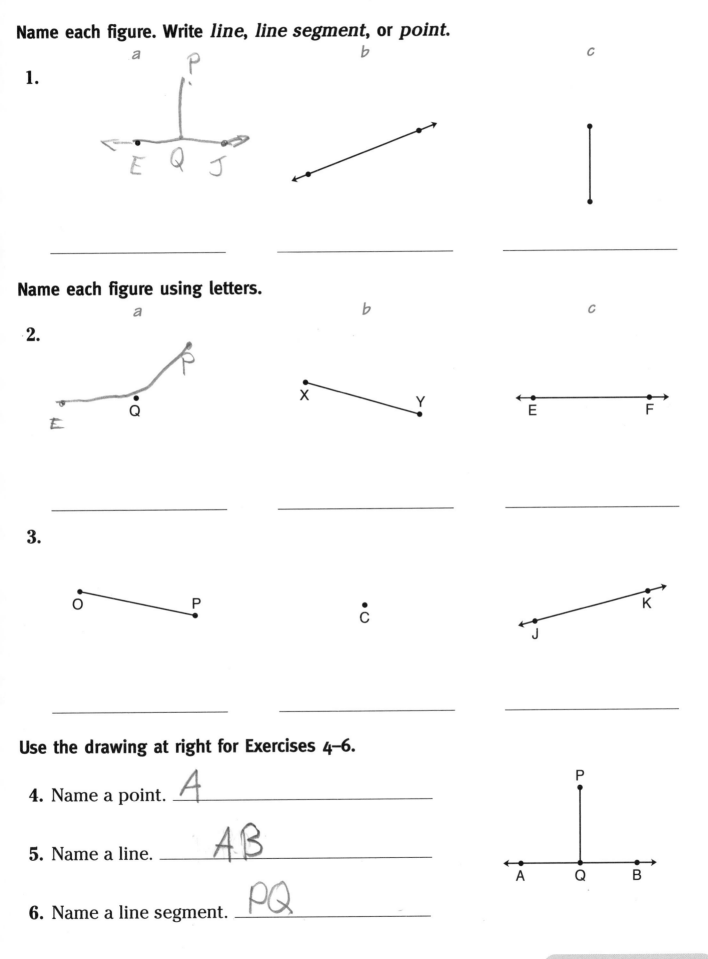

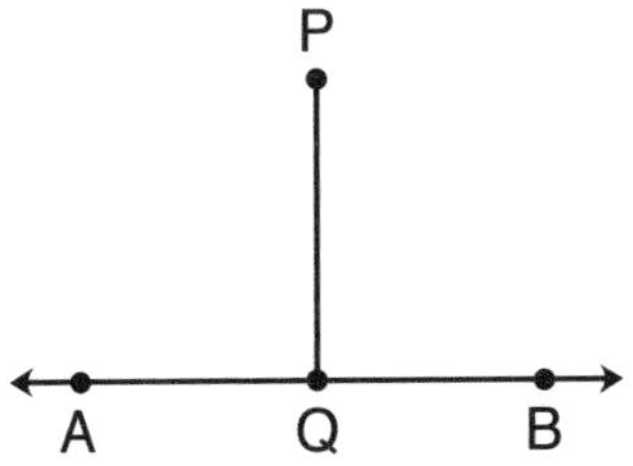

4. Name a point. A

5. Name a line. AB

6. Name a line segment. PQ

Angles

An **angle** is formed when two lines meet at one point.

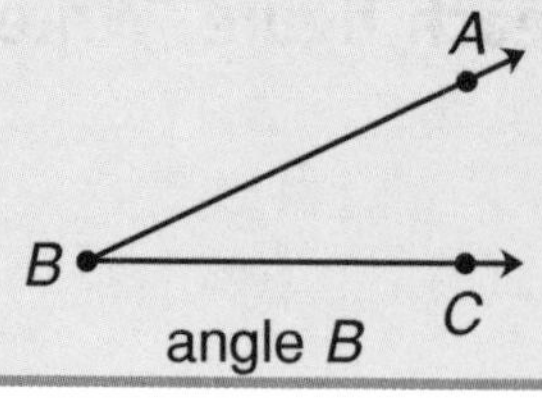

Name an angle by the point where the lines meet: angle *B*

Angles are measured in **degrees** (°).

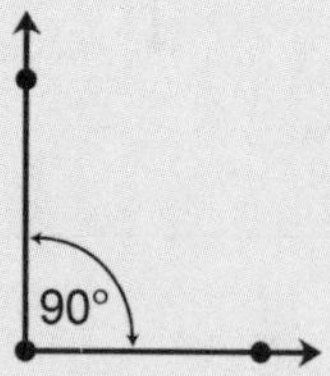

A **right angle** is exactly 90°.

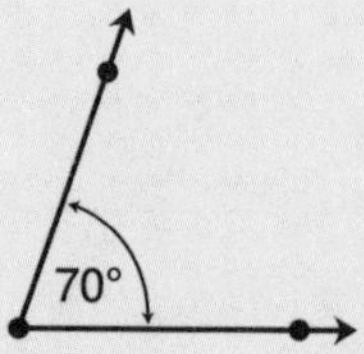

An **acute angle** is less than 90°.

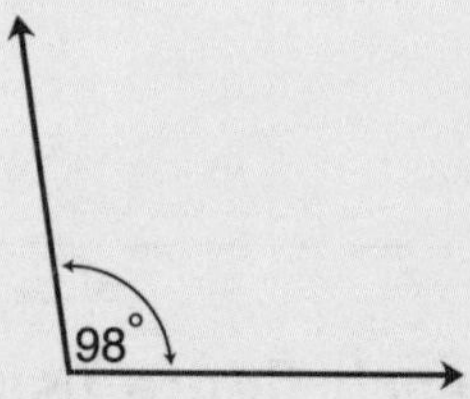

An **obtuse angle** is greater than 90°.

Name each angle.

1.

a

angle M

b

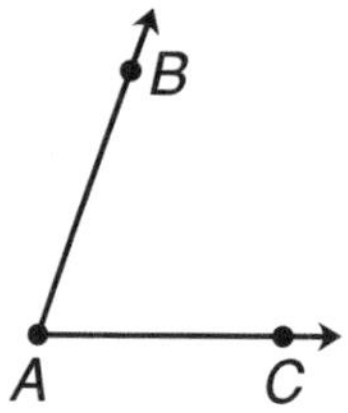

____

c

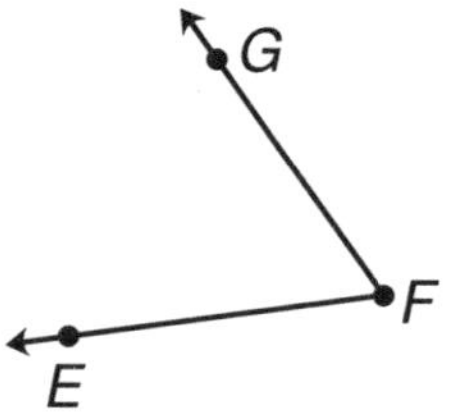

____

Name each angle. Write *right angle*, *acute angle*, **or** *obtuse angle*.

2.

a

acute angle

b

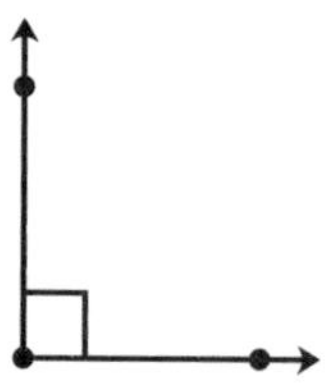

____

c

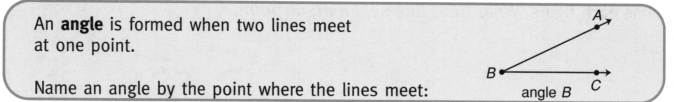

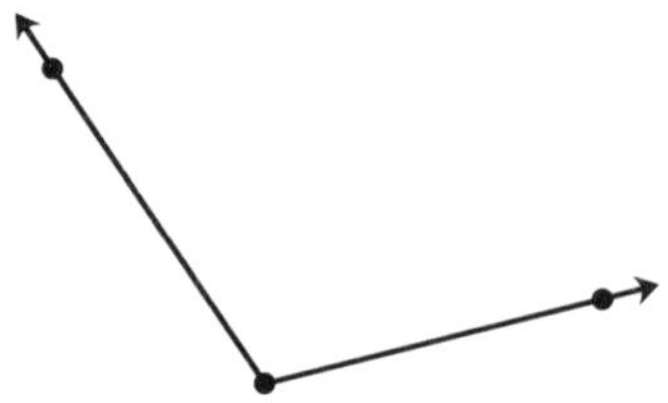

____

Name each angle.

	a	b	c
1.	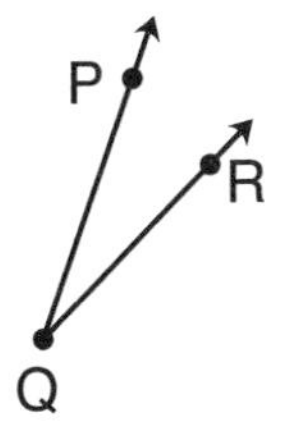	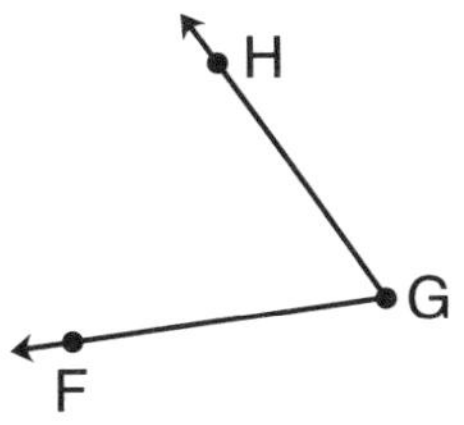	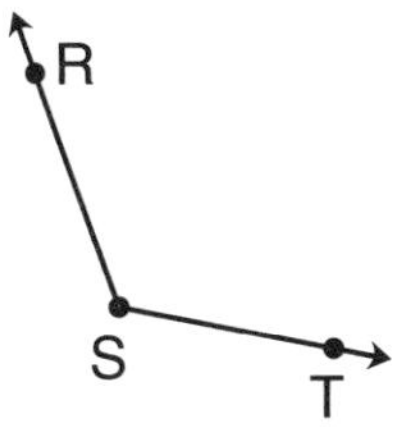

Name each angle. Write *right angle*, *acute angle*, or *obtuse angle*.

	a	b	c
2.	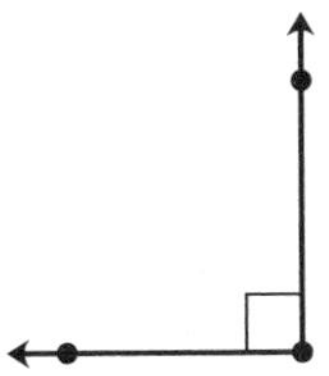		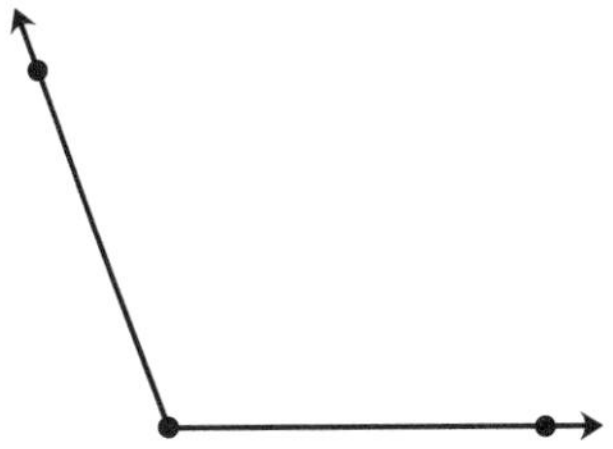
3.	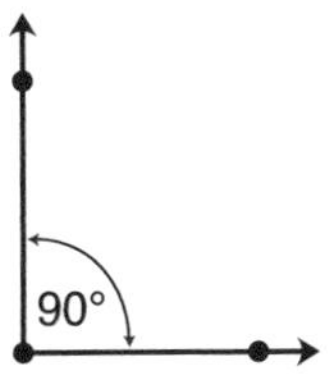	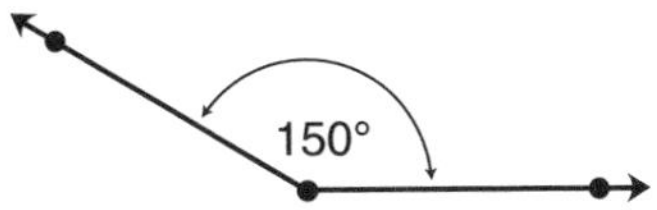	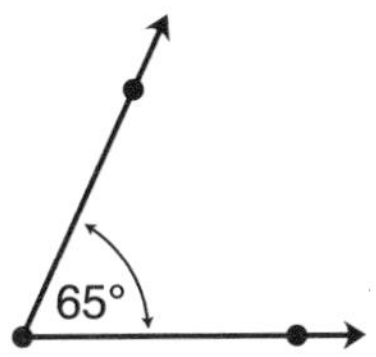

Use the drawing at right for Exercises 4–6.

4. Name a right angle. ______________

5. Name an acute angle. ______________

6. Name an obtuse angle. ______________

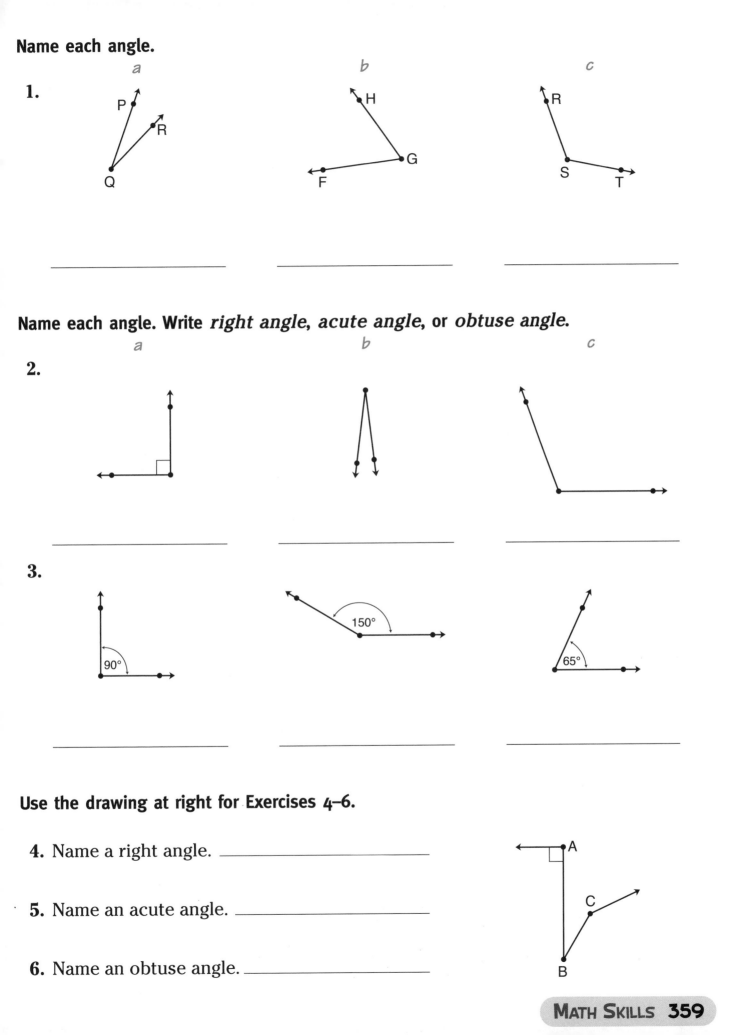

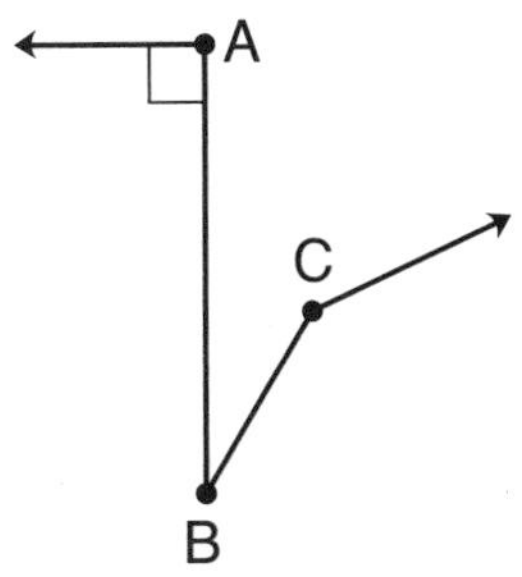

Perimeter

Perimeter is the distance around a figure.

To find the perimeter of a figure, count the number of units around the figure.

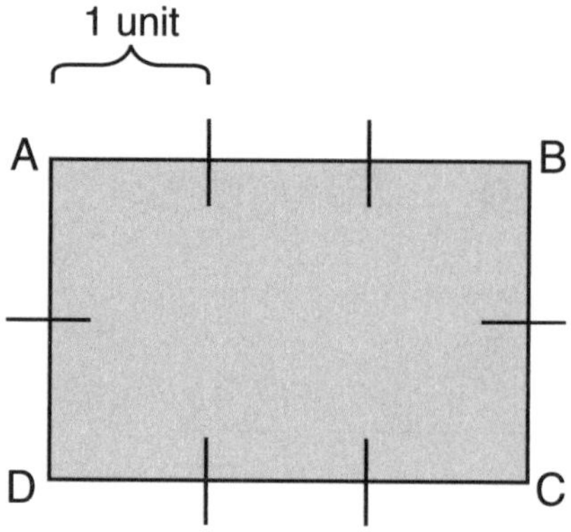

Find the perimeter of this rectangle by counting units.

Start at point *A*. Move clockwise and count the units:

A to *B* (3), to *C* (5), to *D* (8), to *A* (10).

The perimeter of this rectangle is 10 units.

Find the perimeter of each figure.

a | *b*

1. 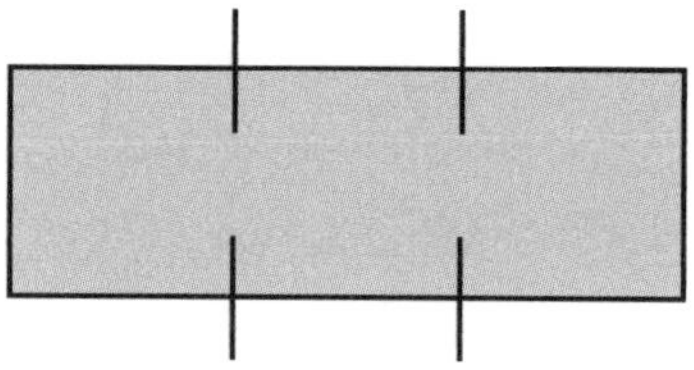

8 units

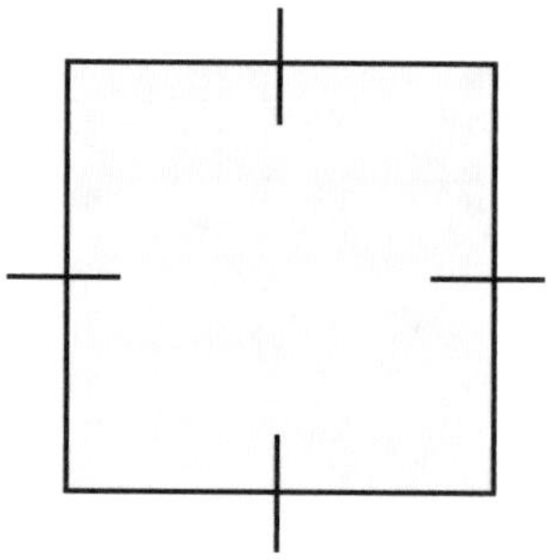

____

2. 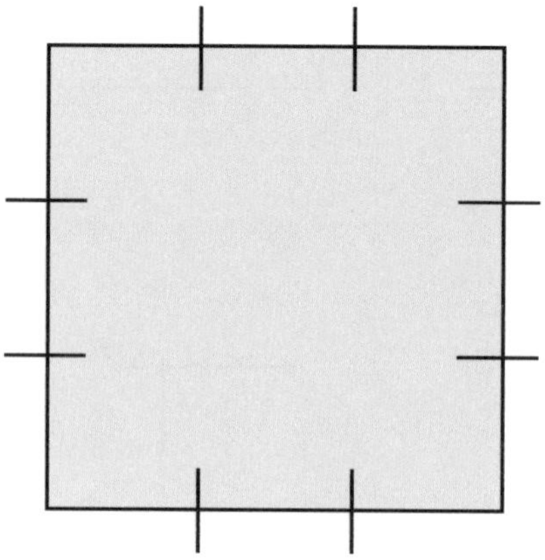

____

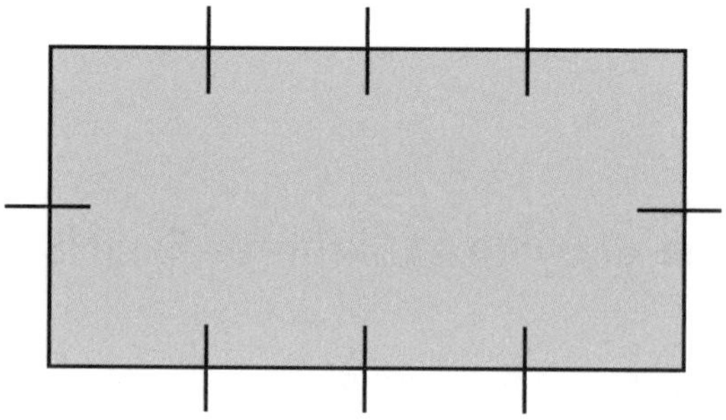

____

Area

The area of a figure is the number of **square units** that cover its surface.

This is 1 square unit.

Count the number of square units to find the area of a figure.

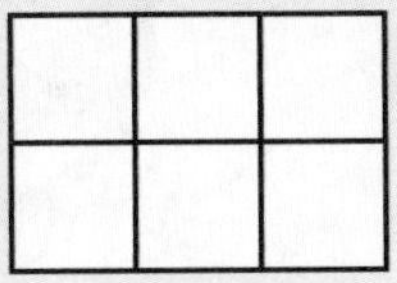

The area of this figure is 6 square units.

Find the area of each figure.

a | *b*

1.

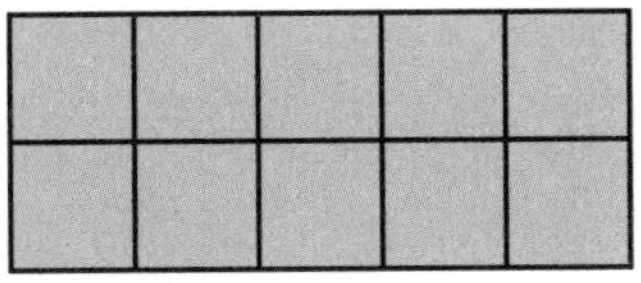

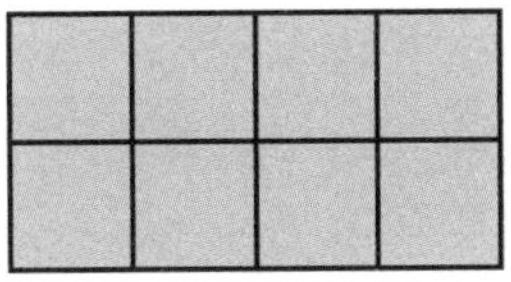

10 square units ____________ | ____________

2.

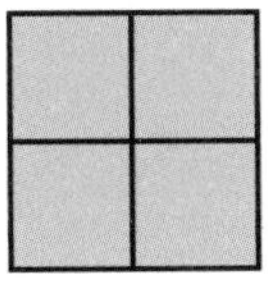

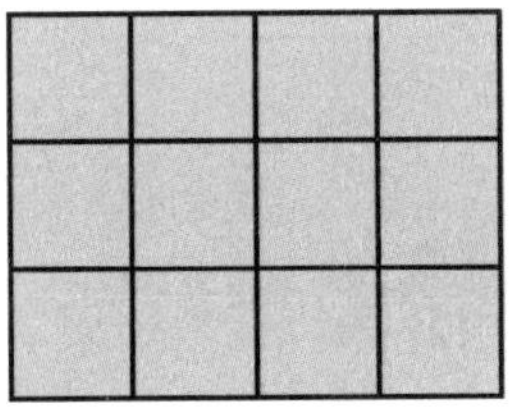

____________ | ____________

3.

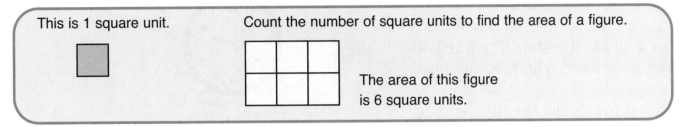

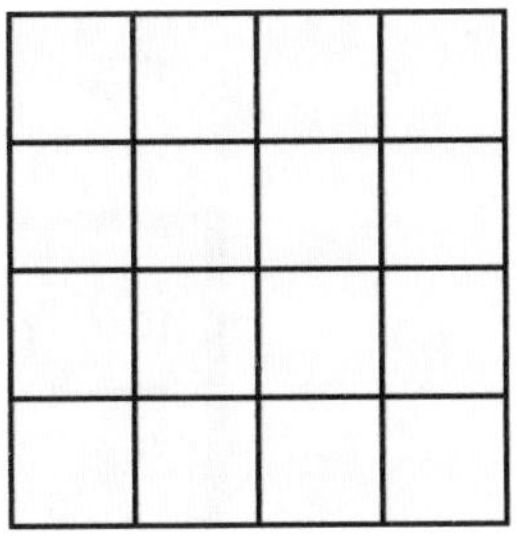

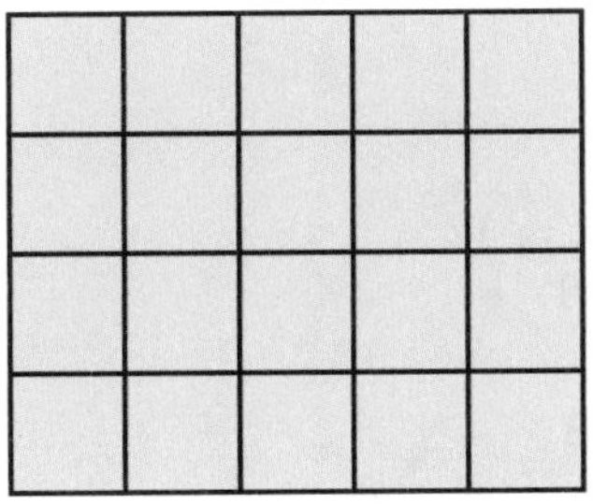

____________ | ____________

Telling Time: Minutes

Time is divided into **hours** and **minutes**.
There are 60 minutes in 1 hour.

On a clock, the short hand tells the hour.
The long hand tells the minutes.

This clock shows the time is 2:40.
Read: 40 minutes after 2
or 20 minutes before 3

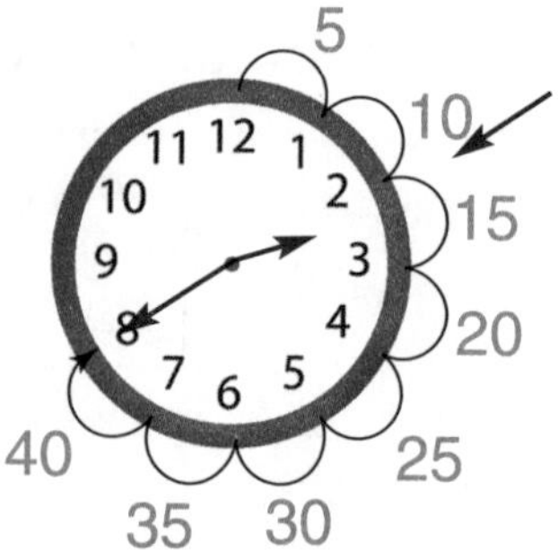

Count by fives to find the minutes. Start at 12.

Write the time shown on each clock.

	a	*b*	*c*
1.			
	9:15	______	______
2.			
	______	______	______
3.			
	______	______	______

Elapsed Time

Elapsed time is the amount of time that passes from the start of an event to its end.

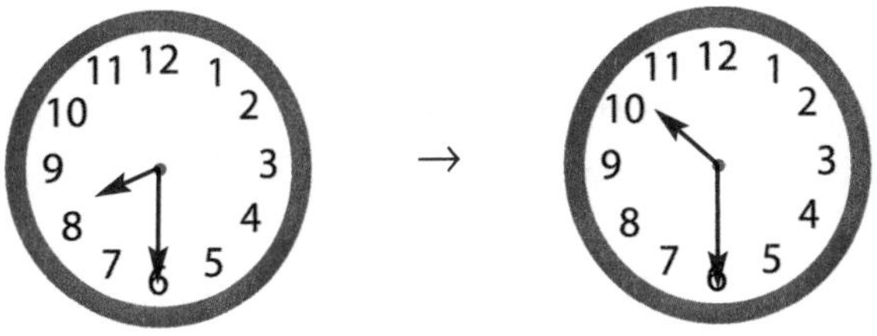

Start End

The start clock shows 8:30.
The end clock shows 10:30.

The elapsed time is 2 hours.

Tell the elapsed times.

a

1. 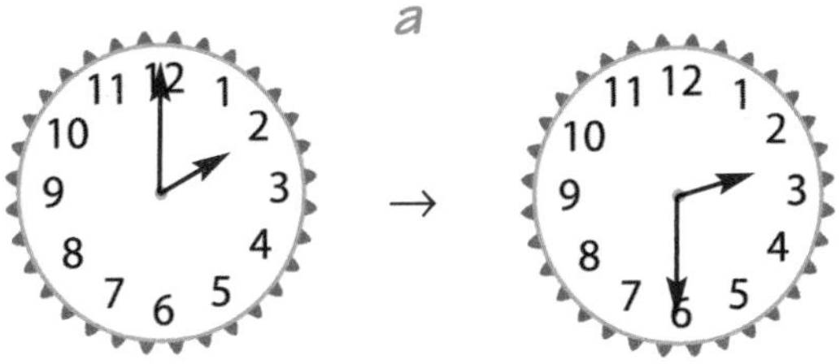

30 minutes

b

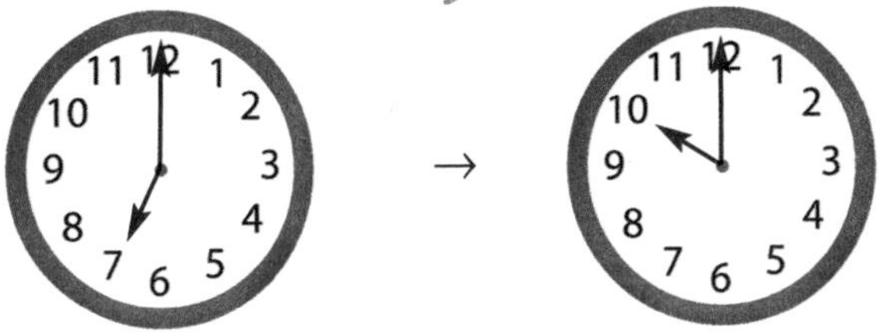

____

2. 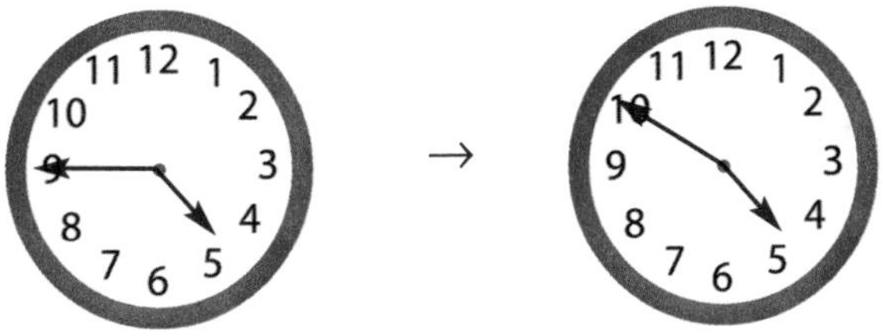

____

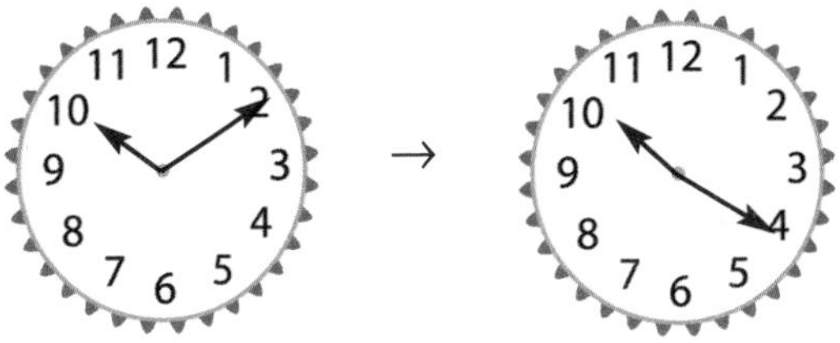

____

3. 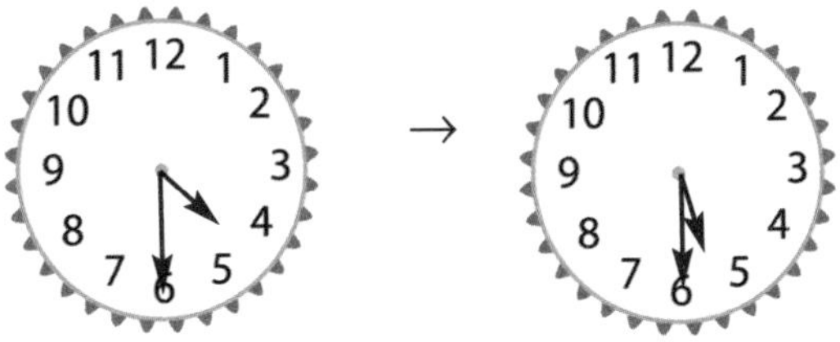

____

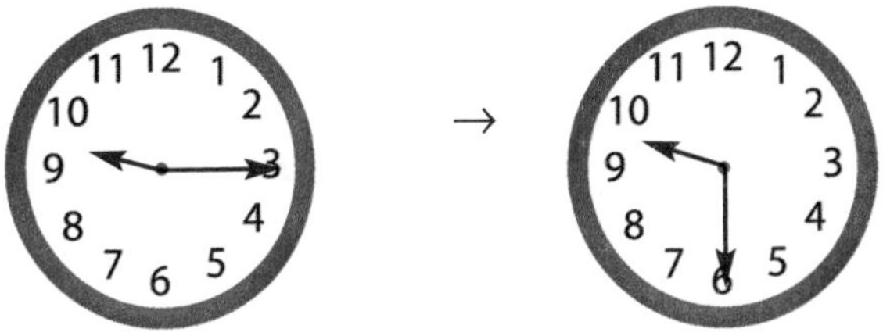

____

Customary Length

The customary units that are used to measure length are **inch, foot, yard,** and **mile.** The chart gives the relationship of one unit to another.

- A safety pin is about 1 inch long.
- A football is about 1 foot long.
- A baseball bat is about 1 yard long.
- A mile is about 18 football fields long.

larger ←□→ smaller	
1 foot (ft.)	= 12 inches (in.)
1 yard (yd.)	= 3 ft.
	= 36 in.
1 mile (mi.)	= 1,760 yd.
	= 5,280 ft.

Choose the best unit of measure. Write *in., ft.,* or *mi.*

	a	b
1.	length of a pen in.	height of a ladder ______
2.	distance an airplane flies ______	width of a notebook ______
3.	length of a butterfly ______	distance across a city ______
4.	height of a person ______	length of a kitchen table ______

Circle the best measurement.

	a		b	
5.	distance between train stations		height of a door	
	115 ft.	115 mi.	7 ft.	7 yd.
6.	length of a caterpillar		distance walked in one hour	
	2 in.	2 ft.	4 mi.	4 yd.
7.	length of a football field		width of your hand	
	100 mi.	100 yd.	3 ft.	3 in.

Use the chart to complete the following.

	a	b	c
8.	36 in. = 1 yd.	12 in. = ______ ft.	1 yd. = ______ ft.
9.	1,760 yd. = ______ mi.	1 yd. = ______ in.	1 mi. = ______ ft.

Metric Length

The metric units that are used to measure length are **centimeter, meter,** and **kilometer.** The chart gives the relationship of one unit to another.

├─┤ 1 cm

- An ant is about 1 centimeter long.
- A door is about 1 meter wide.
- The Golden Gate Bridge is about 1 kilometer long.

larger ← → smaller
1 meter (m) = 100 centimeters (cm)
1 kilometer (km) = 1,000 meters

Choose the best unit of measure.
Write *cm, m,* or *km.*

	a	b
1.	length of a safety pin ___cm___	height of a basketball hoop ______
2.	distance between cities ______	width of a book ______
3.	length of a sofa ______	height of a room ______
4.	length of a car race ______	length of a pencil ______

Circle the best measurement.

	a		b	
5.	length of a chalkboard		length of a fishing pole	
	8 m	8 cm	2 m	2 km
6.	distance walked in 15 minutes		length of a worm	
	1 km	1 m	3 cm	3 m
7.	length of a swimming pool		height of an apartment building	
	50 m	50 km	400 cm	400 m

Use the chart to complete the following.

	a	b	c
8.	1 m = ___100___ cm	1 km = ______ m	2 m = ______ cm
9.	1,000 m = ______ km	100 cm = ______ m	2 km = ______ m

Problem-Solving Method: Make a Drawing

Karen takes her dog for a walk around the whole park every morning. The park is shaped like a square. Each side is 3 blocks long. How many blocks in all do Karen and her dog walk each morning?

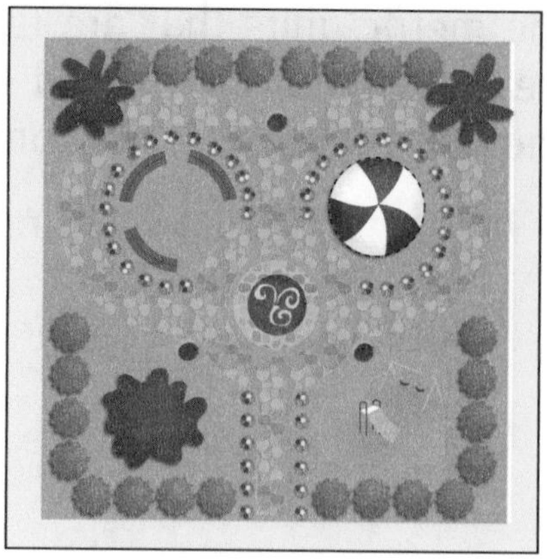

Understand the problem.

- **What do you want to know?**
  how many blocks Karen and her dog walk

- **What information is given?**
  The park is shaped like a square.
  Each side is 3 blocks long.
  They walk around the whole park.

Plan how to solve it.

- **What method can you use?**
  You can make a drawing of the park.

Solve it.

- **How can you use this method to solve the problem?**
  You can count the blocks to find the perimeter of the park.

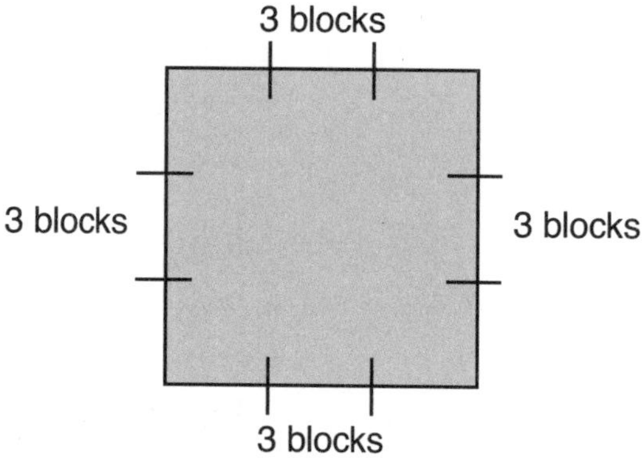

- **What is the answer?**
  Karen and her dog walk 12 blocks each morning.

Look back and check your answer.

- **Is your answer reasonable?**
  You can check your count by adding the number of blocks on each side of the park.

$$3 + 3 + 3 + 3 = 12$$

The sum matches the count.
The answer is reasonable.

Make a drawing to solve each problem.

1. Ben got on the elevator on the first floor. He rode it up to the twenty-first floor. Then he went down 8 floors. What floor is he on now?

21 − 8 = 14
20 − 8 = 13 + 1 = 14

14

_____ floor

2. Oak Street runs straight up town. Elm Street runs straight across town. What kind of angle is formed when the two streets meet?

90°

_____ angle

3. Andre left home and rode his bike 4 miles down Main Street. Then he turned right and rode 2 miles. Then he turned right again and rode 4 miles. How many miles was Andre from home?

4 + 2 + 4 = 10

10

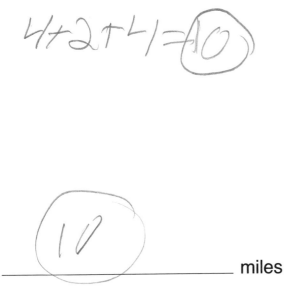

_____ miles

4. Tim, Anne, and Lita work in three different corners of the park. There are paths connecting each of their corners. How many paths are there in all?

3

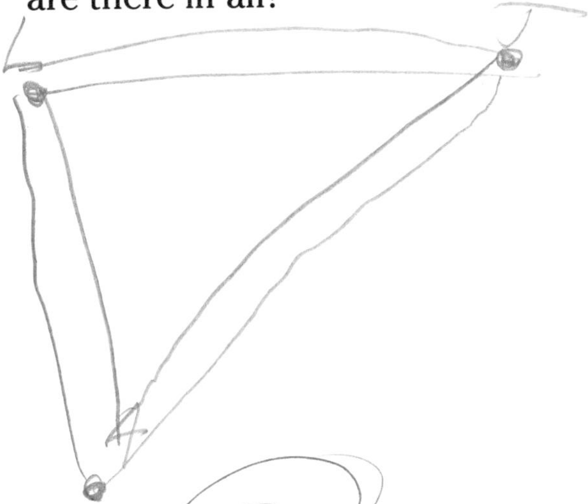

_____ paths

Unit 6 Review

Name each figure using letters.

1.

a

b

c

______________ ______________ ______________

Name each angle. Write *right angle, acute angle,* or *obtuse angle.*

2.

a

b

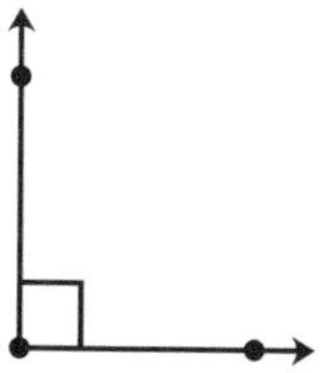

c

______________ ______________ ______________

Find the perimeter and area of each figure.

3.

a

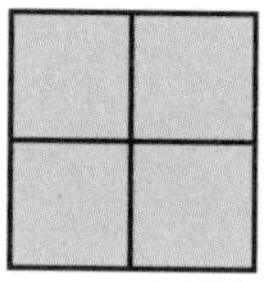

perimeter ______________

area ______________

b

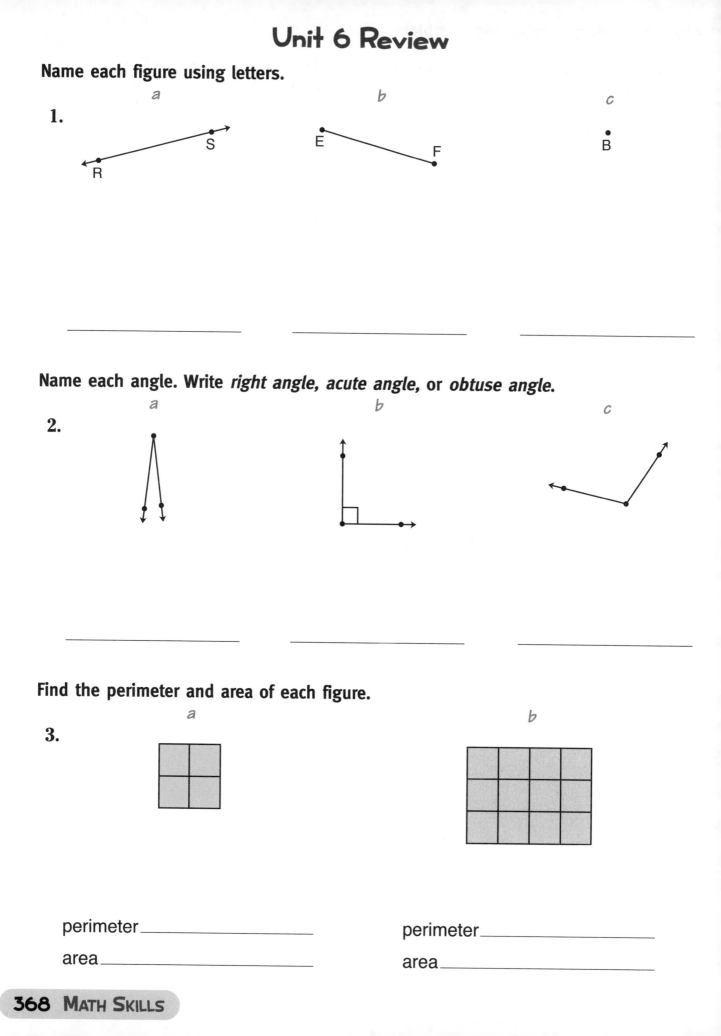

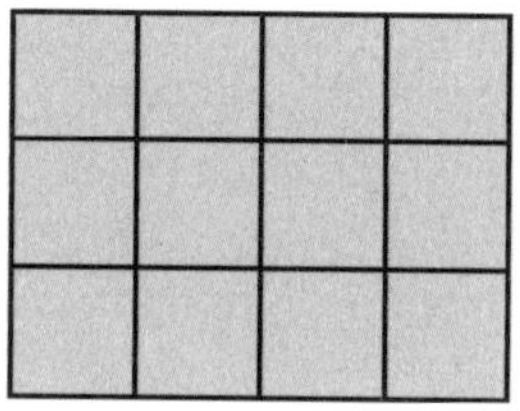

perimeter ______________

area ______________

Unit 6 Review

Write the time shown on each clock.

4.

a  ______________

b  ______________

c  ______________

Tell the elapsed times.

5.

a 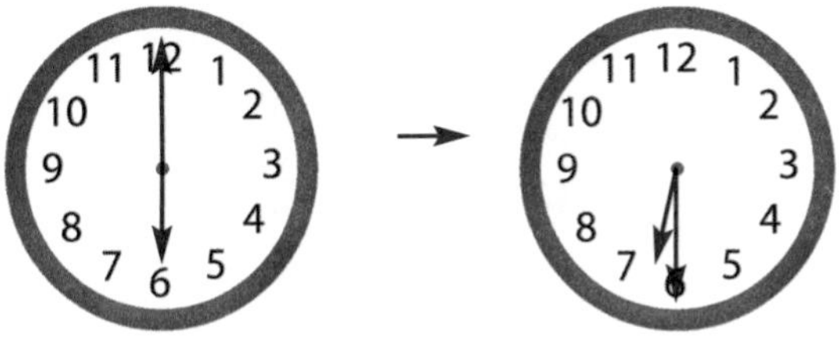 ______________

b 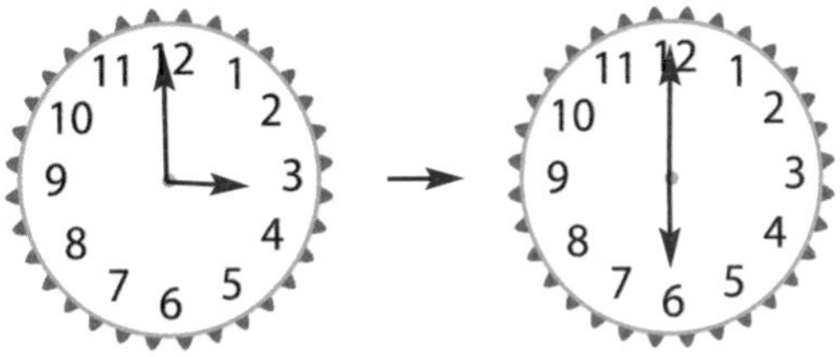 ______________

Choose the best unit of measure. Write *cm, m,* or *km.*

	a	b
6.	length of a toothpick ______	height of a street light ______
7.	distance between states ______	width of a postage stamp ______
8.	width of a swimming pool ______	height of a spider ______

Circle the best measurement.

	a		b	
9.	distance between Dallas and Houston		height of a flower	
	243 ft.	243 mi.	6 in.	6 ft.
10.	length of a whale		width of a butterfly	
	90 ft.	90 mi.	2 in.	2 yd.

unit 7
Fractions

$\frac{1}{2}$: Parts of a Whole

A **fraction** is **part of a whole.**

The fraction $\frac{1}{2}$ shows what part of the circle is shaded blue and what part of the square is shaded blue.

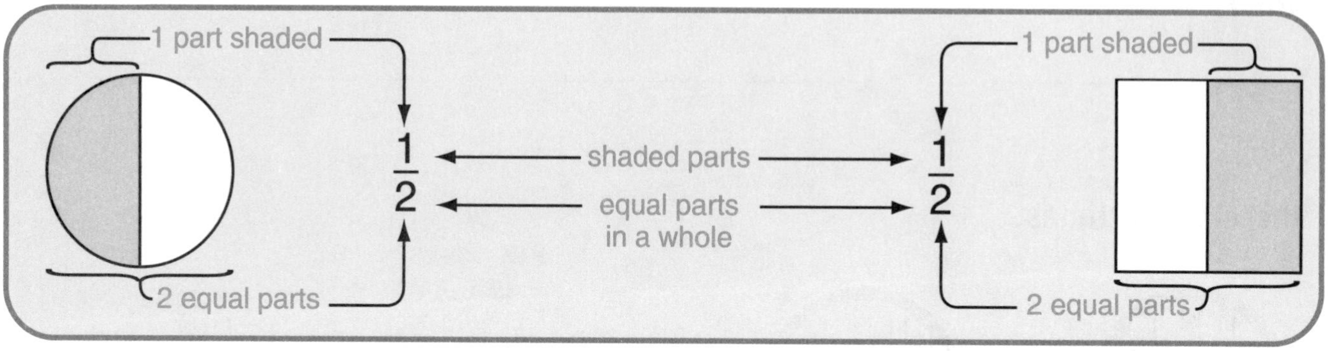

Circle the figures that show $\frac{1}{2}$ shaded.

1. 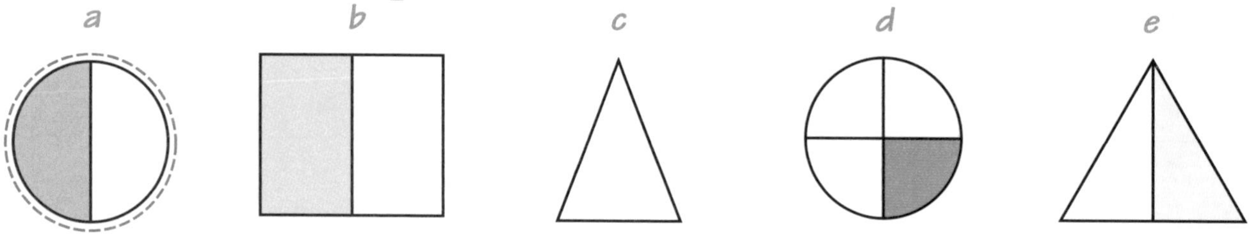

Shade $\frac{1}{2}$ of each figure.

2. 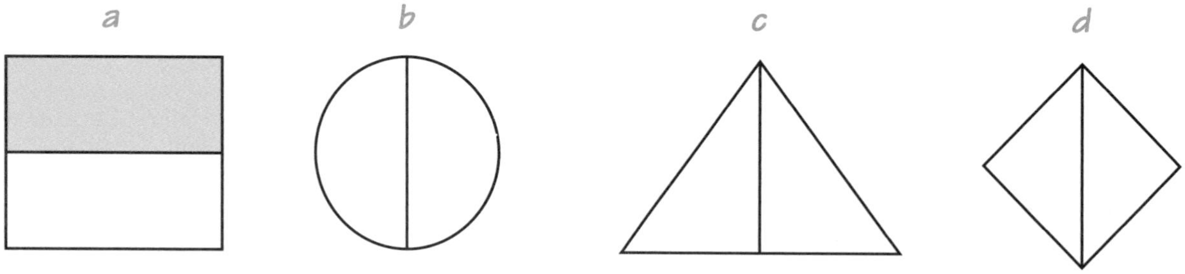

Write a fraction for the shaded part.

3. 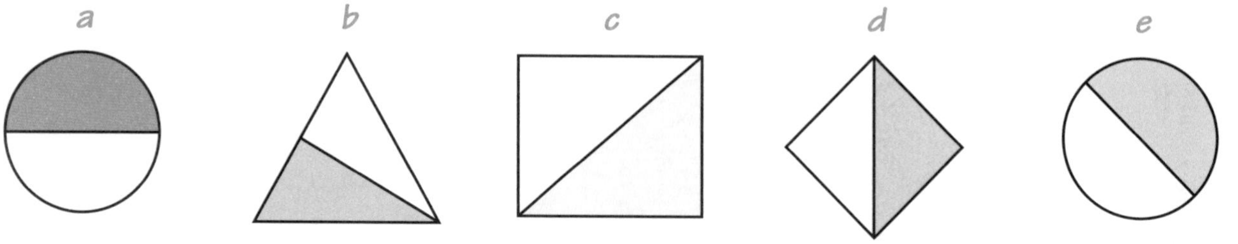

_____ _____ _____ _____ _____

$\frac{1}{2}$: Parts of a Group

A **fraction** may be **part of a group**.

The fraction $\frac{1}{2}$ shows what part of the group of circles and what part of the group of squares are shaded blue.

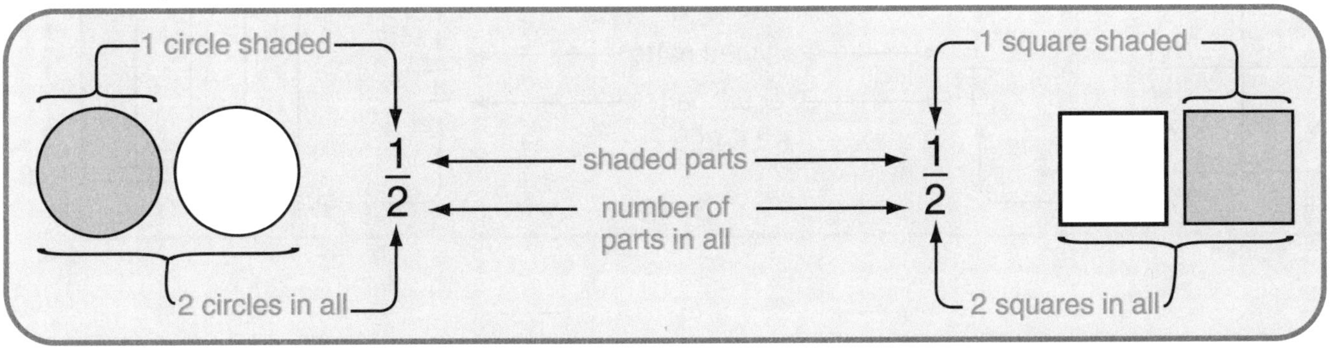

Circle the groups that show $\frac{1}{2}$ shaded.

1.

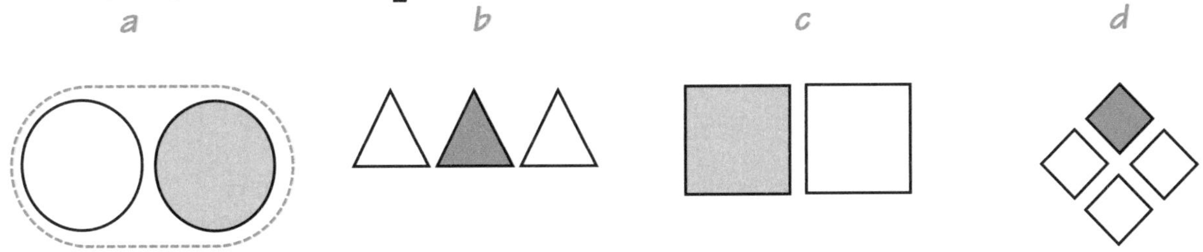

Shade $\frac{1}{2}$ of each group.

2.

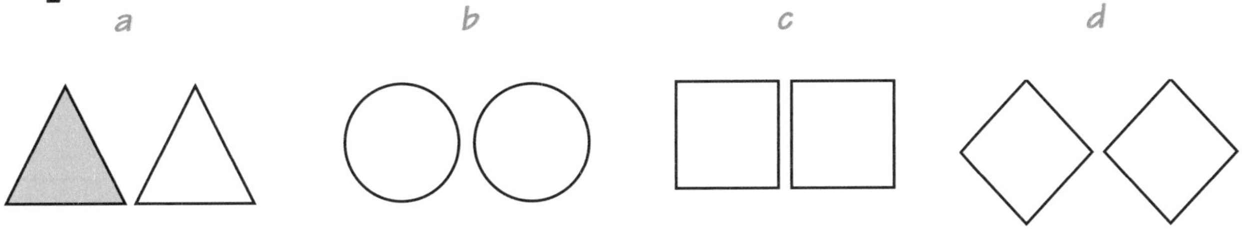

Write a fraction for the shaded part of each group.

3.

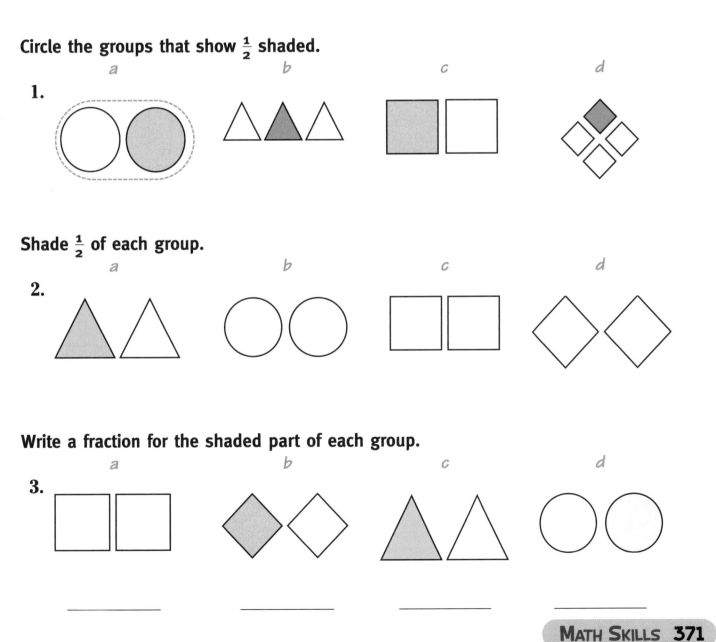

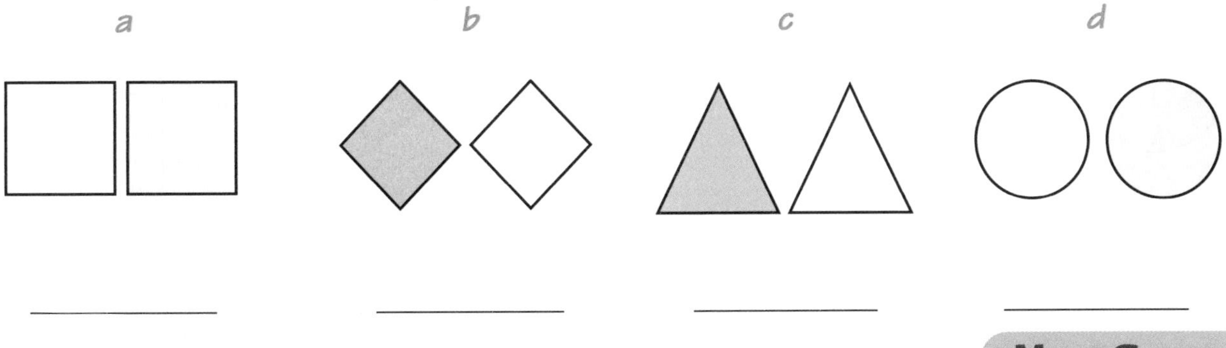

$\frac{1}{4}$: Parts of a Whole

The fraction $\frac{1}{4}$ shows what part of the circle is shaded blue and what part of the square is shaded blue.

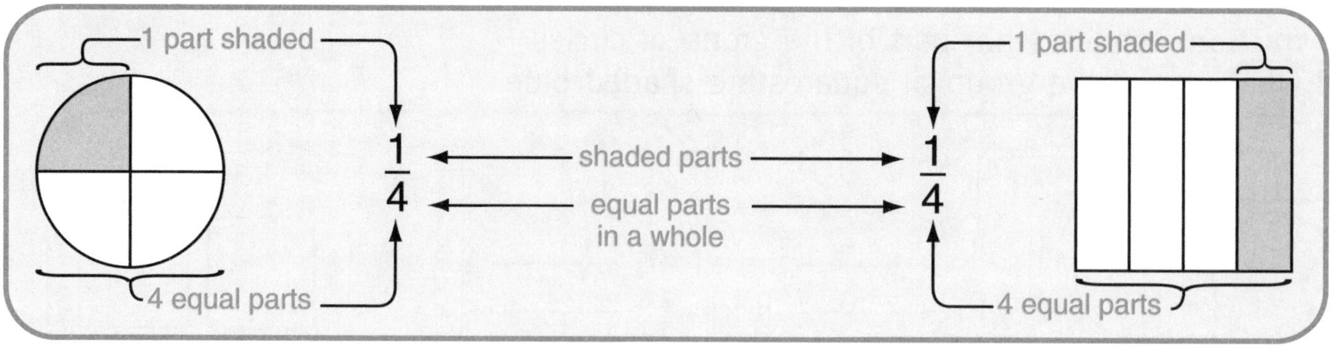

Circle the figures that show $\frac{1}{4}$ shaded.

a b c d e

1.

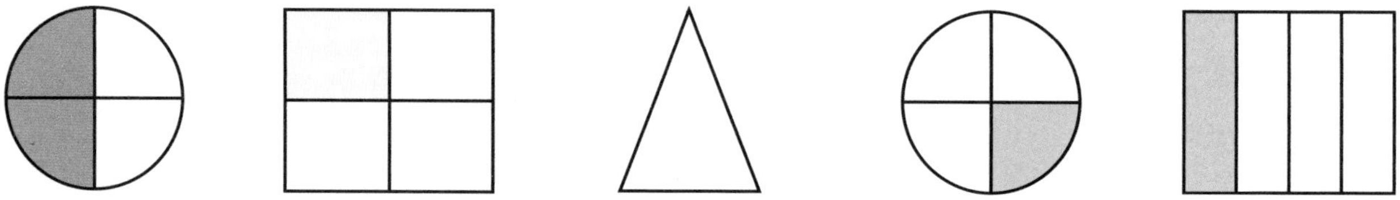

Shade $\frac{1}{4}$ of each figure.

a b c d

2.

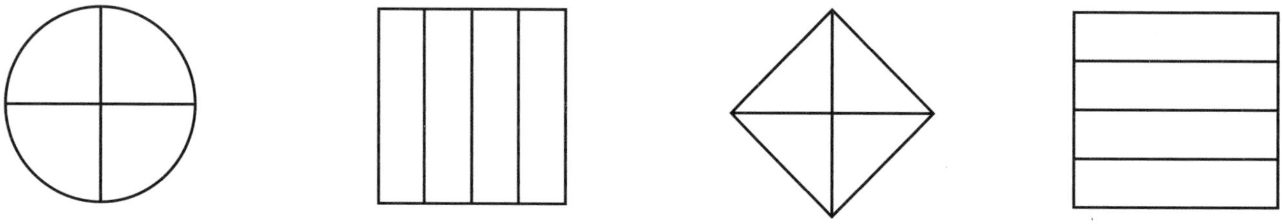

Write a fraction for the shaded part.

a b c d e

3.

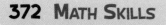

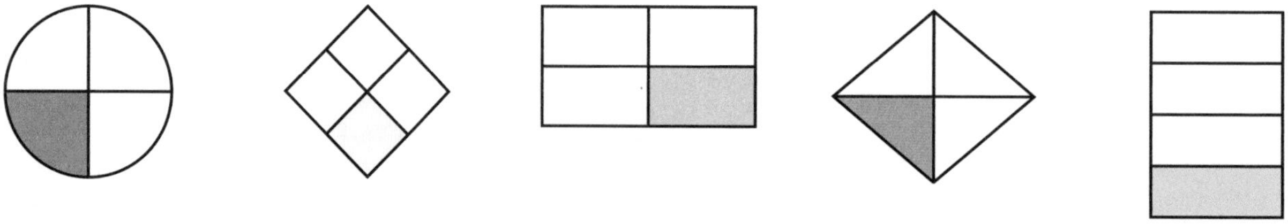

$\frac{1}{4}$: Parts of a Group

The fraction $\frac{1}{4}$ shows what part of the group of circles and what part of the group of squares are shaded blue.

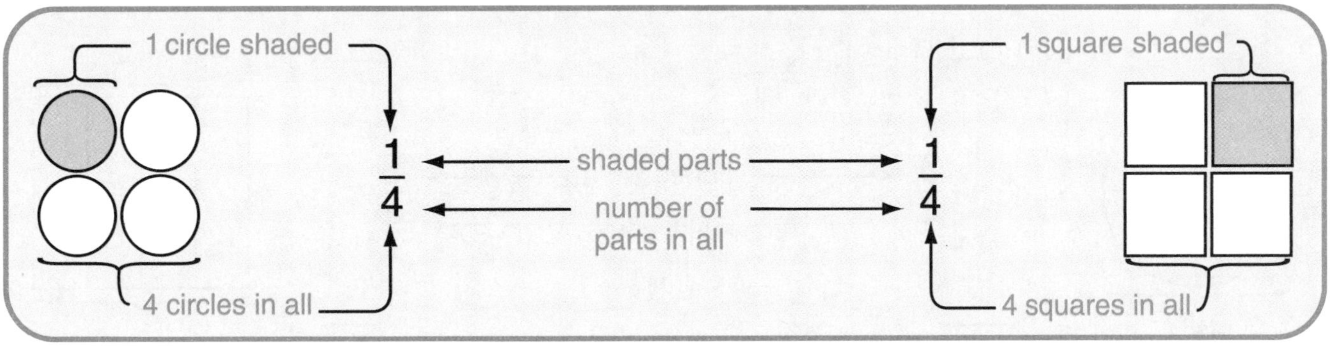

Circle the groups that show $\frac{1}{4}$ shaded.

1.

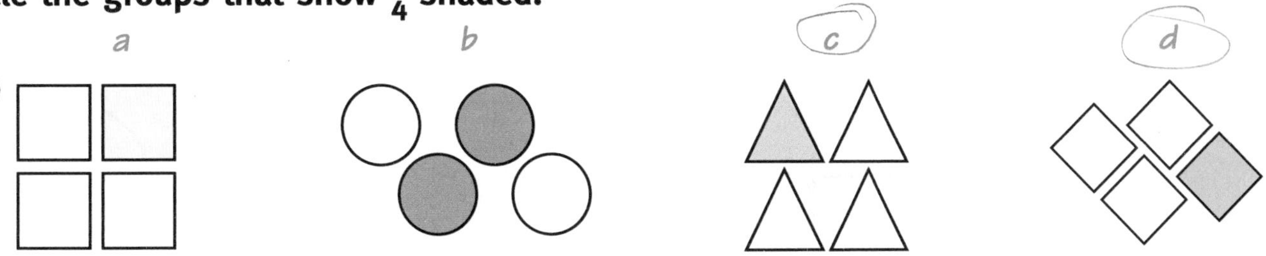

Shade $\frac{1}{4}$ of each group.

2.

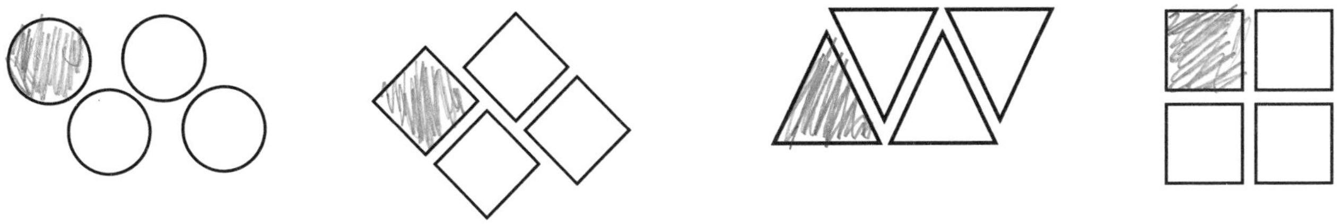

Write a fraction for the shaded part of each group.

3.

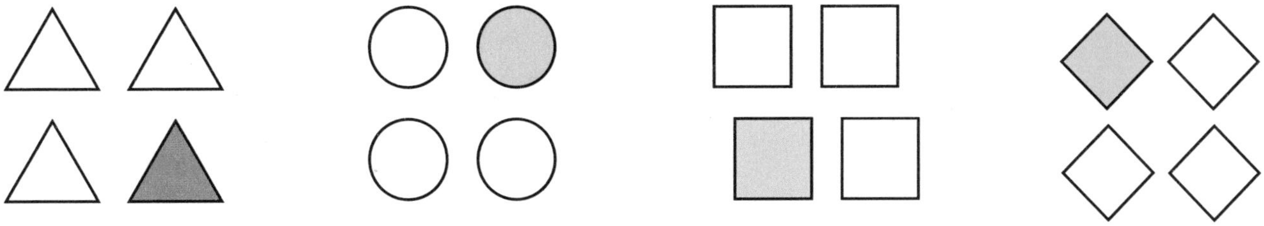

________ ________ ________ ________

$\frac{3}{4}$: Parts of a Whole

The fraction $\frac{3}{4}$ shows what part of the circle is shaded blue and what part of the square is shaded blue.

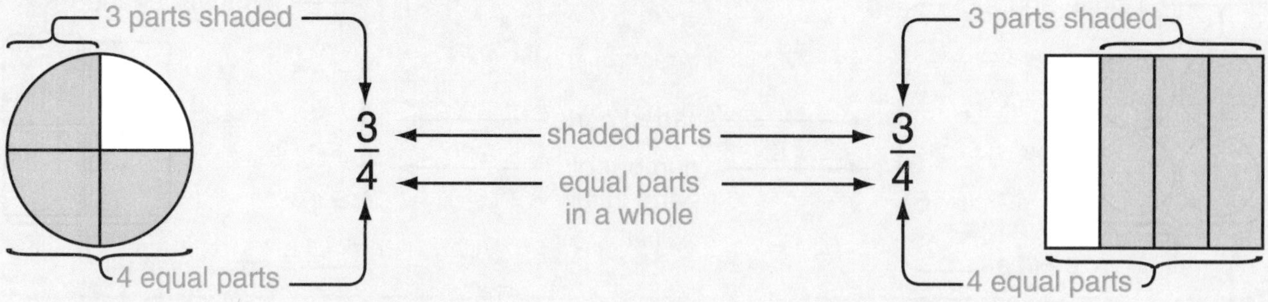

Circle the figures that show $\frac{3}{4}$ shaded.

a *b* *c* *d*

1.

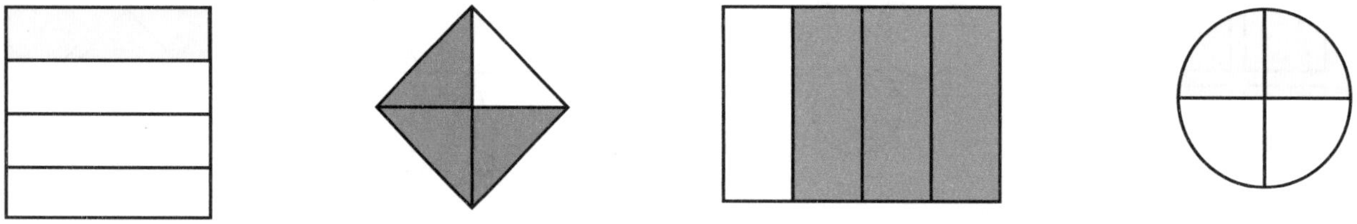

Shade $\frac{3}{4}$ of each figure.

a *b* *c* *d*

2.

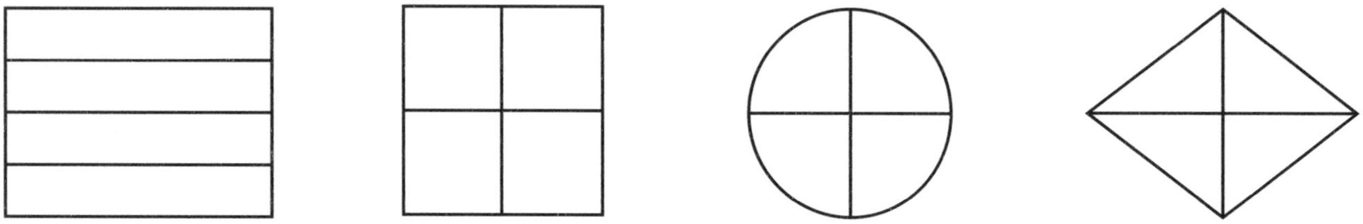

Write a fraction for the shaded part.

a *b* *c* *d* *e*

3.

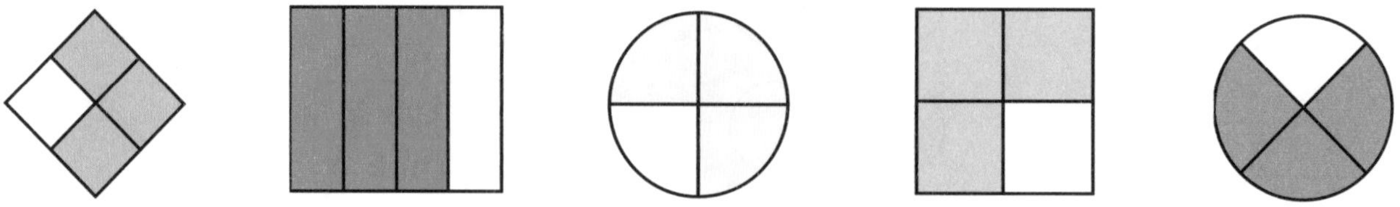

$\frac{3}{4}$: Parts of a Group

The fraction $\frac{3}{4}$ shows what part of the group of circles and what part of the group of squares are shaded blue.

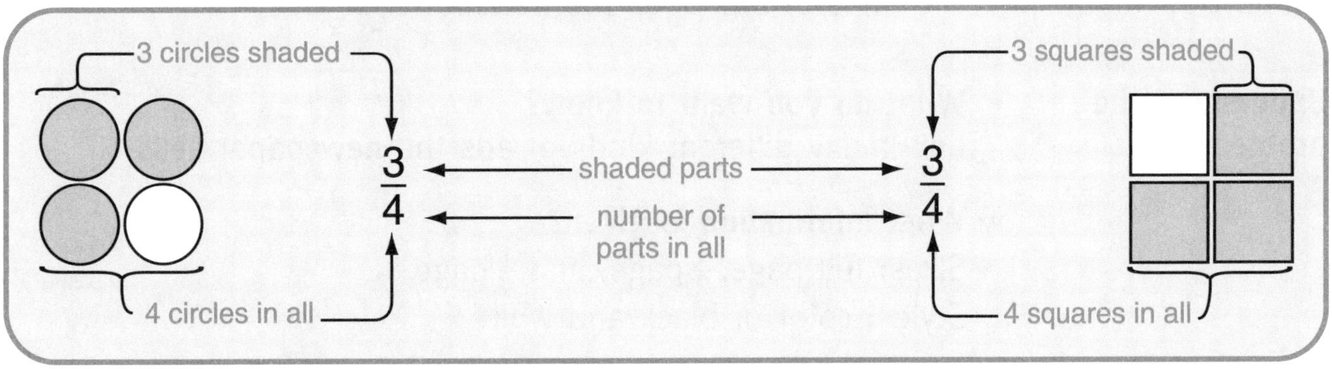

Circle the groups that show $\frac{3}{4}$ shaded.

a *b* *c* *d*

1.

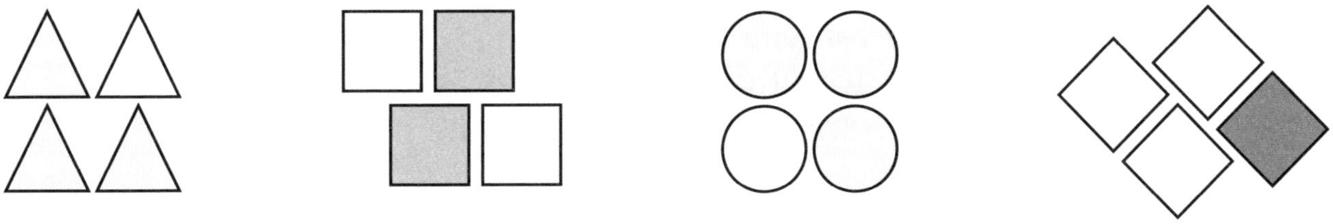

Shade $\frac{3}{4}$ of each group.

a *b* *c* *d*

2.

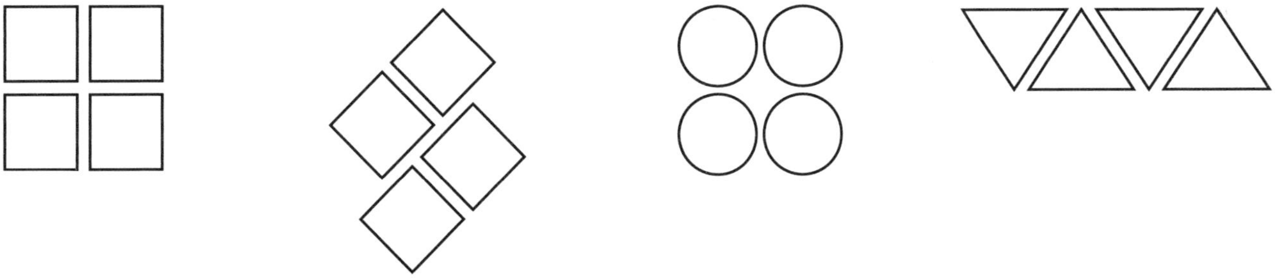

Write a fraction for the shaded part of each group.

a *b* *c* *d*

3.

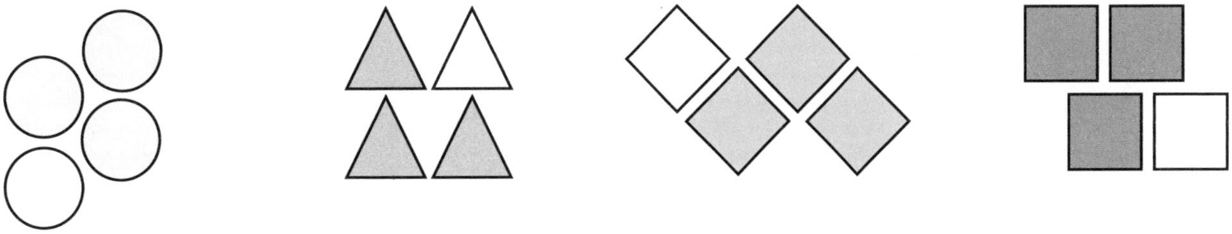

Problem-Solving Method: Make an Organized List

The newspaper sells ads in three different sizes. One covers the full page. One covers $\frac{1}{2}$ of the page. One covers $\frac{1}{4}$ of the page. Ads can be color or black and white. How many different kinds of ads does the newspaper sell?

Understand the problem.

- **What do you want to know?**
  how many different kinds of ads the newspaper sells
- **What information is given?**
  Sizes: full page, $\frac{1}{2}$ page, and $\frac{1}{4}$ page
  Styles: color or black and white

Plan how to solve it.

- **What method can you use?**
  You can make a list of all the combinations of sizes and styles. Then count the combinations.

Solve it.

- **How can you use this method to solve the problem?**
  Start with the first style and list all of its sizes. Then do the same thing for the other style.

Style	Size	Combination
color	full page	full-page color
	$\frac{1}{2}$ page	$\frac{1}{2}$-page color
	$\frac{1}{4}$ page	$\frac{1}{4}$-page color
b&w	full page	full-page b&w
	$\frac{1}{2}$ page	$\frac{1}{2}$-page b&w
	$\frac{1}{4}$ page	$\frac{1}{4}$-page b&w

- **What is the answer?**
  The paper sells 6 different kinds of ads.

Look back and check your answer.

- **Is your answer reasonable?**
  Read the problem again to see if you missed any styles or sizes.

  All of the information is listed.
  The answer is reasonable.

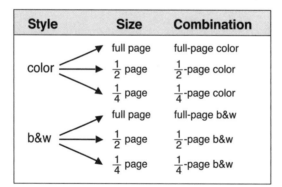

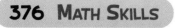

Write an organized list to solve each problem.

1. The gym offers classes in aerobics and yoga. Some classes are 1 hour long and others are $\frac{1}{2}$ hour long. How many different kinds of classes does the gym offer?

_______________ classes

2. John has a red shirt and a blue shirt. He has blue jeans, black jeans, and tan jeans. In how many different ways can he wear these clothes?

_______________ ways

3. Jeff, Lorri, and Dan had a race. In how many different ways could they come in first, second, and third?

_______________ ways

4. The snack shop has white, rye, and wheat bread. It has tuna salad, chicken salad, egg salad, and sliced turkey for sandwiches. In how many different ways can sandwiches be made?

_______________ ways

$\frac{1}{3}$: Parts of a Whole

The fraction $\frac{1}{3}$ shows what part of the circle is shaded blue and what part of the square is shaded blue.

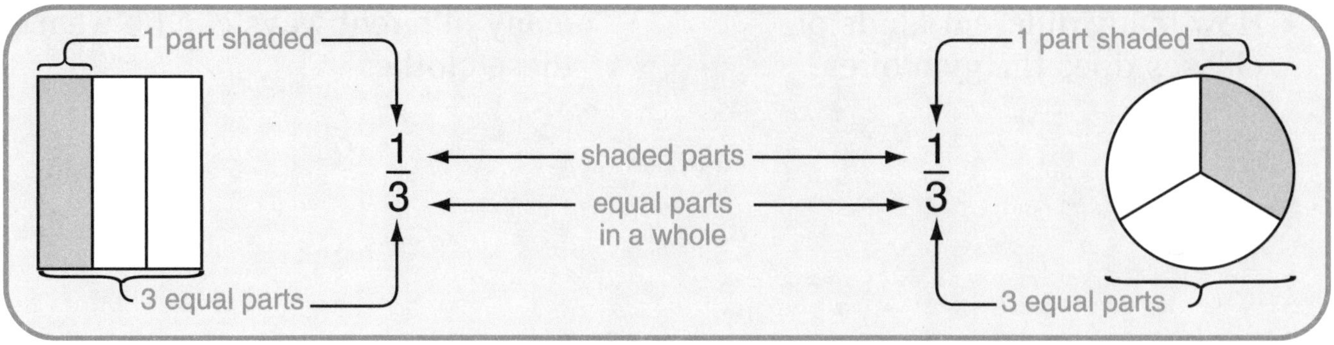

Circle the figures that show $\frac{1}{3}$ shaded.

a *b* *c* *d* *e*

1.

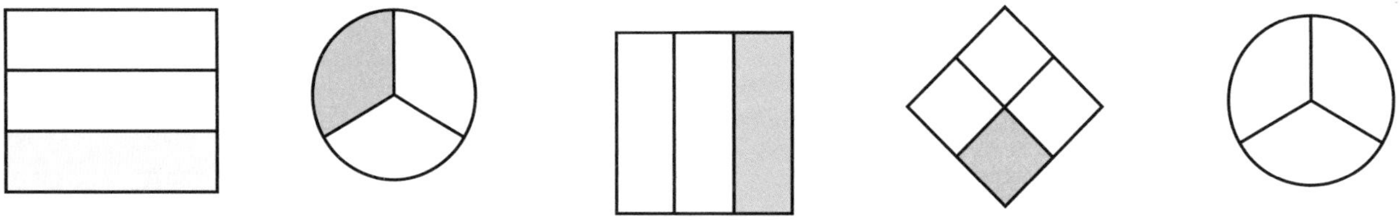

Shade $\frac{1}{3}$ of each figure.

a *b* *c* *d*

2.

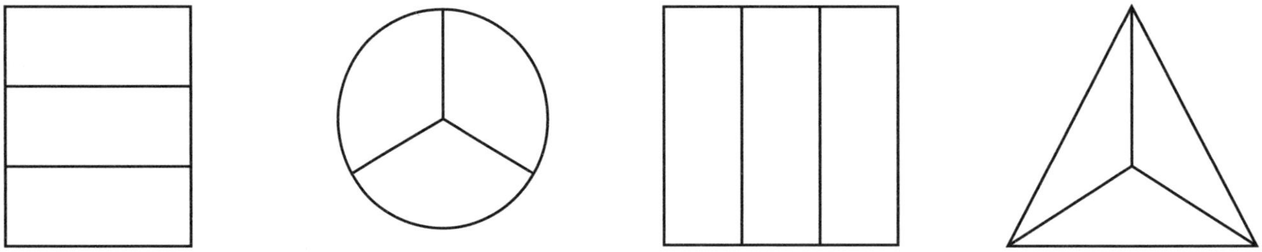

Write a fraction for the shaded part.

a *b* *c* *d* *e*

3.

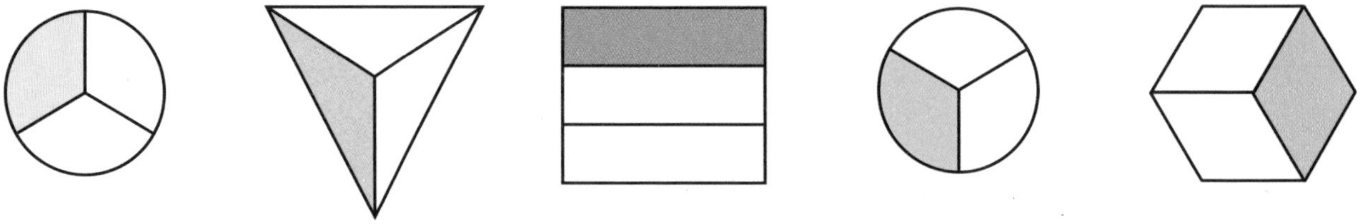

________ ________ ________ ________ ________

$\frac{1}{3}$: Parts of a Group

The fraction $\frac{1}{3}$ shows what part of the group of circles and what part of the group of squares are shaded blue.

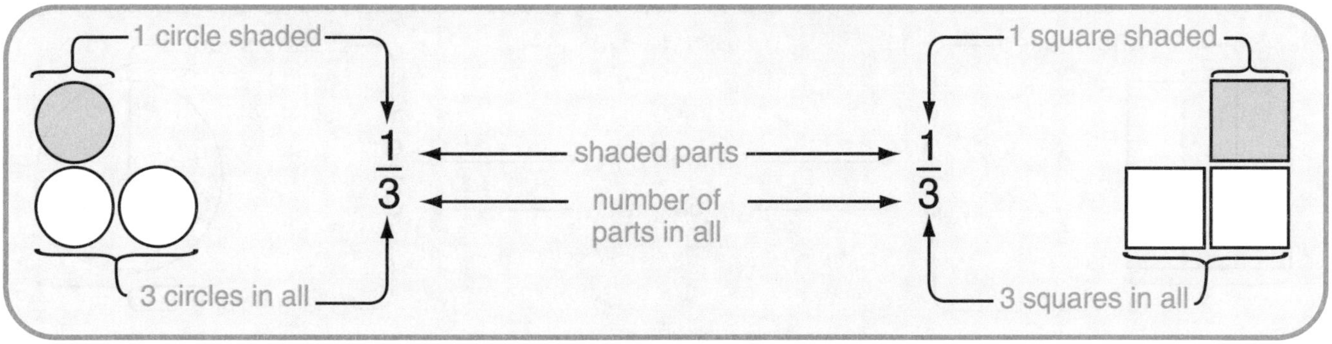

Circle the groups that show $\frac{1}{3}$ shaded blue.

a *b* *c* *d*

1.

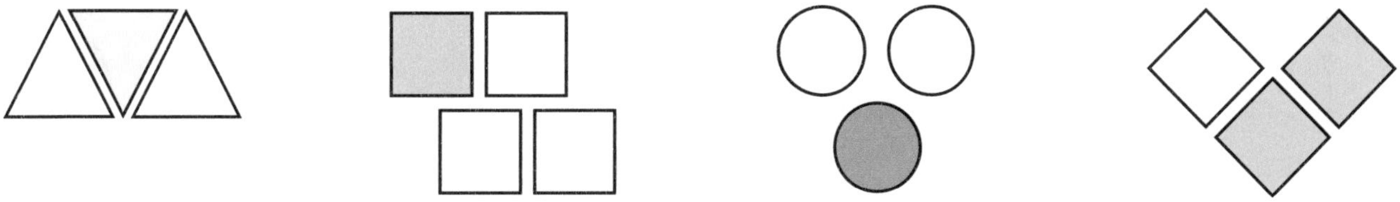

Shade $\frac{1}{3}$ of each group.

a *b* *c* *d*

2.

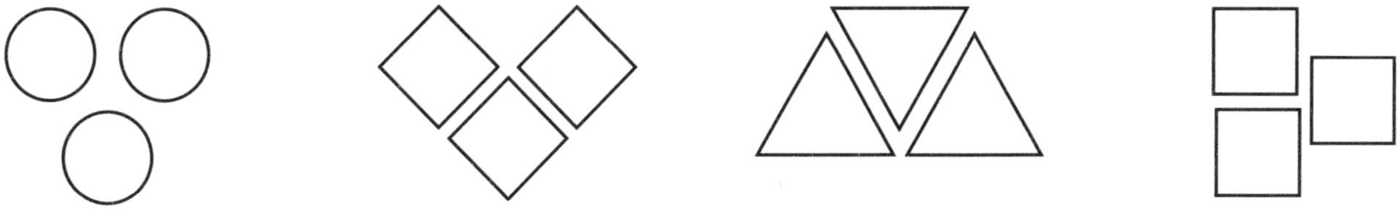

Write a fraction for the shaded part of each group.

a *b* *c* *d*

3.

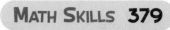

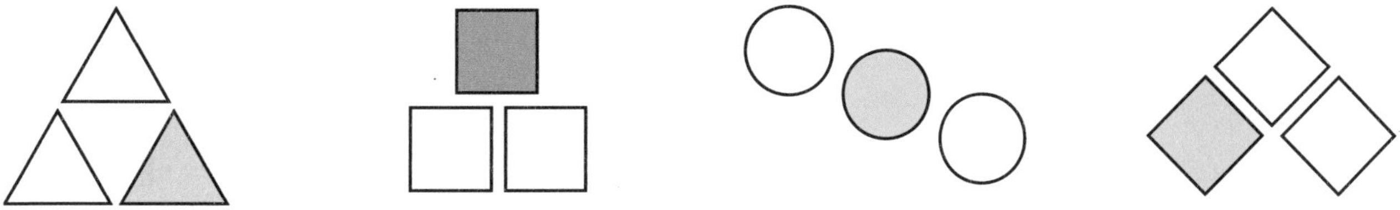

________ ________ ________ ________

$\frac{2}{3}$: Parts of a Whole

The fraction $\frac{2}{3}$ shows what part of the rectangle is shaded blue and what part of the circle is shaded blue.

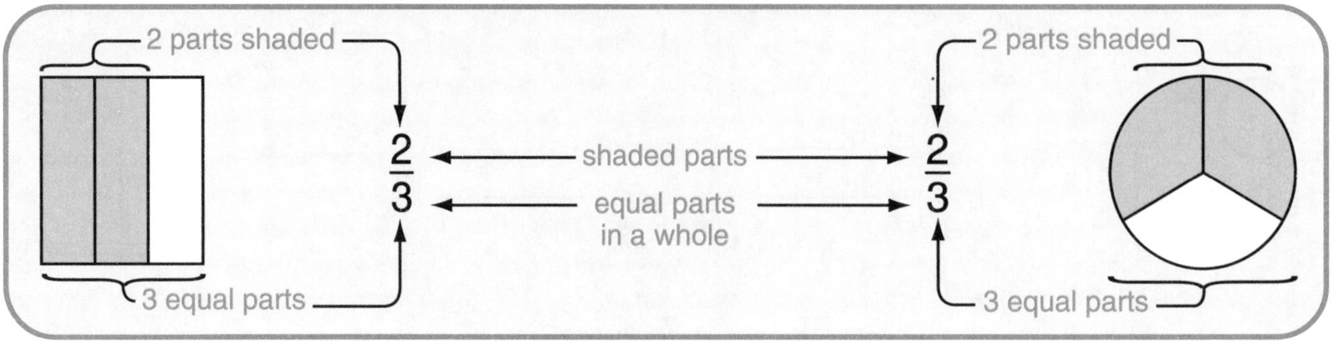

Circle the groups that show $\frac{2}{3}$ shaded.

1.

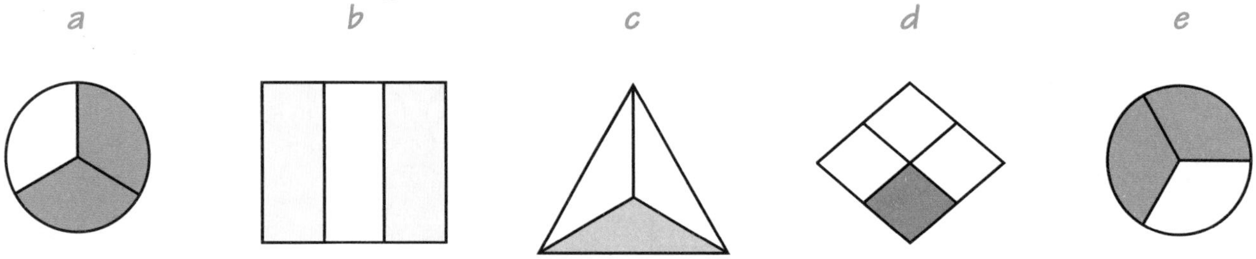

Shade $\frac{2}{3}$ of each figure.

2.

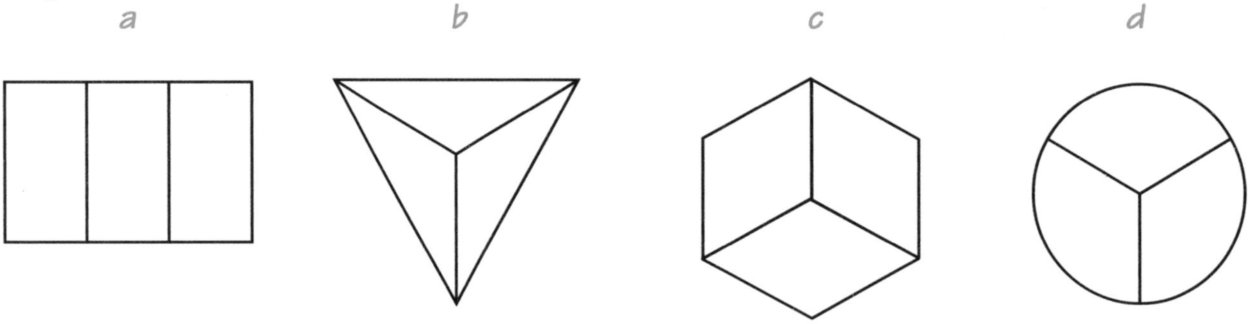

Write a fraction for the shaded part.

3.

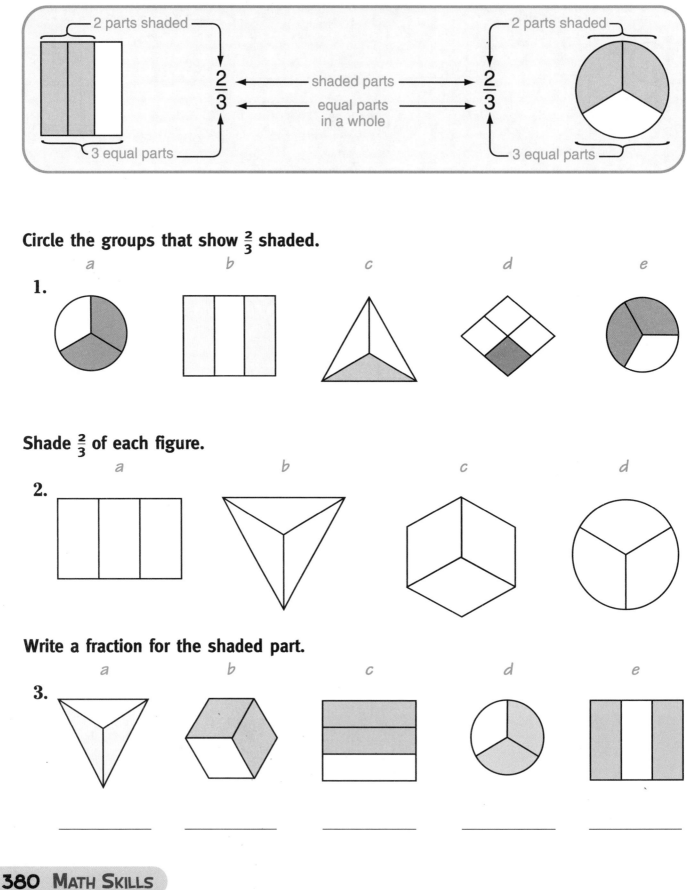

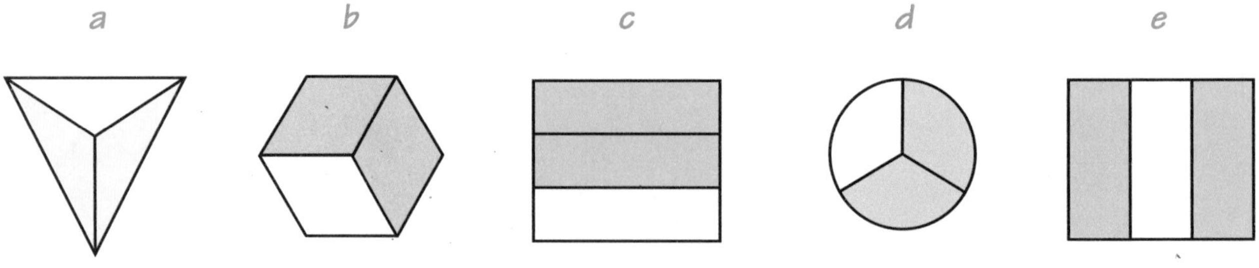

______ ______ ______ ______ ______

$\frac{2}{3}$: Parts of a Group

The fraction $\frac{2}{3}$ shows what part of the group of circles and what part of the group of squares are shaded blue.

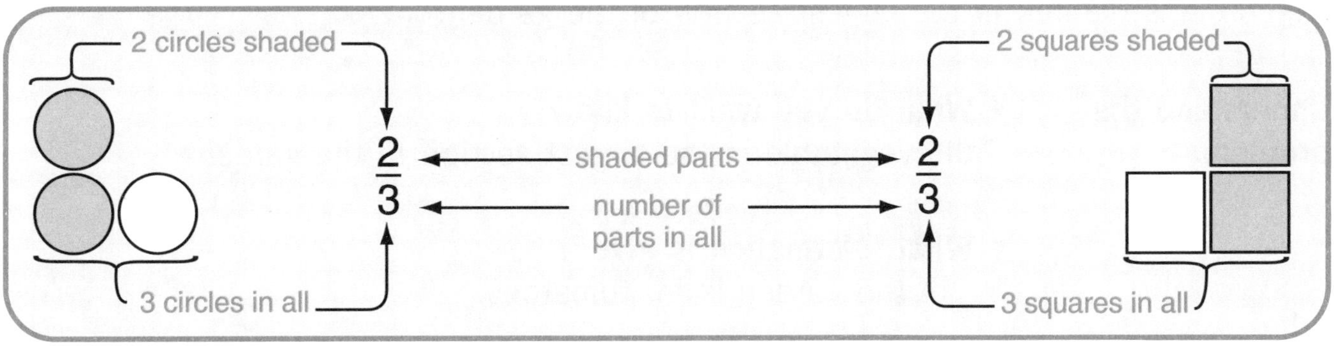

Circle the groups that show $\frac{2}{3}$ shaded.

a *b* *c* *d*

1.

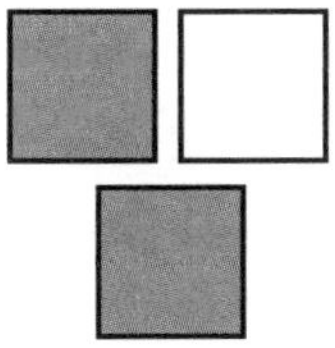
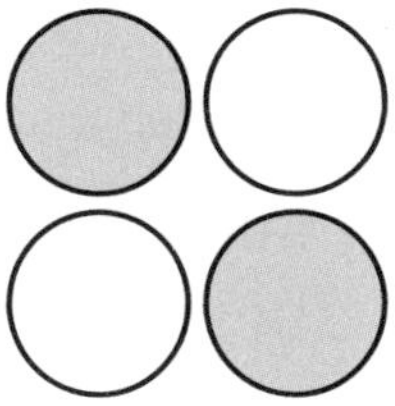

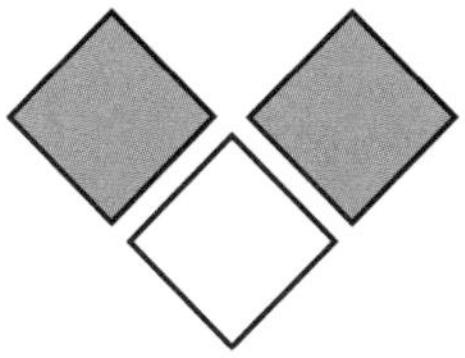

Shade $\frac{2}{3}$ of each group.

a *b* *c* *d*

2.

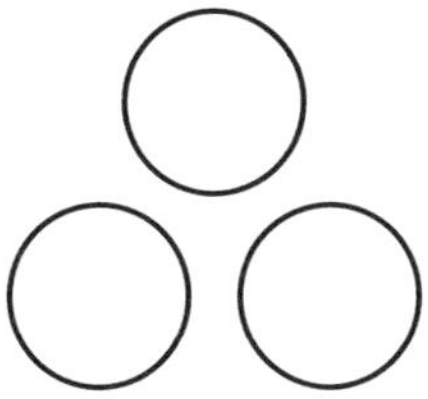
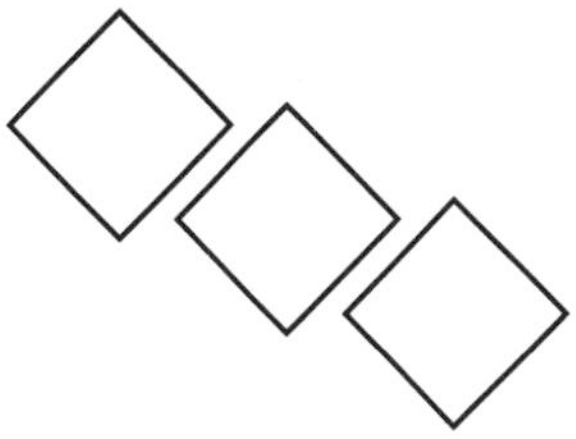
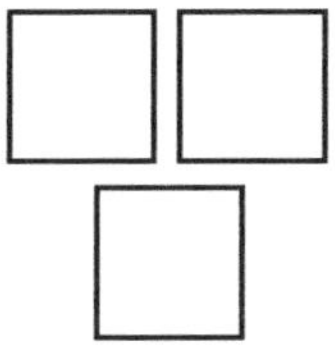

Write a fraction for the shaded part of each group.

a *b* *c* *d*

3.

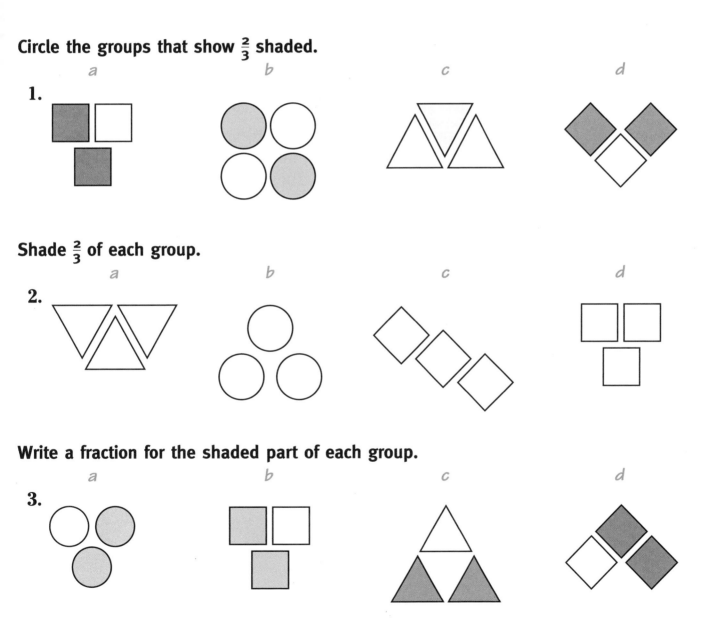

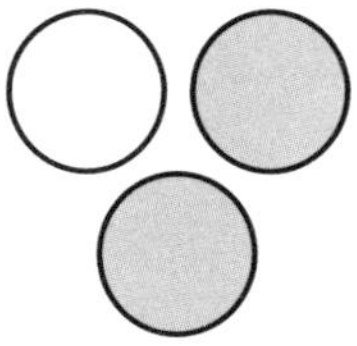
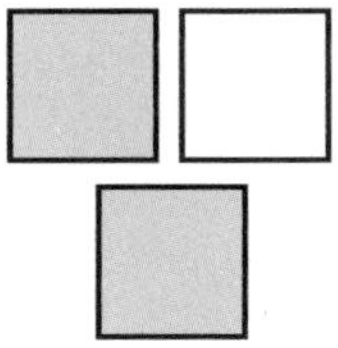
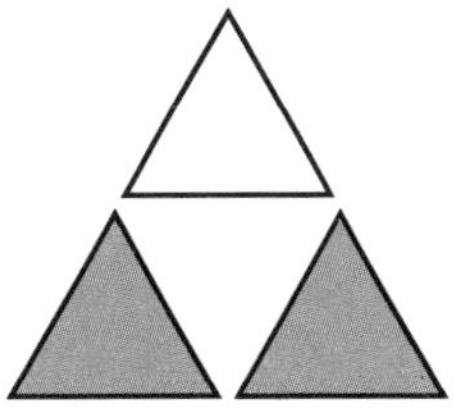
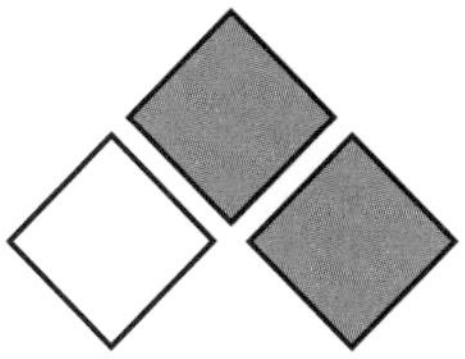

Problem-Solving Method: Make a Drawing

Mr. Lee planted a square vegetable garden. He used $\frac{1}{2}$ of the garden for tomatoes. Then he planted peppers in $\frac{1}{4}$ of the garden and carrots in $\frac{1}{4}$ of the garden. Which vegetable is planted in the largest section of the garden?

Understand the problem.

- **What do you want to know?**
  the vegetable in the largest section of the garden

- **What information is given?**
  $\frac{1}{2}$ of the garden is for tomatoes.
  $\frac{1}{4}$ of the garden is for peppers.
  $\frac{1}{4}$ of the garden is for carrots.

Plan how to solve it.

- **What method can you use?**
  You can draw the garden and compare the sections.

Solve it.

- **How can you use this method to solve the problem?**
  Draw a square for the garden. Divide it into four sections. Label two of these "Tomatoes" to show $\frac{1}{2}$ of the garden. Then label one section "Peppers" and one section "Carrots."

Carrots

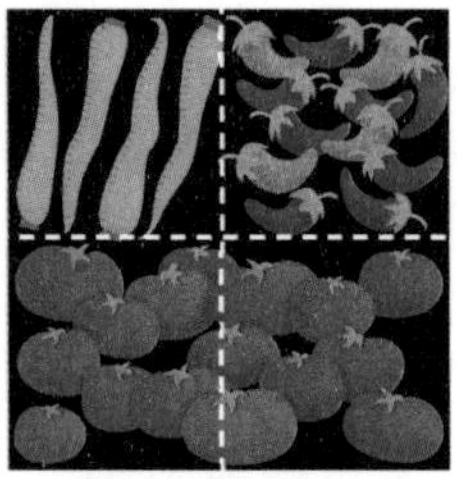

Peppers

Tomatoes

- **What is the answer?**
  Tomatoes have the largest section of the garden.

Look back and check your answer.

- **Is your answer reasonable?**
  You can check by comparing fraction strips.

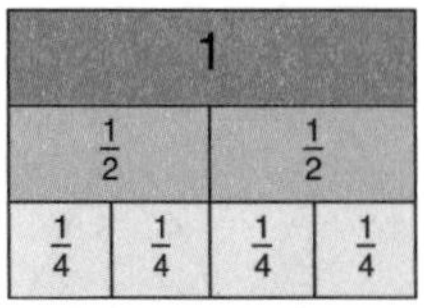

The strips show that $\frac{1}{2}$ is larger than $\frac{1}{4}$.
The answer is reasonable.

Make a drawing to solve each problem.

1. Darrel made two pies for the bake sale. He sold $\frac{1}{3}$ of the apple pie. He sold $\frac{2}{3}$ of the blueberry pie. Which pie did he sell more of?

Answer: ______________________

2. At swim practice, Brent swam $\frac{1}{2}$ mile. Shaneeka swam $\frac{3}{4}$ mile. Who swam farther?

Answer: ______________________

3. Jerry and Paco began riding their bikes at the same time from the same place. After 20 minutes, Jerry had ridden 3 miles to the right. Paco had ridden 4 miles to the left. How far apart were the two boys?

Answer: __________________ miles

4. Rudy and Alicia each brought \$4 to the snack bar. Rudy spent $\frac{1}{2}$ of his money on a hot dog. Alicia spent $\frac{1}{4}$ of her money on a drink. How much money do they each have left?

Rudy \$ ______________________

Alicia \$ ______________________

Naming a Whole

The fractions $\frac{2}{2}$, $\frac{3}{3}$, and $\frac{4}{4}$ all name a whole.

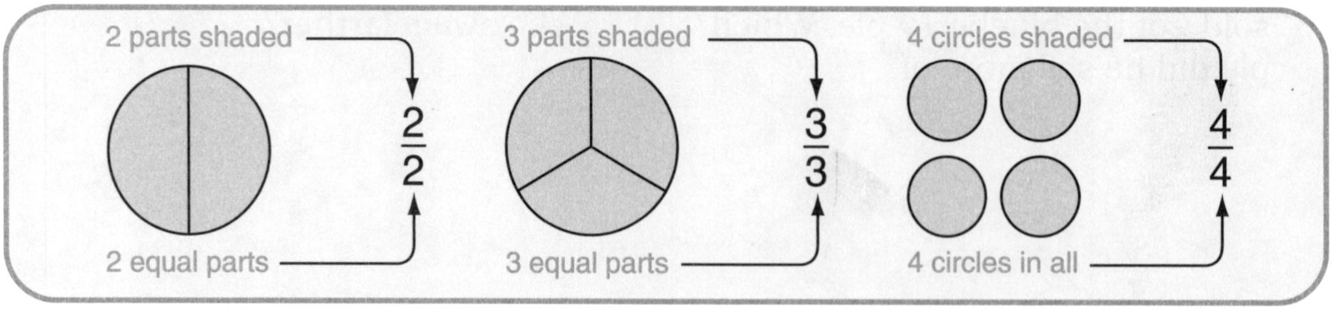

Circle the figures that show $\frac{2}{2}$, $\frac{3}{3}$, or $\frac{4}{4}$ shaded.

a b c d e

1.

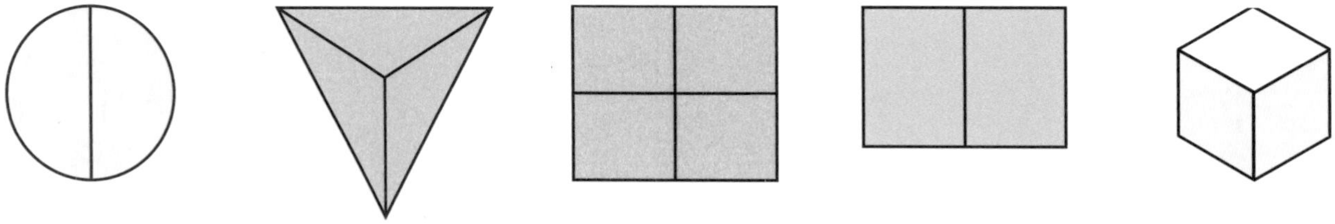

Shade $\frac{2}{2}$, $\frac{3}{3}$, or $\frac{4}{4}$ of each figure.

a b c d

2.

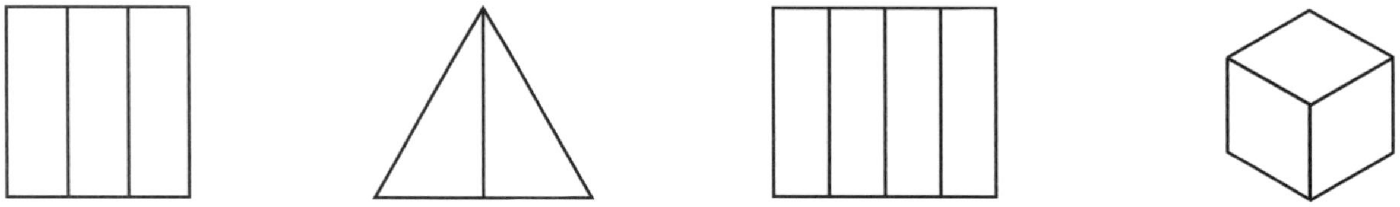

3.

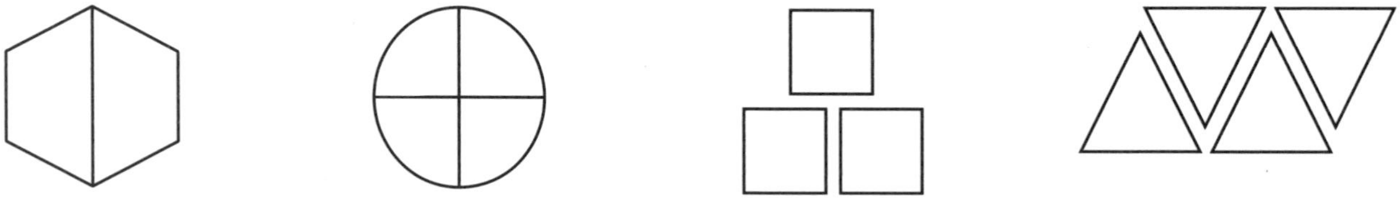

Write a fraction for the shaded part.

a b c d e

4.

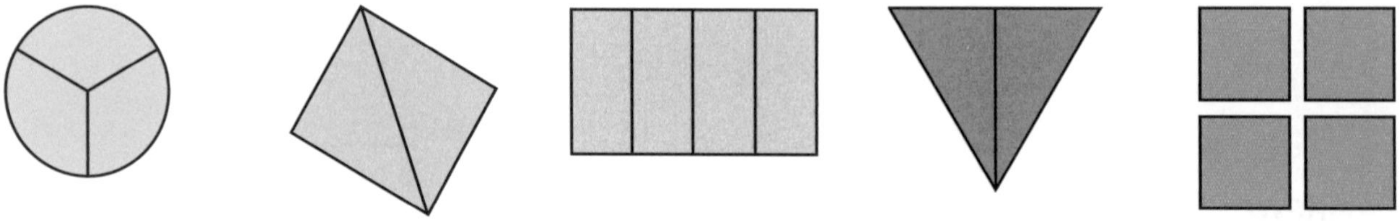

_______ _______ _______ _______ _______

Unit 7 Review

Shade the figure to show the fraction.

a b c d

1.

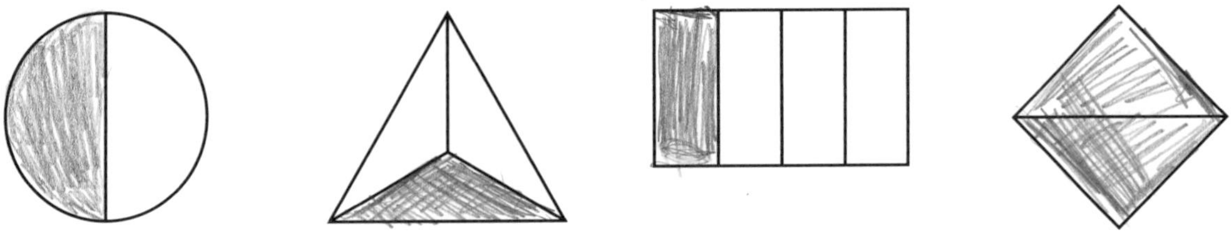

$\frac{1}{2}$ $\frac{1}{3}$ $\frac{1}{4}$ $\frac{2}{2}$

2.

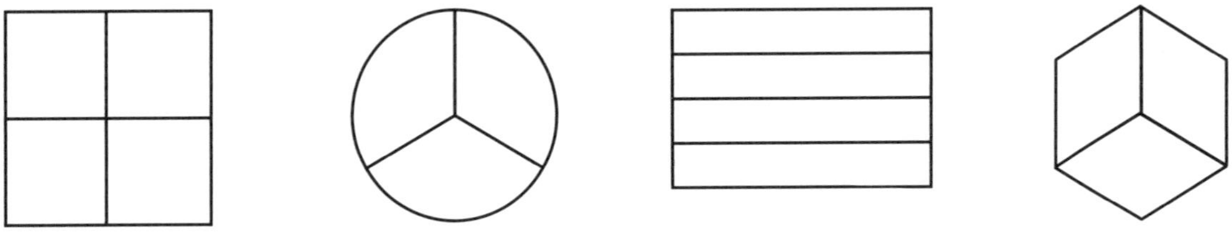

$\frac{3}{4}$ $\frac{2}{3}$ $\frac{4}{4}$ $\frac{3}{3}$

Write a fraction for the shaded part.

a b c d e

3.

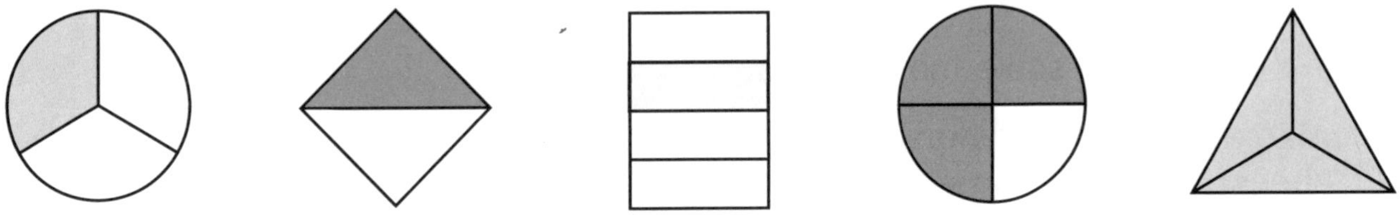

______ ______ ______ ______ ______

4.

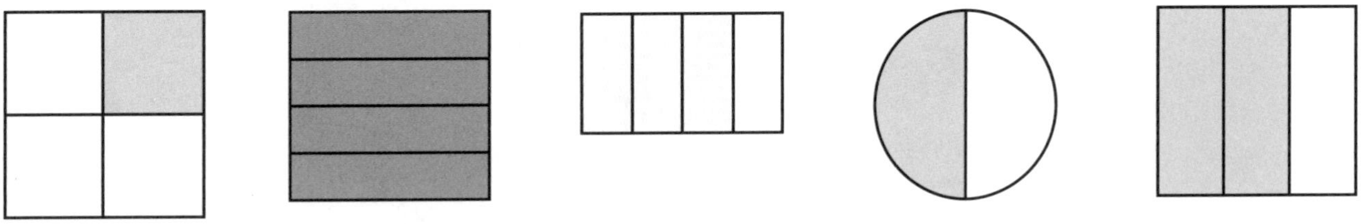

______ ______ ______ ______ ______

5.

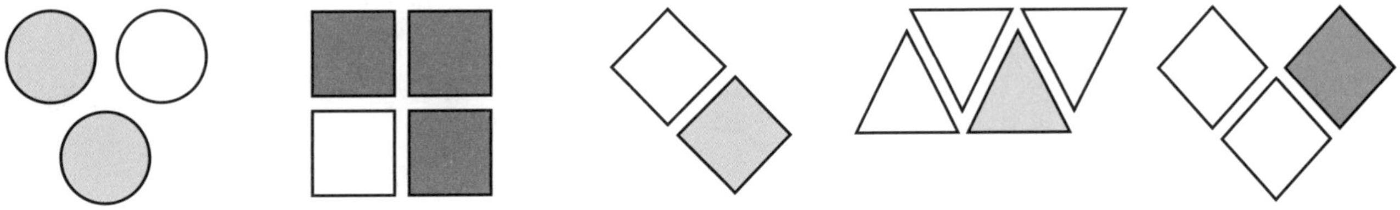

______ ______ ______ ______ ______

Unit 7 Review

Make an organized list to solve each problem.

6. Ellen is buying ribbon for a dress. She can choose either silk or cotton. The ribbon comes in two sizes, $\frac{1}{4}$ inch wide or $\frac{1}{3}$ inch wide. How many different ribbon choices does Ellen have?

_______________ choices

7. Carmen wants to make a picture. She can choose crayon, paint, chalk, or ink. She can use paper or cardboard. How many different ways can she make the picture?

_______________ ways

Make a drawing to solve the problem.

8. Aiko and his friends ordered a cheese pizza and a pepperoni pizza. They ate $\frac{1}{4}$ of the cheese and $\frac{1}{2}$ of the pepperoni. Which pizza did they eat more of?

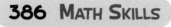

_______________ pizza

Language Arts

Nouns

A **noun** is a word that names a person, place, or thing.
Examples:

person = boy **place** = store **thing** = book

DIRECTIONS **Complete each sentence with a noun from the box.**

musician	forest	girl	stage	tree	flute

1. The sound of a ____________ (thing) floated through the theater.

2. Another ____________ (person) began to play a horn.

3. Then, a boy appeared on the ____________ (place).

4. The boy hid behind a tall ____________ (thing).

5. A young ____________ (person) in a red dress walked onto the stage.

6. The boy pretended he was in a ____________ (place).

DIRECTIONS **Think of a person, a place, and a thing. Write a sentence about each one on the line below.**

7. (person) ____________________

8. (place) ____________________

9. (thing) ____________________

Common Nouns and Proper Nouns

A **common noun** names any person, place, or thing. It begins with a lowercase letter.

Examples:

inventor city month

A **proper noun** names a particular person, place, or thing. Each important word of a proper noun begins with a capital letter.

Examples:

Thomas Alva Edison Seattle July

DIRECTIONS **Read the paragraph below. Circle the common nouns. Underline the proper nouns.**

Maren wants to join the Kona Kai Swim Team, but she has a problem. She goes to Collins School on Miller Avenue. The school is three miles from the pool. That is too far for her to walk. Besides, she has to feed her dog after school. The Kona Express Bus goes only halfway to the pool. Her brother Leif has a car, but he works at the Burger Pit Restaurant until late in the evening. He can't drive her to practice.

DIRECTIONS **Think of a common noun and a proper noun. Write a sentence about each one on the lines below.**

(common noun) ____

(proper noun) ____

Common Nouns and Proper Nouns, page 2

Remember that a common noun names any person, place, or thing. It begins with a lowercase letter.
A proper noun names a particular person, place, or thing. Each important word of a proper noun begins with a capital letter.

DIRECTIONS **Read the sentences below. Circle the common nouns. Underline the proper nouns.**

1. Levi Hutchins was a clockmaker.
2. This young person lived in Concord, New Hampshire.
3. Hutchins always started to work early.
4. This fellow was awake before the sun came up.
5. Some people don't like to get up when the sky is dark.
6. The man had an idea for a new clock.
7. This machine would have a bell in it.
8. The owner would set the piece for a certain time.
9. A chime would ring then.
10. What invention did Hutchins create?

Common Nouns and Proper Nouns, page 3

DIRECTIONS **Read the paragraph below. Find all the common nouns and proper nouns. List them on the chart where they belong.**

Serena and Riane were very good musicians. They practiced at school and at home. One day they were invited to play at the Vallco Concert Hall. Mr. Williams was the leader of the Shadygrove Band. He thought that they had talent. He asked them to join his group.

	PROPER NOUNS	
Person	Place	Thing

	COMMON NOUNS	
Person	Place	Thing

Singular and Plural Nouns

A **singular noun** names one person, one place, or one thing.
Examples: friend house apple
A **plural noun** names more than one person, place, or thing.
Make most nouns plural by adding *s*.
Examples: friends houses apples

DIRECTIONS **Read the sentences below. Circle the singular nouns. Underline the plural nouns.**

1. Badgers are skillful diggers.

2. A badger can dig a deep hole very quickly.

3. This mammal uses its front claws to dig.

4. A frightened animal might dig to get away from an enemy.

5. The mole also digs with powerful paws.

6. Its front legs work like shovels that scoop.

7. It digs long tunnels under bushes and trees.

8. This creature is very nearly blind.

9. This furry digger does not need to see well in its dark world.

10. Both badgers and moles are very good diggers.

Singular and Plural Nouns, page 2

Remember to use a **singular noun** to name one person, one place, or one thing. Use a **plural noun** to name more than one person, place, or thing. Add *s* to most singular nouns to form the plural.

DIRECTIONS **Write the plural form of the noun in ( ) to finish each sentence.**

1. You can see many ________________ on this farm.
(animal)

2. The ________________ take good care of them.
(farmer)

3. The ________________ are clucking loudly.
(chicken)

4. There are ________________ on the little lake.
(duck)

5. You may see a few ________________ there, too.
(swan)

6. In the fields you will see ________________.
(cow)

7. The ________________ are in the barn now.
(horse)

8. Two ________________ are following that sheep.
(lamb)

9. Beyond the fence are some noisy ________________.
(goat)

10. Five big ________________ are rolling in the mud.
(pig)

11. The little ________________ are just watching.
(piglet)

Plural Nouns with *es*

Add *es* to form the plural of a noun ending with *s*, *x*, *ch*, or *sh*.
Examples:

bus	buses	box	boxes
branch	branches	brush	brushes

DIRECTIONS **Write the plural form of each noun.**

1. glass ____________________

2. dish ____________________

3. fox ____________________

4. patch ____________________

5. match ____________________

6. dress ____________________

7. lunch ____________________

8. tax ____________________

9. class ____________________

10. bush ____________________

DIRECTIONS **Choose five of the plural nouns you wrote. Write your own sentences using those nouns on the lines.**

11. ____

12. ____

13. ____

14. ____

15. ____

Plural Nouns with *ies*

If a noun ends in a consonant and *y*, change the *y* to *i* and add *es* to form the plural.

Examples:

buddy buddies jelly jellies

DIRECTIONS **Write the plural form of the noun in ( ) to finish each sentence.**

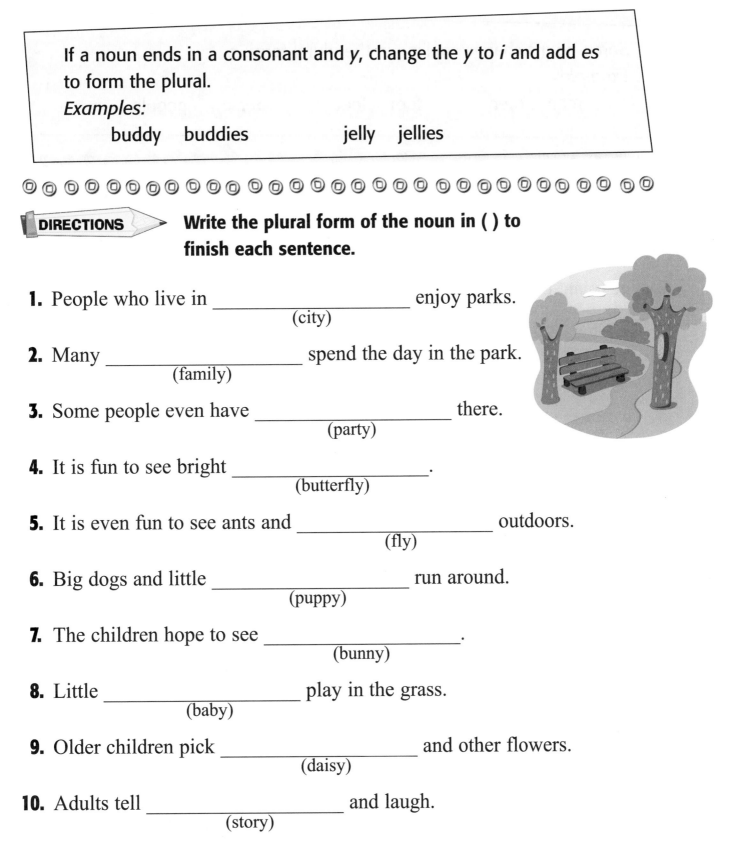

1. People who live in ______________ (city) enjoy parks.

2. Many ______________ (family) spend the day in the park.

3. Some people even have ______________ (party) there.

4. It is fun to see bright ______________ (butterfly).

5. It is even fun to see ants and ______________ (fly) outdoors.

6. Big dogs and little ______________ (puppy) run around.

7. The children hope to see ______________ (bunny).

8. Little ______________ (baby) play in the grass.

9. Older children pick ______________ (daisy) and other flowers.

10. Adults tell ______________ (story) and laugh.

Special Plural Nouns

Some nouns change spelling in the plural form.
Examples:

man men   foot feet   person people

DIRECTIONS **Read each sentence. Circle the noun in ( ) that fits best.**

1. Keisha has gone to Dr. Chun since she was a small (child, children).
2. The (man, men) who lives next door goes to Dr. Chun, too.
3. Dr. Chun is a fine dentist and a friendly (woman, women).
4. She has toys, including a wind-up (goose, geese), in her office.
5. Two of the toys are dancing (mouse, mice).
6. A big stuffed (ox, oxen) sits on a chair.
7. A cartoon about a little country (mouse, mice) hangs on the wall.
8. Two plastic (goose, geese) stand in the corner.
9. Many (child, children) like Dr. Chun.
10. She keeps her patients happy and their (tooth, teeth) healthy.

Singular Possessive Nouns

A **singular possessive noun** shows ownership by one person or thing. Add an apostrophe (') and *s* to most singular nouns to show possession.

Examples:

Bob's dog   the dog's tail

DIRECTIONS **Change each sentence. Replace the underlined words with a possessive noun. Write the new sentence.**

1. The kite <u>that belongs to Hope</u> is bright yellow.

____

2. The tail <u>of the kite</u> is much too long.

____

3. It will get stuck in the branches <u>of that tree</u>.

____

4. The parents <u>of the girl</u> have kites, too.

____

5. The kite <u>that belongs to her mother</u> looks like a dragon.

____

6. The kite <u>that belongs to her dad</u> is shaped like a box.

____

7. Hope wants to fly the kite that <u>belongs to her friend</u>.

____

8. The fields <u>of the park</u> made flying kites fun.

____

Plural Possessive Nouns

A **plural possessive noun** shows ownership by more than one person or thing. To form most plural possessive nouns, add an apostrophe (') to the end of a plural noun.

Examples:

cars' engines   grandparents' ranch   children's lunches

DIRECTIONS **Read the paragraph below. Circle the plural nouns that show ownership.**

The chickens' clucking woke Jason. In the distance, he heard a fox's high bark. Jason and his grandfather checked all the animals' pens. By the chicken coop, they saw several foxes' paw prints. Luckily, none of the chickens had been harmed.

DIRECTIONS **Write the possessive form of each plural noun shown in ( ) below.**

1. Oscar followed the ______________ (squirrels) footprints to the pond.

2. He found his four ______________ (brothers) shoes by the pond.

3. The ______________ (dogs) loud barks made him look up into the trees.

4. His brothers were sitting high up on the ______________ (trees) limbs.

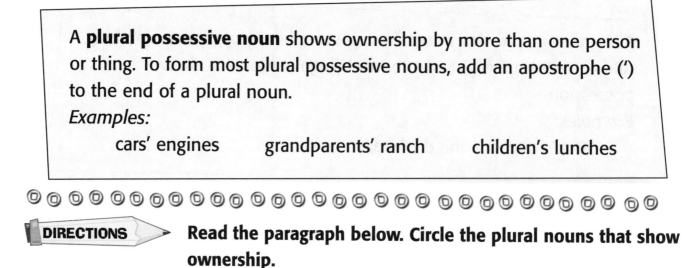

Singular and Plural Possessive Nouns

Remember that a possessive noun shows ownership.
Add an apostrophe (') and *s* to most singular nouns to show possession.
To form most plural possessive nouns, add an apostrophe (') to the end of a plural noun.

DIRECTIONS **Underline the possessive noun in each sentence. On the line, write whether it is singular or plural.**

1. The table's leg was loose. ____________________
2. The dog's wagging tail thumped against the table. ____________________
3. The families' homemade cookies fell to the ground. ____________________
4. The picnickers' dessert was ruined! ____________________
5. The ripe blackberries' smell was sweet. ____________________
6. Danny borrowed Adam's bowl. ____________________
7. The children filled their grandparents' buckets with berries. ____________________
8. The bike's tire was flat. ____________________

Pronouns

A **pronoun** is a word that takes the place of one or more nouns.

Examples:

Little Elk had a gift for painting.
He had a gift for painting.
He takes the place of *Little Elk*.

The warriors admired Little Elk.
They admired Little Elk.
They takes the place of *the warriors*.

DIRECTIONS **Read each pair of sentences. Circle the pronoun in the second sentence. Write which word or words from the first sentence it replaces.**

1. Little Elk loved to look at clouds.
   He felt joy from studying the sky.

   ____

2. Sometimes Little Elk's mother worried. She knew Little Elk was different.

   ____

3. One day Little Elk found some soil. He mixed the soil with rain water.

   ____

4. Little Elk later made a blue paint. It was the color of the sky.

   ____

Singular Pronouns

A **singular pronoun** replaces a singular noun. The words *I*, *me*, *you*, *he*, *she*, *him*, *her*, and *it* are singular pronouns. Always capitalize the pronoun *I*.

Examples:

Jorge, have *you* ever seen picture writing?
You stands for *Jorge*.

I learned about picture writing from my grandfather.
I replaces the speaker's name.

He studied *it* in Arizona.
He stands for *my grandfather*. *It* replaces *picture writing*.

DIRECTIONS **Read each pair of sentences. Write the singular pronoun that fits with the meaning of the second sentence.**

1. Ned was going to a soccer match. ____________________ wore a jacket.

2. Ned's mom had been reading. She had brought a newspaper with ____________________.

3. Ned got on the train. Ned's mom followed __________________.

4. Ned's mom studied a map. ____________________ told Ned they would get off at the next stop.

5. A moment later, the train slowed down. _______ was at the station.

6. Ned held tight as the train stopped. Soon, ____________________ got off the train.

Plural Pronouns

A **plural pronoun** replaces a plural noun. The words *we*, *you*, *they*, *us*, and *them* are plural pronouns.

Examples:

People use colors in many ways.
They use colors in many ways.
They replaces *people*.

Artists use colors in paintings.
Artists use *them* in paintings.
Them replaces *colors*.

DIRECTIONS **Revise each sentence. Replace each word or group of words in ( ) with a plural pronoun.**

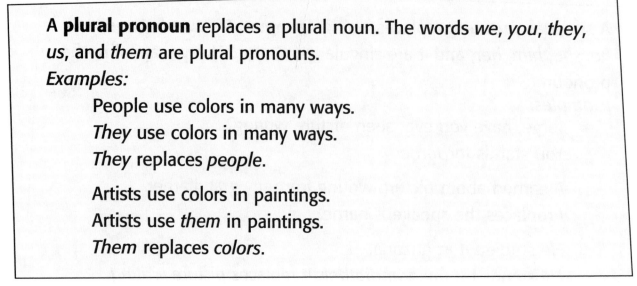

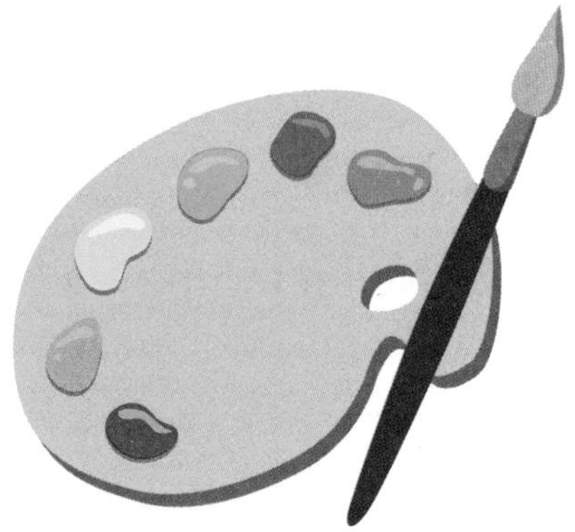

1. (My dad and I) ____________________ like the work of early American artists.

2. My dad knows a lot about (many early American artists) ____________________.

3. (Early American painters) ____________________ sometimes painted on wooden boards.

4. The artists made (paints) ____________________ from plants and rocks.

5. (A master and a student) ____________________ often worked together.

6. Going to museums is fun for (my dad and me) ____________________.

Singular and Plural Pronouns

Remember, a singular pronoun replaces a singular noun. The words *I, me, you, he, she, him, her,* and *it* are singular pronouns. Always capitalize the pronoun *I*.

A plural pronoun replaces a plural noun. The words *we, you, they, us,* and *them* are plural pronouns.

DIRECTIONS **Read each pair of sentences. Write the pronoun that fits best in the second sentence of each pair. Use the clue in ( ) to help you.**

1. Piñatas are popular in Mexico.

____________________ are hollow toys made from paper.
(plural)

2. Piñatas come in many shapes.

Often ____________________ are shaped like animals.
(plural)

3. The piñata hangs from the ceiling.

____________________ contains gifts and treats.
(singular)

4. Anita tries to hit the piñata with a stick.

____________________ has been blindfolded.
(singular)

5. The children cheer when the piñata breaks.

____________________ rush to collect the prizes.
(plural)

Subject Pronouns

A **subject pronoun** takes the place of one or more nouns in the subject of a sentence. The words *I*, *you*, *he*, *she*, *it*, *we*, and *they* are subject pronouns.

Examples:

They brought a snake to school.

I do not like snakes.

You can hold the snake.

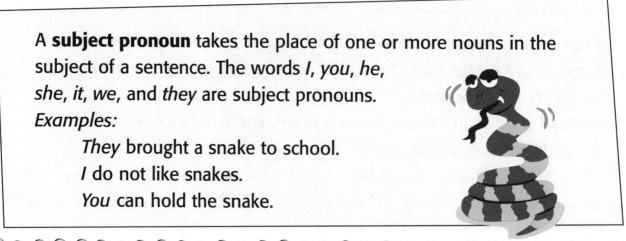

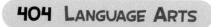

DIRECTIONS **Read the paragraph below. Look at the words in dark letters. Circle the ones that are singular subject pronouns. Underline the one that is a plural subject pronoun.**

My name is Meredyth. **I** love to paint. My mother helped me set up an easel. **She** hangs my pictures around the house. "**They** brighten up the walls," Mom says. My father thinks that **I** am a good artist, too. "**You** will be famous someday," Dad says. **He** is my biggest fan.

DIRECTIONS **Write each pronoun you circled or underlined in the chart below. Next to it, write the word or words the pronoun replaces.**

Subject Pronoun	Word or Words It Replaces

Object Pronouns

An **object pronoun** follows an action verb, such as *see* or *tell*, or a word such as *about, at, for, from, near, of, to,* or *with*.
The words *me, you, him, her, it, us,* and *them* are object pronouns.
Examples:

Sam took *it* home.
Mom had a surprise for *me*.
My friend saw *you*.

DIRECTIONS **Complete this story. Write an object pronoun that replaces the underlined word or words.**

Mom left my brother and me at home. She trusted ____________________. Our mother went to see her parents. She had some presents for ____________________. Mom waved from the car window. We stood on the porch and waved back to ____________________. My older brother was in charge. I had to listen to ____________________.

After a while, we heard a knock on the door. I asked my brother to open ____________________.

"I hope that's not your silly friends," my brother said. "I don't want to see ____________________ on our porch."

I knew my brother wouldn't really be mad. So I asked ____________________ again to open the door. My friends were there. ____________________ were wearing big wolf masks. For just a minute, my brother was afraid of ____________________.

I and *Me*

Use the word *I* as a subject pronoun.
Use the word *me* as an object pronoun.
Examples:
I could not find my lunch.
My brother helped *me*.

DIRECTIONS **Finish each sentence. Write the correct word or words in ( ).**

1. ______________________ play baseball every day.
(My friends and me, My friends and I)

2. Sometimes students from other schools play with ______________.
(I, me)

3. ______________________ take turns pitching.
(Nell and me, Nell and I)

4. Usually, ______________________ are the first batters up.
(Casey and me, Casey and I)

5. My parents like to practice with ______________.
(I, me)

6. Mom pitches the ball to ______________.
(I, me)

7. Then ______________ hit it as hard as I can.
(I, me)

8. Dad always runs after the ball for ______________.
(I, me)

9. He tosses the ball back to ______________________.
(Mom and me, Mom and I)

10. ______________________ have fun playing baseball.
(My parents and me, My parents and I)

Possessive Pronouns

A **possessive pronoun** shows ownership. Some possessive pronouns are *my, your, his, her, its, our*, and *their*.

Examples:

Chipper is *my* horse.

He lives in *our* barn.

Where is *your* pet?

DIRECTIONS **Read each sentence. Circle the possessive pronoun.**

1. Tonya shouted to her friends.
2. "Please come to our apartment this afternoon," she said.
3. Tonya explained, "My family is having a party."
4. Victor asked, "Will your grandfather be there?"
5. "Yes," said Tonya, "and he's bringing two of his brothers."
6. "Mom and Dad are having the party for their anniversary," she said.
7. She went on, "I get to wear my new red shoes."
8. "Even the dog will be wearing its shiny new collar," Tonya said.

DIRECTIONS **Finish each sentence. Write a possessive pronoun that makes sense.**

9. Victor said to Tonya, "I like seeing ____________________ grandfather."
10. Victor explained, "____________________ grandparents live far away, and I hardly ever see them."
11. Tonya smiled and nodded ____________________ head.

Contractions with Pronouns

A **contraction** is a short way of writing two words together. Some of the letters are left out. An apostrophe (') takes the place of the missing letters.

Form some contractions by joining pronouns and verbs.

Examples:

I + am = *I'm*   you + are = *you're*   she + is = *she's*

DIRECTIONS **Write each sentence. Replace the underlined words with a contraction.**

1. <u>It is</u> dark and cold outside.

____

2. <u>You are</u> in a hurry.

____

3. You hear noises, but <u>they are</u> far away.

____

4. Now <u>they have</u> become louder.

____

5. Something is behind you, and <u>it is</u> getting closer.

____

6. "<u>I will</u> just go a little faster," you think.

____

7. Now <u>you are</u> almost running.

____

8. <u>You will</u> be home in just a few minutes.

____

Adjectives

An **adjective** is a word that describes a noun. Adjectives can tell how many, what color, or what size or shape. They can also describe how something feels, sounds, tastes, or smells.
Use exact adjectives to paint clear word pictures.

Examples:

Three birds were in the nest.
The *red* ball was in a *small* box.
The *smooth* soap has a *sweet* smell.

DIRECTIONS **Write the adjective that describes each underlined noun.**

1. The Vikings lived in small <u>villages</u>. ______________________
2. Many <u>houses</u> were built around a main house. ______________________
3. The main <u>building</u> was like a barn. ______________________
4. The roof was held up by heavy <u>beams</u>. ______________________
5. The walls were made of split <u>trunks</u> of trees. ______________________
6. These trunks were set in a double <u>layer</u>. ______________________
7. One end of the central <u>house</u> was for people. ______________________
8. The other <u>half</u> of the building was for cattle. ______________________
9. A wooden <u>screen</u> divided the house. ______________________
10. In the middle of the hall was a big <u>fire</u>. ______________________

Adjectives That Tell How Many

Remember that some adjectives tell how many.
Some adjectives that tell how many do not tell an exact number.
Examples:

A horse runs on *four* legs.
That horse has been in *many* shows.

DIRECTIONS **Read each sentence. Write the adjective that tells how many.**

1. Two monkeys were in the room. ____________________
2. Several boxes were also in the room. ____________________
3. Some bananas were hanging from the ceiling. ____________________
4. After a few hours, the monkeys piled up the boxes. ____________________
5. They were able to reach the eight bananas. ____________________

DIRECTIONS **Write an exact number word to complete each sentence. Then, write the sentence again, using an adjective that does not tell an exact number.**

6. Anna wanted ____________________ pets.

____

7. She asked for ____________________ monkeys.

____

8. We saw ____________________ monkeys at the zoo.

____

Adjectives That Tell What Kind

Remember that some adjectives tell what kind.
They can describe size, shape, or color. They can help you know how something looks, sounds, feels, tastes, or smells.

Examples:

A *tall* woman stands on the corner.
She wears a *red* hat.
This *quiet* detective is Madame Girard.
Tiny cameras are hidden in her hat.

DIRECTIONS **In each sentence, circle the adjective that tells what kind. Write the noun it describes.**

1. Madame Girard also uses tiny computers. ____________________

2. She keeps them in her secret pouch. ____________________

3. She takes careful notes on her cases. ____________________

4. Notes help her solve difficult mysteries. ____________________

5. She once found lost diamonds. ____________________

6. Yesterday she found Lulu's famous parrot. ____________________

7. Today Madame Girard lost an important key. ____________________

8. Lulu helped her embarrassed friend find it. ____________________

DIRECTIONS **Write a sentence using each adjective below.**

9. (green) ______________________________

10. (huge) ______________________________

Predicate Adjectives

An adjective is a word that describes a noun. A **predicate adjective** follows a verb such as *is*, *seems*, or *looks*.

Examples:

That whale is *huge*.

That lion looks *scary*.

DIRECTIONS **Circle the adjective in each sentence. Tell which noun it describes.**

1. Yosemite Park is beautiful. ______________________________
2. The views there are incredible! __________________________
3. This mountain is difficult to climb. ______________________
4. This tree seems taller than the other one. _______________
5. The sky was blue. ____
6. From an airplane, houses look tiny. _______________________
7. The man feels sick. _______________________________________
8. That dog was mean. _______________________________________
9. The flower smelled sweet. __________________________________
10. The cat feels soft. ____

Articles

The words *a*, *an*, and *the* are called **articles**.
Use *a* before a word that begins with a consonant sound.
Use *an* before a word that begins with a vowel sound.
Use *the* before a word that begins with a consonant or a vowel.
Examples:

Have you ever seen *an* owl?
The owl is *a* nocturnal animal.

DIRECTIONS **Read the following paragraph. Circle the articles.**

Last week my mother and I saw an owl in the trees behind our house. It was evening, and the air was just beginning to turn cool. We were walking down a gravel path from the shed to our house. Suddenly, we heard a strange sound. My mother froze, her eyes on an old pine tree. I followed her eyes and caught a glimpse of the owl as it took off.

DIRECTIONS **Complete each sentence by circling the correct article in ( ).**

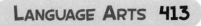

1. My teacher assigned (a / an) report about wild animals.
2. I'm going to write about (a / an) bald eagle.
3. I once saw (a / an) eagle when I was camping with my family.
4. My mother says that bald eagles are (a / an) endangered species.
5. (A / An) cat next door likes to watch birds.

Adjectives That Compare: *er*, *est*

Add *er* to most short adjectives to compare two nouns or pronouns.
Add *est* to most short adjectives to compare more than two nouns or pronouns.
Change the *y* to *i* before adding *er* or *est* to adjectives that end in a consonant and *y*.

Examples:

This tree is *greener* than that one.
The whale is the *largest* of all animals.
She was the *happiest* student in class.

DIRECTIONS **Choose the correct form of the adjective in ( ) to complete each sentence. Write the adjective on the line.**

1. Town Mouse was ______________________ than his cousin.
(richer, richest)

2. One day he visited Country Mouse in the ______________________
(poorer, poorest)
village of the land.

3. Town Mouse was ______________________ than his cousin,
(younger, youngest)
but he was used to much better cooking.

4. Town Mouse said, "I want you to visit my house. It's
______________________ than yours."
(fancier, fanciest)

5. Town Mouse said, "I'm ______________________ than a bear after a
(hungrier, hungriest)
long winter!"

6. The two mice went into the ______________________ dining room
(grander, grandest)
Country Mouse had ever seen.

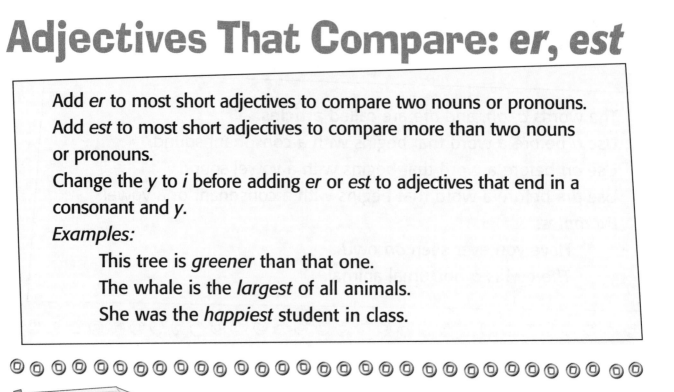

Adjectives That Compare: *more, most*

Use *more* with some adjectives to compare two nouns or pronouns. Use *most* with some adjectives to compare more than two nouns or pronouns.

Examples:

Parrots are *more talkative* than parakeets.

I am the *most athletic* of everyone in my family.

DIRECTIONS **Write *more* or *most* to complete each sentence.**

1. Diving may be the ______________________ difficult of all sports.
2. It is ______________________ interesting to watch than golf.
3. A diver hits the water in the ______________________ graceful way possible.
4. A high dive is ______________________ dangerous than a low one.
5. I saw the ______________________ amazing dive at a meet.

6. That was the ______________________ skillful dive I have ever seen.
7. This year's swimming meet was ______________________ exciting than last year's.
8. The winner was perhaps the ______________________ powerful swimmer I have ever seen.
9. I am ______________________ skilled at diving than my sister.
10. He is the ______________________ talented diver I know.

More about Adjectives That Compare

Adjectives can describe by comparing people, animals, places, or things. Add *er* to adjectives to compare two things, or use the word *more*. Add *est* to adjectives to compare more than two things, or use the word *most*.

DIRECTIONS **Read the following paragraph. Underline the adjectives that make comparisons.**

I think a walk outside is more interesting than an hour of TV. I enjoy trying to spot different birds in the forest. Some birds are rarer than others. For example, owls are the most difficult birds to find. Blue jays are bolder than many birds, so they are easier to spot.

DIRECTIONS **Circle the correct form of the adjective in ( ).**

1. I think dogs are (friendlier / friendliest) than cats.
2. My dog looks (happier / happiest) than my cat when I get home.
3. Dogs are (most / more) obedient than cats.
4. On the other hand, cats are (easier / easiest) to hold in your lap than dogs are.
5. I don't like birds because they are the (noisiest / noisier) kind of pet to have.

Verbs

A **verb** is a word that shows action.
A verb is the main word in the predicate of a sentence. A verb and its subject should agree.
Examples:
Frogs *live* the first part of their lives as water animals.
They *spend* the rest of their lives as land animals.

DIRECTIONS **Circle the verb in each sentence.**

1. Tadpoles begin their lives underwater.
2. A tadpole's body changes over time.
3. Its tail grows long.
4. The back legs kick.
5. Next, the front legs develop.
6. Tadpoles breathe through gills.
7. An older tadpole loses its gills and its tail.
8. The change becomes complete.
9. A tiny frog climbs onto land.
10. The new frog appears as a land animal.

Action Verbs

An **action verb** is a word that shows action.
An action verb is the main word in the predicate of a sentence. An action verb is a word that tells what the subject of a sentence does.
Examples:

Many fruits *grow* in the United States.
My dad *eats* bananas for lunch.

DIRECTIONS **Read each sentence. Write the action verb.**

1. I peek through the curtains at the yard. ______________________
2. The snow covers the ground with a thick white blanket. ______________________
3. Eagerly I go outside. ______________________
4. I close the door quickly behind me. ______________________
5. I walk in the freezing air. ______________________
6. My feet crunch in the new snow. ______________________
7. The cold wind nips my nose. ______________________
8. I build a huge snow castle. ______________________
9. Then, I return to my warm house. ______________________
10. I remove my coat and mittens. ______________________

Main Verbs

Sometimes the predicate has two or more verbs. The **main verb** is the most important verb in a sentence.

Examples:

One type of bird has *become* an excellent swimmer.

Those penguins have *dived* many times to the ocean floor.

DIRECTIONS **Circle the main verb in each sentence.**

1. That squirrel has floated through the air!
2. It has landed safely in a tree.
3. Juan has disappeared inside the house.
4. He had passed his video camera to me.
5. We have taped some amazing animals.
6. This flying squirrel had played a starring role.
7. Have you noticed this picture?
8. The squirrel's body has changed into a glider.
9. It had soared from tree to tree.
10. We have waited for the squirrel's next flight.

Helping Verbs

A **helping verb** can work with the main verb to tell about an action. The helping verb always comes before the main verb. The words *have*, *has*, and *had* are often used as helping verbs.

Examples:

My dad *had* studied all kinds of flight.

We *have* gone on a balloon flight together.

DIRECTIONS **In each sentence, circle the helping verb. Then, write the verb it is helping.**

1. My dad has owned many types of flying machines.

   ____

2. We have traveled in most of them together. ____________________
3. We had soared over the land in hot-air balloons and gliders.

   ____

4. We have wanted a very special plane. ____________________
5. I had looked at pictures of this plane in history books.

   ____

6. Our plane has finally landed at the town airport! ____________________
7. We have replaced many of its parts. ____________________
8. Dad had painted it. ____________________
9. People have called us from all over the country. ____________________
10. Dad has planned a party in honor of the special old plane.

    ____

Main and Helping Verbs

Remember that the main verb is the most important verb in a sentence. The helping verb works with the main verb to tell about an action.

DIRECTIONS **Circle the main verb and underline the helping verb in each sentence.**

Troy has traveled to Mexico. I have visited that country, too. Troy and I have read many books about Mexican history together. I had planned a trip there with Troy. But my teacher has given me too much work, and I have stayed home. Troy has written me a postcard.

DIRECTIONS **Circle the correct helping verb in ( ).**

1. Teo (has / have) lived in Amarillo for ten years.
2. He (have / has) built a house at the edge of the city.
3. Teo's parents also (has / have) built a nice home there.
4. I (have / has) sent a letter to Teo.

DIRECTIONS **Write a sentence about a place you have visited. Use a helping verb in your sentence.**

____

____

____

Present-Tense Verbs

A **present-tense verb** tells about actions that are happening now. Add *s* or *es* to most present-tense verbs when the subject of the sentence is *he*, *she*, *it*, or a singular noun.
Do not add *s* or *es* to a present-tense verb when the subject is *I*, *you*, *we*, *they*, or a plural noun.
Examples:

She *flies* a jet.

Many women *fly* planes today.

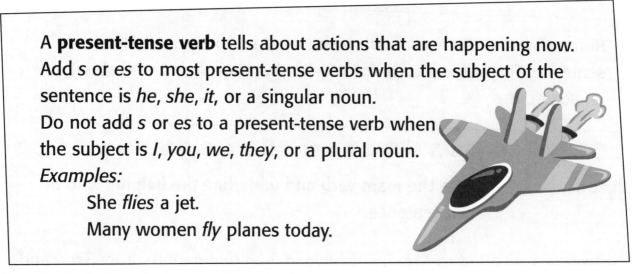

DIRECTIONS **Complete each sentence with a present-tense verb from the box.**

take	takes	drive	drives	chase	chases
play	plays	drink	drinks	watch	watches

1. My grandparents ____________________ to our vacation cabin.

2. My aunt ____________________ her car there, too.

3. I ____________________ icy lemonade.

4. Mom ____________________ iced tea.

5. Eddie and I ____________________ catch.

6. Then we ____________________ each other around the yard.

7. Our dog Mondo ____________________ us silently.

8. He ____________________ the ball from us.

9. Alicia ____________________ a game of checkers with Mom.

10. We ____________________ the sun go down.

Past-Tense Verbs

A **past-tense verb** tells about actions that happened in the past.
Add *ed* or *d* to most present-tense verbs to make them show past tense.
Examples:

Last winter it *snowed* heavily.
The snow *covered* the ground.
We *played* in the snow.

DIRECTIONS **Write the past-tense verb from each sentence on the line. Circle the ending that makes the verb show past tense.**

1. It rained last night. ____________________
2. We closed all the windows quickly. ____________________
3. Thunder crashed outside. ____________________
4. The dog barked at the loud noise. ____________________
5. I watched the lightning. ____________________
6. Rain poured from the roof. ____________________
7. The roof leaked in two places. ____________________
8. We placed buckets under the leaks. ____________________
9. My mother started a fire in the fireplace. ____________________
10. We listened to the storm. ____________________

Present-Tense and Past-Tense Verbs

Remember that a present-tense verb tells about actions that are happening now.
A past-tense verb tells about actions that happened in the past.

DIRECTIONS **Complete each sentence by circling the correct form of the verb in ( ).**

1. Seals (eat / eats) squid and fish.
2. Most seals (lives / live) along the coast.
3. The northern fur seal (spend / spends) the summer near Alaska.
4. Soft fur (covers / cover) the body of a seal pup.
5. A seal (swim / swims) by using both its front and rear flippers.

DIRECTIONS **Change the verb in ( ) to tell about the past, and then write it on the line.**

6. Last summer I ____________________ (visit) my cousin's farm.
7. Every morning I ____________________ (help) feed their cows and pigs.
8. I ____________________ (enjoy) working with animals.
9. My aunt ____________________ (cook) a big breakfast.
10. I ____________________ (like) the smell of bacon and eggs.

Irregular Verbs

An **irregular verb** is a verb that does not end with *ed* to show past tense.
Examples:

Present	Past	Past with Helping Verb
do, does	did	(have, has, had) done
drive, drives	drove	(have, has, had) driven
eat, eats	ate	(have, has, had) eaten
go, goes	went	(have, has, had) gone

DIRECTIONS **Circle the correct verb in ( ) to complete each sentence.**

1. We had (drives / driven) for hours.
2. We (came / comes) to a picnic area in a little valley.
3. We (ate / eats) lunch at the base of Mount St. Helens.
4. Mom (go / went) to get her guidebook.
5. People (drove / driven) away fast when the volcano erupted in 1980.
6. After the eruption, many (come / came) back to rebuild.
7. The eruption of Mount St. Helens (do / did) things to help the ecosystem.
8. I want to (went / go) back one day.

More Irregular Verbs

Remember that an irregular verb is a verb that does not end with *ed* to show past tense. Use special forms of the verbs *eat, give, grow, know, take,* and *write* to show past tense.

DIRECTIONS **Finish each sentence. Write the correct form of the irregular verb in ( ).**

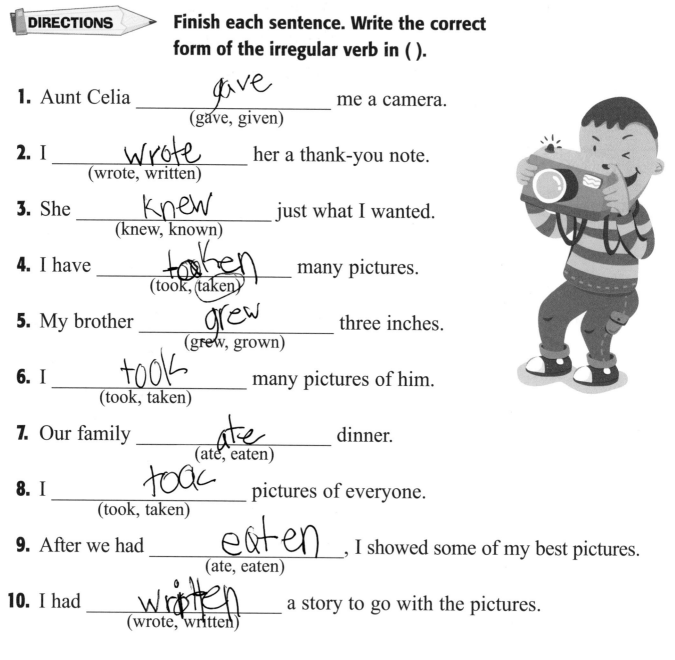

1. Aunt Celia ____gave____ me a camera.
(gave, given)

2. I ____wrote____ her a thank-you note.
(wrote, written)

3. She ____knew____ just what I wanted.
(knew, known)

4. I have ____taken____ many pictures.
(took, taken)

5. My brother ____grew____ three inches.
(grew, grown)

6. I ____took____ many pictures of him.
(took, taken)

7. Our family ____ate____ dinner.
(ate, eaten)

8. I ____toac____ pictures of everyone.
(took, taken)

9. After we had ____eaten____, I showed some of my best pictures.
(ate, eaten)

10. I had ____written____ a story to go with the pictures.
(wrote, written)

Linking Verbs

A **linking verb** connects the subject with words in the predicate of a sentence. It tells what the subject is or is like.
Forms of the verb *be* are often used as linking verbs.
Use *am*, *is*, and *are* to show present tense.
Use *was* and *were* to show past tense.
Examples:
That girl *is* a kind person.
The man *was* lonely.

DIRECTIONS **Read each sentence. Circle the verb. Then write *be* if the verb is a form of *be*. Write *action* if the verb is an action verb.**

1. Many kinds of animals live in trees. ______________________
2. That huge nest is a home for chimpanzees. ______________________
3. Those bird nests are empty now. ______________________
4. Sometimes squirrels use old bird nests. ______________________
5. Hollow trees are also good homes for squirrels. ______________________
6. The hummingbirds were away all winter. ______________________
7. One hummingbird is back now.______________________
8. I am very happy about that. ______________________
9. Hummingbirds are tiny. ______________________
10. They build very small nests. ______________________

Adverbs

An **adverb** is a word that describes a verb.
An adverb may tell *when* or *where* an action happens.
Examples:

Today we visited a theme park.
We ran *ahead*, and our parents followed.

DIRECTIONS **Circle the adverb in each sentence. Then, write if the adverb tells *when* or *where*.**

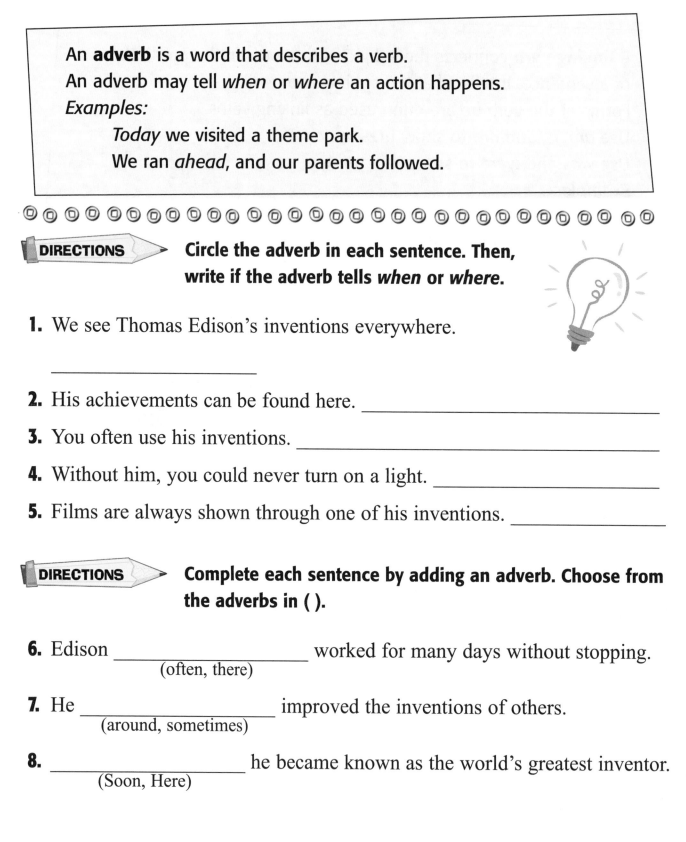

1. We see Thomas Edison's inventions everywhere.

____

2. His achievements can be found here. _______________
3. You often use his inventions. _______________
4. Without him, you could never turn on a light. _______________
5. Films are always shown through one of his inventions. _______________

DIRECTIONS **Complete each sentence by adding an adverb. Choose from the adverbs in ( ).**

6. Edison _______________ worked for many days without stopping.
(often, there)
7. He _______________ improved the inventions of others.
(around, sometimes)
8. _______________ he became known as the world's greatest inventor.
(Soon, Here)

More Adverbs

Remember that an adverb is a word that describes a verb.
Some adverbs tell *how* about a verb. Many adverbs that tell how end in *ly*.

Examples:

My sister screamed *loudly*.

We ran *quickly* to the cave.

DIRECTIONS **Write the adverb in each sentence.**

1. Edith and Carol ran swiftly to the train. ____________________
2. They climbed on board quickly. ____________________
3. Breathlessly, they took the nearest seats. ____________________
4. Luckily, they had arrived on time. ____________________
5. They had excitedly planned this little trip. ____________________
6. They had foolishly waited until the last minute to go to the station.

    ____
7. The train ran exactly on time. ____________________
8. Fortunately, there had been little traffic.

    ____
9. Carol and Edith had barely made it.

    ____
10. They looked happily out the window.

    ____

Using Adverbs

DIRECTIONS **Choose the adverb from the box that best fits in each blank below. Use the clues in ( ) to help you.**

often	carefully	cleverly	downstairs

My grandmother is a woodcarver. She keeps her tools

__________________ (Where?) in the basement. She __________________ (When?)

works on her carving after we eat dinner. With a carving tool in hand, she

__________________ (How?) cuts the wood. After a week or two, she has

__________________ (How?) carved something beautiful.

DIRECTIONS **Finish each sentence by writing an adverb that tells *where, when,* or *how*. Use your own words.**

1. Our family listens to the radio __________________ (When?).
2. Sometimes we listen to the radio __________________ (Where?).
3. We heard a new commercial for milk __________________ (When?).
4. Five cows were singing __________________ (How?).
5. Dad started laughing __________________ (How?).

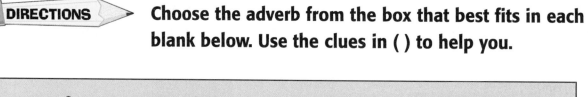

Good and *Well*

Students often have trouble with *good* and *well*.
Use *good* as an adjective.
Use *well* most often as an adverb.
Examples:
I did a *good* job on my report.
I write *well*.

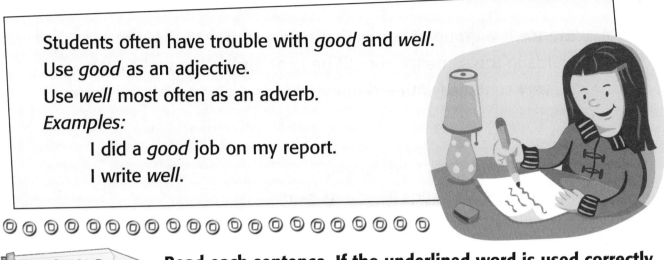

DIRECTIONS **Read each sentence. If the underlined word is used correctly, write *correct*. If not, write the sentence correctly.**

1. Doris went with her mother to see a good movie.

____

2. They sat in the middle so they could see and hear good.

____

3. The actors in the movie played their parts good.

____

4. Doris and her mother shared some very well popcorn.

____

5. The movie was based on a good book Doris had read.

____

DIRECTIONS **Write *good* or *well* to complete each sentence.**

6. Doris and her mother had a _______________ time that day.

7. Doris and her mother always got along _______________.

8. They had especially _______________ times on Saturdays.

What Is a Sentence?

A **sentence** is a group of words that tells a complete thought. The words in the sentence should be in an order that makes sense. Begin every sentence with a capital letter, and end it with the correct end mark.

Examples:

Most plants grow from seeds.

A strawberry's seeds are on its skin.

DIRECTIONS **Read each group of words. If the group is a sentence, draw a line under it.**

1. Dinosaurs lived long ago.
2. The biggest dinosaur of all.
3. Some dinosaurs were small.
4. No bigger than a chicken.
5. Not all dinosaurs ate meat.
6. Leaves and other parts of plants.
7. Tyrannosaurus Rex had big teeth.
8. Dinosaur bones in museums.

DIRECTIONS **Choose two groups of words you did not underline. Add words to make each group a sentence. Write the sentences you make.**

9. ______________________________

____

10. ______________________________

____

Parts of a Sentence

A sentence has several parts.
The **subject** names something or someone in the sentence.
The **predicate** tells what the subject is or does.
Examples:

Birds eat fruit from trees and vines. (subject)

They *drop the seeds onto the ground.* (predicate)

DIRECTIONS **Read each sentence. Write *subject* if the subject is underlined. Write *predicate* if the predicate is underlined.**

1. Our class made flowers out of paper. ______________________
2. Mr. Sanchez brought us many kinds of paper. ______________________
3. Brad folded a yellow handkerchief. ______________________
4. He tied it with a green wire. ______________________
5. His flower was a carnation. ______________________
6. Three girls cut circles out of tissue paper. ______________________
7. Nina glued the circles together. ______________________
8. Her friends curled the edges. ______________________
9. The girls added green paper stems. ______________________
10. Everyone likes our paper garden. ______________________

Subjects

Every sentence has a **subject**. The subject is the part of the sentence about which something is said.
The subject is usually at the beginning of a sentence.
Examples:

Seeds travel in different ways.

Some of these seeds grow into plants.

DIRECTIONS **Write the subject of each sentence.**

1. Some seeds are carried by the wind.

____

2. Dandelion seeds are light and puffy.

____

3. The wind carries them a long way.

____

4. They float through the air.

____

5. Pioneers carried seeds with them.

____

6. These settlers planted the seeds.

____

7. Some families planned orchards.

____

8. The wilderness disappeared slowly.

____

Predicates

Every sentence has a **predicate**. The predicate is the part of the sentence that tells what the subject of the sentence is or does. The predicate is usually the last part of the sentence.

Examples:

Samantha Sanders *is the bravest kid in my class.*

She *thinks of a new adventure every week.*

DIRECTIONS **Write the predicate of each sentence.**

1. Samantha climbed Mount Whitney.

____

2. Mount Whitney is in California.

____

3. Samantha went there with her father.

____

4. They climbed for one whole day.

____

5. Samantha took pictures of snow at the top.

____

6. Samantha went rafting on the Snake River.

____

7. The river bucked like a wild horse.

____

8. She loved the exciting ride.

____

Subjects and Predicates

Remember that every sentence has a subject that names the person or thing the sentence is about.
Every sentence has a predicate that tells what the subject of the sentence is or does.

DIRECTIONS **Underline the subject in each sentence. Circle the predicate in each sentence.**

1. New York City is the largest city in the United States.
2. More than 7 million people live in New York City.
3. New Yorkers come from many different backgrounds.
4. The subway system runs on about 230 miles of track.
5. The city is a center for trade, business, and the arts.
6. Millions of people visit New York City every year.
7. Theater is one of the city's most popular art forms.
8. Many visitors attend Broadway shows.
9. One tall building in New York City is the Empire State Building.
10. The Statue of Liberty stands on an island in New York Harbor.
11. This monument is a symbol of freedom.
12. Tourists take pictures of the statue.

Statements and Questions

A **statement** is a sentence that tells something.
Use a period (.) at the end of a statement.
A **question** is a sentence that asks something.
Use a question mark (?) at the end of a question.
Begin every statement or question with a capital letter.
Examples:
Luther Burbank was a famous gardener.
Where did Luther Burbank live?

DIRECTIONS **Write each statement or question so that it begins and ends correctly. Then circle *S* if the sentence is a statement or *Q* if it is a question.**

1. do you like gardens S Q

____

2. we planted vegetables here S Q

____

3. do the plants need water S Q

____

4. who will pull the weeds S Q

____

5. these tomatoes look good S Q

____

6. are they ripe S Q

____

7. this tomato is bright red S Q

____

Exclamations and Commands

An **exclamation** is a sentence that shows strong feeling.
Use an exclamation point (!) at the end of an exclamation.
A **command** is a sentence that gives an order or a direction.
Use a period (.) at the end of a command.
Examples:

Wow, what a huge blackberry!

Don't pick those berries.

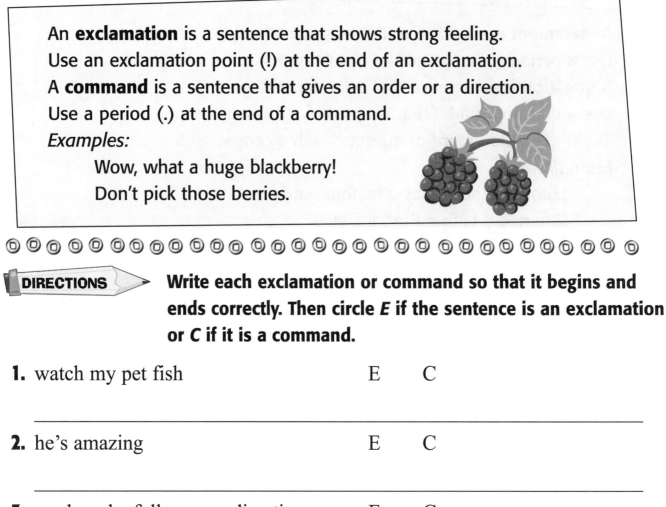

DIRECTIONS **Write each exclamation or command so that it begins and ends correctly. Then circle *E* if the sentence is an exclamation or *C* if it is a command.**

1. watch my pet fish E C

___

2. he's amazing E C

___

3. see how he follows my directions E C

___

4. swim through the hoop, Finny E C

___

5. now dive to the bottom E C

___

6. you're terrific, Finny E C

___

7. swim around in big circles E C

___

Capital Letters and End Marks in Sentences

Begin each sentence with a capital letter.
End statements and commands with a period (.).
End a question with a question mark (?).
End an exclamation with an exclamation point (!).

DIRECTIONS **Add the correct end mark to each sentence.**

1. Do you wonder who made the first comb ______
2. The earliest combs were found in Egyptian tombs 6,000 years old ______
3. Look at that unusual comb ______
4. If you found a 6,000-year-old comb, would you use it ______
5. What an old comb that would be ______

DIRECTIONS **Use capital letters and end marks to separate the sentences in each pair. Write the sentences on the lines.**

6. Most early people used combs the only ones who didn't were the Britons

____

____

7. Does it make you wonder how they looked the Britons left their hair messy

____

____

8. I comb my hair every day do you

____

____

Agreement of Subjects with the Verb *Be*

The predicate of a sentence must agree with the subject in number.
Use *am*, *is*, and *was* with singular subjects.
Use *are* and *were* with plural subjects.

Examples:

The *dog is* gone.

My *friends were* afraid of it.

DIRECTIONS **Write *am*, *is*, or *are* to finish each sentence.**

1. I ____________________ a pet.
2. My ears ____________________ long.
3. My tail ____________________ short and fluffy.
4. My name ____________________ Flopsy.
5. Carrots ____________________ my favorite food.
6. Lettuce ____________________ good for me, too.
7. I ____________________ a rabbit.

DIRECTIONS **Write *was* or *were* to finish each sentence.**

8. We ____________________ tadpoles once.
9. Our mother ____________________ a big green frog.
10. Our home ____________________ in the water.
11. We ____________________ good swimmers.
12. Before long, we ____________________ frogs like our mother.

Combining Sentences with the Same Subject

Good writers sometimes combine sentences to make their writing more interesting.

Two short sentences might have the same subject. The writer writes the subject once and then combines the two predicates in the same sentence.

Example:

Tara *liked crackers*. Tara *liked cheese*.

Tara liked *crackers and cheese*.

DIRECTIONS **Combine the predicates in these sentences. Write the new sentences.**

1. Amir was tired. Amir wanted his lunch.

____

____

2. He turned smoothly in the water. He headed for the other end of the pool.

____

____

3. Amir wanted to win. Amir hoped to set records.

____

____

4. Amir won many races. Amir got many awards.

____

____

Combining Sentences with the Same Predicate

Good writers often combine short sentences to make their writing more interesting.
Two sentences might have the same predicate. The sentences can be combined by joining the subjects with the word *and*.
Example:

Lance likes to play video games. *Raul* likes to play video games.
Lance and Raul like to play video games.

DIRECTIONS **Combine each pair of sentences into one sentence. Remember to join subjects with the word *and*. Write the new sentence.**

1. Guppies are pets for fish tanks. Goldfish are pets for fish tanks.

____

____

2. Catfish help clean the tank. Snails help clean the tank.

____

____

3. Black Bettas are great pets. Goldfish are great pets.

____

4. Guppies have live babies. Black mollies have live babies.

____

5. Zebra fish lay eggs. Angelfish lay eggs.

____

Joining Sentences

Good writers make their writing more interesting by joining sentences that are short and choppy.

Sentences that have ideas that go together can be joined with a comma (,) and the word *and*.

Example:

The river is beautiful. It is also useful.

The river is beautiful, *and* it is also useful.

DIRECTIONS **Use a comma and the word *and* to join each pair of sentences. Write the new sentence.**

1. Inventions make our lives easier. We take them for granted.

____

____

2. We get cold. We turn on a heater.

____

3. Long ago people got cold. They sat around a fire.

____

____

4. A very long time ago, people had no fire. They stayed cold.

____

____

5. Our heater works. We stay warm.

____

Joining Sentences to List Words in a Series

A list of three or more materials or items is called a **series**. Short, choppy sentences can be combined into one long, clear sentence with a series.

Example:

The summer sky *is clear*. The summer sky *is blue*. The summer sky *is beautiful*.

The summer sky *is clear, blue, and beautiful*.

DIRECTIONS **Join each pair of sentences. Write the new sentence.**

1. Pet mice can be black. They can be red or silver.

____

2. Other colors for mice include gray. They also include cream and white.

____

____

3. A mouse can chew on wood. It can chew on nuts and twigs.

____

4. Mice clean their own bodies. They clean their faces and ears.

____

____

5. Soup cans are good resting places for pet mice. They are good for hamsters and gerbils.

____

____

Expanding Sentences

Good writers make sentences clear by using adjectives and adverbs that describe the topic exactly.

Example:

The blue river rolled lazily through the green land.

DIRECTIONS **Add an adjective or an adverb where you see this mark: *. The word or words you add should describe the thing or action. Write your new sentences.**

1. The * hummingbird built a * nest.

____

____

2. She found a * tree in a * place.

____

____

3. She wanted her nest to be * away from * cats.

____

____

4. She laid * eggs and sat on them * .

____

____

5. * the eggs hatched, and the babies cried * for food.

____

____

Avoiding Run-on Sentences

Good writers divide run-on sentences into two or more sentences.
Example:
The sky is blue it is full of clouds.
The sky is blue. It is full of clouds.

DIRECTIONS **Revise each run-on sentence. Write two shorter sentences to make the meaning clearer.**

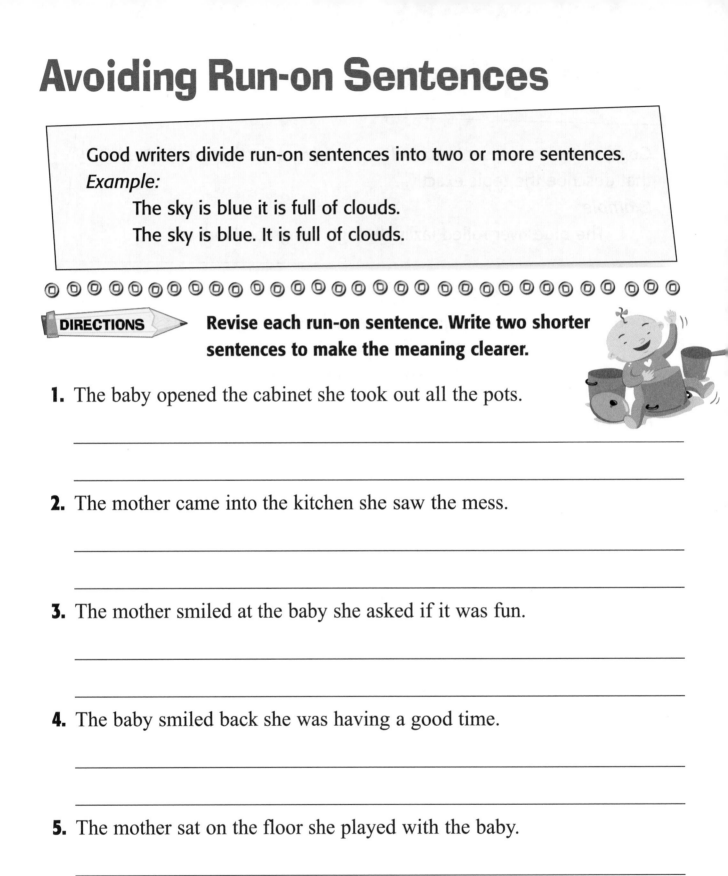

1. The baby opened the cabinet she took out all the pots.

2. The mother came into the kitchen she saw the mess.

3. The mother smiled at the baby she asked if it was fun.

4. The baby smiled back she was having a good time.

5. The mother sat on the floor she played with the baby.

Capital Letters for Names and Titles of People and Pets

Begin a person's name or a pet's name with a capital letter. Begin titles of a person, such as *Ms.*, *Mr.*, and *Dr.*, with a capital letter. Capitalize initials that take the place of names. Always capitalize the word *I*.

Examples:

Bob and *I* took my dog *Zak* to see *Dr*. Edward *D*. Porter.

DIRECTIONS **Write these sentences. Correct each proper noun.**

1. Our dentist is dr ellen j oldham.

____

2. She works with dr karl v swift.

____

3. Dad's friend chan works in the office.

____

4. Sometimes miss kitazawa works there, too.

____

5. My sister leah had her checkup yesterday.

____

6. Today mrs kim and ms ozario will see dr oldham.

____

7. mr kramer sees dr oldham every three months.

____

8. max and i went to visit mrs delgado.

____

Capital Letters for Place Names

Begin the name of a town, city, state, and country with a capital letter.
Begin the name of a street and its abbreviation with a capital letter.
Examples:

Akron, Ohio *Mexico* *Jones Road*

DIRECTIONS **Write each place name correctly.**

1. zion national park ____________________
2. state street ____________________
3. south america ____________________
4. mississippi river ____________________
5. handy hardware store ____________________

DIRECTIONS **Change each sentence. Use a place name for the underlined words. Write your new sentences.**

6. Ms. Bass lived in <u>a city</u>.

____

7. She was a teacher at <u>a school</u>.

____

8. She lived in a building on <u>a street</u>.

____

9. One summer she visited <u>a state</u>.

____

10. Pierre lived in <u>a foreign country</u>.

____

Capital Letters for Days, Months, and Holidays

Begin the name of a day, month, or holiday with a capital letter.

Examples:

Wednesday

January

New Year's Day

January

Sun	Mon	Tues	Wed	Thur	Fri	Sat
			1	2	3	4
5	6	7	8	9	10	11
12	13	14	15	16	17	18
19	20	21	22	23	24	25
26	27	28	29	30	31	

DIRECTIONS **Write each day, month, or holiday correctly.**

1. february ______________________
2. monday ______________________
3. labor day______________________
4. november ______________________
5. saturday ______________________
6. thanksgiving day ______________________

DIRECTIONS **Finish each sentence. Write the name of a day, a month, or a holiday. Be sure to begin the name with a capital letter.**

7. I think ________________ is a good day to play outside.
8. For me, ________________ is the best school day.
9. ________________ is often a day when everything seems to go wrong.
10. I think the best month of the year is ________________.
11. ________________ is the month of my birthday.
12. ________________ is a great month for swimming.

Using Capital Letters

A proper noun names a special person, place, or thing. It begins with a capital letter.

Example:

Pompeii was an ancient city.

DIRECTIONS **The nouns in these sentences are underlined. Write each proper noun. Remember to begin a proper noun with a capital letter.**

1. A terrible thing happened in pompeii long ago.

____

2. The tragedy happened in august.

____

3. One afternoon, the people of italy heard an explosion.

____

4. A volcano named mount vesuvius erupted!

____

5. A few citizens fled toward the mediterranean sea.

____

6. Red-hot lava flowed toward this city near naples.

____

7. The metropolitan museum shows objects the residents used there.

____

8. Families in some parts of europe still worry about volcanoes.

____

Periods

Use a **period (.)** at the end of a statement or a command.
Use a period after an abbreviation.
Use a period after a numeral in the main topic of an outline.
Examples:

Manny and Tony like the beach.
Mr. Smith swims in the summer.

Wind Power

I. Using wind power on the sea
II. Using wind power on land

DIRECTIONS **Read each sentence. Add periods where they are needed.**

1. Manny and Tony go to the beach every day
2. Do not step on the crabs
3. Dr Quick looked at Mr Smith's toe.
4. Mrs Smith found a bandage
5. Dr Quick helped Mr Smith.

DIRECTIONS **Add periods to the outline where they are needed.**

Beach Activities
I Play in the waves
II Look for shells
III Have a picnic

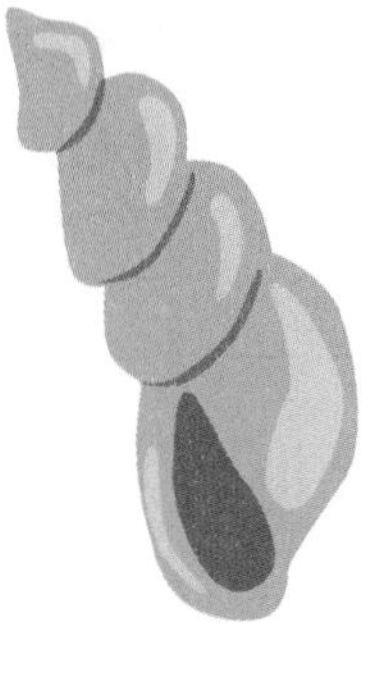

Abbreviations and Initials

An **abbreviation** is a short way of writing a word or words.
Use capital letters and periods to write most abbreviations.
An **initial** is an abbreviation of a name. The initial is the first letter of the name.
Use capital letters and periods to write an initial.

Examples:

Doctor = *Dr.* Street = *St.*
Monday = *Mon.* October = *Oct.*

DIRECTIONS **Write the following items. Use abbreviations or initials wherever possible. Use capital letters correctly.**

1. circle road ____________________
2. july ____________________
3. doctor Homer amos mancebo ____________________
4. tuesday ____________________
5. 493 dinosaur avenue ____________________
6. Mister willard Ambrose ____________________
7. saturday, april 13 ____________________
8. angela phyllis mills ____________________

DIRECTIONS **Each of these items has at least one error. Correct the item, and write it on the line.**

9. mon ____________________
10. Miss Cynthia a forbes ____________________
11. feb. 28 ____________________
12. deerpath rd. ____________________

Commas in Sentences

Use a **comma (,)** after *yes*, *no*, and *well* at the beginning of a sentence.
Use a comma before the word *and* when two sentences are joined.
Examples:

Well, that was a strange place.

Yes, it was scary, *and* I don't want to go back.

DIRECTIONS **Write a sentence to answer each question. Begin each sentence with *Yes*, *No*, or *Well*.**

1. Did you ever give a dog a bath?

____

2. What do you need in order to give a dog a bath?

____

____

3. Would you like to give a dog a bath this afternoon?

____

____

4. Do you have a favorite book?

____

5. What is that funny animal?

____

6. Is the big game on Friday?

____

Commas in a Series

Use a **comma (,)** after each item except the last one in a series of three or more items.

Examples:

The desert is *hot, dry, and sandy.*

Snakes, lizards, and tortoises live there.

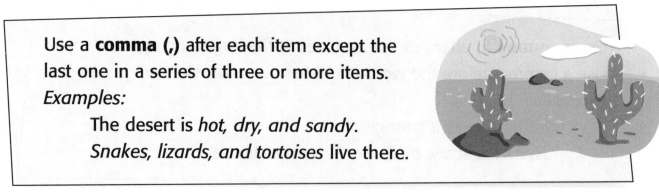

DIRECTIONS **Rewrite each sentence. Add commas where they belong.**

1. An octopus has eight legs large eyes and strong jaws.

2. An octopus eats clams crabs and lobsters.

3. Octopuses live along the coasts of Hawaii Australia and China.

4. The desert seems to shimmer shine and bubble in the hot sun.

5. Sometimes the wind will blow swirl or whip the sand around.

More Uses for Commas

Use a **comma (,)** between a city and a state or a city and a country.
Use a comma between the day and the year.
Use a comma after the greeting in a friendly letter and after the closing of any letter.

Examples:

Topeka, Kansas *Osaka, Japan*

September 17, 2005

Dear Mr. Wong, *Your friend,*

DIRECTIONS **Read this friendly letter. Add commas where they are needed.**

New Delhi India

May 3 2005

Dear Chandra

Today I watched the sun rise from beside the river in our city. As I watched the sun, a beautiful paper boat floated toward the shore. I caught the boat and read your name and address. The shiuli flowers were still fresh. They reminded me of the beauty of the morning. Thank you for sending your boat. It helped me to appreciate the new day and reminded me of forgotten dreams.

May your boats find many new friends for you.

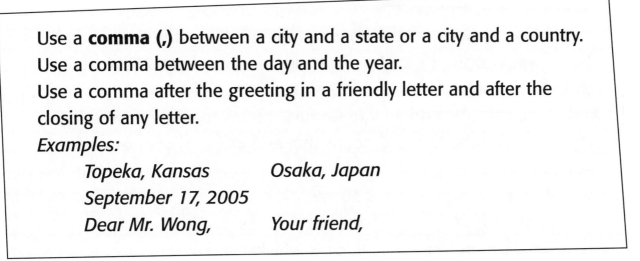

Sincerely

Sadar Rangairi

Colons and Apostrophes

Use a **colon (:)** between the hour and the minute in the time of day.
Use an **apostrophe (')** to show that one or more letters have been left out in a contraction.
Add an apostrophe and an *s* to singular nouns to show possession.
Add an apostrophe to plural nouns that end in *s* to show possession.

Examples:

1:15 P.M.	6:30 A.M.
is not = *isn't*	have not = *haven't*
Amelia's project	the *cat's* whiskers
girls' laughter	*parents'* plan

DIRECTIONS **Complete each sentence correctly. Add colons and apostrophes where they are needed.**

1. Meghan and her family took the 8 30 P.M. train.
2. At 7 15 the next morning, they ate breakfast.
3. The train pulled into Union Station at 8 45 A.M.
4. Meghan didn t want to waste time.
5. She wasn t interested in looking at the city from their windows.
6. Meghan s cousins met them at the hotel.
7. Her cousins rooms overlooked the lake.
8. Meghan s father took them to the fair.
9. They stayed at the fair until 9 00 P.M.
10. Meghan couldn t stay awake on the ride home.

Contractions with *Not*

A **contraction** is a short way of writing two words together. Some of the letters are left out. An apostrophe takes the place of the missing letters.
Use verbs and the word *not* to form some contractions.
Examples:

were + not = *weren't*   have + not = *haven't*
will + not = *won't*   could + not = *couldn't*

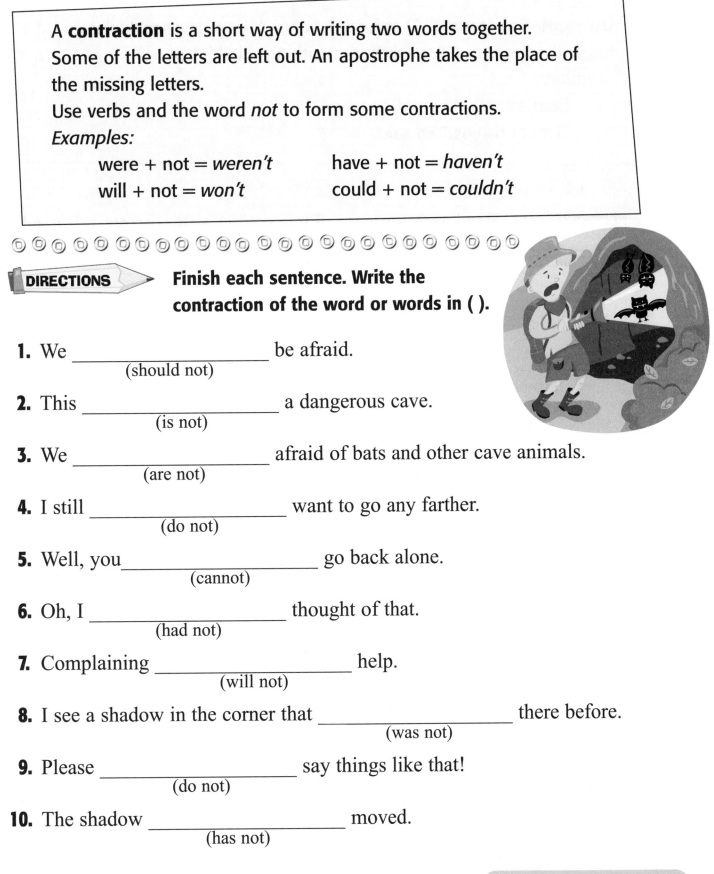

DIRECTIONS **Finish each sentence. Write the contraction of the word or words in ( ).**

1. We ____________________ be afraid.
(should not)

2. This ____________________ a dangerous cave.
(is not)

3. We ____________________ afraid of bats and other cave animals.
(are not)

4. I still ____________________ want to go any farther.
(do not)

5. Well, you ____________________ go back alone.
(cannot)

6. Oh, I ____________________ thought of that.
(had not)

7. Complaining ____________________ help.
(will not)

8. I see a shadow in the corner that ____________________ there before.
(was not)

9. Please ____________________ say things like that!
(do not)

10. The shadow ____________________ moved.
(has not)

Direct Quotations and Dialogue

Use **quotation marks (" ")** before and after the words a speaker says. Begin the first word a speaker says with a capital letter.
Examples:

Sam asked, "Where did you go?"
"I went fishing," Ed said.

DIRECTIONS **Read each sentence. If it is correct, write *correct*. If it needs quotation marks and a capital letter, write the sentence correctly.**

1. Lily said, let's go to the beach.

____

2. Jeff exclaimed, that's a great idea!

____

3. Dad said that he would rather stay home.

____

4. Uncle Bill said, well, I'd love to go to the beach.

____

5. Jeff asked, where is our big beach ball?

____

6. Uncle Bill said that he would pack a picnic lunch.

____

7. Dad reminded them, don't forget your towels.

____

8. Lily shouted, this is great!

____

Titles

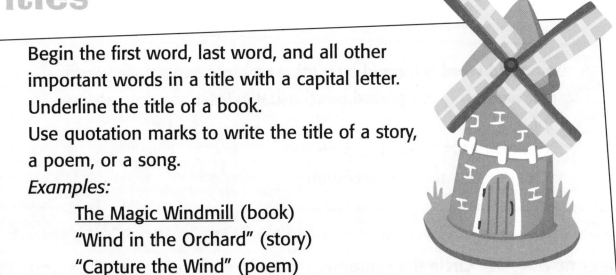

Begin the first word, last word, and all other important words in a title with a capital letter.
Underline the title of a book.
Use quotation marks to write the title of a story, a poem, or a song.

Examples:

The Magic Windmill (book)
"Wind in the Orchard" (story)
"Capture the Wind" (poem)

DIRECTIONS **Write each sentence correctly. Add underlines, quotation marks, and capital letters where they are needed.**

1. Chet got a book called the story of baseball from the library today.

____

____

2. The first story, titled in the beginning, starts in 1846.

____

____

3. The last story is called why is baseball so popular?

____

____

4. Last week Chet read a book called pioneers of baseball by Robert Smith.

____

____

5. His favorite story, the one and only, is about Babe Ruth.

____

Compound Words

A **compound word** is formed by putting together two smaller words. The first word in a compound word usually describes the second.
Examples:

black + berry = *blackberry*
bed + room = *bedroom*

DIRECTIONS **Circle the compound word in each sentence. Then, write the two words that form the compound word, and write the meaning of the compound word.**

1. "Let's play an outdoor game," said Penny.

____

2. "The playground is open," said Paul, "so let's go there."

____

3. "Maybe you should wear an overcoat," said Penny's mom.

____

4. "A lightweight jacket is all I need," said Penny.

____

5. "All right, but be back by mealtime," said Penny's mom.

____

6. "It's a beautiful afternoon," said Paul.

____

7. "Even the mockingbird in that tree likes it," Paul declared.

____

8. "Look at the pretty leaves in the treetop," said Penny.

____

Synonyms

A **synonym** is a word that has almost the same meaning as another word.
Examples:
Afraid is a synonym of *scared*.
Begin is a synonym of *start*.

DIRECTIONS **Read each sentence. Choose the word in ( ) that is a synonym for each underlined word. Then, rewrite the sentence using the synonym.**

1. The pyramids of Egypt have stood for <u>almost</u> 5,000 years. (nearly, over, exactly)

____

____

2. Because the pyramids are so <u>huge</u>, strong, and old, people find them interesting. (small, heavy, large)

____

____

3. To <u>understand</u> anything about the pyramids, we have to learn about Egypt of that time. (write, forget, know)

____

____

4. The rulers of ancient Egypt ruled over a <u>complete</u> country, not just a town or a tribe. (whole, small, growing)

____

____

Antonyms

An **antonym** is a word that means the opposite of another word.
Examples:

Up is an antonym of *down*.
Fast is an antonym of *slow*.

DIRECTIONS **Read each pair of sentences. Find two antonyms and write them on the line.**

1. Getting started with soap carving is the hardest part. The easiest thing is to talk about it.

____

2. Do not cut soap toward yourself. It is best to cut slowly away from yourself.

____

3. Keep your knife clean. A dirty blade is hard to use.

____

4. Remember to keep your soap dry. Don't forget that soap and water make soap suds.

____

5. If you paint the soap, it is a good idea to test a small part. If it looks bad, try a different color.

____

6. A fresh cake of soap is best. An old cake of soap might be partly dried out.

____

7. A small cake of soap is very difficult to work with. It's best to use a large piece.

____

Prefixes

A **prefix** is a letter or group of letters added to the beginning of a base word. A prefix changes the meaning of a word.

Examples:

I *agree* that the pet needs a name.

I *disagree* with your ideas for names.

Prefix	Meaning	Example
dis	not	dislike
im	not	impossible
re	again	redo
re	back	repay
un	not	unlucky
un	opposite of	unwrap

DIRECTIONS **Read each sentence. Change the meaning of each sentence by adding a prefix from the list above to each underlined word. Rewrite the sentence using the new word.**

1. Lexi was a very usual animal.

____

2. She was patient to get out into the world.

____

3. Lexi liked the pet store.

____

4. Every night she felt lucky to be there.

____

5. Lexi thought it was possible to find a new home.

____

Suffixes

A **suffix** is a letter or group of letters added to the end of a base word. A suffix changes the meaning of a word.
Examples:

Amelia made the roller coaster work<u>able</u>.

She was a very good think<u>er</u>.

Suffix	Meaning	Example
able	able to be	wear<u>able</u>
er	one who	build<u>er</u>
ful	full of	hope<u>ful</u>
ible	able to be	flex<u>ible</u>
less	without	care<u>less</u>
or	one who	visit<u>or</u>

DIRECTIONS **Read each sentence. Choose a suffix from the above list to write a single word that has the same meaning as the words in ( ). Write the new word on the line.**

1. When Amelia Earhart was a girl, she was the (person who invents) of a roller coaster. ____________________

2. It was a (full of use) ride. ____________________

3. Her sister Muriel was her (person who helps). ____________________

4. Amelia was (without fear) and rode on it. ____________________

5. She felt (full of joy) as she flew down. ____________________

6. Her first (full of success) ride ended at her grandmother's feet.

____

Homographs

Homographs are words that have the same spelling but different meanings.
Some homographs are pronounced differently.
Examples:

felt: a soft kind of cloth
felt: sensed something on the skin
wind: moving air
wind: to turn a knob on something

DIRECTIONS **Read each sentence. Circle the correct meaning of the underlined word.**

1. While Buddy counted to 20, Buster ran to hide.
a. get out of sight
b. the skin of an animal

2. Buddy looked all over, but he couldn't find Buster.
a. finished, done
b. around

3. After a long time, Buddy gave up.
a. to want something very much
b. lot of

4. "Come out!" shouted Buddy, but Buster stayed under the house.
a. a building where people live
b. an audience

5. Buddy began to worry because the weather was turning cold.
a. changing
b. spinning

6. It felt like fall.
a. a tumble to the ground
b. autumn

DIRECTIONS **Read the sentence. Then, write another sentence using the underlined word as a noun.**

7. "Don't throw the ball so hard!" said Buster.

____

Homophones

Homophones are words that sound alike but are spelled differently and have different meanings.

Example:

A *pair* of girls sat at the table.
They were sharing a *pear*.

DIRECTIONS **Read each sentence. Choose the homophone in ( ) that correctly completes it. Circle the correct homophone.**

1. For seven (daze, days), Julie has been trying to bake a good fruit pie.
2. She has three (pears, pairs) and three apples.
3. She will have to sift the (flower, flour) for the crust.
4. She can never (seam, seem) to get the crust right.
5. The (dough, doe) is always just a little too dry.
6. This is day number (ate, eight).
7. Jan and (I, eye) are hoping this one is good.
8. If Julie gets it (write, right) this time, we will be happy for her.
9. I tasted a (piece, peace) of Julie's first pie.
10. That time it was (fare, fair), but not really excellent.

DIRECTIONS **Underline the pair of homophones in each sentence.**

11. One time Julie won a cooking contest.
12. Twice in the past year, the judges passed over her dishes.
13. Did you ever find a cook who was fined for bad cooking?

Troublesome Words: *to, too, two*

Use *to* when you mean "in the direction of."
Use *too* when you mean "also."
Use *two* when you mean the number 2.
Examples:
I am going *to* a movie.
My friends are going, *too*.
Each ticket costs *two* dollars.

DIRECTIONS **Complete each sentence correctly by writing *to, too,* or *two*.**

1. We went ____________________ the theater.

2. The mayor came, ____________________.

3. An usher showed us ____________________ our seats.

4. "Welcome ____________________ the best show ever!" an announcer said.

5. The first ____________________ performers did a number of good tricks.

6. They sang songs, ____________________.

7. Then, ____________________ actors told some funny jokes.

8. I had never been ____________________ a vaudeville show before.

9. There were ____________________ songs in the finale.

10. "I know this song and the last one, ____________________," the mayor said.

Troublesome Words: *its*, *it's*

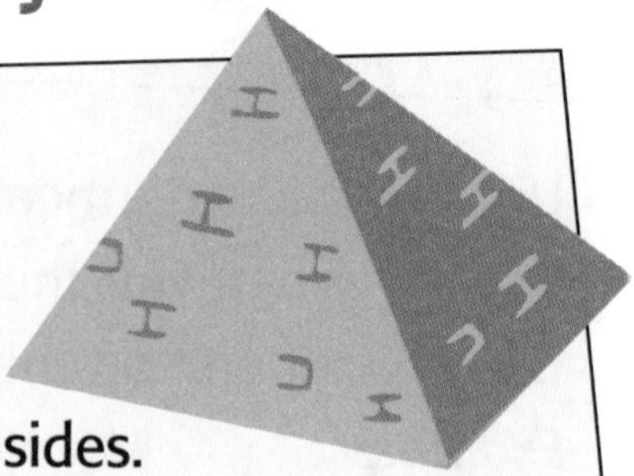

Use *its* when you mean "belonging to it."
Use *it's* when you mean "it is."
Examples:

The pyramid is huge. We climbed *its* steep sides.
It's fun to explore.

DIRECTIONS **Use *its* or *it's* to complete each sentence. Write the correct word on the line.**

1. What is that? ____________________ a mummy!
2. ____________________ thousands of years old.
3. ____________________ wrapped tightly in strips of cloth.
4. The inner chamber of the pyramid is large. Ancient drawings cover ____________________ walls.
5. In one picture, a dog follows ____________________ owner.
6. ____________________ teeth are long and sharp.
7. Look at this mask. ____________________ made of solid gold!
8. ____________________ important to keep careful records.
9. Photograph each item, and write down ____________________ exact location.
10. ____________________ a job that is certain to take many weeks.

Troublesome Words: *your, you're*

Use *your* when you mean "belonging to you."
Use *you're* when you mean "you are."
Examples:
Do you have *your* homework?
You're in trouble now.

DIRECTIONS **Use *your* or *you're* to complete each sentence. Write the correct word on the line.**

1. ____________________ my best pupil, Eric.
2. Pull ____________________ laces tight.
3. Now ____________________ ready to skate safely.
4. Were ____________________ legs this wobbly when you started, Grandpa?
5. Yes, but ____________________ getting better, Eric.
6. ____________________ skates flash like silver.
7. ____________________ saying I'm a fast skater?
8. What was ____________________ greatest race, Grandpa?
9. I won a medal once, but ____________________ too young to remember that.
10. Grandpa, ____________________ the best skater I know.

Troublesome Words: *their, there, they're*

Use *their* when you mean "belonging to them."
Use *there* to tell where.
Use *they're* when you mean "they are."
Examples:

Pirates sailed in *their* ships.
The captain hid his jewels over *there*.
They're beautiful jewels!

DIRECTIONS **Use *their, there,* or *they're* to complete each sentence. Write the correct word on the line.**

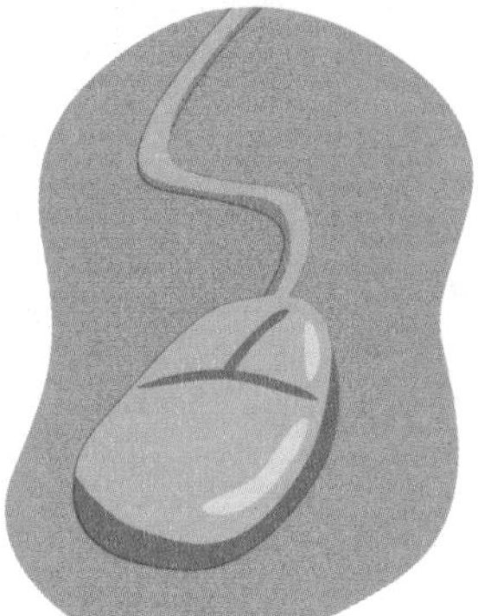

1. Liz and Han are working on ____________________ new computer program.
2. ____________________ staying after school today.
3. ____________________ going to be in the computer lab.
4. They can use one of the computers ____________________.
5. They might be able to ask ____________________ teacher some questions.
6. She's often ____________________, too.
7. Today she can't answer ____________________ questions.
8. "Maybe you'd like to talk with the teachers sitting over ____________________," she says.
9. "____________________ talking about computers."
10. Han and Liz ask the teachers ____________________ questions.

Using Sensory Words

Good writers use sensory words to tell how someone or something looks, feels, sounds, smells, or tastes.

Examples:

The old coin was *shiny* and *bright*.

The cat's fur was *soft* and *smooth*.

DIRECTIONS **Read each sentence. Decide which one of the senses is being used. Write *look, feel, sound, taste,* or *smell* on the line.**

1. The chimneys were outlined against a pale, pink sky.

____

2. The morning air was very chilly. ____________________

3. Suddenly, a loud cry broke the silence. ____________________

4. A young boy poked his head out of one chimney.

____

5. The boy called "All up!" in a loud voice. ____________________

6. He waved his cleaning tools. ____________________

7. Then he slid into the chimney to clean it. ____________________

8. Later he had some spicy cider to drink. ____________________

9. He warmed his hands on the hot cup. ____________________

10. The smell of roast pork filled the air. ____________________

Choosing Words to Paint a Vivid Picture

Good writers choose words that paint a vivid picture. Sometimes, writers compare two things so that you can understand one of them better.

Examples:

Paul Bunyan was as big as *a tree*.

His feet smelled like *dead fish*.

DIRECTIONS **Read each word picture. Underline the two things that are being compared. Then, tell how they are alike.**

1. The fog comes in like a cat.

____

2. The fog covered the top of the hill like a blanket.

____

3. The tree, like an umbrella, protected us from the rain.

____

4. The moon smiled down on us, just as Grandma always did.

____

5. The light reflected off the lake as if the lake were a mirror.

____

6. The grasshoppers called back and forth to each other like an echo in the mountains.

____

7. Like a knife through butter, the boat went through the water.

____

Subject and Verb Agreement

A subject and its verb must agree in number.
To make most verbs agree with singular subjects, add *s*.
To make verbs that end in *sh*, *ch*, *ss*, or *x* agree with singular subjects, add *es*.
To make most verbs agree with plural subjects, do not change the ending.
Examples:

She walks along a sandy trail.
The *rain washes* the flowers of the cacti.
The *birds sing* after it rains.

DIRECTIONS **Read each sentence. Circle the form of the verb that agrees with the subject of the sentence.**

1. The girl (stroll, strolls) with her grandmother.
2. The girl (watch, watches) everything around her.
3. She (enjoy, enjoys) the quail most.
4. Five quail (pass, passes) in front of her.
5. The girl (see, sees) quail eggs in a nest.
6. They (touch, touches) none of them.
7. Grandmother (take, takes) water from the cacti.
8. They (fill, fills) their basket with fruit.
9. Grandmother (teach, teaches) the girl about the desert.
10. The girl (understand, understands) how beautiful it is.

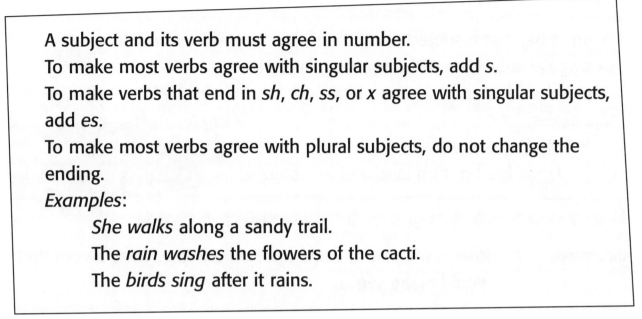

More Subject and Verb Agreement

Remember that a subject and its verb must agree in number.
A singular subject must have a singular verb.
A plural subject must have a plural verb.
Examples:
My *frog is* green.
Frogs live both on land and in water.

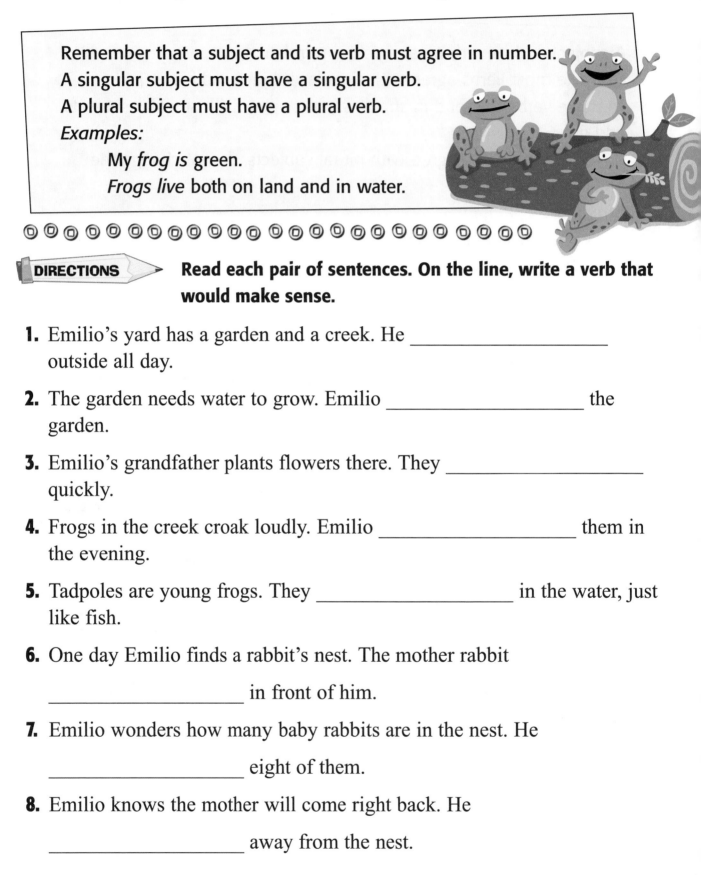

DIRECTIONS **Read each pair of sentences. On the line, write a verb that would make sense.**

1. Emilio's yard has a garden and a creek. He ___________________ outside all day.
2. The garden needs water to grow. Emilio ___________________ the garden.
3. Emilio's grandfather plants flowers there. They ___________________ quickly.
4. Frogs in the creek croak loudly. Emilio ___________________ them in the evening.
5. Tadpoles are young frogs. They ___________________ in the water, just like fish.
6. One day Emilio finds a rabbit's nest. The mother rabbit ___________________ in front of him.
7. Emilio wonders how many baby rabbits are in the nest. He ___________________ eight of them.
8. Emilio knows the mother will come right back. He ___________________ away from the nest.

Paragraphs

A **paragraph** is a group of sentences that tells about one main idea. The first line of a paragraph is indented. This means the first word is moved in a little from the left margin.

The **topic sentence** tells the main idea of the paragraph.

The other sentences in a paragraph are the **detail sentences**.

Detail sentences tell about the main idea.

Example:

Hunter spiders hunt for their food. Some hunters use their teeth to catch food. Other hunters run to trap food. Some jump on insects to catch them.

How to Write a Paragraph

1. Write a topic sentence that clearly tells the main idea of your paragraph.
2. Indent the first line.
3. Write detail sentences that tell about the main idea.

DIRECTIONS **Read the example paragraph. List three details that tell about the main idea.**

Using Enough Details

Good writers give readers interesting details and clear examples. Be sure to use enough details to support your main idea.

DIRECTIONS **Read each paragraph. Answer the questions.**

Owls are best known for their ability to see at night. They can see 100 times better than humans. Their eyes are big and do not move very easily. This is why owls' necks have to turn so far.

Though they can also see well in the daytime, owls are known for seeing at night. They can see 100 times better at night than humans can, but they are color-blind. Owls' eyes are very large, and they control the light coming in by changing the size of the pupils of the eyes. Each pupil acts alone. If you stood in the sunlight and your friend stood in the shade, an owl could see each of you well.

1. Which paragraph is more interesting? Explain your answer.

____

____

2. What is the topic sentence of the second paragraph?

____

____

3. What is one detail given in the second paragraph?

____

____

4. Write one example found in the second paragraph.

____

____

Keeping to the Topic

A good writer plans a paragraph so that it gives details about one main idea.
All the sentences in a paragraph must keep to the topic.

DIRECTIONS **Read the underlined topic sentence below. Choose the sentences that keep to the topic. Write a paragraph, using the topic sentence and the sentences you chose.**

A person who hears can imagine what it is like to be deaf.
Put earplugs in your ears to block out sound.
Try to figure out what people are saying.
Being blind is not easy, either.
Try to call someone on the telephone.
A person who cannot see has different problems.
Deaf people can do all these things and more.

Personal Narrative

In a **personal narrative**, a writer tells about an experience in his or her life.

Example:

Why was I named Cameroon Pele? I never thought about it until a friend asked how I got my name. I didn't know, so I went home to search for answers. First, I sat down to think. Then my sister Helen came in. She was born on the day a volcano named Mount St. Helens erupted. That's how she got her name. I asked her how I had gotten mine. She said that I got my name the same way she did. It's true. I looked it up. I was born on the same day a volcano erupted in Cameroon, Africa.

How to Write a Paragraph That Tells about Yourself

1. Tell about yourself. Use the pronouns *I*, *me*, and *my* to tell about yourself.
2. Write about events in order. Use time-order words.
3. Your narrative should have a beginning, middle, and end.
4. The beginning should introduce the experience.
5. The middle should describe the events in time order.
6. The ending should bring the experience to a close.

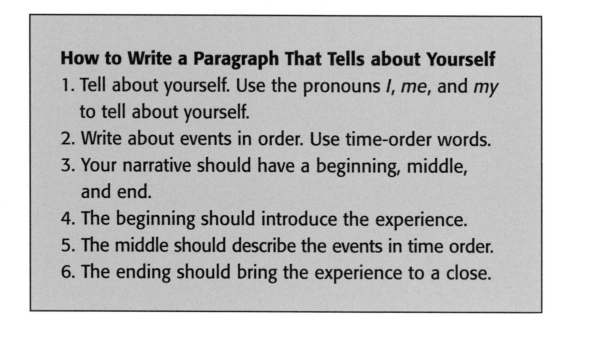

Personal Narrative, page 2

DIRECTIONS **Read the example paragraph on page 478. Then, answer the questions.**

1. Why did the writer write this story?

____

____

2. How do you know this is a personal narrative?

____

____

3. What is the writer's problem?

____

____

DIRECTIONS **Think about something that has happened to you. Use the graphic organizer to plan your personal narrative.**

WRITING PLAN

Beginning	Name the experience you will write about:
Middle	Name three things that happened in the experience:
Ending	Tell how the experience turned out:

Personal Narrative, page 3

Tips for Writing a Personal Narrative:

- Write from your point of view. Use the words *I, me,* and *my* to show your reader that this is your story.
- Think about what you want to tell your reader.
- Organize your ideas into a beginning, middle, and end.
- Write an interesting introduction that "grabs" your reader.
- Write an ending for your story. Tell how the experience ended.

DIRECTIONS **Think about something that has happened to you. Tell about what happened to you in a paragraph. Write at least three sentences. Use your writing plan from page 479 as a guide for writing your personal narrative.**

Poem

In a **poem**, a writer paints a picture with words. Poems often describe something in an unusual or interesting way. Many poems also have rhyming words. The words in a poem often have a definite rhythm, or beat.

Examples:

Rhymed Poem

Cat and Mouse

The mouse poked out her tiny head.
"Look and listen," her mother said.
She heard a bell, and that was that.
The clever mouse escaped the cat.

Unrhymed Poem

Not all poems rhyme. Read how the poem might be written without rhyme.

Cat and Mouse

Like a guard watching for danger,
the mouse peeked around for the cat.

Like an alarm ringing out a warning,
the cat's bell signaled the mouse.

As quick as an eye blink,
the mouse disappeared.

How to Write a Poem

1. Choose a topic for your poem.
2. Give your poem a title.
3. Use colorful words to paint a picture.
4. If you want, use rhyme and rhythm to help you express feelings.

Poem, page 2

DIRECTIONS **Read the example poems on page 481. Then, answer the questions.**

1. Which of the two poems do you like better? Explain why.

____

____

____

2. What are the rhyming words in the first poem?

____

____

3. Read the third and fourth lines of the second poem. What is the cat's bell compared to?

____

____

DIRECTIONS **Finish the poem below. Think of colorful words and words that rhyme. Write another verse for the poem. Then, make up a title for it.**

____

The frog wants a drink.
He hops into the sink.
The ______________ water comes down.
Will the ______________ frog ______________?

____

____

____

Poem, page 3

Tips for Writing a Poem:

- Choose a topic for your poem.
- Use colorful words to paint a picture for your reader.
- Use rhythm and rhyme to express your feelings.
- Use words that begin with the same sound.
- Use words that imitate sounds.
- Make comparisons between things that do not seem alike.
- Give your poem a title.

DIRECTIONS **Think about something that you like to do. Then, think of colorful words that describe it. Use the words in a poem. Write at least eight lines.**

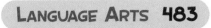

Descriptive Paragraph

In a **descriptive paragraph**, a writer describes a person, place, thing, or event.

A good description lets the reader see, feel, hear, and sometimes taste or smell what is being described.

Example:

Last fall, the air was crisp and cool as Alberto and his big brother waited for the parade to pass. Suddenly, they heard the thump of the big school drum. The parade was coming! Alberto was tall, but even he had trouble seeing over all the people. Beside Alberto, a little girl with a sweet-smelling jelly doughnut was crying. She couldn't see a thing. Alberto lifted the little girl to his shoulders. Then she could see all the high-stepping marchers. The little girl squealed with delight!

How to Write a Descriptive Paragraph

1. Write a topic sentence that clearly tells what the paragraph is about.
2. Add detail sentences. Use colorful words to give information about your topic.
3. Make an exact picture for the reader with the words you choose.

Descriptive Paragraph, page 2

DIRECTIONS **Read the example description on page 484. Then, answer the questions.**

1. In what season does the parade take place? ______________________

2. What are some words the writer uses that appeal to your senses?

____

____

3. What are some descriptions the writer uses to help you imagine what is happening in the story?

____

____

____

DIRECTIONS **Think about something that you would like to describe. It could be a thing, a person you know, or something that has happened to you. Write it in the circle. Then, write words that describe your topic on the lines below. Use the graphic organizer to plan your descriptive paragraph.**

WRITING PLAN

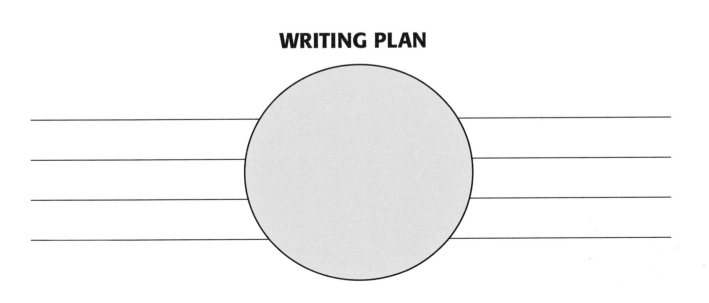

Descriptive Paragraph, page 3

Tips for Writing a Descriptive Paragraph:

- Describe a person, a place, an object, or an event.
- Paint a picture using words.
- Use words that appeal to the reader's senses. Let the reader see, smell, taste, feel, and hear what you are writing about.
- Include a sentence that introduces your topic.
- Write detail sentences that use descriptive words.

DIRECTIONS **Think about something that you would like to describe. Introduce your topic in your first sentence. Then, use the words that you wrote in the graphic organizer on page 485 to describe it. Be sure to appeal to the reader's senses.**

Friendly Letter

A person writes to someone he or she knows in a **friendly letter**. A friendly letter has five parts: a heading, a greeting, a body, a closing, and a signature.

Example:

heading — 27 Green Street
Burlington, NC 27215
April 10, 2005

greeting — Dear Grandma,

body — Sandy and I are fine. Last night he was a busy hamster. He rearranged the wood shavings in his habitat. I love watching him. Please give Aunt Jenny a hug and a kiss for me.

closing — Love,

signature — Mimi

How to Write a Friendly Letter

1. In the heading, include a comma between the name of the city and state and between the day of the month and the year.
2. End the greeting with a comma.
3. Write a friendly message in the body.
4. End the closing with a comma.
5. Sign the letter with your name.

Friendly Letter, page 2

DIRECTIONS **Read the example friendly letter on page 487. Then, answer the questions.**

1. Who wrote this letter? ______________________________
2. What is the writer's address?

   ____

   ____
3. What is the greeting of this letter? ______________________________
4. What is the writer writing about in this letter?

   ____

Address an Envelope

An envelope is used to send a letter or a note.
The receiver's address goes toward the center.
The return address is in the upper left corner.
Postal abbreviations are used for state names.
The ZIP Code goes after the state abbreviation.
Example:

Geraldine Roberts
8 Maple Drive
Camp Hill, PA 17011 — **return address**

stamp

Wendy Garrison
220 Arlington Ave.
Bolivar, NY 14715 — **receiver's name and address**

Friendly Letter, page 3

Tips for Writing a Friendly Letter:
- Think of someone to write to.
- Think of something to write about.
- Write your friendly letter.
- Be sure to include all the parts.
- Fill out the envelope correctly.

heading ______________________________

____

____

greeting ______________________________

body ____

____

____

____

____

____

____

closing ______________________________

signature ______________________________

How-to Paragraph

A **how-to paragraph** gives directions or explains how to do something. Steps are given in time order.
Example:

How to Make a Volcano

You can make a small volcano at home with an adult's help. You will need a pan, a plastic bottle, red food coloring, a bottle of vinegar, baking soda, and some sand. First, add a few drops of food coloring to the vinegar. Next, fill the plastic bottle halfway with baking soda and place it in the middle of the pan. Pile the sand around the bottle. Finally, have an adult quickly pour the vinegar into the hole. Stand back, and let the volcano erupt.

How to Write a How-to Paragraph

1. Write a topic sentence that tells what you are going to explain.
2. Add a detail sentence that tells what materials are needed.
3. Write detail sentences that tell the steps in the directions.
4. Use time-order words such as *first*, *next*, *then*, and *finally* to show correct order.

How-to Paragraph, page 2

DIRECTIONS **Read the example how-to paragraph on page 490. Then, answer the questions.**

1. What does this paragraph tell you how to do? ____________________

   ____

2. What materials are needed to make this thing?

   ____

   ____

3. What is the first step?

   ____

4. What time-order words does the writer use?

   ____

DIRECTIONS **Think about something you want to tell others how to do. Use this writing plan to help you.**

WRITING PLAN

1. What will you tell others how to do?
2. What materials are needed?
3. What steps must the reader follow? Number the steps.
4. What time-order words will you use?

How-to Paragraph, page 3

Tips for Writing a How-to Paragraph:

- Choose one thing to teach someone.
- Think of all the materials that are needed.
- Think of all the steps someone should follow.
- Use time-order words to help the reader follow the steps.

DIRECTIONS **Think about something you want to tell others how to do. Use your writing plan from page 491 as a guide for writing your how-to paragraph.**

Information Paragraph

An **information paragraph** gives facts about one topic. It has a topic sentence that tells the main idea. At least two detail sentences give facts about the main idea.

Example:

The Peak of Perfection — title

Mount Cameroon is a special mountain in Africa. — topic sentence

It is the highest mountain in western Africa and an active volcano. The last time Mount Cameroon erupted was more than 30 years ago. Ash that came out of the volcano turned into rich soil. Farmers now grow tea, rubber trees, and cocoa in that soil. Mount Cameroon is also special because it is one of the wettest places on earth. More than 400 inches of rain fall there each year. — detail sentences

How to Write an Information Paragraph

1. Write a topic sentence that tells your main idea.
2. Write detail sentences that give information about your main idea.
3. Think of a title for your information paragraph.

Information Paragraph, page 2

DIRECTIONS **Read the example information paragraph on page 493. Then, answer the questions.**

1. What is the main idea of the information paragraph?

____

____

2. When did Mount Cameroon last erupt? ______________________

3. Write one detail sentence from the paragraph.

____

____

____

DIRECTIONS **Think about a topic you would like to write about. Use this writing plan to help you.**

WRITING PLAN

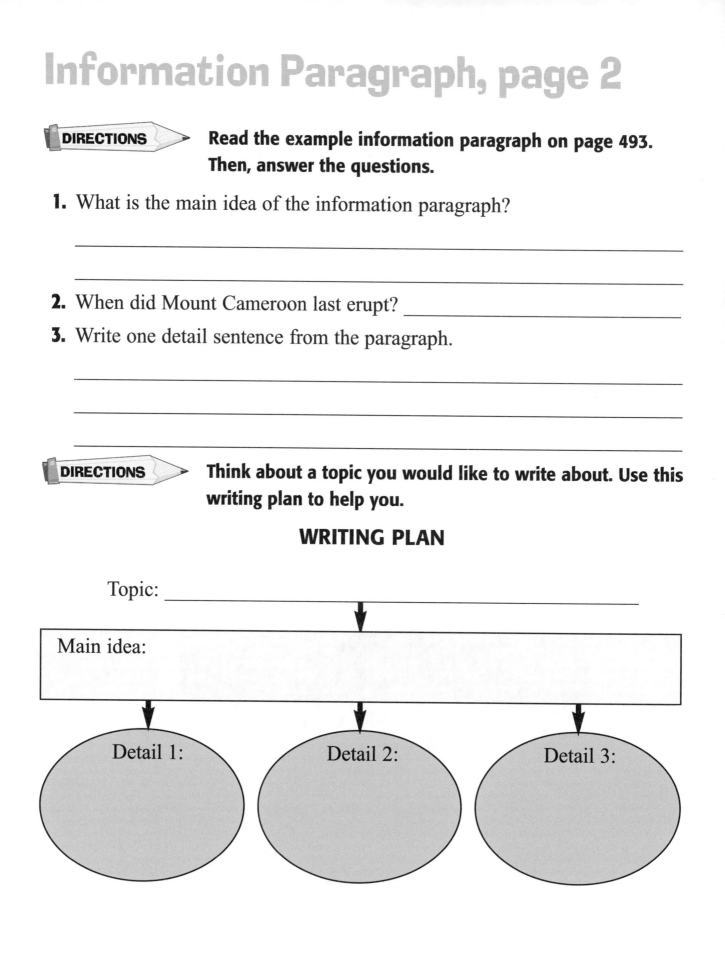

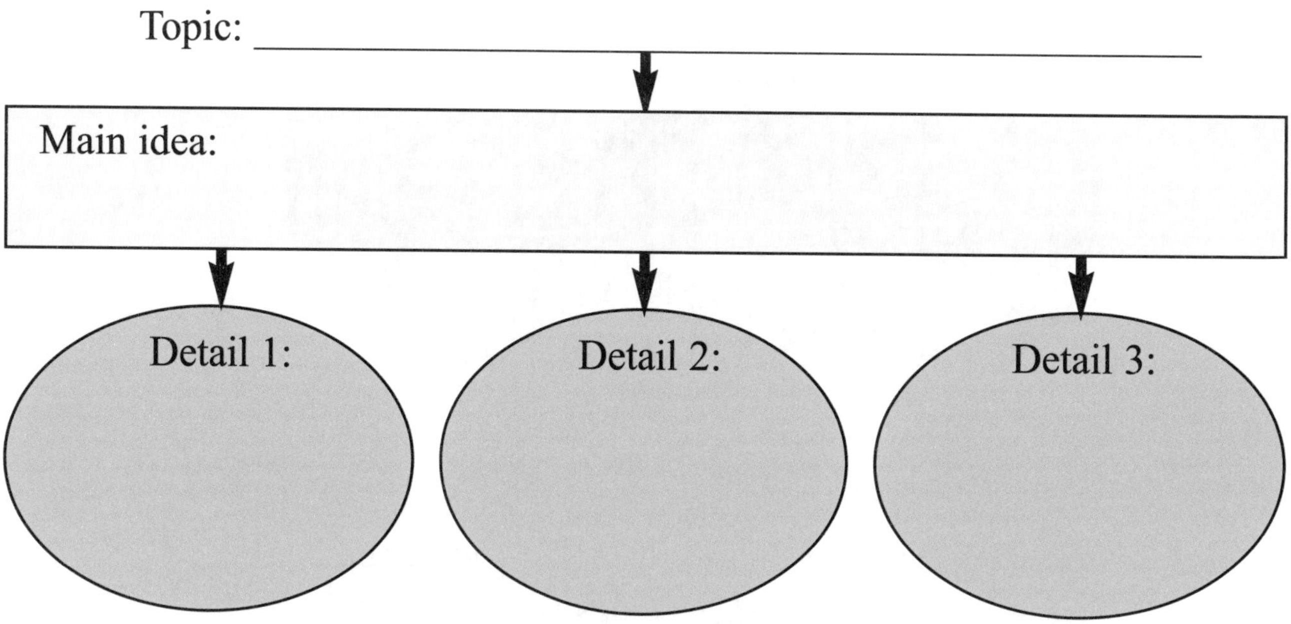

Information Paragraph, page 3

Tips for Writing an Information Paragraph:

- Choose one topic to write about.
- Write a title for your paragraph.
- Write a topic sentence that tells your main idea.
- Write at least two detail sentences that tell facts about the main idea.
- Make sure your facts are correct.

DIRECTIONS **Choose a topic you would like to write about. Use your writing plan from page 494 as a guide for writing your information paragraph.**

Compare and Contrast Paragraph

In a **compare and contrast paragraph**, a writer can show how two people, places, or things are alike or different.

Example:

Geese and whales are different kinds of animals that migrate in large groups. Geese are birds, but whales are mammals. Birds spend much of their time in the air, but whales live in water. These animals are alike, though, because they both migrate thousands of miles. Both geese and whales travel in large groups to reach warmer weather. Geese migrate in groups called flocks. Whales travel in groups called pods.

How to Write a Compare and Contrast Paragraph

1. Write a topic sentence that names the subjects and tells briefly how they are alike and different.
2. Give examples in the detail sentences that clearly tell how the subjects are alike and different.
3. Write about the likenesses or the differences in the same order you named them in the topic sentence.

Compare and Contrast Paragraph, page 2

DIRECTIONS **Read the example compare and contrast paragraph on page 496. Then, answer the questions.**

1. What two things are being compared?

____

2. How are the two things different?

____

____

3. How are the two things alike?

____

____

DIRECTIONS **Choose two things you want to write about. Write them on the lines below. Then, use the Venn diagram to help you plan your writing. List what is true only about A in the A circle. List what is true only about B in the B circle. List what is true about both A and B where the circles overlap.**

A = ____________________

B = ____________________

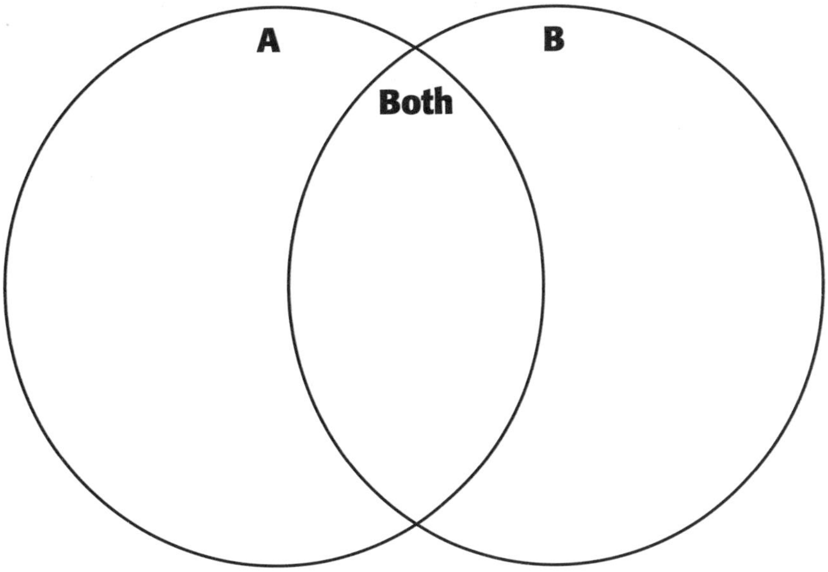

Compare and Contrast Paragraph, page 3

Tips for Writing a Compare and Contrast Paragraph:

- Think about your two subjects.
- Decide how the two subjects are alike and different.
- Write a topic sentence that tells how the two subjects are alike and different.
- Explain how the two subjects are alike.
- Explain how the two subjects are different.
- Write about the likenesses or the differences in the same order you named them in the topic sentence.

DIRECTIONS **Choose two subjects you would like to compare and contrast. Use your Venn diagram from page 497 to write your compare and contrast paragraph.**

Book Report

A **book report** tells about the important events in a book. It does not tell the ending. It also gives the writer's opinion of the book. Finally, it says whether others should read the book.

Example:

A Whale of a Story	**title of report**
The book Humphrey the Lost Whale by Wendy Tokuda and Richard Hall tells the true	**title and author of book**
story of a young whale that took a wrong turn.	**main character**
In the book, people were at first surprised and pleased to see a whale in San Francisco Bay. Then Humphrey headed up the Sacramento	**setting**
River. People soon realized he was lost. Hundreds of people worked together to get Humphrey back to the ocean. This story will	**main idea of book**
make you cheer. Read this book, and share it with a friend.	**whether others should read it**

How to Write a Book Report

1. Tell the title of the book. Underline it.
2. Give the author's name.
3. Tell about the book. Tell the main idea and interesting details. Do not tell the ending.
4. Give your opinion of the book.
5. Think of a title for your report.

Book Report, page 2

DIRECTIONS **Read the example book report on page 499. Then, answer the questions.**

1. What is the title of the book?

____

2. Who wrote the book?

____

3. Who is the main character of the book?

____

4. Where does the book take place?

____

5. Does the writer of the report think others should read the book? ________

DIRECTIONS **Think of a book you would like to tell about. Then, use this writing plan to organize your report.**

Title of book: ________________________________

Author of book: ______________________________

Main character of book: _______________________

Setting of book: ______________________________

Main events of book: __________________________

____

____

____

Should others read this book? __________________

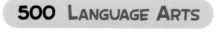

Book Report, page 3

Tips for Writing a Book Report:

- Choose one book to write about.
- Write a title for your report.
- Name the book and the author in your report.
- Name the main character and setting of the book.
- Tell the main events of the book, but do not tell the ending.
- Tell if you think others would like the book.

DIRECTIONS **Choose a book you would like to write about. Use your writing plan from page 500 as a guide for writing your book report.**

Persuasive Paragraph

In a **persuasive paragraph**, a writer tries to make readers agree with his or her opinion.

Example:

Whale watching is good for people and for the environment. Many people have begun working for Earth-friendly causes after sailing near whales. Also, these intelligent animals seem to like the visitors. Tourists excitedly describe how whales come up to the boats to be touched. Most important, whale watching helps people learn how valuable and beautiful these mysterious mammals are. Everyone is helped by a whale-watching trip. Find out more about one today!

opinion in topic sentence

reasons and facts

strongest reason last

restated opinion or call for action

How to Write a Paragraph That Convinces

1. Write a topic sentence that tells your opinion or main idea.
2. Give reasons to support your main idea in the detail sentences. Save your strongest reason for last.
3. At the end of your paragraph, tell your feelings again. Ask your reader to feel the same way.

Persuasive Paragraph, page 2

DIRECTIONS **Read the example persuasive paragraph on page 502. Then, answer the questions.**

1. What is the writer's main idea in this paragraph?

____

____

2. What are two reasons the writer gives to support the main idea?

____

____

____

3. What call for action does the writer use in the last sentence?

____

____

DIRECTIONS **Think of something you feel strongly about. Then, use this writing plan to organize your persuasive paragraph.**

WRITING PLAN

Main idea: ____

Reason 1: ____

Reason 2: ____

Reason 3 (your strongest reason): _______________________________

____

____

Call for action: ____

Persuasive Paragraph, page 3

Tips for Writing a Persuasive Paragraph:

- Choose a topic that you feel strongly about.
- State your opinion in your topic sentence.
- Write good reasons to support your opinion.
- Try to have at least three good reasons.
- Save your strongest reason for last.
- At the end of your paragraph, restate your opinion. Tell the reader to take some action.

DIRECTIONS **Choose a topic that you have an opinion about. Use your writing plan from page 503 as a guide for writing your persuasive paragraph.**

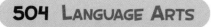

Writing for a Test

Some kinds of test questions ask you to write. These questions check to see if you can organize your thoughts and express your ideas. They also test to see if you can write for a specific purpose and use correct grammar. Here are some tips for writing better on a test.

Before the Test

- Listen carefully to all the directions your teacher or test giver gives you.
- Read all written directions carefully.
- Ask any questions you have. (You might not be allowed to talk once the test starts.)
- Have several pens or sharpened pencils on hand.
- If you are allowed, read each item on the test before you begin.

During the Test

- Take time to identify your task, audience, and purpose.
- Organize your thoughts before you write.
- Write neatly and clearly.
- If you need help, raise your hand. Don't call out or get up.

After the Test

- If you finish before time is up, go back and make final corrections.
- Follow the directions given at the beginning for what to do at the end of the test. You may have to sit quietly while others finish.

Writing for a Test, page 2

Timed Writing

You have probably taken timed tests before. What are some ways to do well during a timed writing test? Follow these tips to make a timed test go more smoothly:

- Stay calm. Take a deep breath and relax.
- For a writing test, remember to check your task and your purpose. (Unless you are told otherwise, your audience is the person who will read the test.)
- Plan how you will use your time. If this is a writing test, decide how much time you need to spend prewriting, drafting, revising, proofreading, and writing the final draft.
- If you begin to run out of time, decide if you can combine some steps. Your goal is to finish.

Written Prompts

A written prompt is a statement or a question that asks you to complete a writing task.

- A narrative prompt asks you to tell a story.
- A persuasive prompt asks you to convince the reader.
- An expository prompt asks you to inform or explain.
- A descriptive prompt asks you to describe something.

Picture Prompts

A picture prompt is a statement or question about a picture. It asks you to tell something about the picture. The prompt also tells the purpose for writing.

Using a Dictionary

The order of letters from *A* to *Z* is called **alphabetical order**. Words in a dictionary are listed in alphabetical order.
When words begin with the same letters, the next letter of the word is used to put the words in alphabetical order: <u>ca</u>pe, <u>cha</u>pel, <u>chi</u>me.
Each word in the dictionary is an **entry word**.
There are two **guide words** at the top of every dictionary page. The word on the left is the first entry word on the page. The word on the right is the last entry word. All the other entry words on the page are in alphabetical order between the guide words.

DIRECTIONS **Use this example dictionary page to answer the questions.**

cherry **chip**

cher·ry [cher′ē] *n., pl.* **cher·ries** **1** A small, round, edible fruit, red, yellow, or nearly black in color, and having a single pit. **2** The tree bearing this fruit. **3** The wood of this tree. **4** A bright red color.

child [chīld] *n., pl.* **chil·dren** [chil′dren] **1** A baby. **2** A young boy or girl. **3** A son or daughter. **4** A person from a certain family.

1. What is the last entry word on this page? ____________________

How do you know? ____________________

2. What are the two guide words on this page? ____________________

____

3. Which of these words would come before *cherry* in the dictionary:

carrot, *corn*, *cactus*, *clover*? ____________________

4. Would the word *chop* be on this page? ____________________

Using a Dictionary, page 2

A **syllable** is a word part that has only one vowel sound. Each entry word in the dictionary is divided into syllables.
A **pronunciation** follows each entry word. It shows how to say the word. It also shows the number of syllables in the word.
Examples:

phlox [fläks]   spinach [spin′ ich]

The **pronunciation key** lists the symbol for each sound. It also gives a familiar word in which the sound is heard. A pronunciation key usually appears on every other page of a dictionary.

a	add	i	it	o͝o	took	oi	oil
ā	ace	ī	ice	o͞o	pool	ou	pout
â	care	o	odd	u	up	ng	ring
ä	palm	ō	open	û	burn	th	thin
e	end	ô	order	yo͞o	fuse	t͟h	this
ē	equal					zh	vision

ə = { a in above, e in sicken, i in possible, o in melon, u in circus }

DIRECTIONS **Read each pronunciation. Choose and circle the word that matches the pronunciation. Then, tell how many syllables are in each word.**

1. klō′ vər   clever   cover   clover   ________

2. bēt   beet   bet   bait   ________

3. pik′ əl   pickle   pocket   pluck   ________

4. pâr   purr   pear   pour   ________

5. (h)wēt   what   wait   wheat   ________

Using a Dictionary, page 3

An **entry** is all the information about an entry word.
A **definition** is the meaning of a word. Many words have more than one definition. Each definition is numbered.
A definition is often followed by an **example** that shows how to use the word.

spin [spin] *v.* **1** To draw out and twist (as cotton or flax) into thread. **2** To make fibers into threads or yarn by spinning. **3** To make something, as a web or cocoon, from sticky fibers from an insect's body: Wolf spiders do not spin webs. **4** To turn or whirl about; rotate: to spin a top. **5** To make up a story or tale.

DIRECTIONS **Use the entry for *spin* to answer the questions.**

1. How many definitions are given for the entry word? ________________

2. For which definition is there an example sentence? ________________

3. How many syllables does the entry word have? ________________

4. What information is given in brackets [ ]? ________________

5. Which definition of *spin* is used in this sentence?

Rumpelstiltskin could spin straw into gold. ________________

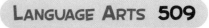

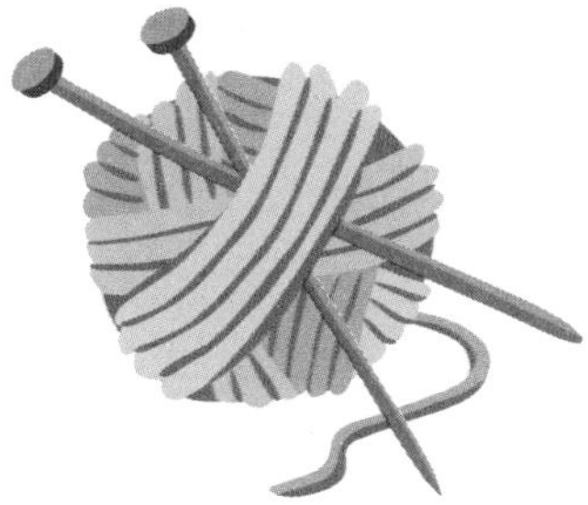

Using a Thesaurus

A **thesaurus** is a book that tells synonyms, words that have nearly the same meaning, and antonyms, words that mean the opposite of a word. Many thesauruses are like dictionaries. The entry words are listed in dark print in alphabetical order. Guide words at the top of the page tell which words can be found on the page. Good writers use a thesaurus to find interesting words.

give **goal**

glad *syn* cheerful, happy, jolly, joyful, lighthearted, merry, pleased
ant blue, downcast, glum, sad, unhappy

DIRECTIONS **Use a thesaurus. Replace the underlined word with a synonym or antonym. Write the new word on the line.**

1. Dan will <u>get</u> a baby duck in the spring.

synonym ____________________

2. Dan is very <u>lucky</u>.

synonym ____________________

3. A baby deer would make a <u>bad</u> pet.

synonym ____________________

4. Baby raccoons are the <u>most</u> popular pets.

antonym ____________________

5. It is very <u>kind</u> to keep raccoons in a cage.

antonym ____________________

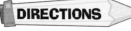

Using an Encyclopedia

An **encyclopedia** is a set of books that has facts on many subjects. Each book in a set is called a volume. The volumes list subjects in alphabetical order.

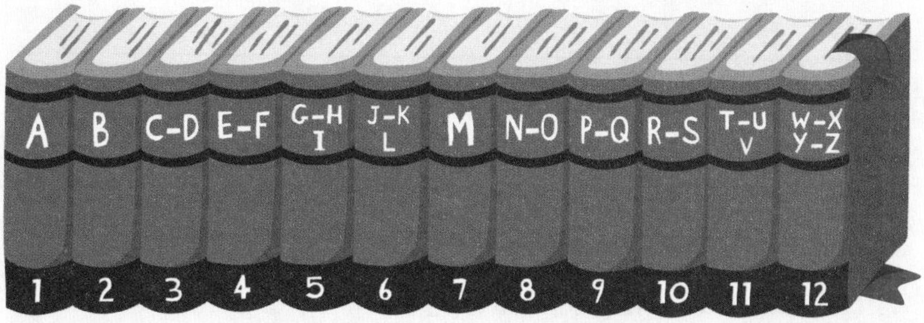

DIRECTIONS **Use the model encyclopedia to write the number of the volume in which you would find each of these subjects.**

1. Mississippi River ____________

2. Explorers ____________

3. Rocky Mountains ____________

4. Barges ____________

5. Colorado River ____________

6. United States ____________

7. Riverboats ____________

8. Farming ____________

DIRECTIONS **Write the word or words you would use to look up the following subjects in an encyclopedia.**

9. the growth of cities ____________

10. the logging business ____________

11. mountains in the United States ____________

12. American ships ____________

13. rivers of America ____________

14. the uses of water ____________

Using the Internet

The computer can help you to do research. You can use the Internet to find almost any information. The key to finding information is to know which keywords to type. Here are some hints to speed up the search.

How to Use the Internet

1. Make a list of keywords or names.
2. Type in two or three keywords.
3. Type in different combinations of keywords until the topic titles focus on the information you need.

DIRECTIONS **Write the keywords you would use to search for these subjects.**

1. author Shel Silverstein ____________________
2. time a movie starts at the theater ____________________
3. the weather ____________________
4. download a new computer game ____________________
5. how to add fractions ____________________
6. where to buy shoes ____________________
7. which Native American groups lived in your area ____________________
8. how to get to a place ____________________
9. what to see in a city you would like to visit ____________________
10. what kind of dog you might like ____________________

Parts of a Book

The **title page** tells the name of a book. It gives the name of the author. It also tells the name of the company that published the book.

The **table of contents** comes after the title page. It lists the titles of the chapters or units in the book. It also lists the page on which each new part begins. Everything in the book is listed in the order in which it appears.

An **index** is a list of all the topics in a book. It is in alphabetical order. It lists the page or pages on which each topic appears.

DIRECTIONS **Use the example book pages to answer the questions.**

title page	table of contents	index
ART PROJECTS AT THE BEACH by Sandy Shore Crafts Books, Inc.	**Contents** Getting Started . . . 8 Shell Art . . . . 10 Sand Art . . . . 32 Sea-Plant and Rock Crafts 50	Beaches, 8–10, 26, 29 Plants, 50–54, 60–62 Rocks, 50–54, 59–62 Sand, 8–12, 32–49 Shells, 8, 10–30

1. What is the title of the book? ____________________

2. Who wrote the book? ____________________

3. What company published this book? ____________________

4. What is the first chapter in the book? ____________________

5. What chapter begins on page 32? ____________________

6. On what pages would you find facts about beaches? ____________________

Kinds of Books

Fiction books tell stories. They tell about make-believe people and things.
Example:
Charlotte's Web, a book about a talking spider

Nonfiction books tell facts about real people, things, or events. A nonfiction book that tells about the life of a real person is called a biography.
Example:
Spider Silk, facts about how spiders spin webs

Reference books are often in a special section in the library. In this section you will find the dictionary, thesaurus, encyclopedia, almanac, atlas, and other books. All these books contain factual information. They are nonfiction books.

DIRECTIONS **Tell if each book below is *fiction* or *nonfiction*.**

1. a book of maps ______________________
2. a true book about a famous scientist's life ______________________
3. a book of facts about insects of the world ______________________
4. a story about Lydia, a hamster that talks ______________________
5. a book of word meanings ______________________
6. a book of poems about dragons ______________________
7. a book about students at a school for wizards ______________________
8. a book of folk tales ______________________

Reading for Information

Skimming is a quick way to read. When you skim a paragraph, you look for its main idea. The main idea is the most important idea in the paragraph.

Scanning is also a quick reading method. When you scan a page, you look it over to find a particular fact.

DIRECTIONS **Skim this paragraph. Then, circle the sentence below that best states the main idea.**

The months of January and March were named after Roman gods long ago. The month of January was named for Janus, the god of beginnings. March was named for Mars, the god of war.

1. Some months are named after Roman gods.
2. The names of the months come from unusual words.
3. The Romans named the months long ago.

DIRECTIONS **Scan this paragraph. Then, answer the questions.**

Other months' names came from Latin words used by Romans. April comes from the Latin word *aperio*, which means "to open." The last four months of the year come from Latin words for numbers: *septem* (seven), *octo* (eight), *novem* (nine), *decem* (ten).

4. What does the Latin word *aperio* mean?

____

5. What Latin word means the number nine?

____

Fact or Opinion

Which of these sentences is a fact? Which is an opinion?

1. There are many different kinds of dogs.
2. I think dogs are the best kind of pets.

If you decided that sentence 1 is a fact, you are right. A **fact** is a statement that can be proved.

Sentence 2 is a nonfact, or an opinion. An **opinion** is what someone thinks, feels, or believes. Words like *think*, *believe*, and *feel* are words often used with opinions. These are clues that what the author is saying is an opinion.

Writers often try to get you to agree with their opinions. It is important for you to know the difference between a fact and an opinion.

DIRECTIONS **Read each statement and decide if it is a fact or an opinion. Write *fact* or *opinion* on the line.**

1. I feel that basketball is the best sport. ______________________

2. A zoo is a place to see many animals. ______________________

3. There are three feet in one yard. ______________________

4. I think math is the hardest subject. ______________________

5. A day is shorter than a week. ______________________

DIRECTIONS **Follow the directions to write complete sentences.**

6. Write a fact about your home. ______________________

____

7. Write an opinion about your home. ______________________

____

Taking Notes

A writer takes good **notes** to remember the facts he or she finds when doing research for a report.

Example:

Wild Travelers, by George Laycock, page 67
Where do male fur seals migrate to?
to Gulf of Alaska
travel 400–500 miles from winter home

How to Take Notes

1. Write a question. Then, find a book to answer the question.
2. List the title of the book, the author, and the pages where you find facts.
3. Write answers to your question. Write only the facts you need for your report.
4. Write the information in your own words. Write sentences or short groups of words.

DIRECTIONS **Read the paragraph. Take notes on the facts you would use in a report about female fur seals.**

Female fur seals do an amazing thing. Each year in the fall, they migrate 3,000 miles. They leave the Pribilof Islands and swim all the way to southern California.

Summary

A **summary** is a short sentence or paragraph that tells the main facts or ideas in a story or selection. To summarize any writing, you must pay attention to the details. Using the question words *who, what, where, when,* and *why* can help you find the important details to include in a summary. A summary table can help you organize the information to write a summary.

DIRECTIONS **Read the paragraph. Then, complete the summary table.**

People who plan to camp should be prepared for some crawly company. Spiders surprise campers by appearing in unusual places. Spiders might be found on early morning canoe trips. They might jump out of boots, drop from trees, or crawl out from under rocks. Spiders crawl into these different spaces looking for a safe place to spin a web to catch food to eat.

Who: What: Where: When: Why:	Summary:

Outline

A writer uses an **outline** to put the notes for a research report in order.

Example:

Migrating Seals

I. Live in Alaska

II. Travel south in fall

How to Write an Outline

1. Write a title telling the subject of your report.
2. Write the main topics. Use a Roman numeral and a period before each topic.
3. Begin each main topic with a capital letter.

DIRECTIONS **Write these main topics in correct outline form. Use the title below for your outline.**

Migrating Monarch Butterflies
migrate south from Canada and northern United States
spend winter in southern United States and Mexico
return home in spring

____

____

____

____

____

____

Rough Draft

A writer quickly puts all of his or her ideas on paper in a **rough draft**.

How to Write a Rough Draft

1. Read your outline and notes. Keep them near you as you write.
2. Follow your outline to write a rough draft. Do not add anything that is not on your outline. Do not leave out anything.
3. Write one paragraph for each Roman numeral in your outline.
4. Write freely. Do not worry about mistakes now. You will make changes later.

DIRECTIONS **Choose one of the outlines below. Write a topic sentence for each paragraph of a rough draft.**

1. Migrating Swallows
   I. Fly long distances to get away from cold
   II. Migrate by day
   III. Travel 10,000 miles

2. Migrating Geese
   I. Live in the United States and Canada
   II. Fly in groups
   III. Fly as far south as Mexico

____

____

____

____

Research Report

First, a writer makes all the changes in the rough draft. Then, he or she writes the final copy of the **research report**.

Example:

Migrating Seals

Seals are migrating animals. Fur seals from the Pribilof Islands near Alaska migrate every fall.

Female and male fur seals migrate to different places. In the fall, female fur seals swim 3,000 miles to southern California. The male fur seals migrate to the Gulf of Alaska. They travel only 400 to 500 miles from their summer homes.

How to Write a Research Report

1. Write the title of your report.
2. Write the report. Use your rough draft.
3. Make all the changes you marked on your rough draft.
4. Indent the first sentence of each paragraph.

DIRECTIONS **On the lines below write some ideas of subjects you would like to research. Take notes on one of the subjects. Write an outline and a rough draft. Then, write a report.**

Analyzing a Research Report

A research report gives facts about one topic.
It usually has more than one paragraph.
It has a title that tells about the topic.

DIRECTIONS **Read this research report. Answer the questions.**

Colds

A cold is caused by a virus. No one really knows how to prevent colds. Getting wet or chilled does not directly give you a cold. A chill, however, might put you in a weaker state than usual. Then, if a cold is going around, you will be more likely to get it.

Colds are usually caught by being near someone who already has one. The easiest way to catch a cold is from someone's sneeze. One person with a cold in a crowd can give it to many other people just by sneezing. If you have a cold, you should stay away from other people.

1. What is the topic of this report? ______________________
2. Write the sentence that states the main idea.

____

____

3. What is one detail about the main idea?

____

____

4. What might the topic of another paragraph in this research paper be?

____

Writing Skills

UNIT 1: Personal Narrative

HOW MUCH DO YOU KNOW?

Read the three sentences. They are out of order. Label each one *beginning, middle,* or *ending*.

1. A patch of lettuce grew under my window.

   ____

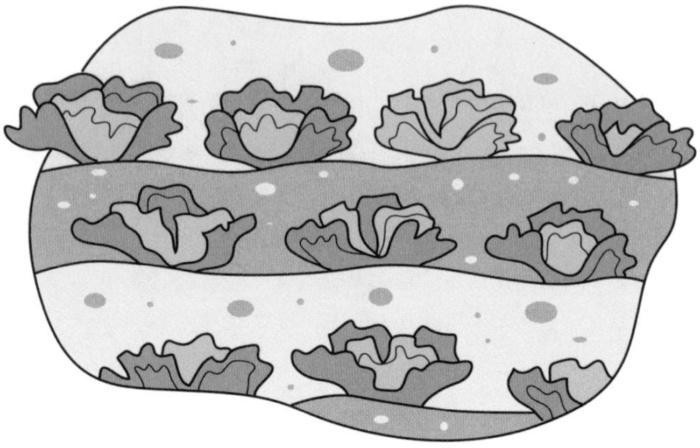

2. I planted seeds under my window.

   ____

3. Mom picked the lettuce for a salad.

   ____

Choose the title you think is more interesting. Draw a line under it. Write a sentence to tell why you think so.

4. A Black Dog   The Tallest Dog in the World

   ____

Write a story about how you got to school today.

____

____

____

____

Analyzing a Personal Narrative

A PERSONAL NARRATIVE
- **has one topic**
- **tells about the writer**
- **has sentences that tell what happens in the beginning, the middle, and the ending**
- **uses the words *I*, *me*, and *my***

Read each group of three sentences. They are out of order. Label each one *beginning*, *middle*, or *ending*.

1. a. I put my palm tree near a window.

   I put apalm tree near my window.

   b. I bought a potted palm tree at the plant store.

   I bought a potted palm tree at the plant store.

   c. I brought the palm tree home.

   I brougt the palm tree home.

2. a. After reading that, I took my palm tree into the shower with me.

   ____

   b. The book said that palm trees should be washed often.

   ____

   c. I read about palm trees in a book about plants.

   ____

Connecting Ideas in a Sequence

To write a personal narrative, good writers tell about things in the order in which they happen.

Read each paragraph. Then number the events below it in the order in which they happened.

1. We looked at the four eggs on the leaves of the tomato plant. Each egg was about as big as the head of a pin. During the week, we watched as the pale green eggs changed to yellowish-green and then almost white. One morning something inside started to cut a hole in one of the eggs. Soon, a tiny caterpillar crawled out of the egg. Within a short time, all the eggs had hatched.

    ____ The eggs changed to yellowish-green, then white.

    ____ The eggs hatched.

    ____ We saw pale green eggs on the tomato leaves.

2. The first thing the pale caterpillars did was start to eat tomato leaves. We watched as they grew and grew. After a few days, the skin of each one split down the back. Each caterpillar crawled out of the old skin. There was a new, bigger skin underneath. Each caterpillar was about four inches long and bright green in color.

____ The caterpillars began to eat the tomato leaves.

____ The caterpillars were four inches long and bright green.

____ The skin of the caterpillars split for the first time.

Capturing the Reader's Interest

Good writers capture the reader's interest by creating
- a catchy title
- a strong beginning sentence

Choose the title you think is more interesting. Circle it. Write a sentence to tell why you think so.

1. Mysteries, Monsters, and Untold Secrets — Things We Don't Understand

____

2. Jim Saves Time — A Wrinkle in Time

____

3. The No-Return Trail — The Country Road

____

4. From the Mixed-Up Files of Mrs. Basil E. Frankenweiler — The Day I Ran Away from Home

____

5. Willie Bea's Day — Willie Bea and the Day the Martians Landed

____

Using the Thesaurus

- A *thesaurus* is a book of *synonyms*, or words that have nearly the same meaning.
- *Antonyms*, or words that mean the opposite of the entry word, follow the synonyms.

Replace the underlined word with a synonym or an antonym. Use a thesaurus or a dictionary to find synonyms and antonyms. Write the new word on the line.

1. Dan will <u>get</u> a baby duck in the spring.

   synonym: ______________________________

2. Dan is very <u>lucky</u>.

   synonym: ______________________________

3. A baby deer would make a <u>good</u> pet.

   antonym: ______________________________

4. Pets <u>need</u> special food and water.

   synonym: ______________________________

5. It is best not to <u>purchase</u> a pet you can't keep.

   synonym: ______________________________

6. Baby raccoons are the <u>most</u> popular wild animal pets.

   antonym: ______________________________

7. It is very <u>kind</u> to keep a raccoon in a cage.

   antonym: ______________________________

Proofreading a Personal Narrative

PROOFREADING HINT

To be a good proofreader, look for one type of error at a time. For example, proofread once for capitalization errors, once for punctuation errors, and once for spelling errors.

Proofread the beginning of the personal narrative, paying special attention to end marks. Use the Proofreading Marks to correct at least seven errors.

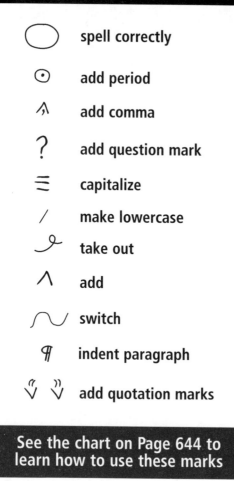

PROOFREADING MARKS

- spell correctly
- ⊙ add period
- add comma
- ? add question mark
- ≡ capitalize
- / make lowercase
- take out
- ^ add
- switch
- ¶ indent paragraph
- add quotation marks

See the chart on Page 644 to learn how to use these marks

Uncle John has always been my favorite uncle What a surprise we all had last summer Late one evening there was a knock at the back door. Can you guess who was standing on our back steps Of course, it was Uncle John He had a backpack, a small suitcase, and an armload of gifts.

Uncle John's present for me was a bright blew T-shirt. it has a picture of an old castle on the back. Uncle John bought the shirt for me when he was traveling in England last year I wore that shirt every day wile Uncle John was staying with us

Uncle John has been to many different parts of the world, and he loved telling us about his adventures. Listening to his stories was almost as much fun as going along on Uncle John's trips

Order a Story

Write one or two sentences of a story in each of the boxes on this page. The boxes should be out of order. Ask a friend to try to put the boxes in order. He or she should read the story aloud to see if it makes sense.

Write Your Own Sentences

Pick your favorite kind of dinosaur. Draw a picture of that dinosaur. Under the picture, write three sentences that tell about it.

Write about Wishes

Talk with a friend about wishes. Make a list of your wishes.

Write four sentences about your wishes. Be sure to revise and proofread your sentences.

A Practice Personal Narrative

SAVE JACK

I remember when I met Danny. He came at just the right time. I was new in town, and I needed a friend. I didn't know that Danny would become my best friend.

The summer I was eight years old, my family moved. We didn't move to a new house down the street. We moved to a new town 500 miles away. I hated leaving my friends. I was so sad when we left.

Here I was in a new town and had no friends. I wouldn't let myself think of the day school would start.

There were lots of people in my class, but I felt lonely. I didn't see any friends. I only saw kids I had never seen before. They all seemed to know and like each other. I wanted someone to notice me, and they did.

One boy called me "Four Eyes" because I wore glasses. "That's an old joke," I thought, but it still bothered me. A second boy called me "Scaredy Cat." I'm not sure why. I guess I looked scared. This wasn't the kind of attention I wanted.

At recess, everyone played ball and ran races. I stood against the building. I saw all of them, but they didn't see me. If I had been younger, I probably would have cried.

When I went home that afternoon, I went straight to my room. I didn't have any homework. I just didn't want Mom to see how unhappy I was.

On Tuesday, I met Danny. "Would you like to play ball at recess?" he asked. At first, I was too surprised to answer. It took a minute to find the word I needed. "Yes," I said gladly. I was happy to play ball with Danny. Suddenly, school was starting to get better. That feeling lasted until I walked home that afternoon.

After school, another boy from my class started to walk home with me. I was still thinking about Danny. Tom wasn't anything like Danny. In fact, he wasn't friendly at all. He started teasing me about being new. "Look at the new kid. Where did you come from? You look green to me." He said more, but I stopped paying attention. A couple of blocks later, Tom got tired and left me alone. By that time, I had almost forgotten how much I liked Danny. All I could think about was how many kids acted like Tom.

When I got to school on Wednesday, Danny was the first person I saw. I couldn't believe it. He was talking to Tom. I decided to go up to them. When I came near, Danny stopped talking. I didn't know what that meant until recess.

At recess, Danny and I were playing soccer. Tom came over and asked if he could play, too. Danny said, "Sure." I didn't know what to say.

On Thursday, more kids came over to play. We had enough people to make two teams. Recess was getting better.

That afternoon, Danny walked home with me even though he lived on a different street. I wondered if he was trying to stop other kids from bothering me. It didn't really matter. I liked

Danny, and he seemed to like me.

On Friday, I learned something about Danny. He was talking to some kids in my class. As I walked up, I heard him say, "Some of us have started a special club called the Save Jack Club. Would you like to join?"

I couldn't believe my ears. Danny had started a club just for me. He had made all the kids in my class part of the club. The kids liked Danny a lot. When they saw that he was my friend, they wanted to be my friends, too. Danny rescued me. I was more than just the new kid now. Danny was my new best friend. He still is.

Respond to the Practice Paper

Write your answers to the following questions or directions.

1. Why did the writer write this story?

2. How did the writer feel in the beginning of the story? How do you know?

3. How did the writer feel at the end of the story? How do you know?

4. Write a paragraph to summarize this story. Use these questions to help you write your summary:
   - What is the story about?
   - What happens first? Second? Third?
   - How does the story end?

Analyze the Practice Paper

Read "Save Jack" again. As you read, think about how the writer wrote the story. Write your answers to the following questions.

1. How do you know that this is a personal narrative?

2. What is Jack's problem?

3. How is the problem solved?

4. How are the first paragraph and the last paragraph alike?

Writing Assignment

Think about the best friend in your life now. Think about writing a personal narrative that tells about your best friend. Use examples and details to show why this person is your best friend. Use this writing plan to help you write a first draft on the next page.

Name your friend:

▼

Tell how you and this person became friends.

▼

Give examples to show why this person is your best friend.

First Draft

TIPS FOR WRITING A PERSONAL NARRATIVE:

- **Write from your point of view. Use the words *I* and *my* to show your readers that this is your story.**
- **Think about what you want to tell your reader.**
- **Organize your ideas into a beginning, middle, and end.**
- **Write an introduction that "grabs" your reader's attention.**
- **Write an ending for your story. Write it from your point of view.**

Use your writing plan as a guide for writing your first draft of a personal narrative. Include a catchy title.

(Continue on your own paper.)

Revise the Draft

Use the chart below to help you revise your draft. Check YES or NO to answer each question in the chart. If you answer NO, make notes to remind yourself how you can revise, or change, your writing to improve it.

Question	YES ✔	NO ✔	If the answer is NO, what will you do to improve your writing?
Does your story describe your best friend?			
Does your story have a strong beginning?			
Do you describe events in the order they happened?			
Does your story have an ending?			
Do you give examples to show why this person is your best friend?			
Do you tell your story from your point of view?			
Have you corrected mistakes in spelling, grammar, and punctuation?			

Use the notes in your chart and your writing plan to revise your draft.

Writing Report Card

Read your revised draft again or ask someone else to read it. Have the person who reads your paper complete the following Report Card. Revise your paper until you have no less than a Very Good Score for each item.

Title of paper: ______________________________

Purpose of paper: *This is a personal narrative. It tells about my best friend.*

Person who scores the paper: ______________________________

Score	Writing Goals
	Does this story have a strong beginning?
	Are the story's main ideas organized into paragraphs?
	Are there details to support each main idea?
	Are the paragraphs organized in a way that makes sense?
	Are there different kinds of sentences that help make the story interesting?
	Is there a strong ending?
	Are the story's grammar, spelling, and punctuation correct?

☺ Excellent Score ☆ Very Good Score + Good Score
✔ Acceptable Score – Needs Improvement

UNIT 2: Informative Writing

HOW MUCH DO YOU KNOW?

Read the paragraph. Draw a line under the sentence that tells the main idea. Then list two details.

Animal tracks can tell you many things. For example, most cat tracks are smaller than dog tracks. Also, cat tracks are more rounded than dog tracks are. Cats usually keep their nails pulled in, but dogs can't do that. So dog tracks show nail marks.

1. ____

2. ____

Read each paragraph. Answer the questions.

A. People who live in cities enjoy parks. Many families spend the day in the park. They do many fun things. Sometimes they bring picnic lunches.

B. People who live in cities enjoy parks. Many families spend the entire day in the park. Sometimes my family begins the morning with a canoe ride on the deep, blue lake. Ducks and turtles watch the canoes go by. At noon, we stop for a picnic of chicken, fruit, and cake. My family spends the afternoon looking for bears, elephants, and dragons in the clouds.

3. Which paragraph is more interesting? Explain your answer.

____

____

4. What is one detail given in the second paragraph?

____

Analyzing an Information Paragraph

AN INFORMATION PARAGRAPH

- is a group of sentences
- tells about one main idea
- has a topic sentence that tells the main idea
- has detail sentences that tell facts about the main idea

Read each paragraph. Draw a line under the sentence that tells the main idea. Then list two details.

1. The squid and the octopus look very different. The octopus has a round head and body. It has eight arms, or tentacles, on the bottom of its body. The squid is torpedo-shaped. All of its tentacles are at one end. Eight of them are the same length. Two are longer, for a total of ten.

   a. ______________________________

   b. ______________________________

2. The squid and the octopus behave very differently. The squid can shoot through the water at great speed. The octopus moves more slowly and spends most of its time on the sea bottom.

   a. ______________________________

   ____

   b. ______________________________

   ____

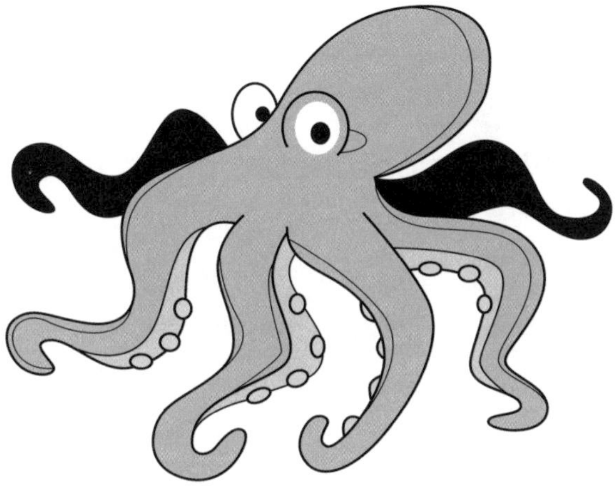

Connecting Main Idea and Details

TO WRITE AN INFORMATION PARAGRAPH, GOOD WRITERS

- think about one main idea
- plan interesting details to tell about the main idea

Read each group of sentences. Write *main idea* or *detail* to tell what each would be in a paragraph.

1. a. If you break off the end, you can make an herb pot.

   ____

   b. You can arrange cracked pieces into a design.

   ____

   c. A person can do a lot of things with an eggshell.

   ____

   d. You can decorate it for certain holidays.

   ____

2. a. Place the egg over a bowl.

   ____

   b. With a safety pin, make a small hole in each end of a raw egg.

   ____

   c. Slowly run water through the hollow egg to clean it out.

   ____

   d. It is easy to hollow out an egg.

   ____

Using Enough Details

GOOD WRITERS GIVE READERS

- interesting details
- clear examples

Read each paragraph. Answer the questions.

A. Owls are best known for their ability to see at night. They can see 100 times better than humans can. Their eyes are big and do not move very easily. This is why owls' necks have to turn so far.

B. Though they can also see well in the daytime, owls are known for seeing at night. They can see 100 times better at night than humans can, but they are color-blind. Owls' eyes are very large, and they control the light coming in by changing the size of the pupil of the eyes. Each pupil acts alone. If you stood in the sun and your friend stood in the shade, an owl could see each of you well.

1. Which paragraph is more interesting? Explain your answer.

____

____

2. What is one detail given in the second paragraph?

____

3. Write one example found in the second paragraph.

____

Keeping to the Topic

- A good writer plans a paragraph so that it shares details about one main idea.
- All the sentences in a paragraph must keep to the topic.

Read the topic sentence below. Choose the sentences that keep to the topic. Write a paragraph, using the topic sentence and the sentences you chose.

A sighted person can only imagine what it is like to be blind.

Put a scarf over your eyes to block out light.

Try to figure out what different foods are.

Being deaf is not easy either.

Pretend to pay for something with coins.

Try to walk into another room and sit at a table.

A person who cannot hear has different problems.

Blind people can do all these things and more.

Proofreading Information Paragraphs

PROOFREADING HINT

To be a good proofreader, look for one type of error at a time. For example, proofread once for capitalization errors, once for punctuation errors, and once for spelling errors.

PROOFREADING MARKS	
◯	spell correctly
⊙	add period
^,	add comma
?	add question mark
≡	capitalize
/	make lowercase
ℓ	take out
∧	add
∿	switch
¶	indent paragraph
∨“ ∨”	add quotation marks

Proofread the information paragraphs, paying special attention to missing words. Use the Proofreading Marks to correct at least six errors.

Pond snails are useful in fish tanks. Pond snails will any extra food your fish leave. They will also eat some the moss that appears on the plants. The snails will eat some of moss on the glass walls of the tank, too If you have sevrel pond snails in fish tank, you will not have to clean the tank as often.

If your pond snails are having babies, be sure to remove the snails the tank. Fish will eat snail eggs. In the same way, if your fish are having babies, be sure remove the snails. Snails will eat fish eggs.

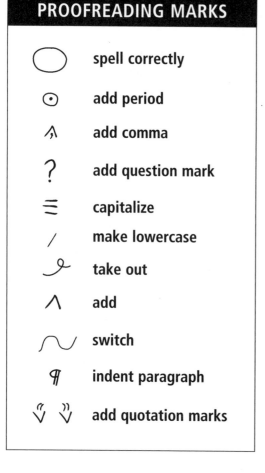

There are many different kinds snails. Their different kinds shells can add grately to the beauty of your fish tank. Not only are snails useful in keeping a tank clean, they also add interest to the tank.

Write about Zoo Animals

Choose one animal you would like to see at the zoo. Draw a picture of the animal. Then write four sentences about the animal. You might write about the animal's looks, food, and special needs.

Make a List and Write a Paragraph

With a friend, make a list of ten interesting topics to write about. Then work alone to pick one of the topics for your paragraph. Write the paragraph. Add one sentence that does not keep to your topic. Ask your friend to read your paragraph and draw a line through the sentence that does not belong.

1. ______________________
2. ______________________
3. ______________________
4. ______________________
5. ______________________
6. ______________________
7. ______________________
8. ______________________
9. ______________________
10. ______________________

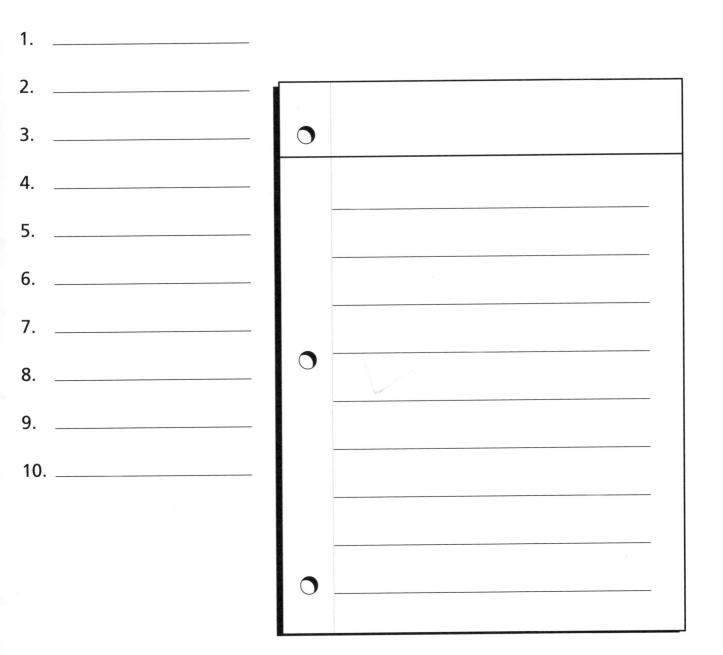

Write about Farm Animals

Write a paragraph about your favorite farm animals. Tell what those animals eat and do. Proofread and revise your paragraph.

A Practice How-to Paper

MAKE A DRUM

You and your friends can each make a drum and drumsticks. Your drum can be simple or fancy. It's up to you.

The most important thing you need to make a drum is a box with a lid. The box should be round and made from cardboard. An empty oatmeal box works well. The box will vibrate, or shake, like a drum.

You will also need these things:

- Two new, unsharpened pencils
- Aluminum foil
- Tempera paint and a small paintbrush
- Colored construction paper
- Glitter, or other shiny things
- Glue
- Heavy cord or string
- Art apron or old shirt
- Old newspapers

Make the drumsticks first. Wrap each pencil in foil. Put the drumsticks away until you have finished making your drum.

Put on your apron. Spread old newspaper on your worktable. Now you are ready to decorate your drum.

First, paint the outside of the box but not the lid. Let the box dry.

Next, cut out a round piece of colored paper to cover the box lid. Glue the paper to the lid. Cut out extra pieces of colored paper to decorate the sides. Glue the pieces to the sides of the drum. You may want to glue glitter or other shiny objects on your drum, too.

Now you need to make a cord for your drum. The cord lets you hang the drum around your neck while you use your drumsticks. Hold one end of the cord at your waist. Pull the other end around your neck. Let it fall to your waist again. Cut the cord.

Ask an adult to help you punch one hole on each side of your box. The holes should be about one inch below the lid. Thread the cord through one hole. Tie two knots in the cord outside the hole. Thread the other end of the cord through the second hole. Tie two knots in the cord.

Hang the drum around your neck. Use your drumsticks to practice drumming.

Together with your friends, plan a parade. Practice tapping a beat for everyone to follow. Beat out a march or a skip. Beat out a run or a walk.

Invite your family to join you. Help them make drums, too. Together, your friends and family can make a neighborhood band.

Respond to the Practice Paper

Write your answers to the following questions or directions.

1. What does this how-to paper teach you to do?

    ____

2. What materials do you need?

    ____

    ____

    ____

    ____

    ____

3. What is the most important thing you need?

    ____

4. Why do you need a cord or a string?

    ____

    ____

5. Write a paragraph to describe a drum you would like to make. On a separate piece of paper, draw a picture to go with your paragraph.

    ____

    ____

    ____

    ____

    ____

Analyze the Practice Paper

Read "Make a Drum" again. As you read, think about how the writer wrote this paper. What did the writer do to help explain how to make a drum? Write your answers to the following questions or directions.

1. Why is this a good example of a how-to paper?

2. What is the first thing the writer tells you to do before you begin to make a drum?

3. Why does the writer list the materials you need to make a drum?

4. Why does the writer use words like *now*, *first*, and *next*?

5. Draw a picture to show one of the steps in making a drum.

Writing Assignment

Think about something you want to tell others how to do. Use this writing plan to help you write a first draft on the next page.

Tell what you want to tell others how to do.

List the materials you will need.

Write the steps someone should follow in order. Number the steps.

Write some sequence words that help the reader know what to do.

First Draft

TIPS FOR WRITING A HOW-TO PAPER:

- Choose one thing to teach someone.
- Think of all the materials you will need.
- Think of all the steps someone will follow.
- Use sequence words.

Use your writing plan as a guide for writing your first draft of a how-to paper. Include a catchy title.

(Continue on your own paper.)

Revise the Draft

Use the chart below to help you revise your draft. Check YES or NO to answer each question in the chart. If you answer NO, make notes to remind yourself how you can revise, or change, your writing to improve it.

Question	YES ✔	NO ✔	**If the answer is NO,** what will you do to improve your writing?
Does your paper teach how to do something?			
Do you include the materials someone needs?			
Do you tell the steps someone must follow?			
Are the steps in order?			
Do you use sequence words?			
Have you corrected mistakes in spelling, grammar, and punctuation?			

Use the notes in your chart and your writing plan to revise your draft.

Writing Report Card

Read your revised draft again or ask someone else to read it. Have the person who reads your paper complete the following Report Card. Revise your paper until you have no less than a Very Good Score for each item.

Title of paper: ______________________________

Purpose of paper: *This is a how-to paper. It explains how to do something.*

Person who scores the paper: ______________________________

Score	Writing Goals
	Does the paper teach how to do something?
	Does the paper tell the materials someone needs?
	Does the paper tell the steps someone will follow?
	Are the steps in order?
	Are there sequence words to help the reader understand?
	Are the story's grammar, spelling, and punctuation correct?

☺ Excellent Score ☆ Very Good Score + Good Score
✔ Acceptable Score – Needs Improvement

UNIT 3: Descriptive Writing

HOW MUCH DO YOU KNOW?

Read the paragraphs. Underline or write the correct answer to each question below them.

Lori picked up Casey's right leg and put it into the green pants. Casey squirmed and his leg came out of the pants.

"Do you not like those green pants?" Lori asked. She picked up the red and white striped pants. Casey lay still while Lori put the pants on him.

Then Lori picked up the blue hat with a red ball on top. She tied the hat under Casey's chin. Casey shook his head. Lori pulled Casey's tail out of the hole she'd cut in the pants.

"You look cute, Casey!" Lori said.

Casey said, "Meow."

1. What color pants would Casey not wear?
   a. green
   b. red and white striped
   c. blue

2. How did Lori make the pants fit Casey?
   a. She picked the pair that fit the best.
   b. She picked the pair Casey liked the best.
   c. She cut a hole for Casey's tail.

3. What two details tell you Casey is a cat?

____

____

____

Analyzing a Descriptive Paragraph

A DESCRIPTIVE PARAGRAPH

- **tells what someone or something is like**
- **paints a clear and vivid word picture**

A. Read each sentence. Write the words that describe colors, shapes, and sizes.

1. Juanita bought a thick red blanket. ____________

____

2. She carried it home in a round basket. ____________

3. Her green basket had an orange pattern on it.

____

4. As she got close to her two-story house, her tiny puppy greeted her.

5. "Hi, Zorba, you huge hound!" Juanita said. ____________

6. Juanita spoiled her little brown dog. ____________

7. The colorful blanket was for Zorba. ____________

B. Read each sentence. Write the words that describe sounds, tastes, smells, and feelings.

8. A loud banging sound came from the kitchen.

____

9. "What a terrific smell!" Juanita thought. ____________

10. "Dad is baking another delicious pie," she said. ____________

11. "It must be a sweet, moist pie," she said. ____________

Observing Details

To write a descriptive paragraph, good writers pay close attention to what they will describe.

Read each paragraph. Underline the correct ending for each numbered sentence or question.

The cactus wren is the largest member of the wren family. Its back is brown with black bars and white streaks. There is a white stripe over each eye. The bird's breast is white, spotted with black.

1. The details in this paragraph tell
   a. about the bird's nest.
   b. about the bird's coloring.
   c. about the bird's life.

2. The colors of the cactus wren are
   a. black and white.
   b. brown and white.
   c. black, brown, and white.

The California poppy is sometimes called the golden poppy. It is a bright yellow color, shading to gold at its center. The flower is two or three inches across. The plant grows two feet tall. In the spring, countless millions of these plants cover California's mountainsides with gold.

3. The details in this paragraph tell
   a. about the poppy's color and size.
   b. about California's ocean.
   c. about California's weather.

4. What name does this plant not have?
   a. golden poppy
   b. mountainside poppy
   c. California poppy

Using Sensory Words and Vivid Language

GOOD WRITERS

- **use sensory words to tell how someone or something looks, feels, sounds, smells, or tastes**
- **use exact verbs to tell how someone or something moves**

Read each sentence. Decide which one of the senses is being used. Write *look*, *feel*, *sound*, *taste*, or *smell* on the line.

1. The chimneys were outlined against a pale pink sky.

   ____

2. The morning air was very chilly. ____________________
3. Suddenly, a loud cry broke the silence. ____________________
4. A young boy poked his head out of one chimney.

   ____

5. The boy called "All up!" in a loud voice.

   ____

6. He waved his cleaning tools.

   ____

7. Then he slid into the chimney to clean it. ____________________
8. Later, he had some spicy cider to drink. ____________________
9. He warmed his hands on the hot cup. ____________________
10. The smell of roast pork filled the air. ____________________

Combining Sentences

- **Good writers often combine short sentences to make writing interesting.**
- **Two sentences might have the same predicate. The sentences can be combined by joining the subjects with the word *and*.**

Combine each pair of sentences into one sentence. Remember to join subjects with the word *and*. Write the new sentence.

1. Guppies are pets for fish tanks. Goldfish are pets for fish tanks.

____

____

2. Catfish clean harmful moss from the tank. Snails clean harmful moss from the tank.

____

____

3. Black mollies are lovely fish. Goldfish are lovely fish.

____

____

4. Guppies have live babies. Black mollies have live babies.

____

____

5. Zebra fish lay eggs. Angelfish lay eggs.

____

Observing Details

PROOFREADING HINT

To be a good proofreader, look for one type of error at a time. For example, proofread once for capitalization errors, once for punctuation errors, and once for spelling errors.

PROOFREADING MARKS

- spell correctly
- add period
- add comma
- add question mark
- capitalize
- make lowercase
- take out
- add
- switch
- indent paragraph
- add quotation marks

Proofread the descriptive paragraphs, paying special attention to the verbs that go with sentence subjects. Use the Proofreading Marks to correct at least seven errors.

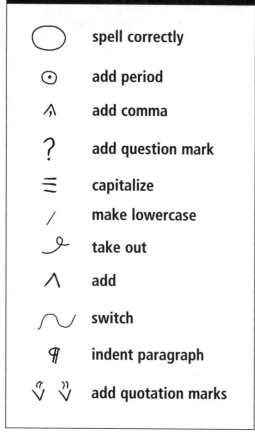

Have you ever heard of a person who likes washing dishes? My friend Dan really enjoy it. In fact, Dan washes dishes whenever he can. Dan pull a chair over to the sink so he can reach everything easily. Dan likes the lemony smell of the liquid detergent He squeezes the bottle gently and watches the liquid soap stream into the water. The soap mix with the hot water. Together, they create a mass of frothy white bubbles. When the bubbles almost reach the top of the sink, Dan turns the water off. then he carefully puts the glasses into the water.

Most of all, Dan like using a brand-new dishcloth. The cloth feel soft in Dan's hands. It has a clean smell, too. Dan rub each glass carefully with the soft, new cloth. Then he rinses the glass and sets it on the drainer.

Write about a Holiday

Choose one special holiday. Draw a picture of the holiday celebration. Write at least four sentences about it. Tell why you like the holiday and what you enjoy doing on the holiday.

Write about the Weather

Choose your favorite kind of weather. Draw a picture showing that weather. Then write four sentences to describe your picture.

Write about Food

Look through old magazines or newspapers and cut out pictures of food. Paste each picture on this page. Write sentences to describe each food.

Describe a Friend

Work with a friend. Look closely at your friend, observing at least five attractive details about him or her. Write five details that your friend would be happy to hear. Draw a picture of your friend.

MY FRIEND

Write about a Pet

Draw a picture of a pet. Write three sentences describing the pet.

A Practice Descriptive Story

MAYBE NEXT YEAR

I sat on the grass behind the field. My parents sat behind me. I watched the batter swing at the ball. "Strike one!" yelled the umpire, raising her right hand. The player got ready to hit again.

The day was hot, and the grass made my skin itch. I didn't care. This was my first live ball game. Matt, a friend from school, was the first pitcher for the White Caps that night. Our team was playing the Green Caps of Pittsfield.

We were playing at home, so the White Caps were on the field. The Green Caps were up at bat. Matt threw the second pitch. "Strike two!" cried the umpire. Matt waited until the player was ready. Then he threw again. The bat whooshed through the air, but I didn't hear it hit the ball. "Strike three!" called the umpire. Matt struck out the Green Cap.

Next, a tall boy put a green batting helmet on his head. He smacked the first ball that Matt pitched. The ball flew toward the third-base line. The Green Cap ran faster than a squirrel to first base. The ball stayed inside the line. The player was safe.

"That was some hit!" roared my father, clapping hard.

"Why are you clapping for him? He's a Green Cap," I said.

"I'm being fair, Jess. I clap for people who do a good job," Dad said. "It doesn't matter what color cap they wear."

The inning went by fast. The Green Caps had two runs. "Wow!" I said to my parents. "They're good. Will we beat them?"

"Never can tell," Mom said.

Two minutes into the second inning, the pitcher struck out our first player. Then came player number two. Player three struck out, too. The Green Caps and their families jumped up and down. They screamed wildly. Their clapping sounded like thunder. My family clapped, too.

The excitement never let up. The air was filled with claps, yells, and moans. Bats cracked, and players ran like swift cats. Their shoes kicked up clouds of dust that moved like storms across the field. Players delivered some hard hits. Umpires called some close strikes. When our team tied the score, the home crowd went wild.

Finally, it was the last inning. A Green Cap hit the ball. I could hear the coach yell, "Run, Jason, run!" Jason flew. No White Cap could keep up. He made it to first base safely. But then, he decided to steal a base. He waited until the pitcher pitched the next ball. Then he ran as fast as his legs could move. Our catcher saw the move. He threw the ball to second base. Jason was caught between first and second base. The player at second base tagged him out. The crowd roared.

That was the end of the last inning for the Green Caps. The score was 2 to 2. Now it was our team's turn. Wham! Tony smacked a long drive to center field. Then Maria hit the ball softly so it wouldn't go far. That helped the player on first base move to second. Paul popped the ball straight up. It went so high that it looked like a small, white bird.

Nancy was our next batter. She clutched the bat like a major-league player. The first two pitches were balls. Then Nancy's bat met the third pitch. The game was won.

What a game! The Green Caps and the White Caps shook hands. They told each other they had done a good job. Families hugged their kids and told them what a great game it had been. My parents and I clapped for everyone. Maybe next year I can be a White Cap.

Respond to the Practice Paper

Write your answers to the following questions or directions.

1. What was Matt's job on the team?

2. Why did Jess's father clap for the Green Caps?

3. How do you know that Jess really liked the game?

4. Write a paragraph to summarize this story. Use these questions to help you write your summary:
    - What is the story about?
    - What happens first? Second?
    - How does the story end?

Analyze the Practice Paper

Read "Maybe Next Year" again. As you read, think about how the writer wrote this story. Write your answers to the following questions.

1. What makes this story descriptive?

___

___

___

2. What are some exciting action words the writer uses?

___

___

___

3. What are some descriptions the writer uses to help you imagine what is happening in the story?

___

___

___

4. The writer says that the players ran like swift cats. What is another way the writer could describe players who run fast?

___

___

___

Writing Assignment

To describe something, a writer tells what he or she sees, hears, feels, tastes, and smells. The writer uses interesting words. The writer also compares things to other things, like a fast runner to a swift cat. Think about something that happened to you that you would like to describe. Use this writing plan to help you write a first draft on the next page.

What experience would you like to describe? Write it in the circle. Then write words that describe the experience on the lines.

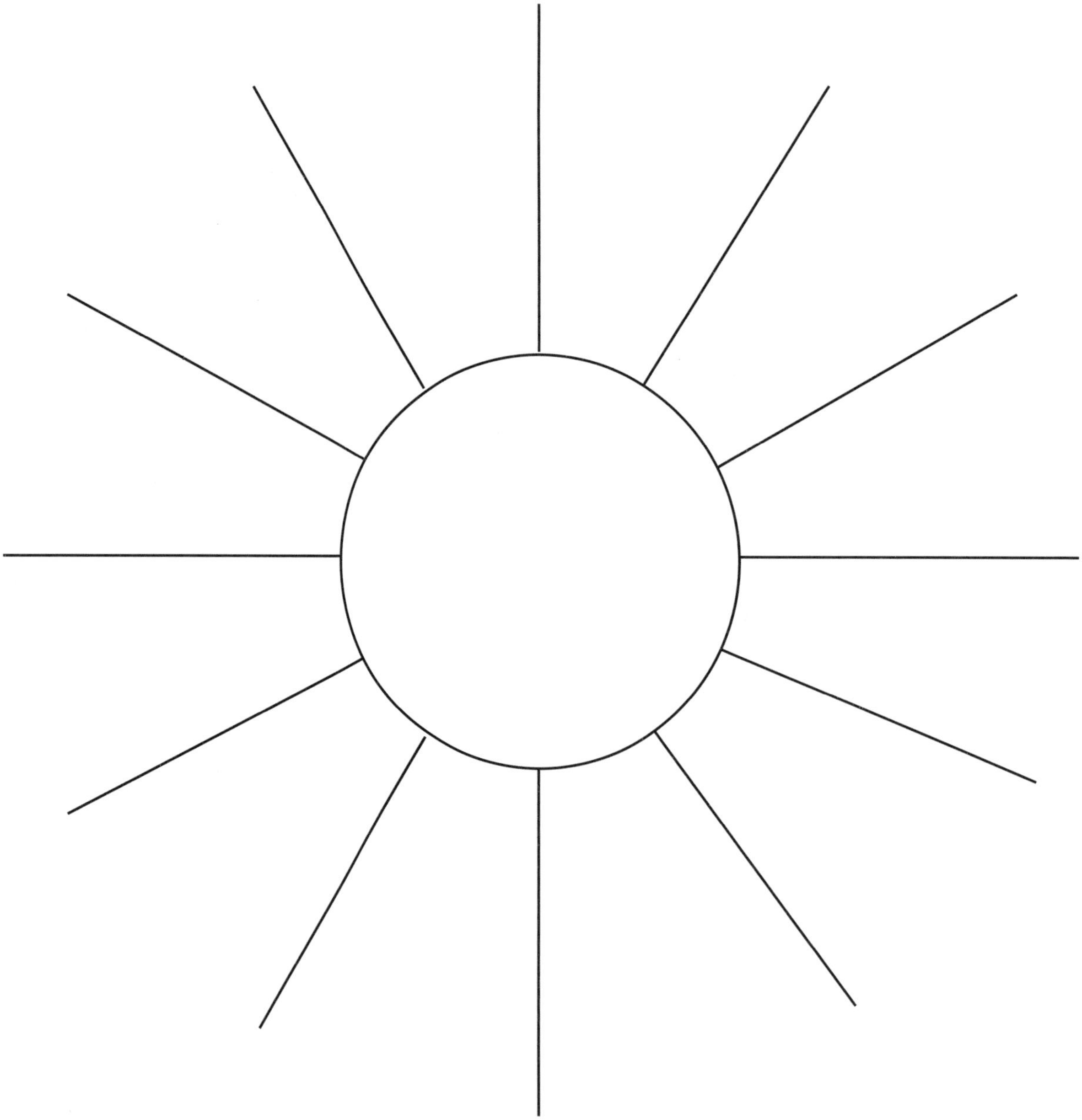

First Draft

TIPS FOR WRITING A DESCRIPTIVE STORY:

- **Help readers see, smell, taste, feel, and hear what you are writing about.**
- **Use interesting words to help you describe.**

Use your writing plan as a guide for writing your first draft of a descriptive story. Include a catchy title.

(Continue on your own paper.)

Revise the Draft

Use the chart below to help you revise your draft. Check YES or NO to answer each question in the chart. If you answer NO, make notes to remind yourself how you can revise, or change, your writing to improve it.

Question	YES ✔	NO ✔	If the answer is NO, what will you do to improve your writing?
Does your story describe something that happened to you?			
Do you describe what happens in order?			
Do you use action words to describe what happens?			
Do you describe what you see, hear, smell, taste, and feel?			
Have you corrected mistakes in spelling, grammar, and punctuation?			

Use the notes in your chart and your writing plan to revise your draft.

Writing Report Card

Read your revised draft again or ask someone else to read it. Have the person who reads your paper complete the following Report Card. Revise your paper until you have no less than a Very Good Score for each item.

Title of paper: ______________________________

Purpose of paper: *This is a descriptive story. It describes something that happened to me.*

Person who scores the paper: ______________________________

Score	Writing Goals
	Does the story describe an experience?
	Are the things that happen in the story in order?
	Does the story describe what the writer sees, hears, tastes, smells, and feels?
	Does the story have action words?
	Are the story's grammar, spelling, and punctuation correct?

☺ Excellent Score ☆ Very Good Score + Good Score

✔ Acceptable Score – Needs Improvement

UNIT 4: Opinion and Comparative Writing

HOW MUCH DO YOU KNOW?

Read the persuasive paragraph. Answer the questions that follow.

The best building material for a house is bricks. A brick house always stays cool in summer and warm in winter. Houses made of wood need to be painted. Bricks never need to be painted. People get wet during the rainy season in a house made of straw. A brick house will keep people dry. Most importantly, a wolf cannot blow down a house made of bricks.

1. Draw a line under the topic sentence.

2. List the three main reasons the writer gives.

____

____

____

____

3. Which reason does the writer think is most important?

____

____

Analyzing a Persuasive Paragraph

A PERSUASIVE PARAGRAPH

- tells the writer's feelings, or opinion
- lists reasons
- asks readers to agree with the writer

Read the persuasive paragraph. Answer the questions that follow.

You should get involved in sports after school. There are many reasons for this. Perhaps the most important one is that exercise is good for your health. Exercise not only helps build strong muscles, it also helps keep your body from storing too much fat. A person who takes part in sports will usually have a healthier heart and lungs than a person who does not. In addition to being good for your health, sports can help you in other ways. Taking part in sports is a good way for you to make friends.

1. Draw a line under the topic sentence.
2. Does the topic sentence tell the writer's opinion?

   ____

3. What are the three main reasons the writer gives?

   ____

   ____

   ____

4. Which reason does the writer think is most important?

   ____

Evaluating to Draw Conclusions

To write a persuasive paragraph, good writers support their feelings with good reasons.

Read each set of statements and the reasons that support it. Draw a line under the three best reasons.

1. Nathan pays for the bus to school, and he also buys his own lunch. Nathan thinks his allowance should be raised.

   a. His friend Orville gets more than he does.

   b. Lunch prices at school went up.

   c. He has been doing extra chores.

   d. Bus fares went up.

   e. He wants to start playing video games after school.

2. Dora's family is moving into a home that has two bedrooms for the three children. Dora thinks she should be the one to get her own room.

   a. She stays up later and doesn't want to disturb the others.

   b. She is the oldest and has more homework to do.

   c. She needs the extra space because she doesn't like to hang up her clothes.

   d. She needs the extra space for slumber parties.

   e. The other two children are boys, and it makes more sense for them to share a room.

Giving Reasons

Good writers give good reasons to convince the reader.

Read each sentence. Write the reason that best supports it. Choose from the reasons in the box below.

1. You should do your homework before watching television.

____

2. You should save part of every allowance.

____

3. After you take your jacket off, hang it up.

____

4. You should try to be on time for appointments.

____

5. It is a good idea to be friendly to new students.

____

REASONS

It's not thoughtful to keep others waiting.

Clothes left lying around make the room messy.

You will have money for something big later.

Television takes time away from studies.

You might make a good friend this way.

Combining Sentences

- Good writers sometimes combine sentences to make their writing more interesting.
- Two short sentences might have the same subject. The writer writes the subject once and then combines the two predicates in the same sentence.

Combine the predicates in these sentences. Write the new sentences.

1. Kathy was tired. Kathy wanted her lunch.

2. She turned smoothly in the water. She headed for the other end of the pool.

3. Kathy wanted to win. Kathy hoped to set records.

4. Kathy won many races. Kathy got many awards.

5. Kathy practiced as much as possible. Kathy competed with stronger swimmers.

Proofreading Persuasive Paragraphs

PROOFREADING HINT

To be a good proofreader, look for one type of error at a time. For example, proofread once for capitalization errors, once for punctuation errors, and once for spelling errors.

Proofread the persuasive paragraphs, paying special attention to words or letters that may be out of order. Use the Proofreading Marks to correct at least seven errors.

PROOFREADING MARKS	
◯	spell correctly
⊙	add period
∧	add comma
?	add question mark
≡	capitalize
/	make lowercase
ℓ	take out
∧	add
∽	switch
¶	indent paragraph
∨ ∨	add quotation marks

Our class play coming is up next month, and everyone should hepl make it a success. It is true that not everyone can act in the play because there are not enough prats. Also, students some do not enjoy appearing on stage. Still, there is something for everyone do to. Those who do not wish to be on the stage can find plenty to do behind the scenes One such job making is scenery. Any student who likes to build can give time to this important job. We'll need staircases, walls, and street lamps for Act I. For Atc II we'll need scenery that looks like a beach

Another important job is making costumes. Students who enjoy different kinds of clothes will have fun this with job. We'll need soem special hats, some jewelry, and some old-fashioned beach clothes.

Write about Pets

Talk with a friend about different kinds of pets. Together, choose a pet you would both like to have. Draw a picture of that pet. Write a paragraph telling why that animal would be a good pet.

Write about Your Home Town

With a friend, make a list of things you like about your town. Then write three sentences that tell why your town is a great place to live.

Things we like about our town

____________________ ____________________

____________________ ____________________

____________________ ____________________

____________________ ____________________

Why Our Town Is a Great Place to Live

____

____

____

____

____

Write Your Opinion

With a friend or two, consider this question: Should third-graders learn to do their own laundry? Write your answer and one reason that supports it. Everyone in the group shares answers. Then, using your reason and others from your group, write a persuasive paragraph to answer the question.

Should third-graders learn to do their own laundry? ____ YES ____ NO

Write about a Movie

With a friend or two, plan and write five sentences about a movie you all like. Revise and proofread your sentences.

Draw a poster for your movie.

Write about Actions People Can Take

Here are statements about actions people can take. Check the statement that you feel the most strongly about and for which you have good reasons. Write a paragraph to convince someone to agree with you.

- ☐ Everyone should learn to cook.
- ☐ Everyone should go camping.
- ☐ Everyone should play a musical instrument.

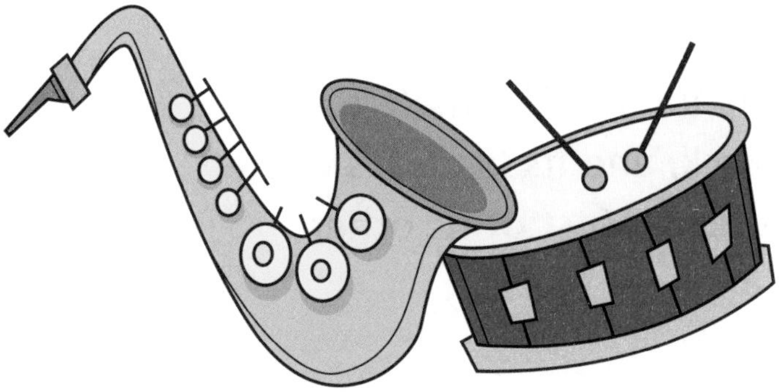

A Practice Alike-and-Different Paper

A BAT AND A BIRD

At night, a bat looks like a bird. Both bats and birds have wings and fly. They are also different in many ways. To understand how they are different, let's look at the Little Brown Bat and the American Robin.

The Little Brown Bat is about three inches long. It is about eight inches wide when its wings are open. The bat's body is covered with dark brown fur. Its ears are black.

The bat has hands with fingers and feet with toes. The wings are hands that have fingers covered with skin. At the ends of the fingers are strong claws. The bats use the claws to hang upside down from rocks. That's the way they like to sleep. They sleep all day. Then they come out when the sun goes down. That's when they fly to feeding grounds to eat.

The bats eat flies and other insects. They use a kind of radar to find their food. The bats let out quick, high sounds. We can't hear these sounds. The sounds bounce off the insects and return to the bats as echoes. Finding food this way is called "echolocation." Echoes let the bats find and catch their food.

Bats are mammals. This means that mother bats give birth to live babies. They also feed the babies milk from their bodies. A mother bat usually has only one baby a year. After it is born, the baby holds onto its mother. It drinks the mother's milk.

The American Robin is a bird, not a mammal. The male robin is colorful. Its beak is yellow. Its head is black, and its throat is white. The feathers on its breast are red like bricks. Most of its other feathers are grayish-brown.

The robin is about ten inches long. Its wings are covered with feathers. Like the bat, the robin has strong claws. It uses its claws to hang onto the branches of trees while it sleeps. Bats sleep during the day, but robins sleep at night. They wake early in the morning to begin singing and searching for food.

Robins like to eat berries and insects. They also eat earthworms.

Like all birds, robins lay eggs. The mother may lay eggs two or three times each year. Each time, she may lay up to six bluish-green eggs. She lays the eggs in a nest made from twigs, roots, grass, and paper. The inside of the nest is lined with mud. Nests are built in trees and on building ledges.

When the eggs hatch, the parents feed their babies. The babies eat food their parents spit up. Robin parents feed the babies until they can leave the nest.

Bats and robins are alike in some ways. They have wings and claws, and they fly. Bats and robins are also different. They look different and eat different foods. They also have and care for their babies in different ways.

Look up in the early evening sky. Do you see something flying? Look closely, listen, and watch. Do you see a Little Brown Bat searching for food? Or is it an American Robin you see, settling on a branch for a night's rest?

Respond to the Practice Paper

Summarize the paper by making a chart. Use the chart below to list ways that Little Brown Bats and American Robins are alike and different.

AN ALIKE-AND-DIFFERENT CHART FOR LITTLE BROWN BATS AND AMERICAN ROBINS

How Little Brown Bats and American Robins Are Alike	How Little Brown Bats and American Robins Are Different

Analyze the Practice Paper

Read "A Bat and a Bird" again. As you read, think about how the writer wrote this paper. Write your answers to the following questions or directions.

1. When did the writer tell you what this paper was going to be about?

____

____

2. The writer tells you many things about Little Brown Bats. In order, list what the writer tells you. The first and last ones are done for you.

- *what Little Brown Bats look like*
- ____
- ____
- *how Little Brown Bats care for their babies*

3. The writer also tells you many things about American Robins. In order, list what the writer tells you. The first one is done for you.

- *what American Robins look like*
- ____
- ____
- ____
- ____

4. What does the writer do in the last two paragraphs?

____

____

____

Writing Assignment

Think about two animals you would like to write about. Think about how they are alike and how they are different. Use this writing plan to help you write a first draft on page 602.

Choose two animals you want to write about. Call them A and B.

A = ____________ B = ____________

With an adult's help, use books or the Internet to learn more about A and B. Learn about these main ideas: 1. how the animals look, 2. where the animals live, and 3. what the animals eat.

The main ideas are written outside each set of circles below. For each main idea, list what is true only about A in the A circle. List what is true only about B in the B circle. List what is true about both A and B where the two circles overlap.

MAIN IDEA:
How they look

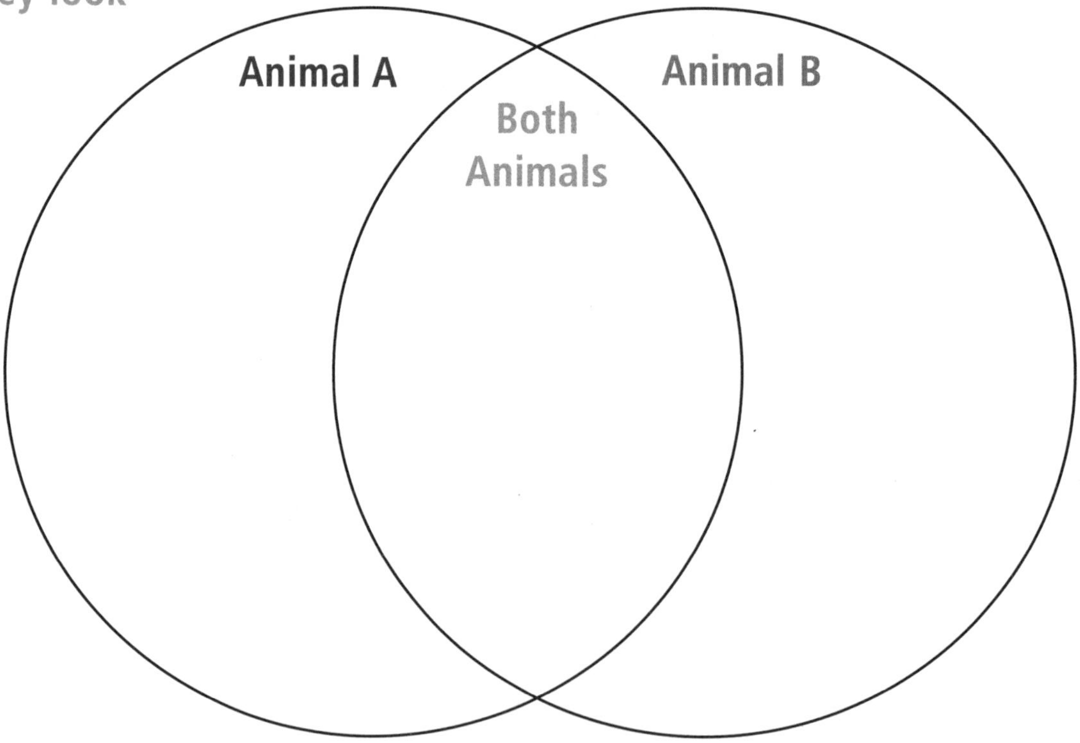

MAIN IDEA:
Where they live

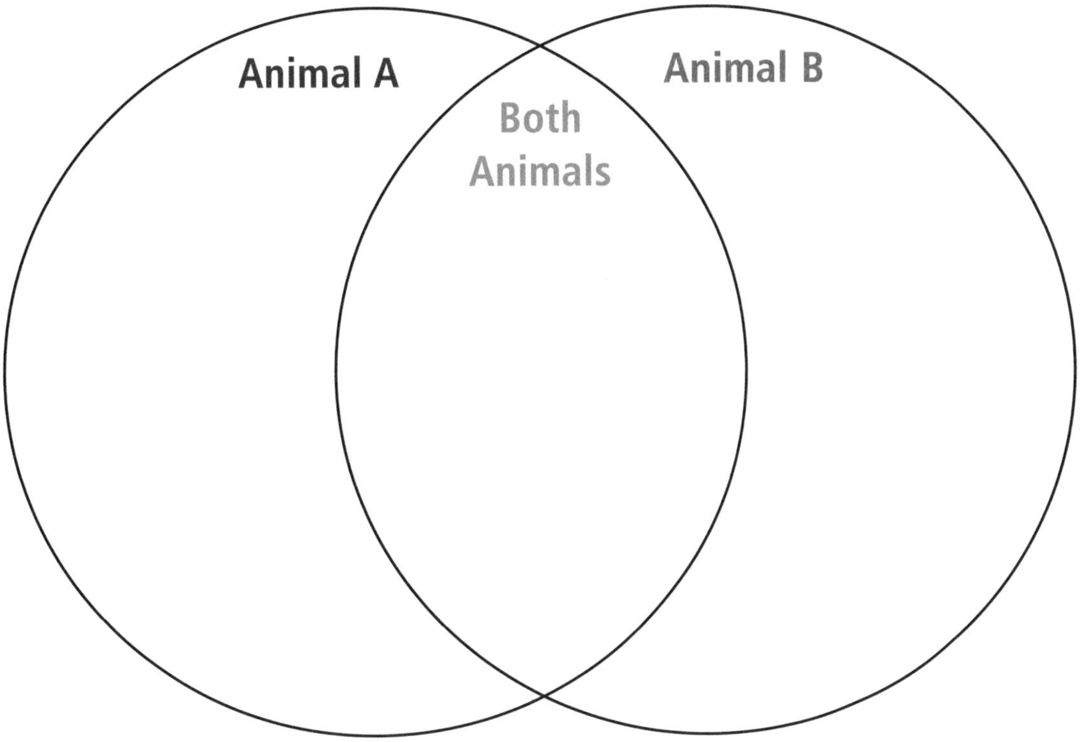

MAIN IDEA:
What they eat

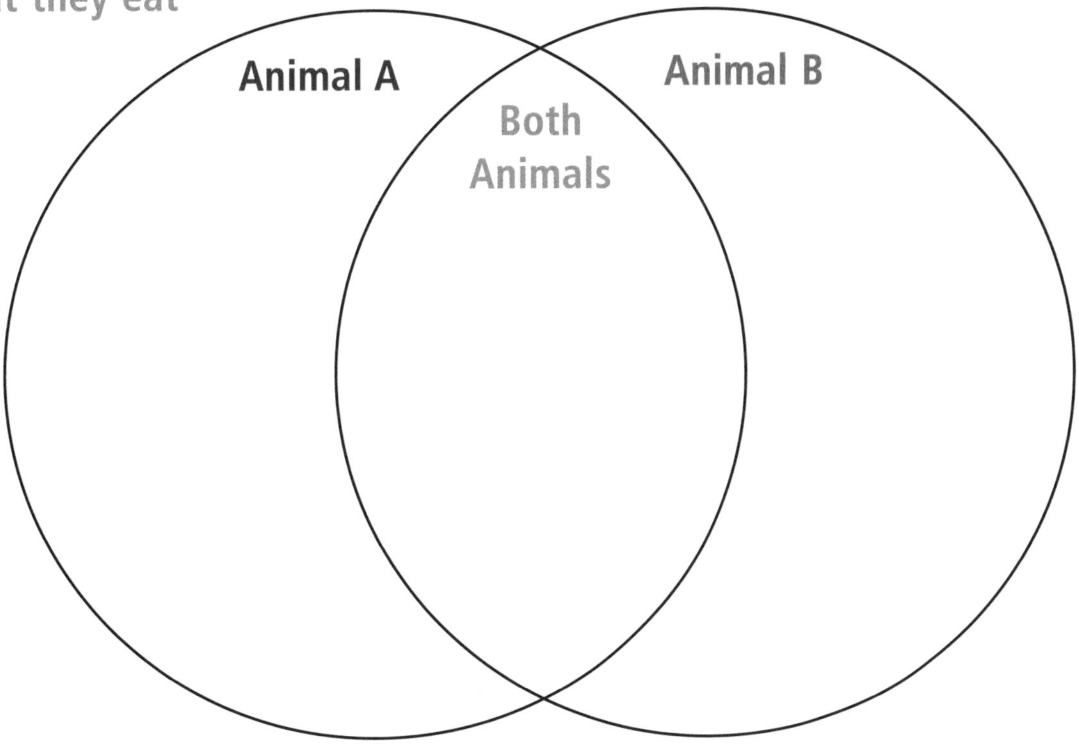

First Draft

TIPS FOR WRITING AN ALIKE-AND-DIFFERENT PAPER:

- Find information about your animals.
- Organize the information you find into main ideas.
- Explain how the animals are alike.
- Explain how the animals are different.
- Use your last paragraph to summarize your main ideas in a new way.

Use your writing plan as a guide for writing your first draft of an alike-and-different paper. Include a catchy title.

(Continue on your own paper.)

Revise the Draft

Use the chart below to help you revise your draft. Check YES or NO to answer each question in the chart. If you answer NO, make notes to remind yourself how you can revise, or change, your writing to improve it.

Question	YES ✔	NO ✔	**If the answer is NO,** what will you do to improve your writing?
Do you introduce the animals you will write about in your first paragraph?			
Do you tell how two animals are alike?			
Do you tell how two animals are different?			
Do you have more than one main idea?			
Do you organize the main ideas into paragraphs?			
Do you use details to explain each main idea?			
Have you corrected mistakes in spelling, grammar, and punctuation?			

Use the notes in your chart and your writing plan to revise your draft.

Writing Report Card

Read your revised draft again or ask someone else to read it. Have the person who reads your paper complete the following Report Card. Revise your paper until you have no less than a Very Good Score for each item.

Title of paper: ______________________

Purpose of paper: *This paper tells how two animals are alike and different.*

Person who scores the paper: ______________________

Score	Writing Goals
	Does the first paragraph tell what the paper will be about?
	Does the paper tell how two animals are alike?
	Does the paper tell how two animals are different?
	Is there more than one main idea?
	Are the main ideas organized into paragraphs?
	Does the last paragraph summarize what the paper is about?
	Are the paper's grammar, spelling, and punctuation correct?

☺ Excellent Score ☆ Very Good Score + Good Score
✔ Acceptable Score – Needs Improvement

UNIT 5: Story

HOW MUCH DO YOU KNOW?

Read the story. Write or underline the answers to the questions that follow.

Pet Day at School

Yesterday we brought our pets to school. They made a lot of noise.

Mr. McGrath said, "Quiet down, dogs! Lie down, cats!"

We tried to help Mr. McGrath. My big dog got excited. She barked and barked. One cat scratched Jose's little dog. Even the ferret was making noise! Jenny didn't have any trouble with her pets. She had three big goldfish.

"You have wonderful pets, Jenny," Mr. McGrath said.

Finally, we all took our pets outside. Except Jenny, of course!

1. What is the setting for this story?

   ____

2. What is the problem Mr. McGrath must solve?

   ____

3. What kind of person is Mr. McGrath?
   a. unhappy
   b. silly
   c. a dog lover

4. Why didn't Jenny's pets cause problems?
   a. Jenny didn't bring any pets.
   b. Fish don't make noise.
   c. Jenny took them outside.

Analyzing a Story

A STORY HAS

- a title
- characters and a setting
- a problem that the characters must solve
- a beginning, a middle, and an ending

Read the story. Answer the questions that follow.

King Midas was a kind but silly man who lived in Greece long ago. One day, in exchange for a kindness, he was granted a wish. Without thinking, King Midas asked that everything he touched would turn to gold. The "golden touch," as it was called, made him very rich. Even his food and drink turned to gold. Midas could not eat or drink. The worst thing was what happened when his daughter ran to hug him. She, too, turned to gold. Finally, King Midas had to beg to have his golden touch taken away.

1. Who is the main character?

   ____

2. What is the setting?

   ____

3. What is the problem the character must solve?

   ____

4. Write one sentence that tells the middle.

   ____

5. Write one sentence that tells the ending.

   ____

Classifying Details as Real or Make-Believe

> To write a make-believe story, good writers use both real and make-believe details.

A. Read the paragraph. Then write three details that are real and three that are make-believe.

Alice sat by the stream with her sister. Just then a white rabbit ran by. The rabbit took a watch out of its vest pocket. It looked at the watch and declared, "I'm late!" Then the rabbit went down a hole in the ground.

Real

1. ____________________

2. ____________________

3. ____________________

Make-Believe

4. ____________________

5. ____________________

6. ____________________

B. Label each sentence *real* or *make-believe* on the line.

7. Alice walked in a garden. ____________________

8. She saw a caterpillar on a leaf. ____________________

9. The caterpillar asked, "Who are you?" ____________________

10. The Queen was a playing card. ____________________

Storytelling: Dialogue and Characters

GOOD WRITERS USE DIALOGUE

- to tell what each character is saying
- to show what each character is like
- to show how a character feels

Read the story with dialogue. Draw a line under the best answer to each question that follows.

"How do you feel?" asked the nurse, looking at the little boy in his hospital bed.

"My ear hurts," the boy answered sadly.

"Does it hurt a lot?" asked the nurse.

"Yes, but I can take it," answered the boy.

The nurse had known children like this before. The child, trying to be brave, would not say how much a pain hurts. The nurse had a special chart for children like this. It showed a ladder. The bottom rung of the ladder meant very little pain, and the top rung meant a lot. The nurse showed her chart to the boy.

"I'm on rung three," said the child, pointing to the middle of the ladder.

"Tell me when you're on rung four," said the nurse, smiling at him. "Then I'll give you some medicine for pain."

1. Who does the talking in this story?

   a. a nurse and a little boy

   b. a nurse

   c. a boy

2. What kind of person is the nurse?

   a. mean

   b. kind

   c. silly

3. What kind of person is the boy?

   a. active

   b. cruel

   c. brave

4. Who says, "I'm on rung three"?

   a. the doctor

   b. the nurse

   c. the boy

Avoiding Run-on Sentences

Good writers divide run-on sentences into two or more sentences.

Revise each run-on sentence. Write two shorter sentences to make the meaning clearer.

1. The little girl opened the drawer she took out all the pots.

   ____

   ____

2. The father came into the kitchen he sighed.

   ____

   ____

3. The father smiled at the girl he asked if she was having a good time.

   ____

   ____

4. The girl smiled back she was having fun.

   ____

   ____

5. The father sat on the floor he played with the girl.

   ____

   ____

Proofreading a Story

PROOFREADING HINT

To be a good proofreader, look for one type of error at a time. For example, proofread once for capitalization errors, once for punctuation errors, and once for spelling errors.

Proofread the stories, paying special attention to capital letters at the beginning of sentences. Use the Proofreading Marks to correct at least six errors.

PROOFREADING MARKS

◯	spell correctly
⊙	add period
∧,	add comma
?	add question mark
≡	capitalize
/	make lowercase
℘	take out
∧	add
∽	switch
¶	indent paragraph
“∨ ”∨	add quotation marks

1. Goldilocks sat down at the bears' table. the first chair she tried was too hard, and the second chair was too soft. the third chair felt just right. Next, Goldilocks tried all the oatmeal on the table The first bowl was too hot, and the second bowl was too cold. The third bowl tasted just right. after she had eaten the whole bowl of oatmeal, Goldilocks went upstairs for a nap.

2. Fox looked up at the grapes on the vine. how delicious they looked! he decided to have some grapes four his lunch. The grapes were quite high, and it was hard for Fox to reach them. he stretched and jumped, but he couldn't get the grapes. Fox tried again and again. the grapes always seemed just out of reach. Finally, Fox gave up. he walked away, asking himself, "Who would want those sour old grapes?"

Write a Story

What might happen when a group of friends goes skating? With a friend or two, plan and write a story about a skating party.

Ideas for story

The Skating Party

Write an Animal Story

Imagine that some mice and some geese become friends. Write three sentences telling what the animals will do. Draw a picture to go with your story.

Write a Story for Younger Children

All kinds of animals make good stories. Here are some animals you may want to write about. Some are real. Some are make-believe. They may make great characters for your story. Add more animals to each list.

Pick one of the animals from the list. Write a make-believe story about that animal to entertain younger children.

____

____

____

____

____

____

A Practice Story

THE MEETING OF THE MICE

Based on a Fable by Abstemius

Martha Mouse was very sad. Clever Cat had caught her brother. Martha wasn't the only sad mouse. Martin Mouse was also sad. Clever Cat had caught his mother and sister.

Martha talked to Martin. "I think," she said, "that we should have a meeting. Let's invite all the mice in town. If we work together, maybe we can find a way to be safe from Clever Cat."

Martin liked the idea. He said, "I think we should meet tonight. How about meeting in the basement of the school?"

Martha answered, "That's a good place. When shall we meet?"

"As soon as it is dark," said Martin. He looked to the left and to the right. "I wouldn't want to lose anyone on the way."

Martha agreed. "You're right. Until we have a plan, we can't be too careful."

Martha and Martin told every mouse they met to come to the meeting. They asked them to tell all their friends, too. That evening, as soon as the sun went down, the mice rushed to the school. Martha and Martin stood by the basement steps. They waved the mice forward. "Come in. It's safe, but hurry."

Hundreds of mice ran down the steps and into the basement.

Martha called the meeting to order. She stood before the other mice and said, "We have come together to discuss a big problem. Many of us have been hurt, and Clever Cat is the reason why. Some of us have lost our tails. Others have lost their fur. Even worse, he has eaten our friends and family."

The other mice squeaked in fright. Each one of them had a story. They wanted to tell how Clever Cat had hurt them, too. The stories took a long time. Finally, all the mice had spoken. Martha squeaked loudly to get everyone's attention. "It is clear. We have all been hurt. Now we have to find a way to keep Clever Cat away from us."

Many mice had ideas. Moby Mouse said, "Let's find a Dog to help us. Dogs chase cats."

Some mice liked the idea. But one said, "That won't help

unless the Dog is willing to chase Clever Cat all day and all night, too."

Another mouse stood up. "My name is Messy," he said. "I think we should hire a Mouse Guard to stand at our holes."

One of Messy's friends stood up to answer. "That won't work," he said. "We have so many holes. We would need too many Mouse Guards."

"That's true," said another mouse. "And besides that, we all have to go out of our holes every day to look for food."

Just then a young mouse stood up. "My name is Tom. I think I have a good idea. Let's hang a bell around Clever Cat's neck. Then we could hear Clever Cat coming. We would have time to run away."

All the mice clapped loudly. They squeaked for joy. They all agreed. This was a wonderful plan.

Just then, an old, old mouse stood up. He had been listening carefully all evening. He introduced himself. Then he said, "The bell is a very good way to keep Clever Cat away. It is a wonderful idea. It would work. But I have one question. Who will hang the bell around Clever Cat's neck?"

The mice were suddenly quiet. They looked at each other. Each mouse asked the next mouse, "Will you hang the bell around Clever Cat's neck?" Not one mouse said yes.

Respond to the Practice Paper

Write your answers to the following questions or directions.

1. A fable is a story that teaches a lesson. What is the lesson of this story?

2. The animals in fables often act like humans. How are the animals in this story like humans?

3. How would you describe the setting for this story?

4. Write a paragraph to summarize this story. Use these questions to help you write your summary:
   - What are the main ideas in the story?
   - How does the story end?
   - What lesson did this story teach?

Analyze the Practice Paper

Read "The Meeting of the Mice" again. As you read, think about how the writer wrote the story. Answer the following questions or directions.

1. Name ways the writer makes the characters seem human.

2. How does the writer make the story exciting?

3. Why does the writer use talking mice to tell the story?

4. Why is the last paragraph important?

Writing Assignment

Sometimes stories help us learn about ourselves. They help us think about what we can be or do. Think about writing a fable. Think about the answers to the questions in the boxes. Use your answers to help you write a first draft on the next page.

What is the lesson of the fable?

▼

Who are the animal characters?

▼

What problem will the characters have?

▼

How will the characters solve their problem? List what will happen in the story. Number each thing that happens.

First Draft

TIPS FOR WRITING A FABLE:

- Think about the lesson you want your fable to teach.
- Make your animal characters seem human.
- Plan a place and time for the story to happen.
- Give your characters a problem to solve.
- Write what happens in order.

Use your writing plan as a guide for writing your first draft of a fable. Include a catchy title.

(Continue on your own paper.)

Revise the Draft

Use the chart below to help you revise your draft. Check YES or NO to answer each question in the chart. If you answer NO, make notes to remind yourself how you can revise, or change, your writing to improve it.

Question	YES ✔	NO ✔	**If the answer is NO,** what will you do to improve your writing?
Does your fable teach a lesson?			
Do your animal characters seem human?			
Do your characters have a problem?			
Do your characters solve their problem?			
Do you describe what happens in order?			
Have you corrected mistakes in spelling, grammar, and punctuation?			

Use the notes in your chart and your writing plan to revise your draft.

Writing Report Card

Read your revised draft again or ask someone else to read it. Have the person who reads your paper complete the following Report Card. Revise your paper until you have no less than a Very Good Score for each item.

Title of paper: ______________________________

Purpose of paper: *This is a fable. It teaches a lesson.*

Person who scores the paper: ______________________________

Score	Writing Goals
	Does the story teach a lesson?
	Do the animals in this story seem human?
	Do the animals have a problem they must solve?
	Do things in the story happen in order?
	Do the animals solve their problem?
	Are the story's grammar, spelling, and punctuation correct?

☺ Excellent Score ☆ Very Good Score + Good Score
✔ Acceptable Score – Needs Improvement

UNIT 6: Short Report

HOW MUCH DO YOU KNOW?

Read this short report. Underline the correct answer to each question.

Thomas Edison, Great Inventor

We see Thomas Edison's inventions everywhere. You often use his inventions. Without him, you could never turn on a light. Films are shown through one of his inventions. Music is listened to on one of his inventions.

Edison invented the electric lamp in 1879. He invented the movie projector and the phonograph. Edison is the greatest inventor who ever lived. He invented over 1,000 things!

1. The topic of this report is
   a. what Thomas Edison invented.
   b. how Thomas Edison invented the electric lamp.
   c. how a movie projector works.

2. What is one detail about the main idea?
   a. Thomas Edison lived in the 1800s.
   b. Edison invented the phonograph.
   c. You cannot turn on a light.

3. Which sentence states an opinion?
   a. Edison is the greatest inventor who ever lived.
   b. Edison invented the electric lamp in 1879.
   c. Films are shown through one of his inventions.

Analyzing a Short Report

A SHORT REPORT

- gives facts about one topic
- usually has more than one paragraph
- has a title that tells about the topic

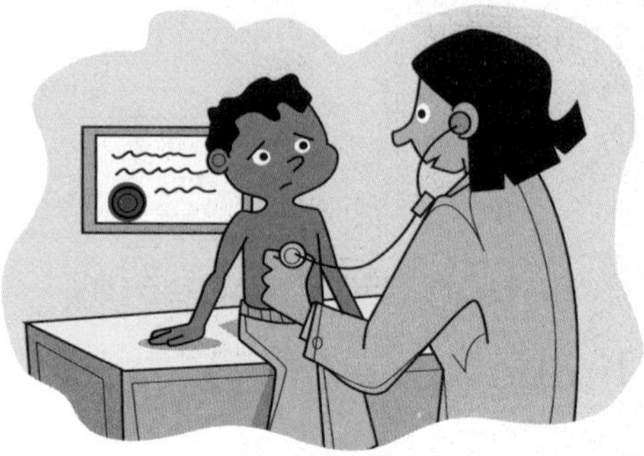

Read this part of a short report.
Answer the questions.

A cold is caused by a virus. No one really knows how to prevent colds. Getting wet or chilled does not directly give you a cold. A chill, however, might put you in a weaker state than usual. Then, if a cold is going around, you will be more likely to get it.

Colds are usually caught by being near someone who already has one. The easiest way to catch a cold is from someone's sneeze. One person with a cold can give it to many other people in a crowd just by sneezing. If you have a cold, you should stay away from other people.

1. What is the topic of this report?

 ____

2. Write the sentence that states the main idea.

 ____

3. What is one detail about the main idea?

 ____

 ____

 ____

4. What might the topic of another paragraph in this short report be?

 ____

Classifying Fact and Opinion

To write a short report, good writers include only facts about the topic.

Read each sentence. Write *fact* or *opinion* to tell what it is.

______________ 1. Liquid is a necessary ingredient of soup.

______________ 2. Chicken soup is better than turkey soup.

______________ 3. Gabriel's Restaurant serves lamb stew.

______________ 4. Gabriel's Restaurant serves good lamb stew.

______________ 5. The dishwasher is broken.

______________ 6. Every home should have a dishwasher.

______________ 7. We eat fish every Sunday.

______________ 8. Fish can be prepared in many ways.

______________ 9. Tuna is the most delicious fish you can buy.

______________ 10. The Japanese people eat a lot of fish.

______________ 11. Gabriel's Restaurant has one high chair.

______________ 12. People should not bring babies to restaurants.

Using Exact Words

Good writers use exact words to tell the facts about a topic.

Read each sentence. From the word list, choose a more exact word or phrase to replace each underlined word or phrase. Write a new sentence with the more exact words.

Word List

1. cat, dog, hamster ... bedroom, living room, kitchen
2. sleeping, napping, dozing ... an hour, about two hours
3. liver, hamburger, spinach ... chopped, grilled, steamed
4. run, walk, exercise
5. ball, stuffed mouse, exercise wheel

1. My <u>pet</u> sat on the sill of the window in the <u>room</u>.

   ____

2. He was <u>resting</u> for <u>a little while</u>.

   ____

3. Soon it would be time to eat some <u>food</u>, which I had <u>fixed</u> for him.

   ____

4. In the afternoon, my pet would want to <u>play</u>.

   ____

5. I need to buy a new <u>toy</u> for my pet.

   ____

Expanding Sentences

Good writers make sentences clear by using adjectives and adverbs that describe the topic exactly.

Add an adjective or an adverb where you see this mark: *
The word or words you add should describe the thing or action.
Write your new sentences.

1. The * robin built a * nest.

2. She found a * branch in a * spot.

3. She wanted her nest to be * away from * animals.

4. She laid * eggs and sat on them *.

5. * the eggs hatched and the babies cried * for food.

Proofreading a Short Report

PROOFREADING HINT

To be a good proofreader, look for one type of error at a time. For example, proofread once for capitalization errors, once for punctuation errors, and once for spelling errors.

PROOFREADING MARKS

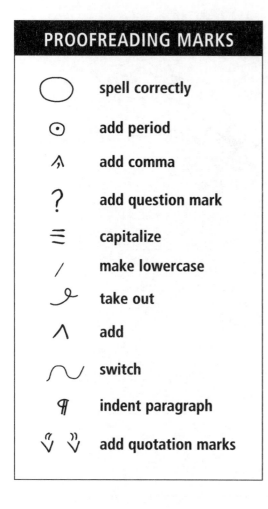

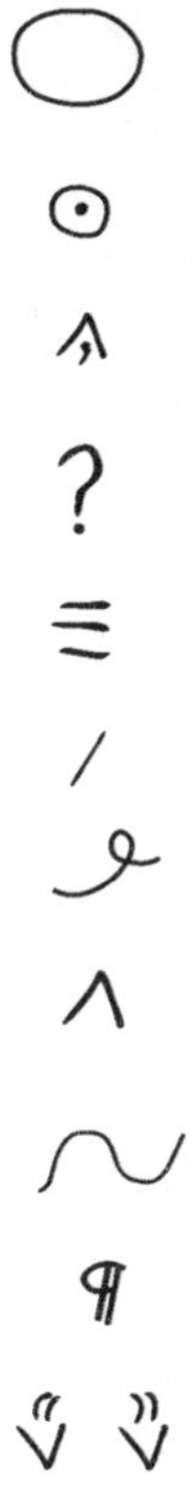

- spell correctly
- add period
- add comma
- add question mark
- capitalize
- make lowercase
- take out
- add
- switch
- indent paragraph
- add quotation marks

Proofread the beginning of a short report, paying special attention to spelling. Use the Proofreading Marks to correct at least six errors.

The Passenger Pigeon

At one time there was a kind of bird called the passenger pigeon. The passenger pigeon was one of the most common birds in the wirld. In fact, their were once so many passenger pigeons that they darkened the skies. One sumar day these birds completely blocked the sunshine in New york. In 1808 poepel saw a flock of passenger pigeons one mile wide and 240 miles long! the flock had more than two billyon birds. The birds in that flock ate about 434,000 bushels of nuts, rice, and berrys every day.

No one now can see even won living passenger pigeon The last wild passenger pigeon was killed in 1906 in connecticut. In 1914 the last passenger pigeon in a zoo died. the passenger pigeon is extinct.

Write about Animal Nests

Many different kinds of animals build nests. With a friend or two, read about one kind of nest. Draw a picture of this nest. Together, write at least four sentences about the animal and its nest.

Make a Bird Book

Work with a friend or two. Together, read about one unusual kind of bird. Draw pictures to show what the bird looks like, where it lives, what it eats, and what is unique about it. Write two sentences to go with each picture.

WHAT IT LOOKS LIKE

____

____

____

WHERE IT LIVES

____

____

____

WHAT IT EATS

____

____

____

WHAT IS UNIQUE ABOUT IT

____

____

____

Write about Robots

With a friend or two, read about robots. Find out what kinds of jobs robots can do. Draw a picture of one type of robot, and write at least five sentences telling what that robot can do.

Write about Birds

With a friend, choose one kind of sea bird to write about. Together, find five facts about this bird. Then write five sentences about it.

SEA BIRD FACTS

A Practice Short Report

THE PONY EXPRESS

Long ago, there were no telephones or radios. There were no televisions or computers. There were no airplanes or cars. It was hard to get news all the way to California.

People who lived in California needed a quick way to get mail and news from the East. People wanted news about their friends and families. They also wanted to know what was happening in other places in the country.

Three people started a company called the Pony Express. The Pony Express carried mail and news throughout the West. On April 3, 1860, one Pony Express rider rode west from St. Joseph, Missouri. St. Joseph was the last stop for trains coming from the East. On the same day, another rider rode east from Sacramento, California. Both young men carried four bags of mail. The Pony Express was a lot faster than the stagecoach. A stagecoach took one month to deliver mail. A Pony Express rider could do it in ten days.

The Pony Express hired young men. They were often younger than 18 years old. They were skinny, too. No rider could weigh more than 120 pounds. That helped their ponies run longer and faster.

The Pony Express ponies were mustangs. These were small, wild horses. The horses were less than five feet tall. They galloped almost twelve miles an hour. The horses were smart. They learned their routes fast.

Besides riders, other people helped run the Pony Express. Some people worked at stations. One of their jobs was to take care of the company's horses. Riders picked up fresh horses when they stopped at stations.

The riders and the people who worked at the stations faced many dangers. One was the weather. Snowstorms slowed riders crossing the high mountains. Sandstorms slowed riders crossing the long, dry deserts. Wild animals like wolves were another danger. The riders also had to protect themselves from bandits. Bandits tried to steal the horses. They also took whatever money the riders were carrying.

Still, there were young men willing to ride for the Pony Express. Together, they covered 2,000 miles of land. A rider would leave one station and gallop to another. At his first stop, he slipped the mail cover off the saddle. He threw it on the saddle of a new horse. Then he was off again. This took about two minutes. Each rider rode 60 to 80 miles. He stopped every 15 to 25 miles to get a fresh horse. At the end of his trip, a fresh rider on a fresh horse took his place. The first rider stayed at his last station until it was time for his next job.

The Pony Express was successful. It delivered the mail faster than stagecoaches. But it only lasted about one and one-half years. It stopped running when telegraph wires reached California. By October 1861, the Pony Express closed its doors. Its riders and horses were no longer needed.

Respond to the Practice Paper

Write your answers to the following questions or directions.

1. What was the Pony Express?

2. Why did the Pony Express start?

3. What dangers did Pony Express riders face?

4. Write a paragraph to summarize information about the Pony Express. Use these questions to help you write your summary:
   - What is the report about?
   - What are some of the main ideas in the report?
   - What are some of the details in the report?

Analyze the Practice Paper

Read "The Pony Express" again. As you read, think about the main ideas the writer tells about. Write your answers to the following questions or directions.

1. When did the writer tell you what this paper was going to be about?

 ____

 ____

2. List the main ideas the writer tells about in order. The first and last ones are done for you.

 - *People in California wanted mail and news.*
 - ____
 - ____
 - ____
 - ____
 - ____
 - ____
 - *The Pony Express ended when telegraph wires reached California.*

3. The writer uses some special words like *mustangs* and *stations*. How does the writer make it easier for the reader to understand these words?

 ____

 ____

4. Why is the last paragraph important? What makes it different from the other paragraphs?

 ____

 ____

Writing Assignment

In a short report, writers write about one topic. They find information about the topic. Then they use the information to choose the main ideas for their report. They also choose details to help explain each main idea.

Think about writing a short report about something in the story you read. You might want to write about a famous Pony Express rider or mustangs. Use this writing plan to help you write a first draft on the next page.

The topic of this paper is:

____

Main Idea of Paragraph 1: ______________________________

Detail: ______________________________

Detail: ______________________________

Detail: ______________________________

Main Idea of Paragraph 2: ______________________________

Detail: ______________________________

Detail: ______________________________

Detail: ______________________________

Main Idea of Paragraph 3: ______________________________

Detail: ______________________________

Detail: ______________________________

Detail: ______________________________

First Draft

TIPS FOR WRITING A SHORT REPORT:

- Find information.
- Take notes about important main ideas.
- Take notes about important details.
- Organize the main ideas and the details into paragraphs.
- Use the last paragraph to summarize your report.

Use your writing plan as a guide for writing your first draft of a short report. Include a catchy title.

(Continue on your own paper.)

Revise the Draft

Use the chart below to help you revise your draft. Check YES or NO to answer each question in the chart. If you answer NO, make notes to remind yourself how you can revise, or change, your writing to improve it.

Question	YES ✔	NO ✔	**If the answer is NO,** what will you do to improve your writing?
Do you write about one topic, or subject, in your report?			
Do you have more than one main idea?			
Do you organize your main ideas into paragraphs?			
Do you include details to help explain your main ideas?			
Do you "stick" to the topic?			
Do you use your last paragraph to summarize your report?			
Have you corrected mistakes in spelling, grammar, and punctuation?			

Use the notes in your chart and your writing plan to revise your draft.

Writing Report Card

Read your revised draft again or ask someone else to read it. Have the person who reads your paper complete the following Report Card. Revise your paper until you have no less than a Very Good Score for each item.

Title of paper: ____________________

Purpose of paper: *This is a short report.*

Person who scores the paper: ____________________

Score	Writing Goals
	Is this paper an example of a short report?
	Does the writer talk about one topic, or subject?
	Are main ideas organized into paragraphs?
	Are there details to explain each main idea?
	Does the report "stick" to the topic?
	Does the last paragraph summarize what the paper is about?
	Are the report's grammar, spelling, and punctuation correct?

☺ Excellent Score ☆ Very Good Score + Good Score
✔ Acceptable Score – Needs Improvement

Proofreading Marks

Use the following symbols to help make proofreading faster.

MARK	MEANING	EXAMPLE
○	spell correctly	like I (liek) dogs.
⊙	add period	They are my favorite kind of pet ⊙
∧,	add comma	I also like cats ∧, birds, and bunnies.
?	add question mark	What kind of pet do you have ?
≡	capitalize	My dog's name is scooter.
/	make lowercase	He has Brown spots.
ℓ	take out	He likes to ~~to~~ run and play.
∧	add	He even likes to get ∧a bath.
∽	switch	Afterward he all shakes over.
¶	indent paragraph	¶ I love my dog, Scooter. He is the best pet I have ever had. Every morning he wakes me with a bark. Every night he sleeps with me.
“ ”	add quotation marks	“You are my best friend,” I tell him.

Test Prep

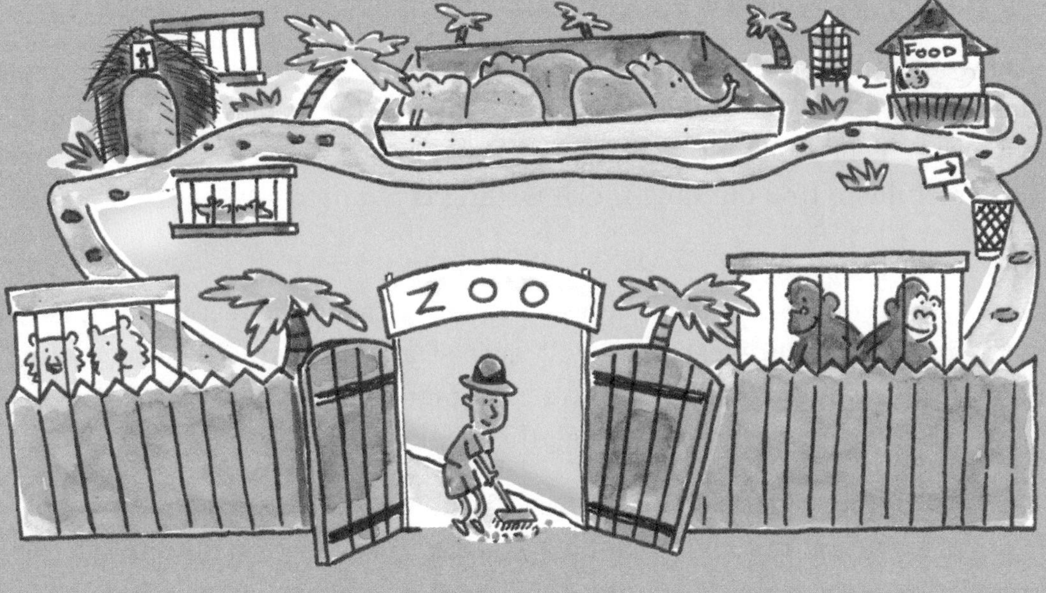

GET READY FOR TESTS

WHAT ARE STANDARDIZED TESTS?

You will take many different tests while at school. A standardized test is a special test that your state gives to every student in your grade. These tests are designed to find out how much you know about subjects like reading and math. They may not be fun, but they do not have to be a nightmare. This workbook can help you prepare!

WHAT CAN YOU EXPECT ON A STANDARDIZED TEST?

All standardized tests are different, but they do have some things in common.

- **Multiple-Choice Questions**
  Most of these tests use multiple-choice questions. You have to pick the best answer from four or five choices. You usually indicate your choice on an answer sheet by filling in or darkening a circle next to the correct answer.

- **Time Limits**
  Standardized tests all have time limits. It is best to answer as many questions as possible before you run out of time. But do not let the time limit make you nervous. Use it to help you keep going at a good pace.

- **Short Answers and Essays**
  Some standardized tests have questions that require writing answers. Sometimes the answer is a word or a sentence. Other times you will write a paragraph or an essay. Always read directions carefully to find out how much writing is required.

HOW CAN THIS BOOK HELP?

Everyone gets a little nervous when taking a test. This book can make test-taking easier by providing helpful tips and practice tests. You will learn strategies that will help you find the best answers. You will also review math, reading, and grammar skills that are commonly needed on standardized tests. Here are some hints for using this book.

- Work in a quiet place. When you take a test at school, the room is very quiet. Try to copy that feeling at home. Sit in a chair at a desk or table, just as you would in school.

- Finish one test at a time. You do not need to finish all of the tests in this book in one session. It is better to complete just one activity at a time. You will learn more if you stop at the end of a practice test to think about the completed questions.

- Ask questions. Talk with a family member or a friend if you find a question you do not understand. These practice tests give you the chance to check your own answers.

How to Be Test Smart

A test-smart student knows what to do when it is test-taking time. You might not know all of the answers, but you will feel relaxed and focused when you take tests. Your test scores will be accurate. They will provide a snapshot of what you have learned during the school year. Here is how you can become test-smart!

Things You Can Do All Year

The best way to get ready for tests is to pay attention in school every day. Do your homework. Be curious about the world around you. Learning takes place all the time, no matter where you are! When test day rolls around, you will be ready to show what you know. Here are some ways you can become a year-round learner.

- Do your schoolwork. Standardized tests measure how much you have learned. If you keep up with your schoolwork, your test scores will reflect all the things you have learned.
- Practice smart study habits. Most people study best when they work in a quiet, clean area. Keep your study area neat. Make sure you have a calculator, dictionary, paper, and pencils nearby.
- Read, read, read. Make reading an everyday habit. A librarian can suggest enjoyable books. Read the newspaper. Subscribe to a children's magazine. Look for empty times in your schedule when you might read, like on a long drive to a ball game. Carry a book with you if you know you will have to wait somewhere.
- Practice. This book is a great start to help you get ready for test day. It provides practice for all of the important skills on the tests.

How to Do Your Best on Test Day

Your teacher will announce a standardized test day in advance. Follow these tips to help you succeed on the big day.

- Plan a quiet night before a test. Trying to study or memorize facts at this point might make you nervous. Enjoy a relaxing evening instead.
- Go to bed on time. You need to be well rested before the test.
- Eat a balanced breakfast. Your body needs fuel to keep your energy high during a test. Eat foods that provide long-term energy, like eggs, yogurt, or fruit. Skip the sugary cereals—the energy they give does not last very long.
- Wear comfortable clothes. Choose a comfortable outfit that you like.
- Do not worry about the other students or your friends. Everyone works at different speeds. Pay attention to answering the questions in a steady fashion. It does not matter when someone else finishes the test.
- Relax. Take a few deep breaths to help you relax. Hold your pencil comfortably and do not squeeze it. Take a break every so often to wiggle your fingers and stretch your hand.

Test-Taking Tips

Here are some hints and strategies to help you feel comfortable with any test. Remember these ideas while taking the tests in this book.

Read the Directions

This sounds obvious. Make sure you read and understand the directions for every test. Never assume that you know what to do. Always read the directions first. They will focus your attention on finding the right answers.

Read the Answers

Read the answers—ALL the answers—for a multiple-choice question, even if you think the first one is correct. Test writers sometimes include tricky answers that seem right when you first read them.

Preview the Questions

Scan each section. This will give you information about the questions. You also can see how many questions there are in the section. Do not spend too much time doing this. A quick glance will provide helpful information without making you nervous.

Use Your Time Wisely

Always follow test rules. On most standardized tests, you can work on only one section at a time. Do not skip ahead or return to another section. If you finish early, go back and check your answers in that section.

- Before the test begins, find out if you can write in the test booklet. If so, add a small circle or star next to those questions that you find difficult. If time allows, come back to these questions before time is up for that section.
- Try not to spend too much time on one question. Skip a difficult question and try to answer it later. Be careful, though! You need to skip that question's number on your answer sheet. When you answer the next question, make sure you carefully fill in or darken the circle for the correct question.
- When finishing a section, look at your answer sheet. Did you answer every question for the section? Erase any extra marks on your answer sheet. Make sure you did not mark two answers for one question.

Make an Educated Guess

Most standardized tests take away points for wrong answers. It might be wise to skip a question if you have no idea about the answer. Leave the answer blank and move on to the next question. But if you can eliminate one or more of the answers, guessing can be a great strategy. Remember, smart guessing can improve your test scores!

- Read every answer choice.
- Cross out every answer you know is wrong.
- Try rereading or restating the question to find the best answer.

Think Before You Switch

When you check your answers, you might be tempted to change one or more of them. In most cases, your first answer is probably the best choice. Ask yourself why you want to make a change. If you have a good reason, pick a new answer. For example, you might have misread the question. If you cannot think of a specific reason, it is probably best to stick with your first answer.

Fill in the Blanks

Fill-in-the-blank questions are found on many tests. The blank is usually in the middle or at the end of a sentence. Use these steps to answer a fill-in-the-blank question.

- Begin with the first answer choice. Try reading the sentence with that word or group of words in place of the blank. Ask yourself, "Does this answer make sense?"
- Then try filling in the blank with each of the other answer choices. Also, use the other words in the sentence as clues to help you decide the correct choice.
- Choose the best answer.

Look for Clue Words

When you read test questions, watch for *clue words* that provide important information. Here are some words that make a difference.

- NOT: Many questions ask you to find the answer that is not true. These questions can be tricky. Slow down and think about the meaning of the question. Then pick the one answer that is not true.
- ALWAYS, NEVER, ALL, NONE, ONLY: These words limit a statement. They often make a generally true statement into a false one.
- SOMETIMES, SOME, MOST, MANY, OFTEN, GENERALLY: These words make a statement more believable. You will find them in many correct answers.
- BEST, MOST LIKELY, SAME, OPPOSITE, PROBABLY: These words change the meaning of a sentence. You often can use them to eliminate choices.

Restate the Question

Short answer or essay questions require writing an answer. Your response must answer the question. Restate the question to make sure your answer stays on target. For example, if the question is "What is a tornado?" your answer should begin with the words "A tornado is . . ."

Be sure to look for the Test Tips throughout this workbook. They will give you more test-taking strategies and help you with certain subject areas.

UNIT 2

SIX READING SKILLS

SKILL 1: DETERMINING WORD MEANINGS

Prefixes and suffixes are parts of some words. A *prefix* is at the start of a word. A *suffix* is at the end of a word. You can use prefixes and suffixes to figure out the meaning of a word.

Whenever Shaquana invited a friend to sleep over, she made sure it was someone who liked to stay up late and tell scary stories. Lately, the only books Shaquana liked to read were about the supernatural.

1 In this paragraph, the word supernatural means —

Ⓐ ghosts and spirits.

Ⓑ people who really like nature.

Ⓒ heroes.

Ⓓ strong people.

Hint: Read the entire paragraph. The prefix "super-" means above or greater than normal.

Sometimes having an older sister drives me crazy. She plays her music really loud while I'm doing my homework. If I ask her to turn it down, she'll make it louder.

2 In this paragraph, the word louder means —

Ⓕ quieter.

Ⓖ more than loud.

Ⓗ almost as loud.

Ⓙ almost the same as it was before.

Hint: The suffix "-er" means more than.

Jeff went into his room to find his sneakers. Just as he got near his closet, he found that he was in darkness.

3 What is meant by darkness?

____

____

____

____

____

____

____

____

Hint: The suffix "-ness" means a state of being.

TEST TIP

When you are asked to write a short answer, be as clear as possible. Stay on track by restating the question. For question 3, you can say to yourself, "Darkness means . . . "

GO ON

The girls were trying to remember what the new girl at camp was like. Joan said she had brown hair and was skinny. Phyllis thought she was on the tallish side.

4 **In this paragraph, the word tallish means —**

Ⓐ that the new girl talked a lot.

Ⓑ that the new girl was shy.

Ⓒ that the new girl was rather tall.

Ⓓ that the new girl was of Irish background.

Hint: The suffix "-ish" means somewhat *or* rather.

My mother asked me to get everything ready. She wanted to make dinner for us when she got home. She told me to take the meat out of the refrigerator and preheat the oven. Then she wanted me to start washing the lettuce.

5 **In this paragraph, the word preheat means —**

Ⓕ check the temperature of.

Ⓖ turn on.

Ⓗ heat beforehand.

Ⓙ clean.

Hint: "Pre-" is a prefix. "Pre-" means before.

Test Tip

Notice that many answer choices are either ABCD or FGHJ. This pattern helps make sure you fill in the correct answer for a question. Make sure you find the circle on the answer sheet that has the letter of your choice.

The boys were planning a garage sale. They had cleaned the toys and found all the pieces for the games. But their old clothes were in such bad shape, they did not think they could resell them.

6 **What does it mean when someone resells something?**

____

____

____

____

____

____

____

____

Hint: "Re-" is a prefix. "Re-" means to do something again.

Test Tip

This list shows some other prefixes you might find in test words. Notice that there are many prefixes that mean "not":

Disappear means "not appear."

Illegal means "not legal."

Impossible means "not possible."

Misspell means "not to spell correctly."

Unfair means "not fair."

GO ON

Sometimes you can figure out the meaning of a new word by using the words around it as clues.

Sherlock Holmes is a great detective. But he lives only in books. The tales about him have been written in 57 languages.

1 In this paragraph, the word tales means —

Ⓐ places.

Ⓑ names.

Ⓒ stories.

Ⓓ pens.

Hint: You get a clue as to what the word tales *means by reading sentences 2 and 3.*

Marie did not know how to operate the compact disc player. She read the manual. She hoped she could find the information she needed in the book.

2 In this paragraph, the word manual means —

Ⓕ a dictionary.

Ⓖ a compact disc.

Ⓗ a recipe book.

Ⓙ a how-to book.

Hint: You get a clue as to what the word manual *means from the sentence after the one in which the word appears.*

Mother ducks often take their ducklings swimming. When a pond is full of mothers and babies, the mother ducks quack and swim around. Whichever mother duck quacks the loudest gets the greatest number of ducklings to swim around her.

3 What are ducklings?

____

____

____

____

____

____

____

____

Hint: You get a clue as to what the word ducklings *means from the second sentence in the paragraph.*

TEST TIP

Using information in the text to figure out the meaning of a word is called *using context clues*. Do not worry if you do not recognize the word. In this type of question, test writers do not expect you to know the word. They want you to use clues to find the meaning. Sometimes a nearby word will have a similar meaning. Other times, the ideas before and after the word should help you figure out or guess the answer. Try to connect ideas. Use logic to see which answer choices make sense and which ones do not.

GO ON

Pat grew up wanting to be a postmaster. As a boy, whenever he went to the post office in his home town in Ohio, he would dream of running it. When he finished school, his dream almost came true. He became a postmaster, but in a different town in Ohio.

4 In this paragraph, the word postmaster means —

Ⓐ someone who likes to collect stamps.

Ⓑ an expert about postage.

Ⓒ a person in charge of a post office.

Ⓓ the person who posts time for runners.

Hint: You get a clue as to what the word postmaster *means from the sentence that tells about Pat's dream.*

Birds perch on a tree even while they sleep. Their toes grab the branch so they don't fall. Three toes point forward. One toe points backward. The toes lock tightly onto the branch.

5 In this paragraph, the word perch means —

Ⓕ fly.

Ⓖ sit.

Ⓗ vanish.

Ⓙ promise.

Hint: You get a clue as to what the word perch *means by reading the sentences after the one in which the word is.*

Doctors studied thousands of people. Some of the people spent a lot of time alone. Many of these people had weak hearts. They were more likely to have a heart attack. Other people spent a lot of time with their families and friends. Most of these social people had strong hearts.

6 Describe someone who is social.

____

____

____

____

____

____

____

____

Hint: You get a clue as to what the word social *means by reading the sentence before the word.*

Test Tip

To answer question 6, you can write one or two sentences. You might begin your answer by restating the question. You could write, "Someone who is social likes to . . ."

GO ON

Specialized or technical words are used in science and social studies. You can use the other information in the passage to help figure out the meaning of these words.

Sometimes, deep in the ocean, an earthquake shakes the ocean floor. The movement starts a tidal wave. At first, the wave is small. But it can move toward the shore at a speed of up to 500 miles per hour. By the time it reaches the coast, it is huge and hits hard.

1 In this paragraph, tidal wave means —

Ⓐ a way of saying hello.

Ⓑ a very big wave sent to shore by an earthquake.

Ⓒ a strong gust of wind.

Ⓓ a group of people that stand up and down in a stadium.

Hint: Tidal wave is a technical word. You get a clue as to what it means by reading the entire paragraph.

There are giant ships more than 700 feet long. These ships were built to carry tons of wheat from place to place. They have a ramp folded up in back. When they get to shore, the ramp unfolds. The cargo is moved off the ship by the ramp.

2 In this paragraph, the word cargo means —

Ⓕ truck.

Ⓖ garbage.

Ⓗ shipment.

Ⓙ flower.

Hint: Cargo is a technical word. You get a clue as to what it means by reading the sentences before the word.

Saliva helps you swallow food by making your throat slippery. Saliva softens food so that the tongue can taste it. Saliva also helps your body break down food.

3 What is saliva and where do you find it?

____

____

____

____

____

____

____

____

Hint: Saliva is a technical word. You can get a clue as to what it means by reading the entire paragraph.

TEST TIP

Think about every choice before you answer a question. To answer question 2, look for a word that means the same as *cargo*. Try replacing the word *cargo* in the paragraph with each answer choice. Find the answer that makes the most sense.

GO ON

Wildflowers grow in many environments. Some are found in woods or fields. Others grow on mountains or in streams and ponds. Wildflowers can grow in the desert, too.

4 In this paragraph, the word environments means —

Ⓐ blossoms.

Ⓑ settings.

Ⓒ oceans.

Ⓓ insects.

Hint: You get a clue as to what environments *means from the sentences after the word.*

Ted couldn't believe that he was on a real television set. Carpenters were working all around him building the scenes where the action would take place. Some painters were working on the rooms of a house, and others were painting a yard. He hoped his parents would let him stay long enough to meet one of the actors or actresses.

5 In this paragraph, the word set means —

Ⓕ a number of tools that are used together.

Ⓖ the number of couples needed for a square dance.

Ⓗ a group of tennis games.

Ⓙ a place where a show is filmed.

Hint: Set *is a technical word. You get a clue as to what it means by reading the entire paragraph.*

Piranhas are fish. They live in South American waters. These fish tend to swim in large groups. They will tear the flesh off an animal or person that is in the water. In just minutes, all that is left is the skeleton.

6 What is a skeleton?

____

____

____

____

____

____

____

____

Hint: Skeleton *is a technical word. You get a clue as to what it means by reading the sentence before the word.*

TEST TIP

Try to form a picture in your mind of what you read. A good picture can help you figure out a word's meaning. When you read the paragraph for question 6, try to "see" what is happening. Which parts of the body do you think fish will not eat? Use your picture to help you define the word *skeleton*.

STOP

Facts or details are important. By noticing them, you will know what the passage is about.

The United States Supreme Court is the highest court of the land. For many years, only men were Supreme Court judges. That was true until 1981. That year, Sandra Day O'Connor became a Supreme Court judge. She was the first woman to do so.

Sandra's first teacher was her mother. Later, Sandra went to school. Sandra finished high school when she was just 16. Then, she followed her dream to study law. She was in law school for five years. When she finished law school, she couldn't find a job. Very few companies wanted women lawyers!

1 Only men served on the Supreme Court —

Ⓐ after 1990.

Ⓑ after 1811.

Ⓒ until 1981.

Ⓓ until 200 years ago.

Hint: Look at sentences 2 and 3.

2 The highest court of the United States is the —

Ⓕ World Court.

Ⓖ State Court.

Ⓗ Supreme Court.

Ⓙ Day Court.

Hint: Look for this sentence in the passage.

3 What was Sandra's dream?

____

____

____

____

____

____

____

____

Hint: Look at sentence 9.

TEST TIP

When you look for details, make sure you read carefully. Take some extra time to check your answer before you fill in or darken the circle. Trick answers might switch two numbers or use a word that makes sense but is not from the paragraph.

GO ON

Sandra married a man she met in law school. They both got jobs as lawyers. For a while, Sandra had her own law office. Then, she and her husband had a son. Sandra decided to stay home. Sandra and her husband had two more sons.

After nine years, Sandra became a judge in Arizona. She was a judge there for seven years. Then, one of the judges from the Supreme Court left. So the Supreme Court needed another judge. The President of the United States heard about Sandra. He asked her to become a judge on the Supreme Court. She eagerly said, "Yes!"

4 **The President asked Sandra Day O'Connor to be a —**

Ⓐ student at a university.

Ⓑ lawyer in Arizona.

Ⓒ judge in an Arizona court.

Ⓓ judge on the Supreme Court.

Hint: Find the section that talks about the President.

5 **Sandra had —**

Ⓕ three sons.

Ⓖ two daughters.

Ⓗ a son and a daughter.

Ⓙ four children.

Hint: Count the number of sons mentioned in the passage.

6 **Sandra and her husband were both —**

Ⓐ doctors.

Ⓑ lawyers.

Ⓒ teachers.

Ⓓ bankers.

Hint: Look at sentence 2.

7 **How long did Sandra stay home with her children?**

____

____

____

____

____

____

____

____

Hint: Look at sentence 7.

TEST TIP

When a question asks you to finish a sentence, remember that both parts of the sentence need to fit together. In question 4, you might be tempted to pick choice C because Sandra was a judge in an Arizona court. But that answer does not go with the first part of the sentence.

GO ON

It is helpful to put events in the order they happened. This may help you to understand a passage.

Long, long ago, the ancient Greeks served a god named Zeus. They honored Zeus by giving grand festivals. The festivals were held in a place called Olympia. During the festivals, athletes showed their strength and speed. These festivals were the first Olympic Games.

In the year 776 B.C., the 200-meter race was won by a young man named Coroebus. He is the first Olympic winner on record. The next festival took place in 772 B.C. This time the Greeks wanted to offer more to their god. So, they held new sporting events. Many people came to watch them. For the next 1,000 years, the Olympics were held every four years. They always took place in Olympia.

At first, only people with money could afford to be Olympic athletes. They had the time to train and get in shape. Some of the events were horse racing, wrestling, boxing, and running. The first Olympics lasted for five days. Prizes were given on the last day. Winning was the most important part of athletics for the ancient Greeks. The winners marched in a parade toward the Temple of Zeus. Along the way, crowds tossed flowers at them. The winners wore olive wreaths. The Greeks gave prizes to the first-place winners only. People teased the losers.

The games were stopped in A.D. 393. At that time, the Romans ruled Greece. The emperor did not like the Greek gods. So, he stopped the Olympic events. The Greek temples stood empty. Over the years, they were buried by floods and earthquakes. In 1892, a Frenchman wanted to start the Olympic Games once again. He thought that the games would bring the people of the world together in peace. In 1896, he succeeded. The first modern games were held in Athens, Greece.

1 When did the Olympic festivals stop?

____

____

____

____

____

____

____

____

Hint: Look at the last paragraph.

TEST TIP

You can write quick notes to help you keep events in order. You might circle dates. You also can watch for *time order words*. Here are some time order words in this paragraph:

long ago
first
next
this time
at first
at that time

GO ON

2 **When were prizes given?**

Ⓐ on the first day

Ⓑ after each event

Ⓒ on the fifth day

Ⓓ every day

Hint: Look at the section mentioning the prizes.

3 **Which of these events happened last in the story?**

Ⓕ Coroebus won a race in Olympia.

Ⓖ A Frenchman wanted to start the Olympic Games once again.

Ⓗ Games were held in Athens, Greece.

Ⓙ Prizes were only given to first-place winners.

Hint: Look at the last paragraph.

TEST TIP

When a question asks you to find the last event, think about the order of events. If you get stuck, try numbering the answer choices. Put a *1* next to the first event and a *2* next to the second event. Keep going until you find the last event.

4 **Which of these happened first in the story?**

Ⓐ The Greeks held a festival in 772 B.C.

Ⓑ The Roman emperor stopped the games in Olympia.

Ⓒ The Greeks held a festival in 776 B.C.

Ⓓ Some events were horse racing, wrestling, boxing, and running.

Hint: Look at the beginning of the story.

5 **When were the first modern Olympic games held?**

____

____

____

____

____

____

____

____

Hint: Look at the section about the modern Olympics.

GO ON

Skill 2: Identifying Supporting Ideas

Written directions tell you how to do something. Every step is important.

My friend told me to meet her at her mother's office at 3 P.M. She told me to walk to building #120 on Liberty Street and then to go in the main entrance and down the flight of stairs on the left. Then, I should turn left at the bottom of the stairs and go down the hall to office #3B. She will be waiting for me inside the office.

1 To get to my friend's mother's office, I should first —

Ⓐ take a bus.

Ⓑ take the elevator right inside the main entrance.

Ⓒ turn right at the bottom of the stairs.

Ⓓ go to #120 Liberty Street.

Hint: Read the directions. They start with the second sentence.

Test Tip

Small details make a big difference on tests. One wrong word makes an answer choice incorrect. In question 1, the first answer is not right because the paragraph does not mention taking a bus.

On these practice tests, think about the wrong answers. Ask yourself, "Why is this answer not right?"

Do the lights ever go out in your neighborhood? They do in ours a lot. Sometimes they go out when it is very hot and everyone is using their air conditioners. Other times, it is during a storm. Luckily, I know what to do when the lights go out. First, I get our flashlight. Then, I go around the house turning off all the lights that were on before, as well as the television and clothes dryer. Next, I call the electric company to find out what's going on. Then I go back to reading my book—using the flashlight!

2 What is the first thing you should do if the lights go out in your house?

____

____

____

____

____

____

____

____

Hint: Read the directions. They start with the word "first."

Test Tip

Pay close attention to *signal words.* The question asks you to name the *first* thing you should do. Make sure you name the first step.

GO ON

I do not like cooking. I do enjoy baking. I think that it is a lot of fun to bake a cake for a party. My favorite cake is plain yellow, because then I can put any kind of icing on it. Here is the recipe:

Step 1: Make a list of all the things you need to get at the store to make the cake.
Step 2: When you have everything, measure the right amount of water.
Step 3: Mix the water with the cake mix and two eggs.
Step 4: Bake it in the oven for about thirty minutes.
Step 5: Take the cake out of the oven and let it cool.
Step 6: Ice the cake with any flavor you like: vanilla, chocolate, or strawberry.

3 When do you put the cake in the oven?

Ⓕ Step 2

Ⓖ Step 3

Ⓗ Step 4

Ⓙ Step 5

Hint: Read the steps in order, starting with Step 1.

TEST TIP

The numbered steps in this paragraph help keep things in order. But the numbers can be easy to confuse. Make sure you choose the correct number of the step to answer question 3. Double-check by rereading each step.

4 Before you start to make a cake, you should —

Ⓐ mix the water with the eggs.

Ⓑ mix the cake mix with the eggs.

Ⓒ make sure you have all the ingredients you need.

Ⓓ take the top off the can of icing you bought at the store.

Hint: Read the steps in order, starting with Step 1.

5 What should you do right after you bake the cake?

____

____

____

____

____

____

____

____

Hint: Read the steps starting with Step 4.

TEST TIP

Restating the question will help you keep track of the order. You can begin, "Right after you bake the cake, you should . . ."

GO ON

The setting of a story lets you know when and where the story is taking place.

Richard Byrd stood outside the small cabin on March 28, 1934. He shook hands with the men who were leaving. They were heading back to the main camp on the east coast of Antarctica. He would stay at the base camp for the winter. There was plenty of food and fuel in the tiny cabin. He felt sure nothing would go wrong.

But something did go wrong. Byrd was burning kerosene for heat, and the fumes were poisoning him. He continued to make his radio messages, because he didn't want anyone to try to rescue him in the dangerous weather. Byrd managed to stay alive until August, when three men arrived at the base camp. They hardly recognized Byrd. He was very thin and looked terrible. Byrd greeted them and then fell to the ground. The men had arrived in the nick of time. After two months of care, Byrd's good health returned.

1 **The story takes place —**

Ⓐ 100 years ago.

Ⓑ within the past 25 years.

Ⓒ over 60 years ago.

Ⓓ in 1943.

Hint: Read the first sentence.

Test Tip

Watch for tricky answers. In question 1, answer D might look familiar, but take a closer look! Why is it wrong?

2 **The story takes place —**

Ⓕ at the main camp.

Ⓖ on the coast of Antarctica.

Ⓗ in a large cabin.

Ⓙ at the base camp.

Hint: Read the first paragraph.

3 **When was Richard Byrd rescued?**

____

____

____

____

____

____

____

____

Hint: Find the section that talks about Byrd's rescue.

Test Tip

When you write a short answer, be as specific as possible. To answer question 3, telling the year is not enough. The paragraph gives a more exact date. Look for the month in which Byrd was rescued.

GO ON

The strongest earthquake in the United States happened in Missouri. It took place in 1811. The center of the earthquake was near a town called New Madrid. Since few people lived near this town, nobody was killed. But the earthquake was quite strong. It changed the course of the Mississippi River.

4 When did the earthquake occur?

Ⓐ in 1911

Ⓑ in 1918

Ⓒ in 1811

Ⓓ in 1981

Hint: Look at the second sentence.

5 Where was the earthquake?

____

____

____

____

____

____

____

____

Hint: Read the first three sentences.

Going to the horse show on that beautiful summer day was a great experience. Before the events started, we were able to get very close to the riders and their horses. Then, after we found our seats, we spent the afternoon watching each rider and horse perform. At the end of the day, the best performers were given ribbons and prizes.

6 When is this story taking place?

Ⓕ in the summer

Ⓖ in the spring

Ⓗ at night

Ⓙ in the morning

Hint: Look at the first sentence.

TEST TIP

Sometimes the obvious choice is right! The answer to question 6 is clearly stated in the first sentence. Be careful not to "overthink" your response. If the answer seems clear to you, it is probably the right one!

STOP

The main idea is the meaning of a passage. Many times it is a sentence in the passage.

A chameleon is a kind of lizard. Its skin is clear, but it can change color. Under its skin are layers of cells. These cells have yellow, black, and red color in them. Anger makes these colors darken. Fear makes them lighten. It also makes yellow spots appear. Temperature and light can also cause the colors to change. These changes make the chameleon hard to see. Changing colors can save a chameleon's life.

1 What is the main idea of this story?

____

____

____

____

____

____

____

____

Hint: What does the whole story talk about?

TEST TIP

When you need to write a main idea, make sure you tell the big idea of what you read. Do not focus on the details. Think about the main meaning of the passage.

To find the main idea of the paragraph for question 3, ask yourself:

- What is this paragraph about?
- What idea connects all of these details?

Don't worry if there are times when you get angry. Getting angry can be both good and bad. Many doctors think that it's all right to show your anger sometimes. People who get angry once in a while may live happier lives. But people must be careful when they are angry. Angry people don't always think clearly. They can do things that they may be sorry about later.

2 What is the main idea of this story?

Ⓐ People can't think straight when they are angry.

Ⓑ People get angry about nothing.

Ⓒ Anger can be both good and bad.

Ⓓ Anger can make you sick.

Hint: Which choice sums up the whole passage?

John Chapman planted apple trees in Ohio in the early 1800s. He carried the seeds all over the country. He sold the seeds or just gave them away to people. Chapman was a very kind man. He loved people, animals, and trees. The story of Johnny Appleseed is the story of his life.

3 What is the main idea of this story?

Ⓕ Apple trees grow from seeds.

Ⓖ We get the story of Johnny Appleseed from the life of John Chapman.

Ⓗ John Chapman lived in Ohio.

Ⓙ John Chapman traveled the country.

Hint: What does the whole story talk about?

GO ON

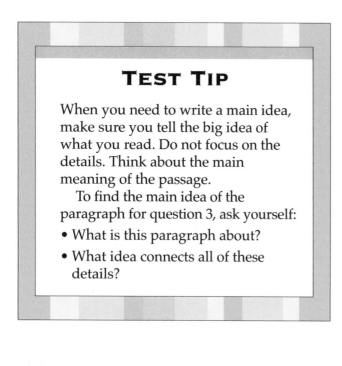

Sometimes, people need help when they get older. Older people may need help walking or cooking food. At night, they count on their families to do these things for them. But during the day, they may be left at home alone. To help them, some cities have built day-care centers. Older people can go to these centers during the day. There they will get the help they need.

4 What is the main idea of this story?

Ⓐ Older people can get the help they need in day-care centers.

Ⓑ Older people cook their lunch.

Ⓒ Families are busy at night.

Ⓓ Older people need help walking.

Hint: All of the sentences in the paragraph give you the main idea.

Test Tip

To choose a main idea, find the answer that states the most important idea. The answer should not focus on small details. It should tell about the whole paragraph.

A man in Florida can talk to fish. He spent a long time learning how to do this. First, he watched fish very closely. Then, he listened to the noises they made. Finally, he learned to make the same sounds. Sometimes, the fish listen to him. At times he can even make them do things. This man thinks that someday fishermen might be able to call fish to their nets.

5 What is the main idea of this story?

Ⓕ Some fish listen to sounds.

Ⓖ Many people like to fish.

Ⓗ Fish never listen.

Ⓙ A man in Florida talks to fish.

Hint: What does the whole story talk about?

Test Tip

Some paragraphs begin or end with the main idea. Read the first sentence in the paragraph for question 5. Do you think this sentence tells the main idea? Which answer choice is like the first sentence?

GO ON

Skill 3: Summarizing Main Ideas

A good summary contains the main idea of a passage. It is short but includes the most important points.

One kind of spider makes a web underwater. It weaves its web in water plants. Then, it carries bubbles of air down to fill the web. The water spider lies still on its web. Soon, a water insect swims near it. The spider dashes out and catches the insect. It brings its catch back to the air-filled web to eat.

1 Which sentence tells what this story is mostly about?

Ⓐ Some spiders look better underwater.

Ⓑ Water spiders build their webs using air bubbles.

Ⓒ Water spiders like water insects.

Ⓓ One kind of spider can live underwater very well.

Hint: Which sentence tells you about the whole passage?

It is hard to think of doctors as artists. But their job of healing people can be beautiful. For instance, doctors help people who can't hear well. In some cases, doctors use a piece of a rib. They carve the rib so that it fits inside the ear. The bone is about a tenth of an inch high. It also has a pretty and interesting shape. With this bone in the ear, the person can hear much better.

2 What is the best summary of this passage?

Ⓕ Some people think that a doctor is a kind of artist because healing people is beautiful.

Ⓖ People who can't hear well need to use their ribs to try to hear better.

Ⓗ Artists know how to carve ribs into pretty shapes.

Ⓙ Doctors help artists hear better using pieces of ribs.

Hint: Which sentence tells you about the whole passage?

Test Tip

Remember that the main idea of a paragraph will not include all of the details. The main idea only tells the most important thing about a paragraph. As you read the answer choices for question 2, you might look for one that includes the word *artists* because that word is in the first sentence. However, the main idea may not include this word.

GO ON

Calamity Jane was a famous woman of the Wild West. She was famous because she was so tough. She lived during the 1800s. She learned to ride a horse and shoot a gun at an early age. People could always hear her coming. She also liked to dress in men's clothes. There weren't many women like her.

3 What is this story mostly about?

Ⓐ It was tough for Calamity Jane to live during the 1800s.

Ⓑ Calamity Jane was famous because she was taught to ride a horse.

Ⓒ Calamity Jane did things that other women in the 1800s did not.

Ⓓ Calamity Jane wore men's clothes.

Hint: Which sentence sums up Calamity Jane?

Cats are very much like lions and tigers. They can jump high in the air. Cats can jump seven feet high. They have padded feet. That way they can sneak up on their prey. Cats have 18 claws on their feet. They can push out and draw back their claws.

4 What is this story mostly about?

____

____

____

____

____

____

____

____

Hint: Which sentence tells you about the whole passage?

Two things make a tree a conifer. One is that it must make seeds in its cones. It must also have needle-like leaves. Conifers are called evergreen trees. They look green all the time. Conifers do lose and replace their leaves. But they never lose all their leaves at the same time.

5 What is this story mostly about?

____

____

____

____

____

____

____

____

Hint: Which sentence tells you about the whole paragraph?

TEST TIP

When you have to write a main idea, try to write one clear sentence. If you write two sentences, you may include too many details.

STOP

Knowing what happened (effect) and what made it happen (cause) helps you to understand what you read.

The big dance was Friday night, and Jodi needed a dress to wear. As she was sorting through her closet, her older sister, Gabriela, tapped her on the shoulder. She knew that Jodi had always liked her blue dress. "How would you like to wear this?" she asked. Jodi's eyes lit up. She hugged Gabriela and ran to try on the dress.

1 Why was Jodi happy?

____

____

____

____

____

____

____

____

Hint: Jodi's eyes lighting up is the effect. What made this happen?

2 Why did Jodi need a dress to wear?

Ⓐ She wanted to be like her older sister, Gabriela.

Ⓑ The big dance was Friday night.

Ⓒ She was tired of blue dresses in her closet.

Ⓓ She couldn't find any dresses in her closet.

Hint: Jodi needing a dress is the effect. What made this happen?

TEST TIP

When you read a question, you might know the answer right away. It is still a good idea to look back at the paragraph. Look for details that support your answer.

If you do not know the answer, reread the choices with the question in mind. To answer question 2, say to yourself, "Jodi needed a new dress because . . . " Look for the detail that completes this sentence.

GO ON

Alex and Vince were spending a week at camp. Tonight was their last night, and it was "skit night." The campers in each cabin had written plays about their camp experiences. Alex had seen how easily Vince made friends with everyone in the camp. When Vince was chosen to be the announcer for skit night, Alex dumped a box of cookie crumbs in Vince's sleeping bag.

3 Why did the campers write plays about their camp experiences?

- Ⓕ They liked to write plays.
- Ⓖ They had so much fun at camp that they had a lot to write about.
- Ⓗ They were going to put on skits.
- Ⓙ Their camp counselors asked them to write plays.

Hint: Writing plays is the effect. What made this happen?

4 Why did Alex dump a box of cookie crumbs in Vince's sleeping bag?

- Ⓐ Vince was chosen to be the announcer for skit night.
- Ⓑ Alex knew how much his friend liked cookies.
- Ⓒ Alex wanted to have a party in the cabin after skit night.
- Ⓓ Vince needed more cookies because he had so many friends.

Hint: Alex dumping a box of cookies in Vince's sleeping bag is the effect. What made this happen?

5 Why was Vince chosen as the announcer for skit night?

____

____

____

____

____

____

____

Hint: Being chosen as announcer is the effect. What made this happen?

Trena's baseball team was not very good. It had not won a game all season. Something had to be done, or else the team would be laughed at by everyone in town. So, Trena promised to eat one bug for every run the team scored. That night, the team scored twenty runs and finally won a game.

6 Why hadn't Trena's baseball team won a game all season?

- Ⓕ Everyone in town laughed at the team.
- Ⓖ The team ate bugs and got sick.
- Ⓗ The team was not very good.
- Ⓙ Something interrupted practices.

Hint: Not winning a game is the effect. What made this happen?

7 Why did the team score twenty runs?

- Ⓐ They ate bugs before the game.
- Ⓑ They had many fans in town.
- Ⓒ There were twenty girls on the team.
- Ⓓ Trena had promised to eat one bug for every run scored.

Hint: Scoring twenty runs is the effect. What made this happen?

GO ON

Many times you can tell in advance what is probably going to happen next. You must think about what would make sense if the story were to go on.

In the morning, Becky came downstairs. "I don't like this house at all," the girl told her parents. "It smells funny." Her mother asked if she had seen the wild strawberries growing in the front yard. Her father mentioned the pony he had seen at the neighboring house. The girl's eyes lit up.

1 What will Becky probably do?

Ⓐ The family will sell the house and move because of the smell.

Ⓑ The father will buy the pony for Becky.

Ⓒ Becky will find some things she likes about that house.

Ⓓ Becky will get angry because her eyes have lit up.

Hint: Think about how Becky feels at the end of the story, before you make your choice.

The man was trying to balance himself. His bicycle was picking up speed on the steep hill. He hit a bump, and one foot lost its grip on the pedal.

2 What will probably happen next?

____

____

____

____

____

____

____

____

Hint: Picture the scene in your mind before writing the answer.

The shaggy animal went up to the back door. It rattled the screen door with its front paw and then sat down. It was quiet for a while. But soon a face appeared at the door, and then there was a scream of joy. "It's Goldie!" a girl's voice said. "She's come back."

3 What will the girl probably do next?

Ⓕ run to get her mother

Ⓖ open the door to let Goldie in

Ⓗ shut and lock the inside door

Ⓙ scream again

Hint: What is most likely to happen next?

TEST TIP

When a test question asks you to make a *prediction*, you should tell the next logical step or event. Base your prediction on clues in the story. To answer question 2, follow the sequence of events. Tell the very next thing you think will happen.

To answer question 3, put yourself in the girl's place. Think about the very next thing you might do in that situation.

GO ON

Valentina Tereshkova was nervous. She knew she'd soon make history. It was a still morning. She sat strapped in her seat. At last, the Soviet spaceship began to shake. Its great engines roared. The ship climbed from the launch pad. It built up speed. Soon, it was racing through the sky. Valentina had become the first woman in space.

4 What will Valentina probably do next?

Ⓐ call her mother

Ⓑ have lunch

Ⓒ follow the steps she was trained to do in space

Ⓓ rest so that she could think clearly

Hint: What seems most likely to happen based on all the sentences?

Cris looked at the window to make sure it was open. Then she marked her place and closed the book. She put it on the table next to her bed. Then she fluffed up the pillow and set the alarm clock.

5 What will Cris most likely do next?

Ⓕ fall asleep

Ⓖ have a snack

Ⓗ get into bed

Ⓙ take a shower

Hint: Read the entire paragraph.

When Sammy woke up, he looked out the window. The slopes were covered with snow. Quickly, he pulled on his long underwear and other warm clothes. He ate a good, hot breakfast so that he'd have plenty of energy. Then he checked his equipment. He walked in his heavy boots toward the door.

6 What is probably going to happen next?

Ⓐ Sammy is going to ski down the slopes.

Ⓑ Sammy is going ice skating.

Ⓒ Sammy is going to play golf.

Ⓓ Sammy is going to stay inside.

Hint: You need to read the whole paragraph, but especially the last sentence.

Test Tip

Remember to picture what is happening as you read. Your picture will help you predict what will happen next.

STOP

The way a character acts tells you about that person's mood.

Al had been standing in line at the counter waiting to pay for the things he had chosen. The store was hot, and the air conditioning didn't work. Al was holding some heavy objects, and he wished the line would move faster. A woman cut to the front of the line. People protested, but the woman didn't budge. Suddenly, Al threw his things into a nearby cart and walked quickly out of the store.

1 How was Al feeling when he left the store?

Ⓐ Al had gotten tired of waiting and planned to come back when the store wasn't so busy.

Ⓑ Al was hungry and looking forward to lunch.

Ⓒ Al was angry that he had waited so long only to have someone cut into the line.

Ⓓ Al felt that he had chosen the wrong items.

Hint: Carefully think about the entire passage, especially the last sentence.

TEST TIP

The things a character does can tell you about that character. If a person jumps up and down and smiles, you can *infer* that the person is happy. Test questions often ask you to *infer* how a character is feeling. You can figure out how a character feels by thinking about what happens in the story.

To answer question 1, you need to infer how Al feels. The paragraph does not say how he feels, but it does give many clues.

Ian and Louise were supposed to be planting corn, beans, and carrots together. While Louise dug up the old garden and turned over the soil, Ian sat under a tree sipping a cool drink. While Louise dug in fertilizer and raked the garden, Ian ate his lunch. When the soil was finally ready for the seeds to be planted, Ian said to Louise, "I'll plant the seeds." Louise yelled back, "No, thanks! I'll plant the seeds!"

2 How did Louise feel?

____

____

____

____

____

____

____

____

Hint: You must read the entire passage and what Louise said at the end of the story to find out how Louise felt.

GO ON

When the baby came home from the hospital, his five-year-old brother, Mike, shouted, "Take it back! You got a new baby because I'm not good enough for you!" Mike's parents talked with him for a long time. They told him that the baby would need special care at first. But that didn't mean they didn't love Mike anymore.

3 How did Mike feel about his new baby brother?

Ⓕ Mike was mad because the baby cried all the time.

Ⓖ Mike was mad because he didn't want to take care of the baby.

Ⓗ Mike felt his parents loved the new baby more than they loved him.

Ⓙ Mike felt that the baby should not get special care.

Hint: Read what Mike said to discover how he felt.

TEST TIP

A character's words often tell about the character. Remember that you will find a character's exact words inside quotation marks. When you come to a quotation in a story, make sure you know who is talking.

To answer question 3, think about Mike's exact words. They give you a clue about how he was feeling.

A fisherman brought a large fish to the king and was paid well for it. As the fisherman left, he picked up a valuable coin from the floor. The angry king called to him, "That is not yours." The man answered, "I did not want someone to step on the king's face. That is why I picked up the coin." The king smiled and let the man keep the coin.

4 How did the king feel after the man said something?

____

____

____

____

____

____

____

____

Hint: Carefully think about the entire passage, especially what the king did at the end of the passage.

STOP

It is important to know the difference between fact and opinion. A fact is real and true. An opinion is a feeling or belief. Words that describe are used to offer opinions.

Stephen Hawking is a famous scientist. He has written books about physics and our universe. But Hawking must do all his work in a wheelchair. In his twenties, he found out that he had Lou Gehrig's disease. Later, he lost his power to speak and write. Now, he does all his work on a special computer. The computer allows him to speak.

1 Why does Stephen Hawking use a computer?

____

____

____

____

____

____

____

____

Hint: A fact is real and true. What is said in the passage?

A sun dog is a bright ring around the sun. Sometimes, the sun dog will also have colors. It may look like a round rainbow. Sun dogs are caused by ice crystals high in the sky. You should never look right at the sun. So wear sunglasses if you want to see a sun dog.

2 Which of these is an OPINION from the passage?

Ⓐ A sun dog is caused by ice crystals.

Ⓑ You should not look right at the sun.

Ⓒ The rainbow colors of a sun dog are beautiful.

Ⓓ A sun dog is a bright ring around the sun.

Hint: Words that describe are opinion words.

TEST TIP

Pay close attention to words that are underlined, in *italics*, or CAPITALIZED. These words give you important information. In question 2, the capitalized word tells you that you need to find an opinion.

GO ON

Did you know that your body shrinks as the day goes by? When you wake up, you are at your tallest. Your body is relaxed. Your muscles are stretched, and your joints are loose. As the day passes, your muscles tighten. Gravity pulls down on your body, too. Your body may be an inch shorter by the end of the day.

3 Which of these is a FACT from the passage?

Ⓕ When you wake up, you feel good because your body is relaxed.

Ⓖ It is good that your muscles tighten so that you don't fall down.

Ⓗ Gravity pulls down on your body.

Ⓙ It's better to be short than tall.

Hint: Words like "feel good," "it is good," and "it is better" are opinion words.

Have you ever watched a pond freeze in winter? The water freezes first on the top. The ice forms a very thin sheet across the water. It takes only about twenty minutes for this sheet to form. Then slowly the ice begins to grow down toward the bottom. It takes an hour for the first sheet to become two times as thick as it was when it started.

4 Which of these is NOT a fact from the passage?

Ⓐ When ice freezes it looks pretty.

Ⓑ It takes about twenty minutes for the first sheet of ice to form.

Ⓒ It takes an hour for the first sheet to become two times as thick.

Ⓓ Ice freezes first on top, forming a very thin sheet across the water.

Hint: Facts are real and true. Which sentence is an opinion?

For years, traveling farm workers were not treated well. At last, Cesar Chavez could stand it no longer. He thought farm workers should be paid more. He wanted better working conditions for them. To gain these, he formed a union. The group went on strike to get what they wanted.

5 Which of these is a FACT from the passage?

Ⓕ It was not fair that farm workers were not treated well.

Ⓖ Better working conditions mean that farm workers will produce more.

Ⓗ To gain better working conditions, Cesar Chavez formed a union.

Ⓙ It is not a good idea to go on strike.

Hint: A fact is real and true. What is actually said in the passage?

Test Tip

Remember that a fact is a true statement. When you are looking for a *fact*, look for a statement that is real and true.

Facts
Dogs have four legs.
Madrid is in Spain.
Squares have four sides.

When you are looking for an *opinion*, look for a statement that tells one person's feelings or beliefs.

Opinions
I love dogs.
Madrid is my favorite city.
Squares are easy to draw.

STOP

READING COMPREHENSION

Directions: Read each story carefully. Then read each question. Darken the circle for the correct answer, or write in the answer.

TRY THIS **More than one answer choice may seem correct. Choose the answer that goes best with the story.**

Sample A **Our Pancakes**

Dad and I made our own breakfast. We made pancakes. They tasted better than Mom's pancakes. Dad and I decided we would keep this as our little secret.

Why will they keep the secret?

Ⓐ They do not want Mom to know they cooked breakfast.

Ⓑ They do not want to hurt Mom's feelings.

Ⓒ They burned the pancakes.

Ⓓ They want to make breakfast again next week.

THINK IT THROUGH **The correct answer is B, They do not want to hurt Mom's feelings. The story states that the pancakes tasted better than Mom's pancakes, but they will keep this secret rather than hurt Mom's feelings.**

STOP

Jill and Jo

Jill and Jo were playing. Jo ran to hide. Jill looked for her. Then it began to rain. Jill and Jo got wet. They ran to the house.

1 **What were the girls playing?**

____

____

____

____

____

____

____

____

2 **Why did Jill and Jo run to the house?**

Ⓐ because they were tired

Ⓑ because it was hot

Ⓒ because it was raining

Ⓓ because it was time for lunch

GO ON

The Girls Get Lost!

Sheila used to live in a large city where she had many friends. When her mother got a job in a small town, Sheila was upset. She didn't want to move. She didn't want to leave her friends, especially her best friend, Katie. Sheila's mother promised that they would arrange a visit with Katie soon.

One day Sheila's mother asked her, "How would you like to go to the zoo on Saturday? I just talked to Mrs. Lee on the phone. She and Katie can meet us there." Sheila was excited. She couldn't think of anything she'd rather do.

The next Saturday was cold and clear. Sheila put on many layers of warm clothing. She had made a book for Katie. It told all about the fun things they had done when they lived next door to each other.

When Sheila and her mother drove up to the zoo, they saw Katie and her mother waiting at the entrance. Sheila and Katie were glad to see each other. They hurried down the path to the monkey house. "Wait for us there," Mrs. Lee said. But the girls were so busy talking that they didn't even hear her.

The girls watched the gorillas for a while. They had never seen such large apes. Then they ran to the area with lions and tigers.

They bought some food for the elephants and fed them. They spent a long time watching a giraffe and its baby.

When they started getting hungry, they turned around to look for their mothers, but they couldn't find them anywhere. "Uh oh! I think we might be in trouble," Sheila said. Katie was worried, too. The girls sat down and tried to think of what to do.

They decided to follow the signs back to the entrance.

When they had walked a long time, they saw their mothers. Their mothers were happy to see them. They had been worried about the girls. "Where have you been? We've been looking everywhere for you!" Sheila's mother said. The girls didn't know what to say. Later Katie whispered to Sheila. "Well, I guess we can add another chapter to the book you wrote. We can write about the time we got lost at the zoo."

GO ON

3 **The boxes below show events that happened in the story.**

The girls met at the zoo.		The girls fed the elephants.
1	2	3

What belongs in the second box?

- Ⓕ The girls watched a giraffe.
- Ⓖ The girls started getting hungry.
- Ⓗ The girls watched the gorillas.
- Ⓙ The girls found their mothers.

4 **Which question does the first paragraph answer?**

- Ⓐ Why was Sheila upset?
- Ⓑ What is the name of the small town where Sheila moved?
- Ⓒ How did the girls get lost?
- Ⓓ What is Katie's favorite food?

5 **Why were the mothers upset?**

____

____

____

____

____

____

____

____

6 **What is this story mainly about?**

- Ⓕ Sheila's move to a small town
- Ⓖ Sheila's mother's new job
- Ⓗ the monkey house
- Ⓙ the girls' day at the zoo

7 **Why did Mrs. Lee tell the girls to wait for their mothers at the monkey house?**

- Ⓐ She liked monkeys.
- Ⓑ She did not want the girls to get lost.
- Ⓒ She was cold.
- Ⓓ She was talking to Sheila's mother.

8 **What was the weather like on the day the girls visited the zoo?**

- Ⓕ hot
- Ⓖ cold and cloudy
- Ⓗ rainy
- Ⓙ cold and clear

9 **A gorilla is a—**

- Ⓐ type of lion.
- Ⓑ type of fish.
- Ⓒ kind of elephant.
- Ⓓ large ape.

TEST TIP

When you read a long story on a test, read the whole story once. Then read the questions one at a time. Check back in the story as you think about each question. If you get stuck, skip that question and return to it later.

GO ON

Making a Clay Pot

With practice, anyone can make a simple pot from clay. Take a piece of clay the size of an apple, and put it on a flat surface. Press and squeeze it until there are no lumps or air bubbles. Then, using both hands, shape the clay into a smooth, round ball.

Now you are ready to begin. Keep the ball in your left hand. With the thumb of your right hand, make an opening in the clay. Press down toward your palm, leaving one half inch of clay at the bottom. This will be the base of your pot. Now keep your thumb inside the pot. Press the clay gently between your thumb and fingers. Turn the pot after each squeeze. This will make the pot thin out evenly. Continue squeezing and turning until the pot is as thin as you want it.

Now the pot must dry. Cover it with plastic so that it won't dry too quickly. After a few days, uncover it. Then wait a few more days. When the pot is completely dry, it is ready to be fired in a special oven called a kiln. After the firing, the pot will keep its shape.

You may want to add color to your pot. In this case, you would put a glaze on the pot and fire it in the kiln a second time.

10 Why is the pot covered with plastic?

____

____

____

____

____

____

____

____

11 In this story, you can tell that a kiln is a—

- Ⓕ cover for the pot.
- Ⓖ glaze for the pot.
- Ⓗ special oven to bake the pot.
- Ⓙ special case to store the pot.

12 The first thing you should do when making a pot is to—

- Ⓐ press and squeeze out all the lumps and air bubbles from the clay.
- Ⓑ cover the clay with plastic.
- Ⓒ shape the clay into a ball.
- Ⓓ make the base of the pot.

13 Why should you turn the pot after each squeeze?

- Ⓕ so the pot will keep its shape
- Ⓖ so the pot will have a base
- Ⓗ so the pot won't be too thick in some spots
- Ⓙ to remove your thumb

GO ON

An Invitation

Holiday Fun!

All members of the Boys and Girls Club of Smithtown are invited to a Fourth of July party on July 4, 2004. The party will be held at the home of club sponsors Frank and Marie Brown.

The party will start at 6:30 P.M. Hamburgers, potato salad, watermelon, and other goodies will be served. Bring your turtle for the annual turtle race. At dark, fireworks will be viewed from the balcony. Sparklers and noisemakers will be provided. A marshmallow roast will be held following the fireworks.

It should be a lot of fun. See you on the 4th!

14 When will the party take place?

____

15 What should the guests bring?

Ⓐ a turtle

Ⓑ watermelon

Ⓒ a swimsuit

Ⓓ potato salad

16 According to the invitation, after the fireworks, the guests will—

Ⓕ eat ice cream.

Ⓖ race turtles.

Ⓗ roast marshmallows.

Ⓙ eat dinner.

17 What time will the party start?

Ⓐ 6:30 P.M.

Ⓑ 2:00 P.M.

Ⓒ 10:00 A.M.

Ⓓ You cannot tell from the invitation.

Test Tip

Remember to write your answers clearly. Also be careful to fill in or darken the entire circle for your answer. Many tests are graded by a computer. The computer has to be able to read your answers clearly.

GO ON

Learning about Apples

People have been eating apples for a very long time. When the first pioneers came to America, there were only small, sour apples called crab apples. These apples were not good to eat. Later, pioneers brought apple seeds from their homes in Europe.

In 1625 a man in Boston planted the first apple orchard in America. After that, when a pioneer family picked a place to live, one of the first things they did was choose an area and plant apple seeds. Soon, there were many apple trees in America.

The pioneers used apples in many ways. They made apple juice, apple butter, and apple pie. Sometimes they used apples as food for their animals.

Today we have refrigerators and grocery stores. We have fresh fruits and vegetables even in the winter. They are trucked in from warm places and sold in our stores. But the pioneers had no trucks or stores. They had no fresh fruits and vegetables during the long winters.

The pioneers soon learned how to preserve fruits and vegetables. They found that if fruit was dried, it would last and would not spoil. They could make apples last through the winter.

In the fall they picked the apples. Then many families would meet for a work party. They would talk and work at the same time. They peeled the apples and cut out the cores. Then they sliced the apples and laid them on a big net. About a week later, the apples were dried. They would keep for many months. The apples could be eaten dried, or they could be soaked in water and made into pies.

GO ON

18 **What does the word orchard mean?**

- Ⓕ a type of apple
- Ⓖ a pioneer
- Ⓗ a group of fruit trees
- Ⓙ a type of store

19 **Why did the pioneers have work parties to dry the apples?**

- Ⓐ to make them dry faster
- Ⓑ to visit and work at the same time
- Ⓒ to earn money
- Ⓓ to find new jobs

20 **Why were apple seeds brought to America by the pioneers?**

____

____

____

____

____

____

____

____

21 **This story was probably written to tell—**

- Ⓕ about pioneer work parties.
- Ⓖ about the first apple orchard in America.
- Ⓗ how to preserve apples.
- Ⓙ about the history of the apple in America.

22 **If the story continued, it would probably be about—**

- Ⓐ other uses for apples.
- Ⓑ how to build a barn.
- Ⓒ the differences between apples and oranges.
- Ⓓ pioneers in New York

23 **The pioneers used apples in all the following ways except as—**

- Ⓕ food for animals.
- Ⓖ juice.
- Ⓗ butter.
- Ⓙ a glue.

24 **You would probably find this story in a book called—**

- Ⓐ *A History of America's Favorite Foods.*
- Ⓑ *Orchard Do's and Don'ts.*
- Ⓒ *Famous Early Americans.*
- Ⓓ *How to Preserve Fruits.*

25 **In this story, the word preserve means—**

- Ⓕ to keep from spoiling.
- Ⓖ to eat quickly.
- Ⓗ to put in a freezer.
- Ⓙ to bury in a trunk in the sand.

26 **In order to answer question 25, the reader should—**

- Ⓐ look for the word preserve in the story.
- Ⓑ reread the last word in each paragraph.
- Ⓒ read other stories about apples.
- Ⓓ reread the first sentence in each paragraph.

GO ON

A Lifelong Love

When Jane Goodall was a young girl, she liked to watch animals. She learned many things about animals by watching them eat, sleep, and play. When she was older, Jane went to Africa to study wild chimpanzees. She had to live in the jungle to be near the chimpanzees all the time. It was hard for Jane at first. The chimpanzees ran whenever she came near. Soon they were more comfortable when she was around. They let her watch them. She learned how they collected vines and made them into beds in the tops of trees. She found that they greeted each other with noises and hugs. Jane also found that the chimpanzees used tools. They poked grass into the dirt to find bugs to eat.

27 What tool did the chimpanzees use?

Ⓕ dirt

Ⓖ bugs

Ⓗ vines

Ⓙ grass

28 Why did the chimpanzees collect vines?

____

____

____

____

____

____

____

____

29 Why did the chimpanzees run from Jane at first?

Ⓐ They were scared of her.

Ⓑ They were playing hide-and-seek.

Ⓒ They were racing each other.

Ⓓ They were looking for food.

30 This story is <u>mainly</u> about—

Ⓕ wild chimpanzees and how they live.

Ⓖ Jane Goodall's study of wild chimpanzees.

Ⓗ foods that chimpanzees eat.

Ⓙ Jane Goodall's life.

TEST TIP

Question 30 asks you to find the main idea of the story. Make sure your answer describes the main idea. Two of the wrong answers are too general. The other wrong answer is too specific. It focuses on one small detail from the story.

STOP

A sample question helps you to understand the type of question you will be asked in the test that follows.

Sample A **Kangaroos**

Kangaroos come in all sizes. The smallest kangaroo is the musky rat. It is about six inches tall. The largest kangaroo is the red kangaroo. It is about six feet tall. It lives in the dry central part of Australia. Red kangaroos are great jumpers.

How tall is a musky rat?

Ⓐ about six feet

Ⓑ about six centimeters

Ⓒ about six inches

Ⓓ very tiny

STOP

Directions: Read each story carefully. Then read each question. Darken the circle for the correct answer, or write in the answer.

The Great Sphinx

The Egyptians made statues of sphinxes to honor kings or queens. A sphinx has the head of a human and the body of a lion. The oldest and largest sphinx is the Great Sphinx. It was built in the desert near Giza, Egypt, thousands of years ago. It is 240 feet long and 66 feet high. At times the Great Sphinx has been buried by sand. Weather has worn away part of the stone. Today scientists are working on ways to save the Great Sphinx. They hope special chemicals will keep it from crumbling.

1 **Why was the Great Sphinx built?**

Ⓐ to honor a king or queen

Ⓑ to honor lions

Ⓒ to protect Giza, Egypt

Ⓓ to attract tourists

TEST TIP

Look in the first sentence to find clues to help you answer question 1. Which detail tells you *why* the Great Sphinx was built?

2 **How do scientists plan to save the Great Sphinx?**

____

____

____

____

____

____

____

____

GO ON

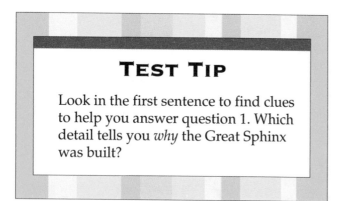

Going to the Store

One day Mrs. Rodriguez was cooking dinner. She called her son Gabriel into the kitchen. "Please ride your bike to the store, and buy a dozen eggs," she said. She gave Gabriel two dollar bills.

On the way to the store, Gabriel passed his friend Eduardo's house. Gabriel stopped to talk for a few minutes. Then he left for the store.

At the store he found the eggs. But when he reached in his pocket, there was no money. The money had fallen out of his pocket. Gabriel got on his bike and retraced his path. He kept his eyes on the street the entire time.

When Gabriel rode up to Eduardo's house, Eduardo came running toward him. "Hey, look what I found!" he said, waving two dollars. "Let's go to the store and buy some ice cream!"

Gabriel grinned. "That's the money I just lost," he said. "I have to buy eggs with it." Eduardo looked disappointed, but he handed the money to Gabriel. "Why don't you ride your bike to the store with me?" Gabriel asked. The two boys raced down the street. They reached the store quickly. Gabriel bought the eggs. But he had forgotten to bring his backpack for carrying them. He decided the safest thing to do was to zip the eggs inside his jacket.

He had just zipped his jacket when Eduardo called out, "Race you to the corner!" Gabriel stood up to get extra speed. But his jacket was not tight enough to hold the eggs. The carton crashed to the street. Gabriel stopped and opened it. "Wow, I sure hope Mom doesn't need more than three eggs," he said to himself.

GO ON

3 **What is this story <u>mainly</u> about?**

- Ⓕ what happened to Eduardo after school
- Ⓖ what Mrs. Rodriguez prepared for dinner
- Ⓗ what Gabriel ate for supper
- Ⓙ what happened to Gabriel on the way to the store

4 **What will probably happen next?**

- Ⓐ Mrs. Rodriguez will be happy to see Gabriel.
- Ⓑ Mrs. Rodriguez will reward Gabriel.
- Ⓒ Mrs. Rodriguez will be unhappy with Gabriel.
- Ⓓ Eduardo will return to the store.

5 **How many eggs were left unbroken?**

- Ⓕ none
- Ⓖ three
- Ⓗ five
- Ⓙ ten

6 **What did Eduardo want to do with the two dollars?**

- Ⓐ buy ice cream
- Ⓑ save it
- Ⓒ give it away
- Ⓓ buy a game

TEST TIP

Check your answers for questions about a story before going to the next page. You might not have time to return to a story. Review your answers while the story is still fresh.

7 **Mrs. Rodriguez sent Gabriel to the store—**

- Ⓕ to return empty pop bottles.
- Ⓖ to pay a bill.
- Ⓗ to buy eggs.
- Ⓙ to meet his father.

8 **What caused the eggs to break?**

____

____

____

____

____

____

____

9 **Eduardo rode to the store with Gabriel—**

- Ⓐ after dinner.
- Ⓑ the second time Gabriel went to the store.
- Ⓒ after lunch.
- Ⓓ the first time Gabriel went to the store.

10 **In this story, the word <u>retraced</u> means—**

- Ⓕ went back over the same path.
- Ⓖ cooked again.
- Ⓗ jumped again.
- Ⓙ laughed again.

GO ON

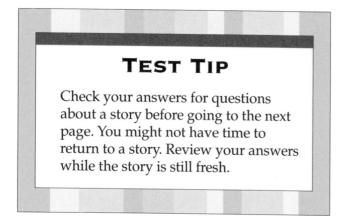

Spaghetti with Meat Sauce

Here's a recipe that is a favorite with many families.

You will need:

1 pound hamburger

2 cans tomato sauce

$\frac{1}{4}$ cup oil

$\frac{1}{2}$ onion, chopped

2 cloves garlic, minced

$\frac{1}{2}$ teaspoon basil

$\frac{1}{2}$ teaspoon oregano

1 package of spaghetti

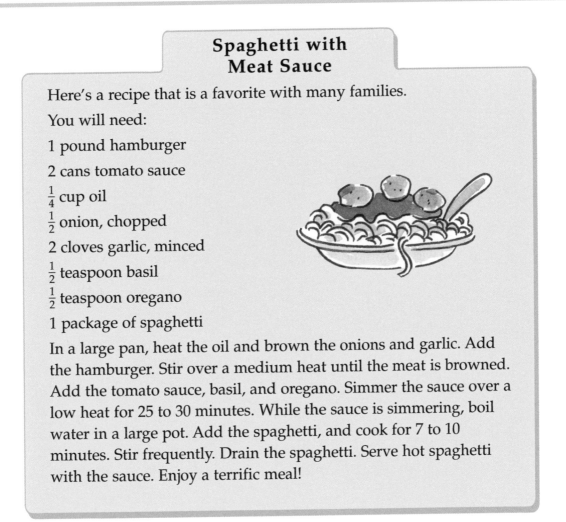

In a large pan, heat the oil and brown the onions and garlic. Add the hamburger. Stir over a medium heat until the meat is browned. Add the tomato sauce, basil, and oregano. Simmer the sauce over a low heat for 25 to 30 minutes. While the sauce is simmering, boil water in a large pot. Add the spaghetti, and cook for 7 to 10 minutes. Stir frequently. Drain the spaghetti. Serve hot spaghetti with the sauce. Enjoy a terrific meal!

11 How should you prepare the onion for cooking?

____

____

____

____

____

____

12 Why is the sauce made before cooking the spaghetti?

Ⓐ The sauce is served first.

Ⓑ The sauce needs time to cook.

Ⓒ It takes more time to cook the spaghetti.

Ⓓ Most people like the sauce better.

13 When making spaghetti with meat sauce, the first step is to—

Ⓕ boil water.

Ⓖ cook the hamburger.

Ⓗ add the tomato sauce.

Ⓙ heat the oil.

14 This recipe tells you to do all the following except—

Ⓐ add basil and oregano.

Ⓑ add sliced mushrooms.

Ⓒ add chopped onions.

Ⓓ add two cans of tomato sauce.

GO ON

A Great Woman

Mae C. Jemison grew up in Chicago, Illinois. Even as a young girl she dreamed of one day becoming an astronaut. She worked hard in school and earned excellent grades.

Mae's extraordinary efforts in grade school and high school gave her the opportunity to go to Stanford University in California. It was there that she received a degree in engineering. Next, Mae enrolled in Cornell University Medical College in New York City. She received a medical degree at this college.

Her dream of becoming an astronaut came true in 1987, when she was accepted in the astronaut program. In 1992, when Jemison was 35 years old, she became the first African-American female astronaut to go into space. She was aboard the space shuttle *Endeavour* along with six other astronauts. The mission of the crew members of the *Endeavour* was to test the effects of weightlessness on certain animals such as frogs and fish.

15 What question does the last paragraph answer?

- Ⓕ How does weightlessness affect certain animals?
- Ⓖ What makes up the astronaut training program?
- Ⓗ How did Mae C. Jemison's dream come true?
- Ⓙ Where is Stanford University?

16 What was the mission of the space shuttle *Endeavour*?

- Ⓐ to take pictures of Earth from space
- Ⓑ to test the effect of weightlessness on animals
- Ⓒ to launch a satellite into space
- Ⓓ to orbit Earth longer than anyone had ever done before

17 What was Mae C. Jemison's lifelong dream?

____

____

____

____

____

____

18 The author probably wrote this story—

- Ⓕ to describe the mission of the space shuttle *Endeavour.*
- Ⓖ to describe the career of Mae C. Jemison.
- Ⓗ to describe the childhood of Mae C. Jemison.
- Ⓙ to explain the astronaut-training program.

TEST TIP

Think about the author's main goal as you read the answer choices.

GO ON

Helping Each Other

Once an ant was crawling lazily down a country path. As the path curved near a stream, the ant realized he was thirsty. The rushing water looked so cool and clear that the ant could hardly wait to take a sip. Suddenly a gust of wind blew the poor ant right into the stream.

"Help! Someone, help! I cannot swim!" he yelled.

Up in a tree not far away, a dove heard the ant's cry for help. She reached up and with her bill plucked a small branch off the tree. In a flash she flew down to where the ant was struggling to stay above water. Carefully she lowered the branch to the water's surface near the ant.

"If you can climb onto the branch, I will carry you to safety," cooed the dove.

The ant gratefully climbed onto the branch. Then the dove lifted the branch from the water and placed it safely on the grassy bank. The ant shook water from his eyes, took a few deep breaths, and looked around to thank the dove. But the dove had flown to the top of a nearby tree.

With a wave of thanks toward the dove, the ant started back down the path. He had only gone a short distance when he noticed a hunter aiming a rifle at the helpful dove.

"This will not do!" exclaimed the ant. He hurried as fast as he could toward the hunter. The angry ant climbed with great purpose over the hunter's large brown shoe and made his way under the hunter's pants leg. Just in the nick of time, the ant took a healthy bite from the hunter's ankle. The hunter let out a loud howl of pain. The noise startled the dove, and she flew from her treetop perch to safety.

GO ON

19 **What did the dove use to save the ant?**

Ⓐ a boat

Ⓑ a branch

Ⓒ her wing

Ⓓ a leaf

20 **What caused the dove to fly to safety?**

Ⓕ a rifle shot

Ⓖ the ant's scream

Ⓗ the hunter's howl

Ⓙ a snapping branch

21 **According to the story, the ant got a drink of water from a—**

Ⓐ puddle of water in the road.

Ⓑ drop of rain on a leaf.

Ⓒ leaf.

Ⓓ stream.

22 **Who heard the ant's cry for help?**

Ⓕ a dove

Ⓖ the hunter

Ⓗ a fish

Ⓙ a butterfly

23 **What most likely would have happened if the ant had not bitten the hunter?**

Ⓐ The hunter would have stepped on the ant.

Ⓑ The dove would have been shot.

Ⓒ The hunter would have fallen into the stream.

Ⓓ The dove would have gone with the ant.

24 **Why did the ant fall into the water?**

____

____

____

____

____

____

____

____

25 **You can tell this story is make-believe because—**

Ⓕ it has a hunter in it.

Ⓖ animals talk in it.

Ⓗ an ant climbs onto a branch.

Ⓙ a dove flies to a treetop.

26 **What lesson can be learned from this story?**

Ⓐ Don't bite the hand that feeds you.

Ⓑ A stitch in time saves nine.

Ⓒ Slow and steady wins the race.

Ⓓ One good turn deserves another.

27 **This story was probably written to—**

Ⓕ teach the reader about ants.

Ⓖ show how ants can survive in water.

Ⓗ discourage people from hunting.

Ⓙ teach a lesson about helping others.

28 **You would most likely find this story in a book called—**

Ⓐ *Country Days.*

Ⓑ *Real-Life Animal Friends.*

Ⓒ *Learning from Animal Tales.*

Ⓓ *How to Hunt.*

STOP

UNIT 4

READING VOCABULARY

UNDERSTANDING WORD MEANINGS

Directions: Darken the circle for the word or words that have the same or almost the same meaning as the underlined word, or write in the answer.

TRY THIS

Choose your answer carefully. The other choices may seem correct. Be sure to think about the meaning of the underlined word.

Sample A

A check is a kind of—

Ⓐ box

Ⓑ picture

Ⓒ dance

Ⓓ mark

THINK IT THROUGH

The correct answer is D, mark. A check is a kind of mark. A check is not a box, a picture, or a dance.

STOP

1 **Slender means—**

Ⓐ quick

Ⓑ shy

Ⓒ thin

Ⓓ lost

2 **What is an ache?**

____

____

____

____

3 **A cap is a kind of—**

Ⓕ lock

Ⓖ hat

Ⓗ head

Ⓙ coat

4 **To connect is to—**

Ⓐ hit

Ⓑ shut

Ⓒ join

Ⓓ belong

5 **Savage means—**

Ⓕ hungry

Ⓖ wild

Ⓗ comfortable

Ⓙ large

6 **To oppose something is to—**

Ⓐ cheer for it

Ⓑ be against it

Ⓒ leave it

Ⓓ want it

STOP

Directions: Darken the circle for the sentence in which the underlined word means the same as it does in the sentence in the box.

TRY THIS

Read the sentence in the box carefully. Decide what the underlined word means. Then look for the sentence in which the underlined word has the same meaning.

Sample A

A wave swept over the beach.

In which sentence does wave have the same meaning as it does in the sentence above?

Ⓐ We saw the flag wave in the wind.

Ⓑ Her hair has a natural wave.

Ⓒ I saw the pilot wave to me.

Ⓓ The fish jumped above the wave.

THINK IT THROUGH

The correct answer is D. In the sentence, The fish jumped above the wave, wave means the same as it does in the sentence in the box. A wave is "a wall of water."

STOP

1 **She wore a circle of flowers in her hair.**

In which sentence does circle have the same meaning as it does in the sentence above?

Ⓐ The plane will circle the field.

Ⓑ Draw a circle on the paper.

Ⓒ Cara belongs to a sewing circle.

Ⓓ Circle your answers.

2 **Let's go out and play.**

In which sentence does play have the same meaning as it does in the sentence above?

Ⓕ The band will play a new song.

Ⓖ My team will play our first game today.

Ⓗ My sister wrote a play.

Ⓙ Please come to my house to play.

3 **That boy lives on our block.**

In which sentence does block have the same meaning as it does in the sentence above?

Ⓐ Use this board to block the hole.

Ⓑ The baby dropped the toy block.

Ⓒ We drove around the block.

Ⓓ She carved that block of marble.

4 **May I borrow some string?**

In which sentence does string have the same meaning as it does in the sentence above?

Ⓕ He helped me string the lights.

Ⓖ I bought a string of pearls.

Ⓗ Cut the string on this package.

Ⓙ My guitar string is broken.

STOP

Directions: Darken the circle for the word or words that give the meaning of the underlined word, or write in the answer.

TRY THIS

Read the first sentence carefully. Look for clue words in the sentence to help you figure out the meaning of the underlined word.

Sample A

A family finally moved into the house that has been vacant for six months. Vacant means—

Ⓐ white

Ⓑ empty

Ⓒ burned

Ⓓ built

THINK IT THROUGH

The correct answer is B, empty. The clue words are finally moved into. All four choices have to do wih a house, but only empty has the same meaning as vacant.

STOP

1 **You should not play with matches because you might harm yourself. Harm means—**

Ⓐ hurt

Ⓑ help

Ⓒ calm

Ⓓ see

2 **Instead of eating french fries, I ate something beneficial to my health. Beneficial means—**

Ⓕ damaging

Ⓖ helpful

Ⓗ equal

Ⓙ thankful

3 **The wagon train couldn't go around the river, so they had to ford it. Ford means—**

Ⓐ drain

Ⓑ paddle

Ⓒ fish

Ⓓ cross

4 **To observe hamsters at play, you must see them at night. Observe means—**

Ⓕ watch

Ⓖ hear

Ⓗ control

Ⓙ do

5 **We need a new song for our play, so our teacher will compose one. Compose means—**

Ⓐ sell

Ⓑ hum

Ⓒ write

Ⓓ use

6 **The instructions on the label say that you should wash that shirt in cold water. What are instructions?**

____

____

____

____

STOP

Sample A

A <u>nursery</u> is a place for—

Ⓐ machines

Ⓑ sleds

Ⓒ nests

Ⓓ babies

STOP

For questions 1–9, darken the circle for the word or words that have the same or almost the same meaning as the underlined word, or write in the answer.

1 <u>Simple</u> means—

Ⓐ smart

Ⓑ cheap

Ⓒ late

Ⓓ easy

2 To <u>trade</u> something is to—

Ⓕ exchange it

Ⓖ collect it

Ⓗ leave it

Ⓙ keep it

3 A <u>kettle</u> is a kind of—

Ⓐ food

Ⓑ pot

Ⓒ chair

Ⓓ basket

4 A <u>policy</u> is a kind of—

Ⓕ plan

Ⓖ sea bird

Ⓗ hood

Ⓙ envelope

5 Something that is <u>accepted</u> is—

Ⓐ received

Ⓑ stolen

Ⓒ pretty

Ⓓ wrapped

6 A <u>meadow</u> is most like a—

Ⓕ vase

Ⓖ garden

Ⓗ store

Ⓙ field

7 A <u>yacht</u> is a kind of—

Ⓐ deer

Ⓑ boat

Ⓒ hat

Ⓓ pickle

8 To <u>tremble</u> means to—

Ⓕ wave

Ⓖ laugh

Ⓗ cough

Ⓙ shake

9 What does it mean to <u>slice</u> something?

____

____

____

____

____

____

____

____

STOP

Sample B

My picture hangs above the fireplace.

In which sentence does above have the same meaning as it does in the sentence in the box?

Ⓐ I had to shout above the noise.

Ⓑ The huge flock of birds filled the skies above.

Ⓒ Your book is on the shelf above the desk.

Ⓓ His scores are above average.

STOP

For questions 10–14, darken the circle for the sentence in which the underlined word means the same as it does in the sentence in the box.

10

The rule was fair to both teams.

In which sentence does fair have the same meaning as it does in the sentence above?

Ⓐ Let's go to the state fair.

Ⓑ Our teacher told us to play fair.

Ⓒ The weather today was fair.

Ⓓ She has very fair hair.

11

We found Grandfather's old sailor's chest in the attic.

In which sentence does chest have the same meaning as it does in the sentence above?

Ⓕ My brother caught a chest cold.

Ⓖ My shirts are in the third drawer of my chest.

Ⓗ The pirates put their treasure in a chest.

Ⓙ The football hit him in the chest.

12

Al will act the hero's part.

In which sentence does act have the same meaning as it does in the sentence above?

Ⓐ I would love to act in a movie.

Ⓑ We liked the third act of the play.

Ⓒ She told us to act like gentlemen.

Ⓓ The soldier performed a brave act.

13

Draw a picture in this space.

In which sentence does space have the same meaning as it does in the sentence above?

Ⓕ It came from outer space.

Ⓖ Space the letters evenly on the line.

Ⓗ A space of two weeks followed.

Ⓙ Leave a space for your name.

14

What time does the show start?

In which sentence does time have the same meaning as it does in the sentence above?

Ⓐ The coach will time my race.

Ⓑ I had a good time at the party.

Ⓒ Try to keep time with the music.

Ⓓ It is now time to return to class.

TEST TIP

These questions focus on words with more than one meaning. First read the sentence. Think about the meaning of the word. Find the answer in which the word has the same meaning as the word in the question box.

STOP

Sample C

The unsafe trail was marked with a warning sign. Unsafe means—

Ⓐ scenic

Ⓑ hilly

Ⓒ dangerous

Ⓓ winding

STOP

For questions 15–21, darken the circle for the word or words that give the meaning of the underlined word, or write in the answer.

15 Instead of dull gray, I wanted to paint my room vivid yellow. Vivid means—

Ⓕ bright

Ⓖ dark

Ⓗ lemon

Ⓙ cool

16 If you don't want to buy a boat, you can charter one for your fishing trip. Charter means—

Ⓐ choose

Ⓑ sail

Ⓒ rent

Ⓓ trade

17 We like everything in the show, but our favorite segment is the pet tricks. Segment means—

Ⓕ actor

Ⓖ song

Ⓗ part

Ⓙ star

18 We tried to open the trunk, but the lid would not budge. Budge means—

Ⓐ slam

Ⓑ rest

Ⓒ move

Ⓓ burn

19 Wild horses roam freely in Nevada. Roam means—

Ⓕ sleep

Ⓖ wander

Ⓗ eat

Ⓙ hide

20 Because I was tired, I neglected to do my exercises. Neglected means—

Ⓐ tried

Ⓑ failed

Ⓒ knew

Ⓓ meant

21 Our kite was broken, but Uncle Victor helped us repair it. Repair means—

____

____

____

____

____

____

____

____

STOP

UNIT 5

MATH PROBLEM-SOLVING PLAN

OVERVIEW

THE PROBLEM-SOLVING PLAN

When solving math problems follow these steps:

STEP 1: WHAT IS THE QUESTION/GOAL?

Decide what must be found. This information is usually presented in the form of a question.

STEP 2: FIND THE FACTS

Locate the factual information in three different ways:

A. **KEY FACTS** are the facts you need to solve the problem.

B. **FACTS YOU DON'T NEED** are those facts that are not necessary for solving the problem.

C. **ARE MORE FACTS NEEDED?** Decide if you have enough information to solve the problem.

STEP 3: SELECT A STRATEGY

Decide what you can do to solve the problem.

STEP 4: SOLVE

Use your plan to solve the problem.

STEP 5: DOES YOUR RESPONSE MAKE SENSE?

Think about your answer. Does it make sense?

Directions: Use the problem-solving plan to solve this math problem.

PROBLEM/QUESTION:

Jackie is going shopping for presents in Green's Toy Store. Mr. Green sells toy bears for $1.98, toy dogs for $1.50, toy cats for $1.45, toy birds for $1.10 and toy snakes for $.88. She can buy only one of each toy animal. Jackie has $5.00 to spend. What is the greatest number of toys she can buy?

STEP 1: WHAT IS THE QUESTION/GOAL?

____

____

____

STEP 2: FIND THE FACTS

____

____

____

STEP 3: SELECT A STRATEGY

____

____

____

STEP 4: SOLVE

____

____

____

STEP 5: DOES YOUR RESPONSE MAKE SENSE?

____

____

____

____

Directions: Use the problem-solving plan to solve this math problem.

PROBLEM/QUESTION:

Eduardo has a choice of 4 possible outfits that he can wear today. He has one striped and one solid shirt. He also has a pair of black pants and a pair of blue pants. Describe the 4 combinations of shirts and pants Eduardo can make.

STEP 1: WHAT IS THE QUESTION/GOAL?

____

____

____

STEP 2: FIND THE FACTS

____

____

____

STEP 3: SELECT A STRATEGY

____

____

____

STEP 4: SOLVE

____

____

____

STEP 5: DOES YOUR RESPONSE MAKE SENSE?

____

____

____

____

____

UNIT 6
MATH PROBLEM SOLVING

UNDERSTANDING NUMERATION

Directions: Darken the circle for the correct answer, or write in the answer.

TRY THIS — **Read each problem carefully. Be sure to think about which numbers stand for hundreds, tens, and ones.**

Sample A

Which is another way to write 238?

Ⓐ 20 + 380

Ⓑ 200 + 30 + 8

Ⓒ 200 + 30 + 80

Ⓓ 2,000 + 30 + 8

THINK IT THROUGH — **The correct answer is B. 200 + 30 + 8 = 238. Therefore, 238 = 200 + 30 + 8.**

STOP

1 **Juanita baked an odd number of muffins to take to the bake sale. How many muffins did she bake?**

Ⓐ 17 muffins

Ⓑ 16 muffins

Ⓒ 12 muffins

Ⓓ 10 muffins

2

Name	Points
Chris	192
Fatima	150
Mike	269
Gwen	148

Which child scored the most number of points in a computer game?

____

____

____

____

3 **Which number belongs in the box on the number line?**

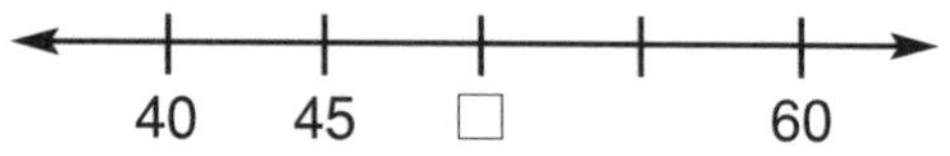

46	50	55	58
Ⓕ	Ⓖ	Ⓗ	Ⓙ

4 **The chart shows how long it takes to grow 4 kinds of plants.**

Corn	Beans	Tomatoes	Peppers
72 days	43 days	60 days	54 days

Which group shows these plants listed in order from shortest to longest growing time?

Ⓐ beans, peppers, tomatoes, corn

Ⓑ peppers, beans, tomatoes, corn

Ⓒ corn, beans, tomatoes, peppers

Ⓓ tomatoes, peppers, beans, corn

STOP

Directions: Darken the circle for the correct answer, or write in the answer.

TRY THIS Read the question twice before choosing your answer. Try using all the answer choices back in the problem. Then choose the answer that you think best answers the question.

Sample A

What is another way to write 4 + 4 + 4 ?

Ⓐ $3 + 4$

Ⓑ 3×4

Ⓒ $4 \times 4 \times 4$

Ⓓ $12 + 4$

THINK IT THROUGH The correct answer is B, 3×4. $4 + 4 + 4 = 12$. Choice B, 3×4, is the only answer that equals 12.

STOP

1 What fraction of the shape is not shaded?

____

____

____

____

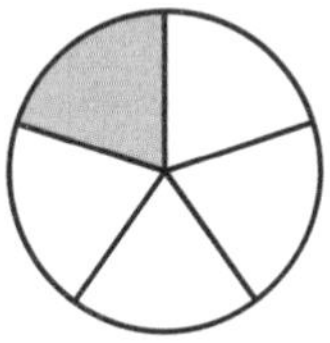

2

Name	Number of Inches
Yoshi	1.9
Penelope	2.1
Marcus	1.7
Felicia	2.4

Which child grew the most inches in a year?

Ⓐ Yoshi

Ⓑ Penelope

Ⓒ Marcus

Ⓓ Felicia

3 Which number belongs in the box to make the number sentence correct?

$7 \times \square = 7$?

7	6	1	0
Ⓕ	Ⓖ	Ⓗ	Ⓙ

4 Which number sentence is in the same fact family as

$8 + 3 = 11$?

Ⓐ $8 \times 3 = 24$

Ⓑ $5 + 6 = 11$

Ⓒ $11 - 3 = 8$

Ⓓ $11 + 3 = 14$

5 Which group of balloons has $\frac{1}{3}$ of the balloons shaded?

Ⓕ Ⓖ Ⓗ Ⓙ

STOP

Directions: Darken the circle for the correct answer, or write in the answer.

TRY THIS

Read each question carefully. Look at each answer choice to see which number or figure will answer the question correctly.

Sample A

What missing number completes the pattern in the boxes?

46	42	38	34	

Ⓐ 30 Ⓒ 33

Ⓑ 32 Ⓓ 35

THINK IT THROUGH

The correct answer is A, 30. The numbers in the pattern decrease by 4. So, the correct answer is 30, because 34 – 4 = 30.

STOP

1 Which of these shows the missing piece of the figure?

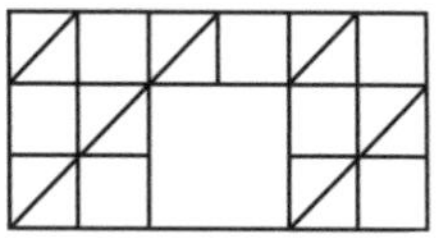

Ⓐ

Ⓑ

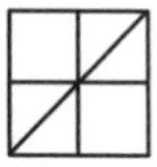

Ⓒ

Ⓓ

2 Which of these shows the missing piece of the figure?

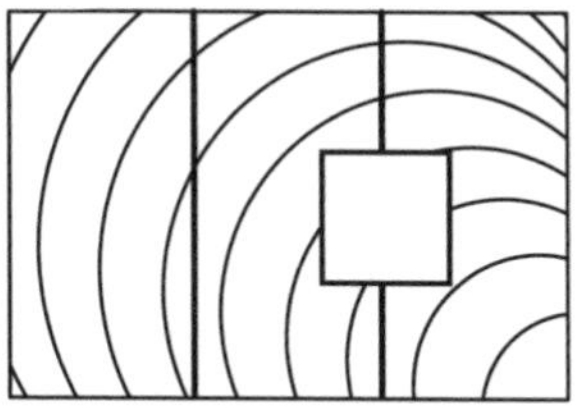

Ⓕ

Ⓖ

Ⓗ

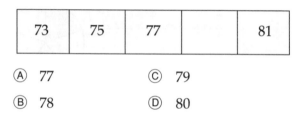

Ⓙ

3 What missing number completes the pattern in the boxes?

73	75	77		81

Ⓐ 77 Ⓒ 79

Ⓑ 78 Ⓓ 80

4 Each juice carton holds 6 drinks. What missing number completes the pattern in the chart?

Number of Drinks	
Number of Cartons of Grape Juice	Number of Drinks
2	12
3	18
4	?
5	30

____

STOP

Directions: Darken the circle for the correct answer, or write in the answer.

TRY THIS

Look at each chart, graph, or picture. Then read the question carefully. Look for words or numbers in the question that tell you what information to find.

Sample A

The tally chart shows the number of pounds of litter Kyle collected on a cleanup project.

How many pounds of paper did Kyle collect?

Ⓐ 2

Ⓑ 7

Ⓒ 8

Ⓓ 10

Litter Collected

Paper	卌 卌
Metal	卌
Plastic	卌 ||
Cloth	||
Other	卌 |

THINK IT THROUGH

The correct answer Is D, 10. Each tally mark stands for 1 pound of paper. Each group of 4 tally marks with a slash stands for 5 pounds of paper. Since there are 2 groups, 5 + 5 = 10 pounds of paper.

STOP

The graph below shows the pets owned by students in Mr. Ito's class. Study the graph and answer questions 1 and 2.

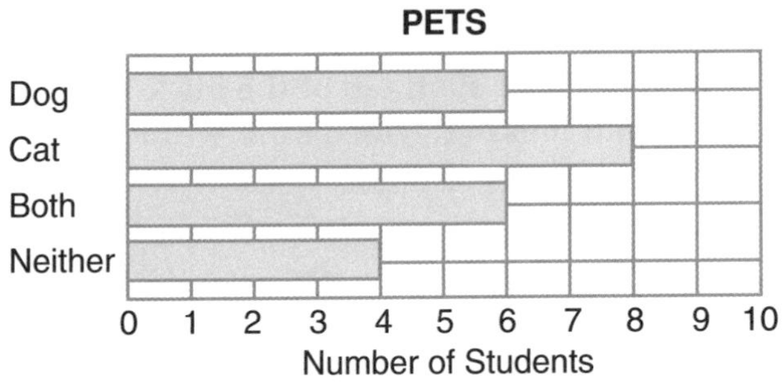

1 Which pet was the most popular?

Ⓐ Dog

Ⓑ Cat

Ⓒ Both

Ⓓ Neither

2 How many more students owned cats than dogs?

Ⓕ 2

Ⓖ 3

Ⓗ 5

Ⓙ 6

3 Dan is using a spinner. Which color will he be the least likely to spin?

____

____

____

____

____

____

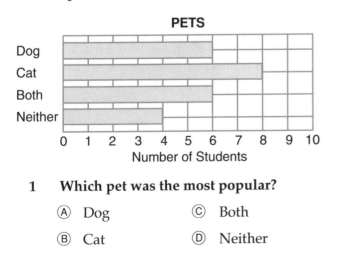

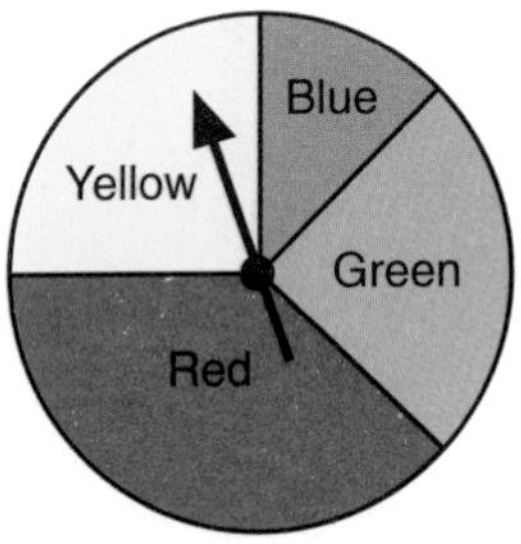

GO ON

4 **The students in Ms. Iannatti's class made this chart to count the fruit they ate in one day.**

Fruit	Number Eaten
Bananas	8
Plums	2
Oranges	12
Apples	16
Peaches	4

Which kind of fruit did students eat exactly 2 times as many of as bananas?

Ⓐ Peaches

Ⓑ Bananas

Ⓒ Oranges

Ⓓ Apples

5 **The tally chart shows the favorite subjects of the students in Mrs. Fine's class.**

Favorite Subject for Third-Grade Students

Science	𝍷𝍷𝍷
Social Studies	𝍸 𝍷
Math	𝍸 𝍷𝍷𝍷𝍷
Language	𝍸 𝍷𝍷𝍷

How many students liked language?

Ⓕ 3

Ⓖ 6

Ⓗ 8

Ⓙ 9

6 **Look at the cards shown here.**

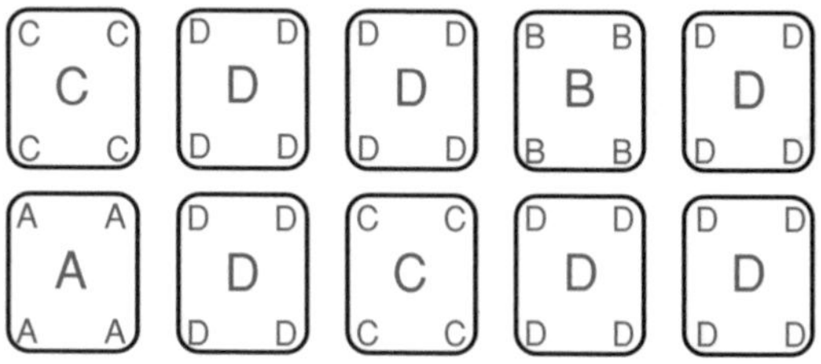

If Kevin picks a card without looking, which will he most likely choose?

Ⓐ A

Ⓑ B

Ⓒ C

Ⓓ D

7 **Ellen collected these shells in a bucket.**

	**3**
	**12**
	**2**
	**4**

If she picks 1 shell out of the bucket without looking, which kind will it most likely be?

Ⓕ

Ⓖ

Ⓗ

Ⓙ

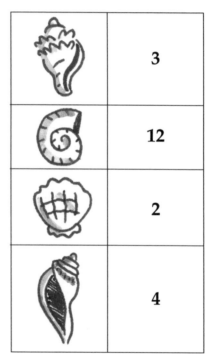

STOP

Directions: Darken the circle for the correct answer, or write in the answer.

TRY THIS Read each question carefully. Study the objects named or shown and use them to help you to choose the correct answer.

Sample A

Which figure will have two halves that match exactly when it is folded on the solid line?

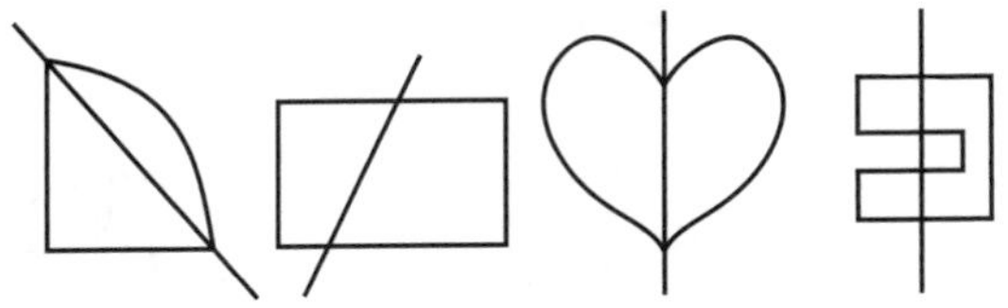

Ⓐ Ⓑ Ⓒ Ⓓ

THINK IT THROUGH The correct choice is C. If the heart is folded on the solid line, each half will match exactly.

STOP

1 Everyone at Shari's birthday party wore a party hat like the one shown here. What shape does the hat have?

Ⓐ cone
Ⓑ pyramid
Ⓒ cube
Ⓓ sphere

2 Look at the numbered shapes. Which two are exactly the same in size and shape?

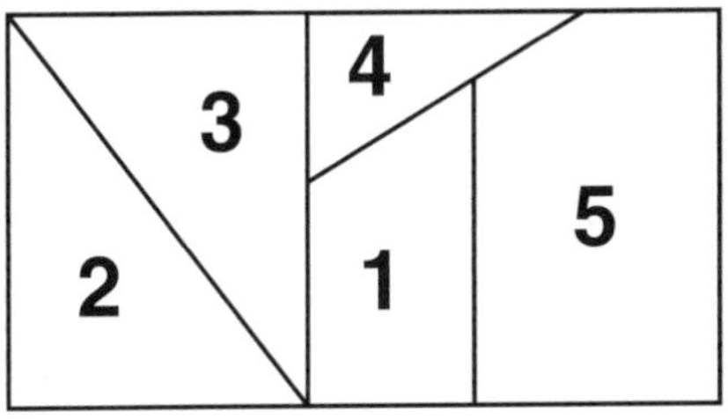

____

____

____

____

3 Which shape has four corners and four sides exactly the same size?

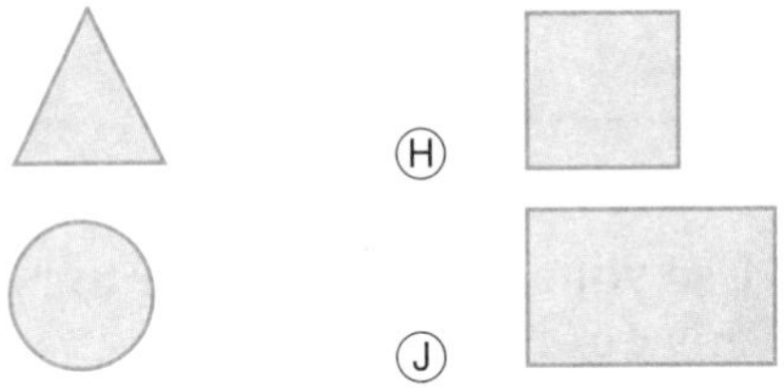

Ⓕ Ⓖ Ⓗ Ⓙ

4 Moira drew this figure on her paper.

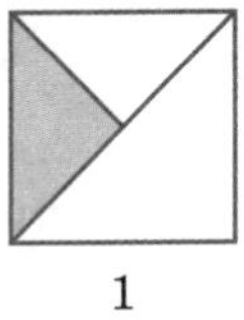

What did it look like when she turned it upside down?

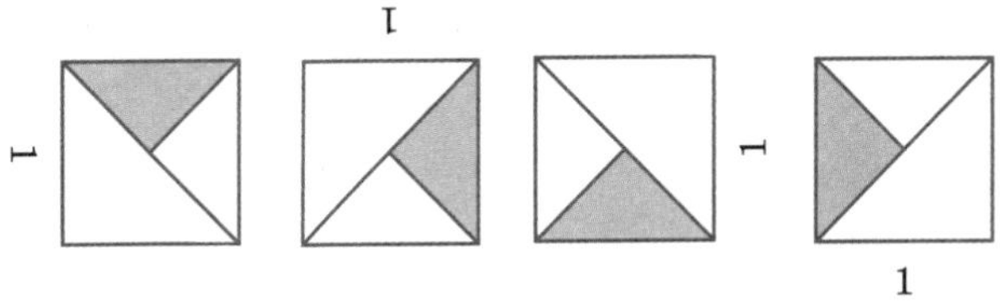

Ⓐ Ⓑ Ⓒ Ⓓ

STOP

Directions: Darken the circle for the correct answer, or write in the answer.

TRY THIS Look at each picture or object shown. Then read the question carefully. Look for words or numbers in the question that tell you what information to find.

Sample A

Cliff ate lunch at 12:00 noon. He went to the park one and one-half hours later. Which clock shows the time Cliff went to the park?

Ⓐ 

Ⓒ 

Ⓑ 

Ⓓ 

THINK IT THROUGH The correct answer is D, 1:30 P.M. If Cliff ate lunch at 12:00 noon, an hour and one-half hour later is 1:30 P.M.

STOP

1 Use your centimeter ruler to help answer this question.

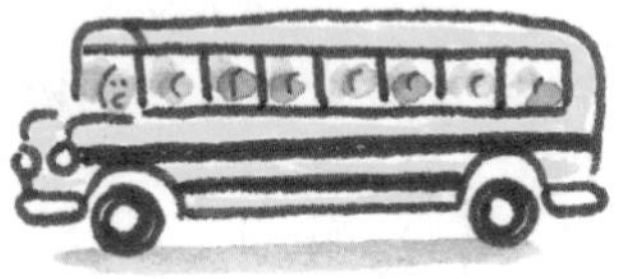

How many centimeters long is the toy bus?

____

____

____

____

____

____

2 Which unit of measurement is best to use to describe the amount of juice in a jar?

Ⓐ cups
Ⓑ inches
Ⓒ pounds
Ⓓ teaspoons

3 Monica found a dime, a nickel, and a quarter in her coat pocket.

What is the value of the money shown?

Ⓕ 45¢
Ⓖ 40¢
Ⓗ 36¢
Ⓙ 31¢

GO ON

4 **Marc bought a package of drawing paper that cost 59¢. He gave the clerk 75¢. How much change should Marc get back?**

Ⓐ 

Ⓑ 

Ⓒ 

Ⓓ 

5 **Jennifer is going to shovel snow off the sidewalk. What is the temperature like outside?**

Ⓕ 92°

Ⓖ 75°

Ⓗ 51°

Ⓙ 30°

Test Tip

For question 5, think about if the choices are hot or cold temperatures. Is the scene in the picture hot or cold?

6 **Mrs. Traub feeds the animals who live behind her house. Which animal lives the shortest distance from Mrs. Traub's house?**

Ⓐ

Ⓑ

Ⓒ

Ⓓ

7 **Terrell drew 2 lines. Use your inch ruler to measure the total length of the lines.**

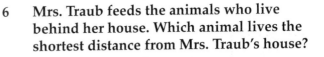

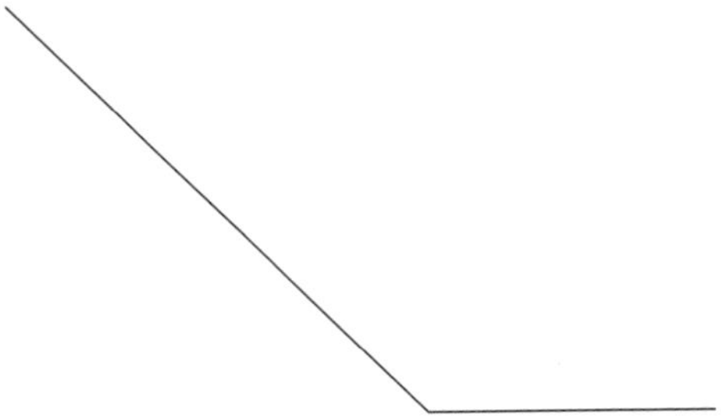

Ⓕ 1 inch

Ⓖ 2 inches

Ⓗ 3 inches

Ⓙ 4 inches

STOP

Directions: Darken the circle for the correct answer, or write in the answer.

TRY THIS Study the words in each problem carefully. Then decide what you have to do to find the answer.

Sample A

Igor blew up 4 fewer balloons than Andy. Andy blew up 6 balloons more than Betsy. Betsy blew up 10 balloons. How many balloons did Igor blow up?

Ⓐ 20

Ⓑ 16

Ⓒ 12

Ⓓ 8

THINK IT THROUGH The correct answer Is C, 12. Betsy blew up 10 balloons. If Andy blew up 6 more than Betsy, he blew up 16 (10 + 6). If Igor blew up 4 fewer than Andy, he blew up 12, since 16 – 4 = 12.

1 Michelle caught 9 fish. She put all of the small fish back into the water. What do you need to know to find out how many fish Michelle took home?

2 There are 4 tour vans at the restaurant. The 32 people on the tour stopped to eat dinner. Which is the most reasonable answer for how many people rode in each van?

Ⓐ 128

Ⓑ 36

Ⓒ 28

Ⓓ 8

3 Marvin collected 45 cans for recycling. Ira collected 39 cans. Which number sentence shows how to find the number of cans they collected altogether?

Ⓕ 39 + □ = 45

Ⓖ 45 – 39 = □

Ⓗ 45 – □ = 39

Ⓙ 45 + 39 = □

4 What number is inside the triangle, inside the square, and is an odd number?

Ⓐ 2

Ⓑ 5

Ⓒ 7

Ⓓ 9

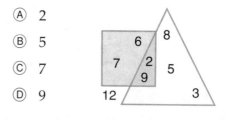

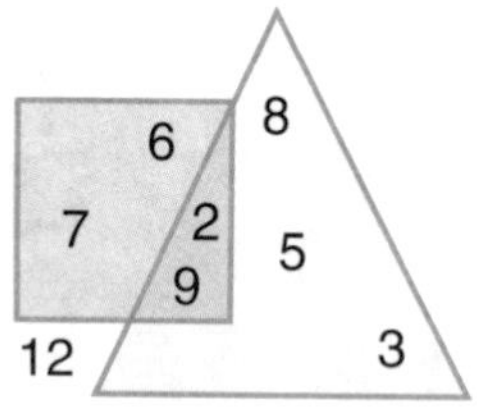

TEST TIP

Be careful to follow every step or rule in a math problem.

Directions: Darken the circle for the correct answer. If the correct answer is not given, darken the circle for NH (Not Here).

TRY THIS

Study each problem carefully. Look at the sign to know if you should add, subtract, multiply, or divide. Then work the problem on scratch paper. Be sure to line up the digits. Remember to regroup where necessary.

Sample A

$15 - \square = 8$

23	10	8	7	NH
Ⓐ	Ⓑ	Ⓒ	Ⓓ	Ⓔ

THINK IT THROUGH

The correct answer is D, 7. To find the missing number, subtract 8 from 15 to get the answer, 7.

STOP

1 $6\overline{)48}$

8	7	6	5	NH
Ⓐ	Ⓑ	Ⓒ	Ⓓ	Ⓔ

2 $9 \div 3 = \square$

6	5	4	3	NH
Ⓕ	Ⓖ	Ⓗ	Ⓙ	Ⓚ

3 $\begin{array}{r} 22 \\ +\ 21 \\ \hline \end{array}$

42	41	39	24	NH
Ⓐ	Ⓑ	Ⓒ	Ⓓ	Ⓔ

4 $\begin{array}{r} 30 \\ 184 \\ +\ 76 \\ \hline \end{array}$

115	124	290	560	NH
Ⓕ	Ⓖ	Ⓗ	Ⓙ	Ⓚ

5 $\begin{array}{r} 6 \\ \times\ 3 \\ \hline \end{array}$

24	18	12	9	NH
Ⓐ	Ⓑ	Ⓒ	Ⓓ	Ⓔ

6 $\begin{array}{r} 92 \\ -\ 57 \\ \hline \end{array}$

35	39	45	149	NH
Ⓕ	Ⓖ	Ⓗ	Ⓙ	Ⓚ

7 $\begin{array}{r} 549 \\ +\ 81 \\ \hline \end{array}$

620	630	720	730	NH
Ⓐ	Ⓑ	Ⓒ	Ⓓ	Ⓔ

8 $\begin{array}{r} 403 \\ \times\ 3 \\ \hline \end{array}$

1,206	1,248	3,208	3,248	NH
Ⓕ	Ⓖ	Ⓗ	Ⓙ	Ⓚ

STOP

Directions: Darken the circle for the correct answer. If the correct answer is not given, darken the circle for NH (Not Here). If no choices are given, write in the answer.

TRY THIS

Read each problem carefully. Think about what the question is asking. Think about which numbers stand for ones, tens, and hundreds. Work the problem on scratch paper. Regroup where necessary.

Sample A

Tracey is reading a book that has 464 pages. She has read 379 pages. How many pages does she have left to read?

Ⓐ 80

Ⓑ 85

Ⓒ 90

Ⓓ 95

Ⓔ NH

THINK IT THROUGH

The correct answer is B, 85. The words "pages left to read" means to subtract 379 from 464 to get 85.

STOP

1 Eric played a computer game for 17 minutes. He played another game for 14 minutes. How many minutes did Eric play the games altogether?

3	21	31	41	NH
Ⓐ	Ⓑ	Ⓒ	Ⓓ	Ⓔ

2 Perry bought 3 boxes of crayons. There were 6 crayons in each box.

How many crayons did Perry buy altogether?

____

____

____

____

____

3 On Saturday, 364 children went to the park to celebrate Earth Day.

What is 364 rounded to the nearest hundred?

Ⓕ 300

Ⓖ 350

Ⓗ 360

Ⓙ 400

Ⓚ NH

4 Mrs. Martin had a pizza party for her class. She wrote down the order for the pizzas.

Cheese	Pepperoni	Vegetable
8	5	2

How many pizzas did she buy altogether?

16	15	14	13	NH
Ⓐ	Ⓑ	Ⓒ	Ⓓ	Ⓔ

STOP

Sample A

$$\begin{array}{r} 51 \\ \times\ 2 \\ \hline \end{array}$$

52 Ⓐ   53 Ⓑ   72 Ⓒ   102 Ⓓ   NH Ⓔ

STOP

Sample B

Jagdesh bought 12 blue balloons and 14 red balloons. How many balloons did she buy in all?

28 Ⓕ   26 Ⓖ   22 Ⓗ   2 Ⓙ   NH Ⓚ

STOP

For questions 1–14, darken the circle for the correct answer. If the correct answer is not here, darken the circle for NH. If no choices are given, write in the answer.

1 $32 \div 8 = \square$

5 Ⓐ   4 Ⓑ   3 Ⓒ   2 Ⓓ   NH Ⓔ

2 $4 \times 21 = \square$

25 Ⓕ   62 Ⓖ   80 Ⓗ   84 Ⓙ   NH Ⓚ

3 $6 \times 5 = \square$

11 Ⓐ   24 Ⓑ   30 Ⓒ   36 Ⓓ   NH Ⓔ

4

$$\begin{array}{r} 315 \\ +\ 23 \\ \hline \end{array}$$

328 Ⓕ   338 Ⓖ   518 Ⓗ   545 Ⓙ   NH Ⓚ

5

$$\begin{array}{r} 200 \\ -\ 164 \\ \hline \end{array}$$

36 Ⓐ   46 Ⓑ   136 Ⓒ   146 Ⓓ   NH Ⓔ

6

$$\begin{array}{r} 460 \\ \times\ 3 \\ \hline \end{array}$$

790 Ⓕ   1,180 Ⓖ   1,380 Ⓗ   1,383 Ⓙ   NH Ⓚ

7 $9\overline{)72}$

____

____

8 **There were 43 pictures sent to an art contest.**

What is this number rounded to the nearest ten?

40 Ⓐ   45 Ⓑ   50 Ⓒ   55 Ⓓ   NH Ⓔ

GO ON

9 At Talfourd Elementary, 687 children ride buses to school. About how many children ride buses if the number is rounded to the nearest hundred?

600	680	690	700	NH
Ⓕ	Ⓖ	Ⓗ	Ⓙ	Ⓚ

10 Dottie sewed buttons on a shirt. There were 5 buttons on each card. She used 3 cards. How many buttons did Dottie sew on the shirt?

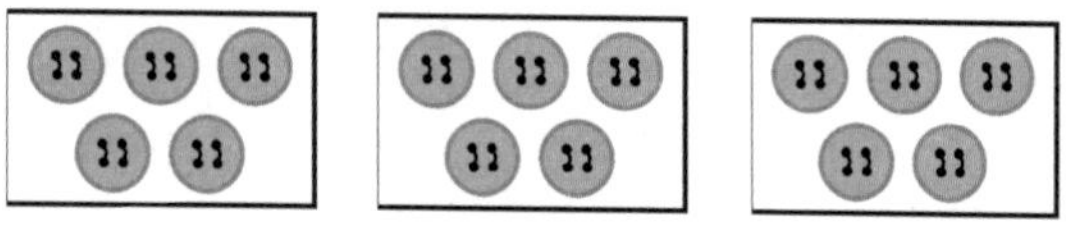

18	15	8	2	NH
Ⓐ	Ⓑ	Ⓒ	Ⓓ	Ⓔ

11 Suki bought a ball for $3.55. She paid $0.20 tax.

How much did Suki spend altogether?

____

____

____

____

____

____

12 Hsu paid $3.29 for a box of paints.

She gave the clerk 5 $1.00 bills.

If there was no tax, how much change should Hsu receive?

$2.81	$2.71	$1.81	$1.71	NH
Ⓕ	Ⓖ	Ⓗ	Ⓙ	Ⓚ

13 Mr. Jones had to drive 380 miles to visit his brother. He had driven 189 miles by lunch. How many more miles does Mr. Jones have to drive?

Ⓐ 211

Ⓑ 201

Ⓒ 191

Ⓓ 91

Ⓔ NH

14 Phoebe had saved $8.50. She earned $3.50 feeding a neighbor's cat. How much money does Phoebe have in all?

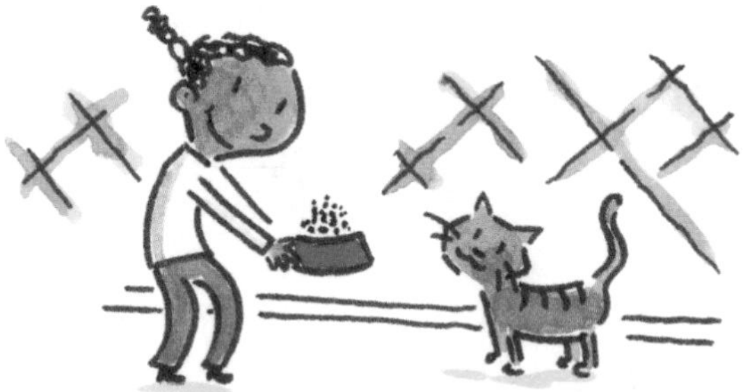

$12.50	$12.00	$11.50	$11.00	NH
Ⓕ	Ⓖ	Ⓗ	Ⓙ	Ⓚ

STOP

Sample A

Which number belongs in the box to make the number sentence correct?

$\square \times 1 = 24$

Ⓐ 2 Ⓒ 23

Ⓑ 4 Ⓓ 24

STOP

For questions 1-44, darken the circle for the correct answer, or write in the answer.

1 **Harvey has 1,354 baseball cards in his collection. What is the value of the 3 in 1,354?**

Ⓐ three thousand

Ⓑ three hundred

Ⓒ thirty

Ⓓ three

2 **The students in Mr. Lee's class are reading books. The table shows the fraction of the book each student has read.**

Name	Amount Read
Amy	$\frac{1}{5}$
Jay	$\frac{1}{4}$

Which student read the most?

Ⓕ Amy Ⓗ Meiko

Ⓖ Jay Ⓙ Ross

3 **Which is another way to write 300 + 50 + 2?**

Ⓐ 352

Ⓑ 3,052

Ⓒ 30,502

Ⓓ 300,502

4 **Which number sentence is in the same fact family as**

11 – 4 = 7

Ⓕ 11 + 4 = 15

Ⓖ 7 + 4 = 11

Ⓗ 7 – 4 = 3

Ⓙ 7 × 4 = 28

5 **Which is another name for eight thousand four hundred ninety-two?**

Ⓐ 8,492 Ⓒ 84,920

Ⓑ 80,492 Ⓓ 840,092

6 **Andy has an odd number of coins in his coin collection. Which is Andy's coin collection?**

Ⓕ Ⓖ Ⓗ Ⓙ

7 **Which number belongs in the box on the number line?**

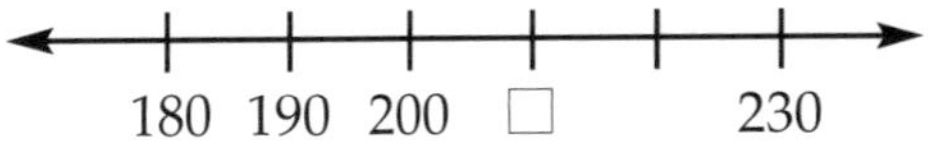

____

____

8 **Which muffin pan is $\frac{1}{2}$ empty?**

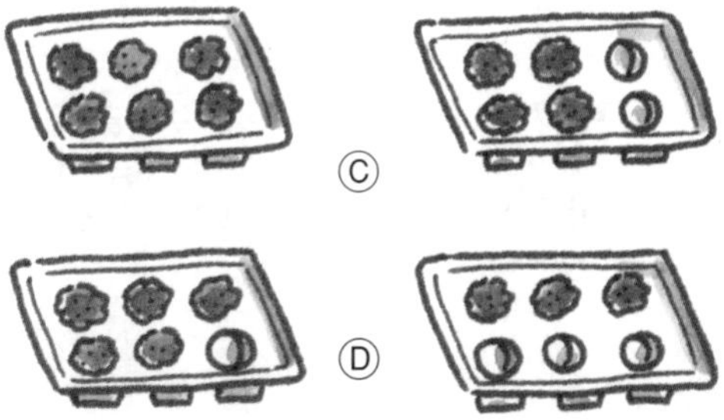

Ⓐ Ⓒ

Ⓑ Ⓓ

GO ON

9 **Which number belongs in the box to make the number sentence correct?**

$6 \times \square = 7 \times 6$

Ⓕ 42　　Ⓗ 7

Ⓖ 13　　Ⓙ 4

10 **What fraction of the shape is shaded?**

Ⓐ $\frac{1}{4}$　　Ⓒ $\frac{3}{3}$

Ⓑ $\frac{3}{4}$　　Ⓓ $\frac{1}{3}$

11 **The table shows the number of lunches sold in the cafeteria in one week.**

Day	Lunches
Monday	298
Tuesday	329
Wednesday	285
Thursday	351
Friday	246

On which day were the most lunches sold?

Ⓕ Monday　　Ⓗ Wednesday

Ⓖ Tuesday　　Ⓙ Thursday

Test Tip

Some math questions ask you to complete a picture. Look for the piece that will match or finish the pattern. Look carefully at the answers for question 14. Imagine placing each one in the empty space in the figure. Which piece will complete the pattern?

12 **The pet store sells 4 fish for $1. What is the missing number that completes the pattern in the chart?**

Fish to Buy	
Number of Dollars	Number of Fish
$ 2	8
$ 3	12
$ 4	?
$ 5	20

Ⓐ 16　　Ⓒ 13

Ⓑ 14　　Ⓓ 4

13 **The chart below shows how much 4 bags of cookies weigh.**

Cookie	Weight
Chocolate chip	2.2 lbs.
Fruit bars	1.7 lbs.
Ginger snaps	2.5 lbs.
Oatmeal	1.9 lbs.

Which cookie bag weighs the least?

Ⓕ Chocolate chip　　Ⓗ Ginger snaps

Ⓖ Fruit bars　　Ⓙ Oatmeal

14 **Which of these shows the missing piece in the figure?**

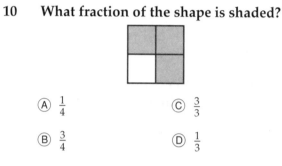

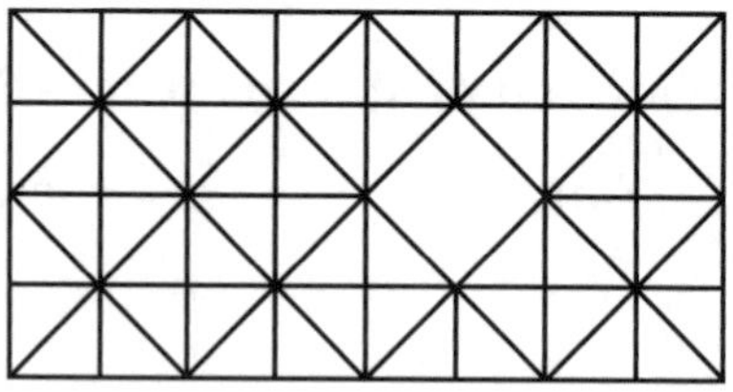

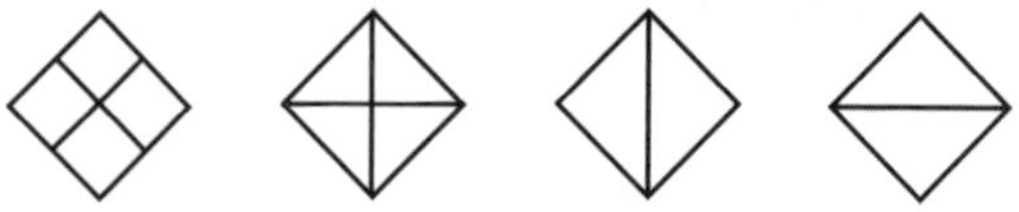

Ⓐ　　Ⓑ　　Ⓒ　　Ⓓ

GO ON

15 The table shows rainfall amounts in 4 cities in Texas.

City	Rain Per Year
Austin	30 inches
Dallas	35 inches
Fort Worth	35 inches
Houston	42 inches

Which two cities together receive a total of 72 inches of rain a year?

Ⓕ Austin and Dallas

Ⓖ Dallas and Houston

Ⓗ Fort Worth and Dallas

Ⓙ Austin and Houston

16 What is the missing number that completes the pattern in the boxes?

19	15	11	7	

Ⓐ 8 Ⓒ 4

Ⓑ 6 Ⓓ 3

17 The tally chart keeps track of the boxes of seeds Rebecca sells.

Kinds of Seeds	Boxes Sold
Flower Seeds	𝍸 𝍸
Vegetable Seeds	𝍸 |||
Herb Seeds	𝍸	
Birdseed	||||

How many boxes of vegetable seeds did Rebecca sell?

Ⓕ 2 Ⓗ 6

Ⓖ 4 Ⓙ 8

The graph below shows the shoes students are wearing in Mrs. Fryman's class. Study the graph and answer questions 18 through 20.

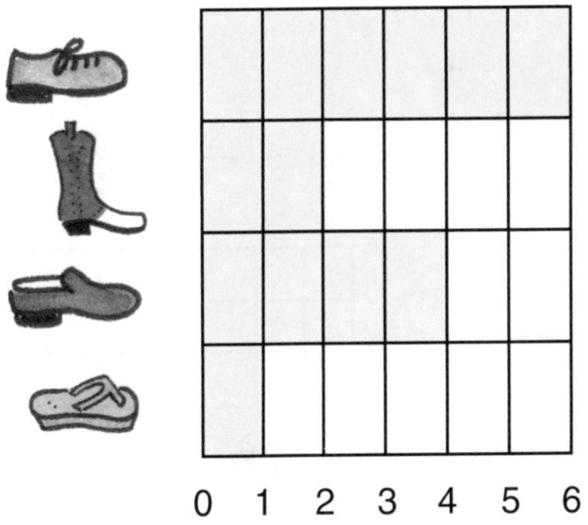

18 How many students are wearing sandals and boots?

Ⓐ 1 Ⓒ 3

Ⓑ 2 Ⓓ 6

19 Which category shows the shoes that 4 students are wearing?

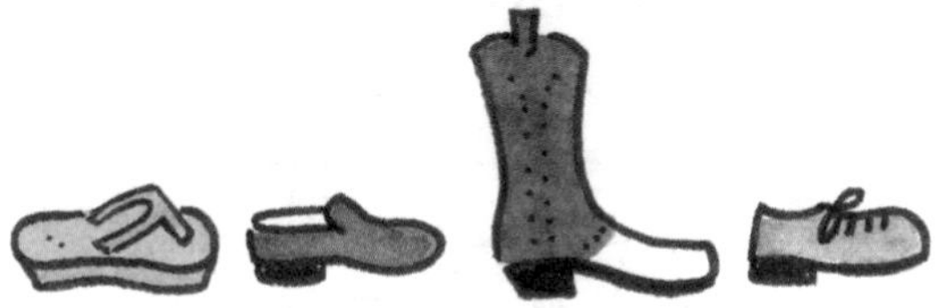

Ⓕ Ⓖ Ⓗ Ⓙ

20 How many more students are wearing lace-up shoes than boots?

____

____

____

____

____

GO ON

21 **What shape does the ball have?**

Ⓐ pyramid

Ⓑ cone

Ⓒ sphere

Ⓓ cube

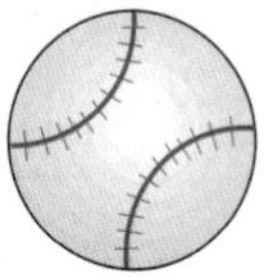

22 **What is the location of the**  **?**

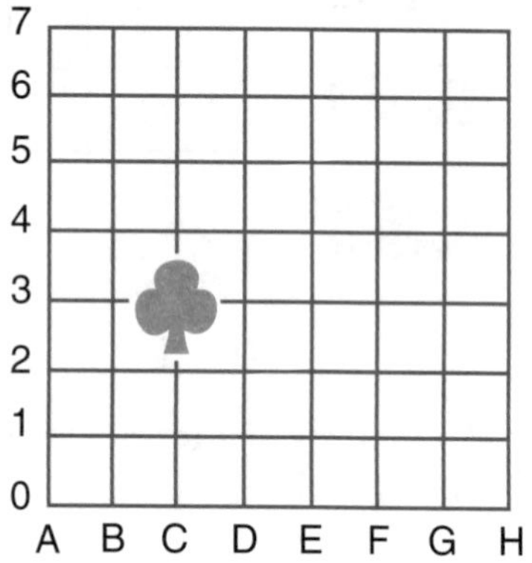

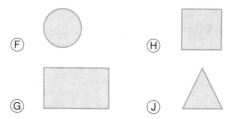

B4	C3	F5	D1
Ⓕ	Ⓖ	Ⓗ	Ⓙ

23 **Look at the numbered shapes. Which two figures are exactly the same in size and shape?**

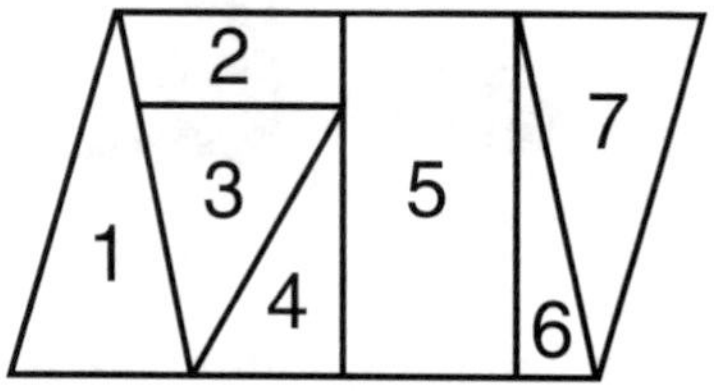

Ⓐ 1 and 4

Ⓑ 2 and 5

Ⓒ 1 and 7

Ⓓ 4 and 6

24 **These shapes were in a box.**

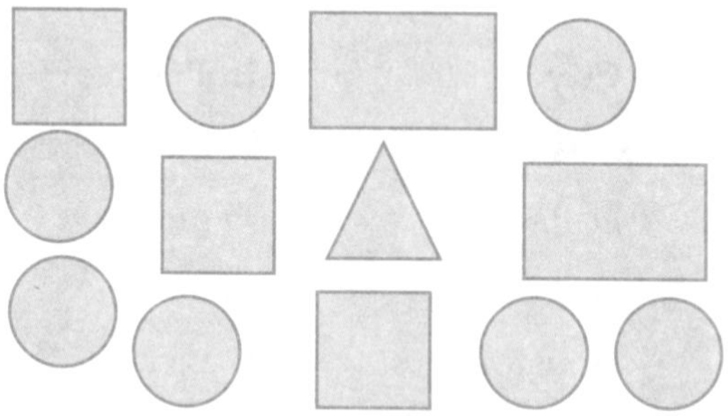

If one shape is picked from the box, which shape will it most likely be?

Ⓕ 

Ⓗ 

Ⓖ 

Ⓙ 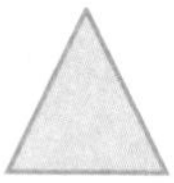

25 **Terry is playing a game with the spinner. Which number will the next spin most likely show?**

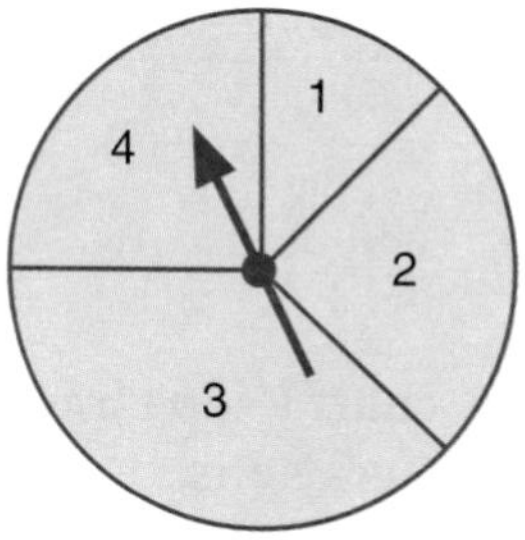

GO ON

26 **How many of the smaller figures are needed to cover the larger figure?**

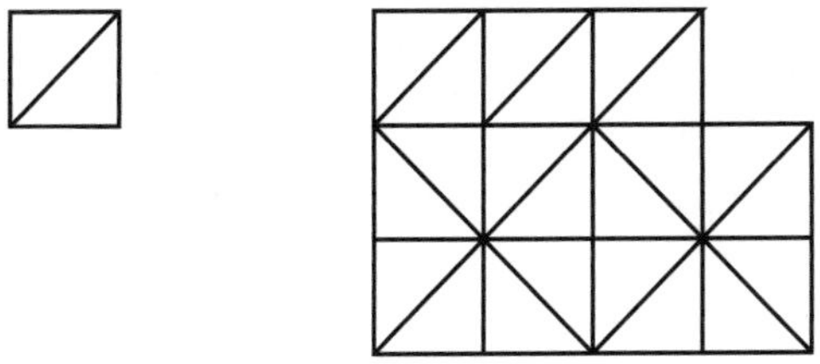

Ⓐ 22

Ⓑ 11

Ⓒ 10

Ⓓ 7

27 **Which figure will have two halves that match exactly when it is folded on the broken line?**

Ⓕ 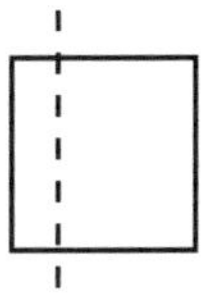

Ⓖ 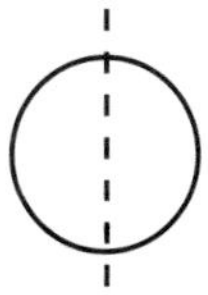

Ⓗ 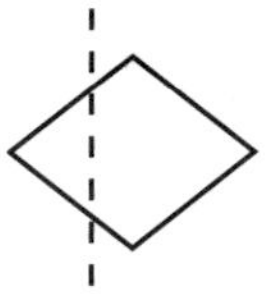

Ⓙ 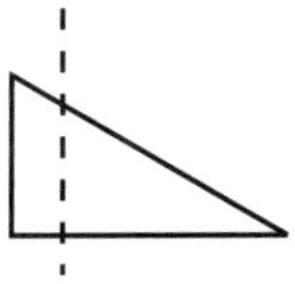

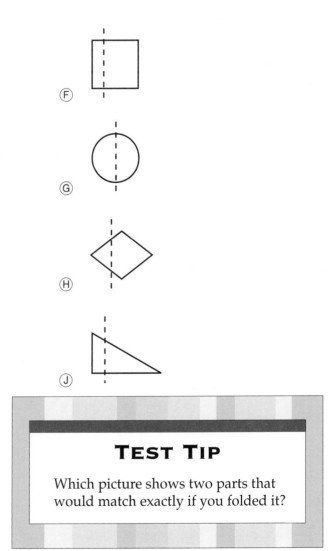

TEST TIP

Which picture shows two parts that would match exactly if you folded it?

28 **Carlos drew a car on a sheet of paper.**

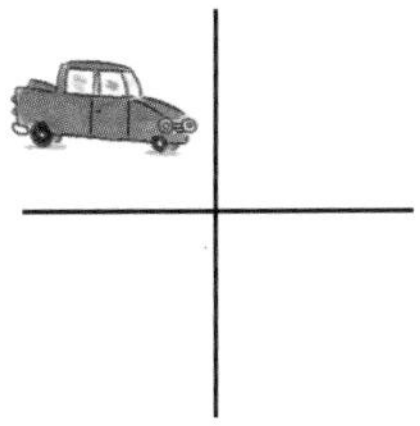

He turns the paper so the car is in the top, right square. What does the car look like now?

Ⓐ 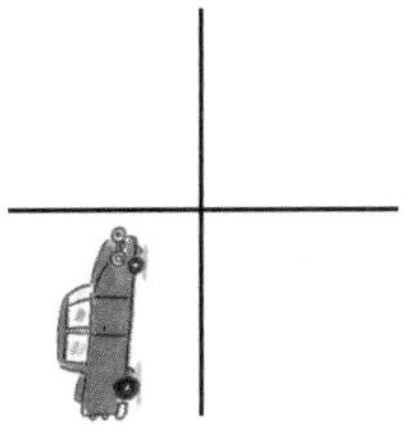

Ⓑ 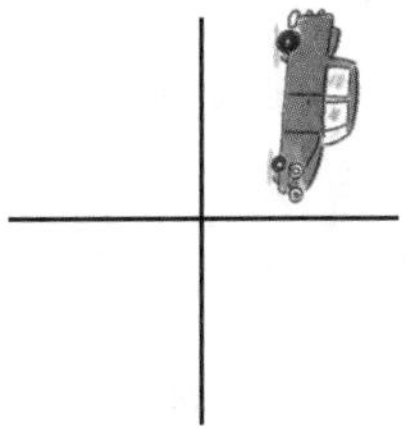

Ⓒ 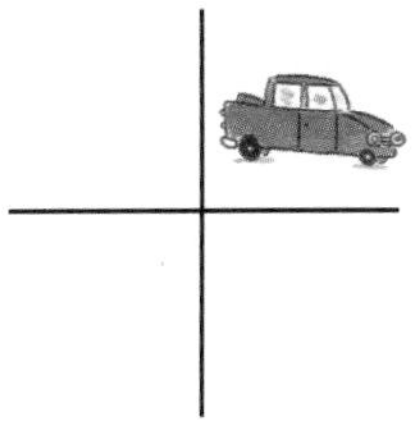

Ⓓ 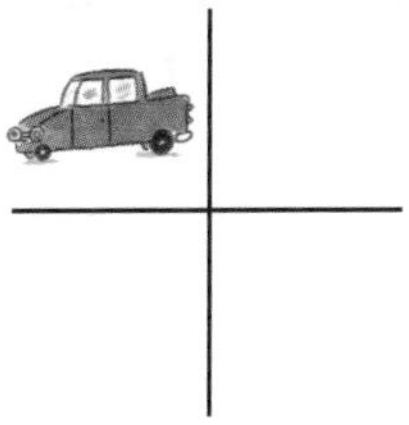

GO ON

29 **Charles found some change in his gym bag. What is the value of the money shown?**

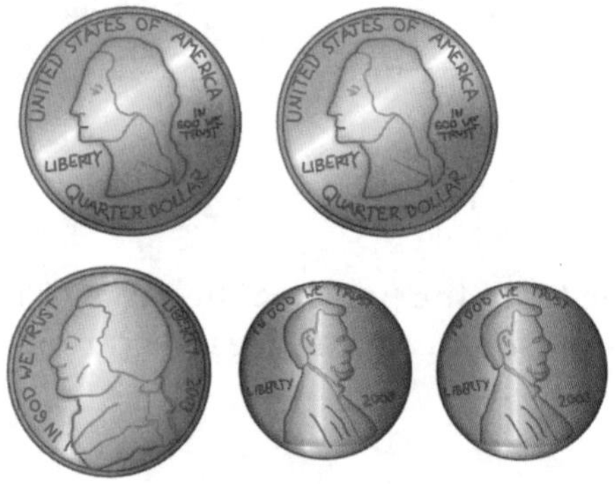

Ⓕ 62¢

Ⓖ 57¢

Ⓗ 27¢

Ⓙ 4¢

30 **<u>About</u> how many leaves long is the rake?**

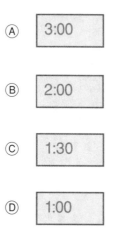

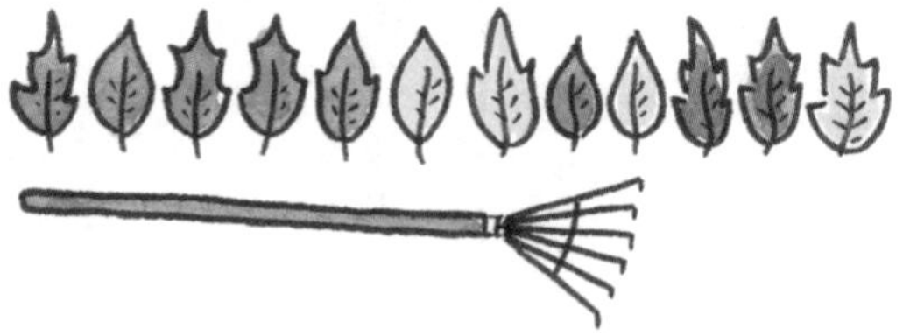

Ⓐ 12

Ⓑ 10

Ⓒ 9

Ⓓ 8

31 **Which unit of measurement is best to use to describe the height of a tree?**

Ⓕ inches

Ⓖ feet

Ⓗ pounds

Ⓙ miles

32 **The table below shows the number of sports cards Artie has in his collection.**

Sports Card Collection

Sport	Number of Cards
Football	16
Basketball	13
Baseball	29
Soccer	18
Hockey	9

Which two categories added together equal the number of baseball cards?

33 **The time is now 9:30. What time will it be four and one-half hours from now?**

Ⓐ 3:00

Ⓑ 2:00

Ⓒ 1:30

Ⓓ 1:00

GO ON

34 **How many small squares in all are needed to fill the large square shown below?**

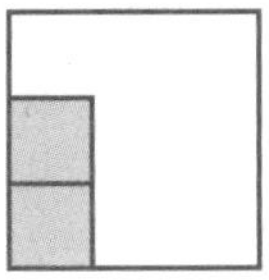

Ⓕ 7 Ⓗ 10

Ⓖ 9 Ⓙ 22

35 **The forest animals come to drink the water in a pond. Which animal lives the shortest distance from the pond?**

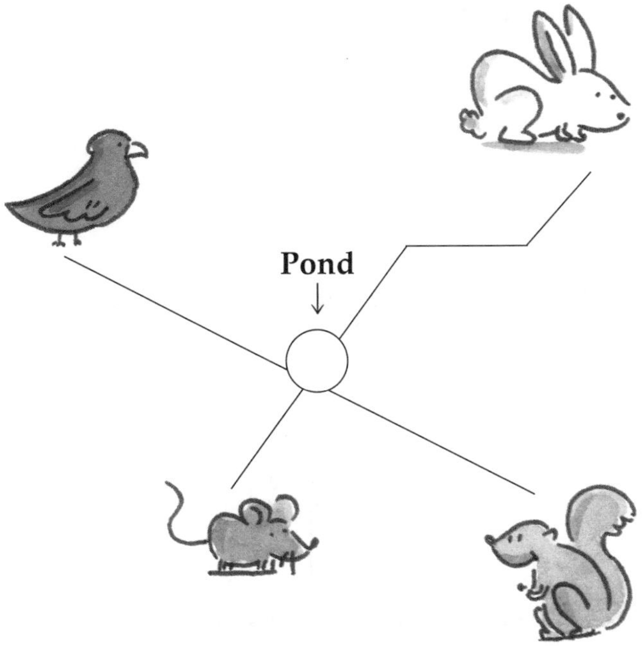

Ⓐ Ⓑ Ⓒ Ⓓ

TEST TIP

To solve question 35, estimate which of the four lines is the shortest one.

36 **Barbara and Ronnie are raking leaves. What is the temperature like outside?**

Ⓕ 21°

Ⓖ 32°

Ⓗ 55°

Ⓙ 98°

37 **Dylan bought some school supplies for $1.67. He gave the clerk $2.00. Which picture shows the coins Dylan should receive in change?**

Ⓐ

Ⓑ

Ⓒ

Ⓓ

GO ON

38 **The table shows the number of animals entered in a farm show.**

Animal	Number of Animals
Cow	29
Goats	22
Pigs	32
Sheep	19

About how many animals were entered altogether?

Ⓕ 100

Ⓖ 80

Ⓗ 70

Ⓙ 40

39 **Jared wants to buy a book for \$3 and a football for \$10. How much money does he need?**

Ⓐ \$1

Ⓑ \$5

Ⓒ \$10

Ⓓ \$20

40 **What number is in the square, is outside the circle, and is an even number?**

Ⓕ 2

Ⓖ 6

Ⓗ 9

Ⓙ 10

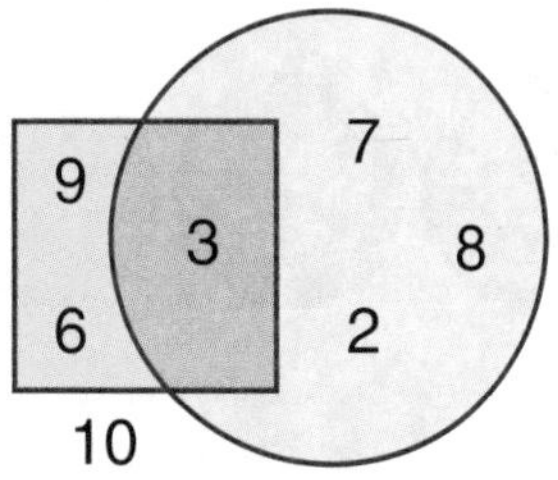

TEST TIP

Make sure your answer for question 40 matches all three rules: It should be inside the square, outside the circle, and even.

41 **Yoshi put 2 stamps on each letter she was going to mail. What do you need to know to find out how many stamps Yoshi used?**

Ⓐ how many letters she was going to mail

Ⓑ how long the envelopes were

Ⓒ how many stamps she bought

Ⓓ how much the stamps cost

42 **Alice has 5 more tickets than Claire. Claire has 3 fewer tickets than Melba. Melba has 7 tickets. How many tickets does Alice have?**

Ⓕ 15

Ⓖ 9

Ⓗ 6

Ⓙ 1

43 **What temperature is shown on the thermometer?**

Ⓐ 52°

Ⓑ 54°

Ⓒ 58°

Ⓓ 60°

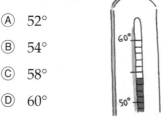

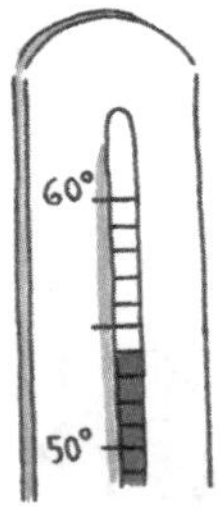

44 **Mark has 4 vases. He put 7 flowers in each vase. Write a number sentence that shows how to find the total number of flowers Mark used.**

STOP

LANGUAGE

PREWRITING, COMPOSING, AND EDITING

Directions: Darken the circle for the correct answer to each question, or write in the answer.

TRY THIS **Pretend that you are writing each sentence. Use the rules you have learned for capitalization, punctuation, and writing clear, correct sentences.**

Rosalina's Trip

Rosalina and her family went to Canada on vacation. They went to many places and had a great time. Rosalina wanted to tell her friend about her trip. So she wrote her a letter.

Sample A

Dear Debbie,

I want to tell you about the great time I had **(1)** in Canada. We visited many places. **(2)** I liked visiting Niagara Falls the best. **(3)** My friend had a great time in Hawaii. **(4)**

Which sentence does <u>not</u> belong in Rosalina's letter?

Ⓐ 1

Ⓑ 2

Ⓒ 3

Ⓓ 4

THINK IT THROUGH **The correct answer is <u>D</u>, <u>4</u>. This sentence does not tell about the topic of the paragraph, which is a vacation in Canada.**

STOP

Here is the next part of Rosalina's letter.

In <u>Ontario, canada,</u> we visited the Welland Ship Canal. **(5)** We watched a huge ship travel through the canal. **(6)**

1 **Write <u>Ontario, canada</u> correctly.**

____

____

____

____

GO ON

The Whale

Alfred's teacher wanted the students in the class to write a report about their favorite animal. Alfred's favorite animal is the whale. So Alfred decided to write his paper about the whale.

2 Alfred put these words in alphabetical *(ABC)* order so he could find them more quickly in the dictionary. Which list is correct?

Ⓐ flippers–flukes–fins–fat

Ⓑ fat–flukes–fins–flippers

Ⓒ fat–fins–flippers–flukes

Ⓓ fins–fat–flippers–flukes

3 If Alfred wanted to find the meaning of the word <u>fluke</u>, where should he look first?

Ⓕ a dictionary

Ⓖ an encyclopedia

Ⓗ an atlas

Ⓙ a language arts book

4 Where could Alfred probably find the most information about whales?

Ⓐ a newspaper

Ⓑ an encyclopedia

Ⓒ a dictionary

Ⓓ a language arts book

Alfred found the book *The Whale* in the library. Use the Table of Contents from this book to answer questions 5–7.

Table of Contents

5 Information about what whales eat begins on page—

____

____

____

6 In which chapter can Alfred find information about the way whales speak to one another?

3	4	5	6
Ⓕ	Ⓖ	Ⓗ	Ⓙ

7 Alfred can find information about the food that whales eat in Chapter—

2	3	4	6
Ⓐ	Ⓑ	Ⓒ	Ⓓ

GO ON

Here is the first part of Alfred's report. Read it carefully. Then answer questions 8–11.

The Whale

It was easy to choose my favorite animal. It is the whale.
(1) (2)
Jerry's favorite animal is the tiger. Did you know that whales did
(3) (4)
not always live in the ocean? Millions of years ago, whales were
(5)
land animals. Walked around on four legs. They lived near the
(6) (7)
oceans. They hunted in the waters near the shore. In time, the
(8) (9)
whales went deeper into the sea. They began to feel more at
(10)
home in the ocean than on land. They became whales as we
(11)
know them today.

8 Which group of words is not a complete sentence? Write the number of the group of words.

____

____

____

____

____

9 What is the best way to write sentence 5?

- Ⓕ The whales millions of years ago were land animals.
- Ⓖ The whales were millions of years ago land animals.
- Ⓗ Land animals were whales millions of years ago.
- Ⓙ As it is written.

10 Which sentence does not belong in Alfred's report?

1	3	5	7
Ⓐ	Ⓑ	Ⓒ	Ⓓ

11 What is the best way to combine sentences 7 and 8 without changing their meaning?

- Ⓕ Living near the ocean, they hunted in waters near the shore.
- Ⓖ They lived near the oceans and hunted in the waters near the shore.
- Ⓗ They hunted near the shore and lived near the ocean.
- Ⓙ They lived and hunted near the waters by the oceans.

GO ON

Here is the next part of Alfred's report. This part has groups of words underlined. Read this part carefully. Then answer questions 12–15.

Whales can be found in all the <u>oceans of the world</u>! Some
(12) **(13)**
whales live in water so deep that they are almost never seen.

Other whales live close to shore, so they're seen often. <u>Most</u>
(14) **(15)**
<u>whales travels</u> from place to place. <u>They moves during</u>
(16)
<u>different times</u> of the year. Whales feed in the cold waters
(17)
near the North and South Poles for part of the year. <u>Ther'es</u>
(18)
<u>much more food</u> for whales there than in warmer waters.

Whales travel to warmer waters to have their babies.
(19)

12 **In sentence 12, <u>oceans of the world!</u> is best written—**

- Ⓐ oceans of the world?
- Ⓑ oceans of the world.
- Ⓒ oceans of the world,
- Ⓓ As it is written.

13 **In sentence 15, <u>Most whales travels</u> is best written—**

- Ⓕ Most whales travel
- Ⓖ Most whales traveling
- Ⓗ Most whales traveled
- Ⓙ As it is written.

14 **In sentence 16, <u>They moves during different times</u> is best written—**

- Ⓐ They moved during different times
- Ⓑ They move'd during different times
- Ⓒ They move during different times
- Ⓓ As it is written.

15 **In sentence 18, <u>Ther'es much more food</u> is best written—**

- Ⓕ Theres' much more food
- Ⓖ There's much more food
- Ⓗ The'res much more food
- Ⓙ As it is written.

GO ON

Time to go Camping!

Millie and her family go camping every summer. This year they will go with Millie's cousin Tara and her family. Millie decides to write Tara a letter to help her get ready for camping.

16 **If Millie wanted to learn more about how to write a letter, she should look in—**

Ⓐ a language arts book.

Ⓑ a dictionary.

Ⓒ an atlas.

Ⓓ an encyclopedia.

Millie made a list of things that Tara should bring for camping. Use her list to answer question 17.

Supplies For Camping

1. a tent
2. a warm sleeping bag
3. a flashlight
4. food for three days
5. plates, cups, spoons, forks, and knives
6. some snacks
7.

17 **Which of these is not something Millie should list as number 7?**

Ⓕ marshmallows to roast

Ⓖ nice jewelry to wear

Ⓗ a bucket to put out a campfire

Ⓙ a cooler to keep food cold

While Millie was writing her letter, she needed to check some words in the dictionary.

18 **What definition best fits the word trail as used in the sentence below? Write the definition.**

We went for a walk on the trail.

____

____

____

____

____

TEST TIP

Pay close attention when the word *not* is included in a question. Make sure your answer for question 17 is *not* a supply for camping.

GO ON

Here is the first page of Millie's letter. Read the letter carefully. Then answer questions 19–21.

> Dear Tara,
>
> I'm so glad that you will be able to go camping with us. I
> **(1)** **(2)**
> can't wait! I know that you have never gone camping. So I
> **(3)** **(4)**
> want to tell you about it. Going camping is so much fun. You'll
> **(5)** **(6)**
> get to be outside for three whole days. You'll get to eat outside.
> **(7)**
> We'll cook food on a stove. We'll cook over a fire. At night you
> **(8)** **(9)** **(10)**
> can see thousands of stars in the sky. Sleeping in a tent is also
> **(11)**
> a lot of fun. All the cousins will be able to sleep in the same tent.
> **(12)**

19 **What is the best way to combine sentences 8 and 9 without changing their meaning?**

Ⓐ We'll cook food on a stove, we'll cook over a fire.

Ⓑ On a stove and over a fire we'll cook food.

Ⓒ On a stove we'll cook food and over a fire we'll cook food.

Ⓓ We'll cook food on a stove and over a fire.

20 **What is the topic sentence of this paragraph?**

____

____

____

____

____

____

21 **What is the best way to write sentence 12?**

Ⓕ In the same tent all the cousins will get to sleep.

Ⓖ All the cousins in the same tent will get to sleep.

Ⓗ All the cousins. Will get to sleep in the same tent.

Ⓙ As it is written.

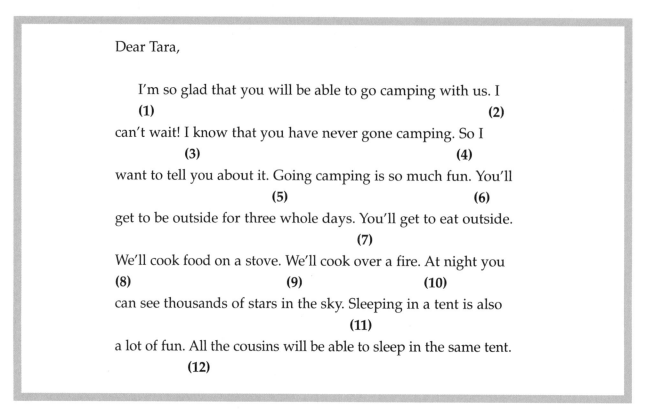

GO ON

Here is the next part of Millie's letter. This part has groups of words underlined. Read this part carefully. Then answer questions 22–25.

You need to get things ready for camping. **(13)** Your parents will bring the tent. **(14)** You should bring an warm sleeping bag. **(15)** You should also bring a flashlight. **(16)** It's so much fun to use flashlights to walk around the camp at night. **(17)** Make sure you bring pots pans, and dishes. **(18)** You'll need them to cook your food. **(19)** Hot dogs and hamburgers taste great when you're camping! **(20)** Make sure you brought a lot of marshmallows. **(21)** We'll be roasting them over the fire. **(22)** I'm also going to bring some fruit and some granola bars. **(23)** You should bring some, too. **(24)**

sincerely yours,
Millie

22 In sentence 15, bring an warm sleeping bag is best written—

Ⓐ brought an warm sleeping bag

Ⓑ bring a warm sleeping bag

Ⓒ brought a warm sleeping bag

Ⓓ As it is written

23 In sentence 18, bring pots pans, and dishes is best written—

Ⓕ bring pots, pans, and dishes

Ⓖ bring pots pans and dishes

Ⓗ bring pots, pans and dishes

Ⓙ As it is written

24 In sentence 21, brought a lot of is best written—

Ⓐ brings a lot of

Ⓑ bringing a lot of

Ⓒ bring a lot of

Ⓓ As it is written

25 At the end of Millie's letter, sincerely yours, is best written—

Ⓕ Sincerely Yours,

Ⓖ Sincerely yours,

Ⓗ sincerely Yours,

Ⓙ As it is written

STOP

Directions: Read each sentence carefully. If one of the words is misspelled, darken the circle for that word. If all the words are spelled correctly, then darken the circle for *No Mistake.*

TRY THIS | Read each sentence carefully. If you are not sure of an answer, first decide which answer choices are spelled correctly. Then see if you can recognize the misspelled word from your reading experience.

Sample A

May played a <u>livly</u> <u>tune</u> on her <u>piano</u>. <u>No mistake</u>
 Ⓐ Ⓑ Ⓒ Ⓓ

THINK IT THROUGH | The correct answer is **A**, for the first underlined word. All of the other words are spelled correctly. <u>Livly</u> should be spelled l-i-v-e-l-y. You should not drop the <u>e</u> when you add <u>-ly</u>.

🛑 STOP

1 In <u>sewing</u> <u>class</u> I am making an <u>aperun</u> for my mom. <u>No mistake</u>
 Ⓐ Ⓑ Ⓒ Ⓓ

2 We saw some <u>unusual</u> <u>butterflies</u> in the <u>woods</u>. <u>No mistake</u>
 Ⓕ Ⓖ Ⓗ Ⓙ

3 Don told the <u>scaryest</u> <u>ghost</u> story at <u>camp</u>. <u>No mistake</u>
 Ⓐ Ⓑ Ⓒ Ⓓ

4 The car <u>startd</u> to <u>slide</u> on the icy <u>highway</u>. <u>No mistake</u>
 Ⓕ Ⓖ Ⓗ Ⓙ

5 The <u>magical</u> king <u>granted</u> the shoemaker three <u>wishs</u>. <u>No mistake</u>
 Ⓐ Ⓑ Ⓒ Ⓓ

🛑 STOP

Sample A

Go Fly a Kite

Leon's scout troop has entered a kite contest. Leon knows how to make and fly a kite. He wants to write a paper to help the other scouts get ready for the contest.

Leon wants to find out when the kite contest in his city will take place. He should look in—

Ⓐ an atlas.

Ⓑ an encyclopedia.

Ⓒ a dictionary.

Ⓓ a newspaper.

STOP

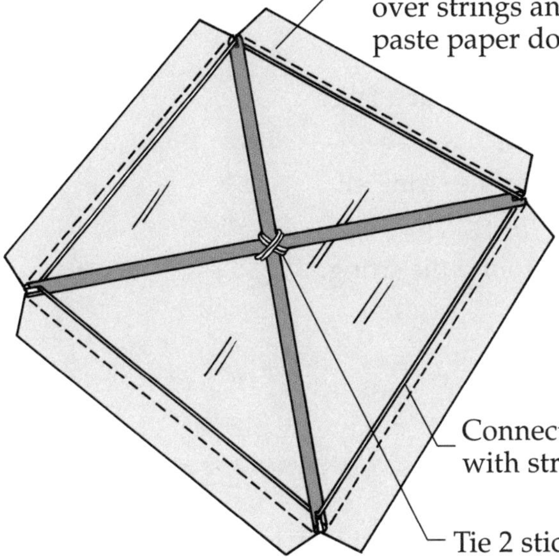
Fold edges of paper over strings and paste paper down.
Connect sticks with string.
Tie 2 sticks together tightly.

1 **Here is a sketch Leon drew of a kite. How will it best help him to write his paper?**

Ⓐ It will help him picture what kind of paper to use.

Ⓑ It will help him picture how to put the kite together.

Ⓒ It will help him remember a kite contest he once entered.

Ⓓ It will help him decide to enter the kite contest.

2 **Leon found the book *How To Fly a Kite*. Where in the book should he look to find the author's name?**

Ⓕ Chapter 1

Ⓖ the title page

Ⓗ the table of contents

Ⓙ the index

3 **If Leon wanted to find out when kites were first made, where should he look?**

Ⓐ a dictionary

Ⓑ an atlas

Ⓒ a language arts book

Ⓓ an encyclopedia

4 **Where should Leon look to find the meaning of the word <u>fasten</u>?**

____

____

____

____

____

____

____

GO ON

Here is the first part of Leon's paper. Read it carefully. Then answer questions 5–7.

How to Make a Kite

I'm going to tell you how to make a flat kite. Make sure that
(1) **(2)**
you have two sticks, string, paper, and glue. Take the two sticks
(3)
and cross them into an *X*. Use the string to tie the sticks together.
(4)
Tie them tightly where the two sticks cross. Then add glue to make
(5) **(6)**
sure the two sticks stay together. Around the ends of the sticks tie
(7)
a string. This will be the outer edge of the kite. Then cut a large
(8) **(9)**
piece of paper. Fold the edges of the paper over the string all
(10)
around the kite. Use paste to glue the paper around the string.
(11)
My sister made a beautiful kite.
(12)

5 What is the topic sentence of this paragraph?

1	2	3	4
Ⓕ	Ⓖ	Ⓗ	Ⓙ

6 What is the best way to write sentence 7?

Ⓐ Around the ends of the sticks a string tie.

Ⓑ Tie a string around the ends of the sticks.

Ⓒ A string tie around the ends of the sticks.

Ⓓ As it is written.

7 Which sentence does <u>not</u> belong in Leon's paper? Write the number.

____

____

____

____

GO ON

Here is the next part of Leon's paper. This part has groups of words underlined. Read this part carefully. Then answer questions 8–11.

The Kite Contest **(13)** will take place in April. The most important **(14)** thing to remember is that your kite has to fly. Then you can enter **(15)** your kite in three events. The first event will decide which kite is **(16)** decorated the best. The judges will look at the colors and designs **(17)** you use. The second event will decide which kite can fly the **(18)** highest. The judges will give you about ten minutes to get your **(19)** kite into the air! The third event will decide how fast you can **(20)** send out your kite to the end of the line and reels it in again.

Lets' all get busy and get our kites ready! **(21)**

8 In sentence 13, The Kite Contest is best written—

Ⓕ The kite contest

Ⓖ The Kite contest

Ⓗ the kite Contest

Ⓙ As it is written.

9 In sentence 19, into the air! is best written—

Ⓐ into the air?

Ⓑ into the air,

Ⓒ into the air.

Ⓓ As it is written.

10 In sentence 20, and reels it in again. is best written—

Ⓕ and reel it in again.

Ⓖ and reeling it in again.

Ⓗ and reel's it in again.

Ⓙ As it is written.

11 In sentence 21, Lets' all get is best written—

Ⓐ Lets all get

Ⓑ Let's all get

Ⓒ Le'ts all get

Ⓓ As it is written.

GO ON

Learning about the Moon

Mary and her class went on a field trip to a planetarium. Her teacher wanted each student to write a paper and tell about one thing they learned. Mary decided to write about the moon.

12 Why is Mary writing the paper?

- Ⓕ to tell about the moon and planets
- Ⓖ to ask her parents to go to the planetarium
- Ⓗ to describe the moon
- Ⓙ to tell what she learned at the planetarium

13 Mary put these words in alphabetical *(ABC)* order so she could find them more quickly in the dictionary. Which list is correct?

- Ⓐ meteors – moonrise – motion – mountains
- Ⓑ moonrise – mountains – meteors – motion
- Ⓒ mountains – motion – moonrise – meteors
- Ⓓ meteors – motion – moonrise – mountains

TEST TIP

Remember the rules for putting two words in *alphabetical*, or ABC, order. If the first letters are the same, look at the second letters. If the second letters also are the same, look at the third letters.

Mary found the book *The Moon* in the library. Use the Table of Contents and Index from the book to answer questions 14–16.

Table of Contents

Index

14 In which chapter could Mary find information about the astronauts who walked on the moon?

2	3	4	5
Ⓕ	Ⓖ	Ⓗ	Ⓙ

15 Mary can find information about moon craters on page—

8	23	25	43
Ⓐ	Ⓑ	Ⓒ	Ⓓ

16 Information about how the moon came to be can be found in Chapter—

____

____

____

____

GO ON

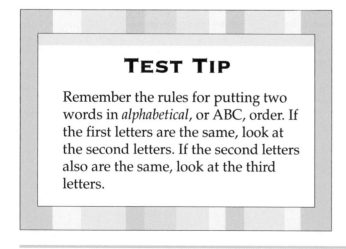

Here is the first part of Mary's report. Read it carefully. Then answer questions 17–20.

Learning about the Moon

I really enjoyed going to the planetarium. **(1)** I learned a lot about the moon. **(2)** The moon is smaller than Earth. **(3)** Jupiter is the largest planet. **(4)** The moon is about 238,000 miles away from Earth. **(5)** That's not very far when you're talking about outer space. **(6)** You cannot live on the moon. **(7)** The moon has no water. **(8)** It has no air. **(9)** During the day the moon is hot. **(10)** Enough to fry an egg. **(11)** At night, the moon is colder than the North Pole. **(12)** The moon is covered with dust–covered flat land. **(13)** It also has many different sizes of craters. **(14)**

17 Which of these is not a complete sentence?

5	7	9	11
Ⓕ	Ⓖ	Ⓗ	Ⓙ

18 What is the best way to combine sentences 8 and 9 without changing their meaning?

Ⓐ The moon, which has no air, has no water.

Ⓑ The moon has no water and the moon has no air.

Ⓒ The moon has no water and no air.

Ⓓ The moon having no water has no air.

19 Which sentence does not belong in Mary's paper?

2	4	6	8
Ⓕ	Ⓖ	Ⓗ	Ⓙ

20 Which of these could be added after sentence 14?

Ⓐ Some of the craters are old volcanoes.

Ⓑ Some planets have more than one moon.

Ⓒ Jamie liked visiting the planetarium, too.

Ⓓ Earth is the third planet from the sun.

GO ON

Here is the next part of Mary's report. This part has groups of words underlined. Read this part carefully. Then answer questions 21–24.

I really liked learning about the people who explored the moon.
(15)

The first people walked on the moon on July 20, 1969? They
(16) **(17)**
take a walk that lasted more than two hours. They gathered
(18)
rocks and soil to bring back to Earth to study. They also took
(19)
many photographs. Before they left for Earth these people set
(20)
up experiments on the moon. More people walk on the moon
(21)
after 1969. Some of them rode in a special kind of car
(22)
called a lunar rover. The work of these people
(23)
helped us learn a lot about the moon.

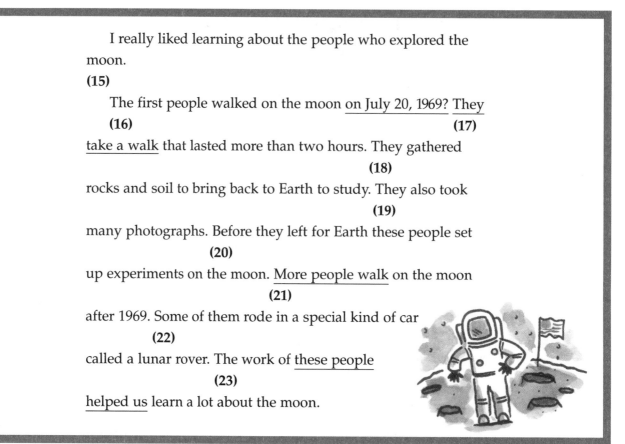

21 **In sentence 16, on July 20, 1969? is best written—**

- Ⓕ on July 20, 1969,
- Ⓖ on July 20, 1969.
- Ⓗ On July 20, 1969?
- Ⓙ As it is written.

22 **In sentence 17, They take a walk is best written—**

- Ⓐ They taking a walk
- Ⓑ They takes a walk
- Ⓒ They took a walk
- Ⓓ As it is written.

23 **In sentence 21, More people walk is best written—**

- Ⓕ More people walked
- Ⓖ More people is walking
- Ⓗ More people walks
- Ⓙ As it is written.

24 **In sentence 23, these people helped us is best written—**

- Ⓐ these people helping us
- Ⓑ these people is helped us
- Ⓒ these people has helping us
- Ⓓ As it is written.

GO ON

For questions 25–32, read each sentence carefully. If one of the words is misspelled, darken the circle for that word. If all the words are spelled correctly, then darken the circle for *No mistake.*

25 Ashley was very lonly in the cabin by the lake. No mistake
 Ⓕ Ⓖ Ⓗ Ⓙ

26 Nick dashd down the street to catch the bus. No mistake
 Ⓐ Ⓑ Ⓒ Ⓓ

27 Flashs of light streaked across the sky during the storm. No mistake
 Ⓕ Ⓖ Ⓗ Ⓙ

28 The plane flew through the clowds. No mistake
 Ⓐ Ⓑ Ⓒ Ⓓ

29 The kitten raced into the alley when the dog barked. No mistake
 Ⓕ Ⓖ Ⓗ Ⓙ

30 Bob walked to the store to buy vegetables. No mistake
 Ⓐ Ⓑ Ⓒ Ⓓ

31 Phil enjoys reading advenchure stories. No mistake
 Ⓕ Ⓖ Ⓗ Ⓙ

32 This is the greasyest pan I've ever washed! No mistake
 Ⓐ Ⓑ Ⓒ Ⓓ

STOP

Sample A

Cathy's Vacation Plans

Cathy is excited about going camping with her family this summer. They plan to go to the Grand Canyon where they will stay for two weeks.

How long will Cathy's family camp?

Ⓐ two days

Ⓑ two weeks

Ⓒ two months

Ⓓ the entire summer

STOP

For questions 1–32, read each story and the questions that follow. Then darken the circle for the correct answer to each question, or write in the answer.

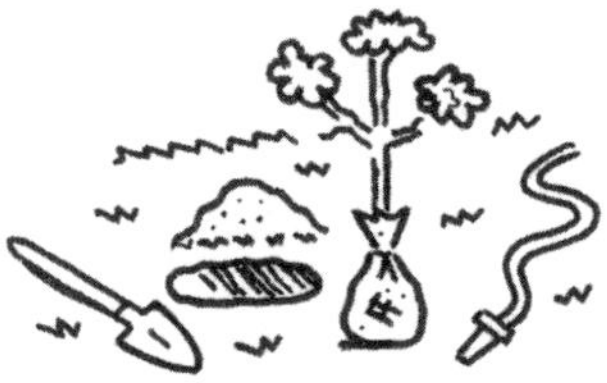

How to Plant a Tree

Planting a tree is a good way to clean the air, provide a home for birds, and make the world more beautiful. You will need a tree, a shovel, and *mulch.*

First, choose a good spot for the tree. It should not be too close to a building or other trees or beneath telephone wires. Dig a two-feet-deep hole with sloping sides.

Second, remove or cut away the container that the tree is in. Pick up the tree by the root ball, not the trunk, and set it in the hole. Then fill the hole with dirt around the root ball. When the hole is a little more than half full, fill the hole with water and stir the mud with your shovel. This will settle the soil and remove air pockets. Then finish filling in the hole with dirt.

Last, place *mulch,* or leaves, straw, or bark, around the tree. Water the tree, and step back to admire your work!

1 **Planting a tree will do all of the following <u>except</u>—**

Ⓐ make the world more beautiful.

Ⓑ save water.

Ⓒ clean the air.

Ⓓ provide a home for birds.

2 **What can be used to make mulch?**

____

____

____

____

GO ON ➡

When Grandma Was a Young Girl

Grandma has told me many stories about what it was like growing up on the farm when she was a girl. Her family lived ten miles from any neighbors. They had little money to buy food in a store. They had to grow most of their food on the farm. They raised cows and chickens for meat. They grew and then canned fruits and vegetables to last the whole winter. Grandma's family stored some of the food in an underground cellar to keep it from spoiling. They also had an underground spring near the house. The water was very cold. They stored milk, butter, and eggs in the spring to keep them fresh.

Grandma and her family had to work very hard. I am glad that we have cars and can go to the grocery store to buy our food.

3 The writer thinks that Grandma's life on the farm was—

Ⓕ difficult.

Ⓖ easy.

Ⓗ fun.

Ⓙ boring.

4 How did the family keep milk and butter fresh?

Ⓐ They canned it.

Ⓑ They stored it in a spring.

Ⓒ They used a refrigerator.

Ⓓ They kept it in a cellar.

5 Why did Grandma's family have to grow most of their food?

____

____

____

____

____

____

6 Which question does the first paragraph answer?

Ⓕ How big was the farm?

Ⓖ What was the grandmother's favorite thing to do?

Ⓗ How did the family get food?

Ⓙ Where did the grandmother go to school?

GO ON

All about Bees

Bees are always busy. Worker bees fly from flower to flower, and then they fly back to the beehive. There the worker bees make honey. They help the queen bee by building nests. They also clean the nests and take care of baby bees. The queen bee lays all the eggs for the beehive. The work that bees do is useful to people. Bees help plants grow in gardens and on farms. The sweet honey that bees make is delicious to eat.

7 **Worker bees do all of the following <u>except</u>—**

Ⓐ make honey.

Ⓑ lay eggs.

Ⓒ clean the nest.

Ⓓ take care of baby bees.

8 **What job does the queen bee have?**

____

____

____

____

____

____

____

____

9 **What is another good title for this story?**

Ⓕ "Busy, Busy Bees"

Ⓖ "How Honey is Made"

Ⓗ "A Day in the Life of a Queen Bee"

Ⓙ "Why Bees Like Flowers"

10 **How is the work that bees do useful to people?**

Ⓐ Bees clean their own nests.

Ⓑ Bees help plants grow in gardens and on farms.

Ⓒ Bees are fun to watch.

Ⓓ Bees are always busy.

GO ON

An Important Food

When you think of bread, what comes to mind? Do you think of a fresh loaf of white bread? Perhaps you picture a nice loaf of wheat bread. If you lived in another country, you might have a very different idea of bread. A boy or girl in Mexico would think of *tortillas*. These are flat, round breads made from corn. People in India would think of *chappatis*. These are heavy pieces of round bread that are fried.

Bread is one of the most important foods. It is eaten more than any other food. It is also eaten in more places than any other food.

Bread has been an important food for a very long time. The first bread was made about 12,000 years ago. People in the Middle East gathered the seeds of wild plants. They used the seeds to make flour. They mixed the flour with water. Then they baked it on hot rocks.

Later people learned how to plant seeds so they could grow their own wheat. People in Egypt learned that if they added yeast to the flour and water, it would make the bread rise. The Egyptians also learned to build ovens in which to bake the bread.

For hundreds of years, bread was made in the same way. But in time, people wanted a light bread. They learned that if flour was sifted through cloth, the rough pieces could be taken out. Then they would have white flour. From white flour, soft white bread could be made. For many years only rich people could buy white bread. Today many people like whole-wheat bread better than white bread. We know that the rough pieces of flour are good for us.

GO ON

11 **You would probably find this story in a book called—**

Ⓕ *Important Foods around the World.*

Ⓖ *Holidays in Many Places.*

Ⓗ *Foods from Mexico.*

Ⓙ *How to Grow Wheat.*

12 **Who first added yeast to bread?**

Ⓐ Egyptians

Ⓑ people in the Middle East

Ⓒ Germans

Ⓓ Mexicans

13 **What are *chappatis*?**

Ⓕ flat, round breads made of corn

Ⓖ sweet biscuits

Ⓗ heavy pieces of fried bread

Ⓙ soft, rye breads

14 **To answer question 13, the reader should—**

Ⓐ reread the first line of each paragraph.

Ⓑ reread the last paragraph of the story.

Ⓒ look for the word *chappatis* in the story.

Ⓓ reread the title of the story.

15 **What is this story mainly about?**

Ⓕ how to make bread

Ⓖ how to eat bread

Ⓗ types of flat bread

Ⓙ the history of bread

16 **If the story continued, it would probably tell about—**

Ⓐ ways bread is made today.

Ⓑ how to eat a healthful diet.

Ⓒ medicines made from plants.

Ⓓ favorite foods of children.

17 **What question does the second paragraph answer?**

Ⓕ How is bread made?

Ⓖ What food is eaten more than any other?

Ⓗ Who made the first bread?

Ⓙ What kind of bread do people like best?

18 **What was bread first made from?**

____

____

____

____

____

____

____

____

GO ON

Visiting Grandmother

Tino loves to visit his grandmother. He doesn't get to visit her very often because his family lives in a city that is six hours away. His grandmother lives in a big wooden house on a farm. It is old and looks like it has secret hiding places.

On the second Sunday of July, Tino's parents took him to his grandmother's. Since it was summer vacation, he was going to stay at Grandmother's for a whole month! His cousins Doug and Barbara would soon be arriving. They would also be staying at their grandmother's this summer.

A big porch wraps around two sides of the house. Tino sat in the porch swing. He could see the trees that circle the house. They had been planted as a *windbreak*. They protect the house from the wind and blowing dirt. The house is in the middle of a large, flat field.

Tino watched the dirt road that leads to the house. He couldn't wait for his cousins to get there! Doug was his age, and Barbara was a year younger. They always had fun together. Last summer they had spent one whole morning making a fort out of sacks of seed that they found in the barn. Then Uncle John had taken them on a tractor ride.

Tino remembered another time with his cousins. They had gone out to explore the fields. Tino touched an electric fence and got a shock. Then they found an old snakeskin. Nothing like that ever happened at home! Tino took the snakeskin to school and showed it to everyone.

Tino could smell the dinner that his mother and grandmother were cooking. He smelled ham, hot rolls, and pumpkin pie. It made him hungry.

Finally he saw a cloud of dust coming up the road. "They're here! They're here!" he shouted.

GO ON

19 After Tino's cousins arrive, what will probably happen next?

Ⓐ They will build a fort on the hill.

Ⓑ They will look for snakeskins.

Ⓒ They will climb the trees in their grandmother's yard.

Ⓓ They will eat dinner at their grandmother's house.

20 The story tells about Tino and his cousins doing all of the following except—

Ⓕ watching old movies.

Ⓖ taking a tractor ride.

Ⓗ finding a snakeskin.

Ⓙ making a fort from seed sacks.

21 How do you think Tino felt when he saw his cousins arriving?

Ⓐ He was worried.

Ⓑ He was excited.

Ⓒ He was angry.

Ⓓ He was sad.

22 Tino's grandmother lives in a—

Ⓕ brick house.

Ⓖ stone house.

Ⓗ wooden house.

Ⓙ new house.

23 What is meant by a *windbreak*?

____

____

____

____

____

____

24 In order to answer question 23, the reader should—

Ⓐ read the title of the story again.

Ⓑ read the first paragraph again.

Ⓒ look in the story for the word *windbreak.*

Ⓓ read the last line of each paragraph again.

25 Tino's grandmother's house was—

Ⓕ on a hill.

Ⓖ in a valley.

Ⓗ in a field.

Ⓙ in a city.

26 These boxes show events that happened in the story.

Tino went to Grandmother's house.		Tino thought about another visit to Grandmother's.
1	**2**	**3**

What belongs in box 2?

Ⓐ Tino's cousins arrived at Grandmother's house.

Ⓑ Tino could smell dinner cooking.

Ⓒ Tino sat in the porch swing.

Ⓓ Tino saw a cloud of dust coming up the road.

GO ON

This poster was placed in the cafeteria at Taft Elementary School.

Help Our Environment!

April is "Help Our Environment!" month at Taft Elementary School. Students can help clean up our planet by collecting used cans, bottles, and newspapers. These things should be put in the recycling bins that have been placed in each classroom. Each class that fills its bin will get a "Clean Class" award. On Earth Day each student in these classes will get to plant a tree in the schoolyard. Let's all help make our school and our world a cleaner place!

27 According to the poster, all of the following activities will happen in April <u>except</u>—

Ⓕ collecting cans, bottles, and newspapers.

Ⓖ filling recycling bins.

Ⓗ planting trees.

Ⓙ taking a trip to the recycling center.

28 What will probably happen after the recycling bins are filled?

Ⓐ The materials will be taken to a recycling center.

Ⓑ The materials will be sent home with students.

Ⓒ The materials will be stored at the school.

Ⓓ The materials will be buried in the schoolyard.

29 Where was this sign posted?

Ⓕ at the neighborhood gym

Ⓖ at Taft Elementary School

Ⓗ at the supermarket

Ⓙ at East High School

30 The recycling bins are for—

Ⓐ bottles and cans.

Ⓑ bottles, plastic, and newspapers.

Ⓒ cans, plastic, and cardboard.

Ⓓ cans, bottles, and newspapers.

31 Who will get to plant trees?

Ⓕ classes who get a "Clean Class" award

Ⓖ students who buy a tree

Ⓗ students who read the most books

Ⓙ classes who make the best grades

32 When will the "Help Our Environment" program be held?

____

____

____

____

____

____

STOP

READING VOCABULARY

Sample A

A parka is a kind of—

Ⓐ warm jacket with a hood

Ⓑ European folk dance

Ⓒ dried meat

Ⓓ sled

STOP

For questions 1-9, darken the circle for the word or words that have the same or almost the same meaning as the underlined word.

1 Familiar means—

Ⓐ old

Ⓑ beautiful

Ⓒ known

Ⓓ strange

2 A lane is most like a—

Ⓕ ladder

Ⓖ road

Ⓗ shack

Ⓙ race

3 To cure means to—

Ⓐ heal

Ⓑ clean

Ⓒ study

Ⓓ correct

4 A tourist is a kind of—

Ⓕ judge

Ⓖ chair

Ⓗ teacher

Ⓙ visitor

5 To recall something is to—

Ⓐ prepare it

Ⓑ clean it

Ⓒ remember it

Ⓓ include it

6 Something that is precise is—

Ⓕ expensive

Ⓖ exact

Ⓗ rare

Ⓙ safe

7 Something that is soaked is—

Ⓐ wet

Ⓑ dirty

Ⓒ soiled

Ⓓ wrinkled

8 A jacket is most like a—

Ⓕ hat

Ⓖ dress

Ⓗ coat

Ⓙ jar

9 A kennel is a place for—

Ⓐ dogs

Ⓑ airplanes

Ⓒ plants

Ⓓ cars

STOP

Sample B

Turn the key to make the car run.

In which sentence does run have the same meaning as it does in the sentence above?

Ⓐ Water will always run downhill.

Ⓑ This fan won't run any more.

Ⓒ Li will run in the race today.

Ⓓ I hit a run at our baseball game.

STOP

For questions 10–14, darken the circle for the sentence in which the underlined word means the same as it does in the sentence in the box.

10

Draw a card and put it on the table.

In which sentence does draw have the same meaning as it does in the sentence above?

Ⓕ We used horses to draw the wagon.

Ⓖ Please draw a picture of a whale for me.

Ⓗ The circus will draw a big crowd.

Ⓙ Each of us will draw a number from the hat.

11

We saw a boat sail on the bay.

In which sentence does bay have the same meaning as it does in the sentence above?

Ⓐ The wolf began to bay at the moon.

Ⓑ The winner was the bay horse.

Ⓒ The water in that bay is icy.

Ⓓ Put a bay leaf in the soup.

12

I ate part of the pie.

In which sentence does part have the same meaning as it does in the sentence above?

Ⓕ I won't part with my favorite jacket.

Ⓖ Joe did part of the work.

Ⓗ Trevor played the part of Peter Pan.

Ⓙ The part in your hair is crooked.

13

Always check your answers.

In which sentence does check have the same meaning as it does in the sentence above?

Ⓐ Dad wrote a check for the clothes.

Ⓑ I put a check beside my name.

Ⓒ My marker is on the red check.

Ⓓ Check to see if you have your ticket.

14

We took a lunch break at noon.

In which sentence does break have the same meaning as it does in the sentence above?

Ⓕ That old chain may break.

Ⓖ At this ranch they break horses.

Ⓗ If you are tired, take a break.

Ⓙ The sun shone through a break in the clouds.

STOP

Sample C

That delicate fruit will bruise easily if it is bumped. Bruise means—

Ⓐ mark

Ⓑ hurt

Ⓒ blossom

Ⓓ taste

STOP

For questions 15–21, darken the circle for the word or words that give the meaning of the underlined word, or write in the answer.

15 He tried to navigate the space shuttle safely through the asteroid field. Navigate means—

Ⓐ dock

Ⓑ chase

Ⓒ land

Ⓓ steer

16 We were astounded by the magician's amazing tricks. Astounded means—

____

____

____

____

____

____

17 That organization works to preserve and protect the environment. Preserve means—

Ⓕ clean up

Ⓖ plant flowers

Ⓗ hunt animals

Ⓙ keep from being lost

18 He was in a hurry and had time for only a brief visit. Brief means—

Ⓐ afternoon

Ⓑ short

Ⓒ casual

Ⓓ lunch

19 He didn't want to lie so he gave him an honest answer. Honest means—

Ⓕ truthful

Ⓖ false

Ⓗ strange

Ⓙ long

20 She inscribed his name on the clay vase with a sharp pen. Inscribed means—

Ⓐ wrote

Ⓑ burned

Ⓒ read

Ⓓ underlined

21 If you plan to attend the party, please send a reply. Reply means—

Ⓕ answer

Ⓖ car

Ⓗ invitation

Ⓙ cake

STOP

PART 1: MATH PROBLEM SOLVING

Sample A

Which is another way to write 700 + 10 + 5?

Ⓐ 700,105 Ⓒ 7,150

Ⓑ 7,001 Ⓓ 715

STOP

For questions 1–43, darken the circle for the correct answer, or write in the answer.

1 **Which number belongs on the number line at point C?**

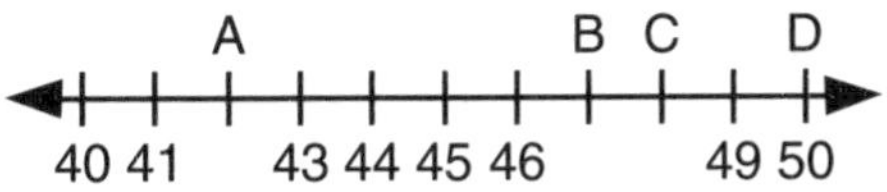

Ⓐ 42 Ⓒ 48

Ⓑ 47 Ⓓ 51

2 **Jean has an even number of stamps in her stamp collection. Which is Jean's stamp collection?**

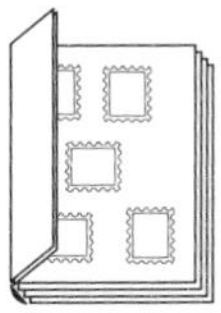

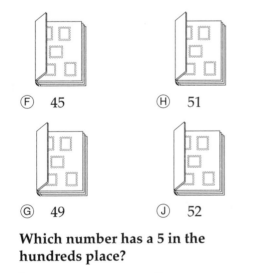

Ⓕ 45

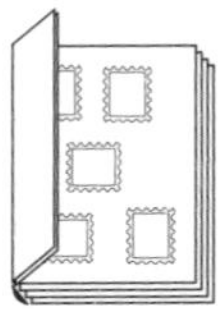

Ⓗ 51

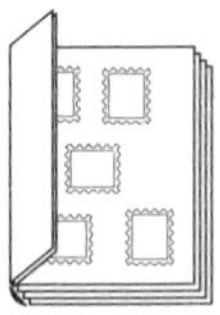

Ⓖ 49

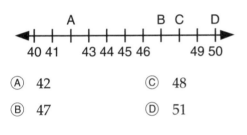

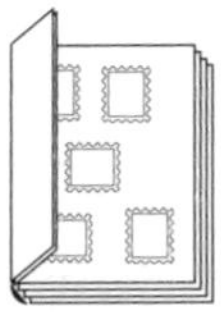

Ⓙ 52

3 **Which number has a 5 in the hundreds place?**

Ⓐ 5,640 Ⓒ 56

Ⓑ 564 Ⓓ 5

4 **The table shows the number of people who go to the movies during the week.**

Day	Number of People
Monday	243
Tuesday	146
Wednesday	297
Thursday	185
Friday	324

On which day did the fewest number of people go to the movies?

Ⓕ Monday Ⓗ Thursday

Ⓖ Tuesday Ⓙ Friday

5 **Which is another name for two thousand one hundred sixty?**

Ⓐ 216 Ⓒ 2,160

Ⓑ 2,106 Ⓓ 21,600

6 **The chart shows the number of students in grades one through four.**

One	Two	Three	Four
290	163	249	312

Which of the following shows the grades listed in order from the fewest number of students to the most students?

Ⓕ Two, three, one, four

Ⓖ Three, two, one, four

Ⓗ Four, two, one, three

Ⓙ One, two, three, four

GO ON

7 **Which number sentence is in the same fact family as**

9 – 6 = 3

?

Ⓐ $6 + 3 = 9$

Ⓑ $9 + 6 = 15$

Ⓒ $6 - 3 = 3$

Ⓓ $6 \geq 3 = 18$

8 **Which number belongs in the box to make the number sentence correct?**

2 × □ = 9 × 2

Ⓕ 2 Ⓗ 11

Ⓖ 9 Ⓙ 18

9 **Which is another way to write 4 × 2?**

Ⓐ $2 \times 2 \times 2 \times 2$

Ⓑ $8 + 2$

Ⓒ $4 + 2$

Ⓓ $2 + 2 + 2 + 2$

10 **Which number belongs in the box to make the number sentence correct?**

5 × □ = 5

Ⓕ 10 Ⓗ 1

Ⓖ 5 Ⓙ 0

11 **What fraction of the shape is not shaded?**

____

____

____

____

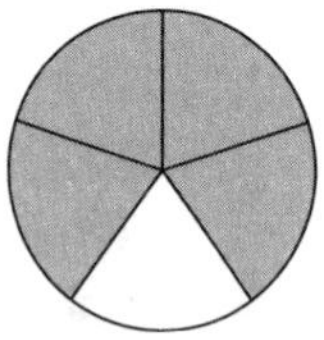

12 **Which picture shows $\frac{2}{3}$ of the flowers shaded?**

Ⓐ 

Ⓒ 

Ⓑ 

Ⓓ 

13 **The pizza restaurant cuts each pizza into 6 slices. What is the missing number that completes the pattern in the chart?**

Pizzas	Number of Slices
1	6
2	?
3	18
4	24

Ⓕ 1 Ⓗ 7

Ⓖ 6 Ⓙ 12

14 **The students in Mrs. James' class must collect 20 leaves. The table shows the fraction of leaves each student has collected so far.**

Name	Fraction Collected
Ken	$\frac{1}{4}$
Dominic	$\frac{1}{5}$
Jenna	$\frac{1}{10}$
Perry	$\frac{1}{2}$

Which student collected the smallest fraction of leaves?

Ⓐ Ken Ⓒ Jenna

Ⓑ Dominic Ⓓ Perry

GO ON➡

The graph below shows the kinds of sports stories students in Ms. Kent's class wrote. Study the graph and answer questions 15 and 16.

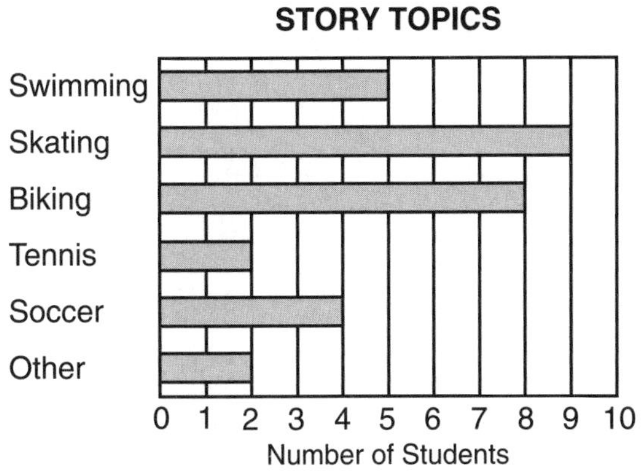

15 **How many students wrote about skating?**

____

____

____

16 **How many more students wrote about skating than soccer?**

Ⓕ 5 Ⓗ 9

Ⓖ 7 Ⓙ 13

17 **The tally chart shows the number of butterflies 4 students spotted during a week.**

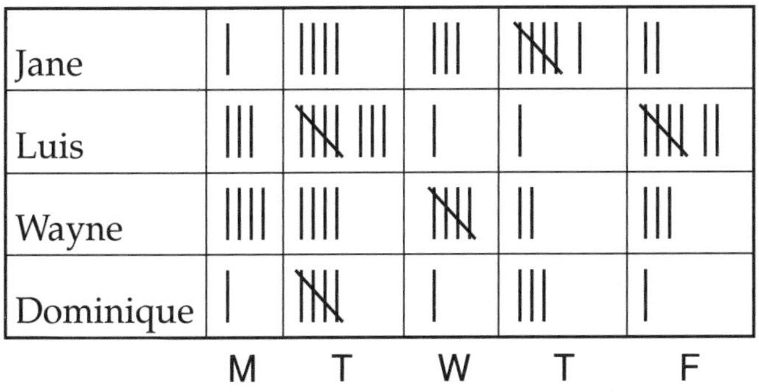

Who spotted more than 5 butterflies but fewer than 10 on Tuesday?

Ⓐ Jane Ⓒ Wayne

Ⓑ Luis Ⓓ Dominique

18 **The chart below shows the number of ounces in cartons of juice.**

Juice	Ounces
Orange	5.3
Apple	5.6
Grape	6.1
Cranberry	4.5

Which juice carton has the most ounces?

Ⓕ Orange Ⓗ Grape

Ⓖ Apple Ⓙ Cranberry

19 **What is the missing number that completes the pattern in the boxes?**

3	9	15	21	

Ⓐ 23 Ⓒ 27

Ⓑ 25 Ⓓ 30

20 **Which shows the piece missing from the figure?**

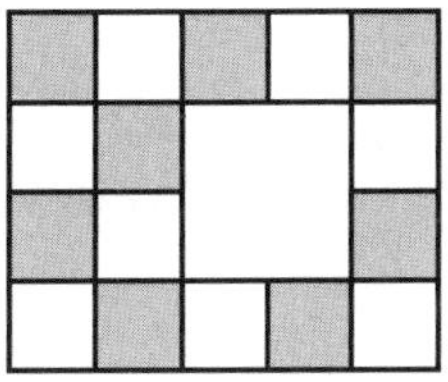

Ⓕ

Ⓗ

Ⓖ

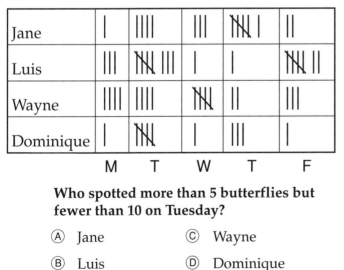

Ⓙ

GO ON ➨

21 **Which names the location of**  **?**

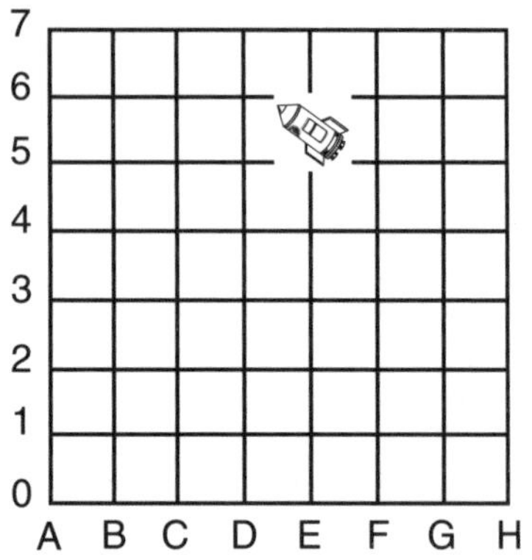

Ⓐ G3 Ⓒ E5

Ⓑ F4 Ⓓ D6

22 **Florence is playing a game with the spinner. Which month will the next spin least likely show?**

23 **The table below shows the number of books students in Mrs. Wallin's class have read.**

Name	Number of Books
Marilyn	18
Penny	27
Lillian	15
Kyle	30
Jim	29

Who read 14 more books than Lillian?

Ⓕ Jim Ⓗ Penny

Ⓖ Kyle Ⓙ Marilyn

24 **Look at the numbered shapes. Which two figures are exactly the same in size and shape?**

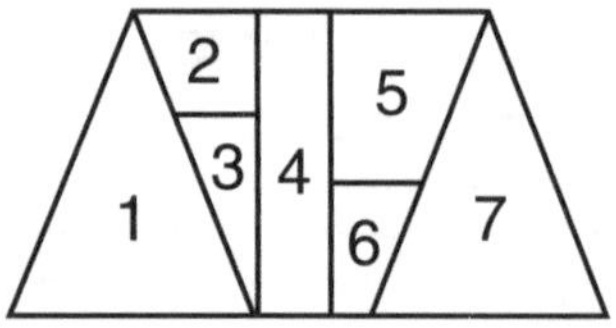

Ⓐ 2 and 5 Ⓒ 3 and 6

Ⓑ 1 and 7 Ⓓ 1 and 4

25 **What shape does the can have?**

Ⓕ cylinder

Ⓖ cube

Ⓗ cone

Ⓙ sphere

26 **These shapes were in a bag.**

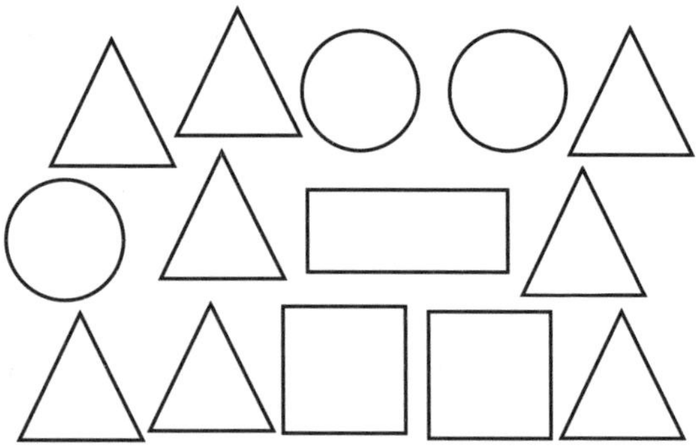

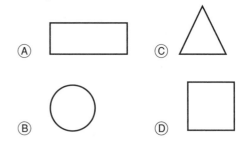

If one shape is picked from the bag, which of these shapes will it most likely be?

Ⓐ 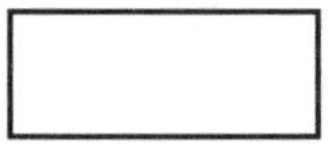 Ⓒ 

Ⓑ 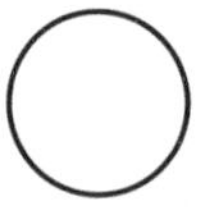 Ⓓ 

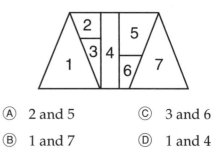

GO ON

27 **Which shape has four corners and four sides that are exactly the same length?**

Ⓕ 

Ⓖ 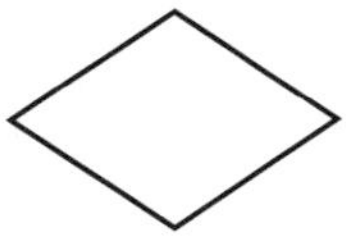

Ⓗ 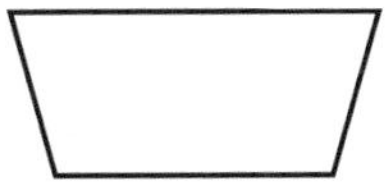

Ⓙ 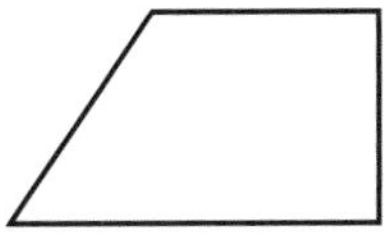

28 **Clara made a card for her mother.**

She turns the card so the words are on the bottom. What does the card look like now?

Ⓐ 

Ⓑ 

Ⓒ 

Ⓓ 

29 **Carmen gets home from school at 3:30. She leaves for baseball practice one and one-half hours later. What time will it be when Carmen leaves for baseball practice?**

Ⓕ 8:00

Ⓖ 5:00

Ⓗ 3:00

Ⓙ 12:00

30 **Which unit of measurement is best to use to measure the weight of an apple?**

Ⓐ pounds

Ⓑ inches

Ⓒ quarts

Ⓓ ounces

31 **Which figure will have two halves that match exactly when it is folded on the solid line?**

Ⓕ 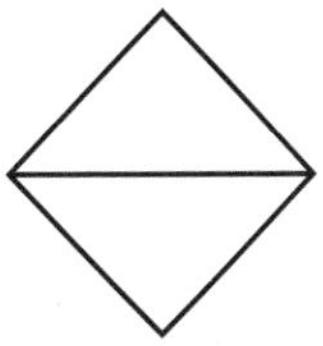

Ⓗ 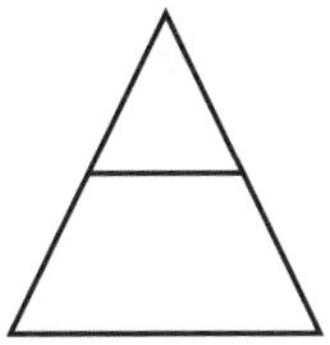

Ⓖ 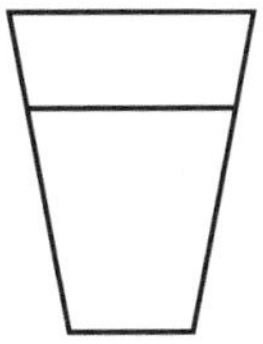

Ⓙ 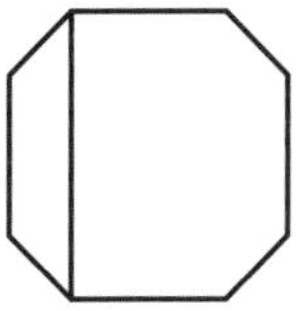

GO ON ➡

32 **Carmine bought a football helmet that cost $9.84. He gave the store clerk $10.00. Which coins should Carmine receive in change?**

Ⓐ 

Ⓑ 

Ⓒ 

Ⓓ 

33 **Aris found these coins in his yard. What is the value of the money shown?**

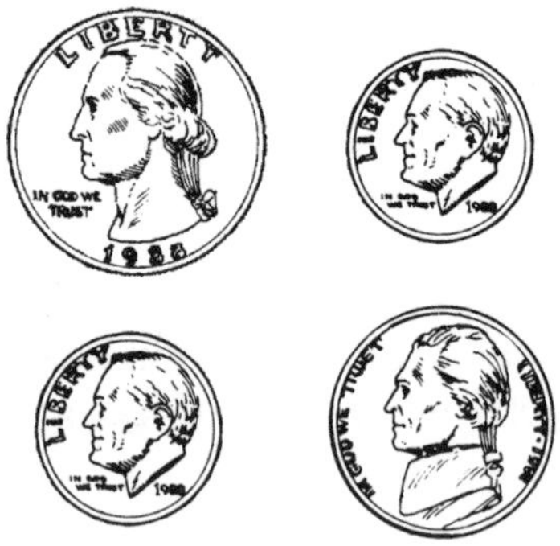

Ⓕ 36¢ Ⓗ 50¢

Ⓖ 41¢ Ⓙ 61¢

34 **What temperature is shown on the thermometer?**

Ⓐ 41°

Ⓑ 48°

Ⓒ 52°

Ⓓ 90°

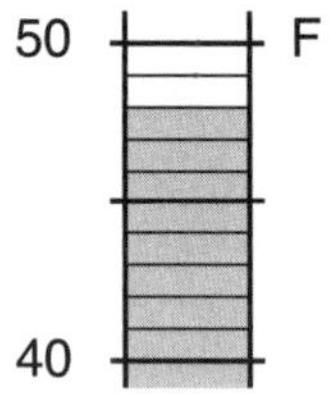

35 **How many inches long is the trail from where the squirrel is to the nuts? Use your inch ruler to answer this question.**

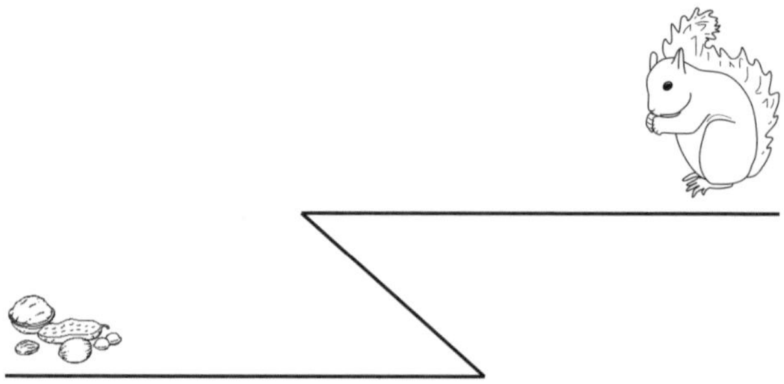

Ⓕ 3 inches Ⓗ 7 inches

Ⓖ 5 inches Ⓙ 9 inches

36 **A bird is building a nest. The lines show how far it flies to get the grass and twigs for the nest. Which line shows the longest distance the bird flies from the nest?**

Ⓐ 1

Ⓑ 2

Ⓒ 3

Ⓓ 4

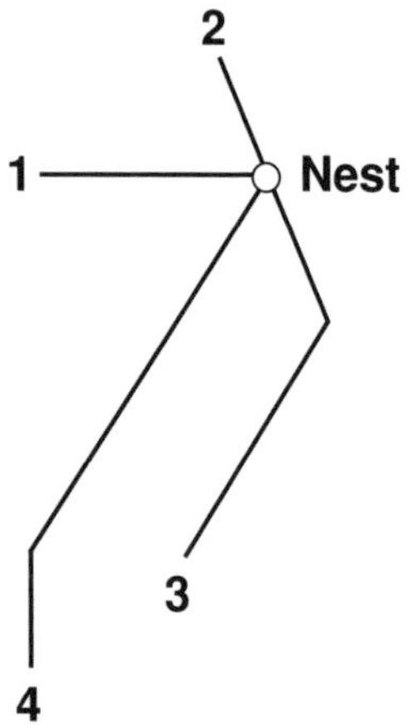

37 **How many small squares in all are needed to fill the rectangle?**

Ⓕ 25

Ⓖ 20

Ⓗ 15

Ⓙ 3

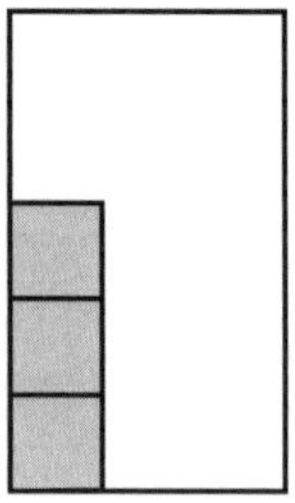

GO ON

38 **Crystal is 5 years younger than Carlos. Carlos is 3 years younger than Don. Don is 13. How old is Crystal?**

Ⓐ 16 Ⓒ 5

Ⓑ 10 Ⓓ 1

39 **The table shows how the third-grade students at Main Street Elementary travel to school.**

Way of Travel	Number of Students
Car	38
Bus	73
Bicycle	9
Walk	9

About how many third-grade students are there altogether?

Ⓕ 80 Ⓗ 130

Ⓖ 100 Ⓙ 140

40 **About how much did Chip spend on 2 shirts and a jacket?**

Ⓐ $10 Ⓒ $30

Ⓑ $20 Ⓓ $40

41 **What number is inside the circle, is outside the square, and is an even number?**

Ⓕ 11

Ⓖ 12

Ⓗ 13

Ⓙ 15

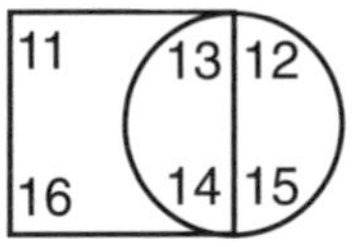

42 **Mr. Takata put the top of his car down before going for a drive. What is the temperature outside like?**

Ⓐ 87°

Ⓑ 41°

Ⓒ 32°

Ⓓ 15°

43 **Dawn sold 15 calendars on Thursday. She sold 30 on Sunday. Which number sentence shows how to find the total number of calendars Dawn sold?**

Ⓕ 30 + 15 = □

Ⓖ 30 – 15 = □

Ⓗ □ + 15 = 30

Ⓙ 30 × 15 = □

STOP

Sample A

$5 \times 7 = \square$

35	30	25	20	NH
Ⓐ	Ⓑ	Ⓒ	Ⓓ	Ⓔ

STOP

For questions 1–22, darken the circle for the correct answer. If the correct answer is not given, darken the circle for NH (Not Here). If no choices are given, write in the answer.

1

$$\begin{array}{r} 711 \\ 28 \\ +\ 84 \\ \hline \end{array}$$

713	722	823	1831	NH
Ⓐ	Ⓑ	Ⓒ	Ⓓ	Ⓔ

2

$$\begin{array}{r} 324 \\ -\ 228 \\ \hline \end{array}$$

94	97	104	106	NH
Ⓕ	Ⓖ	Ⓗ	Ⓙ	Ⓚ

3

$7 + \square = 14$

9	8	7	6	NH
Ⓐ	Ⓑ	Ⓒ	Ⓓ	Ⓔ

4

$$\begin{array}{r} 8 \\ \times\ 8 \\ \hline \end{array}$$

16	56	64	72	NH
Ⓕ	Ⓖ	Ⓗ	Ⓙ	Ⓚ

5

$$\begin{array}{r} 95 \\ -\ 16 \\ \hline \end{array}$$

111	101	89	79	NH
Ⓐ	Ⓑ	Ⓒ	Ⓓ	Ⓔ

6

$$\begin{array}{r} 625 \\ +\ 39 \\ \hline \end{array}$$

654	664	754	764	NH
Ⓕ	Ⓖ	Ⓗ	Ⓙ	Ⓚ

7

$$\begin{array}{r} 648 \\ -\ 63 \\ \hline \end{array}$$

____

____

____

____

8

$$\begin{array}{r} 46 \\ +\ 27 \\ \hline \end{array}$$

____

____

____

____

GO ON

9

$$\begin{array}{r} 57 \\ \times\ 9 \\ \hline \end{array}$$

4,563	453	456	156	NH
Ⓐ	Ⓑ	Ⓒ	Ⓓ	Ⓔ

10

50 × 2 = □

10	52	70	100	NH
Ⓕ	Ⓖ	Ⓗ	Ⓙ	Ⓚ

11

$$\begin{array}{r} 10 \\ \times\ 64 \\ \hline \end{array}$$

74	110	604	640	NH
Ⓐ	Ⓑ	Ⓒ	Ⓓ	Ⓔ

12

$$\begin{array}{r} 123 \\ \times\ 4 \\ \hline \end{array}$$

462	472	492	592	NH
Ⓕ	Ⓖ	Ⓗ	Ⓙ	Ⓚ

13

$5\overline{)35}$

5	6	7	8	NH
Ⓐ	Ⓑ	Ⓒ	Ⓓ	Ⓔ

14

36 ÷ 6 = □

15 **Sally bought a bunch of balloons for $3.59. She paid $0.27 tax. How much did she pay altogether for the balloons?**

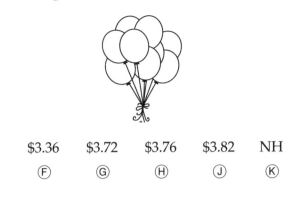

$3.36	$3.72	$3.76	$3.82	NH
Ⓕ	Ⓖ	Ⓗ	Ⓙ	Ⓚ

16 **Harbor Hills Elementary School has 789 students. What is that number rounded to the nearest hundred?**

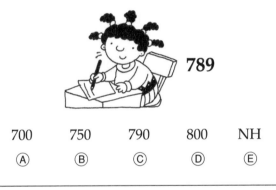

700	750	790	800	NH
Ⓐ	Ⓑ	Ⓒ	Ⓓ	Ⓔ

17 **Amy saw 62 cars in one train. What is that number rounded to the nearest ten?**

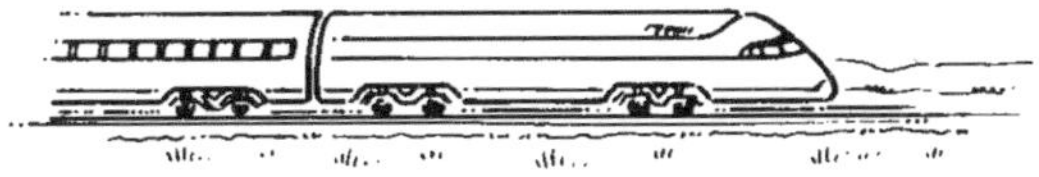

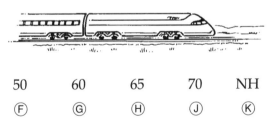

50	60	65	70	NH
Ⓕ	Ⓖ	Ⓗ	Ⓙ	Ⓚ

GO ON

Sample B

Roberto bought 11 pencils. Each pencil cost 7¢. How much did Roberto pay for all the pencils?

18¢	77¢	87¢	88¢	NH
Ⓐ	Ⓑ	Ⓒ	Ⓓ	Ⓔ

STOP

18 **It takes the juice from 3 oranges to make a full glass of orange juice. Ed wants to make 5 glasses of juice. How many oranges does Ed need?**

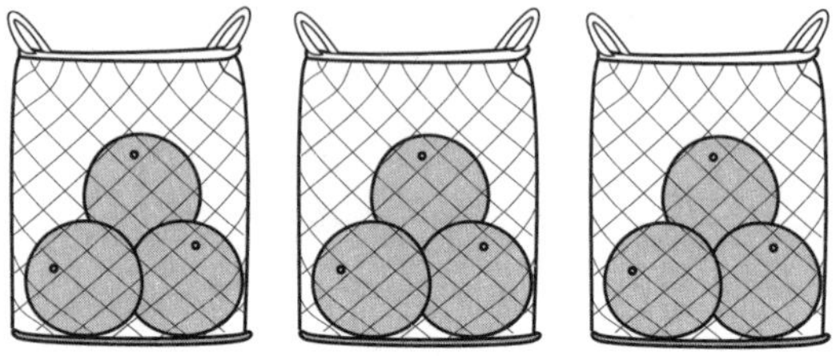

15	12	10	8	NH
Ⓐ	Ⓑ	Ⓒ	Ⓓ	Ⓔ

19 **Fay made a list of all the toy animals she owns.**

Mice	Bears	Dogs
15	3	9

How many toy animals does Fay own altogether?

12	18	24	27	NH
Ⓕ	Ⓖ	Ⓗ	Ⓙ	Ⓚ

20 **Noriko cut 46 fabric squares for a quilt. There were 18 striped squares. The rest were solid colors. How many solid-colored squares did Noriko cut?**

Ⓐ 28

Ⓑ 38

Ⓒ 63

Ⓓ 64

Ⓔ NH

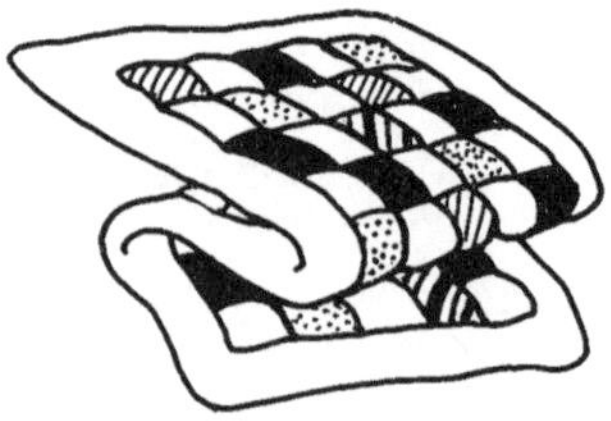

21 **Fran wants to buy this purse, which costs $10.00. She has $2.50. How much more money does she need to buy the purse?**

$10.00

$7.50	$7.75	$8.25	$8.50	NH
Ⓕ	Ⓖ	Ⓗ	Ⓙ	Ⓚ

22 **A group of 561 adults and 804 children went to the circus. How many more children than adults went on the outing?**

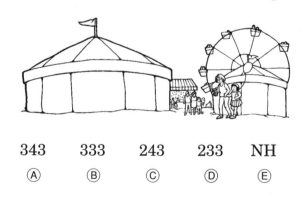

343	333	243	233	NH
Ⓐ	Ⓑ	Ⓒ	Ⓓ	Ⓔ

STOP

Language

Sample A

Let's Get a Pet

Kelly wants to have a pet. She's not sure what kind of pet she wants. Kelly's cousin Maureen has a few pets. Kelly decides to write Maureen a letter to find out which pet she likes best.

Why is Kelly writing this letter?

- Ⓐ to find out more about kittens
- Ⓑ to help her decide what pet to get
- Ⓒ to help her parents learn more about pets
- Ⓓ to learn to write better letters

STOP

For questions 1–4, darken the circle for the correct answer, or write in the answer.

Kelly found the book *Taking Care of a Pet* in the library. Use part of the Index from this book to answer questions 1 and 2.

Index

aquarium pets
  first aid and diseases, 248–249
beds
  for cats, 33
  for dogs, 21–22
cages
  canaries, 62–63
  hamsters, 54–55
  white mice, 51
first aid, 231–254
rabbits
  cleanliness, 42, 44
  handling, 41–42
  teeth, 44–45

1 Information about first aid for pets can be found on all these pages <u>except</u>—

232	245	250	260
Ⓐ	Ⓑ	Ⓒ	Ⓓ

2 Kelly can find information about cages for white mice on which pages?

pages 51

3 Kelly put these words in alphabetical (*ABC*) order so she could find them more quickly in the dictionary. Which list is correct?

- Ⓕ guinea pigs – gerbils – goldfish – guppies
- Ⓖ guppies – guinea pigs – goldfish – gerbils
- Ⓗ guppies – gerbils – goldfish – guinea pigs
- Ⓙ gerbils – goldfish – guinea pigs – guppies

4 Kelly found the book *How to Take Care of a Pet*. Where should she look to find the author's name?

- Ⓐ Chapter 1
- Ⓑ the title page
- Ⓒ the index
- Ⓓ the table of contents

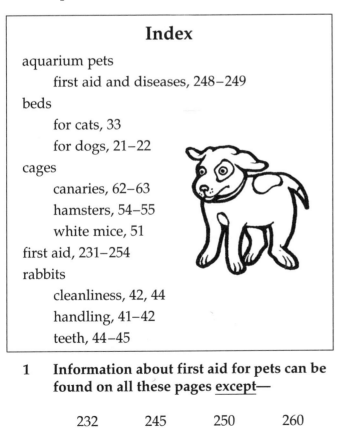

GO ON

Here is the first part of Kelly's letter. Read it carefully. Then answer questions 5–8.

Dear Maureen,

How are you doing? Are your pets doing well? I can get a
(1) **(2)** **(3)**
pet my mom and dad told me. Now I need to decide. Which
(4) **(5)**
one to get. My mom and dad bought me a new bicycle. I think
(6) **(7)**
having a pet will be fun. I know it's a big responsibility. Mom
(8) **(9)**
told me that I would have to take care of it. I'll have to give it
(10)
food and water. I'll have to make it comfortable. I can't wait to
(11) **(12)**
do all this. That's why I'm writing to you.
(13)

5 **The best way to write sentence 3 is—**

- Ⓕ My mom and dad told me that I can get a pet.
- Ⓖ My mom told me that I can get a pet, my dad, too.
- Ⓗ A pet my mom and dad told me I can get.
- Ⓙ As it is written.

6 **Which group of words is <u>not</u> a complete sentence? Write the number of the group of words.**

____

____

____

____

7 **Which of these sentences could be added after sentence 13?**

- Ⓐ Kittens are fun to have as pets.
- Ⓑ Do you have a new bicycle?
- Ⓒ What pet do you think I should get?
- Ⓓ Will you be able to come to my house?

8 **Which sentence does <u>not</u> belong in Kelly's letter?**

6	7	8	10
Ⓕ	Ⓖ	Ⓗ	Ⓙ

GO ON

Here is the next part of Kelly's letter. This part has groups of words underlined. Read the letter carefully. Then answer questions 9–14.

> (14) There are many pets I'd like to get. (15) I would love to have a kitten a puppy, and a hamster. (16) Dad says I have to choose one. (17) A kitten might be a good pet for me. (18) Kittens love to be cuddled. (19) I would be very gentle with it when I held it. (20) Kittens is very playful. (21) They love to play with little balls and string. (22) Kittens needed to be fed every day. (23) Do you think an kitten would be a good pet for me?
>
> sincerely yours,
> Kelly

9 **In sentence 15, a kitten a puppy, and a hamster. is best written—**

Ⓐ a kitten a puppy and a hamster.

Ⓑ a kitten, a puppy and a hamster.

Ⓒ a kitten, a puppy, and a hamster.

Ⓓ As it is written.

10 **In sentence 17, might be a good pet is best written—**

Ⓕ a good pet might be

Ⓖ might a good pet be

Ⓗ be a might good pet

Ⓙ As it is written.

11 **In sentence 20, Kittens is very is best written—**

Ⓐ Kittens are very

Ⓑ Kittens were very

Ⓒ Kittens am very

Ⓓ As it is written.

GO ON

12 **In sentence 22, <u>needed to be fed</u> is best written—**

Ⓕ needs to be fed

Ⓖ need to be fed

Ⓗ needing to be fed

Ⓙ As it is written.

13 **In sentence 23, <u>Do you think an kitten</u> is best written—**

Ⓐ Do you thinks an kitten

Ⓑ Do you thinks a kitten

Ⓒ Do you think a kitten

Ⓓ As it is written.

14 **At the end of Kelly's letter, <u>sincerely yours,</u> is best written—**

Ⓕ Sincerely Yours,

Ⓖ Sincerely yours,

Ⓗ sincerely Yours,

Ⓙ As it is written.

GO ON

Drew is writing a report on his trip to Arizona. Read the following. Then answer questions 15–18.

A Dry Land

Drew's teacher wants the class to write a report about their favorite vacation. Drew enjoyed seeing the desert. So, Drew decided to write his report about his trip to Arizona.

15 **What is the first thing Drew should do before he begins to write his paper?**

Ⓐ Remember what other vacations were like.

Ⓑ Buy books about deserts.

Ⓒ Make a list of what he saw in the desert.

Ⓓ Ask his sister to write about the desert, too.

16 **If Drew wants to find the meaning of the word <u>cactus</u>, where should he look first?**

Ⓕ an encyclopedia

Ⓖ a dictionary

Ⓗ a language arts book

Ⓙ an atlas

17 **If Drew wants to learn more about deserts, he should look in—**

Ⓐ an encyclopedia.

Ⓑ a dictionary.

Ⓒ a newspaper.

Ⓓ a language arts book.

Before Drew begins his report, he looks up some words in the dictionary.

18 **What definition best fits the word dry as used in the sentence below? Write the definition.**

Some plants grow well in a *dry* climate.

____

____

____

____

____

____

____

____

GO ON

Here is the first part of Drew's report. Read it carefully. Then answer questions 19–23.

Sunny Arizona

We stayed in hotels. We visited during the day many places.
(1) (2)
We had to drive many miles. Last year we visited Maine. Most
(3) (4) (5)
of the time we drove through a desert. I couldn't believe how
(6)
big it was. It is very dry in a desert. It is very sunny in a
(7) (8)
desert. A place is called a desert. If it gets less than ten inches
(9) (10)
of rain each year. Staying in a desert makes you thirsty. We
(11) (12)
made sure that we had plenty of water to drink.

19 Which sentence would best begin this paragraph?

- Ⓕ I like to go on vacation.
- Ⓖ My vacation to Arizona was so much fun!
- Ⓗ Next year we plan to visit Texas.
- Ⓙ Summer vacation starts in two weeks.

20 The best way to write sentence 2 is—

- Ⓐ During the day many places we visited.
- Ⓑ During the day we visited many places.
- Ⓒ Many places we visited during the day.
- Ⓓ As it is written.

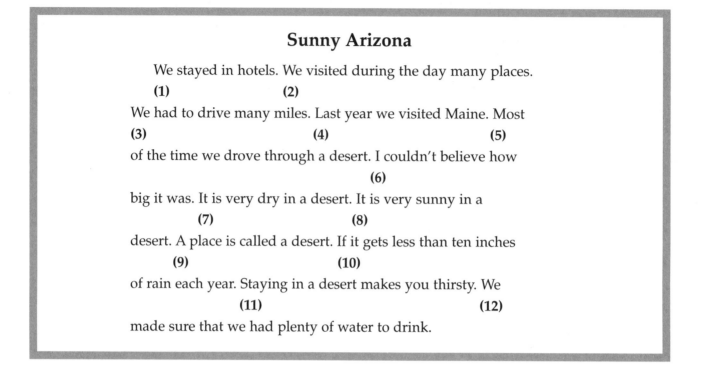

GO ON

21 **Which sentence does <u>not</u> belong in Drew's report? Write the number of the sentence.**

____

____

____

____

22 **Which of these is <u>not</u> a complete sentence?**

5	7	10	12
Ⓕ	Ⓖ	Ⓗ	Ⓙ

23 **What is the best way to combine sentences 7 and 8 without changing their meaning?**

Ⓐ Since it is very sunny it is dry in a desert.

Ⓑ It is very dry in a desert and it is very sunny.

Ⓒ Being very dry it is also very sunny in a desert.

Ⓓ It is very dry and sunny in a desert.

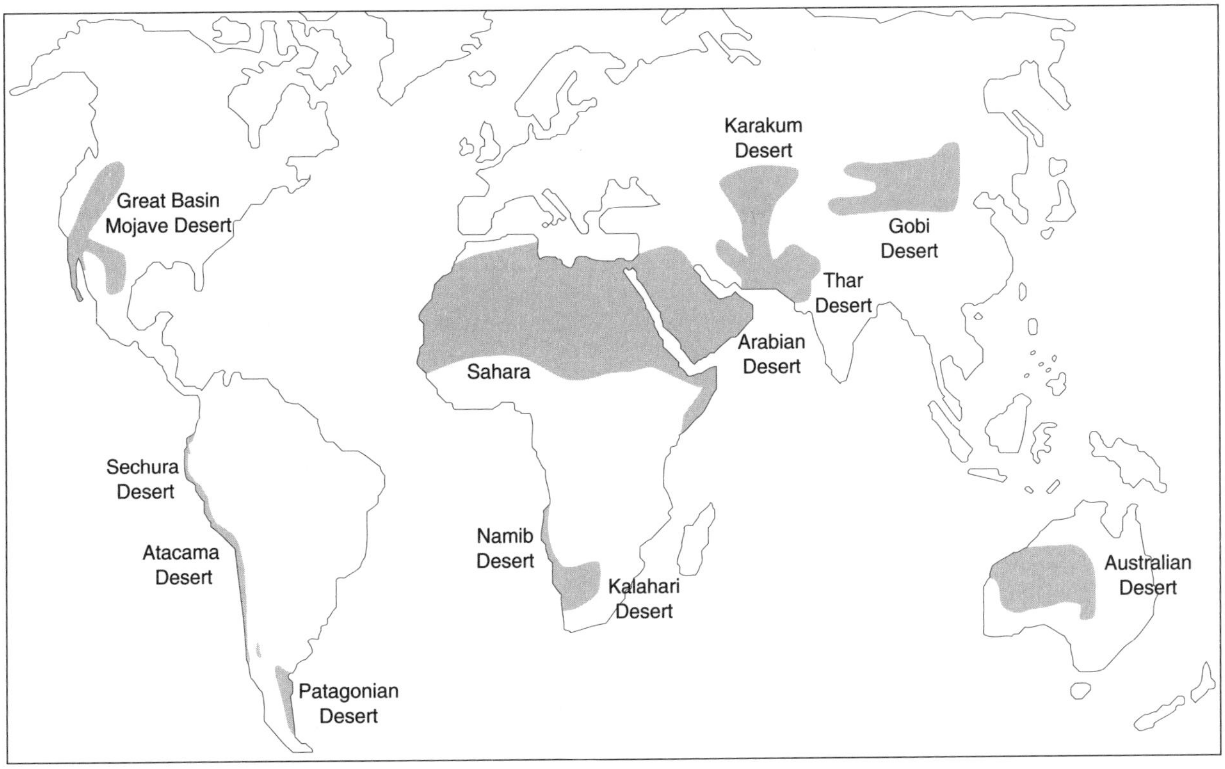

GO ON

Here is the next part of Drew's report. This part has groups of words underlined. Read the draft carefully. Then answer questions 24–27.

(13) I used to think that an desert was just all sand. (14) Some deserts in the world are mostly sand. (15) The desert that I saw in Arizona has some interesting plants. (16) One plant I saw was the cactus. (17) This kind of plant can survive with very little rain. (18) I also seen clumps of grass. (19) At certain times of the year a Desert does get some rain. (20) That's when you can see many colorful flowering plants. (21) I think the desert was a very interesting place to visit. (22) I hope I can visit it again someday.

24 In sentence 13, that an desert is best written—

- Ⓕ that a deserts
- Ⓖ that an deserts
- Ⓗ that a desert
- Ⓙ As it is written.

25 In sentence 18, I also seen is best written—

- Ⓐ I also saw
- Ⓑ I also see
- Ⓒ I also sees
- Ⓓ As it is written.

26 In sentence 19, a Desert does get is best written—

- Ⓕ a desert do get
- Ⓖ a desert does get
- Ⓗ a Desert do get
- Ⓙ As it is written.

27 In sentence 22, I can visit it again is best written—

- Ⓐ I cans visit it again
- Ⓑ i can visit it again
- Ⓒ I, can visit it again
- Ⓓ As it is written.

GO ON

For questions 28–35, read each sentence carefully. If one of the words is misspelled, darken the circle for that word. If all the words are spelled correctly, then darken the circle for *No mistake*.

28 The children laughd at the circus clowns. No mistake
 Ⓕ Ⓖ Ⓗ Ⓙ

29 We watched the snow falling on the mowntan. No mistake
 Ⓐ Ⓑ Ⓒ Ⓓ

30 We collected colorful seashells on the beachs of Hawaii. No mistake
 Ⓕ Ⓖ Ⓗ Ⓙ

31 This apple is sweet and juicy! No mistake
 Ⓐ Ⓑ Ⓒ Ⓓ

32 The family was able to safly leave the burning house. No mistake
 Ⓕ Ⓖ Ⓗ Ⓙ

33 The tinyest kitten is black and white. No mistake
 Ⓐ Ⓑ Ⓒ Ⓓ

34 Birds built nests in the branchs of the oak trees. No mistake
 Ⓕ Ⓖ Ⓗ Ⓙ

35 Lynn threw a penny into the wishing well. No mistake
 Ⓐ Ⓑ Ⓒ Ⓓ

STOP

Answer Key

Reading Skills

p. 8
Fact: Opals are stones that sparkle with many colors.

Fact: Coober Pedy is in South Australia.

p. 9
3. D

p. 10–11
1. D
2. D
3. A
4. C
5. B
6. C
7. D
8. A
9. D
10. B

p. 12–13
1. C
2. B
3. C
4. D
5. B
6. D
7. D
8. D
9. B
10. D

p. 14–15
1. A
2. D
3. A
4. C
5. C
6. D
7. B
8. C
9. C
10. A

p. 16–17
1. C
2. D
3. B
4. A
5. C
6. C
7. A
8. C
9. B
10. D

p. 18–19
1. B
2. A
3. C
4. B
5. C
6. B
7. C
8. A
9. D
10. D

p. 20–21
1. C
2. D
3. B
4. A
5. D
6. C
7. D
8. D
9. B
10. A

p. 22–23
1. D
2. C
3. D
4. A
5. B
6. C
7. C
8. D
9. C
10. A

p. 24–25
1. B
2. B
3. A
4. D
5. B
6. C
7. D
8. C
9. D
10. B

p. 26
Possible answers include:
1. A comet looks like a fuzzy star with a tail.
2. The tail looks long and bright when the comet flies near the Sun.
3. Halley's Comet can be seen about every 77 years.

p. 27
Check that you have four facts in your story.

p. 28
2, 1, 3

p. 29
3. A

p. 30–31
1. 2, 3, 1
2. B
3. A
4. B
5. C

p. 32–33
1. 2, 3, 1
2. A
3. C
4. C
5. B

p. 34–35
1. 2, 1, 3
2. A
3. B
4. B
5. C

p. 36–37
1. 2, 1, 3
2. C
3. A
4. B
5. A

p. 38–39
1. 2, 3, 1
2. C
3. A
4. B
5. C

p. 40–41
1. 3, 2, 1
2. C
3. A
4. B
5. A

p. 42–43
1. 3, 1, 2
2. B
3. C
4. C
5. A

p. 44–45
1. 3, 1, 2
2. C
3. A
4. B
5. B

p. 46
Possible answers include:
1. Leo said he had a rock collection at lunch.
2. Leo smiled and thanked his friends.
3. Jonelle decided to give Leo a rock after he told her about his collection.
4. Leo opened Duane's present second.

p. 47
Check that your story is written in sequence.
Check that you have used time order words, such as first, next, and last.

p. 49
2. A
3. C

p. 50–51
1. D
2. A
3. A
4. B
5. D
6. C
7. B
8. D
9. A
10. B
11. C
12. B
13. A
14. B
15. A
16. D

p. 52–53
1. B
2. A
3. C
4. C
5. D
6. B
7. D
8. B
9. D
10. B
11. A
12. D
13. C
14. B
15. B
16. A

p. 54–55
1. B
2. D
3. A
4. C
5. D
6. B
7. D
8. A
9. D
10. A
11. A
12. C
13. B
14. D
15. C
16. A

p. 56–57
1. B
2. A
3. D
4. A
5. A
6. C
7. B
8. B
9. B
10. A
11. B
12. D
13. A
14. C
15. A
16. D

p. 58–59
1. C
2. C
3. A
4. B
5. D
6. D
7. A
8. C

p. 60–61
1. C
2. C
3. B
4. B
5. C
6. B
7. A
8. D

p. 62–63
1. A
2. B
3. A
4. D
5. A
6. C
7. B
8. D

p. 64–65
1. D
2. B
3. A
4. C
5. D
6. A
7. B
8. D

p. 66
Possible answers include:
1. wet or clean
2. dirt or mud
3. stars or moon
4. day or summer
5. class or school
6. sit or play

p. 67
Possible answers include:
1. picking up litter or planting trees
2. the principal or the mayor
3. make a garden or plant flowers
4. the mall or his favorite store
5. a sale sign or an ad
6. a book or earrings

p. 69
2. The correct answer is B. There are details about the Sahara's location, rainfall, and temperature. If you add these details together, you will get the main idea.

p. 70–71
1. A
2. A
3. C
4. B
5. C

p. 72–73
1. C
2. B
3. C
4. C
5. B

p. 74–75
1. A
2. C
3. B
4. B
5. A

p. 76–77
1. B
2. C
3. A
4. A
5. B

p. 78–79
1. A
2. B
3. C
4. B
5. A

p. 80–81
1. D
2. D
3. B
4. A
5. B

p. 82–83
1. D
2. A
3. A
4. C
5. A

p. 84–85
1. A
2. C
3. B
4. D
5. A

p. 86
Possible answers include:
1. Mary Myers was the first woman balloon pilot.
2. Beto is a famous jockey because he learned to ride horses at his uncle's farm.
3. There's still a lot to learn about oceans.

p. 87
Check that you have underlined your main idea.
Check that you have used three details in your story.

p. 89
zebra, elephant, giraffe, dolphin

p. 90–91
1. B
2. C
3. C
4. C
5. A

p. 92–93
1. C
2. A
3. C
4. B
5. A

p. 94–95
1. A
2. A
3. C
4. C
5. C

p. 96–97
1. C
2. D
3. A
4. B
5. D

p. 98–99
1. C
2. D
3. C
4. A
5. B

p. 100–101
1. D
2. C
3. A
4. B
5. C

p. 102–103
1. B
2. A
3. C
4. A
5. D

p. 104–105
1. B
2. D
3. A
4. D
5. C

p. 106
Possible answers include:
1. Movies didn't always have talking.
2. The English family's goldfish was at least 43 years old.
3. Most people who see the Super Bowl watch it on television.

p. 107
Possible answers include:
1. Raul was not born in America. He came to America from Cuba.
2. Raul did not meet his granduncle in Cuba. He found out about his granduncle after he moved to Florida.
3. Raul and his mom don't live alone. They live with Raul's granduncle.
4. Raul probably doesn't want to move back to Florida. He thinks he will like New Jersey.

p. 110–111
1. B
2. C
3. D
4. A
5. A

p. 112–113
1. A
2. C
3. C
4. D
5. C

p. 114–115
1. D
2. B
3. A
4. A
5. A

p. 116–117
1. B
2. D
3. A
4. C
5. A

p. 118–119
1.
A. F
B. I
C. F
D. F
2.
A. I
B. F
C. F
D. I
3.
A. F
B. I
C. I
D. F
4.
A. I
B. I
C. I
D. F
5.
A. F
B. I
C. I
D. F

p. 120–121
1.
A. I
B. F
C. I
D. F
2.
A. F
B. F
C. I
D. I
3.
A. I
B. I
C. I
D. F
4.
A. F
B. F
C. F
D. I
5.
A. F
B. I
C. F
D. F

p. 122–123
1.
A. F
B. F
C. F
D. I
2.
A. F
B. F
C. I
D. F
3.
A. I
B. F
C. I
D. F
4.
A. I

B. F
C. F
D. F
5.
A. I
B. I
C. I
D. F

p. 124–125
1.
A. F
B. I
C. F
D. I
2.
A. F
B. F
C. F
D. F
3.
A. F
B. F
C. I
D. F
4.
A. F
B. F
C. F
D. I
5.
A. F
B. F
C. I
D. F

p. 126
Possible answers include:
1. Karen kept the pot on a shelf next to a window.
2. Leon's pencil needed sharpening.
3. The dog was a guide dog or Seeing Eye dog.

p. 127
Possible answers include:
1. She thought she wasn't tall enough. She didn't think she played well enough.
2. He needs to be able to catch passes.
3. Mary is willing to learn, hard-working, and serious.
4. Mary is not certain about her skills. She seems to think she has more to learn.

Spelling Skills

p. 132
1. ask, matter, black, add, match, Saturday, class, apple, subtract, thank, catch, January, after, hammer, half
2. laugh

p. 133
1. add
2. matter
3. match
4. class
5. after
6. thank
7. half
8. ask
9. apple
10. subtract
11. hammer
12. black
13. laugh
14. January
15. catch

p. 134
Spell correctly: January, catch, apple, after, half
Capitalize: Did, To, You
Add period after: January, glass

p. 135
1. hammer, January, matter
2. add, class, match
3. ask, Saturday, thank
4. black, laugh, subtract

p. 136
1. page, change, face, save, ate, place, late, safe, came
2. gray, away, pay, May
3. great, break
4. April

p. 137
1. came
2. safe
3. late
4. place
5. page
6. great
7. change
8. gray
9. May
10. ate
11. break
12. pay
13. late
14. save
15. face

p. 138
Spell correctly: safe, place, away, late, break
Capitalize: It, Dig, Then
Take out: from, to

p. 139
Insert words: save, away, gray, May, page, face, great
Capitalize: Heather, Last, Then, He
Add period after: stamps, book, Scooter

p. 140
1. rain, sail, afraid, aid, train, wait, aim, paint
2. fable, danger, table, able, paper
3. eight, weigh
4. they

p. 141
1. aid
2. afraid
3. wait
4. danger
5. able
6. table
7. eight
8. train
9. sail
10. fable
11. rain
12. they
13. weigh
14. paint
15. aim

p. 142
Spell correctly: able, train, eight, They, wait
Capitalize: Sanchez, Each, Our
Take out: with, that

p. 143
1. cable
2. carton
3. coarse
4. black
5. block
6. scheme
7. comb
8. subtract
9. clock
10. card
11. corn
12. socks

p. 144
1. next, egg, end, help, spent, second, forget, dress, address, test
2. ready, read, head
3. again, said
4. says

p. 145
1. address
2. again
3. read
4. forget
5. spent
6. ready
7. help
8. says
9. second
10. test
11. said
12. next
13. end
14. dress
15. egg

p. 146
Spell correctly: forget, says, head, help, second
Capitalize: I, She
Add period after: things, help, finger

p. 147
1. then
2. 3
3. address [page number and number of meanings will vary by dictionary]
4. egg [page number and number of meanings will vary]
5. help [page number and number of meanings will vary]
6. next [page number and number of meanings will vary]

p. 148
1. tests, pages, papers, hammers, tables, clowns, paints, apples, eggs, hands, trains, places
2. dresses, classes, matches, addresses

p. 149
1. paints
2. hammers
3. apples
4. eggs
5. papers
6. pages
7. dresses
8. addresses
9. tests
10. matches
11. trains
12. hands
13. places
14. clowns
15. classes

p. 150
Spell correctly: Pages, clowns, places, eggs, tables
Capitalize: It, They, You
Add period after: world, movie

p. 151
1. addresses, address [number of word forms will vary by dictionary]
2. hands, hand [number of word forms will vary]
3. pages, page [number of word forms will vary]
4. paints, paint [number of word forms will vary]
5. trains, train [number of word forms will vary]

p. 152–153
1. catch
2. half
3. laugh
4. subtract
5. January
6. April
7. place
8. great
9. gray
10. break
11. danger
12. afraid
13. they
14. weigh
15. table
16. ready
17. again
18. says
19. second
20. address
21. apples
22. eggs
23. hammers
24. places
25. matches

p. 154
1. slept, February, them, never, when, sent, kept, September, best, then, cents, Wednesday, better
2. friend
3. many
4. guess

p. 155
1. many
2. friend
3. September
4. Wednesday
5. slept
6. February
7. best
8. sent
9. when
10. then
11. kept
12. them
13. better
14. guess
15. never

p. 156
Spell correctly: friend, them, guess, kept, September
Capitalize: February, Texas, Kim
Add question mark after: did, September

p. 157
1. The book I like best was written by Fred Gibson.
2. It is about a dog called Old Yeller.
3. Travis and Old Yeller have many adventures.
4. Carl Anderson wrote about a horse named Blaze.
5. Blaze was kept by a boy named Billy.
6. A horse named Thunderbolt became friends with Billy and Blaze.

p. 158
1. street, free, wheel, queen, sneeze, meet, need, sleep
2. please, read, each, team, sea, dream, meat
3. people

p. 159
1. sleep
2. street
3. people
4. sneeze
5. read
6. wheel
7. sea
8. meat
9. team
10. dream
11. meet
12. free
13. please
14. each
15. need

p. 160
Spell correctly: team, people, meet, each, Read
Capitalize: One, Each, After
Take out: a, of

p. 161
1. I had a wonderful dream last night.
2. All the people who live on my street were in it.
3. I used a big wheel to steer our big ship out to sea.
4. We had a feast of fruit and roasted meat on an island.

p. 162
1. even
2. only, story, family, sleepy, carry, sunny, funny, very, every, city, penny, happy, busy
3. these
4. key

p. 163
1. carry
2. very
3. key
4. funny
5. every
6. penny
7. these
8. story
9. only
10. happy
11. sunny
12. busy
13. city
14. sleepy
15. even

p. 164
Spell correctly: city, family, happy, busy, very
Capitalize: She, We, Thursday
Add period after: Illinois, morning

p. 165
1–3. [page numbers will vary by dictionary]
4. carry [page number will vary]
5. even [page number will vary]
6. funny [page number will vary]
7. key [page number will vary]

p. 166
1. Sunday, under, summer, sun, lunch, such, much
2. does
3. from, money, nothing, mother, month, front, other, Monday

p. 167
1. front
2. under
3. money
4. such
5. nothing
6. does
7. month
8. Monday
9. from
10. sun
11. Sunday
12. mother
13. much
14. summer
15. other

p. 168
Spell correctly: money, Monday, Summer, front, lunch
Capitalize: Each, Sunday, Does
Add question mark after: it, you

p. 169
1. What comes once in a month, twice in a moment, but never in a hundred years? the letter m
2. What do you lose whenever you stand up? your lap
3. What can you put into the apple pie you have for lunch? your teeth

p. 170
1. they'll, you'll, I'll, we'll, she'll
2. I've, we've, you've, they've
3. I'd, you'd, they'd
4. she's, it's, he's
5. I'm

p. 171
1. It's
2. I've
3. He's
4. You'll
5. You've
6. They'd
7. They've
8. We'll
9. We've
10. I'm
11. She's
12. they'll
13. we'll
14. you'd
15. I'll

p. 172
Spell correctly: I'm, I'd, We've, I've, We'll
Capitalize: Pete, Collins
Add period after: neighborhood, station, owner

p. 173
1. I'll, wi
2. he's, i
3. it's, i
4. they've, ha
5. you'd, ha
6. I'm, a
7. you'd, woul
8. she's, ha

p. 174–175
1. friend
2. Wednesday
3. guess
4. many
5. February
6. queen
7. team
8. people
9. meet
10. please
11. family
12. even
13. every
14. key
15. these
16. does
17. month
18. other
19. lunch
20. such
21. I'm
22. you've
23. she'll
24. they'd
25. it's

p. 176
1. just, hundred, sum, must, butter, supper, number
2. won, cover
3. lovely, something, done, some, shove, none, one

p. 177
1. won
2. cover
3. something
4. some
5. sum
6. one
7. hundred
8. must
9. number
10. none
11. done
12. lovely
13. shove
14. just
15. supper

p. 178
Spell correctly: just, number, lovely, hundred, done
Capitalize: Yesterday, Rocket, Now
Add period after: soon, state

p. 179
1. sail
2. sale
3. ate
4. eight
5. sun
6. son
7. won
8. one
9. sum, some

p. 180
1. thing, little, winter, kick, river, dish, fill, think, spring, which, children
2. pretty, December
3. begin
4. build
5. been

p. 181
1. kick
2. children
3. build
4. river
5. winter
6. dish
7. begin
8. pretty
9. little
10. think
11. which
12. been
13. spring
14. fill
15. thing

p. 182
Spell correctly: build, winter, river, December, spring
Capitalize: Luke, I, Maybe
Add period after: barn, year

p. 183
1. little; circle "simple", "little"
2. many; circle "many", "thick"
3. icy; circle "cold", "icy"
4. dangerous; circle "Thin", "some", "dangerous"
5. pretty; circle "Many", "pretty"
6. hot; circle "hot", "summer"
7. shallow; circle "large", "shallow"
8. brown; circle "red", "brown"
9. every; circle "every"

p. 184
1. alike, while, white, line, size miles, times, nice, drive, write, inside, mine, shine
2. lion, tiny
3. eyes

p. 185
1. drive
2. miles
3. line
4. while
5. size
6. shine
7. nice
8. mine
9. times

10. white
11. eyes
12. write
13. tiny
14. alike
15. inside

p. 186
Spell correctly: miles, line, inside, eyes, tiny
Capitalize: They, Once, Check
Add period after: cheers, disappointed

p. 187
1–4. [guide words and page numbers will vary by dictionary]

p. 188
1. Friday, kind, child, mind, behind
2. fly, why, try, sky, cry, by
3. high, right, light, night
4. buy

p. 189
1. behind
2. fly
3. Friday
4. kind
5. by
6. right
7. light
8. high
9. child
10. cry
11. night
12. try
13. buy
14. mind
15. why

p. 190
Spell correctly: Friday, behind, night, mind, why
Capitalize: Sam, That, Write
Add period after: again, sock

p. 191
1. second
2. k
3. t
4. sky, story
5. behind, buy, by
6. finish, fly, Friday

p. 192
1. wished, asked, dreamed, rained, handed, painted, filled, subtracted, thanked, waited
2. ending, guessing, laughing, meeting, sleeping, reading

p. 193
1. handed
2. thanked
3. waited
4. meeting
5. guessing
6. dreamed
7. rained
8. wished
9. painted
10. reading
11. sleeping
12. asked
13. laughing
14. ending
15. filled

p. 194
Spell correctly: meeting, thanked, wished, asked, ending
Capitalize: This, He, The
Take out: to, it

p. 195
1. Betsy asked Paul, "Who painted this picture?"
2. She saw that Paul was sleeping.
3. Betsy shouted, "Boo!"
4. Paul jumped up fast.
5. "Oh, Betsy," he cried. "Now I'll never know the ending of my dream!"
6. They both started laughing.

p. 196–197
1. lovely
2. hundred
3. won
4. butter
5. done
6. which
7. been
8. pretty
9. build
10. children
11. eyes
12. write
13. lion
14. while
15. tiny
16. Why
17. buy
18. right
19. night
20. behind
21. laughing
22. wished
23. guessing
24. dreamed
25. thanked

p. 198
1. October, shop, block, bottle, o'clock, sorry, socks, problem, jog, lock, bottom, forgot, body
2. what, wash, was

p. 199
1. socks
2. block
3. jog
4. sorry
5. what
6. forgot
7. o'clock
8. was
9. October
10. body
11. bottom
12. shop
13. problem
14. wash
15. bottle

p. 200
Spell correctly: socks, bottom, job, block, problem
Capitalize: Today, They, Sparky
Add period after: school, them

p. 201
1. cap, children, clock, cover
2. salt, shop, sorry, stack
3. wash, west, what, wonder
4. farmer, feed, forgot, funny

p. 202
1. whole, hope, joke, wrote, alone, hole, close
2. slow, blow, show, yellow, snow, know
3. goes, toe
4. November

p. 203
1. goes
2. wrote
3. hope
4. whole
5. know
6. alone
7. yellow
8. close
9. November
10. toe
11. snow
12. blow
13. hole
14. slow
15. show

p. 204
Spell correctly: November, know, hope, yellow, goes
Capitalize: I, Thanks, Why
Add period after: sweater, tablet

p. 205
1. Jack (hurt) his toe.
2. Please (show) me your new shoes.
3. Snow (fell) all night long.
4. We (ate) the whole pizza.
5. Krista (bought) a yellow skateboard
6. Scooter (dug) a hole in the yard.
7. Ming (wrote) a story about a crow.
8. Mrs. Sosa (goes) to lunch with our class.

p. 206
1. most, ago, hold, hello, open, over, comb, almost, both, gold
2. coat, loaf, toast, boat, road
3. cocoa

p. 207
1. comb
2. gold
3. ago
4. both
5. hello
6. hold
7. most
8. almost
9. open
10. over
11. loaf
12. coat
13. toast
14. road
15. boat

p. 208
Spell correctly: Hello, gold, comb, loaf, toast
Capitalize: Adam, We, Do
Add question mark after: beach, jam

p. 209
ACROSS
3. both
4. cocoa
6. road
7. hold
DOWN
1. over
2. coat
3. ago
5. almost
6. boat

p. 210
1. book, took, cook, stood, wood, poor, foot, shook, cookies
2. sure, put, full, pull
3. should, would, could

p. 211
1. pull
2. stood
3. sure
4. poor
5. full
6. took
7. foot
8. should
9. wood
10. cookies
11. could
12. cook
13. put
14. would
15. shook

p. 212
Spell correctly: stood, pull, poor, Could, sure
Capitalize: The, What, If
Take out: an, that

p. 213
1. Many wood products come from Maine.
2. I am sure that the largest state is Alaska.
3. Everyone should visit Chicago, Illinois.
4. Would you like to go to New Orleans?
5. San Francisco shook during an earthquake.
6. My friend from Toronto sent me some cookies.

p. 214
1. sneezed, smiling, hoped, shining, pleased, liked, taking, driving, closed
2. beginning, dropping, stopped, dropped, jogged, hopping, shopping

p. 215
1. jogged
2. beginning
3. closed
4. hoped
5. liked
6. shining
7. stopped
8. smiling
9. hopping
10. sneezed
11. taking
12. dropped
13. driving

14. pleased
15. dropping

p. 216
Spell correctly: stopped, liked, pleased, smiling, driving
Capitalize: I, My, When
Add period after: one, soon

p. 217
1. School closed for vacation on May 28, 2004.
2. On June 25, 1999, Ms. Padden jogged in a race.
3. Old friends dropped in to visit us on February 4, 2003.
4. Ana hoped her party would be on May 17, 2006.

p. 218–219
1. o'clock
2. bottle
3. socks
4. wash
5. hole
6. yellow
7. wrote
8. goes
9. know
10. November
11. toast
12. almost
13. comb
14. road
15. hello
16. cookies
17. poor
18. should
19. shook
20. sure
21. shining
22. dropped
23. hoped
24. stopped
25. hopping

p. 220
1. noon, tooth, school, too
2. blue, Tuesday, true, few, knew, news
3. huge, used, June
4. who, two, move

p. 221
1. noon
2. news
3. who
4. tooth
5. move
6. school
7. blue
8. June
9. few
10. two
11. too
12. huge
13. true
14. used
15. knew

p. 222
Spell correctly: Tuesday, noon, two, blue, who
Capitalize: Here, It, Guess
Add period after: track, race

p. 223
1. few
2. tooth
3. move
4. huge

p. 224
1. curl, turn, Thursday, fur
2. girl, bird, first, dirt, third
3. world, word, work, worm
4. learn, earth
5. were

p. 225
1. worm
2. girl
3. earth or Earth
4. first
5. third
6. turn
7. Thursday
8. word
9. dirt
10. were
11. learn
12. work
13. curl
14. world
15. fur

p. 226
Spell correctly: worm, third, curl, dirt, earth
Capitalize: The, He, The
Add period after: it, morning

p. 227
1. add
2. dirty
3. huge
4. young
5. full, empty
6. turn, spin
7. first, last
8. earth, world

p. 228
1. dark, yard, art, market, garden, hard, father, March, arm, barn, start, star, card, sharp, bark
2. heart

p. 229
1. garden
2. market
3. March
4. card
5. barn
6. yard
7. dark
8. hard
9. father
10. sharp
11. start
12. art
13. star, star
14. heart, heart
15. bark, bark

p. 230
Spell correctly: card, art, start, garden, yard
Capitalize: Are, We, Mary
Add question mark after: sing, us

p. 231
1. Meaning 2
2. Meaning 1 [sentences will vary]

p. 232
1. coin, choice, spoil, boil, voice, soil, noise, point, broil, join, oil
2. boy, royal, toy, joy, enjoy

p. 233
1. royal
2. oil
3. toy
4. joy
5. voice
6. spoil
7. join
8. coin
9. boy
10. enjoy
11. choice
12. noise
13. soil
14. broil
15. point

p. 234
Spell correctly: royal, choice, spoil, joy, voice
Capitalize: Nothing, James, Send
Add period after: want, joy

p. 235
1. We will (enjoy) visiting Minneapolis.
2. My dog Max makes a lot of (noise)!
3. Can you (point) out Mallory Street?
4. This (coin) was made in Colorado.
5. Mrs. Hays bought a (toy) for her baby.
6. Kevin and I want to (join) the baseball team.

p. 236
1. isn't, weren't, doesn't, hadn't, mustn't, wouldn't, won't, shouldn't, aren't, wasn't, don't, couldn't, didn't, hasn't, haven't
2. can't

p. 237
1. won't
2. don't
3. couldn't
4. wouldn't
5. doesn't
6. wasn't
7. hadn't
8. mustn't
9. didn't
10. can't
11. hasn't
12. haven't
13. aren't
14. weren't
15. isn't

p. 238
Spell correctly: couldn't, hasn't, Wouldn't, won't, Doesn't
Capitalize: It, Rose, You Take out: in, like

p. 239
1. isn't
2. aren't
3. weren't
4. wasn't

p. 240–241
1. true
2. used
3. too
4. Two
5. knew
6. Few
7. huge
8. girl
9. were
10. curl
11. earth
12. worm
13. sharp
14. father
15. garden
16. heart
17. voice
18. enjoy
19. royal
20. soil
21. can't
22. aren't
23. haven't
24. won't
25. weren't

p. 242
1. frog, along, long, off, belong, strong
2. walk, water, always, mall, tall, talk
3. bought, brought
4. because
5. draw

p. 243
1. tall
2. off
3. always
4. strong
5. long
6. talk
7. water
8. mall
9. brought
10. draw
11. frog
12. belong
13. along
14. walk
15. bought

p. 244
Spell correctly: always, talk, water, because, along
Capitalize: Jane, I, It's, We
Take out: you, me

p. 245
1. My (sister) <u>hid behind a tall tree</u>.
2. (Ling) <u>bought a baseball</u>.
3. (Mrs. Martinez) <u>took a long vacation</u>.
4. (I) <u>will draw a picture of you</u>.
5. (The old clock) <u>fell off the shelf</u>.

p. 246
1. August, autumn
2. morning, popcorn, before, corner, storm, north, born, fork, sport
3. door, floor, four, pour
4. quart

p. 247
1. popcorn
2. fork
3. storm
4. corner
5. pour
6. north
7. autumn
8. morning
9. before
10. quart
11. floor
12. door
13. four
14. sport
15. born

p. 248
Spell correctly: sport, Before, popcorn, storm, morning
Capitalize: Here, Also, You
Add period after: go, backpack

p. 249
1. August, aunt, autumn
2. point, porch, pour
3. foggy, fond, four
4. money, moon, morning

p. 250
1. house, sound, ground, found, about, hour, around, count, our
2. flower, town, tower, brown, power, down, owl

p. 251
1. house
2. sound
3. hour
4. tower
5. owl
6. down
7. power
8. about
9. flower
10. ground
11. found
12. count
13. brown
14. around
15. our

p. 252
Spell correctly: sound, house, owl, brown, about
Capitalize: We, It, Chris
Take out: our, to

p. 253
1. broth
2. maintain
3. admire
4. dome
5. fire
6. wire
7. starch
8. deer, dear

p. 254
1. near, hear, deer, ear, year, here, dear
2. care, where, stairs, chair, air, hair
3. fire, wire, tire

p. 255
1. hair
2. stairs
3. wire
4. dear
5. air
6. deer
7. hear
8. care
9. ear
10. year
11. near
12. where
13. tire
14. fire
15. here

p. 256
Spell correctly: chair, near, air, care, year
Capitalize: Are, Do, I
Add question mark after: nights, read

p. 257
1. stairs, where, hair
2. fire, wire, tire
3. year, here, near

p. 258
1. taller, tallest, longer, longest, stronger, strongest, greater, greatest, sharper, sharpest
2. dirtier, dirtiest, funnier, funniest
3. hotter, hottest

p. 259
1. hotter
2. sharpest
3. sharper
4. strongest
5. dirtiest
6. taller
7. funniest
8. tallest
9. greater
10. longer
11. stronger
12. longest
13. hottest
14. greatest
15. funnier

p. 260
Spell correctly: greatest, longer, taller, dirtier, greater
Capitalize: Spring, The, Having
Add period after: all, garden

p. 261
1. Sharon tells the funniest jokes we've ever heard.
2. The sun is hotter today than it was yesterday.
3. Gigi is the tallest girl on the basketball team.
4. Twenty is greater than ten.

p. 262–263
1. bought
2. because
3. strong
4. talk
5. draw
6. quart
7. pour
8. autumn
9. before
10. floor
11. hour
12. owl
13. count
14. tower
15. air
16. deer
17. where
18. here
19. wire
20. near
21. care
22. sharpest
23. greater
24. hottest
25. funnier

Math Skills

p. 268

	a		b
	Tens	Ones	
1.	6	4	= 64
2.	4	8	= 48
3.	3	9	= 39
4.	8	1	= 81
5.	9	1	= 91
6.	5	2	= 52

p. 269

		a		b
	Hundreds	Tens	Ones	
1.	1	2	4	= 124
2.	3	4	6	= 346
3.	2	8	9	= 289
4.	4	0	7	= 407

p. 270

		a			b
	Th	H	T	O	
1.	1,	1	2	5	= 1,125
2.	3,	0	4	2	= 3,042
3.	2,	6	0	9	= 2,609
4.	3,	4	2	0	= 3,420

p. 271
1. 3 thousands 0 hundreds 0 tens 3 ones
2. 1 thousand 8 hundreds 0 tens 7 ones
3. 8 thousands 1 hundred 4 tens 0 ones
4. 2 thousands 7 hundreds 9 tens 4 ones
5. 3 thousands 6 hundreds 8 tens 2 ones
6. 4 thousands 0 hundreds 3 tens 6 ones
7. 9 thousands 8 hundreds 0 tens 5 ones
8. 0 thousands 3 hundreds 5 tens 4 ones
9. 5,006
10. 620
11. 5,236
12. 6,571
13. 3,158
14. 7,921
15. 1,320
16. 239

p. 273
Wording for rules may vary.
1. Rule: Skip count by twos. Answer: 8
2. Rule: Add 1 hundred. Answer: 800
3. Rule: Skip count by fives. Answer: 20
4. Rule: Skip count by tens. Answer: 40
5. Rule: Add 1 ten. Answer: 56
6. Rule: Add 1 one. Answer: 113, 114

p. 274
1. 8 ones
2. 2 ones
3. 2 tens
4. 2 hundreds
5. 5 hundreds
6. 1 thousand
7. 2 thousands
8. 188 feet
10. 4,029 points

p. 275

	a	b	c
1.	2,368	1,085	7,654
2.	5,609	9,472	4,961

3. 827
4. 1,413
5. 5,904
6. 732
7. 9,540
8. four thousand, seven hundred fifty-six
9. two hundred seventeen
10. six thousand, fifty-nine
11. eight thousand, one hundred twelve
12. five thousand, ninety-nine

p. 276

	a	b	c
1.	>	<	=
2.	<	<	<
3.	<	>	=
4.	<	>	<
5.	>	<	>

p. 277

		a	
1.	24	36	59
2.	9	17	23
3.	108	116	123
		b	
1.	19	47	75
2.	25	35	42
3.	158	299	759
		c	
1.	22	42	62
2.	88	100	267
3.	238	278	288

p. 278
1. about 50 pencils
2. about 30 gallons
3. about 100 miles

p. 279
a
1. about 8,000 books
2. about 6 inches
3. about 30 students
4. about 4 feet
5. about 8,700 degrees

b
1. about 10 windows
2. about 9,000 pounds
3. about 2,500 miles
4. about 6,000 gallons
5. about 4 miles
6. 4,215
7. 324
8. 9,680

9. 351
10. 79
11. 6,429

p. 281

1. Theodore Roosevelt
2. Elvis Presley: 18 number one songs
Beatles: 20 number one songs
Michael Jackson: 13 number one songs
3. card tricks: Mark
coin tricks: Liz
rabbit tricks: Shawna

p. 282

	a	b	c
1.	81	43	671
2.	267	1,354	283

3. 739
4. 1,580
5. 0 thousands 0 hundreds 4 tens 7 ones
6. 0 thousands 6 hundreds 2 tens 9 ones
7. 7 thousands 8 hundreds 0 tens 9 ones
8. one hundred nineteen
9. three thousand, sixty-five
10. < > <
11. 73
12. 836
13. 5,940
14. 1,091

p. 283

15.
a: 17 31 48
b: 64 72 89
c: 185 267 325

22.
a: about 20 flowers
b: about 500 pounds

Wording for rule may vary.
17. Rule: Skip count by 2 tens.
Answer: 80
18. swim: Mei, baseball: Jamie, Tennis: Anita

p. 284

	a	b	c
1.	5	17	13
2.	9	9	14
3.	8	10	3
4.	15	15	8
5.	12	6	4
6.	12	14	14
7.	11	7	13
8.	18	9	7
9.	5	9	11
10.	11	17	2
11.	9	3	11

p. 285

	a	b	c
1.	9	10	14

	a	b	c	d	e	f	g
2.	8	6	12	9	9	13	11
3.	12	0	16	11	10	7	12
4.	15	14	4	4	3	12	16
5.	6	8	15	6	11	9	10

p. 286

	a	b	c	d	e	f
1.	85	31	47	23	28	56
2.	98	92	89	74	99	91
3.	86	67	53	98	79	99
4.	19	67				

p. 287

	a	b	c	d	e	f
1.	847	591	698	194	487	566
2.	988	993	958	779	629	794
3.	986	156	795	576	749	829
4.	864	997				

p. 288

	a	b	c	d	e	f
1.	30	53	81	38	93	41
2.	43	70	90	37	95	60
3.	61	62	91	94	47	91

p. 289

	a	b	c	d	e	f
1.	637	391	250	551	371	763
2.	871	962	761	697	990	356
3.	750	480	984	891	890	762
4.	185	951				

p. 291

1. Jill: 13 pairs, Dave: 8 pairs
2. hot dog: $5, soda: $3
3. Nita: 15 years old, Joe: 5 years old

p. 292

1. 60 pounds
2. 276 gold medals
3. 273 shells
4. 74 gallons
5. 390 cards

p. 293

	a	b	c	d	e	f
1.	219	620	802	526	706	639
2.	807	807	938	509	829	837
3.	532	227	928	818	988	337
4.	726	408				

p. 294

	a	b	c	d	e	f
1.	962	428	712	305	614	745
2.	454	236	713	553	908	441
3.	934	232	551	943	917	521
4.	315	810				

p. 295

	a	b	c	d	e	f
1.	161	962	86	81	822	196
2.	848	31	82	997	656	173
3.	766	735	332	967	51	82
4.	73	355	42	873	184	485
5.	93	793	91	654	90	944
6.	606	50	80	674	33	633
7.	53	727				

p. 297

1. about 300 roses
2. about 600 pounds
3. about 600 miles
4. about 90 scouts
5. about 110 tons

p. 298

	a	b	c	d	e	f
1.	26	47	97	88	88	98
2.	409	407	846	819	814	556
3.	401	524	543	613	735	851
4.	523	241	332	911	800	779
5.	96	436				
6.	919	808				
7.	652	780				

p. 299

8. Sue: 7 trains; Manuel: 6 trains
9. 11 pepperoni pizzas; 4 cheese pizzas
10. about 130 tons

p. 300

	a	b	c
1.	5	2	3
2.	4	4	4
3.	7	1	7
4.	12	1	2
5.	3	7	5
6.	5	4	9
7.	1	8	3
8.	2	9	5
9.	6	1	3
10.	9	4	3
11.	1	9	2

p. 301

	a	b	c
1.	2	4	3

	a	b	c	d	e	f	g
2.	2	7	6	3	7	7	5
3.	6	6	8	1	3	8	8
4.	8	6	4	7	7	4	3
5.	1	9	2	3	8	5	3

p. 302

	a	b	c	d	e	f
1.	34	73	44	15	82	32
2.	45	57	31	24	24	12
3.	91	46				

p. 303

	a	b	c	d	e	f
1.	513	114	641	255	712	713
2.	422	151	318	421	815	263
3.	232	513				

p. 304

	a	b	c	d	e	f
1.	38	89	27	58	19	49
2.	6	25	37	24	35	13
3.	27	67	13	57	67	25
4.	35	15				

p. 305

	a	b	c	d	e	f
1.	727	226	116	743	604	205
2.	233	602	577	427	315	428
3.	132	318	137	625	226	644
4.	226	608				

p. 307

1. January; 5 days
2. February and March
3. April
4. 10 days
5. May
6. May
7. 8 days
8. 16 days

p. 308

1. 144 bones
2. 109 seats
3. 267 miles
4. 13 men
5. 18 miles per hour

p. 309

	a	b	c	d	e	f
1.	152	474	376	631	42	343
2.	471	663	462	572	250	35
3.	275	653	482	361	870	90
4.	463	782				

p. 310

	a	b	c	d	e	f
1.	15	39	15	535	881	18
2.	138	261	420	56	431	424
3.	281	27	461	126	31	271
4.	870	16	228	57	23	618
5.	435	26	371	19	141	208
6.	17	81				
7.	57	308				

p. 311

	a	b	c	d	e	f
1.	879	473	777	194	187	384
2.	257	581	257	578	184	164
3.	484	127				

p. 312

	a	b	c	d	e	f
1.	212	148	581	780	218	240
2.	533	328	826	471	25	709
3.	258	455	190	65	524	677
4.	550	290	128	373	347	474
5.	347	533	218	491	565	371
6.	654	367	465	23	155	373
7.	465	88				

p. 313

	a	b	c	d	e	f
1.	288	45	659	135	378	547
2.	416	139	377	89	128	639
3.	886	25	568	268	404	156
4.	226	607				

p. 314

	a	b	c	d	e	f
1.	854	432	479	747	453	386
2.	268	778	615	503	328	574
3.	288	569	146	402	233	427
4.	384	745				

p. 315

	a	b	c	d	e	f
1.	283	207	143	335	36	159
2.	143	9	829	763	281	108
3.	146	61	862	22	385	247
4.	264	73	429	238	149	258
5.	278	59				
6.	314	509				
7.	27	139				

p. 317

1. 114 stamps
2. 53 ribbons
3. 57 tadpoles
4. 127 cookies
5. 18 pounds

p. 318

	a	b	c	d	e	f
1.	58	17	16	44	26	68
2.	453	321	133	522	243	202
3.	159	397	449	485	246	178
4.	13	156	249	267	347	322
5.	304	42	111	573	121	256
6.	82	196				
7.	687	259				

p. 319

a	b
8. lion; camel	9. jackal and tiger; 35 mph
10. elephant	
11. 15 mph	12. $53
13. 111 books	

p. 320

	a	b	c	d	e	f	g
1.	0	1	2	3	4	5	6
2.	7	8	9	0	0	0	4
3.	0	8	0	7	5	0	0
4.	0	8	0				
5.	4	0	3				

p. 321

	a	b	c	d	e	f	g
1.	0	2	4	6	8	10	12
2.	14	16	18	2	8	2	12
3.	16	18	4	0	10	6	14
4.	0	4	0	3	0	0	4
5.	7	12	0				

6. 8, 2, 12, 6, 0, 18, 14, 4, 16, 10

p. 322

	a	b	c	d	e	f	g
1.	0	3	6	9	12	15	18
2.	21	24	27	9	18	27	9
3.	3	21	24	12	0	6	15
4.	4	14	18	0	5	0	18

5.

2	9	4	1	6	5	3	8	0	7
4	18	8	2	12	10	6	16	0	14
6	27	12	3	18	15	9	24	0	21

p. 323

	a	b	c	d	e	f	g
1.	0	4	8	12	16	20	24
2.	28	32	36	4	32	28	0
3.	8	20	12	24	36	4	16
4.	14	15	9				
5.	24	4	10				

6. From the top center space, clockwise: 4, 24, 8, 28, 12, 32, 16, 0, 20, 36
7. From the top center space, clockwise: 0, 8, 16, 2, 10, 18, 4, 12, 6, 14

p. 324

	a	b	c	d	e	f	g
1.	0	5	10	15	20	25	30
2.	35	40	45	5	25	20	25
3.	45	10	40	15	35	30	0
4.	21	4	32				
5.	6	24	0				

6.

0	5	10	15	20	25	30	35	40	45
0	1	2	3	4	5	6	7	8	9
0	3	6	9	12	15	18	21	24	27
0	2	4	6	8	10	12	14	16	18
0	4	8	12	16	20	24	28	32	36

p. 325

	a	b	c	d	e	f	g
1.	0	6	12	18	24	30	36
2.	42	48	54	6	36	0	48
3.	18	42	24	54	12	30	42
4.	35	24	32	14	30	8	0
5.	25	48	27				

6. 48, 24, 36, 18
7. 12, 27, 15, 21
8. 40, 30, 20, 35

p. 326

	a	b	c	d	e	f	g
1.	0	7	14	21	28	35	42
2.	49	56	63	35	42	7	63
3.	56	14	42	49	28	0	21
4.	18	36	0				

5. From the top center space, clockwise: 0, 35, 56, 28, 14, 63, 42, 21, 49, 7
6. From the top center space, clockwise: 45, 5, 30, 10, 35, 15, 40, 20, 0, 25

p. 327

	a	b	c	d	e	f	g
1.	0	8	16	24	32	40	48
2.	56	64	72	48	72	64	0
3.	16	8	40	56	72	32	24
4.	30	49	28	3	10	63	24
5.	54	49	9				

6. 48, 32, 72, 40
7. 6, 24, 36, 12
8. 42, 21, 35, 14

p. 328

	a	b	c	d	e	f	g
1.	0	9	18	27	36	45	54
2.	63	72	81	18	63	36	81
3.	45	9	54	72	27	0	63
4.	36	21	20	56	16	20	0
5.	35	42	12				

6.

18	81	36	9	54	45	27	72	0
12	54	24	6	36	30	18	48	0
16	72	32	8	48	40	24	64	0

p. 329

	a	b	c	d	e	f	g
1.	48	16	48	25	56	36	21
2.	5	18	45	0	20	18	42
3.	24	35	32	54	8	30	72
4.	56	30	8	28	54	63	15
5.	49	32	45	9	42	27	40
6.	20	64	12	14	40	72	24
7.	24	36	63	28	36	81	35

p. 331

1. 48 Tiles
2. 20 Squares
3. 36 stamps

p. 332

	a	b	c	d	e	f
1.	40	10	20	30	40	50
2.	60	70	80	90	30	20
3.	500	100	200	300	400	500
4.	200	700	800	600	900	400
5.	100	900	300	700	800	500

p. 333

	a	b	c	d	e	f
1.	128	246	249	146	160	455
2.	106	276	360	328	147	300
3.	66	400	568	216	248	168
4.	188	480				

p. 334

	a	b	c	d	e	f
1.	106	350	216	420	208	128
2.	183	400	186	142	39	360
3.	189	219	168	129	186	147
4.	164	90	164	148	205	276
5.	459	68	189	350	210	279
6.	249	546				
7.	248	648				

p. 335

	a	b	c	d	e	f
1.	384	480	783	225	354	128
2.	445	294	161	312	74	324
3.	200	108	380	134	440	276
4.	332	413				

p. 336

	a	b	c	d	e	f
1.	196	237	864	188	552	112
2.	204	172	344	495	371	608
3.	325	255	567	135	224	228
4.	784	144	90	130	150	378
5.	252	469	54	438	776	64
6.	215	198				
7.	342	574				

p. 337

	a	b	c	d	e	f
1.	48	84	80	195	84	162
2.	450	435	68	300	81	48
3.	468	280	688	148	126	900
4.	280	120	177	126	200	340
5.	539	144	420	425	700	261
6.	246	342				

p. 339

1. Cougars ~~live in North America. They are about 9 feet long. Cougars are one of the best jumpers. They~~ can cover 45 feet in one jump. How many feet can a cougar go in 5 jumps?
225 feet
2. ~~Jupiter is the largest planet.~~ Gravity is different on Jupiter. Things weigh 2 times what they weigh on Earth. Tom weighs 89 pounds. How much would Tom weigh on Jupiter?
178 pounds
3. Giant kelp ~~is a huge seaweed. It~~ can grow 18 inches a day. ~~There are giant kelp forests in the ocean. The forests can be 328 feet tall~~. How many inches can giant kelp grow in 7 days?
126 inches
4. ~~The ostrich is the largest bird in the world. Some ostriches are 9 feet tall. They also lay the biggest eggs.~~ An ostrich egg ~~is 7 inches long. It~~ weighs 3 pounds. How much does a dozen ostrich eggs weigh?
(1 dozen = 12) 36 pounds
5. ~~Little League Baseball started in 1939 in Pennsylvania.~~ There were 3 teams in the first season. Each team had 10 players. ~~By 1998, there were 200,000 teams.~~ How many players were in the first season?
30 players

p. 340

	a	b	c	d	e	f	g
1.	40	80	20	700	900	500	300
2.	480	639	328	188	408	65	69
3.	118	846	104	135	432	290	216
4.	390	435	48	332	483	384	460
5.	80	60	300				
6.	568	129	108				
7.	485	168	222				
8.	720	592	318				

p. 341

9. 24 panes
10. 15 squares
11. Leatherbacks ~~are the largest turtles. They can weigh 1,100 pounds. Leatherbacks are also the fastest turtles. They~~ can swim about 22 miles per hour. How many miles can the turtle swim in 8 hours?
176 miles

p. 342

	a	b	c	d	e
1.	5	2	9	8	3
2.	4	6	2	3	7
3.	9	9	1	8	1
4.	5	7	1	5	6
5.	9	9	7		
6.	5	6	8		

p. 343

	a	b	c	d	e
1.	4	2	3	9	7
2.	2	6	5	4	5
3.	5	6	8	4	9
4.	9	8	7	7	4
5.	4	7	8		
6.	9	6	5		

7. 3, 8, 1, 5, 4, 6, 9, 7
8. 4, 1, 7, 9, 2, 8, 5, 6
9. 3, 9, 2, 7, 5, 4, 6, 1

p. 344

	a	b	c	d	e
1.	7	3	6	7	8
2.	7	5	2	8	8
3.	5	1	9	9	5
4.	4	5	5	7	2
5.	3	6	9		
6.	6	4	1		

7. 3, 7, 8, 4, 9, 5, 2, 6
8. 9, 4, 3, 7, 5, 2, 8, 6

p. 345

	a	b	c	d	e
1.	5	7	4	6	1
2.	3	3	8	1	6
3.	8	8	5	4	4
4.	2	9	4	7	5
5.	9	6	6		
6.	7	8	3		

7. 4, 8, 5, 3, 9, 6, 2, 7
8. 6, 9, 3, 5, 8, 2, 4, 7
9. 7, 5, 2, 6, 3, 9, 4, 8
10. 5, 9, 6, 4, 2, 8, 3, 7

p. 347

1. division; 4 days
2. addition; 734 students
3. multiplication; 280 miles
4. subtraction; 265 pounds
5. division; 7 hamsters

p. 348

	a	b	c	d	e
1.	6	1	7	6	7
2.	9	6	4	6	9
3.	9	5	7	8	3
4.	9	2	8	4	8
5.	9	4	8		
6.	6	7	8		

7. 27 ÷ 3 = 9 = 4)36
49 ÷ 7 = 7 = 5)35
40 ÷ 5 = 8 = 6)48
6 ÷ 3 = 2 = 7)14
21 ÷ 7 = 3 = 5)15
2 ÷ 2 = 1 = 7)7
24 ÷ 6 = 4 = 2)8

p. 349

	a	b	c	d	e
1.	9	4	9	6	8
2.	8	5	7	5	2
3.	6	5	4	8	8
4.	9	1	7	6	3
5.	9	7	9		
6.	6	7	9		
7.	8	8	7		

8. From the top center space, clockwise: 1, 5, 9, 2, 6, 3, 7, 4, 8
9. From the top center space, clockwise: 9, 2, 6, 3, 7, 4, 8, 1, 5

p. 350

	a	b	c	d	e
1.	8	5	6	7	3
2.	5	4	4	5	9
3.	6	6	5	5	8
4.	1	5	8	8	5
5.	7	2	9		
6.	6	7	8		

7. 3, 7, 6, 4, 9, 5
8. 4, 7, 3, 8, 6, 9
9. 6, 8 5, 7, 9, 4
10. 4, 6, 3, 8, 7, 9
11. 6, 8, 4, 7, 9, 5

p. 351

	a	b	c	d	e
1.	1	8	3	6	4
2.	3	3	8	6	7
3.	3	9	5	4	7
4.	2	7	2	5	3
5.	5	8	4		
6.	7	6	9		

7. $81 \div 9 = 9 = 7\overline{)63}$
$42 \div 7 = 6 = 6\overline{)36}$
$56 \div 8 = 7 = 9\overline{)63}$
$18 \div 6 = 3 = 8\overline{)24}$
$40 \div 8 = 5 = 6\overline{)30}$
$36 \div 9 = 4 = 8\overline{)32}$
$12 \div 6 = 2 = 4\overline{)8}$
$48 \div 6 = 8 = 3\overline{)24}$

p. 353

1. $64 \div 8 = 8$, 8 people
2. $5 \times 8 = 40$, 40 slices
3. $68 \div 136 = 204$, 204 bones
4. $107 - 72 = 35$, 35 inches
5. $72 \div 9 = 8$, 8 teams

p. 354

	a	b	c	d	e
1.	3	7	4	4	6
2.	7	2	9	8	9
3.	5	1	3	2	9
4.	6	5	4	3	2
5.	8	8	8	6	1
6.	7	6	4	5	3
7.	7	6	4		
8.	6	5	9		
9.	9	9	2		

p. 355

10. division; 8 bales
11. multiplication; 318 gallons
12. addition: 220 fish
13. subtraction: 12 questions
14. $13 \times 7 = 91$, 91 hours

p. 356

1. **a:** line segment, **b:** point, **c:** line
2. **a:** line *LM or ML*, **b:** line segment *BC or CB*, **c:** point A

p. 357

1. **a:** point, **b:** line, **c:** line segment
2. **a:** point *Q*, **b:** line segment *XY or YX*, **c:** line *EF or FE*
3. **a:** line segment *OP or PO*, **b:** point *C*, **c:** line *JK or KJ*
4. point *A*, point *B*, point *Q*, point *P*
5. line *AB or BA*
6. line segment *PQ*, line segment *AB*, line segment *BA*, line segment *AQ*, line segment *QA*, line segment *QB*, line segment *BQ*, line segment *QP*

p. 358

1. **a:** angle *M*, **b:** angle *A*, **c:** angle *F*
2. **a:** acute angle, **b:** right angle, **c:** obtuse angle

p. 359

1. **a:** angle *Q*, **b:** angle *G*, **c:** angle *S*
2. **a:** right angle, **b:** acute angle, **c:** obtuse angle
3. **a:** right angle, **b:** obtuse angle, **c:** acute angle
4. angle *A*
5. angle *B*
6. angle *C*

p. 360

	a	b
1.	8 units	8 units
2.	12 units	12 units

p. 361

	a	b
1.	10 square units	8 square units
2.	4 square units	12 square units
3.	16 square units	20 square units

p. 362

	a	b	c
1.	9:15	8:30	4:55
2.	1:20	10:05	4:35
3.	11:25	6:10	12:45

P. 363

	a	b
1.	30 minutes	3 hours
2.	5 minutes	10 minutes
3.	1 hour	15 minutes

p. 364

	a	b
1.	in.	ft.
2.	mi.	in.
3.	in.	mi.
4.	ft.	ft.
5.	115 mi.	7 ft.
6.	2 in.	4 mi.
7.	100 yd.	3 in.

	a	b	c
8.	1	1	3
9.	1	36	5,280

p. 365

	a	b	c
1.	cm	m	
2.	km	cm	
3.	m	m	
4.	km	cm	
5.	8 m	2 m	
6.	1 km	3 cm	
7.	50 m	400 m	
8.	100	1,000	200
9.	1	1	2,000

p. 367

1. thirteenth floor
2. right angle
3. 2 miles
4. 3 paths

p. 368

1. **a:** line *RS*; **b:** line segment *EF*; **c:** point *B*
2. **a:** acute angle; **b:** right angle; **c:** obtuse angle
3. **a:** perimeter: 8 units area: 4 square units; **b:** perimeter: 14 units area: 12 square units

p. 369

	a	b	c
4.	7:50	1:25	11:30

	a	b
5.	30 minutes	3 hours
6.	cm	m
7.	km	cm
8.	m	cm
9.	243 mi	6 in.
10.	90 ft	2 in.

p. 370

1. Child should circle a, b, and e.
2. Check shading.
3. All answers are $\frac{1}{2}$.

p. 371

1. Child should circle a and c.
2. Check shading.
3. All answers are $\frac{1}{2}$.

p. 372

1. Child should circle b, d, and e.
2. Check shading.
3. All answers are $\frac{1}{4}$.

p. 373

1. Child should circle a, c, and d.
2. Check shading.
3. All answers are $\frac{1}{4}$.

p. 374

1. Child should circle b and c.
2. Check shading.
3. All answers are $\frac{3}{4}$.

p. 375

1. Child should circle and a and c.
2. Check shading.
3. All answers are $\frac{3}{4}$.

p. 377

1. 4 different classes
2. 6 different ways
3. 6 different ways
4. 12 different ways

p. 378

1. Child should circle a, b, and c.
2. Check shading.
3. All answers are $\frac{1}{3}$.

p. 379

1. Child should circle a and c.
2. Check shading.
3. All answers are $\frac{1}{3}$.

p. 380

1. Child should circle a, b, and e.
2. Check shading.
3. All answers are $\frac{2}{3}$.

p. 381

1. Child should circle a and d.
2. Check shading.
3. All answers are $\frac{2}{3}$.

p. 383

1. blueberry
2. Shaneeka
3. 7 miles
4. Rudy: $2
Alicia: $3

p. 384

1. Child should circle a, b, c, and d.
2. Check shading.
3. Check shading.

	a	b	c	d	e
4.	$\frac{3}{3}$	$\frac{2}{2}$	$\frac{4}{4}$	$\frac{2}{2}$	$\frac{4}{4}$

p. 385

1. Check shading.
2. Check shading.

	a	b	c	d	e
3.	$\frac{1}{3}$	$\frac{1}{2}$	$\frac{1}{4}$	$\frac{3}{4}$	$\frac{3}{3}$
4.	$\frac{1}{4}$	$\frac{4}{4}$	$\frac{3}{4}$	$\frac{1}{2}$	$\frac{2}{3}$
5.	$\frac{2}{3}$	$\frac{3}{4}$	$\frac{1}{2}$	$\frac{1}{4}$	$\frac{1}{3}$

p. 386

6. 4 different choices
7. 8 different ways
8. pepperoni pizza

LANGUAGE ARTS

p. 388

1. flute
2. musician
3. stage
4. tree
5. girl
6. forest
7.–9. Sentences will vary.

p. 389

Common nouns: problem, school, miles, pool, dog, school, pool, brother, car, evening, practice
Proper nouns: Maren, Kona Kai Swim Team, Collins School, Miller Avenue, Kona Express Bus, Leif, Burger Pit Restaurant
Sentences will vary.

p. 390

1. Common: clockmaker; proper: Levi Hutchins, 2. common: person; proper: Concord, New Hampshire, 3. proper: Hutchins, 4. common: fellow, sun 5. common: people, sky 6. common: man, idea, clock, 7. common: machine, bell, 8. common: owner, piece, time 9. common: chime, 10. common: invention; proper: Hutchins

p. 391

Proper Nouns
Person: Serena, Riane, Mr. Williams;
Place: Vallco Concert Hall;
Thing: Shadygrove Band
Common Nouns
Person: musicians, leader;
Place: school, home;
Thing: day, talent, group

p. 392

1. plural: badgers, diggers
2. singular; badger, hole
3. singular: mammal; plural: claws
4. singular: animal, enemy
5. singular: mole; plural: paws
6. plural: legs, shovels
7. plural: tunnels, bushes, trees
8. singular: creature
9. singular: digger, world
10. plural: badgers, moles, diggers

p. 393

1. animals
2. farmers
3. chickens
4. ducks

5. swans
6. cows
7. horses
8. lambs
9. goats
10. pigs
11. piglets

p. 394
1. glasses
2. dishes
3. foxes
4. patches
5. matches
6. dresses
7. lunches
8. taxes
9. classes
10. bushes
11.–15. Sentences will vary.

p. 395
1. cities
2. families
3. parties
4. butterflies
5. flies
6. puppies
7. bunnies
8. babies
9. daisies
10. stories

p. 396
1. child
2. man
3. woman
4. goose
5. mice
6. ox
7. mouse
8. geese
9. children
10. teeth

p. 397
Sentences may vary.
1. Hope's kits is bright yellow.
2. The kite's tail is much too long.
3. It will get stuck in that tree's branches.
4. The girl's parents have kites, too.
5. Her mother's kite looks like a dragon.
6. Her dad's kits is shaped like a box.
7. Hope wants to fly her friend's kite.
8. The park's fields made flying kites fun.

p. 398
Paragraph: chickens', animals', foxes'
1. squirrels'
2. brothers'
3. dogs'
4. trees'

p. 399
1. table's; singular
2. dog's; singular
3. families'; plural
4. picnickers'; plural
5. blackberries'; plural
6. Adam's; singular
7. grandparents'; plural
8. bike's; singular

p. 400
1. He; Little Elk
2. She; Little Elk's mother
3. He; Little Elk
4. It; paint

p. 401
1. He
2. her
3. him
4. She
5. It
6. he

p. 402
1. We
2. them
3. They
4. them
5. They
6. us

p. 403
1. They
2. they
3. It
4. She
5. They

p. 404
Paragraph: singular: I, She, I, You, He; plural: They
Chart: I, Meredyth; She, mother; They, pictures; I, Meredyth; You, Meredyth; He, Dad

p. 405
us, them, her, him, it, them, him, They, them

p. 406
1. My friends and I
2. us
3. Nell and I
4. Casey and I
5. me
6. me
7. I
8. me
9. Mom and me
10. My parents and I

p. 407
1. her
2. our
3. My
4. your
5. his
6. their
7. my
8. its
9. your
10. My
11. her

p. 408
1. It's
2. You're
3. they're
4. they've
5. it's
6. I'll
7. you're
8. You'll

p. 409
1. small
2. Many
3. main
4. heavy
5. split
6. double
7. central
8. other
9. wooden
10. big

p. 410
1. Two
2. Several
3. Some
4. few
5. eight
6.–8. Sentences will vary.

p. 411
1. tiny; computers
2. secret; pouch
3. careful; notes
4. difficult; mysteries
5. lost; diamonds
6. famous; parrot
7. important; key
8. embarrassed; friend
9.–10. Sentences will vary.

p. 412
1. beautiful; Yosemite Park
2. incredible; views
3. difficult; mountain
4. taller; tree
5. blue; sky
6. tiny; houses
7. sick; man
8. mean; dog
9. sweet; flower
10. soft; cat

p. 413
Paragraph: an, the, the, a, the, a, an, a, the
1. a
2. a
3. an
4. an
5. A

p. 414
1. richer
2. poorest
3. younger
4. fancier
5. hungrier
6. grandest

p. 415
1. most
2. more
3. most
4. more
5. most
6. most
7. more
8. most
9. more
10. most

p. 416
Paragraph: more interesting, rarer, most difficult, bolder, easier
1. friendlier
2. happier
3. more
4. easier
5. noisiest

p. 417
1. begin
2. changes
3. grows
4. kick
5. develop
6. breathe
7. loses
8. becomes
9. climbs
10. appears

p. 418
1. peek
2. covers
3. go
4. close
5. walk
6. crunch
7. nips
8. build
9. return
10. remove

p. 419
1. floated
2. landed
3. disappeared
4. passed
5. taped
6. played
7. noticed
8. changed
9. soared
10. waited

p. 420
1. has; owned
2. have; traveled
3. had; soared
4. have; wanted
5. had; looked
6. has; landed
7. have; replaced
8. had; painted
9. have; called
10. has; planned

p. 421
Paragraph
Main verbs: traveled, visited, read, planned, given, stayed, written
Helping verbs: has, have, have, had, has, have, has
1. has
2. has
3. have
4. have
Sentences will vary.

p. 422
1. drive
2. drives
3. drink
4. drinks
5. play
6. chase
7. watches
8. takes
9. plays
10. watch

p. 423
1. rained; ed
2. closed; d
3. crashed; ed
4. barked; ed

5. watched; ed
6. poured; ed
7. leaked; ed
8. placed; d
9. started; ed
10. listened; ed

p. 424
1. eat
2. live
3. spends
4. covers
5 swims
6. visited
7. helped
8. enjoyed
9. cooked
10. liked

p. 425
1. driven
2. came
3. ate
4. went
5. drove
6. came
7. did
8. go

p. 426
1. gave
2. wrote
3. knew
4. taken
5. grew
6. took
7. ate
8. took
9. eaten
10. written

p. 427
1. live; action
2. is; be
3. are; be
4. use; action
5. are; be
6. were; be
7. is; be
8. am; be
9. are; be
10. build; action

428
1. everywhere; where
2. here; where
3. often; when
4. never; when
5. always; when
6. often
7. sometimes
8. Soon

p. 429
1. swiftly
2. quickly
3. Breathlessly
4. Luckily
5. excitedly
6. foolishly
7. exactly
8. Fortunately
9. barely
10. happily

p. 430
Paragraph: downstairs, often, carefully, cleverly
1.–5. Sentences will vary.

p. 431
1. correct
2. well
3. well
4. good
5. correct
6. good
7. well
8. good

p. 432
Students should underline: 1, 3, 5, 7
9.–10. Sentences will vary.

p. 433
1. subject
2. subject
3. predicate
4. subject
5. predicate
6. predicate
7. subject
8. predicate
9. subject
10. predicate

p. 434
1. Some seeds
2. Dandelion seeds
3. The wind
4. They
5. Pioneers
6. These settlers
7. Some families
8. The wilderness

p. 435
1. climbed Mount Whitney
2. is in California
3. went there with her father
4. climbed for one whole day
5. took pictures of snow at the top
6. went rafting on the Snake River
7. bucked like a wild horse
8. loved the exciting ride

p. 436
1. subject: New York City; predicate: is the largest city in the United States.
2. subject: More than 7 million people; predicate: live in New York City.
3. subject: New Yorkers; predicate: come from many different backgrounds.
4. subject: The subway system; predicate: runs on about 230 miles of track.
5. subject: The city; predicate: is a center for trade, business, and the arts.
6. subject: Millions of people; predicate: visit New York City every year.
7. subject: Theater; predicate: is one of the city's most popular art forms.
8. subject: Many visitors; predicate: attend Broadway shows.
9. subject: One tall building in New York City; predicate: is the Empire State Building.
10. subject: The Statue of Liberty; predicate: stands on an island in New York Harbor.
11. subject: This monument; predicate: is a symbol of freedom.
12. subject: Tourists; predicate: take pictures of the statue.

p. 437
1. Do you like gardens?; Q
2. We planted vegetables here.; S
3. Do the plants need water?; Q
4. Who will pull the weeds?; Q
5. These tomatoes look good.; S
6. Are they ripe?; Q
7. This tomato is bright red.; S

p. 438
1. Watch my pet fish.; C
2. He's amazing!; E
3. See how he follows my directions.; C
4. Swim through the hoop, Finny.; C
5. Now dive to the bottom.; C
6. You're terrific, Finny!; E
7. Swim around in big circles., C

p. 439
1. ?
2. .
3. .
4. ?
5. . or !
6. Most early people used combs. The only ones who didn't were the Britons.
7. Does it make you wonder how they looked? The Britons left their hair messy.
8. I comb my hair every day. Do you?

p. 440
1. am
2. are
3. is
4. is
5. are
6. is
7. am
8. were
9. was
10. was
11. were
12. were

p. 441
1. Amir was tired and wanted his lunch.
2. He turned smoothly in the water and headed for the other end of the pool.
3. Amir wanted to win and hoped to set records.
4. Amir won many races and got many awards.

p. 442
1. Guppies and goldfish are pets for fish tanks.
2. Catfish and snails help clean the tank.
3. Bettas and goldfish are great pets.
4. Guppies and black mollies have live babies.
5. Zebra fish and angelfish lay eggs.

p. 443
1. Inventions make our lives easier, and we take them for granted.
2. We get cold, and we turn on a heater.
3. Long ago people got cold, and they sat around a fire.
4. A very long time ago, people had no fire, and they stayed cold.
5. Our heater works, and we stay warm.

p. 444
1. Pet mice can be black, red, or silver.
2. Other colors for mice include gray, cream, and white.
3. A mouse can chew on wood, nuts, and twigs.
4. Mice clean their own bodies, faces, and ears.
5. Soup cans are good resting places for pet mice, hamsters, and gerbils.

p. 445
Sentences will vary. Possible responses are given.
1. The tiny hummingbird built a dainty nest.
2. She found a large tree in a quiet place.
3. She wanted her nest to be far away from curious cats.
4. She laid three eggs and sat on them patiently.
5. Soon the eggs hatched, and the babies cried hungrily for food.

p. 446
1. The baby opened the cabinet. She took out all the pots.
2. The mother came into the kitchen. She saw the mess.
3. The mother smiled at the baby. She asked if it was fun.
4. The baby smiled back. She was having a good time.
5. The mother sat on the floor. She played with the baby.

p. 447
1. Our dentist is Dr. Ellen J. Oldham.
2. She works with Dr. Karl V. Swift.
3. Dad's friend Chan works in the office.
4. Sometimes Miss Kitazawa works there, too.
5. My sister Leah had her checkup yesterday.
6. Today Mrs. Kim and Ms. Ozario will see Dr. Oldham.
7. Mr. Kramer sees Dr. Oldham every three months.
8. Max and I went to visit Mrs. Delgado.

p. 448
1. Zion National Park
2. State Street
3. South America
4. Mississippi River
5. Handy Hardware Store
6.–10. Sentences will vary. Be sure each sentence has a proper noun.

p. 449
1. February
2. Monday
3. Labor Day
4. November
5. Saturday
6. Thanksgiving Day
7.–12. Sentences will vary. Be sure each answer is the name of a day, month, or holiday.

p. 450
1. Pompeii
2. August
3. Italy
4. Mount Vesuvius
5. Mediterranean Sea
6. Naples
7. Metropolitan Museum
8. Europe

p. 451
1. Manny and Tony go to the beach every day.
2. Do not step on the crabs.
3. Dr. Quick looked at Mr. Smith's toe.
4. Mrs. Smith found a bandage.
5. Dr. Quick helped Mr. Smith.
Beach Activities
I. Play in the waves
II. Look for shells
III. Have a picnic

p. 452
1. Circle Rd.
2. July
3. Dr. Homer A. Mancebo or Dr. H. A. Mancebo
4. Tues.
5. 493 Dinosaur Ave.
6. Mr. W. Ambrose
7. Sat., Apr. 13
8. Angela P. Mills or A. P. Mills
9. Mon.
10. Miss Cynthia A. Forbes
11. Feb. 28, 12. Deerpath Rd.

p. 453
Sentences will vary. Be sure each answer begins with Yes, No, or Well.

p. 454
1. An octopus has eight legs, large eyes, and strong jaws.
2. An octopus eats clams, crabs, and lobsters.
3. Octopuses live along the coasts of Hawaii, Australia, and China.
4. The desert seems to shimmer, shine, and bubble in the hot sun.
5. Sometimes the wind will blow, swirl, or whip the sand around.

p. 455
Commas needed after New Delhi, May 3, Chandra, and Sincerely

p. 456
1. Meghan and her family took the 8:30 P.M. train.
2. At 7:15 the next morning, they ate breakfast.
3. The train pulled into Union Station at 8:45 A.M.
4. Meghan didn't want to waste time.
5. She wasn't interested in looking at the city from their windows.
6. Meghan's cousins met them at the hotel.
7. Her cousins' rooms overlooked the lake.
8. Meghan's father took them to the fair.
9. They stayed at the fair until 9:00 P.M.
10. Meghan couldn't stay awake on the ride home.

p. 457
1. shouldn't
2. isn't
3. aren't
4. don't
5. can't
6. hadn't
7. won't
8. wasn't
9. don't
10. hasn't

p. 458
1. Lily said, "Let's go to the beach."
2. Jeff exclaimed, "That's a great idea!"
3. correct
4. Uncle Bill said, "Well, I'd love to go to the beach."
5. Jeff asked, "Where is our big beach ball?"
6. correct
7. Dad reminded them, "Don't forget your towels."
8. Lily shouted, "This is great!"

p. 459
1. Chet got a book called <u>The Story of Baseball</u> from the library today.
2. The first story, titled "In the Beginning," starts in 1846.
3. The last story is called "Why Is Baseball So Popular?"
4. Last week Chet read a book called <u>Pioneers of Baseball</u> by Robert Smith.
5. His favorite story, "The One and Only," is abut Babe Ruth.

p. 460
1. outdoor; out, door; out of a house, outside
2. playground; play, ground; a place to play
3. overcoat; over, coat; a coat worn over a sweater or jacket
4. lightweight; light, weight; not heavy
5. mealtime; meal, time; a time to eat a meal
6. afternoon; after, noon; after 12:00 P.M.
7. mockingbird; mocking, bird; a bird that sounds like other birds
8. treetop; tree, top; the top of a tree

p. 461
Check that the correct synonym is used in the rewritten sentences.
1. nearly
2. large
3. know
4. whole

p. 462
1. hardest; easiest
2. toward; away
3. clean; dirty
4. remember; forget
5. good; bad
6. fresh; old
7. small; large

p. 463
1. unusual
2. impatient
3. disliked
4. unlucky
5. impossible

p. 464
1. inventor
2. useful
3. helper
4. fearless
5. joyful
6. successful

p. 465
1. a
2. b
3. b
4. a
5. a
6. b
7. Sentences will vary.

p. 466
1. days
2. pears
3. flour
4. seem
5. dough
6. eight
7. I
8. right
9. piece
10. fair
11. One; won
12. past; passed
13. find; fined

p. 467
1. to
2. too
3. to
4. to
5. two
6. too
7. two
8. to
9. two
10. too

p. 468
1. It's
2. It's
3. It's
4. its
5. its
6. Its
7. It's
8. It's
9. its
10. It's

p. 469
1. You're
2. your
3. you're
4. your
5. you're
6. Your
7. You're
8. your
9. you're
10. you're

p. 470
1. their
2. They're
3. They're
4. there
5. their
6. there
7. their
8. there
9. They're
10. their

p. 471
1. look
2. feel
3. sound
4. look
5. sound
6. look
7. look
8. taste
9. feel
10. smell

p. 472
1. fog, cat: Both are quiet, and you can't hear them coming.
2. fog, blanket: Both cover something so you can't see what's underneath.
3. tree, umbrella: Both provide shelter.
4. moon, Grandma: Both make the speaker feel good by seeming to smile.
5. lake, mirror: Both the lake and the mirror reflect light.
6. grasshoppers, echo: Both seem to respond right away.
7. knife, boat: Both move quietly and easily.

p. 473
1. strolls
2. watches
3. enjoys
4. pass
5. sees
6. touch
7. takes
8. fill
9. teaches
10. understands

p. 474
Answers will vary. Possible responses are given.
1. plays
2. waters
3. grow
4. hears
5. swim
6. hops
7. counts
8. walks

p. 475
Some hunters use their teeth to catch food.
Other hunters run to trap food.

Some jump on insects to catch them.

p. 476
Answers may vary.
1. The second paragraph is more interesting because there are more details and examples.
2. Though they can also see well in the daytime, owls are known for seeing at night.
3. Responses will vary, but should correctly give a detail from stood in the shade, an owl could see each of you well.

p. 477
Answers may vary.
A person who hears can imagine what it is like to be deaf. Put earplugs in your ears to block out sound. Try to figure out what people are saying. Try to call someone on the telephone. Deaf people can do all these things and more.

p. 479
1. to tell how he got his name
2. The writer tells a story about himself.
3. At first, he does not know how he got his name.

p. 482
1. Answers will vary.
2. head, said; that, cat
3. an alarm.
Poem: Answers will vary.

p. 485
1. fall
2. Answers will vary: crisp, cool, thump, big, tall, little, sweet-smelling jelly, high-stepping, squealed
3. Answers will vary.

p. 488
1. Mimi
2. 27 Green Street, Burlington, NC 27215
3. Dear Grandma
4. her hamster

p. 491
1. how to make a volcano
2. a pan, a plastic bottle, red food coloring, a bottle of vinegar, baking soda, and some sand
3. First, add a few drops of food coloring to the vinegar.
4. First, Next, Finally

p. 494
1. Mount Cameroon is a special mountain in Africa.
2. more than 30 years ago
3. Answers will vary.

p. 497
1. geese and whales
2. They are different kinds of animals, and they live in different places.
3. They both migrate long distances in large groups.

p. 500
1. <u>Humphrey the Lost Whale</u>
2. Wendy Tokuda and Richard Hall
3. Humphrey, a young whale
4. San Francisco Bay
5. yes

p. 503
1. Whale watching is good for people and for the environment.
2. Answers may vary: People work for Earth-friendly causes after watching whales.; People learn how special whales are.
3. Find out more about a whale-watching trip today.

p. 507
1. chip; because it is the second guide word
2. cherry, chip
3. carrot, cactus
4. no

p. 508
1. clover; 2
2. beet; 1
3. pickle; 2
4. pear; 1
5. wheat; 1

p. 509
1. 5
2. 3
3. 1
4. pronunciation
5. 2

p. 510
Answers will vary.
1. purchase
2. fortunate
3. awful
4. least
5. unkind

p. 511
1. 7
2. 4
3. 10
4. 2
5. 3
6. 11
7. 10
8. 4
9. cities
10. logging
11. mountains, United States
12. ships, America
13. rivers, America
14. water

p. 512
1. Silverstein
2. movies
3. weather
4. computers; games
5. math; fractions
6. shoes
7. Native Americans
8. maps
9. the name of the city
10. dogs

p. 513
1. <u>Art Projects at the Beach</u>
2. Sandy Shore
3. Crafts Books, Inc.
4. Getting Started
5. Sand Art
6. 8–10, 26, 29

p. 514
1. nonfiction
2. nonfiction
3. nonfiction
4. fiction
5. nonfiction
6. fiction
7. fiction
8. fiction

p. 515
Students should circle sentence 1., 4. to open, 5. *novem*

p. 516
1. opinion
2. fact
3. fact
4. opinion
5. fact
6.–7. Sentences will vary.

p. 517
Notes should include: each fall, migrate 3,000 miles, Pribilof Islands to southern California

p. 518
Answers may vary.
Who: Campers
What: Spiders
Where: In unusual places, such as in canoes and boots
When: At different times
Why: Looking for a safe place to spin a web to catch food
Summary: Spiders spin webs in unusual places to catch food. Campers may be surprised by spiders at any time.

p. 519
Migrating Monarch Butterflies
I. Migrate south from Canada and northern United States
II. Spend winter in southern United States and Mexico
III. Return home in spring

p. 520
Topic sentences will vary, but should be complete sentences.
Examples for Migrating Swallows:
1. Migrating swallows fly long distances to get away from the cold.
2. Migrating swallows migrate by day.
3. Migrating swallows travel 10,000 miles.
Examples for Migrating Geese:
1. Migrating geese live in the United States and Canada.
2. Migrating geese fly in groups.
3. Migrating geese fly as far south as Mexico.

p. 522
1. colds
2. A cold is caused by a virus.
3. Answers will vary.
4. Answers will vary.

Writing Skills

Answers to the practice paper exercises questions may vary, but examples are provided here to give you an idea of how your child may respond.

p. 524
1. middle
2. beginning
3. ending
4. Responses will vary. Be sure reason given is valid.

p. 525
1. a. ending b. beginning c. middle
2. a. ending b. middle c. beginning

p. 526–527
1. 2, 3, 1
2. 1, 3, 2

p. 528
Responses will vary. Be sure reasons given are valid.

p. 529
1. receive
2. fortunate
3. bad
4. require
5. buy
6. least
7. cruel

p. 530–531

Uncle John has always been my favorite uncle. What a surprise we all had last summer. Late one evening there was a knock at the back door. Can you guess who was standing on our back steps? Of course, it was Uncle John. He had a backpack, a small suitcase, and an armload of gifts.

Uncle John's present for me was a bright blue (blew) T-shirt. It (it) has a picture of an old castle on the back. Uncle John bought the shirt for me when he was traveling in England last year. I wore that shirt every day while (wile) Uncle John was staying with us.

Uncle John has been to many different parts of the world, and he loved telling us about his adventures. Listening to his stories was almost as much fun as going along on Uncle John's trips.

p. 538
1. The writer wrote "Save Jack" to explain how he became friends with Danny. Danny created a club to help Jack make friends at a new school. (Help your child clearly identify the purpose for writing. Guide him or her in supporting the answers with details from the story.)
2. First, Jack says he feels sad about leaving his friends. Later, Jack says he feels lonely, scared, and unhappy.
3. Jack seems happy and grateful to Danny for his help in making friends. For instance, in the last paragraph, Jack says, "Danny rescued me." (Look for a clear understanding of how Jack's feelings changed over time in the answers. Be sure your child includes details from the narrative to support his or her understanding.)
4. Be sure your child correctly summarizes the significant events of the story, paraphrasing as needed. Summaries should be organized in a thoughtful way, with the main ideas and important details clearly presented. Spelling, punctuation, capitalization, and grammar should be correct.

p. 539
1. Jack uses words like *I, me,* and *my* to show that he is writing about his own personal experiences.
2. Jack is the new kid at school, and he feels lonely and scared.
3. Danny, a boy at Jack's new school, actually solves Jack's problem. Danny starts the Save Jack Club. After a few days, the club includes everyone in Jack's class. The club is a way for Danny to get everybody to play soccer together.
4. In the first paragraph, Jack tells that this story is about being new in town and not knowing that Danny would become his best friend. In the last paragraph, Jack says he's more than just a new kid now. He also explains how Danny rescued him and became Jack's best friend.

p. 544–545
Main idea: Animal tracks can tell you many things.
1. , 2. Sentences will vary. Be sure that details refer to the main idea.
3. Paragraph B is more interesting because there are more details and examples.
4. Responses will vary, but should correctly give a detail from the paragraph.

p. 546
1. Main idea: The squid and the octopus look very different. a., b. Sentences will vary. Be sure that details refer to the main idea.
2. The squid and the octopus behave very differently. a., b. Sentences will vary. Be sure that details refer to the main idea.

p. 547
1. a. detail b. detail c. main idea d. detail
2. a. detail b. detail c. detail d. main idea

p. 548
Possible responses:
1. Paragraph B is more interesting because there are more details and examples.
2. Responses will vary but should correctly give a detail from the paragraph.
3. Responses will vary but should correctly give a detail from the paragraph.

p. 549
A sighted person can only imagine what it is like to be blind. Put a scarf over your eyes to block out light. Try to figure out what different foods are. Pretend to pay for something with coins. Try to walk into another room and sit at a table. Blind people can do all these things and more.

p. 550–551

Pond snails are useful in fish tanks. Ponds snails will ^eat any extra food your fish leave. They will also eat some ^of the moss that appears on the plants. The snails will eat some of ^the moss on the glass walls of the tank, too⊙ If you have sevrel [several] pond snails in ^the fish tank, you will not have to clean the tank as often.

If your pond snails are having babies, be sure to remove the snails ^from the tank. Fish will eat snail eggs. In the same way, if your fish are having babies, be sure ^to remove the snails. Snails will eat fish eggs.

There are many different kinds ^of snails. Their different kinds ^of shells can add grately [greatly] to the beauty of your fish tank. Not only are snails useful in keeping a tank clean, they also add interest to the tank.

p. 557
1. This how-to paper teaches how to make a drum and drumsticks.
2. The materials needed to make a drum and drumsticks include a round oatmeal box with a lid; two new, unsharpened pencils; foil; tempera paint and paintbrush; colored construction paper; glitter or other shiny things; glue; cord; an apron or old shirt; and old newspapers.
3. The most important thing is a round cardboard box with a lid.
4. The cord lets you hang the drum around your neck while you play it. (Help your child recognize this answer as an important detail. Discuss the importance of including details such as this in a how-to paper.)
5. Answers will vary, but look for indications of understanding, such as a clear description of the drum and drumsticks and a corresponding illustration. Spelling, punctuation, capitalization, and grammar should be correct.

p. 558
1. The writer states the purpose of the paper clearly, lists materials, gives clear, step-by-step instructions, and gives helpful hints and details.
2. The writer tells what materials to collect and then says to make the drumsticks.
3. The writer lists the materials so they can be collected before starting the project. This saves time and makes the project easier to do.
4. Sequence words help the reader to understand the order of the steps.
5. Pictures and answers may vary. Check pictures to determine if your child understood the instructions.

p. 563
1. a
2. c
3. Casey has a tail. Casey said, "Meow."

p. 564
1. thick, read
2. round
3. green, orange
4. two-story, tiny
5. huge
6. little, brown
7. colorful
8. loud, banging
9. terrific
10. delicious
11. sweet, moist

p. 565
1. b
2. c
3. a
4. b

p. 566
1. look
2. feel
3. sound
4. look
5. sound
6. look
7. look
8. taste
9. feel
10. smell

p. 567
1. Guppies and goldfish are pets for fish tanks.
2. Catfish and snails clean harmful moss from the tank.
3. Black mollies and goldfish are lovely fish.
4. Guppies and black mollies have live babies.
5. Zebra fish and angelfish lay eggs.

p. 568–569

Have you ever heard of a person who likes washing dishes? My friend Dan really enjoy^s it. In fact, Dan washes dishes whenever he can. Dan pull^s a chair over to the sink so he can reach everything easily. Dan likes the lemony smell of the liquid detergent⊙ He squeezes the bottle gently and watches the liquid soap stream into the water. The soap mix^es with the hot water. Together, they create a mass of frothy white bubbles. When the bubbles almost reach the top of the sink, Dan turns the water off. then [Then] he carefully puts the glasses in the water.

Most of all, Dan like^s using a brand-new dishcloth. The cloth feel^s soft in Dan's hands. It has a clean smell, too. Dan rub^s each glass carefully with the soft, new cloth. Then he rinses the glass and sets it on the drainer.

p. 578
1. Matt is the pitcher for the White Caps.
2. The father tells Jess that he is being fair. "I clap for people who do a good job," he says.
3. In the last paragraph, Jess says, "What a game!" Jess also says that next year, maybe she can be a White Cap.
4. Be sure your child correctly summarizes the significant events of the story, paraphrasing as needed.

Main ideas should be organized logically and important details presented clearly. Spelling, punctuation, capitalization, and grammar should be correct.

p. 579
1. The writer uses descriptive action words and comparisons. The bat "whooshed" through the air. The runner "ran faster than a squirrel." The crowd's clapping "sounded like thunder," and the players "ran like swift cats." The ball looked "like a small, white bird."
2. Some of the words the writer uses are "kicked," "tagged," "smacked," and "popped."
3. The writer describes the feelings, sights, and sounds of the game. The writer uses descriptions, such as "The grass made my skin itch," "Their clapping sounded like thunder," and "The air was filled with claps, yells, and moans."
4. The players ran like the wind. The players swept past like locomotives.

p. 584
1. The best building material for a house is bricks.
2. Possible responses: A brick house stays cool in summer and warm in winter. A brick house will keep people dry. A wolf can not blow down a house made of bricks.
3. That a wolf cannot blow down a house made of bricks.

p. 585
1. You should get involved in sports after school.
2. yes
3. Possible responses: Exercise is important for good physical health. Exercise builds strong muscles; exercise keeps the body from storing fat; and exercise builds a healthy heart and lungs.
4. It is important for your health.

p. 586
1. b, c, d
2. a, b, e

p. 587
1. Television takes time away from studies.
2. You will have money for something big later.
3. Clothes left lying around make the room messy.
4. It's not thoughtful to keep others waiting.
5. You might make a good friend this way.

p. 588
1. Kathy was tired and wanted her lunch.
2. She turned smoothly in the water and headed for the other end of the pool.
3. Kathy wanted to win and hoped to set records.
4. Kathy won many races and got many awards.
5. Kathy practiced as much as possible and competed with stronger swimmers.

p. 589–590

Our class play coming is up next month, and everyone should hepl [help] make it a success. It is true that not everyone can act in the play because there are not enough prats [parts]. Also, students some do not enjoy appearing on stage. Still, there is something for everyone do to.
Those who do not wish to be on the stage can find plenty to do behind the scenes⊙ One such job making is scenery. Any student who likes to build can give time to this important job. We'll need staircases, walls, and street lamps for Act I. For Atc [Act] II we'll need scenery that looks like a beach⊙

Another important job is making costumes. Students who enjoy different kinds of clothes will have fun with this job. We'll need soem [some] special hats, some jewelry, and some old-fashioned beach clothes.

p. 598
Guide your child in organizing the information in a clear manner. <u>How Little Brown Bats and American Robins Are Alike</u>: Both fly.; Both have wings.; Both have claws.; Both eat insects.
How Little Brown Bats and American Robins Are Different: The bat is 3 inches long, but the robin is 10 inches long.; The bat has brown fur and black ears. The robin has a yellow beak and feathers that are black, red, and grayish-brown.; The bat has wings made from clawed fingers covered with skin. It uses its claws to hang upside down. The robin has claws it uses to perch in trees.; The bat sleeps all day. The robin is active during the day and sleeps at night.; The bat uses a kind of radar called echolocation to find insects and flies.; The bat is a mammal, gives birth to one live baby at a time, and the baby drinks milk. The robin is a bird, lays 6 bluish-green eggs, and feeds its babies food that the parent spits up.; The robin builds a mud-lined nest out of twigs, roots, grass, and paper in trees or on a ledge.

p. 599
1. The writer tells that the paper is about how bats and birds are alike and different in the first paragraph.
2. What Little Brown Bats look like, What Little Brown Bats eat and how they find their food, What Little Brown Bats are, How Little Brown Bats care for their babies
3. What American Robins look like, When American Robins are awake and asleep, What American Robins like to eat, How American Robins build their nests, and How American Robins care for their babies
4. In the last two paragraphs, the writer tells the reader to notice how birds and bats are alike and different. This is a way for the writer to restate the paper's main ideas and tie the first and last paragraphs together.

p. 605
Possible responses
1. school
2. Mr. McGrath finds the pets too noisy.
3. a
4. b

p. 606
Possible responses:
1. King Midas
2. Greece long ago
3. The golden touch has made his food, drink, and daughter turn to gold.
4. Even his food and drink turned to gold.
5. King Midas had to beg to have his golden touch taken away.

p. 607
1. Girl sits by a stream.
2. Rabbit runs by.
3. Rabbit goes down a hole.
4. Rabbit has a vest on.
5. Rabbit has a watch.
6. Rabbit talks.
7. real
8. real
9. make-believe
10. make-believe

p. 608–609
1. a
2. b
3. c
4. c

p. 610
1. The baby opened the cabinet. She took out all the pots.
2. The mother came into the kitchen. She saw the mess.
3. The mother smiled at the baby. She asked if it was fun.
4. The baby smiled back. She was having a good time.
5. The mother sat on the floor. She played with the baby.

p. 611–612

1. Goldilocks sat down at the bears' table. the first chair she tried was too hard, and the second chair was too soft. the third chair felt just right. Next, Goldilocks tried all the oatmeal on the table⊙ The first bowl was too hot, and the second bowl was too cold. The third bowl tastes just right. after she had eaten the whole bowl of oatmeal, Goldilocks went upstairs for a nap.

2. Fox looked up at the grapes on the vine. how delicious they looked! he decided to have some grapes four [for] his lunch. The grapes were quite high, and it was hard for Fox to reach them. he stretched and jumped, but he couldn't get the grapes. Fox tried again and again. the grapes always seemed just out of reach. Finally, Fox gave up. he walked away, asking himself, "Who would want those sour old grapes?"

p. 619
1. This story teaches that it takes more than just talk to get something done. All the mice had ideas for taking care of their cat problem, but no one had the courage to put the bell on Clever Cat. (Help your child clearly identify the purpose of this story. Guide him or her in supporting the answers with details from the story.)
2. The mice act just like people do. They have different personalities and names. They have many different feelings. For example, the first sentence says that Martha Mouse was very sad. The mice have conversations, and they tell stories. (Look for your child's clear understanding of how the writer gives human traits to the animals in the story.)

3. The story takes place in the dark basement of a school. (Look for your child's understanding of setting. Help your child understand why the mice chose the basement.)
4. Be sure your child correctly summarizes the significant events of the story, paraphrasing as needed. Summaries should be organized in a thoughtful way, with the main ideas and important details clearly presented. Spelling, punctuation, capitalization, and grammar should be correct.

p. 620
1. Abstemius makes the animals seem human by giving them individual personalities. Martha Mouse has a take-charge personality. Martin is helpful but cautious. Also, the writer gives the mice lively conversation and shows them having many feelings, such as sadness, fear, and joy.
2. The writer makes the story exciting by having the meeting take place at night. The reader feels that Clever Cat might find the mice at any moment and pounce.
3. The writer uses the mice to say something about people. The mice are small and full of bustling talk, but not one of them wants to take a risk. The writer is really saying that people can be full of ideas but slow to act.
4. In the last paragraph, the reader sees that despite the mice's experiences, strong feelings, and grand ideas, not one mouse is willing to put the bell on the cat.

p. 625
1. a
2. b
3. a

p. 626
1. colds
2. A cold is caused by a virus.
3. Responses will vary.
4. Responses will vary.

p. 627
1. fact
2. opinion
3. fact
4. opinion
5. fact
6. opinion
7. fact
8. fact
9. opinion
10. fact
11. fact
12. opinion

p. 628
Responses will vary.

p. 629
Accept any reasonable responses.

p. 630–631

At one time there was a kind of bird called the passenger pigeon. The passenger pigeon was one of the most common birds in the wirld (world). In fact, their (there) were once so many passenger pigeons that they darkened the skies. One sumar (summer) day these birds completely blocked the sunshine in New york. In 1808 poepel (people) saw a flock of passenger pigeons one mile wide and 240 miles long! the flock had more than two billyon (billion) birds. The birds in that flock ate about 434,000 bushels of nuts, rice, and berrys (berries) every day.

No one now can see even won (one) living passenger pigeon. The last wild passenger pigeon was killed in 1906 in connecticut. In 1914 the last passenger pigeon in a zoo died. the passenger pigeon is extinct.

p. 638
1. The Pony Express was a service started in 1860 that carried mail and news throughout the West. (Help your child include all the pertinent information in his or her answers.)
2. People who lived in California needed a quick way to get mail and news from the East. A stagecoach took one month to deliver mail. A Pony Express rider could do it in ten days. (Check to see that your child included all significant details.)
3. Pony Express riders had to ride through dangerous weather, such as snowstorms and sandstorms. They also faced wild animals and bandits.
4. Be sure that your child identifies the report's main ideas and includes significant details. Spelling, punctuation, capitalization, and grammar should be correct.

p. 639
1. The writer tells the topic in the title of the report. The first two paragraphs give important information that explains why the Pony Express began. Then, the Pony Express is introduced in the third paragraph.
2. People in California wanted mail and news.; Three people started a company called the Pony Express.; The Pony Express hired young men.; Riders rode wild horses called mustangs.; Other people worked for the Pony Express.; Pony Express workers faced many dangers.; Riders covered 2,000 miles by riding in relays.; The Pony Express ended when telegraph wires reached California.
3. The writer uses examples of simpler words to define each word that the reader might not know.
4. The last paragraph summarizes how the Pony Express was successful and why it ended.

Test Prep

p. 650–651
1. A
2. G
3. There was no light in the room.
4. C
5. H
6. to sell again

p. 652–653
1. C
2. J
3. baby ducks
4. C
5. G
6. A person who is social is someone who spends a lot of time with family and friends.

p. 654–655
1. B
2. H
3. Saliva is something found in your throat that helps you soften, swallow, and break down food.
4. B
5. J
6. an animal's or person's bones

p. 656–657
1. C
2. H
3. Her dream was to study law.
4. D
5. F
6. B
7. 9 years

p. 658–659
1. A.D. 393
2. C
3. H
4. C
5. 1896

p. 660–661
1. D
2. get out a flashlight
3. H
4. C
5. Take the cake out of the oven and let it cool.

p. 662–663
1. C
2. J
3. He was rescued in August.
4. C
5. in Missouri
6. F

p. 664–665
1. A chameleon's ability to change colors can save its life.
2. C
3. G
4. A
5. J

p. 666–667
1. D
2. F
3. C
4. How cats are very much like lions and tigers.
5. What makes a tree a conifer.

p. 668–669
1. Gabriela let Jodi borrow her blue dress.
2. B
3. H
4. A
5. Vince was friends with everyone at camp.
6. H
7. D

p. 670–671
1. C
2. The man will fall off the bicycle.
3. G
4. C
5. H
6. A

p. 672–673
1. C
2. She felt angry because she has to do all the work.
3. H
4. He was happy because the man did not want to keep the coin.

p. 674–675
1. The computer helps him speak.
2. C
3. H
4. A
5. H

p. 676–683
SA. B
1. hide-and-seek
2. C
3. H
4. A
5. They were worried.
6. J
7. B
8. J
9. D
10. to keep moisture in the pot for a while
11. H
12. A
13. H
14. July 4, 1998
15. A
16. H
17. A
18. H
19. B
20. to plant for food
21. J

22. A
23. J
24. A
25. F
26. A
27. J
28. to make beds
29. A
30. G

p. 684–690
SA. C
1. A
2. by using special chemicals to keep it from crumbling
3. J
4. C
5. G
6. A
7. H
8. They fell out of Gabriel's jacket.
9. B
10. F
11. chop it
12. B
13. J
14. B
15. H
16. B
17. to become an astronaut
18. G
19. B
20. H
21. D
22. F
23. B
24. A gust of wind blew him into the water.
25. G
26. D
27. J
28. C

p. 691
SA. D
1. C
2. pain
3. G
4. C
5. G
6. B

p. 692
SA. D
1. B
2. J
3. C
4. H

p. 693
SA. B
1. A
2. G
3. D
4. F
5. C
6. directions

p. 694–696
SA. D
1. D
2. F
3. B
4. F
5. A
6. J
7. B
8. J
9. cut
SB. C
10. B
11. G
12. A
13. J
14. D
SC. C
15. F
16. C
17. H
18. C
19. G
20. B
21. fix

p. 698
Step 1. What is the greatest number of toys Jackie can buy with $5.00?
Step 2. Bears cost $1.98. Dogs cost $1.50. Cats cost $1.45. Birds cost $1.10. Snakes cost $0.88. Jackie has five dollars. She can only buy one of each animal.
Step 3. Buy toys one at a time, starting with the least expensive, until there isn't enough money left to buy another toy.
Step 4. $5.00 − $0.88 = $4.12; $4.12 − $1.10 = $3.02. $3.02 − $1.45 = $1.57. $1.57 − $1.50 = $0.07.
Step 5. Jackie can buy four toys. The answer makes sense because she has only 7 cents left after buying the four least expensive toys.

p. 699
Step 1. Describe the four outfits Eduardo can make.
Step 2. He has 1 striped shirt and 1 solid shirt. He has 1 black pair of pants and 1 blue pair.
Step 3. Make a list of combinations.
Step 4. Striped/Black; Solid/Black; Striped/Blue; Solid/Blue
Step 5. Yes, because it lists the four different outfits.

p. 700
SA. B
1. A
2. Mike
3. G
4. A

p. 701
SA. B
1. $\frac{4}{5}$
2. D
3. H
4. C
5. F

p. 702
SA. A
1. C
2. H
3. C
4. 24

p. 703–704
SA. D
1. B
2. F
3. blue
4. D
5. H
6. D
7. G

p. 705
SA. C
1. A
2. 2 and 3
3. H
4. B

p. 706–707
SA. D
1. 4 cm
2. A
3. G
4. B
5. J
6. C
7. H

p. 708
SA. C
1. how many fish Michelle put into the water
2. D
3. J
4. D

p. 709
SA. D
1. A
2. J
3. E
4. H
5. B
6. F
7. B
8. K

p. 710
SA. B
1. C
2. 18
3. J
4. B

p. 711–712
SA. D
SB. G
1. B
2. J
3. C
4. G
5. A
6. H
7. 8
8. A
9. J
10. B
11. $3.57
12. J
13. C
14. G

p. 713–720
SA. D
1. B
2. J
3. A
4. G
5. A
6. H
7. 210
8. D
9. H
10. B
11. J
12. A
13. G
14. B
15. J
16. D
17. J
18. C
19. J
20. 4
21. C
22. G
23. C
24. F
25. 3
26. B
27. G
28. B
29. G
30. C
31. G
32. football and basketball
33. B
34. G
35. D
36. H
37. B
38. F
39. D
40. G
41. A
42. G
43. B
44. $7 \times 4 = 28$

p. 721–727
SA. D
1. Ontario, Canada
2. C
3. F
4. B
5. 18
6. J
7. C
8. 6
9. J
10. B
11. G
12. B
13. F
14. C
15. G
16. A
17. G
18. a path or track
19. D
20. 5
21. J
22. B
23. F
24. C
25. G

p. 728
SA. A
1. C
2. J
3. A
4. F
5. C

p. 729–735
SA. D
1. B

2. G
3. D
4. a dictionary
5. F
6. B
7. 12
8. F
9. C
10. F
11. B
12. J
13. A
14. J
15. A
16. 2
17. J
18. C
19. G
20. A
21. G
22. C
23. F
24. D
25. F
26. A
27. F
28. C
29. J
30. D
31. G
32. A

p. 736–743

SA. B
1. B
2. leaves, straw, or bark
3. F
4. B
5. There was little money to buy food in a store.
6. H
7. B
8. laying eggs
9. F
10. B
11. F
12. A
13. H
14. C
15. J
16. A
17. G
18. the seeds from wild plants
19. D
20. F
21. B
22. H
23. trees that protect house from wind
24. C
25. H
26. C
27. J
28. A
29. G
30. D
31. F
32. during the month of April

p. 744–746

SA. A
1. C
2. G
3. A
4. J
5. C
6. G
7. A
8. H
9. A
SB. B
10. J
11. C
12. G
13. D
14. H
SC. A
15. D
16. amazed
17. J
18. B
19. F
20. A
21. F

p. 747–753

SA. D
1. C
2. J
3. B
4. G
5. C
6. F
7. A
8. G
9. D
10. H
11. $\frac{1}{5}$
12. C
13. J
14. C
15. 9
16. F
17. B
18. H
19. C
20. J
21. C
22. May
23. F
24. B
25. F
26. C
27. G
28. D
29. G
30. D
31. F
32. A
33. H
34. B
35. G
36. D
37. H
38. C
39. H
40. B
41. G
42. A
43. F

p. 754–756

SA. A
1. C
2. K
3. C
4. H
5. D
6. G
7. 585
8. 73
9. E
10. J
11. D
12. H
13. C
14. 6
15. K
16. D
17. G
SB. B
18. A
19. J
20. A
21. F
22. C

p. 757–765

SA. B
1. D
2. 51
3. J
4. B
5. F
6. 5
7. C
8. F
9. C
10. J
11. A
12. G
13. C
14. G
15. C
16. G
17. A
18. having little or no rainfall.
19. G
20. B
21. 4
22. H
23. D
24. H
25. A
26. G
27. D
28. F
29. C
30. G
31. D
32. G
33. A
34. F
35. D